France

Vintage	Red Bordeaux		White Bordeaux		Alsace
	Médoc/Graves	Pom/St-Ém	Sauternes & sw	Graves & dry	
2018	8–9	8–9	7–9	7–8	7–9
2017	6–8	6–7	8–9	7–8	9–10
2016	8–9	8–9	8–10	7–9	7–8
2015	7–9	8–10	8–10	7–9	7–9
2014	7–8	6–8	8–9	8–9	7–8
2013	4–7	4–7	8–9	7–8	8–9
2012	6–8	6–8	5–6	7–8	8–9
2011	7–8	7–8	8–10	7–8	5–7
2010	8–10	7–10	7–8	7–9	8–9
2009	7–10	7–10	8–10	7–9	8–9
2008	6–8	6–9	6–7	7–8	7–8
2007	5–7	6–7	8–9	8–9	6–8
2006	7–8	7–8	7–8	8–9	6–8
2005	9–10	8–9	7–9	8–10	8–9
2004	7–8	7–9	5–7	6–7	6–8
2003	5–9	5–8	7–8	6–7	6–7
2002	6–8	5–8	7–8	7–8	7–8
2001	6–8	7–8	8–10	7–9	6–8
2000	8–10	7–9	6–8	6–8	8–10

France, continued

Vintage	Burgundy			Rhône	
	Côte d'Or red	Côte d'Or white	Chablis	North	South
2018	8–10	7–8	8–9	7–9	7–8
2017	6–9	8–9	6–8	7–9	7–9
2016	7–8	7–8	7–8	7–9	7–9
2015	7–9	7–8	7–8	8–9	8–9
2014	6–8	7–9	7–9	7–9	6–8
2013	5–7	7–8	6–8	7–9	7–8
2012	8–9	7–8	7–8	7–9	7–9
2011	7–8	7–8	7–8	7–8	6–8
2010	8–10	8–10	8–10	8–10	8–9
2009	7–10	7–8	7–8	7–9	7–8
2008	7–9	7–9	7–9	6–7	5–7
2007	7–8	8–9	8–9	6–8	7–8
2006	7–8	8–10	8–9	7–8	7–9
2005	7–9	7–9	7–9	7–8	6–8

Beaujolais 18 17 15 14 11. Crus will keep. **Mâcon-Villages** (white). Drink 18 17 15 14.
Loire (sweet Anjou and Touraine) best recent vintages: 18 15 10 09 07 05 02 97 96 93 90 89; Bourgueil Chinon Saumur-Champigny: 18 17 15 14 10 09 06 05 04 02. **Upper Loire** (Sancerre Pouilly-Fumé): 18 17 15 14 12. **Muscadet:** DYA.

HUGH
JOHNSON'S
POCKET
WINE
BOOK

2020

MITCHELL BEAZLEY

Hugh Johnson's Pocket Wine Book 2020

Edited and designed by Mitchell Beazley,
an imprint of Octopus Publishing Group Limited,
Carmelite House, 50 Victoria Embankment
London EC4Y 0DZ
www.octopusbooks.co.uk

An Hachette UK Company
www.hachette.co.uk

Distributed in the US by Hachette Book Group
1290 Avenue of the Americas
4th and 5th Floors
New York, NY 10020
www.octopusbooksusa.com

Copyright © Octopus Publishing Group Ltd 2019

First edition published 1977

Revised editions published 1978, 1979, 1980, 1981, 1982,
1983, 1984, 1985, 1986, 1987, 1988, 1989, 1990, 1991, 1992,
1993, 1994, 1995, 1996, 1997, 1998, 1999, 2000, 2001,
2002 (twice), 2003, 2004, 2005, 2006 (twice), 2007, 2008,
2009, 2010, 2011, 2012, 2013, 2014, 2015, 2016, 2017, 2018,
2019

A CIP record for this book is available from
the British Library.

ISBN (UK): 978-1-73472-484-9
ISBN (US): 978-1-73472-612-6

General Editor **Margaret Rand**
Commissioning Editor **Hilary Lumsden**
Senior Editors **Pauline Bache, Alex Stetter**
Proofreader **Jamie Ambrose**
Art Director **Yasia Williams-Leedham**
Designer **Jeremy Tilston**
Deputy Picture Manager **Jennifer Veall**
Senior Production Manager **Katherine Hockley**

Printed and bound in China

Mitchell Beazley would like to acknowledge and thank the following
for supplying photographs for use in this book:

Alamy Stock Photo Westend61 GmbH 325. **Getty Images** Eric Feferberg/
AFF 332. **iStock** BreakingTheWalls 3; gilaxia 7, 11; halbergman 13; igorrr 321;
itakdalee 327 above left; Jeja 14; kaisersosa67 16; mythja 331; Rouzes 327 left;
Savushkin 327 below right; StevanZZ 4; StudioM1 1; wwing 328. **Richard
Brendon** 336. **SEGUIN MOREAU** 323. **Unsplash** Zachariah Hagy 6.

HUGH
JOHNSON'S
POCKET
WINE
BOOK
2020

GENERAL EDITOR
MARGARET RAND

Acknowledgements

This store of detailed recommendations comes partly from my own notes and mainly from those of a great number of kind friends. Without the generous help and cooperation of innumerable winemakers, merchants and critics, I could not attempt it. I particularly want to thank the following for help with research or in the areas of their special knowledge:

Ian D'Agata, Helena Baker, Amanda Barnes, Lana Bortolot, Jim Budd, Michael Cooper, Michael Edwards, Sarah Jane Evans MW, Elizabeth Gabay, Susan Gordon, Caroline Gilby MW, Anthony Gismondi, Paul Gregutt, Michael Karam, Anne Krebiehl MW, James Lawther MW, Konstantinos Lazarakis MW, John Livingstone-Learmonth, Michele Longo, Campbell Mattinson, Adam Montefiore, Jasper Morris MW, Ch'ng Poh Tiong, André Ribeirinho, Margaret Rand, Ulrich Sautter, Eleonora Scholes, Paul Strang, Sean Sullivan, Tim Teichgraeber, Gal Zohar, Philip van Zyl.

Contents

How to use this book

The top line of most entries consists of the following information:

1. Aglianico del Vulture Bas

2. r dr (s/sw sp)

3. ★★★

4. 10' 11 12 13 14' 15 (16)

1. Aglianico del Vulture Bas

Wine name and the region the wine comes from, abbreviations of regions are listed in each section.

2. r dr (s/sw sp)

Whether it is red, rosé or white (or brown), dry, sweet or sparkling, or several of these (and which is most important):

r	red
p	rosé
w	white
br	brown
dr	dry*
sw	sweet
s/sw	semi-sweet
sp	sparkling

( ) brackets here denote a less important wine
* assume wine is dry when dr or sw are not indicated

3. ★★★

Its general standing as to quality: a necessarily rough-and-ready guide based on its current reputation as reflected in its prices:

★	plain, everyday quality
★★	above average
★★★	well known, highly reputed
★★★★	grand, prestigious, expensive

So much is more or less objective. Additionally there is a subjective rating:

★ etc.   Stars are coloured for any wine that, in my experience, is usually especially good within its price range. There are good everyday wines as well as good luxury wines. This system helps you find them.

4. 10' 11 12 13 14' 15 (16)

Vintage information: those recent vintages that are outstanding, and of these, which are ready to drink this year, and which will probably improve with keeping. Your choice for current drinking should be one of the vintage years printed in **bold** type. Buy light-type years for further maturing.

16 etc.   recommended years that may be currently available

14' etc.   vintage regarded as particularly successful for the property in question

11 etc.   years in bold should be ready for drinking (those not in bold will benefit from keeping)

13 etc.   vintages in colour are those recommended as first choice for drinking in 2020. (*See also* Bordeaux introduction, p.100.)

(17) etc.   provisional rating

The German vintages work on a different principle again: *see* p.156.

Other abbreviations & styles

DYA	drink the youngest available
NV	vintage not normally shown on label; in Champagne this means a blend of several vintages for continuity
CHABLIS	properties, areas or terms cross-referred within the section; all grapes cross-ref to Grape Varieties chapter on pp.16–26
Foradori	entries styled this way indicate wine especially enjoyed by Hugh Johnson (mid-2018–19)

Agenda 2020

In case you think the world of wine just plods along year after year, Champagne the same, Bordeaux the same, Burgundy more expensive, Napa ditto, Oz Australier than ever, that's not what it looks like from here. Whether you're talking global or local, climate or grape, or soil, or owner, or machinery, or chemistry, or even language, it's changed.

Most of the changes are organic – not in the sulphur-free sense, but arising naturally from the metabolism of the wine industry. Its interests push and pull each other, as they do in any sprawling business. Marketing tells production what it wants; production tries to oblige, and the result is a compromise – maybe a gem, maybe a turkey, maybe a Yellowtail creature that will sell millions of cases.

Nature forces changes: frost, flood and drought (mostly drought) push wine-growers this way and that. There are producers who shelter themselves from natural fluctuations: canny people in the Champagne business, or Sherry bodegas, or any long-term blenders out to achieve continuity may find their stocks squeezed, but risk less from nature's bloody-mindedness.

Fashion: does it force change, or follow it? Fashion plays a bigger and bigger role in what we drink, but a mysterious one. On the one hand it is fickle, suddenly making a decent obscure wine like Albariño an international hit; on the other it can cast wines as glorious as German Rieslings and the finest Sherries into a limbo that can last for a generation or more.

Obvious cases of individual influence changing tastes are not common; in fact, Robert Parker's push for the sort of wines he enjoys, and its success, remains unique. Why did it do so well?

Because he provided a simple scoring system to go with it, and one that Americans could grasp instinctively. High school marks go up to 100 – but effectively discount the first 50 points, so the real scale is 50–100; a 50-point system ending in an inflated result 95 looks better than 45. In practice no one scores any wine lower than 70 – so really a 30-point scale in which you can score 100! In grade terms 70 is a D – bordering on a Fail. Above 90 is grade A, 80–89 is B, 70–79 is C. In school terms any wine considered worth critical attention gets a B, and any "fine" wine an A. No wonder winemakers liked it. Wines, though, aren't children and don't do exams.

Now that the 100-point system has gone mainstream and is
no longer under Parker's supervision it means less and less.
Sadly, almost every wine magazine and website now feels obliged
to adopt it. Can you take it seriously? We are left juggling 89s,
92s and 94s given by different authorities, until in desperation
we are offered an average of averages. There is a better way:
called the market.

The internet gives us access to real-time wine prices.
Winesearcher.com tells you instantly what price almost any
wine, from any producer, of any available vintage, is fetching
in almost any market. It also tells you how much is available,
auction prices and a wide range of critical opinion. (Even an
averaged 100-point score.) Adam Smith would love it.

Then on the front line there are more and more sommeliers.
Sommeliers have come a long way from the day when in a
three-star Paris restaurant I politely pointed out to the resplendent
functionary that what the château offered as a St-Émilion was in
fact in St-Estèphe. "Oh," said he, "is it?" and producing a stub of
pencil amended the bible-like Carte des Vins. No, your modern
sommelier is formidably qualified. My restaurant policy these
days is to outline my menu, emphasize that tonight is not Gala
Night, and ask him or her (all right, them) to surprise me. I meet
all sorts of Greek gems and Tasmanian treasures this way.

Sommeliers lead to more and more specialist glassware,
demanding a size and a level of fragility that would never do
at home. It was George Riedel from Austria who persuaded
the world that every class and style of wine needed a different
glass – all huge. Cupboards round the world were filled to
bursting with his elegant monsters. But times change; today
the flat-bottomed (still huge) glass seems to be the thing –
and my friend and colleague Jancis Robinson has gone in the
opposite direction, asserting that a single model (hers) is ideal
for all sorts of wine. (It is generous – and has a flat bottom).
But then her domestic practice is one I admire. She eschews
a table covered with glasses: It's one glass per person, however
many different wines. She provides a "tip-bucket" for the
remainders of wines that don't get drunk before she pours the
next. The formula works for wine professionals. My guests,
alas, always want to hang on to all their glasses, sipping away
long after I move to serve the next wine.

The concomitant to super-thin, and super-light, glasses is,
of course, the heavyweight bottle. It probably started in Italy;
a producer wants to emphasize the specialness (and price) of
his wine so he orders bottles that weigh as much empty as a
normal bottle does full. His competitors of course follow suit.
Supermarket customers, perhaps less skilled at reading labels

than weighing bottles, are impressed. Glass factories are happy. Transport costs go up. Only the poor old planet has another burden to bear. The screwcap closure, on the other hand, has my enthusiastic endorsement for all but a few slow-developing wines, certainly for any you open as soon as you get home.

A handful of wine-writers make it their business to coin new wine-words rather than just fruit similes. Andrew Jefford is perhaps the most poetically prolific: who can resist "A wine that leans on the wind and strains at the leash". Tricky for other writers to apply, though. Some words seem to ring bells all round; they get adopted straight away and just as soon, I fear, lose their intended meaning. "Citrus" has become the adjective (though not "citrusy". Like "crispy" – what is wrong with "crisp"?). Any hint of sharpness, as in a lemon or lime, is currently labelled "citrus".

And, of course, "mineral". For a couple of years I tried to ban it from this book as being near to meaningless – which in a literal sense it is. Then someone suggested it evokes the electrical energy arising when two complementary minerals collide. Electricity, or at least energy, made more sense. What about "crystalline", the latest coinage, along with "precise"? I see exactly what their initiators were driving at, but as they join the fruit-salad clichés on back labels and pub menus they will need fresh metaphors to replace them.

The mythology of wine is ever fertile. You find more and more "single-vineyard" wines, as though grapes were automatically better for coming from one patch. It may be so – or not. And *vins de garde*. It is true that the best wines of the "best" regions usually need a few years in bottle to reach their full potential. Sometimes many years. Does it follow that a wine is better for being a slow starter? It could simply mean it is not very agreeable to drink at any age.

Enough is changing, in short, to justify yet another *Pocket Wine Book*, my 43rd. The facts keep changing; the world keeps changing. It is just my good fortune to have hit on that priceless commodity, built-in obsolescence.

The main sound emanating from wine regions this year as picking finished was a sigh of relief. In 2017 there was everything from frost to fires; in 2018, by contrast, some regions would quite like to talk about a vintage of the century. The only reason they don't is because they know that our reaction would be "What? Another one?"

In **England** it shows signs of being the best vintage ever, with a plentiful crop of ripe and healthy grapes. More than one producer plans to make a burgundy-style red Pinot Noir this year, and all the bubbly-makers are cheerful.

Not everything went smoothly everywhere. Northern Europe's wet spring meant that mildew staged some ferocious attacks in **Bordeaux**, and if growers were not quick on their toes they could lose a large part of their crop. One grower blamed *le pont* – the habit of taking life easy on Friday, the bridge to the weekend – for a lot of the damage. This year, if you couldn't get your vineyard teams out on Friday, Saturday or Sunday or whenever they were needed, you paid the price. Even the most conscientious growers, however, are beginning to ask if organic viticulture is really viable in Bordeaux when disease pressure is this great. But those who survived – and not everybody was affected – made splendid wines. Sauternes is happy, as well, with some shrivelling of ripe grapes followed by plentiful botrytis.

Burgundy, by contrast, had a relatively calm year. The usual news stories about hailstones the size of golf balls didn't materialize this year. Mildew was a problem, however, and as ever, detailed vineyard work was the only answer. Quality looks good.

Mildew was a problem in the **Rhône**, too, with the loss of half the Grenache in some parts of the south, though a June mistral helped. Summer was a scorcher, but a bit of rainfall in August kept the ripening process ticking along; even so, acidity is fairly low. Tannins in the reds are velvety; whites were often picked early to retain that precious acidity.

In **Champagne** they're using words like "fabulous", "mind-boggling", "extraordinary" – from which you might infer that they're rather pleased. The pattern was the same: a cold, wet spring, then a hot, dry summer. There was a bit of hail, a bit of mildew and picking started early, hastily bringing more than one chef de cave back from the beach. Even the first tastings of the *vins clairs* confirmed that these are wonderfully ripe, rich and balanced wines, though not completely homogeneous. Expect a good crop of vintage wines and prestige cuvées from 2018

Vintage report 2018

in years to come, and plenty of reserve wines stashed away to replace those they've had to use up recently. Vintage years come round more often than ever these days. Generosity was the word in **Alsace**, as well: after 2017's record low, says Hugel, "It feels good to see grapes on the vines." Pinot Noir looks good, as well as the white grapes.

The wet spring might have been a worry in France, but in the **Douro** it brought an end to 20 consecutive dry months. Nature overcompensated, as usual, with 90mm (3.5in) of rain in less than two hours in Pinhão, and there was massive erosion, with olive trees scarred by the stones flung at them by rainwater gushing down the hillsides. Yields across the country except for the Alentejo are very low, though quality is very good for both Port and Douro table wines.

Northern **Italy** had high yields and healthy ones; Tuscany had mildew but no hail, and results look promising, though the rainy spring "required solid nerves", says Axel Heinz, winemaker at Ornellaia.

Germany seems to have had a vintage weirdly close to perfect: hot, dry, disease-free, pest-free, with good yields, and sweet wines as a sort of *bonne bouche* at the end. They reckon they're getting better at dealing with hot summers: the wines won't be overripe or too heavy. Definitely wines to buy.

South Africa had a generally small harvest in 2018 because of its long-lasting drought, and the smallest of all was in Swartland. In spite of that quality looks good: all those heat-loving grapes – bush-vine Chenin Blanc, Grenache, Marsanne, Viognier – that are Swartland's star turns produced intense, weighty wines.

And **California**? Much of it was rather calm. Drought continues to be a problem, forest fires wreaked (wrought?) terrifying damage, including to the newish Malibu Coast AVA, but most producers reported a hot July and a cool August; drought in Santa Barbara County, but generally good flavours at relatively low sugar levels. Wildfires affected **Oregon** as well, and a pall of smoke hung over Willamette Valley for a few days, but winemakers reported a beautiful year, with record sunshine and high temperatures. Rain arrived just in time to revive the vines and cool the temperatures in time for harvest, and in spite of the heat, the Pinot Noirs seem to have good acidity. **Washington** was warm, too, and like Oregon it cooled in the nick of time. Cabernet Sauvignon looks good, as does Syrah. In **New York**'s Finger Lakes, however, it was a summer of rain, and the threat of rot that goes with it. There was hot weather too, though again it eased off in time for picking, but nobody would have called it an easy vintage. Sugar levels are lower than usual, but flavour and ripeness are all there.

How many wines these days really need to be aged? It always used to be a joke about Australian wines, that the only ageing they got was in the car going home from the bottle shop. Take a look around now and you'll find that the rest of the world is quietly following.

Take the 2017 vintage in **Burgundy**. These are such succulent, aromatic, taut wines, both white and red, that they cry Drink Me! Now! They are simply delectable; and of course, for the first time for a couple of years, there are plenty of them. Quantities of individual crus from individual producers might be small – that's the way Burgundy is – but overall, if you want to make this the year you start investigating Pinot Noir in its heartland, you can hardly go wrong. Yes, the Grands Crus from top growers will all be sold by now, to the big-hitter buyers: the same ones go round all the major merchants, getting what allocations they can from each. But by the time this book appears there will still be simpler wines – Bourgogne Rouge and Blanc, some Premiers Crus, some wines from the Mâconnais and Côte Chalonaise, on merchants' lists. Buy them. The whites are looking terrific – they're the best white burgundies for some years. The reds are perhaps a shade behind the whites, but they are delicious, all black fruit and crunchy textures, very pure and tense.

The truth is, many merchants will be delighted to get your telephone call. They need buyers like you: the lesser wines are in much more generous supply than the top ones, and the big spenders probably can't be bothered with them. Which leaves the field open for you. Go to a burgundy specialist, because they'll have had the prettiest wines from the get-go. And enjoy. But remember the reds of a good vintage like this keep getting better for years.

Other 2017s? Much of the **rest of Europe** had a tough time of it. The wines are good, and of course for every producer hit by frost or hail there's another who got away with it. There are good wines everywhere, and many of them can be drunk right now.

Yes, red **Bordeaux** can need longer, just as burgundy will close up after a couple of years and need longer to emerge. But **Riesling** doesn't seem to do that now; it's drinkable all the way through. **Grüner Veltliner** too. **Garnacha**, from new-wave producers who don't kill it with oak and overextraction, is wonderful young. Young **Rhône**, young **Nebbiolo**: same story. **Barolo** needs time.

Vintage Port: 2017s, opened young, before they've had time to close up, will be divine. Forget dusty-old-bottle stuff. Honestly.

A closer look at 2017

If you like Rhône whites, try Verdicchio

This is not an exact comparison. Rhône blends of Marsanne and Roussanne are redolent of *garrigue* flowers and herbs, with an embracing breadth and suppleness coupled with some enlivening phenolic bitterness. Verdicchio has plenty of tannic briskness – it's one of those whites that Italians regard as substitute reds – allied to citrus and melon fruit with notes of chamomile and apple. It's quite a gutsy wine, rich but dry, excellent with food, and it ages to honey and beeswax flavours. Standards are high in the Marches region, and you'll find the names of the very best producers on p.152. Lugana from Garda is the same grape.

If you like Rheingau Riesling, try New Zealand Riesling

I wouldn't have written that a couple of years ago. But the latest crop of NZ Rieslings suggests that they're getting the grape completely right: tense, linear and concentrated. Riesling doesn't work if you're afraid of that tension: you have to go for it. In Germany's Rheingau, they know exactly what they're doing, and are adept at reflecting the differences of each vineyard site. NZ is still on a learning curve in that respect, but the linearity and the tension are there in the glass. Felton Road is the estate in the lead, making characterful, pungent, detailed wines that will stand against any in the world, from biodynamically farmed vineyards.

If you like Loire whites, try Swartland

The more I taste Swartland whites, the more I wonder why I ever drink anything else. I could say the same for the reds, it's true, but let's focus on the whites here. They tend to be based on Chenin Blanc, and for years Chenin Blanc here was regarded as only fit for cheap bottlings. Then a few imaginative winemakers came along, looked at the old dry-farmed bush-vines growing there and the concentrated fruit they produced, and wondered if the world was missing a trick. The result is some of the finest whites around anywhere, with tense concentration, herbal, salty freshness, great elegance and complexity and the ability to age. Everything you'd expect from top Loire Chenin, in fact, except the tendency to sweetness.

If you like Sauternes, try Vin de Constance

It might seem perverse to point you from an entire region to a single producer, but a bit of perversity never hurt anyone. Vin de Constance has been around since 1685 but has had its ups and downs, and at the moment it's on a very impressive up. The 2015 is the best I've ever tasted, all citrus and pineapple, orange peel and pith, acidity and structure with a very fine line of tannin running through a tense, linear structure. It has great concentration and weightless weight. It's sweet and refreshing, perhaps narrower in profile than Sauternes, and made from different grapes: Muscat de Frontignan instead of Sauternes' blend of Sémillon and Sauvignon Blanc. I can imagine it with treacle tart.

If you like Southern Rhône reds, try Lebanon

Okay, the grapes are different, but you'll recognize the feel of the wine – and the French heritage. Southern Rhône relies on Grenache, Mourvèdre and the rest of a substantial Mediterranean crew, for lavender- and herb-scented blends that combine breadth and tightness, and that mature to notes of leather and undergrowth. Lebanon blends red grapes in whatever way it pleases: you'll find Cabernet Sauvignon with Syrah and/or Grenache and/or Cinsault, or Cinsault on its own, or Mourvèdre with Cabernet Sauvignon – you get the picture. Rules do not intrude when it comes to blends. The wines vary in quality, it's true, but where there are faults they're usually ones of overoaking. The best wines (for which *see* p.239) are supple, complex and aromatic with leather, earth, spice, balsamic cherries, flowers and herbs, with moderate alcohol of under 14%.

If you like Beaujolais, try Okanagan Gamay

I could also say, if you like Gamay, drink more of it. Beaujolais the region is not flourishing, even though its wines are better than ever: more characterful, finer, more precise. (No, I'm not talking about Nouveau; let's forget about Beaujolais Nouveau.) Gamay at its best has all the freshness, juiciness and expression you could want, and the crus are like burgundy for beginners. But should you happen on some Gamay from Canada's Okanagan region, from the steep and beautiful hills surrounding the lake of the same name, seize it. Okanagan doesn't grow that much Gamay, but should grow more, to make more of this wonderfully silky, supple, spicy red. There's even a bit of pét-nat Gamay, all rose petals and sourdough.

If you like St-Émilion, try Napa Cabernet

Napa Cabernet is changing. Yes, there are still producers stuck in the "luxury goods" mindset, who can't or won't escape overripeness, overextraction and overoaking. But gradually they're moving from being fruit bombs to being something more serious. As the oak retreats so the fruit is exposed – and it can turn out to be supple, silky, spicy, sweetly ripe, rather seductive, and definitely alliterative. Napa has always told us that it has wonderful terroir, and now it's starting to show us too. Its Cabernet is not exactly like anything from Bordeaux, but the ripe, Merlot-driven fruit-cakiness of St-Émilion is the nearest comparison. And not a bad one.

Grape varieties

In the past two decades a radical change has come about in all except the most long-established wine countries: the names of a handful of grape varieties have become the ready-reference to wine. In senior wine countries, above all France and Italy, more complex traditions prevail. All wine of old prestige is known by its origin, more or less narrowly defined – not just by the particular fruit juice that fermented. For the present the two notions are in rivalry. Eventually the primacy of place over fruit will become obvious, at least for wines of quality. But for now, for most people, grape tastes are the easy reference point – despite the fact that they are often confused by the added taste of oak. If grape flavours were really all that mattered, this would be a very short book. But of course they *do* matter, and a knowledge of them both guides you to flavours you enjoy and helps comparisons between regions. Hence the originally Californian term "varietal wine", meaning, in principle, made from one grape variety. At least seven varieties – Cabernet Sauvignon, Pinot Noir, Riesling, Sauvignon Blanc, Chardonnay, Gewurztraminer and Muscat – taste and smell distinct and memorable enough to form international wine categories. To these add Merlot, Malbec, Syrah, Sémillon, Chenin Blanc, Pinots Blanc and Gris, Sylvaner, Viognier, Nebbiolo, Sangiovese, Tempranillo. The following are the best and/or most popular wine grapes.

All grapes and synonyms are cross-referenced in small capitals throughout every section of this book.

Grapes for red wine

Agiorgitiko Greek; the grape of Nemea, now planted almost everywhere. Versatile and delicious, from soft and charming to dense and age-worthy. A must-try.

Aglianico S Italian, the grape of Taurasi; dark, deep and fashionable.

Alicante Bouschet Used to be shunned, now stylish in Alentejo, Chile, esp old vines.

Aragonez *See* TEMPRANILLO.

Auxerrois *See* MALBEC, if red. White Auxerrois has its own entry in White Grapes.

Băbească Neagră Traditional "black grandmother grape" of Moldova; light body and ruby-red colour.

Babić Dark grape from Dalmatia, grown in stony seaside v'yds round Šibenik. Exceptional quality potential.

Baga Portugal. Bairrada grape. Dark and tannic. Great potential but hard to grow.

Barbera Widely grown in Italy, best in Piedmont: high acidity, low tannin, cherry fruit. Ranges from barriqued and serious to semi-sweet and frothy. Fashionable in California and Australia; promising in Argentina.

Blauburger Austrian cross between BLAUER PORTUGIESER and BLAUFRÄNKISCH. Makes simple wines.

Blauburgunder *See* PINOT N.

Blauer Portugieser Central European, esp Germany (Rheinhessen, Pfalz, mostly for rosé), Austria, Hungary. Light, fruity reds: drink young, slightly chilled.

Blaufränkisch (Kékfrankos, Lemberger, Modra Frankinja) Widely planted in Austria's Mittelburgenland: medium-bodied, peppery acidity, a characteristic salty note, berry aromas and eucalyptus. Often blended with CAB SAUV or ZWEIGELT. Lemberger in Germany (speciality of Württemberg), Kékfrankos in Hungary, Modra Frankinja in Slovenia.

Boğazkere Tannic and Turkish. Produces full-bodied wines.

Bonarda Ambiguous name. In Oltrepò Pavese, an alias for Croatina, soft fresh *frizzante* and still red. In Lombardy and Emilia-Romagna an alias for Uva Rara. Different in Piedmont. Argentina's Bonarda can be any of these, or something else. None are great.

Bouchet St-Émilion alias for CAB FR.

Brunello SANGIOVESE, splendid at Montalcino.

Cabernet Franc [Cab Fr] The lesser of two sorts of Cab grown in B'x, but dominant in St-Émilion. Outperforms CAB SAUV in Loire (Chinon, Saumur-Champigny, rosé), in Hungary (depth and complexity in Villány and Szekszárd) and often in Italy. Much of ne Italy's Cab Fr turned out to be CARMENÈRE. Used in B'x blends of Cab Sauv/MERLOT across the world.

Cabernet Sauvignon [Cab Sauv] Grape of great character: slow-ripening, spicy, herby, tannic, with blackcurrant aroma. Main grape of the Médoc; also makes some of the best California, S American, E European reds. Vies with SHIRAZ in Australia. Grown almost everywhere, and led vinous renaissance in eg. Italy. Top wines need ageing; usually benefits from blending with eg. MERLOT, CAB FR, SYRAH, TEMPRANILLO, SANGIOVESE, etc. Makes aromatic rosé.

Cannonau GRENACHE in its Sardinian manifestation; can be v. fine, potent.

Carignan (Carignane, Carignano, Cariñena) Low-yielding old vines now v. fashionable everywhere from s of France to Chile; best: Corbières. Lots of depth and vibrancy. Overcropped Carignan is wine-lake fodder. Common in North Africa, Spain (as Cariñena) and California.

Carignano *See* CARIGNAN.

Cariñena *See* CARIGNAN.

Carmenère Old B'x variety now a star, rich and deep, in Chile (where it's pronounced *carmeneary*). B'x looking at it again.

Castelão *See* PERIQUITA.

Cencibel *See* TEMPRANILLO.

Chiavennasca *See* NEBBIOLO.

Cinsault (Cinsaut) A staple of s France, v.gd if low-yielding, wine-lake stuff if not. Makes gd rosé. One of parents of PINOTAGE.

Cornalin du Valais Swiss speciality with high potential, esp in Valais.

Corvina Dark and spicy; one of best grapes in Valpolicella blend. Corvinone, even darker, is a separate variety.

Côt *See* MALBEC.

Dolcetto Source of soft, seductive dry red in Piedmont. Now high fashion.

Dornfelder Gives deliciously light reds, straightforward, often rustic, and well-coloured in Germany, parts of the USA, England. German plantings have doubled since 2000.

Duras Spicy, peppery, structured; exclusive to Gaillac and parts of Tarn Valley, Southwest France.

Fer Servadou Exclusive to Southwest France, aka Mansois in Marcillac, Braucol in Gaillac and Pinenc in St-Mont. Redolent of red summer fruits and spice.

Fetească Neagră Romania: "black maiden grape" with potential as showpiece variety; can give deep, full-bodied wines with character. Acreage increasing.

Frühburgunder An ancient German mutation of PINOT N, mostly in Ahr but also in Franken and Württemberg, where it is confusingly known as Clevner. Lower acidity than Pinot N.

Gamay The Beaujolais grape: v. light, fragrant wines, best young, except in Beaujolais crus (see France) where quality can be high, wines for 2–10 yrs. Grown in the Loire Valley, in central France, in Switzerland and Savoie. California's Napa Gamay is Valdiguié.

Gamza *See* KADARKA.

Garnacha (Cannonau, Garnatxa, Grenache) Widespread pale, potent grape fashionable with *terroiristes*, because it expresses its site. The base of Ch-du-Pape. Also gd for rosé and *vin doux naturel* – esp in the s of France, Spain and California – but also the mainstay of beefy Priorat. Old-vine versions prized in South Australia. Usually blended with other varieties. Cannonau in Sardinia, Grenache in France.

Garnatxa *See* GARNACHA.

Graciano Spanish; part of Rioja blend. Aroma of violets, tannic, lean structure, a bit like PETIT VERDOT. Difficult to grow but increasingly fashionable.

Grenache *See* GARNACHA.

Grignolino Italy: gd everyday table wine in Piedmont.

Kadarka (Gamza) Spicy, light East Europe reds. In Hungary revived, esp for Bikavér.

Kalecik Karasi Turkish: sour-cherry fruit, fresh, supple. A bit like GAMAY. Drink young.

Kékfrankos Hungarian BLAUFRÄNKISCH.

Lagrein N Italian, dark, bitter finish, rich, plummy. DOC in Alto Adige (*see* Italy).

Lambrusco Productive grape of the lower Po Valley; quintessentially Italian, cheerful, sweet and fizzy red.

Lefkada Rediscovered Cypriot variety, higher quality than MAVRO. Usually blended as tannins can be aggressive.

Lemberger *See* BLAUFRÄNKISCH.

Malbec (Auxerrois, Côt) Minor in B'x, major in Cahors (alias Auxerrois), the star in Argentina. Dark, dense, tannic but fleshy wine capable of real quality. High-altitude versions in Argentina are bee's knees. Bringing Cahors back into fashion.

Maratheftiko Deep-coloured Cypriot grape with quality potential.

Marselan CAB SAUV x GRENACHE, 1961. Gd colour, structure, supple tannins, ages well.

Mataro *See* MOURVÈDRE.

Mavro Most planted black grape of Cyprus but only moderate quality. Best for rosé.

Mavrodaphne Greek; means "black laurel". Sweet fortifieds, speciality of Patras, also in Cephalonia. Dry versions too, great promise.

Mavrotragano Greek, almost extinct but now revived; on Santorini. Top quality.

Mavrud Probably Bulgaria's best. Spicy, dark, plummy late-ripener native to Thrace. Ages well.

Melnik Bulgarian grape from the region of the same name. Dark colour and a nice dense, tart-cherry character. Ages well.

Mencía Making waves in Bierzo, N. Spain. Aromatic with steely tannins and lots of acidity.

Merlot The grape behind the great fragrant and plummy wines of Pomerol and (with CAB FR) St-Émilion, a vital element in the Médoc, soft and strong (and *à la mode*) in California, Washington, Chile, Australia. Lighter, often gd in n Italy (can be world-class in Tuscany), Italian Switzerland, Slovenia, Argentina, S Africa, NZ, etc. Perhaps too adaptable for own gd: can be v. dull; less than ripe it tastes green. Much planted in Eastern Europe, esp Romania.

Modra Frankinja See BLAUFRÄNKISCH.

Modri Pinot See PINOT N.

Monastrell See MOURVÈDRE.

Mondeuse Found in Savoie; deep-coloured, gd acidity. Related to SYRAH.

Montepulciano Deep-coloured grape dominant in Italy's Abruzzo and important along Adriatic coast: Marches to s Puglia. Also name of a Tuscan town, unrelated.

Morellino SANGIOVESE in Maremma, s Tuscany. Esp Scansano.

Mourvèdre (Mataro, Monastrell) A star of s France (eg. Bandol, growing influence Châteauneuf-du-Pape), Australia (aka Mataro) and Spain (aka Monastrell). Excellent dark, aromatic, tannic grape, gd for blending. Enjoying new interest in eg. South Australia and California.

Napa Gamay Identical to Valdiguié (s of France). Nothing to get excited about.

Nebbiolo (Chiavennasca, Spanna) One of Italy's best red grapes; makes Barolo, Barbaresco, Gattinara and Valtellina. Intense, nobly fruity, perfumed wine with steely tannin: improves for yrs.

Negroamaro Puglian "black bitter" red grape with potential for either high quality or high volume.

Nerello Mascalese Characterful Sicilian red grape, esp on Etna; elegance potential.

Nero d'Avola Dark-red grape of Sicily, quality levels from sublime to industrial.

Nielluccio Corsican; plenty of acidity and tannin. Gd for rosé.

Öküzgözü Soft, fruity Turkish grape, usually blended with BOĞAZKERE, rather as MERLOT in B'x is blended with CAB SAUV.

País Pioneer Spanish grape in Americas. Rustic; some producers now trying harder.

Pamid Bulgarian: light, soft, everyday red.

Periquita (Castelão) Common in Portugal, esp round Setúbal. Originally nicknamed Periquita after Fonseca's popular (trademarked) brand. Firm-flavoured, raspberryish reds develop a figgish, tar-like quality.

Petite Sirah Nothing to do with SYRAH; gives rustic, tannic, dark wine. Brilliant blended with ZIN in California; also found in South America, Mexico, Australia.

Petit Verdot Excellent but awkward Médoc grape, now increasingly planted in CAB areas worldwide for extra fragrance. Mostly blended but some gd varietals, esp in Virginia.

Pinotage Singular S African cross (PINOT N x CINSAULT). Has had a rocky ride, getting better from top producers. Gd rosé too. "Coffee Pinotage" is espresso-flavoured, sweetish, aimed at youth.

Pinot Crni See PINOT N.

Pinot Meunier (Schwarzriesling) [Pinot M] 3rd grape of Champagne, better known as Meunier, great for blending but transformed into a surprisingly fine wine in its own right as now it's better understood as a bridge between PINOT N and CHARD Best still chalky sites (Damery, Leuvigny, Festigny) nr Épernay.

Pinot Noir (Blauburgunder, Modri Pinot, Pinot Crni, Spätburgunder) [Pinot N] Glory of Burgundy's Côte d'Or: scent, flavour, texture unmatched anywhere. Fine in Alsace. Recent German efforts revolutionary. V.gd in Austria, esp in Kamptal, Burgenland, Thermenregion. Light in Hungary; mainstream, light to weightier in Switzerland (aka Clevner). Splendid in Sonoma, Carneros, Central Coast, also Oregon, Ontario, Yarra Valley, Adelaide Hills, Tasmania, NZ's Central Otago, S Africa's Walker Bay. Some v. pretty Chileans. Promise New French clones promise improvement in Romania. Modri Pinot in Slovenia; probably country's best red. In Italy, best in ne, gets worse as you go s. PINOTS BL and GR mutations of Pinot N.

Plavac Mali (Crljenak) Croatian, and related to ZIN, like so much round here. Lots of quality potential, can age well, though can also be alcoholic and dull.

Primitivo S Italian grape, originally from Croatia, making big, dark, rustic wines, now fashionable because genetically identical to ZIN. Early ripening, hence the name. The original name for both seems to be Tribidrag.

Refosco (Refošk) Various DOCs in Italy, esp Colli Orientali. Deep, flavoursome and age-worthy wines, particularly in warmer climates. Dark, high acidity. Refošk in Slovenia and pointe e, genetically different, tastes similar.

Refošk See REFOSCO.

Roter Veltliner Austrian; unrelated to GRÜNER V. There is also a Frühroter and a Brauner Veltliner.

Rubin Bulgarian cross NEBBIOLO X SYRAH. Peppery, full-bodied.

Sagrantino Italian grape grown in Umbria for powerful, cherry-flavoured wines.

St-Laurent Dark, smooth, full-flavoured Austrian speciality. Can be light and juicy or deep and structured. Also in Pfalz.

Sangiovese (Brunello, Morellino, Sangioveto) Principal red grape of Tuscany and central Italy. Hard to get right, but sublime and long-lasting when it is. Dominant in Chianti, Vino Nobile, Brunello di Montalcino, Morellino di Scansano and various fine IGT offerings. Also in Umbria (eg. Montefalco and Torgiano) and across the Apennines in Romagna and Marches. Not so clever in the warmer, lower-altitude v'yds of the Tuscan coast, nor in other parts of Italy despite its nr-ubiquity. Interesting in Australia.

Sangioveto See SANGIOVESE.

Saperavi Main red of Georgia, Ukraine, etc. Blends well with CAB SAUV (eg. in Moldova). Huge potential, seldom gd winemaking.

Schiava See TROLLINGER.

Schioppettino NE Italian, high acidity, high quality. Elegant, refined, can age.

Schwarzriesling PINOT M in Württemberg.

Sciacarello Corsican, herby and peppery. Not v. tannic.

Shiraz See SYRAH.

Spanna See NEBBIOLO.

Spätburgunder German for PINOT N.

Syrah (Shiraz) The great Rhône red grape: tannic, purple, peppery wine that matures superbly. Important as Shiraz in Australia, increasingly gd under either name in Chile, S Africa, terrific in NZ (esp Hawke's Bay). Widely grown.

Tannat Raspberry-perfumed, highly tannic force behind Madiran, Tursan and other firm reds from Southwest France. Also rosé. Now the star of Uruguay.

Tempranillo (Aragonez, Cecibel, Tinto Fino, Tinta del País, Tinta Roriz, Ull de Llebre) Aromatic, fine Rioja grape, called Ull de Llebre in Catalonia, Cencibel in La Mancha, Tinto Fino in Ribera del Duero, Tinta Roriz in Douro, Tinta del País in Castile, Aragonez in s Portugal. Now Australia too. V. fashionable; elegant in cool climates, beefy in warm. Early ripening, long maturing.

Teran (Terrano) Close cousin of REFOSCO, esp on limestone (karst) in Slovenia.

Teroldego Rotaliano Trentino's best indigenous variety; serious, full-flavoured wine, esp on the flat Campo Rotaliano.

Tinta Amarela *See* TRINCADEIRA.

Tinta del País *See* TEMPRANILLO.

Tinta Negra (Negramoll) Until recently called Tinta Negra Mole. Easily Madeira's most planted grape and the mainstay of cheaper Madeira. Now coming into its own in Colheita wines (*see* Portugal).

Tinta Roriz *See* TEMPRANILLO.

Tinto Fino *See* TEMPRANILLO.

Touriga Nacional [Touriga N] The top Port grape, now widely used in the Douro for floral, stylish table wines. Australian Touriga is usually this; California's Touriga can be either this or Touriga Franca.

Trincadeira (Tinta Amarela) Portuguese; v.gd in Alentejo for spicy wines. Tinta Amarela in the Douro.

Trollinger (Schiava, Vernatsch) Popular pale red in Württemberg; aka Vernatsch and Schiava. Covers group of vines, not necessarily related. In Italy, snappy, brisk.

Vernatsch *See* TROLLINGER.

Xinomavro Greece's answer to NEBBIOLO. "Sharp-black"; the basis for Naoussa, Rapsani, Goumenissa, Amindeo. Some rosé, still or sparkling. Top quality, can age for decades. Being tried in China.

Zinfandel [Zin] Fruity, adaptable grape of California with blackberry-like, and sometimes metallic, flavour. Can be structured and gloriously lush, ageing for decades, but also make "blush" pink, usually sweet, jammy. Genetically the same as s Italian PRIMITIVO.

Zweigelt (Blauer Zweigelt) BLAUFRÄNKISCH X ST-LAURENT, popular in Austria for aromatic, dark, supple, velvety wines. Also found in Hungary, Germany.

Grapes for white wine

Airén Bland workhorse of La Mancha, Spain: fresh if made well.

Albariño (Alvarinho) Fashionable, expensive in Spain: apricot-scented, gd acidity. Superb in Rías Baixas; shaping up elsewhere, but not all live up to the hype. Alvarinho in Portugal just as gd: aromatic Vinho Verde, esp in Monção, Melgaço.

Aligoté Burgundy's 2nd-rank white grape. Sharp wine for young drinking, perfect for mixing with cassis (blackcurrant liqueur) to make Kir. Widely planted in East Europe, esp Russia.

Alvarinho *See* ALBARIÑO.

Amigne One of Switzerland's speciality grapes, traditional in Valais, esp Vétroz. Total planted: 43 ha. Full-bodied, tasty, often sweet but also bone-dry.

Ansonica *See* INSOLIA.

Arinto Portuguese; the mainstay of aromatic, citrusy wines in Bucelas; also adds welcome zip to blends, esp in Alentejo.

Arneis Nw Italian. Fine, aromatic, appley-peachy, high-priced grape, DOCG in Roero, DOC in Langhe, Piedmont.

Arvine Rare but excellent Swiss *spécialité*, from Valais. Also Petite Arvine. Dry or sweet, fresh, long-lasting wines with salty finish.

Assyrtiko From Santorini; one of the best grapes of the Mediterranean, balancing power, minerality, extract and high acid. Built to age. Could conquer the world...

Auxerrois Red Auxerrois is a synonym for MALBEC, but white Auxerrois is like a fatter, spicier PINOT BL. Found in Alsace and much used in Crémant; also Germany.

Beli Pinot *See* PINOT BL.

Blanc Fumé *See* SAUV BL.

Boal See BUAL.

Bourboulenc This and the rare Rolle make some of the Midi's best wines.

Bouvier Indigenous aromatic Austrian grape, esp gd for Beerenauslese and Trockenbeerenauslese, rarely for dry wines.

Bual (Boal) Makes top-quality sweet Madeira wines, not quite so rich as MALMSEY.

Carricante Italian. Principal grape of Etna Bianco, regaining ground.

Catarratto Prolific white grape found all over Sicily, esp in w in DOC Alcamo.

Cerceal See SERCIAL.

Chardonnay (Morillon) [Chard] The white grape of Burgundy and Champagne, now ubiquitous worldwide, partly because it is one of the easiest to grow and vinify. Also the name of a Mâcon-Villages commune. The fashion for overoaked butterscotch versions now thankfully over. Morillon in Styria, Austria.

Chasselas (Fendant, Gutedel) Swiss (originated in Vaud). Neutral flavour, takes on local character: elegant (Geneva); refined, full (Vaud); exotic, racy (Valais). Fendant in Valais. Makes almost 3rd of Swiss wines but giving way, esp to red. Gutedel in Germany; grown esp in s Baden. Elsewhere usually a table grape.

Chenin Blanc [Chenin Bl] Wonderful white grape of the middle Loire (Vouvray, Layon, etc). Wine can be dry or sweet (or v. sweet), but with plenty of acidity. Formerly called Steen in S Africa; many ordinary but best noble. California can do it well but doesn't bother.

Cirfandl See ZIERFANDLER.

Clairette Important Midi grape, low-acid, part of many blends. Improved winemaking help.

Colombard Slightly fruity, nicely sharp grape, makes everyday wine in S Africa, California and Southwest France. Often blended.

Dimiat Perfumed Bulgarian grape, made dry or off-dry, or distilled. Far more synonyms than any grape needs.

Ermitage Swiss for MARSANNE.

Ezerjó Hungarian, with sharp acidity. Name means "thousand blessings".

Falanghina Italian: ancient grape of Campanian hills. Gd dense, aromatic, dry.

Fendant See CHASSELAS.

Fernão Pires See MARIA GOMES.

Fetească Albă / Regală Romania has two Fetească grapes, both with slight MUSCAT aroma. F. Regală is a cross of F. Albă and GRASĂ; more finesse, gd for late-harvest wines. F. NEAGRĂ is dark-skinned.

Fiano High-quality grape giving peachy, spicy wine in Campania, s Italy.

Folle Blanche (Gros Plant) High acid/little flavour make this ideal for brandy. Gros Plant in Brittany, Picpoul in Armagnac, but unrelated to true PICPOUL. Also respectable in California.

Friulano (Sauvignonasse, Sauvignon Vert) N Italian: fresh, pungent, subtly floral. Used to be called Tocai Friulano. Best in Collio, Isonzo, Colli Orientali. Found in nearby Slovenia as Sauvignonasse; also in Chile, where it was long confused with SAUV BL. Ex-Tocai in Veneto now known as Tai.

Fumé Blanc See SAUV BL.

Furmint (Šipon) Superb, characterful. The trademark of Hungary, both as the principal grape in Tokaji and as vivid, vigorous table wine, sometimes mineral, sometimes apricot-flavoured, sometimes both. Šipon in Slovenia. Some grown in Rust, Austria for sweet and dry.

Garganega Best grape in Soave blend; also in Gambellara. Top, esp sweet, age well.

Garnacha Blanca (Grenache Blanc) The white version of GARNACHA/Grenache, much used in Spain and s France. Low acidity. Can be innocuous, or surprisingly gd.

Gewurztraminer (Traminac, Traminec, Traminer, Tramini) [Gewurz] One of the most pungent grapes, spicy with aromas of rose petals, face cream, lychees, grapefruit. Wines are often rich and soft, even when fully dry. Best in Alsace; also gd in Germany (Baden, Pfalz, Sachsen), Eastern Europe, Australia, California, Pacific Northwest and NZ. Can be relatively unaromatic if just labelled Traminer (or variants). Italy uses the name Traminer Aromatico for its (dry) "Gewurz" versions. (The name takes an Umlaut in German.) Identical to SAVAGNIN.

Glera Uncharismatic new name for Prosecco vine: Prosecco is now wine only in EU, but still a grape name in Australia.

Godello Top quality (intense, mineral) in nw Spain. Called Verdelho in Dão, Portugal, but unrelated to true VERDELHO.

Grasă (Kövérszőlő) Romanian; name means "fat". Prone to botrytis; important in Cotnari, potentially superb sweet wines. Kövérszőlő in Hungary's Tokaj region.

Graševina See WELSCHRIESLING.

Grauburgunder See PINOT GR.

Grechetto Ancient grape of central and s Italy noted for the vitality and stylishness of its wine. Blended, or used solo in Orvieto.

Greco S Italian: there are various Grecos, probably unrelated, perhaps of Greek origin. Brisk, peachy flavour, most famous as Greco di Tufo. Greco di Bianco is from semi-dried grapes. Greco Nero is a black version.

Grenache Blanc See GARNACHA BLANCA.

Grillo Italy: main grape of Marsala. Also v.gd full-bodied dry table wine.

Gros Plant See FOLLE BLANCHE.

Grüner Veltliner [Grüner V] Austria's fashionable flagship white grape. V. diverse: from simple, peppery, everyday, to great complexity, ageing potential. Found elsewhere in Central Europe and outside.

Gutedel See CHASSELAS.

Hárslevelú Other main grape of Tokaji, but softer, peachier than FURMINT. Name means "linden-leaved". Gd in Somló, Eger as well.

Heida Swiss for SAVAGNIN.

Humagne Swiss speciality, older than CHASSELAS. Fresh, plump, not v. aromatic. Humagne Rouge is not related but increasingly popular: same as Cornalin du Aosta. Cornalin du Valais is different. (Keep up at the back, there.)

Insolia (Ansonica, Inzolia) Sicilian; Ansonica on Tuscan coast. Fresh, racy wine at best. May be semi-dried for sweet wine.

Irsai Olivér Hungarian cross; aromatic, MUSCAT-like wine for drinking young.

Johannisberg Swiss for SILVANER.

Kéknyelú Low-yielding, flavourful grape giving one of Hungary's best whites. Has the potential for fieriness and spice. To be watched.

Kerner Quite successful German cross. Early ripening, flowery (but often too blatant) wine with gd acidity.

Királyleanyka Hungarian; gentle, fresh wines (eg. in Eger).

Koshu Supposedly indigenous Japanese grape/wine, much hyped. Fresh, harmless.

Kövérszőlő See GRASĂ.

Laski Rizling See WELSCHRIESLING.

Leányka Hungarian. Soft, floral wines.

Listán See PALOMINO.

Longyan (Dragon Eye) Chinese original; gd substantial, aromatic wine.

Loureiro Best Vinho Verde grape after ALVARINHO: delicate, floral. Also in Spain.

Macabeo See VIURA.

Maccabeu See VIURA.

Malagousia Rediscovered Greek grape for gloriously perfumed wines.

Malmsey See MALVASIA. The sweetest style of Madeira.

Malvasia (Malmsey, Malvazija, Malvoisie, Marastina) Italy, France and Iberia. Not a single variety but a whole stable, not necessarily related or even alike. Can be white or red, sparkling or still, strong or mild, sweet or dry, aromatic or neutral. Slovenia's and Croatia's version is Malvazija Istarka, crisp and light, or rich, oak-aged. Sometimes called Marastina in Croatia. "Malmsey" (as in the sweetest style of Madeira) is a corruption of Malvasia.

Malvoisie See MALVASIA. A name used for several varieties in France, incl BOURBOULENC, Torbato, VERMENTINO. Also PINOT GR in Switzerland's Valais.

Manseng, Gros / Petit Gloriously spicy, floral whites from Southwest France. The key to Jurançon. Superb late-harvest and sweet wines too.

Maria Gomes (Fernão Pires) Portuguese; aromatic, ripe-flavoured, slightly spicy whites in Barraida and Tejo.

Marsanne (Ermitage) Principal white grape (with ROUSSANNE) of the Northern Rhône (Hermitage St-Joseph, St-Péray). Also gd in Australia, California and (as Ermitage Blanc) the Valais. Soft, full wines that age v. well.

Melon de Bourgogne See MUSCADET.

Misket Bulgarian. Mildly aromatic; the basis of most country whites.

Morillon CHARD in parts of Austria.

Moscatel See MUSCAT.

Moscato See MUSCAT.

Moschofilero Pink-skinned, rose-scented, high-quality, high-acid, low-alcohol Greek grape. Makes white, some pink, some sparkling.

Müller-Thurgau [Müller-T] Aromatic wines to drink young. Makes gd sweet wines but usually dull, often coarse, dry ones. In Germany, most common in Pfalz, Rheinhessen, Nahe, Baden, Franken. Has some merit in Italy's Trentino-Alto Adige, Friuli. Sometimes called Ries x Sylvaner (incorrectly) in Switzerland.

Muscadelle Adds aroma to white B'x, esp Sauternes. In Victoria used (with MUSCAT, to which it is unrelated) for Rutherglen Muscat.

Muscadet (Melon de Bourgogne) Makes light, refreshing, v. dry wines with a seaside tang around Nantes in Brittany. Also found (as Melon) in parts of Burgundy.

Muscat (Moscatel, Moscato, Muskateller) Many varieties; the best is Muscat Blanc à Petits Grains (alias Gelber Muskateller, Rumeni Muškat, Sarga Muskotály, Yellow Muscat). Widely grown, easily recognized, pungent grapes, mostly made into perfumed sweet wines, often fortified, as in France's *vin doux naturel*. Superb, dark and sweet in Australia. Sweet, sometimes v.gd in Spain. Most Hungarian Muskotály is Muscat Ottonel except in Tokaj, where Sarga Muskotály rules, adding perfume (in small amounts) to blends. Occasionally (eg. Alsace, Austria, parts of s Germany) made dry. Sweet Cap Corse Muscats often superb. Light Moscato fizz in n Italy.

Muskateller See MUSCAT.

Narince Turkish; fresh and fruity wines.

Neuburger Austrian, rather neglected; mainly in the Wachau (elegant, flowery), Thermenregion (mellow, ample-bodied) and n Burgenland (strong, full).

Olaszriesling See WELSCHRIESLING.

Païen See SAVAGNIN.

Palomino (Listán) The great grape of Sherry; with little intrinsic character, it gains all from production method. As Listán, makes dry white in Canaries.

Pansa Blanca See XAREL·LO.

Pecorino IGT: not a cheese but alluring dry white from a recently nr-extinct variety. IGT in Colli Pescaresi.

Pedro Ximénez [PX] Makes sweet brown Sherry under its own name, and used in Montilla and Málaga. Also grown in Argentina, the Canaries, Australia, California and S Africa.

Picpoul (Piquepoul) Southern French, best known in Picpoul de Pinet. Should have high acidity. Picpoul Noir is black-skinned.

Pinela Local to Slovenia. Subtle, lowish acidity; drink young.

Pinot Bianco *See* PINOT BL.

Pinot Blanc (Beli Pinot, Pinot Bianco, Weißburgunder) [Pinot Bl] A cousin of PINOT N, similar to but milder than CHARD. Light, fresh, fruity, not aromatic, to drink young. Gd for Italian *spumante*, and potentially excellent in the ne, esp high sites in Alto Adige. Widely grown. Weißburgunder in Germany and best in s: often racier than Chard.

Pinot Gris (Pinot Grigio, Grauburgunder, Ruländer, Sivi Pinot, Szürkebarát) [Pinot Gr] Ultra-popular as Pinot Grigio in n Italy, even for rosé, but top, characterful versions can be excellent (from Alto Adige, Friuli). Cheap versions are just that. Terrific in Alsace for full-bodied, spicy whites. Once important in Champagne. In Germany can be alias Ruländer (sw) or Grauburgunder (dr): best in Baden (esp Kaiserstuhl) and s Pfalz. Szürkebarát in Hungary, Sivi P in Slovenia (characterful, aromatic).

Pošip Croatian; mostly on Korčula. Quite characterful and citrusy; high-yielding.

Prosecco Old name for grape that makes Prosecco. Now you have to call it GLERA.

Renski Rizling Rhine RIES.

Rèze Super-rare ancestral Valais grape used for *vin de glacier*.

Ribolla Gialla / Rebula Acidic but characterful. In Italy, best in Collio. In Slovenia, traditional in Brda. Can be v.gd, even made in eccentric ways.

Rieslaner German cross (SILVANER x RIES); low yields, difficult ripening, now v. rare (less than 50 ha). Makes fine Auslesen in Franken and Pfalz.

Riesling Italico *See* WELSCHRIESLING.

Riesling (Renski Rizling, Rhine Riesling) [Ries] The greatest, most versatile white grape, diametrically opposite in style to CHARD. Offers a range from steely to voluptuous, always positively perfumed, with far more ageing potential than Chard. Great in all styles in Germany; forceful and steely in Austria; lime-cordial and toast fruit in South Australia; rich and spicy in Alsace; Germanic and promising in NZ, NY State, Pacific Northwest; has potential in Ontario, S Africa. In warmer climates soon smells of petrol.

Rkatsiteli Found widely in Eastern Europe, Russia, Georgia. Can stand cold winters and has high acidity: protects to a degree from poor winemaking. Also in ne US.

Robola In Greece (Cephalonia) a top-quality, floral grape, unrelated to RIBOLLA GIALLA.

Roditis Pink grape, all over Greece, usually making whites. Gd when yields low.

Roter Veltliner Austrian; unrelated to GRÜNER V. There is also a Frühroter and an (unrelated) Brauner Veltliner.

Rotgipfler Austrian; indigenous to Thermenregion. With ZIERFANDLER, makes lively, lush, aromatic blend.

Roussanne Rhône grape of real finesse, now popping up in California and Australia. Can age many yrs.

Ruländer *See* PINOT GR.

Sauvignonasse *See* FRIULANO.

Sauvignon Blanc [Sauv Bl] Distinctive aromatic, grassy-to-tropical wines, pungent in NZ, often minerally in Sancerre, riper in Australia. V.gd in Rueda, Austria, n Italy (Isonzo, Piedmont, Alto Adige), Chile's Casablanca and S Africa. Blended with SÉM in B'x. Can be austere or buxom (or indeed nauseating). Sauvignon Gris is a pink-skinned, less aromatic version of Sauv Bl with untapped potential.

Sauvignon Vert *See* FRIULANO.

Savagnin (Heida, Païen) Grape for *vin jaune* from Jura: aromatic form is GEWURZ. In Switzerland known as Heida, Païen or Traminer. Full-bodied, high acidity.

Scheurebe (Sämling) Grapefruit-scented German RIES x SILVANER (possibly). In Pfalz v. successful, esp for Auslese and up. Can be weedy: must be v. ripe to be gd.

Sémillon [Sém] Contributes lusciousness to Sauternes but decreasingly important for Graves and other dry white B'x. Grassy if not fully ripe, but can make soft dry wine of great ageing potential. Superb in Australia; NZ and S Africa promising.

Sercial (Cerceal) Portuguese: makes the driest Madeira. Cerceal, also Portuguese, seems to be this plus any of several others.

Seyval Blanc [Seyval El] French-made hybrid of French and American vines. V. hardy and attractively fruity. Popular and reasonably successful in e US and England but dogmatically banned by EU for "quality" wines.

Silvaner (Johannisberg, Sylvaner) Can be excellent in Germany's Rheinhessen, Pfalz, esp Franken: plant/earth flavours and mineral notes. V.gd (and powerful) as Johannisberg in the Valais, Switzerland. The lightest of the Alsace grapes.

Šipon See FURMINT.

Sivi Pinot See PINOT GR.

Spätrot See ZIERFANDLER.

Sylvaner See SILVANER.

Tămâioasă Românească Romanian: "frankincense" grape, with exotic aroma and taste. Belongs to MUSCAT family.

Torrontés Name given to a number of grapes, mostly with an aromatic, floral character, sometimes soapy. A speciality of Argentina; also in Spain. DYA.

Traminac Or Traminec. See GEWURZ.

Traminer Or Tramini (Hungary). See GEWURZ.

Trebbiano (Ugni Blanc) Principal white grape of Tuscany, found all over Italy in many different guises. Rarely rises above the plebeian except in Tuscany's Vin Santo. Some gd dry whites under DOCs Romagna or Abruzzo. Trebbiano di Soave, aka VERDICCHIO, only distantly related. T di Lugana now called Turbiana. Grown in southern France as Ugni Blanc, and Cognac as St-Émilion. Mostly thin, bland wine; needs blending (and more careful growing).

Ugni Blanc [Ugni Bl] See TREBBIANO.

Ull de Llebre See TEMPRANILLO.

Verdejo Grape of Rueda in Castile, potentially fine and long-lived.

Verdelho Great quality in Australia (pungent, full-bodied); rare but gd (and medium-sweet) in Madeira.

Verdicchio Potentially gd, muscular, dry; central-e Italy. Wine of same name.

Vermentino Italian, sprightly with satisfying texture, ageing capacity. Potential here.

Vernaccia Name given to many unrelated grapes in Italy. Vernaccia di San Gimignano is crisp, lively; Vernaccia di Oristano is Sherry-like.

Vidal French hybrid much grown in Canada for Icewine.

Vidiano Most Cretan producers love this. Powerful, stylish. Lime/apricot, gd acidity.

Viognier Ultra-fashionable Rhône grape, finest in Condrieu, less fine but still aromatic in the Midi. Gd examples from California, Virginia, Uruguay, Australia.

Viura (Macabeo, Maccabéo, Maccabeu) Workhorse white grape of n Spain, widespread in Rioja and Catalan Cava country. Also found over border in Southwest France. Gd quality potential.

Weißburgunder PINOT BL in Germany.

Welschriesling (Graševina, Laski Rizling, Olaszriesling, Riesling Italico) Not related to RIES. Light and fresh to sweet and rich in Austria; ubiquitous in Central Europe, where it can be remarkably gd for dry and sweet wines.

Xarel·lo (Pansa Blanca) Traditional Catalan grape, for Cava (with Parellada, MACABEO). Neutral but clean. More character (lime cordial) in Alella, as Pansa Blanca.

Xynisteri Cyprus's most planted white grape. Can be simple and is usually DYA, but when grown at altitude makes appealing, minerally whites.

Zéta Hungarian; BOUVIER X FURMINT used by some in Tokaji Aszú production.

Zierfandler (Spätrot, Cirfandl) Found in Austria's Thermenregion; often blended with ROTGIPFLER for aromatic, orange-peel-scented, weighty wines.

Wine & food

Has food fashion ever changed faster? As wines evolve (and today's wine fashion items weren't on the market five years ago) food gets more fused than ever. Today's menu is frequently just a list of ingredients. Of course there remains a list of classics, dishes where the main ingedient is still the main ingredient. There's no call to be original choosing the wine for these; the well-tried formula is no secret. Beat Chablis with oysters if you can. If you want to be original, almost futuristically on-trend, and yet enjoy your dinner, choose Sherry. Fino first, then Oloroso.

Before the meal – apéritifs

Cocktail addicts can look away now. The conventional and most effective appetite-creating apéritif wines are either sparkling (epitomized by Champagne) or fortified (epitomized by Sherry). You have to be French to understand how Port could spur the appetite. A glass of a light table wine before eating is the easy choice. **Warning** Avoid peanuts; they destroy wine flavours. Olives are too piquant for many wines. Don't serve them with Champagne; they need Sherry or a Martini. With Champagne, nibble almonds, pistachios, cashews, cheese straws or succulent gougères straight from the oven.

First courses

Aïoli Its garlic heat demands a thirst-quencher. Cold young Rhône white, Picpoul, Provence rosé, VERDICCHIO, Loire SAUV BL. Beer, marc or grappa... you'll hardly notice.

Antipasti With the classic ham, olives and pickled bits: dry or medium white, Italian (ARNEIS, VERDICCHIO, PINOT GRIGIO, VERMENTINO, GRECHETTO); light but gutsy red, eg. Valpolicella. Or Fino Sherry; sadly unobtainable in Italy.

Artichokes Not great for wine. Incisive dry white: NZ SAUV BL; Côtes de Gascogne or a modern Greek (precisely, 4-yr-old MALAGOUSIA, but easy on the vinaigrette); maybe Côtes du Rhône, red or white.

Asparagus is lightly bitter (white more so), so wine needs plenty of flavour. VIOGNIER can work. Rheingau RIES is classic; Ries generally gd to try. SAUV BL echoes the flavour. SÉM beats CHARD, esp Australian, but Chard gd with melted butter, hollandaise. Alsace PINOT GR, dry MUSCAT, or Jurançon Sec. Argument for trying a really sweet wine too, maybe not Yquem.

Aubergine (Melitzanosalata or Imam Bayildi) Crisp New World SAUV BL; or modern Greek or Sicilian dry white. Baked aubergine dishes (eg. *imam bayildi*) need sturdy reds: SHIRAZ, ZIN, or indeed Turkish. Or Med whites (incl Fino).

Avocado Not a wine natural. Dry to slightly sweet white with gd acidity: Rheingau or Pfalz Kabinett, GRÜNER V, Wachau RIES, Sancerre, PINOT GR, Australian CHARD (unoaked), or dry rosé.

Burrata Forget mozzarella; this is the crème de la crème. So a top Italian white, FIANO or Cusumano's GRILLO. I'll try Sauternes one day.

Carpaccio, beef or fish The beef version works well with most wines, incl reds. Tuscan is appropriate, but fine CHARDS are gd. So are vintage and pink Champagnes. Give Amontillado a try. **Salmon** Chard or Champagne. **Tuna** VIOGNIER, California Chard, Marlborough SAUV BL. Or sake.

Caviar Iced vodka (and) full-bodied Champagne (eg. Bollinger, Krug). Don't (ever) add raw onion.

Ceviche Australian RIES or VERDELHO, Chilean SAUV BL, TORRONTÉS. Manzanilla.

Charcuterie / salami High-acid, unoaked red works better than white. Simple

Valpolicella, REFOSCO SCHIOPPETINO, TEROLDEGO, BARBERA. If you must have white, it needs acidity. Chorizo makes wines taste metallic. Don't waste anything fine on it.

Dim sum Classically, China tea. PINOT GR or classic German dry RIES; light PINOT N. For reds, soft tannins are key. Bardolino, Rioja; Côtes du Rhône. Also NV Champagne or English fizz.

Eggs *See also* SOUFFLÉS. Not easy: eggs have a way of coating your palate. Omelettes: follow the other ingredients; mushrooms suggest red. With a truffle omelette, vintage Champagne. As a last resort I can bring myself to drink Champagne with scrambled eggs or eggs Benedict. Florentine, with spinach, is not a winey dish.

quails' eggs Blanc de blancs Champagne; VIOGNIER.

gulls' eggs Push the luxury: mature white burgundy or vintage Champagne.

oeufs en meurette Burgundian genius: eggs in red wine with a glass of the same.

Escargots (or frogs' legs) Rhône reds (Gigondas or Vacqueyras). Burgundy: white St-Véran or Rully. Midi: *petits-gris* with local white, rosé or red. Alsace: PINOT BL or dry MUSCAT. Loire: frogs' legs and semi-dry CHENIN BL.

Fish terrine or fish salad (incl crab) Calls for something fine. Pfalz RIES Spätlese Trocken, top GRÜNER V, Premier Cru Chablis, Clare Valley RIES, Sonoma CHARD; or Manzanilla.

Foie gras Sweet white: Sauternes, Tokaji Aszú 5 Puttonyos, late-harvest PINOT GR or RIES, Vouvray, Montlouis, Jurançon *moelleux*, GEWURZ. Old dry Amontillado can be sublime. With hot foie gras, mature vintage Champagne. But never CHARD, SAUV BL, or (shudder) red.

Haddock, smoked, mousse, soufflé or brandade Wonderful for stylish, full-bodied white: Grand Cru Chablis or Pessac-Léognan; Sonoma, S African or NZ CHARD.

Herrings, raw or pickled Dutch gin (young, not aged) or Scandinavian akvavit, and cold beer. If you must, try MUSCADET, but it's a waste (of the wine).

Mezze A selection of hot and cold vegetable dishes. Fino Sherry is in its element. So are Greek whites.

Mozzarella with tomatoes, basil Fresh Italian white, eg. Soave, Alto Adige. VERMENTINO from Liguria or Rolle from the Midi. *See also* AVOCADO.

Oysters, raw NV Champagne, Chablis, MUSCADET, white Graves, Sancerre, or Guinness. Experiment with Sauternes. Manzanilla is excellent. Flat oysters are worth gd wine. Pacific ones drown it.

Stewed, grilled or otherwise cooked Puligny-Montrachet or gd New World CHARD. Champagne is gd with either.

Pasta Red or white according to the sauce:

cream sauce (eg. carbonara) Orvieto, GRECO di Tufo. Young SANGIOVESE.

meat sauce MONTEPULCIANO d'Abruzzo, Salice Salentino, MALBEC.

pesto (basil) sauce BARBERA, Ligurian VERMENTINO, NZ SAUV BL, Hungarian FURMINT.

seafood sauce (eg. vongole) VERDICCHIO, Lugana, Soave, GRILLO, Cirò, unoaked CHARD.

tomato sauce Chianti, Barbera, Sicilian red, ZIN, S Australian GRENACHE.

Pastrami Alsace RIES, young SANGIOVESE or St-Émilion.

Pâté, chicken liver Calls for pungent white (Alsace PINOT GR or MARSANNE), a smooth red eg. light Pomerol, Volnay or NZ PINOT N. More strongly flavoured pâté (duck, etc.) needs Gigondas, Moulin-à-Vent, Chianti Classico or gd white Graves. Amontillado can be a marvellous match.

Pipérade Navarra rosado, Provence or Midi rosé, dry Australian RIES. Or red: Corbières or La Clape.

Prosciutto (also with melon, pears or figs) Full, dry or medium white: Orvieto, GRECHETTO, FIANO, GRÜNER V, Tokaji FURMINT, Australian SEM or Jurançon Sec. SERCIAL Madeira. Manzanilla.

Risotto Follow the flavour: **with vegetables** (eg. Primavera) PINOT GR from Friuli, Gavi, youngish SÉM, DOLCETTO or BARBERA d'Alba; **with fungi porcini** Finest mature

Barolo or Barbaresco; **with seafood** A favourite dry white. **Nero** A rich dry white: VIOGNIER or even Corton-Charlemagne.

Salads Any dry and appetizing white or rosé wine.

NB Vinegar in salad dressings *destroys* the flavour of wine. Why don't the French know this? If you want salad at a meal with fine wine, dress it (gingerly) with wine or lemon juice instead of vinegar. Sea salt and lots of good oil are the key.

Salmon, smoked Dry but pungent white: Fino (esp Manzanilla), Condrieu, Alsace PINOT GR, Grand Cru Chablis, Pouilly-Fumé, Pfalz RIES Spätlese, vintage Champagne. Vodka, schnapps or akvavit.

Soufflés As show dishes these deserve ★★★wines; **with cheese** Mature red burgundy or B'x, CAB SAUV (not Chilean, Australian), etc. Or fine mature white burgundy; **with fish (esp smoked haddock with chive cream sauce)** Dry white: ★★★Burgundy, B'x, Alsace, CHARD, etc.; **with spinach (tough on wine)** Mâcon-Villages, St-Véran or Valpolicella. Champagne (esp vintage) can also spark things with the texture of a soufflé.

Tapas Perfect with cold fresh Fino Sherry, which can cope with the wide range of flavours, hot and cold. Or sake.

Tapenade Manzanilla or Fino Sherry, or any sharpish dry white or rosé. Definitely not Champagne.

Taramasalata A Med white with personality, Greek if possible. Fino Sherry works well. Try Rhône MARSANNE.

Trout, smoked More delicate than smoked salmon. Mosel RIES Kabinett or Spätlese. Chablis or Champagne Blanc de Blancs.

Whitebait Crisp dry whites, eg. FURMINT, Greek, Touraine SAUV BL, VERDICCHIO, white Dão, Fino Sherry. Or beer.

Fish

Abalone Dry or medium white: SAUV BL, Meursault, PINOT GR, GRÜNER V. In Hong Kong: Dom Pérignon (at least).

Anchovies, marinated It scarcely matters. In eg. salade Niçoise: Provence rosé.

Bass, sea V.gd for any fine/delicate white, eg. Clare dry RIES, Chablis, white Châteauneuf, WEISSBURGUNDER from Baden, Pfalz. But rev wine up for more seasoning, eg. ginger, spring onions; more powerful Ries, not necessarily dry.

Beurre blanc, fish with A top-notch MUSCADET *sur lie*, a SAUV BL/SÉM blend, Premier Cru Chablis, Vouvray, ALBARIÑO or Rheingau RIES.

Brandade Premier Cru Chablis, Sancerre Rouge or NZ PINOT N.

Brill More delicate than turbot: hence a top fish for fine old Puligny and the like. With the richness of hollandaise you could go up to Montrachet.

Cod, roast Gd neutral background for fine dry/medium whites: Chablis, Meursault, Corton-Charlemagne, Cru Classé Graves, GRÜNER V, German Kabinett or Grosses Gewächs, or gd lightish PINOT N. Persuade the chef not to add chorizo.

black cod with miso sauce NZ or Oregon Pinot N, Meursault Premier Cru or Rheingau RIES Spätlese. Vintage Champagne.

Crab (esp Dungeness) and RIES together are part of the Creator's plan. But He also created Champagne.

Chinese, with ginger and onion German Ries Kabinett or Spätlese Halbtrocken. Tokaji FURMINT, GEWURZ.

cioppino SAUV BL; but West Coast friends say ZIN. Also California sparkling.

cold, dressed Top Mosel Ries, dry Alsace or Australian Ries or Condrieu.

softshell Unoaked CHARD, ALBARIÑO or top-quality German Ries Spätlese.

Thai crabcakes Pungent Sauv Bl (Loire, S Africa, Australia, NZ) or Ries (German Spätlese or Australian).

with black bean sauce A big Barossa SHIRAZ or SYRAH. Even a tumbler of Cognac.

with chilli and garlic Quite powerful Ries, perhaps German Grosses Gewächs or Wachau Austrian.

Curry *See* Indian dishes (Meat, poultry, game).

Eel, smoked 1st choice is Fino Sherry. RIES, Alsace, or Austrian, or GRÜNER V. Vintage Champagne. Schnapps.

Fish and chips, fritto misto, tempura Anything white goes, as long as there's no vinegar. Chablis, white B'x, SAUV BL, PINOT BL, Gavi, Fino, white Dão, Koshu, sake, or NV Champagne or Cava.

Fish pie (creamy) ALBARIÑO, Soave Classico, RIES Erstes Gewächs, Spanish GODELLO.

Gravadlax SERCIAL Madeira (eg. 10-yr-old Henriques), Amontillado, Tokaji FURMINT, orange wine. Or NV Champagne.

Haddock Rich, dry whites: Meursault, California CHARD, MARSANNE or GRÜNER V. **smoked** as for KIPPERS, but *see* EGGS, SOUFFLÉS.

Hake SAUV BL or any fresh fruity white: Pacherenc, Tursan. **cold with mayonnaise** fine CHARD.

Halibut As for TURBOT.

Herrings, fried / grilled Need a sharp white to cut their richness. Rully, Chablis, MUSCADET, Bourgogne ALIGOTÉ, Greek, dry SAUV BL. Or Indian tea. Or cider. A Speyside malt with a raw kipper is memorable.

Ikan bakar This classic Indonesian/Malay dish works well with GRÜNER V.

Kedgeree Full white, still or sparkling: Mâcon-Villages, S African CHARD, GRÜNER V, German Grosses Gewächs or (at breakfast) Champagne.

Kippers A gd cup of tea, preferably Ceylon (milk, no sugar). Scotch? Dry Oloroso Sherry is surprisingly gd.

Lamproie à la Bordelaise Glorious with 5-yr-old St-Émilion or Fronsac. Or Douro reds with Portuguese lampreys.

Lobster with a rich sauce, eg. Thermidor Vintage Champagne, fine white burgundy, Cru Classé Graves. Alternatively, for its inherent sweetness, Sauternes, Pfalz Spätlese, even Auslese. **plain grilled, or cold with mayonnaise** NV Champagne, Alsace RIES, Premier Cru Chablis, Condrieu, Mosel Spätlese or a local fizz.

Mackerel, grilled Hard or sharp white to cut the oil: SAUV BL from Touraine, Gaillac, Vinho Verde, white Rioja or English white. Or Guinness. **smoked** An oily wine-destroyer. Manzanilla, Vinho Verde or Schnapps, peppered or bison-grass vodka.

Monkfish Succulent but neutral; full-flavoured white or red, according to sauce.

Mullet, grey VERDICCHIO, Rully or unoaked CHARD.

Mullet, red A chameleon, tasty and delicate, adaptable to gd white or a delicate red, esp PINOT N.

Mussels marinières MUSCADET *sur lie*, Premier Cru Chablis, unoaked CHARD. **Curried** Something semi-sweet; Alsace RIES. **With garlic/parsley** *See* ESCARGOTS.

Paella, shellfish Full-bodied white or rosé, unoaked CHARD, ALBARIÑO or GODELLO. Or local Spanish red.

Perch, sandre Exquisite fish for finest wines: top white burgundy, Grand Cru Alsace RIES or noble Mosels. Or try top Swiss CHASSELAS (eg. Dézaley, St-Saphorin).

Prawns with mayonnaise Menetou-Salon. **With garlic** Keep the wine light, white or rosé, and dry. **With spices** Up to and incl chilli, go for a bit more body, but not oak: dry RIES or Italian, eg. FIANO, Grillo.

Salmon, seared or grilled PINOT N is fashionable, but CHARD is better. MERLOT or light claret not bad. Best is fine white burgundy: Puligny- or Chassagne-Montrachet, Meursault, Corton-Charlemagne, Grand Cru Chablis; GRÜNER V, Condrieu, California, Idaho or NZ CHARD, Rheingau Kabinett/Spätlese, Australian RIES. **fishcakes** Call for similar, but less grand, wines.

Sardines, fresh grilled V. dry white: Vinho Verde, MUSCADET or modern Greek.

Sashimi The Japanese preference is for white wine with body (Chablis Premier Cru, Alsace RIES) with white fish, PINOT N with red. Both need acidity: low-acidity wines don't work. Simple Chablis can be too thin. If soy is involved, then low-tannin red (again, Pinot). Remember sake (or Fino). As though you'd forget Champagne.

Scallops An inherently slightly sweet dish, best with medium-dry whites.

    in cream sauces German Spätlese, Montrachets or top Australian CHARD.

    grilled or seared Hermitage Blanc, GRÜNER V, Pessac-Léognan Blanc, vintage Champagne or PINOT N.

    with Asian seasoning NZ Chard, CHENIN BL, GODELLO, Grüner V, GEWURZ.

Scandi food Scandinavian dishes often have flavours of dill, caraway, cardamom and combine sweet and sharp flavours. Go for acidity and some weight: GODELLO, FALANGHINA, VERDELHO, Australian, Alsace or Austrian RIES. Pickled/fermented/raw fish is more challenging: beer or akvavit. *See also* entries for smoked fish, etc.

Shellfish Dry white with plain boiled shellfish, richer wines with richer sauces. RIES is the grape. **With plateaux de fruits de mer** Chablis, MUSCADET de Sèvre et Maine, PICPOUL de Pinet, Alto Adige PINOT BL.

Skate / raie with brown butter White with some pungency (eg. PINOT GR d'Alsace or ROUSSANNE) or a clean, straightforward wine, ie. MUSCADET or VERDICCHIO.

Snapper SAUV BL if cooked with oriental flavours; white Rhône or Provence rosé with Med flavours.

Sole, plaice, etc., plain, grilled or fried Perfect with fine wines: white burgundy or its equivalent. **With sauce** According to the ingredients: sharp, dry wine for tomato sauce, fairly rich for creamy preparations.

Sushi Hot wasabi is usually hidden in every piece. German QbA Trocken wines, simple Chablis, ALVARINHO or NV Brut Champagne or Koshu. Obvious fruit doesn't work. Or, of course, sake or beer.

Swordfish Full-bodied, dry white (or why not red?) of the country. Nothing grand.

Tagine, with couscous North African flavours need substantial whites to balance – Austrian, Rhône – or crisp, neutral whites that won't compete. Go easy on the oak. VIOGNIER or ALBARIÑO can work well.

Teriyaki A way of cooking, and a sauce, used for meat as well as fish. Germans favour off-dry RIES with weight: Kabinett can be too light.

Trout, grilled or fried Delicate white wine, eg. Mosel (esp Saar or Ruwer), Alsace PINOT BL, FENDANT.

Tuna, grilled or seared Best served rare (or raw) with light red wine: young Loire CAB FR or red burg. Young Rioja is a possibility.

Turbot Best rich, dry white: Meursault, Chassagne-Montrachet, Corton-Charlemagne, mature Chablis or its California, Australian or NZ equivalent. Condrieu. Mature Rheingau, Mosel or Nahe Spätlese or Auslese (not Trocken).

Meat, poultry, game

Barbecues The local wine: Australian, S African, Chilean, Argentina are right in spirit. Reds need tannin and vigour. Or the freshness of cru Beaujolais.

Beef (see also Steak) boiled Red: B'x (eg. Fronsac), Roussillon, Gevrey-Chambertin or Côte-Rôtie. Medium-ranking white burgundy is gd, eg. Auxey-Duresses. In Austria you may be offered skin-fermented TRAMINER. Mustard softens tannic reds, horseradish kills your taste: can be worth the sacrifice.

    roast An ideal partner for your fine red wine of any kind. Even Amarone. *See* above for mustard. The silkier the texture of the beef (wagyu, Galician eg.), the silkier the wine.

    stew, daube Sturdy red: Pomerol or St-Émilion, Hermitage, Cornas, BARBERA, SHIRAZ, Napa CAB SAUV, Ribera del Duero or Douro red.

Beef stroganoff Dramatic red: Barolo, Valpolicella Amarone, Priorat, Hermitage, late-harvest ZIN. Georgian SAPERAVI or Moldovan Negru de Purkar.

Boudin blanc (white pork sausage) Loire CHENIN BL, esp when served with apples: dry Vouvray, Saumur, Savennières; mature red Côte de Beaune if without.

Boudin noir (blood sausage) Local SAUV BL or CHENIN BL (esp in Loire). Or Beaujolais cru esp Morgon. Or light TEMPRANILLO. Or Fino.

Brazilian dishes Pungent flavours that blend several culinary traditions. Sherry would add another. Rhônish grapes work for red, or white with weight: VERDICCHIO, Californian CHARD. Or Caipirinhas. And a ten-mile run afterwards..

Cabbage, stuffed Hungarian KADARKA; village Rhône; Salice Salentino, PRIMITIVO and other spicy s Italian reds. Or Argentine MALBEC (no oak, if you can find one).

Cajun food Fleurie, Bouilly or New World SAUV BL. **With gumbo** Amontillado.

Cassoulet Red from Southwest France (Gaillac, Minervois, Corbières, St-Chinian or Fitou) or SHIRAZ. But best of all Fronton, Beaujolais cru or young TEMPRANILLO.

Chicken Kiev Alsace RIES, Collio, CHARD, Bergerac rouge.

Chicken / turkey / guinea fowl, roast Virtually any wine, incl v. best bottles of dry to medium white and finest old reds (esp burgundy). Sauces can make it match almost any fine wine (eg. coq au vin; the burgundy can be red or white, or *vin jaune* for that matter). **Fried** Sparkling works well.

Chilli con carne Young red: Beaujolais, TEMPRANILLO, ZIN, Argentine MALBEC, Chilean CARMENÈRE. Many drink beer.

Chinese food To the purist there's no such thing: food in China is regional – like Italian, only more confusing. I often serve both whites and reds concurrently during Chinese meals; no one wine goes with the whole affair. Peking duck is pretty forgiving. Champagne becomes a thirst quencher. Beer, too.

    Cantonese Rosé or dry to dryish white – Mosel RIES Kabinett or Spätlese Trocken. Ries should not be too dry; GEWURZ is often suggested but rarely works; GRÜNER V is a better bet. You need wine with acidity. Dry sparkling (esp Cava) works with the textures. Reds can work, but they should have worked off young tannins and not be too dry, or overtly oaky. PINOT N 1st choice; ★★St-Émilion or Châteauneuf.

    Shanghai Richer and oilier than Cantonese, not one of wine's natural partners. Shanghai tends to be low on chilli but high on vinegar of various sorts. German and Alsace whites can be a bit sweeter than for Cantonese. For reds, try MERLOT – goes with the salt. Or mature Pinot N, but a bit of a waste.

    Szechuan style VERDICCHIO, Alsace PINOT BL or v. cold beer. Mature Pinot N can also work; but see above. The Creator intended tea.

    Taiwanese LAMBRUSCO works with traditional Taiwan dishes if you're tired of beer.

Choucroute garni Alsace PINOT BL, PINOT GR, RIES or lager.

Cold roast meat Generally better with full-flavoured white than red. Mosel Spätlese, Hochheimer, Côte Chalonnaise v.gd, as is Beaujolais. Leftover Champagne too.

Confit d'oie / de canard Young, tannic red B'x, California CAB SAUV and MERLOT, Priorat cuts richness. Alsace PINOT GR or GEWURZ match it.

Coq au vin Red burgundy. Ideal: one bottle of Chambertin in the dish, two on the table. *See also* Chicken.

Dirty (Creole) rice Rich, supple red: NZ PINOT N, GARNACHA, BAIRRADA, MALBEC.

Duck or goose Rather rich white, esp for the strong flavour of goose: Pfalz Spätlese or off-dry Grand Cru Alsace. Or mature, gamey red: Morey-St-Denis, Côte-Rôtie, Pauillac, Bairrada. With oranges or peaches, the Sauternais propose drinking Sauternes, others Monbazillac or RIES Auslese. Mature, weighty vintage Champagne is gd too, and handles accompanying red cabbage surprisingly well. **Peking** *See* CHINESE FOOD.

    wild duck Big-scale red: Hermitage, Bandol, California or S African CAB SAUV, Australian SHIRAZ – Grange if you can afford it.

with olives Top-notch Chianti or other Tuscans.

roast breast & confit leg with Puy lentils Madiran (best), St-Émilion, Fronsac.

Game birds, young, roast The best red wine you can afford, but not too heavy.

older birds in casseroles Red (Gevrey-Chambertin, Pommard, Châteauneuf-du-Pape, Dão, or Grand Cru Classé St-Émilion, Rhône). Don't forget game birds can be even better cold the next day esp with fine German wines.

well-hung game Vega Sicilia, great red Rhône, Château Musar.

cold game Best German RIES; or mature vintage Champagne.

Game pie, hot Red: Oregon PINOT N, St-Émilion Grand Cru Classé. **Cold** Gd-quality white burgundy or German Erstes Gewächs, cru Beaujolais, Champagne.

Goat As for lamb. **Jamaican curry goat** *See* Indian dishes.

Goulash Flavoursome young red: Hungarian Kékoportó, ZIN, Uruguayan TANNAT, Douro red, MENCÍA, young Australian SHIRAZ, SAPERAVI. Or dry white from Tokaj.

Grouse *See* GAME BIRDS; but push the boat right out. Top burgundy or Châteauneuf.

Haggis Fruity red, eg. young claret, young Portuguese red, New World CAB SAUV or MALBEC or Châteauneuf-du-Pape. Or, of course, malt whisky.

Ham, cooked Softer red burgundies: Volnay, Savigny, Beaune; Chinon or Bourgueil; sweetish German white (RIES Spätlese); lightish CAB SAUV (eg. Chilean), or New World PINOT N. And don't forget the heaven-made match of ham and Sherry.

Hamburger Young red: Australian CAB SAUV, Chianti, ZIN, Argentine MALBEC, Chilean CARMENÈRE or SYRAH, TEMPRANILLO. Or full-strength Coke (not diet). If you add cheese and stuff, heaven help you; you're on your own.

Hare Jugged hare calls for flavourful red: not-too-old burgundy or B'x, Rhône (eg. Gigondas), Bandol, Barbaresco, Ribera del Duero, Rioja Res. The same for saddle or for hare sauce with pappardelle.

Indian dishes Various options: dry Sherry is brilliant. Choose a fairly weighty Fino with fish, and Palo Cortado, Amontillado or Oloroso with meat, according to the weight of the dish; heat's not a problem. The texture works too. Otherwise, medium-sweet white, v. cold, no oak: Orvieto *abboccato*, S African CHENIN BL, Alsace PINOT BL, TORRONTÉS, Indian sparkling, Cava or NV Champagne. Rosé is gd all-rounder. For tannic impact Barolo or Barbaresco, or deep-flavoured reds – ie. Châteauneuf-du-Pape, Cornas, Australian GRENACHE or MOURVÈDRE, or Valpolicella Amarone – will emphasize the heat. Hot-and-sour flavours need acidity.

Sri Lankan More extreme flavours, coconut. Sherry, rich red, rosé, mild white.

Japanese dishes A different set of senses come into play. Texture and balance are key; flavours are subtle. Gd mature fizz works well, as does mature dry RIES; you need acidity, a bit of body, and complexity. Dry FURMINT can work well. Umami-filled meat dishes favour light, supple, bright reds: Beaujolais perhaps, or mature PINOT N. Full-flavoured *yakitori* needs lively, fruity, younger versions of the same reds. Koshu with raw fish; orange Koshu with wagyu beef. *See also* SUSHI, SASHIMI, TERIYAKI.

Kebabs Vigorous red: modern Greek, Corbières, Chilean CAB SAUV, ZIN or Barossa SHIRAZ. SAUV BL, if lots of garlic.

Korean dishes Fruit-forward wines seem to work best with strong, pungent Korean flavours. PINOT N, Beaujolais, Valpolicella can all work: acidity is needed. Non-aromatic whites: GRÜNER V, SILVANER, VERNACCIA. But I drink beer.

Lamb, roast One of the traditional and best partners for v.gd red B'x, or its CAB SAUV equivalents from the New World. In Spain, finest old Rioja and Ribera del Duero Res or Priorat, in Italy ditto SANGIOVESE.

slow-cooked roast Flatters top reds, but needs less tannin than pink lamb.

Liver Young red: Beaujolais-Villages, St-Joseph, Médoc, Italian MERLOT, Breganze CAB SAUV, ZIN, Priorat, Bairrada.

calf's Red Rioja Crianza, Fleurie. Or a big Pfalz RIES Spätlese.

Mexican food Californians favour RIES: Calavera restaurant in Oakland lists 33 RIES, mostly German.

Moussaka Red or rosé Naoussa, SANGIOVESE, Corbières, Côtes de Provence, Ajaccio, young ZIN, TEMPRANILLO.

Mutton A stronger flavour than lamb, and not usually served pink. Needs a strong sauce. Robust red, top-notch, mature CAB SAUV, SYRAH. Sweetness of fruit (eg. Barossa) suits it.

'Nduja Calabria's spicy, fiery spreadable salumi needs a big, juicy red: young Rioja, Valpolicella, CAB FR, AGLIANICO, CARIGNAN, NERELLO MASCALESE.

Osso bucco Low-tannin, supple red such as DOLCETTO d'Alba or PINOT N. Or dry Italian white such as Soave.

Ox cheek, braised Superbly tender and flavoursome, this flatters the best reds: Vega Sicilia, St-Émilion. Best with substantial wines.

Oxtail Rather rich red: St-Émilion, Pomerol, Pommard, Nuits-St-Georges, Barolo, or Rioja Res, Priorat or Ribera del Duero, California or Coonawarra CAB SAUV, Châteauneuf-du-Pape, mid-weight SHIRAZ, Amarone.

Paella Young Spanish red, dry white, rosé: Penedès, Somontano, Navarra, or Rioja.

Pigeon or squab PINOT N perfect; young Rhône, Argentine MALBEC, young SANGIOVESE. Try Franken SILVANER Spätlese. With luxurious squab, top quite tannic red.

Pork, roast A perfect rich background to a fairly light red or rich white. It deserves ★★★ treatment: Médoc is fine. Portugal's suckling pig is eaten with Bairrada Garrafeira; S America's with CARIGNAN; Chinese is gd with PINOT N.

    pork belly Slow-cooked and meltingly tender, this needs a red with some tannin or acidity. Italian would be gd: Barolo, DOLCETTO or BARBERA. Or Loire red, or lightish Argentine MALBEC.

Pot au feu, bollito misto, cocido Rustic reds from region of origin; SANGIOVESE di Romagna, Chusclan, Lirac, Rasteau, Portuguese Alentejo or Spain's Yecla, Jumilla.

Quail Succulent little chick deserves tasty red or white. Rioja Res, mature claret, PINOT N. Or a mellow white: Vouvray or St-Péray.

Quiche Egg and bacon are not great wine matches, but one must drink something. Alsace RIES or PINOT GR, even GEWURZ, is classical. Beaujolais could be gd too.

Rabbit Lively, medium-bodied young Italian red, eg. AGLIANICO del Vulture, REFOSCO; Chiroubles, Chinon, Saumur-Champigny or Rhône rosé. **With prunes** Richer, fruitier red. **With mustard** Cahors. **As ragu** Medium-bodied red with acidity.

Satay McLaren Vale SHIRAZ, Alsace, NZ GEWURZ. Peanut sauce: problem for any wine.

Sauerkraut (German) Franken SILVANER, lager or Pils. (But *see also* CHOUCROUTE GARNI.)

Sausages *See also* CHARCUTERIE/SALAMI. The British banger requires a young MALBEC from Argentina (a red wine, anyway).

Singaporean dishes Part Indian, part Malay and part Chinese, Singaporean food has big, bold flavours that don't match easily with wine – not that that bothers the country's many wine-lovers. Off-dry RIES is as gd as anything. With meat dishes, ripe, supple reds: Valpolicella, PINOT N, DORNFELDER, unoaked MERLOT or CARMENÈRE.

Steak au poivre A fairly young Rhône red or CAB SAUV.

    filet, ribeye or tournedos Any gd red, esp burgundy (but not old wines with Béarnaise sauce: too New World PINOT N is better).

    Fiorentina (bistecca) Chianti Classico Riserva or BRUNELLO. Rarer the meat, more classic the wine; the more cooked, the more you need New World, sweet/strong wines. Argentine MALBEC is perfect for steak Argentine-style, ie. cooked to death.

    Korean *yuk whe* (world's best steak tartare) Sake.

    tartare Vodka or light young red: Beaujolais, Bergerac, Valpolicella. Aussies drink GAMAY with kangaroo tartare, charred plums, Szechuan pepper.

    T-bone Reds of similar bone structure: Barolo, Hermitage, Australian CAB SAUV or SHIRAZ, Chilean SYRAH, Douro.

Steak-&-kidney pie or pudding Red Rioja Res or mature B'x. Pudding (with suet) wants vigorous young wine. Madiran with its tannin is gd.

Stews & casseroles Burgundy such as Nuits-St-Georges or Pommard if fairly simple; otherwise lusty, full-flavoured red: young Côtes du Rhône, BLAUFRÄNKISCH, Corbières, BARBERA, SHIRAZ, ZIN, etc.

Sweetbreads A rich dish, so grand white wine: Rheingau RIES or Franken SILVANER Spätlese, Grand Cru Alsace PINOT GR or Condrieu, depending on sauce.

Tagines Depends on what's under the lid, but fruity young reds are a gd bet: Beaujolais, TEMPRANILLO, SANGIOVESE, MERLOT, SHIRAZ. Amontillado is great.
    chicken with preserved lemon, olives VIOGNIER.

Tandoori chicken RIES or SAUV BL, young red B'x or light n Italian red served cool. Also Cava and NV Champagne, or of course Palo Cortado or Amontillado Sherry.

Thai dishes Ginger and lemon grass call for pungent SAUV BL (Loire, Australia, NZ, S Africa) or RIES (Spätlese or Australian). Most curries suit aromatic whites with a touch of sweetness: GEWURZ is also gd.

Tongue Gd for any red or white of abundant character. Alsace PINOT GR or GEWURZ, gd GRÜNER V. Also Beaujolais, Loire reds, BLAUFRÄNKISCH, TEMPRANILLO, full, dry rosés.

Veal, roast A friend of fine wine. Gd for any fine old red that may be fading with age (eg. a Rioja Res, old Médoc or Côte de Nuits) or a German or Austrian RIES, Vouvray, Alsace PINOT GR.

Venison Big-scale reds, incl MOURVÈDRE, solo as in Bandol or in blends. Rhône, Languedoc, B'x, NZ Gimblett Gravels or California CAB SAUV of a mature vintage; or rather rich white (Pfalz Spätlese or Alsace PINOT GR). With a sweet and sharp berry sauce, try a German Grosses Gewächs RIES, or a Chilean CARMENÈRE or SYRAH.

Vietnamese food Slanted Door, famous San Fran Vietnamese restaurant, favours RIES, dry or up to Spätlese, German, Austrian, NZ. Also GRÜNER V, SEM; for reds, PINOT N, CAB FR, BLAUFRÄNKISCH.

Vitello tonnato Full-bodied whites: CHARD; light reds (eg. Valpolicella) served cool. Or a rosé.

Wild boar Serious red: top Tuscan or Priorat. NZ SYRAH. I've even drunk Port.

Vegetable dishes (*See also* FIRST COURSES)

Agrodolce Italian sweet-and-sour, with pine kernels, sultanas, capers, vinegar and perhaps anchovies. Points to fresh white: VERDICCHIO, unoaked CHARD. Or orange.

Baked pasta dishes *Pasticcio*, lasagne and cannelloni with elaborate vegetarian fillings and sauces: an occasion to show off a grand wine, esp finest Tuscan red, but also claret and burgundy.

Beetroot Mimics a flavour found in red burgundy. You could return the compliment. New-wave (ie. light) Grenache/GARNACHA is gd, as well.

Cauliflower, roast, etc. Go by other (usually bold) flavours. Try Austrian GRÜNER V, Valpolicella, NZ PINOT N.
    cauliflower cheese Crisp, aromatic white: Sancerre, RIES Spätlese, MUSCAT, ALBARIÑO, GODELLO. Beaujolais-Villages. No, go on; comfort wine with comfort food.
    with caviar – yes, really. Vintage Champagne.

Chimichurri A sauce found with steak or anything else. Complicated with wine: SAUV BL or TEMPRANILLO, according to context. Or try Fino.

Couscous with vegetables Young red with a bite: SHIRAZ, Corbières, Minervois; rosé; orange wine; Italian REFOSCO or SCHIOPPETTINO.

Fennel-based dishes SAUV BL: Pouilly-Fumé or NZ; SYLVANER or English SEYVAL BL; or young TEMPRANILLO.

Fermented foods *See also* SAUERKRAUT, CHOUCROUTE, KOREAN. *Kimchi* and *miso* are being worked into many dishes. Fruit and acidity are generally needed. If in sweetish veg dishes, try Alsace.

Grilled Mediterranean vegetables Italian whites, or for reds Brouilly, BARBERA, TEMPRANILLO or SHIRAZ.

Harissa A flavouring, but a powerful one. Juicy Med red or weighty (not oaky) white will work, according to context.

Lentil dishes Sturdy reds such as Corbières, ZIN or SHIRAZ.

    dhal, with spinach Tricky. Soft light red or rosé is best, and not top-flight.

Macaroni cheese As for CAULIFLOWER CHEESE.

Mushrooms (in most contexts) A boon to most reds and some whites. Context matters as much as species. Pomerol, California MERLOT, Rioja Res, top burgundy or Vega Sicilia. Button or Paris mushrooms with cream: fine whites, even vintage Champagne. On toast: best claret – even Port. Ceps/porcini: Ribera del Duero, Barolo, Chianti Rufina, Pauillac or St-Estèphe, NZ Gimblett Gravels.

Onion / leek tart / flamiche Fruity, off-dry or dry white: Alsace PINOT GR or GEWURZ is classic; Canadian, Australian or NZ RIES; Jurançon. Or Loire CAB FR.

Peppers or aubergines (eggplant), stuffed Vigorous red: Nemea, Chianti, DOLCETTO, ZIN, Bandol, Vacqueyras.

Pumpkin / squash ravioli or risotto Full-bodied, fruity dry or off-dry white: VIOGNIER or MARSANNE, demi-sec Vouvray, Gavi or S African CHENIN.

Ratatouille Vigorous young red: Chianti, NZ CAB SAUV, MERLOT, MALBEC, TEMPRANILLO; young red B'x, Gigondas or Coteaux du Languedoc. Fino Sherry can work too.

Roasted root vegetables Sweet potatoes, carrots, etc., often mixed with eg. beetroot, cabbage, garlic, onions and others have plenty of sweetness. Rosé, esp with some weight, or orange wine. Pesto will tilt it towards white.

Saffron Found in sweet and savoury dishes, and wine-friendly. Rich white: ROUSSANNE, VIOGNIER, PINOT GR. With desserts, Sauternes or Tokaji. *See also* TAGINES.

Seaweed Depends on context. *See also* SUSHI. The iodine notes go well with Austrian GRÜNER V, RIES.

Spiced vegetarian dishes *See* INDIAN DISHES, THAI DISHES (MEAT, POULTRY, GAME).

Sweetcorn fritters Often with a hot, spicy sauce. Rosé, orange or mild white all safe.

Tahini Doesn't really affect wine choice. Go by rest of dish.

Truffles Black truffles are a match for finest Right Bank B'x, but even better with mature white Hermitage or Châteauneuf. White truffles call for best Barolo or Barbaresco of their native Piedmont. With buttery pasta, Lugana. Or at breakfast, on fried eggs, BARBERA.

Watercress, raw Makes every wine on earth taste revolting.

Wild garlic leaves, wilted Tricky: a fairly neutral white with acidity will cope best.

Desserts

Apple pie, strudel or tarts Sweet German, Austrian or Loire white, Tokaji Aszú, or Canadian Icewine.

Apples, Cox's Orange Pippins Vintage Port (and sweetmeal biscuits, with or without Cheddar cheese) is the Saintsbury [wine] Club plan.

Bread-&-butter pudding Fine 10-yr-old Barsac, Tokaji Aszú, Australian botrytized SEM.

Cakes & gâteaux *See also* CHOCOLATE, COFFEE, RUM. BUAL or MALMSEY Madeira, Oloroso or Cream Sherry, Asti, sweet Prosecco.

Cheesecake Sweet white: Vouvray, Anjou, or Vin Santo – nothing too special.

Chocolate A talking point. Generally only powerful flavours can compete. Texture matters. BUAL, California Orange MUSCAT, Tokaji Aszú, Australian Liqueur Muscat, 10-yr-old Tawny or even young Vintage Port; Asti for light, fluffy mousses. Experiment with rich, ripe reds: SYRAH, ZIN, even sparkling SHIRAZ. Banyuls for a weightier partnership. Médoc can match bitter black chocolate, though it's a bit of a waste of wine, and Amarone is more fun. Armagnac, or a tot of gd rum.

    and olive oil mousse 10-yr-old Tawny Port or as for black chocolate, above.

Christmas pudding, mince pies Tawny Port, Cream Sherry or that liquid Christmas pudding itself, PEDRO XIMÉNEZ Sherry. Tokaji Aszú. Asti, or Banyuls.

Coffee desserts Sweet MUSCAT, Australia Liqueur Muscats, or Tokaji Aszú.

Creams, custards, fools, syllabubs *See also* CHOCOLATE, COFFEE, RUM. Sauternes, Loupiac, Ste-Croix-du-Mont or Monbazillac.

Crème brûlée Sauternes or Rhine Beerenauslese, best Madeira, or Tokaji Aszú. (With concealed fruit, a more modest sweet wine, eg. Monbazillac.)

Ice cream and sorbets Give wine a break.

Lemon flavours For dishes like tarte au citron, try sweet RIES from Germany or Austria or Tokaji Aszú; v. sweet if lemon is v. tart.

Meringues (eg. Eton Mess) Recioto di Soave, Asti, mature vintage Champagne.

Nuts (incl praliné) Finest Oloroso Sherry, Madeira, Vintage or Tawny Port (nature's match for walnuts), Tokaji Aszú, Vin Santo, or Setúbal MOSCATEL. Cashews and Champagne. Pistachios with Fino. **Salted nut parfait** Tokaji Aszú, Vin Santo.

Orange flavours Experiment: old Sauternes, Tokaji Aszú, California Orange MUSCAT.

Panettone Vinsanto. Jurançon *moelleux*, late-harvest RIES, Barsac, Tokaji Aszú.

Pears in red wine Rivesaltes, Banyuls, or RIES Beerenauslese.

Pecan pie Orange MUSCAT or Liqueur Muscat.

Raspberries (no cream, little sugar) Excellent with fine reds which themselves taste of raspberries: young Juliénas, Regnié.

Rum flavours (baba, mousses, ice cream) MUSCAT – from Asti to Australian Liqueur, according to weight of dish.

Strawberries, wild (no cream) With red B'x (most exquisitely Margaux) poured over. **With cream** Sauternes, Vouvray *moelleux*, Vendange Tardive Jurançon.

Summer pudding Fairly young Sauternes of a gd vintage.

Sweet soufflés Sauternes or Vouvray *moelleux*. Sweet (or rich) Champagne.

Tiramisú Vin Santo, young Tawny Port, MUSCAT de Beaumes-de-Venise, Sauternes, or Australian Liqueur Muscat. Better idea: skip the wine.

Trifle Should be sufficiently vibrant with its internal Sherry (Oloroso for choice).

Zabaglione Light-gold Marsala or Australian botrytized SEM, or Asti.

Wine & cheese

The notion that wine and cheese were married in heaven is not borne out by experience. Fine red wines are slaughtered by strong cheeses; only sharp or sweet white wines survive. Principles to remember (despite exceptions): first, the harder the cheese, the more tannin the wine can have; second, the creamier the cheese, the more acidity is needed in the wine – and don't be shy of sweetness. Cheese is classified by its texture and the nature of its rind, so its appearance is a guide to the type of wine to match it. Below are examples. I always try to keep a glass of white wine for my cheese.

Bloomy-rind soft cheeses, pure-white rind if pasteurized, or dotted with red: Brie, Camembert, Chaource, Bougon (goats milk "Camembert") Full, dry white burgundy or Rhône if the cheese is white and immature; powerful, fruity St-Émilion, young Australian (or Rhône) SHIRAZ/SYRAH or GRENACHE if it's mature.

Blue cheeses The extreme saltiness of Roquefort or most blue cheeses needs the sweetness of Sauternes (or Tokaji), esp old Stilton, and Port, (youngish) Vintage or Tawny, is a classic. Intensely flavoured old Oloroso, Amontillado, Madeira, Marsala and other fortifieds go with most blues. Never gd claret, please.

Cooked cheese dishes Frico Traditional in Friuli. Cheese baked or fried with potatoes or onions; high-acid local REFOSCO (r), OR RIBOLLA GIALLA (w).

Mont d'Or Delicious baked, and served with potatoes. Fairly neutral white with freshness: GRÜNER V, Savoie.

fondue Trendy again. Light, fresh white as above.

macaroni or cauliflower cheese Easy-drinking red or dry white.

Fresh, no rind – cream cheese, crème fraîche, mozzarella Light crisp white: Chablis, Bergerac, Entre-Deux-Mers; rosé: Anjou, Rhône; v. light, young, fresh red: B'x, Bardolino, Beaujolais.

Hard cheeses, waxed or oiled, often showing marks from cheesecloth – Gruyère family, Manchego and other Spanish cheeses, Parmesan, Cantal, Comté, old Gouda, Cheddar and most "traditional" English cheeses Hard to generalize; Gouda, Gruyère, some Spanish, and a few English cheeses complement fine claret or CAB SAUV and great SHIRAZ/SYRAH. But strong cheeses need less refined wines, preferably local ones. Sugary, granular old Dutch red Mimolette, Comté or Beaufort gd for finest mature B'x. Also for Tokaji Aszú. But try tasty whites too.

Natural rind (mostly goats cheese) with bluish-grey mould (the rind becomes wrinkled when mature), sometimes dusted with ash – St-Marcellin Sancerre, light SAUV BL, Jurançon, Savoie, Soave, Italian CHARD; or young Vintage Port.

Semi-soft cheeses, thickish grey-pink rind – Livarot, Pont l'Evêque, Reblochon, Tomme de Savoie, St-Nectaire Powerful white B'x, even Sauternes, CHARD, Alsace PINOT GR, dryish REIS, s Italian and Sicilian whites, aged white Rioja, dry Oloroso Sherry. Strongest of these cheeses kill almost any wines. Try marc or Calvados.

Washed-rind soft cheeses, with rather sticky, orange-red rind – Langres, mature Époisses, Maroilles, Carré de l'Est, Milleens, Münster Local reds, esp for Burgundian cheeses; vigorous Languedoc, Cahors, Côtes du Frontonnais, Corsican, s Italian, Sicilian, Bairrada. Also powerful whites, esp Alsace GEWURZ, MUSCAT.

Food & your finest wines

With v. special bottles, the wine guides the choice of food rather than vice versa. The following is based largely on gastronomic conventions, some bold experiments and much diligent and ongoing research.

Red wines

Amarone Classically, in Verona, risotto all'Amarone or pastissada. But if your butcher doesn't run to horse, then shin of beef, slow-cooked in more Amarone.

Barolo, Barbaresco Risotto with white truffles; pasta with game sauce (eg. pappardelle alla lepre); porcini mushrooms; Parmesan.

Great Syrahs: Hermitage, Côte-Rôtie, Grange; Vega Sicilia Beef (such as the super-rich, super-tender, super-slow-cooked ox cheek I had at Vega Sicilia), venison, well-hung game bone marrow on toast; English cheese (esp best farm Cheddar) but also hard goats milk and ewes milk cheeses such as England's Berkswell or Ticklemore. I treat Côte-Rôtie like top red burgundy.

Great Vintage Port or Madeira Walnuts or pecans. A Cox's Orange Pippin and a digestive biscuit is a classic English accompaniment.

Red Bordeaux v. old, light, delicate wines, (eg. pre-59) Leg or rack of young lamb, roast with a hint of herbs (not garlic); entrecôte; simply roasted (and not too well-hung) partridge or roast chicken never fails.

    fully mature great vintages (eg. 59 61 82 85) Shoulder or saddle of lamb, roast with a touch of garlic; roast ribs or grilled rump of beef.

    mature but still vigorous (eg. 89 90) Shoulder or saddle of lamb (incl kidneys) with rich sauce. Fillet of beef marchand de vin (with wine and bone marrow). Grouse. Avoid beef Wellington: pastry dulls the palate.

    Merlot-based Beef (fillet richest), well-hung venison. In St-Émilion, lampreys.

Red burgundy Consider the weight and texture, which grow lighter/more velvety with age. Also the character of the wine: Nuits is earthy, Musigny flowery, great Romanées can be exotic, Pommard is renowned for its four-squareness. Roast chicken or (better) capon is a safe standard with red burgundy; guinea fowl for slightly stronger wines, then partridge, grouse or woodcock for those progressively more rich and pungent. Hare and venison (chevreuil) are alternatives.

great old burgundy The Burgundian formula is cheese: Époisses (unfermented); a fine cheese but a terrible waste of fine old wines. *See* above.

vigorous younger burgundy Duck or goose roasted to minimize fat. Or faisinjan (pheasant cooked in pomegranate juice). Coq au vin, or lightly smoked gammon.

Rioja Gran Reserva, Top Duero reds Richly flavoured roasts: wild boar, mutton, saddle of hare, whole suckling pig.

White wines

Beerenauslese / Trockenbeerenauslese Biscuits, peaches, greengages. Desserts made from rhubarb, gooseberries, quince, apples. But TBAs don't need or want food.

Condrieu, Château-Grillet, Hermitage Blanc V. light pasta scented with herbs and tiny peas or broad beans. Or v. mild tender ham. Old white Hermitage loves truffles.

Grand Cru Alsace: Ries Truite au bleu, smoked salmon, or choucroute garni.

    Pinot Gr Roast or grilled veal. Or truffle sandwich (slice a whole truffle, make a sandwich with salted butter and gd country bread – not sourdough or rye – wrap and refrigerate overnight. Then toast it in the oven. Thanks, Dom Weinbach).

    Gewurztraminer Cheese soufflé (Münster cheese).

    Vendange Tardive Foie gras or tarte tatin.

Old vintage Champagne (not Blanc de Blancs) As an apéritif, or with cold partridge, grouse, woodcock. The evolved flavours of old Champagne make it far easier to match with food than the tightness of young wine. Hot foie gras can be sensational. Don't be afraid of garlic or even Indian spices, but omit the chilli.

    late-disgorged old wines have extra freshness plus tertiary flavours. Try with truffles, lobster, scallops, crab, sweetbreads, pork belly, roast veal, chicken.

Sauternes Simple crisp buttery biscuits (eg. langues de chat), white peaches, nectarines, strawberries (without cream). Not tropical fruit. Pan-seared foie gras. Lobster or chicken with Sauternes sauce. Ch d'Yquem recommends oysters (and indeed lobster). Experiment with blue cheeses. Rocquefort is classic, but needs one of the big Sauternes.

Tokaji Aszú (5–6 puttonyos) Foie gras recommended. Fruit desserts, cream desserts, even chocolate can be wonderful. Roquefort. It even works with some Chinese, though not with chilli – the spice has to be adjusted to meet the sweetness. Szechuan pepper is gd. Havana cigars are splendid. So is the naked sip.

Top Chablis White fish simply grilled or meunière. Dover sole, turbot, halibut are best; brill, drenched in butter, can be excellent. (Sea bass is too delicate; salmon passes but does little for the finest wine.)

Top white burgundy, top Graves, top aged Riesling Roast veal, farm chicken stuffed with truffles or herbs under the skin, or sweetbreads; richly sauced white fish (turbot for choice) or scallops, white fish as above. Lobster, poached wild salmon.

Vouvray moelleux, etc. Buttery biscuits, apples, apple tart.

Fail-safe face-savers

Some wines are more useful than others – more versatile, more forgiving. If you're choosing restaurant wine to please several people, or just stocking the cellar with basics, these are the wines: red – Alentejo, BARBERA d'Asti/d'Alba, BLAUFRÄNKISCH, Beaujolais, Chianti, GRENACHE/GARNACHA if not overextracted/overoaked, MALBEC (easy on the oak), PINOT N, Valpolicella; white – Alsace PINOT BL, Entre-Deux-Mers, ASSYRTIKO, unoaked or v. lightly oaked CHARD, Fino Sherry, GRÜNER V, RIES from Alsace, Germany (dry, fruity), Sancerre, gd Soave, VERDICCHIO.

France

More heavily shaded areas are
the wine-growing regions.

Abbreviations used in the text:

Al	Alsace
Beauj	Beaujolais
Burg	Burgundy
B'x	Bordeaux
Cas	Castillon-Côtes de Bordeaux
Chab	Chablis
Champ	Champagne
Cors	Corsica
C d'O	Côte d'Or
Fron	Fronsac
L'doc	Languedoc
Lo	Loire
Mass C	Massif Central
Prov	Provence
N/S Rh	Northern/Southern Rhône
Rouss	Roussillon
Sav	Savoie
SW	Southwest
AC	appellation contrôlée
ch, chx	château(x)
dom, doms	domaine(s)

Map labels: Le Havre, Caen, Brest, LOIRE, Loire, Nantes, Muscadet, Anjou-Saumur, La Rochelle, BORDEA, Médoc, Bordeaux, Pomerc, St-Émi, Graves, Ent Deu, Sauternes, Côtes du Marman, Buze, Tursan, Côtes St-M, Biarritz, Madi, Jurançon

I've been accused of bias, prejudice, even of getting too long in the
tooth, but nothing has come my way to change my mind. France
belongs here, in the front of the book and at the head of any list of wine
countries. Not only is it the original of most of the world's favourite
wines, having invented their grape varieties; it just does them better, in
more instances, with an eye – I won't say an unerring eye – for style,
scale, value and sheer drinkability. If you read these French pages right
through you'd be amazed. Is it geography? Is it genius? Both, of course.

Now France is at the forefront of a debate over wine styles: whether
wine should be perfect, or whether it should be unique. It's embodied
in the contrast between Bordeaux and burgundy: both extremely
fashionable, both in great demand worldwide. But Bordeaux seeks to
be perfect, while burgundy, fixated on the details of terroir, seeks to be
unique. Bordeaux, too, wants to express its terroir in ever-greater detail.
As we discuss in this year's supplement, good wine is supposed to
express its terroir – terroir is the calling card of good wine. If it doesn't
express that, then what does it express? Cellar technology, is the answer.

France entries also cross-reference to Châteaux of Bordeaux

Yes, you can have terroir expression massaged and polished by cellar technology – that's top Bordeaux. The luxury-goods market does not allow for imperfections.

Elsewhere in France you can see the same dichotomy. In Champagne, the big houses seek perfection while the growers seek uniqueness. (Both, I should stress, produce stellar quality – but in different ways.) The Rhône and the Midi have both kinds – as soon as the winemaker seeks to express him- or herself in the wine rather than the terroir, the style of the wine changes, usually in the direction of more extraction, more power. The Loire and Alsace? Mostly about uniqueness, again partly because of the lack of international brands. Industrial wine is something else again: cheap (usually), cheerful (hopefully), reliable. It's produced in many countries across the globe, including France; it's one of the great benefits of our age, in some ways; in other ways not, industrial wines come from industrially farmed agribusiness vineyards.

Red Bordeaux

Médoc / Red Graves For many wines, bottle-age is optional: for these it is indispensable. Minor chx from light vintages need only 2 or 3 yrs, but even modest wines of great years can improve for 15 or so, and the great chx of these yrs can profit from double that time.

2018 Pure, aromatically intense Cab Sauv. Rich, powerful (alcs high) but balance there. Long-term potential, but yields uneven due to mildew, hail.

2017 Attractive wines gd balance, fresh, fairly early-drinking. Volumes often small.

2016 Cab Sauv with colour, depth, structure. Vintage to set aside.

2015 Excellent Cab Sauv, not structure of 05 10. Some variation. Keep.

2014 Cab Sauv bright, resonant. Gd to v.gd; classic style, beginning to open.

2013 Worst since 92. Patchy success at Classed Growth level. Early-drinking.

2012 Difficulties ripening Cab Sauv but early-drinking charm.

2011 Mixed quality, better than its reputation. Classic freshness, moderate alc. After an awkward phase beginning to open.

2010 Outstanding. Magnificent Cab Sauv, deep-coloured, concentrated, firm. Keep for yrs.

2009 Outstanding yr. Structured, with exuberant fruit. Accessible or keep.

2008 Much better than expected; fresh, classic flavours. Drinking now

Fine vintages: 06 05 00 98 96 95 90 89 88 86 85 82 75 70 66 62 61 59 55 53 49 48 47 45 29 28.

St-Émilion / Pomerol

2018 Powerful but pure. Best from limestone, clay soils. Mildew affected yields.

2017 Gd balance, classic fruit-cake flavours. Will be quite early-drinking.

2016 Conditions as Méd. Some young vines suffered in drought but overall excellent.

2015 Great yr for Merlot. Perfect conditions. Colour, concentration, balance.

2014 More rain than the Méd so Merlot variable. V.gd Cab Fr. Drinking now.

2013 Difficult flowering (so tiny crop), rot in Merlot. Modest yr, early-drinking.

2012 Conditions as Méd. Merlot marginally more successful. Drinking now.

2011 Complicated, a Méd. Gd Cab Fr. Pomerol best overall? Don't shun it.

2010 Outstanding. Powerful wines, high alc. Concentrated. Time in hand.

2009 Again, outstanding. Powerful wines (high alc) but seemingly balanced. Hail in St-Ém cut production at certain estates.

2008 Similar conditions to Méd. Tiny yields, quality surprisingly gd. Drinking now best will age.

Fine vintages: 05 01 00 98 95 90 89 88 85 82 71 70 67 66 64 61 59 53 52 49 47 45.

Red burgundy

Côte d'Or Côte de Beaune reds generally mature sooner than grander wines of Côte de Nuits. Earliest drinking dates for lighter commune wines, eg. Volnay, Beaune; latest for GCs, eg. Chambertin, Musigny. Even the best burgundies are more attractive young than equivalent red Bordeaux. It can seem magical when they really blossom yrs later.

2018 Wow: this may join the legends with sumptuous ripe reds throughout. Sugar merchants unhappy, vignerons grinning for (y)ear to (y)ear.

2017 Survived frosts. Big crop, attractive wines, mostly ripe enough, stylish lighter wines, slight preference for Côte de Nuits.

2016 Short frosted crop but some spectacular reds with great energy, fresh acidity. Keep them locked away, though.

2015 Dense, concentrated wines, as 05, but with the additional juiciness of 10. Earning a stellar reputation; don't miss them. Lesser appellations attractive now.

2014 Beaune, Volnay, Pommard hailed once again. Attractive fresh reds, medium density, lovely fragrance. Take a look soon.

2013 Côte de Beaune hailed again. Small crop for Nuits, delicious perfumed wines for those who waited, with crunchy energy. Lesser wines ready.

2012 Côte de Beaune lost crop to hail. Small crop of fine wines in Côte de Nuits, exuberant yet classy. Still to be kept, though.

2011 Some parallels with 07. Early harvest, lighter wines, now accessible. Start bringing them out of the cellar.

2010 Turning into a great classic: pure, fine-boned yet also with impressive density. Village wines and some Premiers Crus open for business.

2009 Beautiful, ripe, plump reds. Well past the puppy-fat stage and some a bit overcooked, but the rest will be long-term keepers.

2008 Lean but lively, will suit more ascetic palates than hedonists. Best wines show Pinot purity, opening up nicely. Now to early 2020s.

Fine vintages: 05 03 02 99 96 (drink or keep) 95 93 90 88 85 78 71 69 66 64 62 61 59 (mature).

White burgundy

Côte d'Or White wines are now rarely made for ageing as long as they were 20 yrs ago, but top wines should still improve for 10 yrs or more. Most Mâconnais and Chalonnais (St-Véran, Mâcon-Villages, Montagny) usually best drunk early (2–3 yrs).

2018 Huge crop, ripened well; forward, attractive, less intensity than Chablis.

2017 Turning out really well, a decent crop of ripe, balanced, consistent wines with enough acidity. Best since 14.

2016 Small, frosted crops, inconsistent results. Undamaged v'yds did well, others lacking balance for the long term.

2015 Rich, concentrated; warm, dry summer. Most picked early, have done well, later wines may be too heavy. Similar to 09 but more successes.

2014 Finest, most consistent vintage for a generation. White fruit flavours, ripe but fresh, elegant, balanced. Start drinking, but keep best for later.

2013 Tricky, often flabby. Drink soon, be careful.

2012 Tiny production, poor flowering, hailstorms. Decent weather later; wines full of energy, showing well. Gd tip for 2020.

2011 Fine potential for conscientious producers, some flesh, gd balance, but easy to overcrop. Attractive early, start drinking up.

2010 Exciting; gd fruit-acid balance, now developing exotic aromatics. Safest to drink soon.

2009 Full crop, healthy grapes, two styles: 1st-rate, to keep from early pickers; others can be flabby.

Fine vintages (all ready): 05 02 99 96 93 92 85 79 73 59.

Chablis

GC Chablis of vintages with both strength and acidity really need at least 5 yrs, can age superbly for 15 or more; PCs proportionately less, but give them 3 yrs at least. Then, for the full effect, decant them. Yes, really.

2018 Looks like we may have something exceptional; v. concentrated wines.

2017 Despite frost again, classical style, much more exciting than 16.

2016 Hail, frost, more hail, hardly any wine, and often unbalanced.

2015 Hot, dry summer; rich, ripe wines with a concentrated core. Keep GCs.

2014 Excellent early crop, ideal balance, saline notes. Drink Chablis, keep crus.
2013 Small crop, late harvest, rot issues. Mixed bag, drink up.

Beaujolais

18 Hot summer, another one of the big beasts 17 Large crop but hideous
hail, esp Fleurie, Moulin-à-Vent. 16 Large crop of juicy wines, unless hailed
(Fleurie). 15 Massive wines, best outstanding, others alc monsters. 14 Fine
crop, enjoyable now. 13 Late vintage with mixed results. 12 Tiny crop, economic
misery, v'yds abandoned.

Southwest France

2018 Fruity, rich wines. Dry whites and rosés mostly ready 2020. Most reds
     (esp oaked) and sweet whites 2021 on. Heftier styles will need longer.
2017 Finesse not power; all ready, reds will keep c.3 yrs, Madiran, Cahors longer.
2016 Satisfactory rather than brilliant; drinkable now, though bigger styles
     will keep.
2015 Outstanding: full, fruity, fine. Blockbusters will keep for many yrs.
2014 Well-balanced sweet whites; rest are much admired, can be drunk now.
2013 Best avoided unless you have a gd tip for exceptions rather than rule.
2012 Mostly drink up. Most beginning to look tired, except Cahors, Madiran.

The Midi

2018 Mildew, but vibrant (r w), if picked at right time after along hot summer.
     Pic St-Loup: powerful, rich, v.gd reds.
2017 Small, but v.gd quality: Roussillon possibly better than 15. Powerful, rich
     Pic St-Loup reds, fine tannins. Cabardes reds balanced, will age, whites
     excellent acidity, fruit.
2016 Generally excellent. Reds balanced, will age; whites fresh, fruity.
2015 Reds: ripe fruit, elegant tannins. Some whites v.gd, some low acidity.
2014 Most early-drinking. Roussillon: pleasant, light reds. Whites better.

Northern Rhône

Depending on site and style, these can be as long-lived as burgundies. White
Hermitage can keep for as long as red. Impossible to generalize, but don't be
in a hurry (r or w).
2018 V.gd; enormous wines, some headiness. Astonishing, v. rich Hermitage
     (r). Whites fat, sustained, low acidity, drink early except for Hermitage.
2017 V.gd, esp Côte-Rôtie. Full reds, deeper than 16, show sunshine, packed-in
     tannins. Whites for hearty food, Condrieu variable.
2016 Gd–v.gd, reds pure, harmonious, Côte-Rôtie classics. NB Cornas, Crozes-
     Hermitage reds. Marvellous Hermitage whites, other whites gd, clean.
2015 Excellent, v. deep reds everywhere, wonderful, v. long-lived Hermitage,
     Côte-Rôtie. Full whites, can be heady.
2014 Plump reds, gained depth over time. Excellent whites: style, freshness.
2013 V.gd reds, with tight body, crisp tannin, freshness. 15–20 yrs life.
     Exceptional whites (Hermitage, St-Joseph, St-Péray).
2012 V.gd Hermitage, open-book Côte-Rôtie. Fresh reds come together well,
     will last 15 yrs+ Whites have style, freshness.
2011 Gd Hermitage, Cornas. Côte-Rôtie more body recently. Whites satisfactory.
2010 Wonderful. Reds: marvellous depth, balance, freshness. Long-lived.
     Côte-Rôtie as gd as 78. V.gd Condrieu, rich whites elsewhere.
2009 Excellent, sun-packed wines. Some rich Hermitage, v. full Côte-Rôtie.
     Best Crozes, St-Joseph have aged well. Rather big whites: can live.

Southern Rhône

2018 Can be v.gd. Shocking crop loss Châteauneuf, esp organic. Deep reds from hot sun. Gd Gigondas, Valréas, Visan, Vinsobres: higher, later v'yds. V. full whites.

2017 V.gd, can be variable. Rich, bold reds, tannins normally ripe despite drought. Most strict top domaines did best. Gd Rasteau. Full s whites.

2016 Wonder yr, excellent for all (Châteauneuf, old-vines Grenache triumph). Rich, sensuous, long reds: fruit bonanza. Sun-filled whites, plenty of body; keep some to mature.

2015 V.gd: rich, dark, lots of body, firm tannins, often enticing flair. Quality high across board (Gigondas); cheap reds value. V.gd, full whites.

2014 Gd in places, aromatic finesse returns to Châteauneuf. Stick to best names; dilution issue. NB Gigondas, Rasteau, Cairanne. Fresh whites.

2013 Tiny crop. Vibrant, slow-burn reds, v. low Grenache yields: atypical wines. Châteauneuf best from old vines. Gd-value Côtes du Rh. V.gd whites.

2012 Full reds, lively, gd tannins. Open-book vintage. Food-friendly whites.

2011 Sunny, supple, can be fat, drink quite soon. Alc issue. Decent whites.

2010 Outstanding. Full-bodied, balanced reds. Tiptop Châteauneuf. Clear-fruited, well-packed tannins. Whites deep, long.

2009 Dense reds. Drought: some grainy tannins. Gd Rasteau. Sound whites.

Champagne

2018 Exceptional vintage, possibly sky-high quality: virtually no rot, v. hot dry summer. Could recall 59 76.

2017 Chard from blue-chips (Roederer, Krug) gd but Pinots N, esp M suffered in rain.

2016 Purity of fruit and elegance, best for Pinot N.

2015 Great Pinot N, refined M, some overripe Chard others sumptuous.

2014 Chard best; unlikely to be vintage yr. Maybe for some Blanc de Blancs.

2013 Potentially brilliant Côte des Blancs Chard. Pinot N hit, miss: glorious in Äy.

2012 Exquisite Pinot N, best since 52, fine Pinot M, Chard stolid, some lack verve. Gd NV yr.

2011 Lack of proper structure, maturity; a few fine growers' wines.

Fine vintages: 09' 08' 06 04 02' 00 98 96' 95 92 90 89 88' 82 76.

The Loire

2018 Exceptional quality, quantity: dry, hot summer/autumn after June rain. 5th gd–v.gd vintage, a unique run. Some comparing with 47.

2017 Gd-quality, but April frosts again (Muscadet, Savennières, parts of Touraine, Pouilly-Fumé). Bourgueil, Menetou-Salon, Sancerre spared.

2016 Low quantity, but quality gd for those who had a crop. Sancerre spared.

2015 Gd–v.gd across range. Fine sweet wines in Layon and L'Aubance.

2014 Well-balanced dry whites, ripe reds delicious now but will age further. Outstanding Muscadet.

Alsace

2018 Warm, but fresh wines. Gewurz, Pinot Gr, Ries top from high-altitude GCs.

2017 One of best since World War Two, with 47 71 08.

2016 Classic finely balanced vintage and plenty of it, unlike 13 14 15.

2015 Rich vintage, one of driest ever. Great Pinot N, if not much of it.

2014 Gewurz, Pinot Gr attacked by Suzuki fruit fly. Ries wonderful, great acidity.

2013 Becoming a classic vintage, now opening up. Great potential (Ries).

2012 Small crop of concentrated wines, in dry style of 10.

Abymes Sav w ★→★★ Hilly zone s Chambéry, next to APREMONT. DYA Vin de SAV AC (1973) cru (261 ha). Jacquère grape (80% min) Try: des Anges, Ducret, Giachino, Labbe, Perrier, Ravier, Sabots de Venus.

Ackerman Lo r p w (dr) (sw) sp ★→★★★ First SAUMUR sparkling house (1811). On acquisition trail. Négociant and estates: Celliers du Prieuré, Donatien-Bahuaud and Drouet Frères (Pays Nantais), Monmousseau, Perruche, Rémy-Pannier, Varière, CH de SANCERRE.

AC or AOC (Appellation Contrôlée) / AOP Government control of origin and production (but not quality) of most top French wines; around 45% of total. Now being converted to AOP (Appellation d'Origine Protegée – which is much nearer the truth than Contrôlée).

Agenais SW Fr r p w ★ DYA IGP of Lot-et-Garonne. Prunes better bet than grapes, though a few DOMS (Boiron, Campet, Lou Gaillot) exception to the rule. Oh, for better co-ops.

Alain Chabanon, Dom L'doc ★★★ Once-pioneering MONTPEYROUX producer keeps up with Campredon, Esprit de Font Caude, MERLOT-based Merle aux Alouettes. Delicious whites Le Petit Trélans, pure VERMENTINO, age-worthy Trélans Vermentino/CHENIN BL.

Allemand, Thierry N Rh r ★★★→★★★★ 90' 91' 95' 99' 01' 05' 06' 07' 08' 09' 10' 12' 13' 15' 16' 17' 18' Magnificent CORNAS 5-ha DOM, low sulphur, organic. Two v. deep, smoky wines. Top is Reynard (profound, complex; 20 yrs+), Chaillot (v.gd fruit) drinks sooner.

Alliet, Philippe Lo r w ★★★→★★★★ 05' 09' 10' 11 14' **15'** 16 17 18' V. respected CHINON producer with son Pierre. Tradition, VIEILLES VIGNES and two steep s-facing v'yds e of Chinon: l'Huisserie and Coteau de Noiré. Wines need time. V.gd 18 (quality, quantity).

Aloxe-Corton Burg r w ★★→★★★ 05' 09' 10' 12' 14 **15'** 17 18' The n end of CÔTE DE BEAUNE, famous for GC CORTON, CORTON-CHARLEMAGNE, but less interesting at village or PC level. Reds attractive but not overextracted. Best DOMS: Follin-Arbelet, Rapet, Senard, Terregelesses, TOLLOT-BEAUT.

Alquier, Jean-Michel L'doc r w ★★★ Stellar FAUGÈRES producer. MARSANNE/ROUSSANNE/GRENACHE Des Vignes au Puits; SAUV Pierres Blanches. Reds: emphasis on SYRAH benefitting from 340m (1115ft) altitude and schist for finesse; Les Bastides (old higher-altitude Syrah) more structured and Syrah-based Les Grandes Bastides d'Alquier longer in new oak. Les Premières (younger vines); Maison Jaune, only in gd Grenache yrs.

Alsace (r) w (sw) (sp) ★★→★★★★ Sheltered e slope of Vosges and 1800 sun hrs make France's Rhine wines: aromatic, fruity, full-strength, drier styles back in vogue. Still much sold by variety (PINOT BL, GEWURZ). Yet rich diversity of 13 geological formations (incl granite, gneiss, limestone) shapes best terroir wines for ageing. RIES up to 20 yrs for GC. *Pinot reaching high levels* (esp 16 17 18). *See* VENDANGE TARDIVE, SÉLECTION DES GRAINS NOBLES.

Alsace Grand Cru Al ★★★→★★★★ 06 07 08' 10 12 13 (esp RIES) 15' 17' AC. Restricted to 51 of best-named v'yds (approx 1600 ha, 800 in production) and four noble grapes (PINOT GR, RIES, GEWURZ, MUSCAT). Production rules require higher min ripeness. Concept of local management allows extra rules specific to each cru. PINOT N's GC status imminent. Also plans for PC in gd sites.

Amiel, Mas Rouss r w sw ★★★ Leading MAURY, CÔTES DU ROUSS, IGP. Look for Vol de

---

AOP and IGP: what's happening in France

The Europe-wide introduction of AOP (Appellation d'Origine Protegée) and IGP (Indication Géographique Protegée) means that these terms may now appear on labels. AC/AOC will continue to be used, but for simplicity and brevity this book now uses IGP for all former VDP.

Nuit from v. old CARIGNAN, GRENACHE-based Vers le Nord, Origine, Altaïr, others. Plus young *grenat* (Maury version of RIMAGE), venerable RANCIO VDN 20- to 40-yr-old Maury dramatically aged in 1000 60-litre glass demijohns for 12 mths in full sun.

Amirault, Yannick Lo ★★★→★★★★ 05' 08' 09' 10' 11 12 14' 15' 16' 17' 18' Organic. Impeccable BOURGUEIL (20 ha)/ST-NICOLAS-DE-BOURGUEIL (10 ha). Top wines: La Mine (St-Nicolas), La Petite CAVE, Le Grand Clos, Les Quartiers (Bourgueil). Yannick amazed by 18.

Angerville, Marquis d' C d'O r w ★★★★ Bio superstar in VOLNAY, not just classy but classical too, esp legendary CLOS des Ducs (MONOPOLE). Enjoy Champans, Taillepieds as well. *See also* DOM DU PÉLICAN for Jura interests.

Anglès, Ch d' L'doc ★★★ Stellar LA CLAPE estate renovated by Eric Fabre, ex-technical director of CH LAFITE, captivated by MOURVÈDRE. Unoaked Classique (r p w), ageworthy oaked *grand vin* (r w).

Anjou Lo r p w (dr) (sw) (sp) ★→★★★★ Both region and AC encompassing ANJOU, SAUMUR. Poor reputation holds region back. CHENIN BL dry whites: wide range of styles from light quaffers to complex – pressure for dry crus, esp Chaume; juicy reds, incl GAMAY; fruity CAB FR-based Anjou Rouge; robust but tannic ANJOU-VILLAGES, incl CAB SAUV. Mainly dry SAVENNIÈRES; lightly sweet to rich COTEAUX DU LAYON Chenin Bl; rosé (dr s/sw), sparkling mainly CRÉMANT. Many natural wines often VIN DE FRANCE. 18 may well be great.

Anjou-Coteaux de la Loire Lo w sw s/sw ★★→★★★★ 09 10' 11' 14 15' 16 17 18 Small (30 ha, 15 producers) AC for sweet CHENIN BL w of Angers; more racy than COTEAUX DU LAYON. Esp CH de Putille, Delaunay, Fresche, VIGNOBLE Musset-Roullier (excellent).

Anjou-Villages Lo r ★→★★★★ 09' 10' 14' 15' 16' 17 (18') Structured red AC (CAB FR/CAB SAUV, a few pure Cab Sauv). Grippy tannins can be a problem; needs bottle-age. Top wines gd value, esp Bergerie, Branchereau, Brizé, CADY, CH Pierre-Bise, CLOS de Coulaine, Delesvaux, Ogereau, Sauveroy, Soucherie. Sub-AC Anjou-Villages-Brissac same zone as COTEAUX DE L'AUBANCE; look for Bablut, CH de Varière (part of ACKERMAN), Haute Perche, Montigilet, Princé, Richou, Rochelles. 18 v. promising.

Apremont Sav w ★★ Largest cru of Savoie (378 ha, 20.6% of volume) just s of Chambéry. Jacquère only grape. Keep up to 5 yrs. Producers: Aphyllantes, Blard, Boniface, Dacquin, Giachino, Masson, Perrier, Rouzan.

Arbin Sav r ★★ SAV cru 39 ha. Deep-coloured, spicy red, solely from MONDEUSE grapes, ideal après-ski. Drink to 8 yrs+. Try: l'Idylle, Magnin, Quenard, Tosset.

Arbois Jura r p w (sp) ★★→★★★★ 10' 12 14' 15' 16 (17) Heart of n Jura, great spot for wine, cheese, chocolates, walking and Louis Pasteur museum. CHARD, and/or SAVAGNIN whites, VIN JAUNE, reds from Poulsard, Trousseau or PINOT N. Try terroir-true Stephane TISSOT, fresh *ouillé* styles from DOM DU PÉLICAN, oxidative (*typés*) whites from Overnoy/Houillon, plus all-rounders AVIET, Pinte, Renardières, Rolet.

Ariège SW Fr r r p w ★ 17 18 Locally popular IGP on way to Andorra. Try DOM des Coteaux d'Engravies (esp varietal SYRAH), Swiss-owned Dom Beau Regard.

Arjolle, Dom de l' L'doc ★★★ Large CÔTES de THONGUE family-run estate. Range incl Equilibre, Equinoxe, Paradoxe, varietals and blends, and two original Vins de France: Z for ZIN, K for CARMÉNÈRE.

Arlaud C d'O r ★★★→★★★★ Leading MOREY-ST-DENIS estate energized by Cyprien A and siblings. Beautifully poised, modern wines with depth and class from exceptional BOURGOGNE Roncevie up to GCS. Fine range of Morey PCS, esp Ruchots.

Arlay, Ch d' Jura r p w sw ★★ One of bigger JURA players with aristocratic history and sound wines. VIN JAUNE of interest.

Arlot, Dom de l' C d'O r w ★★→★★★ AXA-owned NUITS-ST-GEORGES estate, stylish fragrant Nuits in both colours, esp red CLOS des Forêts St Georges. Calmer approach to whole-bunch vinification now. Top wine ROMANÉE-ST-VIVANT.

Armand, Comte C d'O r ★★★★ Sole owner of exceptional CLOS des Epeneaux, most graceful wine of POMMARD. Great wines, esp since 99, poise, finesse, longevity. Solid AUXEY, VOLNAY too.

Arnoux-Lachaux C d'O r ★★★ →★★★★ Long-est BURG DOM enjoying renaissance with new generation. Cakily concentrated wines replaced by lighter-coloured ethereal gems. All gd, esp Vosne Suchots.

Aube Champ S v'yds of CHAMP, aka Côte des Bar. V.gd PINOT N used by houses elsewhere in Champ. NB Drappier Grande Sendrée.

Aupilhac, Dom d' L'doc ★★★ MONTPEYROUX. Sylvain Fadat cultivates s-facing old-vine MOURVÈDRE, CARIGNAN: old-vine Le CARIGNAN (his 1st wine, 1989), as well as n-facing, higher-altitude SYRAH and whites in Les Cocalières.

Auxey-Duresses C d'O r w ★★→★★★ (r) 09' 10' 12 15' **16** 17 18' (w) 14' 15' 17' 18 CÔTE DE BEAUNE village in valley behind MEURSAULT. Fresh *whites offer value*, reds now ripen in most yrs. Best: (r) COCHE-DURY, COMTE ARMAND, DOMS LEROY (Les Boutonniers) and ROULOT, Gras, Moulin aux Moines, Paquet, Prunier; (w) Lafouge, LEROUX, Piquet.

Aveyron SW Fr r p w ★ IGP DYA. Handful of keen local growers, eg. ★★Nicolas Carmarans, developing a local market for wines from rare local grapes. Try ★DOMS Bertau, Bias (PINOT N), Pleyjean and cf. AOPS ENTRAYGUES, ESTAING, MARCILLAC.

Aviet, Lucien Jura ★★ Fine ARBOIS grower, nicknamed Bacchus. Gd-value, eg. attractive light Poulsard and tangy SAVAGNIN.

Avize Champ ★★★★ Côte des Blancs GC CHARD village home to finest growers Agrapart, Corbon, De Sousa, Selosse; Co-op Union CHAMP provides base wines to major houses.

Aÿ Champ Revered PINOT N village, home of BOLLINGER, DEUTZ. Mix of merchants and growers' wines, either made in barrel, eg. Claude Giraud, master of Argonne oak, or in tanks. *Gosset-Brabant* Noirs d'Aÿ excels. Aÿ Rouge (Coteaux Champenois) now excellent in ripe yrs (esp 15').

Ayala Champ Reborn AŸ house, owned by BOLLINGER. Fine BRUT Zéro, BLANC DE BLANCS. Ace Prestige Perle d'Ayala **08'** 09 12' 13 15' 16. Precision, purity. Energy under Caroline Latrine, chef de CAVE.

Bachelet Burg r w ★★ →★★★★ Widespread family name in s c D'O. Look for: B-Monnot (esp PULIGNY, BÂTARD-MONTRACHET), Bernard B (Maranges), Jean-Claude B (CHASSAGNE, St-Aubin, etc). No relation to Denis B (great GEVREY-CHAMBERTIN).

Bandol Prov r p (w) ★★★ Compact coastal AC; Superb barrel-aged reds; ageing potential enormous, MOURVÈDRE the key, with GRENACHE, CINSAULT; drop of white from CLAIRETTE, UGNI BL, occasionally SAUV BL. Mourvèdre-based *rosés* often have gd ageing potential. Several stars: DOMS de la Bégude, du Gros'Noré, La Bastide Blanche, Lafran Veyrolles, La Suffrène, Mas de la Rouvière, *Pibarnon*, Pradeaux, TEMPIER, Terrebrune, Vannières.

Banyuls Rouss r p w ★★→★★★ Deliciously original and underappreciated VDN, based on old GRENACHES NOIR, BLANC, Gris. Young vintage RIMAGE is fresh, fruity. Traditional RANCIOS, aged for many yrs, much more rewarding. Serious alternative to fine old Tawny Port. Best: DOMS du Mas Blanc (★★★), la Rectorie (★★★), la Tour Vieille (★★★), Les CLOS de Paulilles, Coume del Mas (★★), Madeloc, Vial Magnères. See also MAURY.

Baronne, Ch La L'doc ★★★ Bio family estate in CORBIÈRES; min intervention in cellar. Barrels, amphoras, eggs... Corbières Alaric, Les Chemins, Les Lanes and (CARIGNAN planted 1892) Pièce de Roche. IGP Hauterive. Sulphur-free Les Chemins de Traverse, and VIN DE FRANCE VERMENTINO/Grenache Gris (w).

Barrique B'X (and Cognac) term for oak barrel holding 225 litres. Used globally, but global mania for excessive new oak now thankfully fading. Average price €750/barrel.

Barsac Saut w sw ★★→★★★★ 90' 01' 05 09' 11' 15' 16' Neighbour of SAUT with v. similar botrytized wines from lower-lying limestone soil; fresher, less powerful. Badly hit by frost in 2017. Top: CAILLOU, CLIMENS, COUTET, DOISY-DAËNE, DOISY-VÉDRINES, NAIRAC.

Barthod, Ghislaine C d'O r ★★★ →★★★★ A reason to fall in love with CHAMBOLLE-MUSIGNY, if you haven't already. Wines of perfume, delicacy, yet depth, concentration. Impressive range of nine PCS, incl Charmes, Cras, Fuées, Les Baudes.

Bâtard-Montrachet C d'O w ★★★★ 04' 07' 08' 09' 10 11 12 14' 15 17' 18 12-ha GC downslope from LE MONTRACHET itself. Grand, hefty whites that need some time; more power than neighbours BIENVENUES-B-M and CRIOTS B-M. Seek out: BACHELET-Monnot, BOILLOT (both H and JM), CARILLON, DOMS DE LA VOUGERAIE, LEFLAIVE, FAIVELEY, GAGNARD, LATOUR, LEROUX, MOREY, OLIVIER LEFLAIVE, Pernot, Ramonet, SAUZET.

Baudry, Dom Bernard Lo r p w ★★→★★★ 09' 10' 14' 15' 16' 17' (18') 32 ha Cravant-les-Coteaux, gravel and limestone; Mathieu Baudry in charge. V.gd CHINONS, from CHENIN BL whites to CAB FR (r p); drink Les Granges early; CLOS Guillot, Croix Boissée, Les Grézeaux more complex. Organic. Consistent, age-worthy.

Baudry-Dutour Lo r p w (sp) ★★→★★★ 14' 15' 16' 17' (18') CHINON's largest producer, incl CHX de St Louans (r w), La Grille, La Perrière, La Roncée. Run by J-M Dutour and Christophe Baudry. Modern, functional winery in Panzoult. Consistently reliable: light, early-drinking to age-worthy (r w). IGP SAUV BL.

Baumard, Dom des Lo r p w sw sp ★★→★★★ 14 15 16 17 (18') 40 ha ANJOU dom, esp CHENIN BL whites, incl SAVENNIÈRES (CLOS St Yves, Clos du Papillon), Clos Ste Catherine. Apostle of cryoextraction for QUARTS DE CHAUME (illegal from 2020). New winery.

Baux-en-Provence, Les Prov r p w ★★→★★★ V'yds around dramatic bauxite outcrop of Alpilles that divides cooler n from hotter s. White: CLAIRETTE, GRENACHE BL, Rolle, ROUSSANNE. Red: CAB SAUV, SYRAH, GRENACHE. Most v'yds organic. Best estate remains *Trévallon*: IGP Cab/Syrah blend. Also CHX d'Estoublon, Romanin, DOM Hauvette, Mas de la Dame, Mas Ste Berthe, Terres Blanches, Valdition and atypical Milan.

Béarn SW Fr r p w ★→★★ AOP (r) 15 17 18 (p w) DYA. Pinks from co-op at ★Bellocq hit the spot in summer. Reds from ★DOMS de la Callabère, Lapeyre/Guilhémas. Whites from local Ruffiat de Moncade grape.

Beaucastel, Ch de S Rh r w ★★★★ 90' 95' 99' 05' 06' 07' 09' 10' 12' 13' 15' 16' 17' 18' Large, organic CHÂTEAUNEUF estate: old MOURVÈDRE, 100-yr-old ROUSSANNE. Darkly fruited, recently smoother wines, drink at 3 or from 7–8. Intense,brilliant, top-quality 60% Mourvèdre Hommage à Jacques Perrin (r). *Wonderful old-vine Roussanne*: enjoy over 5–25 yrs. Genuine, serious own-vines CÔTES DU RH Coudoulet de Beaucastel (r, v.gd 16'), lives 10 yrs+. Famille Perrin GIGONDAS (v.gd), RASTEAU, VINSOBRES (best) all gd, authentic. Note organic Perrin Nature Côtes du Rh (r w). Growing N Rh merchant venture, Maison Les Alexandrins (elegant). (*See also* Tablas Creek, California.)

Beaujolais r (p) (w) ★ DYA. Basic appellation of huge Beauj region. Often dull but doesn't need to be – try those from hills around Bois d'Oingt. Can now be sold as COTEAUX BOURGUIGNONS.

Beaujolais Primeur / Nouveau Beauj More of an event than a drink. The BEAUJ of the new vintage, hurriedly made for release at midnight on the 3rd Wednesday in Nov. Enjoy juicy fruit but don't let it put you off real thing.

Beaujolais-Villages Beauj r ★★ 15' 17 18' Next best v'yds after the ten named crus, eg. MOULIN-À-VENT. May specify best village such as Lantigné. Burgaud, Chemarin, Lacarelle top sources.

Beaumes-de-Venise S Rh r (p) (w) br ★★ (r) 09' 10' 12' 13' 15' 16' 17' (MUSCAT) DYA. Village nr GIGONDAS, high v'yds, popular for VDN Muscat apéritif/dessert. Serve v. cold: grapey, honeyed, can be stylish, eg. DOMS Beaumalric, Bernardins (musky,

> **Beaulolais stars**
>
> BEAUJ is one of greater Burg's most dynamic regions, where prices remain relatively affordable, so much so that many C D'O producers are investing in land down here: JADOT, Louis BOILLOT, Thibault LIGER-BELAIR in MOULIN À Vent; BOUCHARD, DROUHIN, LAFARGE-Vial in FLEURIE. Others sniffing around... Alternatively look to hungry "new kid in town" producers, eg. Julie Balagny or Julien Sunier in Fleurie, P-H Thillardon in CHÉNAS, Richard Rottiers in Moulin à Vent. It's still GAMAY, though; you may still prefer PINOT N.

traditional), Coyeux Durban (rich, long life), Fenouillet (brisk), JABOULET, Pigeade (fresh, v.gd), VIDAL-FLEURY, co-op Rhonéa. Also punchy, grainy reds. CH Redortier, de Fenouillet, Dom Cassan, Durban, la Ferme St-Martin (organic), St-Amant (gd w). Leave for 2– yrs. Simple whites (some dry MUSCAT, VIOGNIER).

Beaumont des Crayères Champ Côte d'Épernay co-op making model PINOT M-based Grande Rés NV. Vintage Fleur de Prestige top value 12' 13 14 15'. Great CHARD-led CUVÉE Nostalgie 02' 13. New Fleur de Meunier BRUT Nature 12' 15'. More Chard planting planned.

Beaune C d'O r (w) ★★★ 05' 09' 10' 11 12 14 15' 16 17 18' Centre of Burg wine trade, classic merchants: BOUCHARD, Champy, CHANSON, DROUHIN, JADOT, LATOUR, Remoissenet and young pretenders Gambal, Lemoine, LEROUX, Roche de Bellene; top DOMS Croix, DE MONTILLE, LAFARGE, plus iconic HOSPICES DE BEAUNE. Graceful, perfumed PC reds offering value, eg. Bressandes, Cras, VIGNES Franches; more power from Grèves. Try Aigrots, CLOS St Landry, and esp *Clos des Mouches (Drouhin)* for whites.

Becker, Caves J Al r w ★ ★★★ Organic estate certified bio since 1999. Stylish wines, incl poised, taut GC Froehn in Zellenberg, prime RIES country between Riquewihr and Ribeauvillé. Interesting contrast with Ries GC Mandelberg.

Belargus, Dom Lo Ambitious new 26-ha venture by Parisian financier and CHENIN-lover, Ivan Massonnat, who has bought Pithon-Paillé (10 ha QUARTS DE CHAUME) from Laffourcade and 3 ha in SAVENNIÈRES.

Bellet Prov r p w ★★ Minute AC, under 70 ha within city of Nice; rarely seen elsewhere. Rewarding white from Rolle surprisingly age-worthy. Folle Noire for red (DYA). Braquet for rosés. Ten producers: CH de Bellet, oldest, now owned by property company REM. Also Ch de Cremat, CLOS St Vincent, Collet de Bovis, DOMS de la Source, de Toasc, Via Julia Augusta.

Bellivière, Dom de Lo r w sw (sp) ★★–★★★ 15' 16 17 18' 15-ha, bio. Fine JASNIÈRES, COTEAUX DU LOIR, peppery red Pineau d'Aunis. Les Arches de Bellivière (NÉGOCIANT).

Bergerac SW Fr r p w dr sw ★ ★★★ 15' 16 17 18 AOP Bargains from Bx's neighbour. Disparate styles, huge quality variation. ★★★CLOS des Verdots, ★★★*Tour des Gendres*, ★★CH Cluzeau, DOMS du Cantonnet, *Fleur de Thénac*, Jonc-Blanc, Julien Auroux. *See* growers in sub-AOPS MONBAZILLAC, MONTRAVEL, PÉCHARMANT, ROSETTE, SAUSS GNAC for some of best.

Berlioz, Gilles Sav V.gd tiny bio DOM (3.5 ha) in CHIGNIN. Four small parcels: Altesse, JACQUÈRE, MONDEUSE, Persan. Wines incl: El Hem, La Deuse, Le Jaja, Les Christine, Les Filles, Les Fripons.

Berthet-Bondet, Jean Jura r w ★★ Biggest producer (still small) of CH-CHALON VIN JAUNE but covers all bases for Jura red, white and CRÉMANT reliably. COTES DU JURA tradition v.gd value.

Bertrand, Gérard L'doc r p w ★★ Ambitious grower and NÉGOCIANT, now one of biggest in MIDI; Villemajou (CORBIÈRES cru Boutenac), Laville-Bertou (MINERVOIS-La Livinière), l'Aigle (LIMOUX), IGP Hauterive Cigalus, la Sauvageonne (v.gd rosé) (Terrasses du Larzac), recently bought CH de la Soujeole (Malepère), DOM du Temple and Deux Rocs in Cabrières. Flagship: *Ch l'Hospitalet* (LA CLAPE) with top wine Hospitalis. Aspirational, expensive CLOS d'Ora (Minervois-La Livinière). Also Prima Nature: zero sulphur. Converting to bio.

Besserat de Bellefon Champ ★★ Épernay house specializing in gently sparkling CHAMP (old CRÉMANT style). Part of LANSON-BCC group. Respectable rising quality, always gd value, esp 13 14 15, tiny but excellent 17'.

Beyer, Léon Al r w ★★→★★★ Top family AL house, arch-traditionalists delivering intense, dry gastronomic wines listed by many Michelin-starred restaurants. Best, and calling card, is lovely RIES Comtes d'Eguisheim 14 17'. With climate change, Beyer PINOT N is startlingly gd in poised burgundian style, esp 16 17.

Bichot, Maison Albert Burg r w ★★→★★★ Major BEAUNE merchant/grower. Impressive wines in a sturdy style, more concentrated than perfumed. Best wines from own DOMS, Adélie (MERCUREY), CLOS Frantin (NUITS), du Pavillon (Beaune), LONG-DEPAQUIT (CHAB).

Bienvenues-Bâtard-Montrachet C d'O ★★★→★★★★ 04 07 08 09 10 12 14' 15 17' 18 Fractionally lighter, earlier-maturing version of BÂTARD, more initial grace, super-succulence. Best: BACHELET, CARILLON, FAIVELEY, LEFLAIVE, Ramonet, VOUGERAIE.

Billaud Chab ★★★→★★★★ DOM Billaud-Simon is a long-time leader in CHAB, now back to best under FAIVELEY ownership. Equally brilliant are Samuel B's wines, esp Vaillons, CLOS, etc.

Billecart-Salmon Champ ★★★ New generation at helm of family house. New chef de CAVE trained by retiring maestro François Domi. Brilliant multi-vintage 200th Anniversary CUVÉE for long cellarage to 2035. Cuvée Louis Bl de Blancs probably best CHARD in 06. Superb 60s St Hilaire 98 99 02. NF Billecart perhaps greatest 02. Exquis Elisabeth Salmon Rosé 02 06 07.

Bize, Simon C d'O r w ★★★ High-class SAVIGNY grower (r w), great range of PCS. NB Aux Guettes, Vergelesses. tasty generic BOURGOGNES too.

Blagny C d'O r w ★★→★★★ 05' 09' 10' 12 14 15' 16' 17 18' Hamlet on hillside above MEURSAULT and PULIGNY. Own AC for austere yet fragrant reds, volumes falling. Whites sold as Meursault-Blagny PC. V'yds: La Jeunelotte, Pièce Sous le Bois, Sous le Dos d'Ane. Growers: (r) LEROUX, Matrot; (w) de Cherisey, JOBARD, LATOUR, Matrot.

Blanc de Blancs Any white wine made from white grapes only, esp CHAMP. Indication of style, not of quality.

Blanc de Noirs White (or slightly pink or "blush", or "gris") wine from red grapes, esp CHAMP: generally rich, even blunt, in style. But many now more refined; better PINOT N and new techniques.

Blanck, Paul & Fils Al r w ★★→★★★★ Grower at Kientzheim. Finest from 6-ha GC Furstentum (RIES, GEWURZ, PINOT GR), GC SCHLOSSBERG (great Ries 14 16 17'). Excellent Classique generics: tiptop, great value.

Blanquette de Limoux L'doc w sp ★★ Great-value bubbles from cool hills sw of Carcassonne; older history than CHAMP. 90% Mauzac with a little CHARD, CHENIN BL. AC CRÉMANT de Limoux, more elegant with Chard, Chenin Bl, PINOT N, and less Mauzac. Large *Sieur d'Arques co-op.* Also Antech, Delmas, Laurens, RIVES-BLANQUES, Robert and several newcomers: DOMS La Coume-Lumet, Les Hautes Terres, Jo Riu, Monsieur S.

Blaye B'x r ★→★★★ 10' 11 12 14 15 16 Designation for better reds (lower yields, higher v'yd density, longer maturation) from AC BLAYE-CÔTES DE B'x.

Blaye-Côtes de Bordeaux B'x r w ★→★★ 10' 12 14 15 16' Mainly MERLOT-led red AC on right bank of Gironde. A little dry white (mainly SAUV BL). Best CHX: Bel Air la Royère, Bourdieu, Cailleteau Bergeron, Cantinot, des Tourtes, Gigault (CUVÉE Viva), Haut-Bertinerie, Haut-Grelot, Jonqueyres, Monconseil-Gazin, Mondésir-Gazin, Montfollet, Roland la Garde, Segonzac. Also CAVE des Hauts de Gironde (Tutiac) co-op for whites. Bad hail 18.

Boeckel, Dom Al ★★★→★★★★ VIGNERONS since the 1600s; DOM started 1853, now

23 ha, organic cultivation. RIES Wibbelsberg, CLOS Eugenie is rich, rounded 13 16 17. GC Zotzenberg unique site for top *Sylvaner*. Exemplary CRÉMANT D'AL.

Boillot C d'O r w Leading Burg family. Look for ★★★Jean-Marc (POMMARD), esp for fine, long-lived whites; ★★→★★★★Henri (MEURSAULT), potent whites and modern recs; ★★★Louis (CHAMBOLLE, married to GHISLAINE BARTHOD) for ever-improving recs, and his brother ★★→★★★Pierre (GEVREY).

Boisset, Jean-Claude Burg Ultra-successful merchant/grower group created over last 50 yrs. Boisset label and esp own v'yds *Dom de la Vougeraie* excellent. Recent additions to empire are the brands VINCENT GIRARDIN (Burg) and HENRI MAIRE (JURA). Also projects in California (Gallo connection), Canada, Chile, Uruguay.

Boizel Champ ★★★ Exceptional value, rigorous quality, family-run. Well-aged BLANC DE BLANCS is a steal. CUVÉE Sous Bois shows expression without woodiness. Prestige Cuvée Joyau de France, esp Rosé 12, drink sublimely in 2020.

Bollinger Champ ★★★★ Great classic house, ever-better quality and much fresher now. BRUT Special NV on top form since 2012; RD 04; underrated Grande Année 07 08'. PINOT N-led, innovative Vintage Rosé 06, lush, powerful, with high 30% of Côte aux Enfants rouge, brilliant with game. Change of MD, now a Burgundian, in 20 17/18. *See also* LANGLOIS-CH.

Bonneau du Martray, Dom C d'O (r) ★★★ (w) ★★★★ Reference producer for CORTON-CHARLEMAGNE, bought 2016 by Stanley Kroenke, owner of Screaming Eagle (California) and Arsenal football club (UK). Intense wines designed for long (c.10 yrs) ageing, glorious mix of intense fruit, underlying minerals. Small amount of fine red CORTON.

Bonnes-Mares C d'O r ★★★★ 90' 93 96' 99' 02' 05' 09' 10' 12' 15' 16' 18' GC between CHAMBOLLE-MUSIGNY and MOREY-ST-DENIS with some of latter's wilder character. Sturdy, long-lived wines, less fragrant than MUSIGNY. Best: ARLAUD, Bernstein, BRUNO CLAIR, Drouhin-Laroze, DE VOGÜÉ, Dujac, Groffier, JADOT, MORTET, MUGNIER, ROUMIER, VOUGERAIE.

Bonnezeaux Lo w sw ★★★→★★★★ 05' 09 10' 11' 14 15' 16 17 18' 80 ha; 40 producers. Can be top Lo sweet CHENIN BL from three sw-facing slopes in COTEAUX DU LAYON. Esp: CHX de Fesles, La Variète (ACKERMAN), DOMS de Mihoudy, du Petit Val, Les Grandes VIGNES. Lasts decades.

Bordeaux r (p) w ★→★★★ 16 (18) Catch-all AC for generic B'x (represents nearly half region's production). Most brands (*Dourthe*, Michel Lynch, MOUTON CADET, *Sichel*) are in this category. *See* CHX Barreyre, Bauduc, Bonhoste, BONNET, Reignac, Tour de Mirambeau. Quantity hit by mildew, hail 18.

Bordeaux Supérieur B r r →★★★ 10' 14 15 16 (18) Superior denomination to above. Higher min alc, lower yield, longer ageing. Mainly bottled at property. Mildew depleted yields in 13. Consistent CHX: Camarsac, Fleur Haut Gaussens, Grand Village, Grée-Larocque, Jean Faux, Landereau, Parenchère (CUVÉE Raphaël), Perrin, *Pey la Tour* (Rés), Reignac, *Thieuley*, Turcaud (Cuvée Majeure).

Borie-Manoux B'x Admirable B'x shipper, CH-owner: BATAILLEY, BEAU-SITE, DOM DE L'EGLISE, LYNCH-MOUSSAS, TROTTEVIEILLE. Also owns NÉGOCIANT Mähler-Besse.

Bouchard Père & Fils Burg r w ★★→★★★★ Top BEAUNE merchant, quality v. sound all round, robust style. Whites best in MEURSAULT and GC, esp CHEVALIER-MONTRACHET. Flagship reds: Beaune VIGNE de l'Enfant Jésus, CORTON, *Volnay Caillerets Ancienne Cuvée Carnot*. Same group as WILLIAM FÈVRE (CHAB), CH de Poncié (BEAUJ).

Bouches-du-Rhône Prov r p w ★ IGP from Marseille environs. Simple, hopefully fruity, reds from s varieties, plus CAB SAUV, SYRAH, MERLOT.

Bourgeois, Henri Lo r p w ★★→★★★ 10 12 14' 15' 16' 17' 18' Model SANCERRE grower/merchant in Chavignol. Dynamic, close-knit family always to improve. V.gd: CHÂTEAUMEILLANT, COTEAUX DU GIENNOIS, MENETOU-SALON, POUILLY-FUMÉ, QUINCY, IGP Petit Bourgeois. Best: Etienne Henri, Jadis, La Bourgeoise (r w), MD de

Bourgeois, Sancerre d'Antan. Top wines v. age-worthy. Also Clos Henri in Marlborough, NZ.

Bourgogne Burg r (p) w ★→★★ (r) 15' 16 **17** 18' (w) 14' 15 17' 18 Ground-floor AC for Burg, ranging from mass-produced to bargain beauties. Sometimes comes with subregion attached, eg. CÔTE CHALONNAISE, HAUTES-CÔTES and latest addition, C D'O. Whites from CHARD unless B. ALIGOTÉ. Reds from PINOT N unless declassified BEAUJ crus (sold as Bourgogne GAMAY) or B. Passetoutgrains (Pinot/Gamay mix, must have 30%+ of former).

Bourgueil Lo r (p) ★★→★★★ 10' 14' 15' **16 17' 18'** 1400 ha, full-bodied, long-lived TOURAINE reds, rosés based on CAB FR. Gd vintages age 50 yrs+. Incl: AMIRAULT, Ansodelles, Audebert, Chevalerie, Courant, de la Butte, Gambier, Lamé Delisle Boucard, Ménard, Minière, Nau Frères, Omasson, Revillot, Rochouard. Frosted 16, largely escaped 17. Excellent 18.

Bouscassé, Dom SW Fr r w ★★★ 12 14 15' (17) (18) King of MADIRAN. BRUMONT lives here in Napa Valley style. Reds a shade quicker to mature than oaky flagship MONTUS. ★★★Petit Courbu-based dry PACHERENC best of its kind.

Bouvet-Ladubay Lo (r) p w sp ★★→★★★ SAUMUR sparkling and CRÉMANT DE LO now run by Monmousseau family. Patrice M (president), daughter Juliette (CEO). CUVÉE Trésor (p w), BRUT Extra Zéro, SAUMUR-CHAMPIGNY Les Nonpareils best.

Bouzereau C d'O r w ★★→★★★ The B family infest MEURSAULT, in a gd way. Try whites from Jean-Baptiste (DOM Michel B), Vincent B or B-Gruère & Filles.

Bouzeron Burg (r) w ★★ 15' 17' 18 CÔTE CHALONNAISE village with unique AC for ALIGOTÉ; stricter rules and greater potential than straight BOURGOGNE Aligoté. BOUCHARD PÈRE, Briday, FAIVELEY, Jacqueson gd; *A & P de Villaine* outstanding.

Bouzy Rouge Champ r ★★★ 09 12 15' Still red of famous PINOT N village. Formerly like v. light burg, now with more intensity (climate change, better viticulture), also refinement. VCP CLOS, Colin and Paul Bara best producers.

Boxler, Albert Al ★★★★ Compact DOM, 13.5 ha, classic AL as complex as great burg. Artisan precepts, brillant RIES GC Sommerberg and PINOT GR Res 10 both ready but will hold well.

Brocard, J-M Chab w ★★→★★★ Successful quality grower/merchant. Julien B has added bio methods to father Jean-Marc's flair. Sustainable mix of volume/value CHAB lines and high-class individual bottlings. Try GC Les Preuses.

Brouilly Beauj r ★★ 15' **16 17** 18' Largest of ten BEAUJ crus: solid, rounded wines with some depth of fruit, approachable early but can age 3–5 yrs. Top growers: CHX de la Chaize, Thivin, Piron, DOM Chermette, JC Lapalu, L&R Dufaitre.

Brumont, Alain SW Fr r w ★★★ MADIRAN's star still makes blockbusting BOUSCASSÉ, Le Tyre, MONTUS, but also easier-drinking wines eg. ★Torus and range of quaffable IGPS. ★★★PACHERENCS (dr sw) outstanding.

Brut Champ Term for dry classic wines of CHAMP. Most houses have reduced dosage (adjustment of sweetness) in recent yrs. But great Champ can still be made at 8–9g residual sugar.

Brut Ultra / Zéro Term for bone-dry wines (no dosage) in CHAMP (also known as Brut Nature); back in fashion, quality generally improving. Needs ripe yr, old vines, max care, eg. POL ROGER Pure, ROEDERER Brut Nature, Veuve Fourny Nature.

Bugey Sav r p w sp ★→★★ AC 490 ha for light, fresh sparkling (56%), *pétillant*, still. Three sectors: Belley, Cerdon, Montagnieu. Eight associated Bugey ACs. Whites (50% incl sp) mainly CHARD also incl ALIGOTÉ, Jacquère, Roussette. Rosé (33%) Reds (17%): GAMAY, MONDEUSE, PINOT N. Growers: Angelot, Lingot-Martin, Monin, Peillot, Pellerin, Trichon.

Buxy, Caves de Burg r (p) w ★→★★★ Leading CÔTE CHALONNAISE co-op for decent CHARD, PINOT N, source of many merchants' own-label ranges. Easily largest supplier of AC MONTAGNY.

Buzet SW Fr r (p) (w) ᴀᴏᴘ ★★ **15′** 17 18 Plummy cousin of ʙ'x. Bio ★★★ᴅᴏᴍ du Pech (natural wines) was ahead of field, incl ᴄʜx du Frandat, bio ᴅᴏᴍ Salisquet and co-op's Ch de Guèze.

Cabernet d'Anjou Lo p s/sw ★→★★ DYA. 5485 ha Lo's largest-volume appellation. ᴅᴇᴍɪ-ꜱᴇᴄ to sweet rosé. Bablut, Bergerie, ᴄᴀᴅʏ, ᴄʜ ᴘɪᴇʀʀᴇ-ʙɪꜱᴇ, Chauvin, Clau de Nell, de Sauveroy, Grandes ᴠɪɢɴᴇꜱ, Montgilet, Ogereau, Varière.

Cadillac-Côtes de Bordeaux B'x r ★→★★ **10′ 14** 15 16 (18) Long, narrow, hilly zone on right bank of Garonne. Mainly ᴍᴇʀʟᴏᴛ with ᴄᴀʙꜱ ꜱᴀᴜᴠ, ꜰʀ. Medium-bodied, fresh reds; quality v. varied. Best: Alios de Ste-Marie, Biac, Carignan, *Carsin*, ᴄʟᴏꜱ Chaumont, Clos Ste-Anne, de Ricaud, Grand-Mouëys, Lamothe de Haux, Laroche, Le Doyenné, Mont-Pérat, Plaisance, Réaut (Carat), *Reynon*, Suau.

Cady, Dom Lo r p w sw sp ★★→★★★ 14′ 15′ 16′ 17′ (18′) V.gd organic family in St Aubin de Luigné, now Alexandre in charge. Range of ᴀɴᴊᴏᴜ with accent on ᴄʜᴇɴɪɴ, incl ᴄᴏᴛᴇᴀᴜx ᴅᴜ ʟᴀʏᴏɴ, esp Chaume, Les Varennes. V. promising 18.

Cahors SW Fr r ★★→★★★★ **12** 15′ 16 (17) (18) ᴀᴏᴘ now reasserting claim to be ᴍᴀʟʙᴇᴄ's true home. All red (some w ɪɢᴘꜱ). Wide variation of styles between eg. traditional ★★★ᴄʟᴏꜱ de Gamot, modern ᴄʜ ᴅᴜ ᴄèᴅʀᴇ and trendy ★★★★ᴅᴏᴍ Cosse-Maisonneuve. Early-drinking from ★★ᴄʜx Paillas, ᴄʟᴏꜱ Coutale, Combella-Serre. Wait longer for ★★★ᴄʜx Chambert, Haut-Monplaisir, Clos Triguedina, Clos Troteligotte, ᴅᴏᴍ de la Bérengeraie, Lo Domeni; ★★ᴄʜx Armandière, de Gaudou, La Coustarelle, Vincens. Range of styles from ★★★ᴄʟᴏꜱ d'Un Jour, Dom du Prince, Lamartine, La Reyne, Les Croisille, Mas La Périé, ★★Eugénie, La Caminade. Influential Vigouroux family empire incl ★★ᴄʜx de Mercuès, Hautes-Serres and Léret-Monpézat under Argentinian influence.

Cailloux, Les S Rh r (w) ★★★ 78′ 81′ 90′ 98′ 03′ 05′ 09′ 10′ 16′ 18-ha ᴄʜâᴛᴇᴀᴜɴᴇᴜꜰ ᴅᴏᴍ; elegant, benchmark, handmade reds, v.gd value. Special wine Centenaire, oldest ɢʀᴇɴᴀᴄʜᴇ 1889 noble, dear. Also ᴅᴏᴍ André Brunel (esp gd-value ᴄôᴛᴇꜱ ᴅᴜ ʀʜ red Est-Ouest), round Féraud-Brunel Côtes du Rh merchant range.

Cairanne S Rh r p w ★★→★★★ 10′ 15′ **16′** 17′ 18′ Excellent choice from *garrigue* soils, wines of character, dark fruits, mixed herbs, esp ᴄʟᴏꜱ Romane, ᴅᴏᴍꜱ Alary (stylish), *Amadieu* (pure, bio), Boisson (punchy), Brusset (deep), Cros de Romet, Escaravailles (flair), Féraud-Brunel, Grands Bois (organic), Grosset, Hautes Cances (true, traditional), Jubain, *Oratoire St Martin* (detail, classy), Présidente, Rabasse-Charavin (punchy), *Richaud* (great fruit). Food-friendly, 3D *whites*.

Cal Demoura, Dom L'doc r p w ★★★ Estate to follow in ᴛᴇʀʀᴀꜱꜱᴇꜱ ᴅᴜ ʟᴀʀᴢᴀᴄ. Meticulous winemaking by Vincent Goumard: Paroles de Pierre, L'Etincelle with six different grapes (w); ʟ'ᴅᴏᴄ blends (r) Combariolles, predominantly ɢʀᴇɴᴀᴄʜᴇ Feu Sacré, Terres de Jonquières and Fragments, mainly old ꜱʏʀᴀʜ.

Canard-Duchêne Champ House owned by ᴀʟᴀɪɴ ᴛʜɪéɴᴏᴛ. Now run by his childen, Frederic and Garance. ʙʀᴜᴛ Vintage 09 12′ 13, Charles VII Prestige multivintage. ★★★ᴄᴜᴠéᴇ Léonie. Improved Authentique Cuvée (organic) 09 12′. Single-v'yd Avize Camin 12 13 16′.

Canon-Fronsac B'x r ★→★★★ 09′ 10′ **14** 15 16 (18) Small enclave within ꜰʀᴏɴ, otherwise same wines. 47 growers. Best: rich, full, finely structured. Try ᴄʜx Barrabaque, Canon Pécresse, Cassagne Haut-Canon la Truffière, ᴅᴜ ɢᴀʙʏ, GrandRenouil, La Fleur Cailleau, ᴍᴏᴜʟɪɴ ᴘᴇʏ-ʟᴀʙʀɪᴇ, Pavillon, Vrai Canon Bouché.

Carillon C d'O ★★★ Contrasting ᴘᴜʟɪɢɴʏ producers: Jacques unchangingly classical; Referts best ᴘᴄ. Brother François wider range and more modern approach. Try Folatières, Combettes. Village Puligny great from both.

Cassis Prov (r) (p) w ★★ DYA. Pleasure port in hills e of Marseille best-known for savoury dry whites based on ᴄʟᴀɪʀᴇᴛᴛᴇ, ᴍᴀʀꜱᴀɴɴᴇ, eg. ᴄʟᴏꜱ Ste Magdeleine, ᴅᴏᴍ de la Ferme Blanche, Fontcreuse, Paternel. Growers fight with property developers, so prices high, but quality interesting.

FRANCE

Castelnau, De Champ Rising co-op with fine v'yds/contracts. Cellarmaster Elisabeth Sarcelet insists on longer lees-ageing in excellent BLANC DE BLANCS and vintage 02. Innovative Prestige Collection Hors d'Age blended from best wines in cellar, different each yr. current release CCF2067 is led by fine PINOT M.

Castillon-Côtes de Bordeaux B'x r ★★ →★★★ 09' 10' 14 15 16 (18) Appealing e neighbour of ST-ÉM with improved quality; similar wines, usually less plump. Plenty of new investors from POMEROL and St-Ém. Top: Alcée, Ampélia, Cap de FAUGÈRES, CLOS Les Lunelles, Clos Louie, Clos Puy Arnaud, Côte Montpezat, *d'Aiguilhe*, *de l'A*, Joanin Bécot, *La Clarière-Laithwaite*, l'Aurage, l'Hêtre, Montlandrie, Poupille, Veyry, Vieux CH Champs de Mars.

Cathiard, Dom Sylvain C d'O r ★★★★ Sébastien C makes wines of astonishing quality from VOSNE-ROMANÉE, esp Malconsorts, Orveaux, Reignots, plus NUITS-ST-GEORGES Aux Thorey, Murgers. Seductive young, will develop well over time.

Cave Cellar, or any wine establishment.

Cave coopérative Wine-growers' co-op winery; over half of all French production. Often well-run, well-equipped; wines gd value, but many closing down.

Cazes, Dom Rouss r p w sw ★★ →★★★ Historic DOM, family-run, now part of Advini, largest bio producer in ROUSS. Pioneered B'X varieties, now favours MIDI: Le Canon du Maréchal GRENACHE/SYRAH; Crédo CÔTES DU ROUSS-VILLAGES with Ego, Alter. Sensational aged RIVESALTES CUVÉE Aimé Cazes. CLOS de Paulilles BANYULS, COLLIOURE. New sulphur-free Hommage, powerful SYRAH; MAURY SEC. Ambre (sw w) made with GRENACHE BL. Great value.

Cédre, Ch du SW Fr r w ★★ →★★★ 12 14 15' 16 (17) Best-known of modern CAHORS school. ★★★Le Prestige lighter on purse and palate than ★★more serious top growths. Delicious ★★VIOGNIER IGP. Substantial NÉGOCIANT business.

Cépage Grape variety. *See* pp.16–26 for all.

Cérons B'x w sw ★★ 10' 11 13 14 15' 16 Tiny 23-ha sweet AC next to SAUT. Less intense wines, eg. CHX de Cérons, du Seuil, Grand Enclos, Haura.

Chablis ★★ →★★★ 12' 14' 15 17 18' Wine, region full of energy. Transcends CHARD grape with marine mineral infusion from kimmeridgian soil. Saliva-sur-mer.

Chablis Grand Cru Chab w ★★★ →★★★★ 07' 08' 09 10' 12' 14' 15 17 18' Contiguous s-facing block overlooking River Serein, most concentrated CHAB, needs 5–15 yrs to show detail. Seven v'yds: Blanchots (floral), Bougros (incl Côte Bouguerots), CLOS (usually best), Grenouilles (spicy), Preuses (cashmere), Valmur (structure), Vaudésir (plus brand La Moutonne). Many gd pupils.

Chablisienne, La Chab r w ★★ →★★★ Exemplary co-op responsible for huge slice of CHAB production, esp supermarket-own labels. Gd individual CUVÉES too, eg. GC Grenouilles.

Chablis

There is no better expression of the all-conquering CHARD than the full but tense, limpid but stony wines it makes on the heavy limestone soils of CHAB. Best makers use little or no new oak to mask the precise definition of variety and terroir: Barat, B Defaix, ★Bessin, ★Billaud-Simon, ★Boudin, ★C moreau, ★Dampt family, dom des Malandes, ★Droin, ★DROUHIN, Duplessis, E Vocoret, G Robin, ★J Collet, J DURUP, J-M BROCARD, ★J-P Grossot, LAROCHE, LONG-DEPAQUIT, ★L Michel, MOREAU-Naudet, N Fèvre, ★Picq, ★Pinson, Piuze, ★RAVENEAU, ★Samuel Billaud, Servin, Temps Perdu, Tribut, ★V DAUVISSAT, ★W FÈVRE. Simple, unqualified "Chab" may be thin, and PETIT CHAB thinner; well worth premiums for PC or GC, and essential to mature them 3–15 yrs. Co-op, LA CHABLISIENNE, has high standards (esp ★Grenouille) and many different labels. (★ = outstanding.)

Chablis Premier Cru Chab w ★★★ 09 10' 12' 14' 15 17 18' Well worth small premium over straight CHAB: better sites on rolling hillsides. Mineral favourites: Montmains, Vaillons, Vaucoupin, greater opulence from Mont de Milieu, *Montée de Tonnerre*, Vaulorent.

Chambertin C d'O r ★★★★ 90' 93 96' 99' 02' 05' 09' 10' 12' 14 15' 16 17 18' Candidate for Burg's most imperious wine; amazingly dense, sumptuous, long-lived, expensive. Producers who match potential incl: Bernstein, BOUCHARD PÈRE & FILS, Charlopin, Damoy, DOM LEROY, DUGAT-Py, DROUHIN, MORTET, ROSSIGNOL-TRAPET, ROUSSEAU, TRAPET.

Chambertin-Clos de Bèze C d'O r ★★★★ 90' 93 96' 99' 02' 03 05' 09' 10' 12' 14 15' 16 17 18' Splendid neighbour to CHAMBERTIN, slightly more accessible in youth, velvet texture, deeply graceful. Best: Bart, B CLAIR, Damoy, D Laurent, DROUHIN, Drouhin-Laroze, Duroché, FAIVELEY (incl super-CUVÉE Les Ouvrées Rodin), Groffier, JADOT, Prieuré-Roch, ROUSSEAU.

Chambolle-Musigny C d'O r ★★★ →★★★★ 93 99' 02' 05' 09' 10' 12' 15' 16 17 18' Silky, velvety wines from CÔTE DE NUITS: Charmes for substance, more chiselled from Cras, Fuées and majesty from Amoureuses, plus GCs BONNES MARES, MUSIGNY. Superstars: BARTHOD, DE VOGÜÉ, MUGNIER, ROUMIER with Felletig, HUDELOT-Baillet and Sigaut on rise. Gd wines from producers outside village: DROUHIN, Groffier, Pousse d'Or, RION.

Champagne Sparkling wines of PINOTS N, M and CHARD: 33,805 ha, heartland c.145km (90-miles) e of Paris. Some PINOT BL in AUBE adds freshness. Other sparkling wines, however ace, cannot be called Champ.

Champagne le Mesnil Champ ★★★ Top-flight co-op in greatest GC CHARD village. Exceptional CUVÉE Sublime 08' 09 13 15 17 from finest sites. Majestic Cuvée Prestige 05 triumphs against odds. Real value.

Chandon de Briailles, Dom C d'O r w ★★★ DOM known for fine, lighter style yet perfumed reds, esp PERNAND-VERGELESSES, Île de Vergelesses, CORTON Bressandes. Style defined by BIO farming, min sulphur, lots of stems, no new oak.

Chanson Père & Fils Burg r w ★ →★★★ Resurgent BEAUNE merchant, quality whites and fine if idiosyncratic reds (whole-cluster aromatics). Try Beaunes, esp CLOS des Fèves (r), CLOS DES MOUCHES (w). Great CORTON-Vergennes (w).

Chapelle-Chambertin C d'O r ★★★ 99' 02' 05' 09' 10' 12' 14' 15' 16 18' Lighter neighbour of CHAMBERTIN; thin soil does better in cooler, damper yrs. Fine-boned wine, less meaty. Top: Damoy, DROUHIN-Laroze, JADOT, ROSSIGNOL-TRAPET, TRAPET, Tremblay.

Chapoutier N Rh ★★ →★★★★ Vocal bio grower/merchant at HERMITAGE. Broadly stylish reds via low-yield, plot-specific, expensive CUVÉES. Dense GRENACHE CHÂTEAUNEUF – Barbe Rac, Croix de Bois (r); CÔTE-RÔTIE La Mordorée; Hermitage – L'Ermite (outstanding r w), Le Pavillon (deep r), Cuvée de l'Orée (w), Le Méal (w). Also ST-JOSEPH Les Granits (r w). *Hermitage whites* outstanding, 100% old-vine MARSANNE. Gd-value *Meysonniers Crozes*. V'yds in COTEAUX D'AIX-EN-PROV, CÔTES DU ROUSS-VILLAGES (gd DOM Bila-Haut), RIVESALTES. Also own Ferraton at Hermitage, BEAUJ house Trenel, CH des Ferrages (PROV), has AL v'yds and Australian joint ventures, esp Doms Tournon and Terlato & Chapoutier (fragrant); also Portuguese Lisboa project, Douro too: hotel, wine bar in Tain, list gets longer every yr.

Charbonnière, Dom de la S Rh r (w) ★★★ 05' 09' 10' 16' 17-ha CHÂTEAUNEUF estate run by sisters. Sound Tradition (r), deep, special wines: distinguished, authentic

---

Champagne domaines to watch in 2020
ANSELME SELOSSE, Armand (Arnaud) Margaine, Didier Doué, Lancelot-Pienne, Lilbert et Fils, Nathalie Falmet, Nicolas Maillart, Philppe Brun, Veuve Fourny, Vilmart.

FRANCE

Mourre des Perdrix, also Hautes Brusquières, new L'Envol, VIEILLES VIGNES. V. elegant, tasty white. Also peppery, small-quantity VACQUEYRAS red.

Chardonnay As well as a white wine grape, also the name of a MÂCON-VILLAGES commune, hence Mâcon-Chardonnay.

Charlemagne C d'O w ★★★★ 13 14' 15' 17' 18 Almost extinct sister appellation to CORTON-CHARLEMAGNE (same rules), revived by DOM DE LA VOUGERAIE from 2013.

Charmes-Chambertin C d'O r ★★★★ 99' 02' 03 05' 09' 10' 12' 15' 16 17 18' GEVREY GC, 31 ha, incl neighbour MAZOYÈRES-CHAMBERTIN. Raspberries and cream plus dark-cherry fruit, sumptuous texture, fragrant finish at best. Try ARLAUD, BACHELET, Castagnier, Coquard-Loison-Fleurot, DUGAT, DUJAC, Duroché, LEROY, MORTET, Perrot-Minot, Roty, ROUSSEAU, Taupenot-Merme, VOUGERAIE.

Chartogne-Taillet Champ A disciple of SELOSSE, Alexandre Chartogne is a new star in CHAMP. Exceptional BRUT Ste Anne NV and single-v'yds Le Chemin de Reims and Les Barres; striking energy.

Charvin, Dom S Rh ★★★ 98' 99' 01' 06' 07' 09' 10' 12' 15' 16' 17' Terroir-focused 8-ha CHÂTEAUNEUF estate, 85% GRENACHE, no oak, only one handmade CUVÉE. Spiced, mineral, high-energy red, with vintage accuracy. V.gd-value, genuine, long-lived CÔTES DU RH (r).

Chassagne-Montrachet C d'O r w ★★★→★★★★ (w) 02' 04 05' 08' 09' 12' 14' 15 17 18' Large village at s end of CÔTE DE BEAUNE. Great whites from eg. Blanchot, Cailleret, La Romanée GCS. Best reds: CLOS St Jean, Morgeot, others more rustic. Try: Coffinet, COLIN, GAGNARD, MOREY, Pillot families plus DOMS Heitz-Lochardet, MOREAU, Niellon, Ramonet (reds too). But too much indifferent village white grown on land better suited to red.

Château (Ch) Means an estate, big or small, gd or indifferent, particularly in B'X (see pp.100–21). Means, literally, castle or great house. In Burg, DOM is usual term.

Château-Chalon Jura w ★★★★ 96 99' 00 05' 09 10' 12 Not a CH but AC and village, the summit of VIN JAUNE style from SAVAGNIN grape. Min 6 yrs barrel-age, not cheap. A sharper, more winey version of Sherry, not fortified. Ready to drink (or cook a chicken in) when bottled, but gains with further age. Fervent admirers search out BERTHET-BONDET, MACLE, Mossu, TISSOT or Bourdy for old vintages.

Château-Grillet N Rh w ★★★★ 01' 04' 07' 09' 10' 12' 14' 15' 16' 17' France's smallest AC. 3.7-ha curved amphitheatre v'yd nr CONDRIEU, sandy-granite terraces. Bought by F Pinault of CH LATOUR in 2011, prices up, wine en finesse, if less deep than before. Smooth, precise VIOGNIER: drink at cellar temperature, decanted, with new-wave food.

Châteaumeillant Lo r p ★→★★ Dynamic 76-ha AC sw Bourges. 23 producers. GAMAY, PINOT N for light reds (75%), VIN GRIS (25%). Pinot N potentially best red but pure versions idiotically banned. BOURGEOIS, Chaillot, Gabrielle, Goyer, Joffre, Joseph Mellot, Lecomte, Nairaud-Suberville, Roux, Rouzé, Siret-Courtaud. V. promising 18.

Châteauneuf-du-Pape S Rh r (w) ★★★→★★★★ 78' 81' 90' 95' 01' 07' 09' 10' 16' Nr Avignon, about 50 gd DOMS (remaining 85 uneven to poor). Up to 13 grapes (r w), headed by GRENACHE, plus SYRAH, MOURVÈDRE (increasing), Counoise. Warm, spiced, floral, textured, long-lived; can be fine, pure, magical, but till mid-2010s too many heavy, sip-only Parker-esque wines. Small, traditional names can be gd value. Prestige old-vine wines (v.gd GRENACHE 16'). To avoid: late-harvest, new oak, 16% alc, too pricey. Whites fresh, fruity, or sturdy, best can age 15+ yrs. Top names: CHX DE BEAUCASTEL, Fortia, Gardine (lovely modern, also w), Mont-Redon, RAYAS (unique, marvellous), Sixtine, Vaudieu; DOMS Barroche, Beaurenard, Bois de Boursan (value), Bosquet des Papes (value), Chante Cigale, Chante Perdrix, CHARBONNIÈRE, CHARVIN (terroir), CLOS du Caillou, Clos du Mont-Olivet, CLOS DES PAPES (ace), Clos St-Jean (sip), Cristia, de la Biscarelle (racy fruit), de la Janasse

> **Châteauneuf as it should be**
> CHÂTEAUNEUF-DU-PAPE should be a seductive wine of finesse, pedigree, suave tannins, floral touches with notes of cedar, Provençal herbs – as opposed to a fruit-bomb. The shape should be spherical. Praise be that in the fabulous 16 vintage, some (often younger) growers knew not to overextract, and instead go with nature's flow: DOMS Chante Cigale VIEILLES VIGNES, de la Solitude Cornelia Constanza, Font de Michelle Étienne Gonnet, Marcoux Vieilles Vignes, Raymond Usseglio Impériale.

(bold), de la Vieille Julienne (bio), du Banneret (traditional), Font-de-Michelle (stylish), Grand Tinel (value), Grand Veneur (oak), Henri Bonneau, LES CAILLOUX, Marcoux (fantastic VIEILLES VIGNES), Mas du Boislauzon (full), Pegaü (da Capo is cult), Pierre André (bio, traditional), Porte Rouge (2.5 ha) P Usseglio, R Usseglio (bio), Roger Sabon, Sénéchaux (modern), CH Sixtine, St-Préfert (sleek), Vieux Donjon, VIEUX TÉLÉGRAPHE.

Chave, Dom Jean-Louis N Rh r w ★★★★ 99' 00 01' 03' 04 05' 07' 09' 10' 11' 12' 13' 15' 16' 17' 18 Excellent family DOM at heart of HERMITAGE. Classy, silken, long-lived reds (more rich recently), incl expensive, v. occasional Cathelin. V.gd, complex white (mainly MARSANNE); occasional VIN DE PAILLE. ST-JOSEPH reds smoky, deep, plot-specific CLOS Florentin (since 2015) v. stylish; also fruity J-L Chave brand St-Joseph Offerus, jolly CÔTES DU RH Mon Coeur, sound merchant Hermitage Farçonnet (r w).

Chavignol Lo r p w SANCERRE village, v. steep v'yds Cul de Beaujeu (largely white), Les Monts Damnés + Grande Côte (also in Amigny). Clay-limestone soil gives full-bodied, mineral whites and reds that age 15 yrs+. V. fine young producers: Matthieu Delaporte (Vincent Delaporte), Pierre Martin. Other producers: ALPHONSE MELLOT, Boulay (v.gd), BOURGEOIS, Cotat, DAGUENEAU, Paul Thomas, Thomas Laballe.

Chénas Beauj r ★★★ 14' 15' 16 18' Smallest BEAUJ cru, between MOULIN-À-VENT and JULIÉNAS, gd-value, meaty, age-worthy, merits more interest. Thillardon is reference DOM, but try also Janodet, LAPIERRE, Pacalet, Piron, Trichard, co-op.

Chêne Bleu Prov ★★ Ambitious part-bio DOM high in hills e of SÉGURET. Extravagant, expensive wines, mainly Ventoux. Stylish part-oaked rosé.

Chevalier-Montrachet C d'O w ★★★★ 04 08 09' 10 12 14' 15 17' 18 Just above MONTRACHET on hill just below in quality, yet makes brilliant crystalline wines. Long-lived but can be accessible early. Top grower is LEFLAIVE, special CUVÉES Les Demoiselles from JADOT, LOUIS LATOUR and La Cabotte from BOUCHARD; try also: CH de Puligny, Chartron, COLIN (P), Dancer, Niellon.

Cheverny Lo r p w ★ ★★★ 16 17 18' LO AC (532 ha) s Blois. White from SAUV BL (majority)/CHARD blend. Light reds mainly GAMAY, PINOT N (also CAB FR, CÔT). **Cour-Cheverny** (48 ha): Romorantin – needs bottle-age. Esp Cazin, CLOS Tue-Boeuf, de Montcy, Gendrier, Huards, Tessier; DOMS de la Desoucherie, du Moulin, Veilloux, Villemade. Fine 18

Chevillon, R C d'O r ★★★ Fabulous range of accessible but age-worthy NUITS-ST-GEORGES PCS: Les St-Georges Vaucrains for power, but try Pruliers, Chaignots, etc. too.

Chidaine, François Lo (r) w dr sw sp ★★★ 14 15 16 17 18' Bio champion. Brilliantly precise MONTLOUIS 20 ha) single v'yds, VIN DE FRANCE, VOUVRAY (10 ha), TOURAINE (7 ha). Owns historic CLOS Baudoin (Vouvray). Accent on SEC and DEMI-SEC. Also Le Chenin d'ailleurs (LIMOUX) to compensate Lo frosts, plus red and white from Spain.

Chignin Sav (r) w ★ DA. AC, 108 ha (95 ha w, 13 ha r). Light white Jacquère grapes, MONDEUSE, GAMAY, PINOT N. Chignin-Bergeron (92 ha) is 100% ROUSSANNE.

Chinon Lo r p (w) ★★ ★★★ 14' 15' 16' 17' 18' 2300 ha (10% p, 2% w); 200 producers.

Sand, gravel, limestone: light to rich TOURAINE CAB FR. Best age 30 yrs+. A little dry CHENIN BL (some wood). Best: ALLIET, BAUDRY, BAUDRY-DUTOUR, Coulaine, Couly-Dutheil, Dozon, Grosbois, JM Raffault, Jourdan-Pichard, Landry, L'R, Moulin à Tan, Noblaie, Pain, Petit Thouars, P & B Couly; now extensive frost protection. Excellent 18.

Chiroubles Beauj r ★★ 15' 17 18' BEAUJ cru in hills above FLEURIE: fresh, fruity, savoury wines. Growers: Ch de Javernand, Cheysson, Lafarge-Vial, Métrat, Passot, Raousset, or merchants DUBOEUF, Trenel.

Chorey-lès-Beaune C d'O r (w) ★★ 09' 10' 12 15' 17 18 TOLLOT-BEAUT is reference for this affordable, uncomplicated AC. Try also Arnoux, DROUHIN, Dublère, Guyon, JADOT, Rapet.

Chusclan S Rh r p w ★ →★★ 16' 17' CÔTES DU RH-VILLAGES with above-average Laudun-Chusclan co-op, incl gd fresh whites. Soft reds, cool rosés. Best co-op labels (r) Chusclan DOM de l'Olivette, CÔTES DU RH Femme de Gicon (r), Enfant Terrible (w), Excellence, LIRAC Dom St Nicolas. Also full CH Signac (best Chusclan, can age), Dom La Romance (fresh, organic), special CUVÉES from *André Roux*.

Clair, Bruno C d'O r p w ★★★ →★★★★ Top-class CÔTE DE NUITS estate for supple, subtle, savoury wines. Gd-value MARSANNAY, old-vine SAVIGNY La Dominode, GEVREY-CHAMBERTIN (CLOS ST-JACQUES, Cazetiers) and standout CHAMBERTIN-CLOS DE BÈZE. Best whites from MOREY-ST-DENIS, CORTON-CHARLEMAGNE.

Clairet B'x Between rosé/red. B'x Clairet is AC. Try CHX Fontenille, Penin, Turcaud.

Clairette de Die N Rh w dr s/sw sp ★★ NV NRh/low Alpine bubbles: flinty or (better) semi-sweet MUSCAT sparkling, beautiful setting. Underrated, muskily fruited, gd value; or dry CLAIRETTE, can age 3–4 yrs. NB: Achard-Vincent, Carod, Jaillance (value), Poulet et Fils (terroir, gd Chatillon-en-Diois r), J-C Raspail (organic, gd IGP SYRAH). Must try.

Clape, Dom Pierre, Olivier N Rh r (w) ★★★ →★★★★ 89' 90' 91' 95' 99' 01' 03' 05' 06' 07' 09' 10' 12' 13' 14' 15' 16' 17' 18 The kings of CORNAS. Great location SYRAH v'yds, many old vines, gd soil work. Profound, lingering reds, vintage accuracy, need 6 yrs+, live 25+. Clear fruit in youngish-vines label Renaissance. Superior CÔTES DU RH, VIN DE FRANCE (r), *St-Péray* (gd style, improved). Auguste C RIP 2018.

Clape, La L'doc r p w ★★ →★★★ Dramatic limestone massif twixt Narbonne and Mediterranean; once an island. High sunshine hours for warm, spicy reds, esp MOURVÈDRE. Sea air gives deliciously salty, herbal whites, based on BOURBOULENC, with ageing potential. New appellation and also Cru du L'doc. CHX ANGLÈS, Camplazens, La Négly, *l'Hospitalet*, Mire l'Etang, Pech-Céleyran, *Pech-Redon*, Ricardelle, *Rouquette-sur-Mer* and Mas du Soleila, Sarrat de Goundy.

Climat Burg Refers to individual named v'yd at any level, esp in CÔTE D'OR, eg. MEURSAULT Tesson, MAZOYÈRES-CHAMBERTIN. UNESCO World Heritage status.

Clos A term carrying some prestige, reserved for distinct (walled) v'yds, often in one ownership (esp AL, Burg, CHAMP).

Clos de Gamot SW Fr r ★★★ 12 15' 16 Textbook examples (still gaining plaudits) of traditional CAHORS before outsiders started messing about with it. ★★★★low-yield CUVÉE VIGNES Centenaires (best yrs only) miraculously survives recent Cahors fashions, deer and wild boar; vines sadly facing retirement. Drink while you can.

Clos de la Roche C d'O r ★★★★ 90' 93' 96' 99' 02' 05' 08 09' 10' 15' 16' 17 18 Maybe finest GC of MOREY-ST-DENIS, as much grace as power, more savoury than sumptuous, blueberries. Needs time. DUJAC and PONSOT references but also try Amiot, ARLAUD, Bernstein, Castagnier, Coquard, H LIGNIER, LEROY, LIGNIER-Michelot, Pousse d'Or, Remy, ROUSSEAU.

Clos des Fées Rouss r w Small, highly-individual estate. Barrel-fermented SYRAH/GRENACHE/MOURVÈDRE/CARIGNAN. De Battre mon Coeur s'est Arrêté is high-altitude Syrah. Gd IGP COTES DE CATALANES (w) old-vine GRENACHE BL.

Clos des Lambrays C d'O r ★★★ 99' 02 05' **09'** 10' 12' 15' 16' 17 18' All but MONOPOLE GC v'yd at MOREY-ST-DENIS, now belongs to LVMH. Early-picked, spicy, stemmy style may evolve with new winemaker from 2018.

Clos des Mouches C d'O r w ★★★ (w) 02 05' 09' 10' 15 17' 18 PC v'yd in several Burg ACS. Mouches = honeybees; *see* label of DROUHIN's iconic BEAUNE bottling. Also BICHOT, CHANSON (Beaune), plus CLAIR, MOREAU, Muzard (SANTENAY), Germain (MEURSAULT).

Clos des Papes S Rh r w ★★★★ 99' 01' 03' 04' **05'** 07' 09' 10' **14'** 15' 16' 17' Always classy CHÂTEAUNEUF DOM of Avril family, v. small yields. Rich, intricate, textured red (mainly GRENACHE, MOURVÈDRE, drink at 2–3 yrs or from 8+); **great white** (six varieties, complex, allow time, deserves rich cuisine; 2–3 yrs, then 10–20).

Clos de Tart C d'O r ★★★★ 02' 03 05' 08' **10'** 13' 14 15' 16' 17 18' Expensive MOREY-ST-DENIS GC. Sylvain Pitiot (director 1996–2014) made a powerful, late-picked style. Made with a lighter touch since. Now part of Pinault/Artemis empire (CH LATOUR, CH GRILLET, etc.).

Clos de Vougeot C d'O r ★★ →★★★★ 90' 99' 02' 03' 05' 09' 10' 12' 13' 15' 16 17 18' CÔTE DE NUITS GC with many owners. Occasionally sublime, needs 10 yrs+ to show real class. Style, quality depend on producer's philosophy, technique, position. Top: ARNOUX-LACHAUX, BOUCHARD, Castagnier, CH de la Tour (stems), DROUHIN, EUGÉNIE (intensity), *Faiveley*, Forey, GRIVOT, *Gros*, HUDELOT-Noëllat, JADOT, LEROY, LIGER-BELAIR (both), MÉO-CAMUZET, MONTILLE, MORTET, MUGNERET, *Vougeraie*.

Clos du Mesnil Champ ★★★★ KRUG's famous walled v'yd in GC Le Mesnil. Long-lived, pure CHARD vintage, great mature yrs like 95 *à point* till 2020+; **02** and remarkable 03 cB' 13' will be classics, as will 17'.

Clos du Roi C d'O r ★★→★★★ Frequent Burg v'yd name. The king usually chose well. Best v'yd in GRAND CRU CORTON (DE MONTILLE, Pousse d'Or, VOUGERAIE); top PC v'yd in MERCUREY; future PC (?) in MARSANNAY. Less classy in BEAUNE.

Clos Rougeard Lo r w (sw) ★★★★ 14 15 16 17 18' Legendary/ICONIC small DOM of Nady and late Charly Foucault. Since 2017 Martin and Olivier Bouygues (CH MONTROSE; *see* B'X). Great finesse, age brilliantly: SAUMUR Blanc, SAUMUR-CHAMPIGNY, COTEAUX DE SAUMUR. Now stratospheric prices.

Clos St-Denis C d'O r ★★★ 90' **93'** 96' 99' 02' 03 05' 09' 10' 12' 15' 16' 17 18' GC at MOREY-ST-DENIS. Sumptuous in youth, silky with age. Try ARLAUD, Bertagna, Castagnier, Coquard-Loison-Fleurot, DUJAC, JADOT, Jouan, LEROUX, PONSOT (Laurent from 2016).

Clos Ste-Hune Al w ★★★★ Legendary TRIMBACH single site from GC ROSACKER. Greatest RIES in AL? Super 10 13 16 17. Initially austere, needs a decade ageing; complex wine for gastronomy. Recent acquisition GC SCHLOSSBERG more luxuriant, floral.

Clos St-Jacques C d'O r ★★★★ 90' 93 96' 99' 02' 05' 09' 10' 12' 15' 16 17 18' Hillside PC in GEVREY-CHAMBERTIN with perfect se exposure. Excellent producers: CLAIR, ESMONIN, FOURRIER, JADOT, ROUSSEAU; powerful, velvety reds often ranked and priced above many GC.

Clovallon, Dom de L'doc r w ★★ Haute Vallée de l'Orb. Catherine Roque made name with elegant PINOT N Pomarèdes, original white blend Aurièges. Now run by daughter Alix; new CUVÉE Les Indigènes. Mother at Mas d'Alezon, FAUGÈRES for ★★★Presbytère Montfalette, (w) Cabretta.

Coche-Dury C d'O r w ★★★★ Superb MEURSAULT DOM led by Jean-François Coche and son Raphaël. Exceptional whites from ALIGOTÉ to CORTON-CHARLEMAGNE; v. pretty reds too. Hard to find at sensible prices. Gd-value cousin Coche-Bizouard (eg. Meursault Goutte d'Or) is sound, but not same style.

Colin C d'O (r) w ★★★ →★★★★ Leading CHASSAGNE-MONTRACHET and ST-AUBIN family; new generation turning heads with brilliant whites, esp Pierre-Yves C-MOREY, DOM Marc C, Joseph C (new!) and their cousins Philippe C and Bruno C.

Colin-Morey Burg ★★★ Pierre-Yves C-M has struck a chord with his vibrant tingling whites, esp from *St-Aubin* and CHASSAGNE-MONTRACHET PC, with their characteristic gun-flint bouquets. Great wines in youth and for ageing.

Collines Rhodaniennes N Rh r w ★★ N Rh IGP has character, quality, incl v.gd Seyssuel (schist), sparky granite hillside reds v.gd value, often from top estates. Can contain young-vine CÔTE-RÔTIE. Mostly SYRAH (best), plus MERLOT, GAMAY, mini-CONDRIEU VIOGNIER (best). Reds: A Paret, A Perret, Bonnefond, E Barou, *Jamet* (v.gd), Jasmin, J-M Gérin, L Chèze, Monier-Pérreol (bio), N Champagneux, S Ogier (v.gd), S Pichat, ROSTAING. Whites: Alexandrins, A Perret (v.gd), Barou, F Merlin, *G Vernay (v.gd)*, P Marthouret, X Gérard, Y Cuilleron.

Collioure Rouss r p w ★★ Table-wine twin of BANYULS from same terraced coastal v'yds. Characterful reds, mainly GRENACHE, enjoy the sea air. Gd whites based on GRENACHE BLANC and better Gris. Top: DOMS Bila-Haut, de la Rectorie, du Mas Blanc, La Tour Vieille, Madeloc, Vial-Magnères; Coume del Mas; Les CLOS de Paulilles. Co-ops Cellier des Templiers, l'Étoile.

Comté Tolosan SW Fr r p w ★ IGP covering most of sw and multitude of sins. ★★DOM de Ribonnet (all colours, huge variety of CÉPAGES) stands out among huge variety of mostly moderate wines, mostly DYA. *See* PYRENEES-ATLANTIQUES.

Condrieu N Rh w ★★★→★★★★★ 14' 16' Home of VIOGNIER; floral, musky airs, pear, apricot flavours from sandy granite slopes. Best: pure, precise (16 over 15 17 18); but beware excess oak, sweetness, alc, v. hot yrs a problem. Rare white match for asparagus. 75 growers; quality varies. Best: A Paret, A Perret (all three wines gd), Boissonnet, CHAPOUTIER, Clos de la Bonnette (organic), C Pichon, DELAS, Faury (esp La Berne), F Merlin, F Villard (lighter recently), Gangloff (great style), GUIGAL (big), *G Vernay* (fine, classy), Monteillet, Niéro, ROSTAING, St Cosme, X Gérard, Y Cuilleron.

HypoCondrieu: excessive worry about Viognier. **MitaCondrieu**: Viognier in every cell.

Corbières L'doc r (p) (w) ★★→★★★ Largest AC of L'DOC, with cru of Boutenac in s hills and ten subzones. Almost all red; styles reflect varying terroir from coastal lagoons to hot dry foothills of Pyrenees. CARIGNAN significant. Try: CHX Aiguilloux, *Aussières*, Borde-Rouge, LA BARONNE, Lastours, la Voulte Gasparets, Les CLOS Perdus, Les Palais, *Ollieux Romanis*, Pech-Latt; DOMS de Fontsainte, de Villemajou, du Grand Crès, du Vieux Parc, Trillol, Villerouge; Clos de l'Anhel, Grand Arc, SERRES-MAZARD. Castelmaure an outstanding co-op.

Cornas N Rh ★★★ 99' 01' 05' 09' 10' 12' 15' 16' 17' 18' Top-quality N Rhô SYRAH, *très à la mode* (incl crazed thirst for wines of departed growers). Deep, strongly fruited, always mineral-lined. Can drink some for vibrant early fruit, really need 5 yrs+. Stunning 10 15. Top: ALLEMAND (top two), Balthazar (traditional), *Clape* (benchmark), Colombo (new oak), Courbis (modern), *Delas*, *Dom du Tunnel*, Dumien Serrette, G Gilles, J&E Durand (racy fruit), Lemenicier, M Barret (bio, improved), P&V Jaboulet, Tardieu-Laurent (deep, oak), Voge (oak), V Paris.

Corsica / Corse r p w ★→★★★ ACS Ajaccio, PATRIMONIO; plus crus Calvi, Coteaux du Cap Corse, Sartène. IGP: Île de Beauté and Mediterranée. Altitude, sea winds moderate heat. Lots of variety. SCIACARELLO gives elegant spicy reds. Less widely planted NIELLUCCIO makes more structured reds; gd rosés; *tangy, herbal Vermentino* whites. Also sweet MUSCATS. Top: Abbatucci, Alzipratu, Canarelli, CLOS Capitoro, Clos d'Alzeto, Clos Poggiale, Fiumicicoli, *Peraldi*, Pieretti, *Nicrosi*, Saperale, *Torraccia*, Vaccelli. Hard to find, but it today's passion for the rare and indigenous.

Corton C d'O r (w) ★★★→★★★★★ 90' 99' 02' 03' 05' 09' 10' 12' 15' 16 17 18' Overpromoted GC, but can be underrated from best v'yds CLOS DU ROI, Bressandes, Renardes, Rognet. Wines can be fine, elegant, not all blockbusters. Reference:

BONNEAU DU MARTRAY, BOUCHARD, CHANDON DE BRIAILLES, DRC, Dubreuil-Fontaine, FAIVELEY (Clos des Cortons), Follin-Arbelet, MÉO-CAMUZET, Senard, TOLLOT-EEAUT, but try also Camille Giroud, DOM des Croix, H & G Buisson, Mallard, Rapet, Terregelesses. Occasional whites, eg. HOSPICES DE BEAUNE, CHANSON from Vergennes v'yd.

Corton-Charlemagne C d'O w ★★★ →★★★★ 04 05' 09' 10' 14' 15' 17' 18 Potentially scintillating GC, invites mineral descriptors, should age well. Sw- and w-facing limestone slopes, plus band round top of hill. Top: *Bonneau du Martray*, EOUCHARD, CLAIR, *Coche-Dury*, FAIVELEY, HOSPICES DE BEAUNE, JADOT, LATOUR, Mallard, MONTILLE, P Javillier, Rapet, Rollin. *See also* CHARLEMAGNE.

Costières de Nîmes S Rh r p w ★→★★ N of Rhône delta, sw of CHÂTEAUNEUF, similar stony soils, gd quality, value. Red (GRENACHE, SYRAH) is robust, spicy, ages well. Best: CHX de Grande Cassagne, de Valcombe, d'Or et des Gueules, L'Ermitage, Mas Carlot (gd fruit), Mas des Bressades (top fruit), Mas Neuf, Montfrin (organic), Mourgues-du-Grès, Nages, Roubaud, Tour de Béraud Vessière (w) DOMS de la Patience (organic), du Vieux Relais, Galus, M KREYDENWEISS, Petit Romain. Gd, *lively rosés, stylish whites* (ROUSSANNE).

Côte Chalonnaise Burg r w sp ★★ Region immediately s of C D'O; always threatening to be rediscovered. Lighter wines, lower prices. BOUZERON for ALIGOTÉ, *Rully* for accessible, juicy wines in both colours; *Mercurey* and GIVRY have more structure and can age; MONTAGNY for leaner CHARD.

Côte d'Or Burg Département name applied to central and principal Burg v'yd slopes: CÔTE DE BEAUNE and CÔTE DE NUITS. Not used on labels except for BOURGOGNE C d'O AC, finally introduced for 2017 vintage.

Côte de Beaune C d'O r w ★★→★★★★ S half of C D'O. Also a little-seen AC in its own right applying to top of hill above BEAUNE itself. Try from DROUHIN: largely declassified Beaune PC. Also VOUGERAIE.

Côte de Beaune-Villages C d'O r ★★ 10' 12 15' 16 17 18 Reds from lesser villages of s half of C D'O. Nowadays usually NÉGOCIANT blends.

Côte de Brouilly Beauj r ★★ 15' 16 17 18' Variety of styles as soils vary on different flanks of Mont Brouilly. Merits a premium over straight BROUILLY. Reference is CH Thivin, but try also Blain, Brun, Dufaitre, Pacalet.

Côte de Nuits C d'O r (w) ★★→★★★★ N half of C D'O. Nearly all red, from CHAMBOLLE-MUSIGNY, MARSANNAY, FIXIN, GEVREY-CHAMBERTIN, MOREY-ST DENIS, NUITS-ST GEORGES VOSNE-ROMANÉE, VOUGEOT.

Côte de Nuits-Villages C d'O r (w) ★★ 05' 09' 10' 12' 15' 16 17 18' Junior AC for extreme n/s ends of CÔTE DE NUITS; can be bargains. Chopin, Gachot-Monot, Jourdan (specialists); Arduy, Arlot, D BACHELET, FOURNIER (gd). Single-v'yds appearing.

Côte Roannaise Lo p ★★→★★★ 16' 17' 18' Exciting AC, lower slopes of granite hills w of Roanne. Vgd GAMAY. Try: Bonneton, Désormière, Fontenay, Giraudon Paroisse, Plasse Pothiers, Sérol, Vial. V.gd white IGP Urfé: ALIGOTÉ, CHARD ROUSSANNE, VIOGNIER. Run of gd vintages.

Côte-Rôtie N Rh r ★★★ →★★★★ 99' 01' 05' 09' 10' 12' 15' 16' 17' 18' Finest Rh red mainly SYRAH, some VIOGNIER, style connects to Burg. Violet airs, pure (esp 2016) complex, v. fine with age (5–10 yrs+). Exceptional, v. long-lived 10 15. Top: *Barge* (traditional), B Chambeyron, Benetière, Billon, Bonnefond (oak), Bonserine (esp La Garde), Burgaud, CHAPOUTIER, Clusel-Roch (organic), DELAS, DOM de Rosiers Duclaux, Gaillard (oak), Garon, GUIGAL (long oaking), *Jamet* (wonderful), Jasmin Jean-Luc Jamet, J-M Gérin, J-M Stéphan (organic), Lafoy, Levet (traditional) *Rostaing* (fine), S Ogier (racy, oak), VIDAL-FLEURY (La Chatillonne).

Côtes Catalanes Rouss r p w ★★ IGP; quality belies humble status. Some of ROUSS' best. Innovative growers working with venerable bush vines, esp GRENACHE CARIGNAN (r w and Gris). Best: DOMS *Casenove, Dom of the Bee*, GÉRARD GAUBY, *Jones*

L'Horizon, La Préceptorie Centernach, Le Soula, Matassa, Olivier Pithon, Padié, Roc des Anges, Soulanes, TRELOAR, Vaquer.

Côtes d'Auvergne Mass C r p (w) ★→★★ AC 17 18' (410 ha). Scattered AC. GAMAY, some PINOT N, CHARD. Best reds improve 3–4yrs. Villages: Boudes, Chanturgue, Châteaugay, Corent (p), Madargues (r). Producers: Bernard, CAVE St-Verny (v.gd), Goigoux, Maupertuis, Montel, Pradier, Sauvat.

Côtes de Bordeaux B'x ★ AC launched in 2008 for reds. Embraces and permits cross-blending between CAS, FRANCS, BLAYE, CADILLAC, Ste-Foy. Growers who want to maintain *the identity of a single terroir* have stiffer controls (NB) but can put Cas, CADILLAC, etc. before Côtes de B'x. BLAYE-CÔTES DE B'X, FRANCS-CÔTES DE B'X and Ste-Foy-Côtes de B'x also produce a little dry white. Around 1000 growers in group. Represents 10% B'x production. Try CHX Dudon, Lamothe de Haux, Malagar.

Côtes de Bourg B'x r w ★→★★ 09' 10' 14 15 16 (18) Solid, savoury reds, a little white from e bank of Gironde. Mainly MERLOT but 10% MALBEC. Hail in 2018. Top CHX: Brûlesécaille, Bujan, Civrac, *Falfas*, Fougas-Maldoror, Grand-Maison, Grave (Nectar VIEILLES VIGNES), Haut-Guiraud, Haut-Macô, Haut-Mondésir, Macay, Mercier, Nodoz, *Roc de Cambes*, Rousset, Sociondo.

Côtes de Duras SW Fr r p w ★→★★★ 15' 16 17' 18' Affordable AOP, s of BERGERAC, home to nest of passionate organic growers. ★★★DOM Mouthes-les-Bihan leads from Mont Ramé, Nadine Lusseau, Petit Malromé (excellent value); ★★La Fon Longue, La Tuilerie la Brille, Les Cours, Les Hauts de Riquet, Mauro Guicheney. ch Condom's ★★★sweet still outstanding. Other gd growers: ★★Doms Chater, de Laulan, Grand Mayne.

Côtes de Gascogne SW Fr (r) (p) w ★★ DYA IGP. ★★Giants PRODUCTEURS PLAIMONT, esp 900-ha+ DOM Tariquet, have most market share for these bar-style wines, light, often aromatic, fun. Boiled sweet and nail-polish-remover flavours seem popular. ★★Doms Chiroulet, d'Arton, d'Espérance, de l'Herré, Horgelus, Ménard, Millet, Miselle, Pellehaut and CH des Cassagnoles. Or ★Chx de Lauroux, de Magnaut, Papolle, St Lannes. Tariquet's best product is Armagnac.

Côtes de Millau SW Fr r p w IGP ★ from scenic upper Tarn Valley, locally very popular. DYA. Lord Foster's Millau viaduct celebrated in wines from worthy co-op. ★DOM du Vieux Noyer probably best of independents.

Côtes de Montravel SW Fr sw sw ★★ 15 16' 17 18' Sub-AOP of BERGERAC; Attractive, unfashionable off-dry wines usually SÉM-based. Better with foie gras than most stickies. Attractive as apéritif.

Côtes de Provence Prov r p w ★→★★★ (p w) DYA. Huge AC concentrating on rosé, 90%, with research improving quality; sets trend for pale dry rosés elsewhere. Mainly GRENACHE, CINSAULT. Satisfying reds, mainly SYRAH, Grenache, MOURVÈDRE nearer coast. Dry whites, increasingly 100% Rolle. Fréjus, La Londe, Pierrefeu, STE-VICTOIRE, NOTRE DAME DES ANGES are subzones. Leaders: *Gavoty* (superb), CLOS Cibonne (primarily Tibouren); CHX d'Esclans, de Selle, Estandon VIGNERONS, Gasqui. *See* BANDOL, COTEAUX D'AIX, COTEAUX VAROIS.

Côtes de Thongue L'doc r p w ★★ (p w) DYA. Top HÉRAULT IGP, in Thongue Valley, close to Med. Original blends and single varietals. Best reds age. DOMS Condamine l'Evèque, DE L'ARJOLLE, l'Horte, la Croix Belle.

Côtes de Toul Al r p w ★ DYA. V. light wines from Lorraine; mainly VIN GRIS.

Côtes du Brulhois SW Fr r p (w) ★→★★ 15' 16 17 18 Lively AOP nr Agen; borrows its "black wine" tag from CAHORS. Some TANNAT obligatory, Prunelard also making an appearance. Handful of independents: ★★Doms Bois de Simon, des Thermes, du Pountet, CH la Bastide, unusually enjoy support from gd co-op.

Côtes du Forez Lo r p (sp) ★→★★ 17 18' Most s Lo AC (147 ha), on latitude of CÔTE-RÔTIE. V.gd GAMAY (r p). Bonnefoy, CLOS de Chozieux, Guillot, Mondon &

Demeure, Real, Verdier/Logel. Excellent AC, exciting IGP: CHARD, CHENIN BL, PINOT GR, RIES, ROUSSANNE, VIOGNIER. Gd 17, v.gd 18.

Côtes du Jura Jura r p w (sp) ★★→★★★ 05' 09 10 12 14 15' 16 18' Revitalized region, big on natural wines and trendy with sommeliers, so pricey. Light perfumey reds from PINOT N, Poulsard, Trousseau. Try J-M Petit, Pignier. Whites from fresh, fruity CHARD to deliberately oxidative SAVAGNIN or blends. Great food wines. NB: BERTHET-BONDET, Bourdy, CH D'ARLAY, DOM DU PÉLICAN, DOM LABET, Ganevat, LUCIEN AVIET, STÉPHANE TISSOT. *See also* ARBOIS, CH CHALON, L'ÉTOILE ACS.

Côtes du Rhône S Rh r p w ★ →★★ 16' 18' The wide base of S Rh, 170 communes. Incl gd SYRAH of Brézème, St-Julien-St-Alban (N Rh). Split between enjoyable, handmade, high quality (note CHÂTEAUNEUF estates, numbers rising) and dull, mass-produced. Lively fruit more emphasized; 2016 ace. Mainly GRENACHE, also SYRAH, CARIGNAN. Usually best drunk young. Vaucluse best, then GARD (Syrah).

Côtes du Rhône-Villages S Rh r p w ★ →★★★ 16' 17' 18 Full-bodied, spiced reds from 7700 ha, incl 21 named S Rh villages (St-Andéol new in 2018). A rising tide. Best are generous, lively, gd value. Red heart is GRENACHE, plus SYRAH, MOURVÈDRE. Improving *whites*, often incl VIOGNIER, ROUSSANNE added to rich base CLAIRETTE, GRENACHE BL – *gd with food. See* CHUSCLAN, LAUDUN, PLAN DE DIEU, ST-GERVAIS, SABLET, SÉGURET (QUALITY), VALRÉAS, VISAN (improving). New villages from 16 vintage: Ste-Cécile (gd range DOMS), Suze-la-Rousse, Vaison la Romaine. NB: Gadagne, MASSIF D'UCHAUX, Plan de Dieu, PUYMÉRAS, SIGNARGUES. Try: CHX Fontségune, Signac; Doms Aphillanthes, Aure, Bastide St Dominique, *Biscarelle*, Bois St Jean, Cabotte (bio), Coulange, Coste Chaude, Crève Coeur, Grand Veneur, Grands Bois (organic), Gravennes, *Janasse*, Jérome, Mas de Libian (bio), Montbayon, Montmartel, *Mourchon*, Pasquiers, Pique-Basse, Rabasse-Charavin, Réméjeanne, Renjarde, Romarins, Saladin, St-Siffrein, Ste-Anne, Valériane, Viret; CAVE de RASTEAU, Les VIGNERONS d'Estézargues.

Côtes du Roussillon-Villages Rouss r ★→★★★ 32 villages in n part of ROUSS with Caramany, Latour de France, Lesquerde, Tauravel, Les Aspres singled out on label. Best v'yds Pyrenees foothills. CARIGNAN key. Co-ops inevitably important, but quality and character from independent estates: Boucabeille, *Cazes*, CLOS des Fées, Clot de l'Oum, des Chênes, *Gauby*, Les VIGNES de Bila-Haut, Mas Becha, *Mas Crémat*, Modat, Piquemal, Rancy, Roc des Anges, Thunevin-Calvet. Côtes du Rouss to s for simple warming reds. *See also* CÔTES CATALANES.

Côtes du Tarn SW France r p w ★ DYA. IGP roughly co-extensive with GAILLAC AOP, but with growers further s. *Moelleux* SAUV BL from ★★DOM d'en Segur and Lou Bio range from Dom IGNES de Garbasses outstanding.

Top Côtes du Rhône producers

Put on your specs and study this; there's an ocean of gd wine out there: CHX Fonsalette (beauty), Gigognan, Hugues, La Borie, La Courançonne, Montfaucon (w also), Mont-Redon, Mourre du Tendre (rich, long life), Rochecolombe (organic), St Cosme, St-Estève, Trignon (incl VIOGNIER); DOMS André Brunel (stylish), Bastide St Dominique, Bramadou, Carabiniers (bio) Charvin (terroir, v.gd, ages), Chaume-Arnaud (organic), Combebelle, Coudoulet de BEAUCASTEL (classy r), Corinne Depeyre (organic), Cros de la Mûre (great value), Espigouette, Famille Lançon, Ferrand (full), Gramenon (bio), Grand Nicolet (genuine), Haut-Musiel, Janasse (old GRENACHE), Jaume, M-F Laurent (organic), Manarine, M Dumarcher (organic), Réméjeanne (w also), Romarins, Soumade, Vieille Julienne (classy, ages); CAVE Estézargues, CLOS des Cîmes (v. high v'rds), DELAS, E GUIGAL (great value), Famille Perrin, GEORGES DUBOEUF, Mas Poupéras; co-ops CAIRANNE, RASTEAU.

Côtes du Vivarais S Rh r p w ★ 16′ 18 Mostly DYA. Across hilly Ardèche country w of Montélimar. Marked improvement: cool fruit, easy-drinking, based on GRENACHE, SYRAH; some more sturdy, oak-aged reds. NB: Gallety (best, depth, lives well), Mas de Bagnols, *Vignerons de Ruoms* (v.gd value).

Coteaux Bourguignons Burg ★ DYA. Mostly reds, GAMAY, PINOT N. New AC since 2011 to replace BOURGOGNE Grand Ordinaire and to sex up basic BEAUJ. Rare whites ALIGOTÉ, CHARD, MELON, PINOTS BL, GR.

Coteaux Champenois Champ r (p) w ★★★ (w) DYA. AC for still wines of CHAMP, eg. BOUZY. Vintages as for Champ. Better reds with climate change, and viticulture (12′).

Coteaux d'Aix-en-Provence Prov r p w ★★ Extensive AC with Aix at centre, from Durance River to Med, from STE-VICTOIRE mtn, with wide range of styles: more CAB SAUV in cooler n. DOM du CH, Bas Chx Beaupré, Calissanne, La Realtière, Les Bastides, Les Béates, Eole (on Alpilles), Revelette, *Pigoudet*. *See also* LES BAUX-EN-PROV, PALETTE.

Coteaux d'Ancenis Lo r p w (sw) ★→★★ 16 17 18′ AOP (150 ha e of Nantais). 40 producers, Dry, DEMI-SEC, sweet CHENIN BL whites, age-worthy *Malvoisie* (PINOT GR); light reds, rosés mainly GAMAY, plus CABS SAUV, FR, esp Guindon, Landron Chartier, Paonnerie, Pléiade, Quarteron.

Coteaux de Chalosse SW Fr r p w ★ DYA. Local IGP from Les Landes. Local grape varieties incl Arriloba, Baroque, Egiodola. Active co-op at Tursan. ★DOMS de Labaigt, Tastet. Rare outside region.

Coteaux de Glanes SW Fr r p ★★ DYA IGP from Upper Dordogne. Nine-man co-op can't make enough wine to satisfy thirst of locals. Ségalin grape distinguishes it from other mainstream blends.

Coteaux de l'Ardèche *See* IGP ARDÈCHE.

Coteaux de l'Aubance Lo w sw ★★→★★★ 10′ 11′ 13 14′ 15′ 16 17 18′ Small AC (209 ha; 40 producers) for long-ageing sweet CHENIN BL. Nervier, less rich than COTEAUX DU LAYON except SÉLECTION DES GRAINS NOBLES. S of LO nr Angers, less steep than Layon. Esp Bablut, CH Princé, Haute-Perche, Montgilet, Richou, Rochelles, Varière. Potentially v.gd 18.

Coteaux de Saumur Lo w sw ★★→★★★ 14′ 15′ 16 17 18′ Late-harvest CHENIN BL (12 ha depending on yr). Like COTEAUX DU LAYON but less rich, more delicate, citrus. Esp Champs Fleuris, Nerleux, St Just, Targé, Vatan. Best with cheese or on its own.

Coteaux des Baronnies S Rh r p w ★→★★ DYA. Rh IGP in high hills e of VINSOBRES, nr Nyons. SYRAH (best), CAB SAUV, MERLOT, CHARD (for once gd value), plus GRENACHE, CINSAULT, etc. Genuine, fresh country wines: improving easy reds, also clear VIOGNIER. NB: DOMS du Rieu-Frais, Le Mas Sylvia, Rosière.

Coteaux du Giennois Lo r p w ★→★★ 17 18′ Small AC (194 ha), spread-out v'yds along n Lo, Cosne to Gien. Frost 16 17, 18 (v.gd). Bright, lemony SAUV BL (103 ha) lighter style of SANCERRE or POUILLY-FUMÉ; can be v.gd. Light reds blend GAMAY/PINOT N. Best: Berthier (esp L'Inédit), BOURGEOIS, Catherine & Michel Langlois, Charrier, Émile Balland, Paulat, Treuillet, Villargeau.

Coteaux du Layon Lo w sw ★★→★★★★ 10′ 11′ 14′ 15′ 16 17 18′ Heart of ANJOU: long-lived sweet CHENIN BL. Seven villages can add name to AC. Chaume now Layon PC. Top ACs: BONNEZEAUX, QUARTS DE CHAUME. Growers: Baudouin, BAUMARD, Breuil, *Ch Pierre-Bise*, Chauvin, Delesvaux, Forges, Guegniard, Juchepie, Ogereau, *Pithon-Paillé*, Soucherie. Frost again 17. Often great quality but difficult to sell.

Coteaux du Loir Lo r p w dr sw ★→★★★ 15′ 16 17 18′ N tributary of Loire, Le Loir; scenic, exciting region with Coteaux du Loir (80 ha), *Jasnières* (65 ha). Frost-prone. Steely, fine, precise, long-lived CHENIN BL, GAMAY, peppery Pineau d'Aunis, some fizz, plus Grolleau (rosé), CAB, CÔT. Best: Ange Vin, Breton, DOM DE BELLIVIÈRE (v.gd), Fresneau, Gigou, Janvier, Le Briseau, Les Maisons Rouges, Roche Bleue.

Coteaux du Lyonnais Beauj r p (w) ★ DYA Junior BEAUJ. Best en PRIMEUR.

Coteaux du Quercy SW Fr r p ★ 15' 16 17 (18) AOP s of CAHORS. CAB FR at heart of hearty winter-proof wines. Will keep. Active co-op challenged by independents ★★DOMS du Guillau Merchien (IGP) and ★Doms d'Ariès, Mazuc, Mystère d'Éléna (Dom de Revel).

Coteaux du Vendômois Lo r p w ★→★★ 16 17 18' AC, 28 communes, c.150 ha: Vendôme to Montoire in Le Loir Valley. Mostly VIN GRIS from Pineau d'Aunis (Chenin Noir) reds typically peppery, also blends of CAB FR, PINOT N, GAMAY. Whites: CHENIN BL, CHARD. Best: Brazilier, Four à Chaux, J Martellière, Montrieux, Patrice Colin; CAVE Li Vendômois (200 ha total).

Coteaux et Terrasses de Montauban SW Fr r p w ★→★★ DYA IGP Created and still dominated by DOM le Montels (also in CAHORS) with range of easy, gd-value wines often found in local markets. Look out too for ★Dom Biarnès, Mas des Anges.

Coteaux Varois-en-Provence Prov r p w ★→★★ Small AC, on cooler higher slopes, between bigger COTEAUX d'AIX and CÔTES de PROV. Warming reds, fresh rosés from usual s varieties. Potential being realized esp SYRAH. Try CHX la Calisse, Duvivier, Margüi, Trians; DOs du Deffends, du Loou, Les Terres Promises, St Mitre.

Coulée de Serrant Lo w dr sw ★★★ 10' 11 12 13 14 15 16 18' Historic, steep CHENIN BL monopole 7-ha bio v'yd overlooking Lo in heart of AC SAVENNIÈRES. Virginie Joly in charge. V. oxidative style sharply divides opinions – best decanted; bottle variation. Severe frost 17, promising 18.

Courcel, Dom de C d'O r ★★★ Leading POMMARD estate, fine floral wines using ripe grapes and whole bunches. Top, age-worthy, PCS Rugiens and Épenots, plus interesting Croix Noires.

The Hermitage hill is mostly organic or bio; Crozes-Hermitage mostly neither. Odd.

Crémant In CHAMP, used to mean "creaming" (half-sparkling): now called *demi-mousse/perle*. Since 1975, AC for quality classic-method fully sparkling from AL, B'X, BOURGOGNE, Die, Jura, LIMOUX, Lo and Luxembourg. Many gd examples.

Crépy Sav w ★★ Sav ∠ 35 ha. Light, soft white from s shore of Lake Geneva. 100% CHASSELAS. Try: Grande CAVE de Crépy Mercier, Fichard.

Criots-Bâtard-Montrachet C d'O ★★★ 09 10 12 14' 15 17' 18 Tiny MONTRACHET satellite, 1.57 ha. Less concentrated than BÂTARD. Try Belland, Blain-GAGNARD, Caroline MOREY, Fontaine G, LAMY, or d'Auvenay if you're v. rich.

Cros Parantoux Burg ★★★★ Cult PC in VOSNE-ROMANÉE made famous by the late Henri Jayer. Now made to great acclaim and greater price by DOMS ROUGET and MÉO-CAMUZET. But Brûlées better?

Crozes-Hermitage N Rh r w ★★→★★★ 10' 15' 16' 17' 18 SYRAH from mainly flat v'yds nr River Isère: dark-berry, liquorice, tar; mostly early-drinking (2–5 yrs). Often more stylish, complex, cooler from granite hills nr HERMITAGE: fine, red-fruited, can age; 16 fun wines. Best simple CUVÉES) ideal for grills, parties. Some oaked, older-vine wines cost more. Top: *A Graillot*, Aléofane (r w), Belle (organic), *Chapoutier,* Dard & Ribo (organic), *Delas* (Le CLOS v.gd, DOM des Grands Chemins), E Darnaud, G Robin; DOMS Combier (organic), de *Thalabert* of JABOULET, des Entrefaux (oak), des Hauts-Châssis, des Lises (fine), *du Colombier*, Dumaine (organic), Fayolle Fils & Fille (stylish), Habrard (organic), Les Bruyères (bio, big fruit), Machon, Melody, Mucyn, Remizières (oak), Rousset, Ville Rouge, Vins de Vienne, Y Chave. Drink *white* (MARSANNE) early, v.gd vintages recently. Value.

Cuve close Quicker method of making sparkling wine in a tank. Bubbles die away in glass much quicker than with *méthode traditionnelle*.

Cuvée Wine contained in a *cuve* or vat. A word of many uses, incl synonym for "blend" and 1st-press wines (as in CHAMP). Often just refers to a "lot" of wine.

Dagueneau, Didier Lo w ★★★→★★★★ 12' 13 14' 15' 16' 17 18' Best producer of

POUILLY-FUMÉ (12 ha); precise, age-worthy SAUV BL. Run by Didier's siblings Louis-Benjamin (name on label) and Charlotte. Immaculate v'yds/winery. CUVÉES incl Buisson Renard, Pur Sang, Silex. Also SANCERRE (Le Mont Damné, CHAVIGNOL), Les Jardins de Babylone (JURANÇON).

Dauvissat, Vincent Chab w ★★★★ Imperturbable bio producer, uses old barrels and local 132-litre *feuillettes* for CHAB. Grand, age-worthy wines similar to RAVENEAU cousins. Best: La Forest, Les CLOS, Preuses, Séchet. Try DOM Jean D (no relation).

Deiss, Dom Marcel Al r w ★★★ Bio grower at Bergheim. Favours blended wines from individual v'yds, often different varieties co-planted, mixed success, variable. Best wine RIES Schoenenbourg 13 14 17.

Delamotte Champ BRUT, BLANC DE BLANCS, brilliant 07 08' 13 17 CUVÉE Nicholas Delamotte. Fine, small, CHARD-dominated house at Le Mesnil. One of few genuine SAIGNÉE rosés. Managed with SALON by LAURENT-PERRIER. Called "the poor man's Salon" but sometimes surpasses it, as in 85' 02.

Delas Frères N Rh r p w ★★ →★★★★ Steady quality N Rh v'yd owner/merchant, with CONDRIEU, CROZES-HERMITAGE, CÔTE-RÔTIE, HERMITAGE v'yds. Best: *Côte-Rôtie Landonne*, Hermitage DOM des Tourettes (r w), Les Bessards (r, terroir, v. fine, smoky, long life), ST-JOSEPH Ste-Épine (r). S Rh: esp CÔTES DU RH St-Esprit (r), Grignan-les-Adhémar (r, value). Whites lighter recently. Owned by ROEDERER.

Demi-sec Half-dry: but in practice more like half-sweet (eg. CHAMP is typically 45g/l dosage).

Derenoncourt, Stéphane B'x Leading international consultant; self-taught, focused on terroir, fruit, balance. Own property, *Dom de l'A* in CAS.

Deutz Champ Once among greatest Grandes Marques, now steady revival. Improved BRUT Classic NV; Brut 06 08 lovely, harmonious; 12 new release. Top-flight CHARD CUVÉE Amour de Deutz 06, Amour de Deutz Rosé 06. One of top small CHAMP houses, ROEDERER-owned. *Superb Cuvée William Deutz* 95. New Parcelles d'Ay 12.

Dirler-Cadé, Dom Al 23 ha in warm s of AL: wines of weight and personality. Gd % GCS. Marvellous old-vines MUSCAT GC Saering 13 16 17. Excellent Saering RIES, rich yet finely sketched 10 14.

Domaine (Dom) Property. *See* under name, eg. TEMPIER, DOM.

Dom Pérignon Champ Vincent Chaperon now chef de CAVE of this luxury CUVÉE of MOËT & CHANDON. Ultra-**consistent quality in incredible quantities**, creamy character, esp with 10–15 yrs bottle age; v. tight in youth. *Oenothèque* concept (long bottle age, recent disgorgement, boosted price) renamed Plénitude; at 7, 16, 30 yrs+ (P1, P2, P3); superb P2 98; still vibrant P3 70. Superb 02 will be 2nd Plenitude. More PINOT N focus in DP since 2000, esp exquisite 06 in both Blanc and Rosé.

Dopff au Moulin Al w ★★★ →★★★★ Ancient, top-class family producer. Class act in GEWURZ GCS Brand, Sporen 09 12 15 ' 16 17'; lovely RIES SCHOENENBOURG 13 exceptional rose 2020; *Sylvaner de Riquewihr 14*. Pioneer of AL CRÉMANT; v.gd CUVÉES: Bartholdi, Julien, Bio. Specialist in classic dry wines. Blue-chip.

Dourthe B'x Sizeable merchant/grower; wide range, quality emphasis. CHX: BELGRAVE, LA GARDE, LE BOSCQ, Grand Barrail Lamarzelle Figeac, PEY LA TOUR, RAHOUL, REYSSON. *Dourthe No 1* (esp white) well-made generic B'X.

Drappier, Michel Champ Great family-run AUBE house. DOM of fine PINOT N, now 60 ha+, 15 certified bio; *Pinot-led NV*, BRUT ZÉRO, Brut *sans souffre* (no sulphur), Millésime d'Exception 12 of great potential; ace Prestige CUVÉE Grande Sendrée 12 17 18. Cuvée Quatuor (four *cépages*). Superb older wines 95' 85 82 (magnums).

DRC (Dom de la Romanée-Conti) C d'O r w ★★★★ Grandest estate in Burg. MONOPOLES ROMANÉE-CONTI and LA TÂCHE, major parts of ÉCHÉZEAUX, GRANDS-ÉCHÉZEAUX, RICHEBOURG, ROMANÉE-ST-VIVANT and a tiny part of MONTRACHET. Also

CORTON from 200? CORTON-CHARLEMAGNE from 2019. Crown-jewel prices. Keep top vintages for decades.

Drouhin, Joseph & Cie Burg r w ★★★→★★★★ Fine family-owned grower/NÉGOCIANT in BEAUNE; v'yds (all bio) incl (w) Beaune *Clos des Mouches*, MONTRACHET (Marquis de LAGUICHE) and large CHAB holdings. Stylish, fragrant reds from pretty CHOREY LÈS-BEAUNE to majestic *Musigny*, GRANDS-ÉCHÉZEAUX, etc. Also DDO (Domaine Drouhin Oregon) see US.

Duboeuf, Georges Beauj r w ★★→★★★ From hero – saviour of BEAUJ – to less so (too much BEAUJ NOUVEAU), always major player and still v. sound source for multiple Beauj crus and MÂCON bottlings.

Dugat C d'O r ★★★ Cousins Claude and Bernard (Dugat-Py) made excellent deep-coloured GEVREY-CHAMBERTIN, respective labels. Both flourishing with new generation. Tiny volumes, esp GCS, huge prices, esp Dugat-Py.

Dujac, Dom C d'O r w ★★★→★★★★ MOREY-ST-DENIS grower noted for sensual, smoky reds, from unbeatable village Morey to outstanding GCS, esp CLOS DE LA ROCHE, CLOS ST-DENIS, ÉCHÉZEAUX. Slightly more mainstream these days. Lighter merchant wines as D Fils & Père and DOM Triennes in COTEAUX VAROIS.

Dureuil-Janthial Burg r w ★★ Top DOM in RULLY in capable hands of Vincent D-J with *fresh, punchy whites*; cheerful, juicy reds: Maizières (r w), PC Meix Cadot (w)

Durup, Jean Chab w ★★ Volume CHAB producer as DOM de l'Eglantière and CH de Maligny, allied by marriage to Dom Colinot in IRANCY.

Duval-Leroy Champ Dynamic Vertus CHAMP house, family-owned. 200 ha of mainly fine CHARD crus. New shift to vegan-friendly Champ, ie. natural clarification and settling, avoiding milk-protein fining agents. V.gd Fleur de Champagne NV. Top Blanc de Prestige *Femme 13*.

Échézeaux C d'O r ★★★ 99' 02' 05' 09' **10'** 12' 15' 16 17 18' GC next to CLOS DE VOUGEOT, but totally different style: lacy, ethereal, scintillating. Can vary depending on exact location. Best: ARNOUX-LACHAUX, Berthaut-Gerbet, Coquard-Loison-Fleurot, DRC, DUJAC, EUGÉNIE, GRIVOT, GROS, Guyon, Lamarche, LIGER-BELAIR, Mongeard-MUGNERET, MUGNERET-GIBOURG, ROUGET, Tardy, Tremblay.

Ecu, Dom de l' LC r) w dr (sp) ★★★ 12 14' 15' **18'** Bio MUSCADET-SÈVRE-ET-MAINE (Granite, Taurus) GROS PLANT, VIN DE FRANCE. Guy Bossard made reputation, now run by dynamic Fred Niger. Gd CAB FR, PINOT N. Big range, large collection of amphorae. Frost 16, 17. Relief in 18.

Edelzwicker Al w ★ DYA. Blended light white. CH d'Ittenwiller, HUGEL Gentil gd.

Eguisheim, Cave Vinicole d' Al r w ★★ Impeccable co-op. Excellent value: fine GCS Hatschbourg, Hengst, Ollwiller, Spiegel. Owns Willm. Top label: WOLFBERGER. Best: Grande Res 10, Sigillé, Armorié. Gd CRÉMANT, PINOT N, esp 15' 17 18.

Emmanuel Brochet Champ Bijou producer, exceptional CHAMP from a steep hill, Mont Bernard Extra Brut pure, exhilarating, winemaking slow and patient resting in barrel for 9 mths. Certified organic, no fining or filtration.

Entraygues et du Fel and Estaing SW Fr r p w ★→★★ DYA. Two tiny AOP neighbours in almost vertical terraces above Lot Valley. Bone dry CHENIN BL for whites, esp ★★DOMS Laurent Mousset (gd reds, esp ★★La Pauca, excellent rosé) Méjanassère. ★★Nicolas Carmarans making wines in and out of AOP.

Entre-Deux-Mers B'x w ★→★★ DYA. Often gd-value dry white B'x (drink *entre deux huitres*) from between the Rivers Garonne and Dordogne. Best: CHX Beauregard Ducourt, BONNET Chantelouve, Fontenille, Haut-Rian, Landereau, *Le Coin* (for SAUV Gris), Les Arromans, Lestrille, Marjosse, Martinon, Nardique-la-Gravière, Ste-Marie, *Tour de Mirambeau*, Turcaud.

Esmonin, Dom Sylvie C d'O r ★★★ Rich, dark wines from fully ripe grapes, whole-bunch vinification and new oak. Best: GEVREY-CHAMBERTIN VIEILLES VIGNES, CLOS ST-JACQUES. Cousin Frédéric has gd Estournelles St-Jacques.

Étoile, L' Jura w ★★ AC of Jura best-known for elegant CHARD grown on limestone and marl. VIN JAUNE and VIN DE PAILLE also allowed but not reds. DOM de Montbourgeau is reference, esp En Banode. Also try: Cartaux-Bougaud, Philippe Vandelle.

Eugénie, Dom C d'O r (w) ★★★→★★★★ Former DOM Engel in VOSNE, now owned by Artemis Estates. Powerful, dark-coloured wines. CLOS VOUGEOT, GRANDS-ÉCHÉZEAUX best, but try village Clos d'Eugenie.

Faiveley, J Burg r w ★★ →★★★★ More grower than merchant, making high-class reds and sound whites. Leading light in CÔTE CHALONNAISE, but save up for top wines from CHAMBERTIN-CLOS DE BÈZE, CHAMBOLLE-MUSIGNY, CORTON **Clos des Cortons**, NUITS. Ambitious recent acquisitions throughout C D'O and DOM Billaud-Simon (CHAB).

Faller, Théo / Weinbach, Dom Al w ★★★→★★★★ Probably finest v'yds in AL, wines of great **character and elegance**. The late Laurence Faller made wines in a drier gastronomic style, supremely expressed in GC SCHLOSSBERG 10. Also RIES L'inedit 13 mineral complexity. SELECTION DES GRAINS NOBLES GEWURZ as gd as it gets.

Faugères L'doc r (p) (w) ★→★★★ One of earliest, and now Cru du L'doc. Compact, seven villages, defined by schist, on s-facing foot-ills of the Cevennes. Majority reds, fresh, spicy, age-worthy. Elegant whites: MARSANNE, ROUSSANNE, VERMENTINO, GRENACHE BL. Est families plus newcomers. Drink DOMS Cébène, Chaberts, Chenaie, des Trinités, JEAN-MICHEL ALQUIER, LÉON BARRAL, Mas d'Alezon, Ollier-Taillefer, St Antonin, **Sarabande**, many others. High proportion of organic growers.

Fèvre, William Chab w ★★★→★★★★ Biggest owner of CHAB GCS; Bougros Côte Bougerots and Les CLOS outstanding. Small yields, no expense spared, priced accordingly, top source for rich, age-worthy wines and some more humble.

Fiefs Vendéens Lo r p w ★→★★★ 15' 16 17 18' Mainly DYA AC. From the Vendée nr Sables d'Olonne, from tourist quaffers to serious age-worthy wines. CHARD, CHENIN BL, MELON, SAUV BL (w), CAB FR, CAB SAUV, GAMAY, Grolleau Gris, Négrette, PINOT N (r p). Esp: Coirier, DOM St-Nicolas (bio – v.gd producer), Mourat (122 ha), Prieuré-la-Chaume (bio). Frost 16, 17. V. promising 18.

Fitou L'doc r ★★ 12 13 14 15 16 17 Characterful rugged red from inland hills s of Narbonne as well as tamer coastal v'yds. MIDI's oldest AC for table wine, created in 1948. 11 mths' ageing, benefits from bottle-age. Seek out CH de Nouvelles, Champs des Soeurs, DOM **Bergé-Bertrand**, de Rolland, **Jones**, Lérys.

Fixin C d'O r (w) ★★★ 05' 09' 10' 12' 14 15' 16 17 18' Worthy, under-valued n neighbour of GEVREY-CHAMBERTIN. Sturdy, sometimes splendid reds but can be rustic. Best v'yds: Arvelets, CLOS de la Perrière, Clos du Chapitre, Clos Napoléon. Top locals: Berthaut-Gerbet, Gelin, Joliet plus v.gd Bart, Bichot, CLAIR, FA. VELEY, MORTET.

Fleurie Beauj r ★★★ 14 15' 18' Top BEAUJ cru for perfumed, strawberry fruit, silky texture. Racier from La Madone hillside, richer below. Horribly hailed on in 16, 17, sadly. Classic names: CH de Poncié, Beauregard, Chatelard, DOM Chignard, CLOS de la Roilette, Depardon, DUBOEUF, Métrat, co-op. Naturalists: Balagny, Dutraive, Métras, Sunier. Newcomers: Clos de Mez, Dom de Fa, Lafarge-Vial.

Fourrier, Domaine C d'O r ★★★★ Jean-Marie F has taken a sound GEVREY-CHAMBERTIN DOM to new levels, with cult prices to match. Sensual vibrant reds at all levels. Best CLOS ST-JACQUES, Combe aux Moines, GRIOTTE-CHAMBERTIN

Francs-Côtes de Bordeaux B'x r w ★★ 10' 14 15 16 (18) Tiny b'x AC next to CAS. Fief of Thienpont (PAVIE-MACQUIN) family. Mainly red from MERLOT but some gd white (eg. Charmes-Godard). Reds can age a little. Top CHX: Francs, La Prade, Le Puy (Emilien), Marsau, Puyfromage, Puyanché, **Puygueraud**.

Fréjus Prov r p ★★ Subzone of CÔTES DE PROV. Most e zone on volcanic soils. Tight when young, ages well. Try CH de Rouet. Ch d'Esclans is here, but does not use Fréjus label.

Fronsac B'x r ★★→★★★ 09' 10' 14 15 16 (18) Underrated hilly AC w of ST-ÉM; great-value MERLOT-dominated red, some ageing potential. Top CH: Arnauton, DALEM Fontenil, *la Dauphine*, la Grave, la Rivière, la Rousselle, LA VIEILLE CURE, LES TROIS CROIX, Haut-Carles, Mayne-Vieil (CUVÉE Alienor), *Moulin-Haut-Laroque*, Tour du Moulin, Villars. See also CANON-FRON.

Fronton SW Fr r p ★★ 15 16 18 AOP n of Toulouse. Compulsory use of Négrette grape (often unblended and rare elsewhere) yields flavours of violets, cherries, liquorice. Best known ★★CHX *Bellevue-la-Forêt*, *Bouissel*, but try CHX Baudare, Boujac, Caze, du Roc, Fayet, Laurou, Plaisance (esp sulphur-free Alabets), DOMS des Pradelles, Viguerie de Belaygues. No AOP for whites as yet.

Fuissé, Ch Burg w ★★→★★★ Both commercial and quality leader in POUILLY-FUISSÉ. Top terroirs Le Clos, Combettes. Also BEAUJ crus, eg. JULIÉNAS.

Gagnard C d'O (r) ★ ★★★→★★★★ Clan in CHASSAGNE-MONTRACHET. Long-lasting wines, esp Caillerets, BÂTARD from Jean-Noël G; while Blain-G, Fontaine-G have full range inc rare CRIOTS-BÂTARD, MONTRACHET itself. Gd value offered by all Gagnards. Decent Chassagne reds all round.

Gaillac SW Fr r p w dr sw sp ★→★★ 15' 16 18' Thrusting historic AOP w of Albi based on rare grapes Len de l'El, Duras, Braucol, Prunelard, Mauzac. Worth investigating. Young bio producers stealing march on establishment. Look for ★★★Causse-Marines, La Ramaye, La Vignereuse, Le Champ d'Orphée, Peyres-Roses, PLAGEOLES ★★L'Enclos des Braves, L'Enclos des Roses, La Ferme du Vert; DOMS Brin, Escausses, du Moullin, Mayragues, Rotier. More traditional from CHX Larroque, Palvié; Doms Labarthe, La Chanade, Mas Pignou. ★★Ch Bourguet (w sw)

Ganevat Jura r w ★★★→★★★★ CÔTES DU JURA superstar. Single-v'yd CHARD (eg. Chalasses, Grand Teppes), pricey but fabulous. Also innovative reds.

Gauby, Dom Gérard Rouss r w ★★★ Exemplary ROUSS producer, attracted several others to village of Calce. Bio and increasingly natural. Both IGP CÔTES CATALANES, CÔTES DU ROUSS-VILLAGES. High-altitude v'yds up to 550m (1804ft), chalk for fresh acidity. Muntada, Les Calcinaires VIEILLES VIGNES. Associated with DOM Le Soula. Dessert wine Le Pain du Sucre.

Gers SW Fr r p w LYA IGP usually sold as CÔTES DE GASCOGNE; indistinguishable.

Gevrey-Chambertin C d'O r ★★★ 99' 02' 05' 09' 10' 12' 15' 16 17 18' Major AC for interesting savoury reds at all levels up to great CHAMBERTIN and GC cousins. Top PCS Cazetiers, Combe aux Moines, Combottes, CLOS ST-JACQUES. Value from single-v'yd village wines (En Champs, La Justice) and VIEILLES VIGNES bottlings. Top: BACHELET, BOILLOT, Burguet, Damoy, DROUHIN, Drouhin-Laroze, DUGAT, Dugat-Py, Duroché, ESMONIN, FAIVELEY, FOURRIER, Géantet-Pansiot, Harmand-Geoffroy, Heresztyn-Mazzini, JADOT, LEROY, Magnien, MORTET, ROSSIGNOL-TRAPET, Roty, ROUSSEAU, Roy, SERAFIN, TRAPET.

Gigondas S Rh r p→★ ★★★ 01' 05' 06' 09' 10' 12' 13' 15' 16' 17' 18' Top S Rh red. Handsome v'yds on stony clay-sand plain rise to Alpine limestone hills e

---

Prunelard: father of the more famous Malbec

Officially declared MALBEC's true father, this GAILLAC grape, lost following phylloxera, has now taken off. In 2000 PLAGEOLES was the only grower with just 4 ha; today there are at least 15. It's late-ripening and tastes of plums, hence probably part of the name. The other part, "lard" or sometimes "lan", is said to derive from the white bloom that forms on the mature fruit. The style of its wines is as variable as that of Malbec, but on the whole they're deep-coloured, well-balanced, strongly built and of medium alc. Most suggest wild black fruits, some mint and others liquorice, violets too. Other growers incl DOMS de la Ramaye, Carcenac, Labarthe and the CAVE CO-OP at Labastide-de-Lévis.

of Avignon; GRENACHE, plus SYRAH, MOURVÈDRE. Robust, clear, smoky, wines; best offer fine dark-red fruit. Top 10 15 16. More oak recently, higher prices, but genuine local feel in many. Try: Boissan, Bosquets (gd modern), Bouïssière (punchy), Brusset, Cayron, CH de Montmirail, Ch de St Cosme (swish), *Clos des Cazaux* (value), CLOS du Joncuas (organic, traditional), DOM St Gayan (long-lived), *Famille Perrin*, Goubert, Gour de Chaulé (fine), Grapillon d'Or, Longue Toque, Moulin de la Gardette (stylish), Notre Dame des Pallières, *Les Pallières*, P Amadieu (v. consistent), Pesquier, Pourra (robust), *Raspail-Ay*, Roubine, Santa Duc (now stylish), Semelles de Vent, Teyssonières. Heady rosés.

Gimonnet, Pierre Champ ★★→★★★ 28 ha of GCs and PCs on n Côte des Blancs. New v'yd in Oger. Enviably consistent CHARD. Ace CUVÉE Gastronome for seafood 13 16 17. Not a fan of single-v'yd Champ.

Girardin, Vincent C d'O r w ★★→★★★ White-specialist MEURSAULT-based grower/NÉGOCIANT, now under BOISSET ownership. Original coming back to Meursault as DOM Pierre Vincent.

Givry Burg r (w) ★★ 15' 16 17 18' Top tip in CÔTE CHALONNAISE for tasty reds that can age. Better value than MERCUREY. Rare whites nutty in style. Best (r): JOBLOT, CLOS Salomon, *Faiveley*, F Lumpp, Masse, Thénard.

Goisot Burg r w ★★★ Guilhem & J-H G, outstanding bio producers of single-v'yd bottlings of ST-BRIS (SAUV BL) and Côtes d'Auxerre for CHARD, PINOT N. Nobody else comes close.

Gonon, Dom N Rh r w ★★★ 10' 13' 15' 16' 17' 18' Top-name ST-JOSEPH, organic, tremendous v'yd care, old vines around Tournon. Red, exciting dark fruit, lives well; white, Les Oliviers, rich, seductive, also ages well.

Gosset Champ Odilon de Varine, formerly at HENRIOT, now chef de CAVE here: passionate about terroir. New Grand Blanc de Meunier is 1st solo-variety from a Grande Marque, mainly 07, elegant, aged on CHARD lees. Prestige Celebris Bris Extra BRUT one of best. Classic in 04, sublime 95.

Gouges, Henri C d'O r w ★★★ Grégory G at helm for meaty, long-lasting NUITS-ST-GEORGES from several PC v'yds. Some find them too tannic in youth. Try CLOS des Porrets, Vaucrains, iconic Les St-Georges. Interesting *white Nuits*, incl PINOT BL.

Grand Cru (GC) Official term neaning different things in different areas. One of top Burg v'yds with its own AC. In AL, one of 51 top v'yds, each now with its own rules. In ST-ÉM, 60% of production is St-Ém GC, often run-of-the-mill. In MÉD there are five tiers of GC CLASSÉS. In CHAMP 17 villages are GCs. Since 2011 in Lo for QUARTS DE CHAUME, and emerging system in L'DOC. Take with pinch of salt in PROV.

Grande Rue, La C d'O r ★★★ 02' 03 05' 06 09' 10' 12' 15' 16 17 18' MONOPOLE of DOM Lamarche, GC between LA TÂCHE, ROMANÉE-CONTI. Quality, consistency improved under Nicole L.

Grands-Échézeaux C d'O r ★★★★ 90' 93 96' 99' 02' 03 05' 09' 10' 12' 15' 17 18' Superlative GC next to CLOS de VOUGEOT, but with a MUSIGNY silkiness. More weight than most ÉCHÉZEAUX. Top: BICHOT (CLOS Frantin), Coquard-Loison-Fleurot, DRC, DROUHIN, EUGÉNIE, G NOËLLAT, Lamarche.

Grange des Pères, Dom de la L'doc r w ★★★ IGP Pays l'Hérault. Cult estate neighbouring MAS DE DAUMAS GASSAC, 1st vintage 1992. Red wines from SYRAH, MOURVÈDRE, CAB SAUV; white 80% ROUSSANNE, plus MARSANNE, CHARD. Stylish wines with ageing potential.

Gratien, Alfred and Gratien & Meyer Champ ★★★ BRUT 93 12 13 15' 18' Small but beautiful; Brut NV. CHARD-led Prestige CUVÉE Paradis Brut, Rosé (multi-vintage). Excellent quirky CHAMP and Lo house, owned by Henkell Freixenet. Fine, v.dry, lasting, oak-fermented wines incl *The Wine Society's house Champagne*. Careful buyer of top crus from favourite growers. Also Gratien & Meyer in SAUMUR.

Graves B'x r w ★→★★ 10' 14 15 16 (18) Gravel soils provide the name. Appetizing grainy reds from MERLOT and CAB SAUV, fresh SAUV/SÉM dry whites. One of best values in B'x today. Top CHX: ARCHAMBEAU, Brondelle, de Cérons, CHANTEGRIVE CLOS Bourgelat, *Clos Floridène*, CRABITEY, Ferrande, Fougères, Grand Enclos du CH de Cérons, Haura, Magneau, Pont de Brion, RAHOUL, *Respide-Médeville* Roquetaillade La Grange, St-Robert CUVÉE Poncet Deville, Vieux Ch Gaubert Villa Bel Air.

Graves de Vayres B'x r w ★ DYA. Tiny AC within E-2-M zone. Red, white, *moelleux*.

Grignan-les-Adhémar S Rh r (p) w ★→★★ 16' 17' 18 Mid-Rh AC; best reds hearty tangy, herbal. Leaders: Baron d'Escalin, DELAS (value), La Suzienne (value); CHX Bizard, La Décelle (incl w Côtes du Rh), Mas Théo (bio); DOMS de Bonetto-Fabrol de Montine (stylish r, gd p w, also r CÔTES DU RH), Grangeneuve best (esp VIEILLES VIGNES), St-Luc.

Griotte-Chambertin C d'O r ★★★★ 90' 96' 99' 02' 03 05' 09' 10' 12' 15' 16 17 18 Small GC next to CHAMBERTIN; nobody has much volume. Brisk red fruit, with depth and ageing potential, from DROUHIN, DUGAT, FOURRIER, *Ponsot (Laurent)*.

Grivot, Jean C d'O r w ★★★→★★★★ Huge improvements at this VOSNE-ROMANÉE DOM in past decade, reflected in higher prices. Superb range topped by GCS CLOS DE VOUGEOT, ÉCHÉZEAUX, RICHEBOURG.

Gros, Doms C d'O w ★★★→★★★★ Family of VIGNERONS in VOSNE-ROMANÉE with stylish wines from Anne (sumptuous RICHEBOURG), succulent reds from Michel (CLOS de Réas), Anne-Françoise (now in BEAUNE) and Gros Frère & Soeur (CLOS VOUGEOT En Musigni). Not just GCS; try value HAUTES-CÔTES DE NUITS. Also Anne's DOM Gros-Tollot in MINERVOIS.

Gros Plant du Pays Nantais Lo w (sp) ★→★★ DYA. Much-improved AC from GROS PLANT (FOLLE BLANCHE), best racy, saline, perfect with oysters. Try: Basse Ville, ECU, Haut-Bourg, Luneau-Papin, Poiron-Dabin, Preuille. Sparkling: either pure or blended. April frost 17, fine 18.

Guigal, Ets E N Rh r ★ ★★→★★★★ Celebrated grower-merchant: CÔTE-RÔTIE mainly, plus CONDRIEU, CROZES-HERMITAGE, HERMITAGE, ST-JOSEPH, 53-ha CHÂTEAUNEUF DOM de Nalys v'yds. Merchant: Condrieu, Côte-Rôtie, Crozes-Hermitage, Hermitage, S Rh. Owns DOM de Bonserine (sturdy Côte-Rôtie), VIDAL-FLEURY (fruit, quality on up). Top, v. expensive Côte-Rôties La Mouline, La Landonne, La Turque (ultra rich, new oak for 42 mths, so atypical), also v.gd Hermitage, St-Joseph VIGNES de l'Hospice; all reds dense. Standard wines: gd, esp *top-value Côtes du Rh* (r p w). Best whites: Condrieu, Condrieu La Doriane (oaky), Hermitage.

Hautes-Côtes de Beaune / Nuits C d'O r w ★★ (r) 15' 17 18' (w) 14' 15' 17' 18 ACS for villages in hills behind CÔTE DE BEAUNE/NUITS. Attractive lighter reds, whites for early drinking. Best whites: Devevey, MÉO-CAMUZET, Montchovet, Thevenot-le-Brun. Top reds: Carré, Duband, Féry, GROS, Jacob, Jouan, LIGER-BELAIR, Magnien, Naudin-Ferrand, Parigot, Verdet. Also useful large co-op in BEAUNE.

Haut-Médoc B'x r ★★→★★★ 09' 10' 14 15 16' (18) Prime source of dry, digestible CAB/MERLOT reds. Usually gd value. Plenty of CRUS BOURGEOIS. Wines usually sturdier in n; finer in s. Five Classed Growths (BELGRAVE, CAMENSAC, *Cantemerle*, LA LAGUNE, LA TOUR-CARNET). Other top CHX: Arnauld, BELLE-VUE, CAMBON LA PELOUSE, Charmail, CISSAC, CITRAN, Clément-Pichon, COUFRAN, D'AGASSAC, *de Lamarque*, Gironville, Lamothe-Bergeron, LANESSAN, Larose Perganson, *Malescasse*, SÉNÉJAC, *Sociando-Mallet*.

Haut-Montravel SW Fr w sw ★★ 15 16' 17 18' Sweetest of three MONTRAVEL white AOPS, best (★★★CH Puy-Servain-Terrement, ★★DOMS Moulin Caresse, bargain Libarde) should not be overlooked for better-known MONBAZILLAC, SAUSSIGNAC.

Haut-Poitou Lo r p w sp ★→★★ 16 17 18' Best age 5–6 yrs+. AC (around 750 ha) nw of Poitiers from CAB SAUV, CAB FR, GAMAY, CHARD, PINOT N, SAUV BL. Dynamic *Ampelidae*

(Frédéric Brochet) dominates with IGP wines 120 ha. Also La Tour Beaumont, Morgeau La Tour.

Heidsieck, Charles Champ Iconic house, smaller than before, wines more brilliant than ever. *Brut Ré* all purity and subtle ripe complexity. Peerless Blanc des Millénaires 04. Older BRUT Vintage in prime mature form, esp 83 81; CHAMP Charlie Prestige CUVÉE likely to be reintroduced from 2023. New BLANC DE BLANCS NV, nicely priced, delicious.

Heidsieck Monopole Champ Once-great CHAMP house. Fair-quality, gd-price Gold Top 09 12 15. Part of VRANKEN group.

Hengst Al GC. Gives powerful wines. Excels with top GEWURZ from JOSMEYER, ZIND-HUMBRECHT; also AUXERROIS, CHASSELAS, PINOT N.

Henri Abelé Champ New name for Abel Lepitre, oldest house, now focusing on exports. Best CUVÉE Sourire de Reims 12, new Sourire Rosé 15 voluptuous, from Les Riceys (AUBE), expansive burgundian style. Gd value.

Henriot Champ Fine family CHAMP house. BRUT Souverain NV much improved; ace BLANC DE BLANCS de CHARD NV; Brut 98' 02' 08; Brut Rosé 06 09. New long-aged *Cuve 38*, a solera of GC Chard since 1990. Exceptional new prestige CUVÉE Hemera 05. Still stocks of long-lived prestige cuvée Les Enchanteleurs 90. Also owns BOUCHARD PÈRE & FILS, FÈVRE.

Hermitage N Rh r w ★★★ →★★★★ 99' 01' 05' 06' 07' 09' 10' 11' 12' 13' 15' 16' 17' 18' (2010, 15 both brilliant). Part granite hill on e Rhône bank with grandest, fullest, most stylish SYRAH and complex, nutty/white-fruited, fascinating, v.-long-lived white (MARSANNE, some ROUSSANNE) best left for 6–7 yrs+. Best: Alexandrins, Belle, *Chapoutier* (bio), Colombier, DELAS, Faurie (pure), GUIGAL, Habrard (w), *J-L Chave* (rich, elegant), M Sorrel (mighty Le Gréal r), *Paul Jaboulet Aîné*, Philippe & Vincent Jaboulet (r w), Tardieu-Laurent (oak). TAIN co-op gd (esp Gambert de Loche r, VIN DE PAILLE w).

Hortus, Dom de l' L'doc r w ★★★ Four siblings taking over at this extended family-run PIC ST-LOUP reds. Fine SYRAH-based reds: elegant Bergerie and oak-aged Grande CUVÉE (r). Intriguing Bergerie IGP Val de Montferrand (w) with seven grapes. Also CLOS du Prieur (r) in cooler TERRASSES DU LARZAC.

Hospices de Beaune C d'O Spectacular medieval foundation with grand charity auction of CUVÉES from its 61 ha for Beaune's hospital, 3rd Sunday in Nov, run since 2005 by Christie's. Individuals can buy as well as trade. Winemaker Ludivine Griveau making fine consistent wines. Try BEAUNE cuvées, VOLNAYS or expensive GCS, (r) CORTON, ÉCHÉZEAUX, MAZIS-CHAMBERTIN, (w) BÂTARD-MONTRACHET. Bargains unlikely, charity is the point.

Hudelot C d'O r w ★★★ VIGNERON family in CÔTE DE NUITS. New life breathed into H-NOËLLAT (VOUGEOT), while H-Baillet (CHAMBOLLE) challenging hard. Former more stylish, latter more punchy.

Huet Lo w ★★★★ 09' 10' 11' 14 15' 16' 17 18' Most famous VOUVRAY estate, long-time bio; CHENIN BL benchmark. Anthony Hwang also owns Királyudvar in Tokaji (*see* Hungary). Winemaker: Jean-Bernard Berthomé. Single v'yds: CLOS du Bourg, Le Haut Lieu, Le Mont. Almost immortal, esp sweet: 1919 21 24 47 59 89 90 96 97 03 05. Well worth decanting. Also *pétillant*.

Hugel & Fils Al r w sw ★★ →★★★★ Revered AL house at Riquewihr, led by 12th-generation Jean-Philippe Hugel, no longer opposed to GC designation. Famed for late-harvest, esp RIES, GEWURZ VENDANGE TARDIVE, SÉLECTION DE GRAINS NOBLES. Superb Ries Schoelhammer 07 10 13 17 from GC site.

IGP (Indication Géographique Protégée) Potentially most dynamic category in France (with over 150 regions), allowing scope for experimentation. Successor to VDP, from 2009 vintage, but position unchanged and new terminology still not accepted by every area. Zonal names most individual: eg. CÔTES DE GASCOGNE,

CÔTES DE THONGUE, Pays des Cévennes, Haute Vallée de l'Orb, among others. Enormous variety in taste and quality, but never ceases to surprise.

IGP Ardèche S Rh r p w ★ →★★★ 16' 17' 18 (Was Coteaux de l'Ardèche.) Rocky hills w of Rh, gd selection, quality up, often gd value. New DOMS; fresh reds, some oaked (unnecessary); VIOGNIER (eg. CHAPOUTIER, Mas de Libian), MARSANNE. Best from SYRAH, also GAMAY (often old vines), CAB SAUV (Serret). Restrained, burg-style Ardèche CHARD by LOUIS LATOUR (Grand Ardèche v. oaky). Doms du Colombier, du Grangeon, du Mazel, de Vigier, Flacher, JF Jacouton; CH de la Selve; Ferraton, Mas d'Intras (organic).

Irancy Burg r (p) ★★ 05 14' 15' 16 18 Light though structured red made nr CHAB from PINOT N and more rustic local César. Elbows-on-table stuff. Best v'yds: Palotte, Mazelots. Best: Cantin, **Colinot, Dauvissat**, Goisot, Renaud, Richoux.

Irouléguy SW Fr r p (w) ★ →★★★ 15' 16 18 Basque AOP (only one). Can't go wrong here. Hearty reds based on TANNAT softened by CAB FR. Best from ★★★Ameztia, Arretxea, Bordaxuria, Brana, Mourguy, Ilarria. Fruity whites based on Petit Courbu and the two Mansengs; ★★★Xuri d'Ansa (from gd co-op), DOM Xubialdea. Rosés make perfect summer drinking.

Jaboulet Aîné, Paul N Rh r w Grower-merchant at Tain. V'yds well worked, wines polished, modern. Once-leading producer of HERMITAGE, esp ★★★★La Chapelle (fabulous 61 78 90), quality varied since 90s, some revival since 2010 on reds. Also CORNAS St-Pierre, **Crozes Thalabert** (can be stylish), Roure (sound); owns DOM de Terre Ferme CHÂTEAUNEUF, merchant of other Rh, notably CÔTES DU RH *Parallèle 45*, CONDRIEU, VACQUEYRAS, VENTOUX (r, quality/value). Whites lack true Rh body, drink most young, range incl new v. expensive La Chapelle white (not made every yr).

L'doc has five winds: Tramontane, Cers, Scirocco, Autan, Marin. Draughty spot.

Jacquart Champ Simplified range from co-op-turned-brand, concentrating on what it does best: PC Côte des Blancs CHARD from member growers. Fine range of Vintage BLANC DE BLANCS 08 13 for restaurants. V.gd Vintage Rosé 06.

Jacquesson Champ ★★★★ Bijou Dizy house for precise, v. dry wines. Outstanding single-v'yd Avize CHAMP Caïn 08 12'. Corne Bautray, all CHARD. Dizy 09, excellent **numbered NV cuvées** 730' 731' 732 733 734 735 738 739 740 (12 base: best yet) 741, 742.

Jadot, Louis Burg r p w ★★ →★★★★ Dynamic BEAUNE merchant making powerful whites (DIAM corks) and well-constructed age-worthy reds with significant v'yd holdings in BEAUJ, CÔTE, MÂCON; esp POUILLY-FUISSÉ (DOM Ferret), MOULIN-À-VENT (CH des Jacques, **Clos du Grand Carquelin**).

Jamet, Dom N Rh r w ★★★ →★★★★ 99' 05' 10' 13' 15' 16' 17' 18' Top CÔTE-RÔTIE estate. Jean-Paul J's 8 ha cover 16 different sites, integrating into a wonderful, complex, intricate, long-lived vine. Rare Côte Brune, mostly 1940s SYRAH, is magical, deep lives 30 yrs+. Also gd-value, genuine CÔTES DU RHÔNE (r w), VIN DE PAYS.

Jasnières Lo w dr (sw) ★★ →★★★★ 14' 15' 16 17' 18' CHENIN BL, lively, sharp, dry to sweet, AC (70 ha), s-facing slopes Loir Valley. Esp Breton, DE BELLIVIÈRE, Gigou, Janvier, J-B Métais, L'Ange Vin (also VIN DE FRANCE), Le Briseau, Les Maisons Rouges, Roche Bleue, Ryke. V. age-worthy. Early, v. promising 18.

Jobard C d'O r w VIGNERON family in MEURSAULT. Top DOMS are Antoine J, esp long-lived Poruzots, Genevrières, CHARMES; and Rémi Jobard for immediately classy Meursaults plus reds from MONTHÉLIE, VOLNAY.

Joblot Burg r w ★★ Reference DOM for GIVRY, new CUVÉES Empreinte, Mademoiselle from 2016, plus classics La Servoisine and CLOS du Cellier Aux Moines.

Joseph Perrier Champ Fine family-run CHAMP house with v.gd PINOTS N, M v'yds, esp in own Cumières DOM. Ace Prestige CUVÉE Joséphine 02 08' 09 12'. Excellent BRUT

Royale NV, as generous as ever but more precise with less dosage. Distinctive, tangy BLANC DE BLANCS 08 13' 15', fine food wine. 15'; now drier, finer Cuvée Royale BRUT NV; distinctive tangy Blanc de Blancs 02 04 06 08 13' 15'.

Josmeyer Al w ★★→★★★ Exceptional family AL house, pioneer of bio viticulture, centered on RIES GC Hengst 13 14 16 17. Intriguing single-v'yd Pinot Auxerrois and entry-level Ries Dragon.

Juliénas Beauj r ★★★ 15' 16 17 18' Deserves to be better known for deep-fruited BEAUJ, esp for CLIMATS Beauvernay, etc. DOM Perrachon leads the way, try also Aufranc, Burrier, CH BEAUREGARD, CH FUISSÉ, Chignard, Trenel.

Jurançon SW Fr w dr sw ★→★★★ (sw) 12 13 15' 16' (18) (dr) 16' 17' 18' Separate AOPS for sweet and dry whites. Balance of richness, acidity the key to quality. DAGUENEAU's tiny ★★★★Jardins de Babylon sets the benchmark for best-known ★★★DOMS *Cauhapé*, de Souch, Lapeyre, Larrédya. ★★CH Jolys, Doms Bellauc, Bellegarde, Bordenave, Capdevielle, Castéra, Guirardel, Nigri, Uroulat, CLOS Benguères. ★Gan co-op gd value.

Kaefferkopf Al w dr (sw) ★★★ The 51st GC of AL at Ammerschwihr. Permitted to make blends as well as varietal wines, possibly not top-drawer.

Kientzler, Andre Al w sw ★★→★★★★ 5th-generation family DOM. Lush sensual GEWURZ GC Kirchberg 09 16 17, classic VENDANGE TARDIVE dessert wines. Exemplary care in v'yds.

Kreydenweiss, Marc Al w sw ★★→★★★★ Bio since 1968. Rich diversity of soils: GC Moenchberg on limestone for PINOT GR and majestic RIES Kastelberg on black schist, ages for up to 20 yrs 07 10. Also in COSTIÈRES de NÎMES.

Krug Champ Supremely prestigious de luxe house. ★★★★Grande CUVÉE, esp 160th Edition based on 04; 164th Edition (08 base) still young. Vintage 98 00 02 04; Rosé; CLOS DU MESNIL 00' 02 03; CLOS D'AMBONNAY 95' 98' 00; Krug Collection 69 76' 81 85. Rich, nutty wines, oak-fermented; highest quality, ditto price. Vintage 03 a fine surprise, 02 magnificent in 2020.

Kuentz-Bas Al w sw ★★→★★★ Great improvements since Jean-Baptiste Adam bought DOM in 2004. Among highest AL v'yds, organic/bio, serious yet accessible wines: drier RIES 13 16 17'. Fine PINOT GR, GEWURZ VENDANGE TARDIVE 09 12 17.

Labet, Dom Jura ★★★ Key CÔTES DU JURA estate in s part of region (Rotalier). Best-known for range of single-v'yd CHARD whites, eg. En Billat, En Chalasse, La Bardette; gd PINOT N, VIN JAUNE.

Ladoix C d'O r w ★★ (r) 09' 10' 12 15' 16 17 18' (w) 14' 15 17' 18 Explore here for fresh, exuberant whites, eg. Grechons, and juicy reds, esp Les Joyeuses from local DOMS Chevalier, Loichet, Mallard, Ravaut. Those with more cash try Le Cloud from Prieuré-Roch.

Ladoucette, de Lo (r) (p) w ★★★ 14 15 16 17 18' Largest POUILLY-FUMÉ estate at CH du Nozet (165 ha). Prestige brand Baron de L. SANCERRE Comte Lafond, owns La Poussie (Bué's most impressive site: r p w) and Marc Brédif: CHINON, MUSCADET, TOURAINE, VOUVRAY etc.

Lafarge, Michel C d'O r (w) ★★★★ Classic VOLNAY bio estate run by Frédéric L, son of ever-present Michel, 110 vintages between them. Outstanding, long-lived PCS *Clos des Chênes*, Caillerets, CLOS du CH des Ducs. Also fine BEAUNE, esp Grèves (r) and Clos des Aigrots (w). New FLEURIE project, Lafarge-Vial.

Lafon, Dom des Comtes Burg r w ★★★★ Fabulous bio MEURSAULT DOM, back to reliable best with long-lasting red VOLNAY *Santenots* equally outstanding. Value from excellent Mâconnais wines under Héritiers L label, while Dominique L makes his own COTE DE BEAUNE wines separately.

Laguiche, Marquis de C d'O ★★★★ Largest owner of Le MONTRACHET and a fine PC CHASSAGNE, both excellently made by DROUHIN.

Lalande de Pomerol B'x r ★★ 08 09' 10' 14 15 16 (18) Improving satellite neighbour

---

> **Languedoc rising stars**
> Keen drinkers now scan L'DOC with rising expectations. We haven't seen the half yet. NB: all founded since 2008, and looking gd: **Cabardès** Guilhem Barré; **Corbières** L'Espérou, Olivier Mavit; **Faugères** Grain Sauvage, Mas Lou, Les Serrals; **Fitou** Sarrat d'en Sol; **La Clape** La Combe de St Paul **Limoux** Cathare, Monsieur S; **Pézenas** La Grange des Bouys, Ste Cécile au Parc; **Pic St-Loup** CH Fontanès, Mas Gourdou, Mas Peyrolle; **St-Chinian** La Lauzeta, Les Païssels, Lanye Barrac; **Terrasses du Larzac** Clos Maïa, Les Chemins de Carabote, Mas Combarèla. There's a bit of work for you.

of POM. MERLOT-driven. Varied terroir: clay, gravel, sand. Top CHX: Arne de Musset, Bertineau St-Vincent, Chambrun, Garraud, Grand Ormeau, Haut-Chaigneau, Jean de Gué, Laborderie-Mondésir, La Chenade, LA FLEUR DE BOÜARD, La Sergue, Les Cruzelles, *Les Hauts Conseillants*, Pavillon Beauregard, Perron (La Fleur), Sabines, Siaurac, TOURNEFEUILLE.

La Londe Prov r p ★★ Subzone of CÔTES DE PROV on coastal schist: maritime influence. Try St Marguerite, Léoube, CLOS Mireille.

Lamy C d'O (r) w ★★★ DOM Hubert Lamy is go-to address for ST-AUBIN. Breathtakingly fresh, concentrated whites, often from higher density plantings. Sound reds too.

Landron, Doms Lo w dr sp ★★→★★★ 14' 15' 16 17 18 V.gd producer (46 ha) of organic/bio MUSCADET-SÈVRE-ET-MAINE: La Louvetrie, Fief du Breil.

Langlois-Château Lo (r) (w) sp ★★→★★★ SAUMUR, SANCERRE (Fontaine-Audon). BOLLINGER-owned (incl 89 ha). Gd CRÉMANT de Lo. Still wines incl Saumur Blanc VIELLES VIGNES 14 15, SAUMUR-CHAMPIGNY, POUILLY-FUMÉ.

Languedoc r p w Large regional AC incl CORBIÈRES, MINERVOIS, ROUSS from Cabardès to Sommières, but not Malepère, replaced AC Coteaux L'Doc in 2007. Rules the same. Bottom of pyramid of Midi ACs. Hierarchy of superior crus is work in progress. Subregions incl Cabrières (historic rosé AC with high % CINSAULT), Grès de Montpellier, Pézenas, Quatourze, St-Saturnin: usual L'doc grapes. Tiny Cabardès and Malepère where B'X meets Midi. CLAIRETTE du L'doc tiny, once-fashionable white. Not all ACs have much specific identity: go by grower.

Lanson Champ Black Label NV; Rosé NV; Vintage BRUT on a roll, esp 02 08 12' 15. Renewed house, part of LANSON-BCC group. Ace prestige NV Lanson Père et Fils Noble CUVÉE BLANC DE BLANCS, rosé and vintage; new Brut vintage single-vyd CLOS Lanson 08 09 12. Extra Age multi-vintage, Blanc de Blancs esp gd. Experienced new winemaker Hervé Dantan (since 15) starting to allow some malo (*see* A Little Learning) for a rounder style.

La Peira L'doc r w English-owned, AL winemaker, rich intense reds. La Peira (SYRAH/GRENACHE), las Flors de la Peira (Syrah/Grenache/MOURVÈDRE), Obriers de la Peira (CARIGNAN/CINSAULT).

Lapierre, Marcel Beauj r ★★★ Mathieu and Camille L continue cult DOM making sulphur-free MORGON. Range of styles and CUVÉES on offer.

Laplace, Dom SW Fr From basic family farm to smart modern enterprise: the oldest MADIRAN DOM famous for ★★★*Ch d'Aydie*, which needs lots of time. Odie d'Aydie less so. More commercial, lighter, all-TANNAT IGPS ★★Les Deux Vaches, ★Aramis. Excellent ★★★PACHERENCS (dr sw). Sweet fortified Maydie (think BANYULS) gd with chocolate.

Laroche Chab w ★★ Major player in CHAB with quality St Martin blend, Vieille Voye special CUVÉE, exceptional GC *Res de l'Obedience* named for historic HQ (worth a visit). Also Mas La Chevalière in L'DOC.

Latour, Louis Burg r w ★★→★★★★ Famous traditional family grower/merchant making full-bodied whites from C D'O v'yds (esp CORTON-CHARLEMAGNE),

Mâconnais, Ardèche (all CHARD); reds looking classier: CORTON, ROMANÉE-ST-VIVANT. Also owns Henry Fessy in BEAUJ.

Latricières-Chambertin C d'O r ★★★★ 90' 93 96' 99' 03 05' 09' 10' 12' 15' 16 17 18' GC next to CHAMBERTIN, rich if not quite as intense. Does well in warm dry yrs. Best: ARNOUX-LACHAUX, BIZE, Drouhin-Laroze, Duband, FAIVELEY, LEROY, Remy, ROSSIGNOL-TRAPET, TRAPET.

Laudun S Rh r p w ★→★★ 16' 17' Sound CÔTES DU RH-VILLAGE, w bank. Fresh, dashing whites. Red fruit/peppery reds (much SYRAH), lively rosés. Immediate flavours from CHUSCLAN-Laudun co-op. **Dom Pelaquié** best, esp elegant white. Also CHX Courac, de Bord, Juliette, St-Maurice; DOMS Duseigneur (bio), Carmélisa, Maravilhas (bio, r w), Olibrius.

Laurent-Perrier Champ Important house; family presence less obvious, ripe for a change of ownership? BRUT NV (CHARD-led) still perfect apéritif. V.gd skin-contact Rosé. Fine vintages: **02 08 09 12**. Grand Siècle CUVÉE multi-vintage on form, peerless Grand Siècle Alexandra Rosé 09. Ultra-Brut less impressive than under family aegis.

Laurent Vervesin Champ Young grower rejoins family DOM. Organic principles in original BLANC DE BLANCS GC, 15% oak, clear, precise. Aubeline GC is fuller, and liked in Scandinavia.

Leflaive, Dom Burg w ★★★★ Reference PULIGNY-MONTRACHET DOM heading back to top. Steps being taken to restore longevity of great wines from GC, incl LE MONTRACHET, CHEVALIER and *fabulous PC*: Pucelles, Combettes, Folatières, etc. Value from developing s Burg range, eg. MÂCON Verzé.

Leflaive, Olivier C d'O r w ★★→★★★ White specialist NÉGOCIANT at PULIGNY-MONTRACHET. Smart wines of late, spot on with BOURGOGNE Les Setilles as with own GC v'yds. Also La Maison d'Olivier, hotel, restaurant, tasting room.

Léon Barral Rouss r w FAUGÈRES bio producer. Focus on concentrated MOURVÈDRE, SYRAH, CARIGNAN. Valinière and Jadis top blends. Terret Blanc main white.

Leroux, Benjamin C d'O r w ★★★ Growing reputation as BEAUNE-based NÉGOCIANT equally at home in red or white. Poised, honest wines. CÔTE D'OR only, esp GEVREY, MEURSAULT, VOLNAY.

Leroy, Dom C d'O r w ★★★★ Lalou Bize Leroy, bio pioneer, delivers extraordinary quality from tiny yields in VOSNE-ROMANÉE and from DOM d'Auvenay. Both fiendishly expensive even ex-dom. As is amazing treasure trove of mature wines from family NÉGOCIANT, Maison L.

Liger-Belair, Comte C d'O r ★★★★ Comte Louis-Michel L-B makes brilliantly ethereal wines in VOSNE-ROMANÉE. Ever-increasing stable headed by LA ROMANÉE. Try village La Colombière, PC Reignots, NUITS-ST-GEORGES crus. Also in Oregon, Chile.

Liger-Belair, Thibault C d'O r ★★★→★★★★ New winery in NUITS-ST-GEORGES, for succulent bio burg from generics up to Les St-Georges and GC RICHEBOURG. Also range of stellar old-vine single-v'yd MOULIN-À-Vent.

Lignier C d'O r w ★★★ Family in MOREY-ST-DENIS. Hubert L (eg. CLOS DE LA ROCHE) on form under son Laurent. V.gd PCS from Virgile L-Michelot, esp Faconnières, but DOM Georges L divides opinion.

Limoux L'doc r w ★★ Interesting still wine AC to complement bubbly BLANQUETTE, CRÉMANT de Limoux. Obligatory oak-ageing for white, from CHARD, CHENIN, Mauzac, as varietal or blend. Red AC based on MERLOT, plus SYRAH, GRENACHE, CABS. PINOT N, illogically for a cool climate, only allowed in CRÉMANT and for IGP Haute Vallée de l'Aude. Growers: DOMS de Baronarques, de Fourn, Mouscaillo, RIVES-BLANQUES and Cathare, *Jean-Louis Denois*.

Lirac S Rh r p w ★★ 10' 15' 16' 17' 18 Four villages nr TAVEL, stony, quality soils. Spicy red (can live 5 yrs+), impetus from CHÂTEAUNEUF owners via clearer fruit, more flair. Reds best, esp DOMS *de la Mordorée* (best, r w), Carabiniers (bio), Duseigneur (bio), Giraud, Jonquer (bio, character), Lafond Roc-Epine, La Lôyane, La Rocalière (gd fruit), Maby (Er-made, gd w), Marcoux (stylish), Plateau des Chênes; CHX de Bouchassy (gd w), de Manissy, de Montfaucon (v.gd w CÔTES DU RH), Mont-Redon, St-Roch; Mas Isabelle (handmade), Rocca Maura, R Sabon. Whites improving fast, project freshness, body, go 5 yrs.

Listrac-Médoc H-Méd r★★★★ 09' 10' 14 **15 16**' (18) Up-and-coming AC for savoury red B'x; now more fruit, depth and MERLOT due to clay soils. Growing number of gd whites under AC B'x. Best CHX: Cap Léon Veyrin, CLARKE, Ducluzeau, FONRÉAUD, Fourca-Borie, FOURCAS-DUPRÉ, FOURCAS-HOSTEN, l'Ermitage, Liouner, Mayne-Lalande, Reverdi, SARANSOT-DUPRÉ.

Long-Depaquit Chab ★★★ Sound CHAB DOM, famous flagship brand, La Moutonne. Part of BICHOT empire.

Lorentz, Gustave Al ★★→★★★ Grower/merchant at Bergheim. RIES is strength in GCS Altenburg de Bergheim, Kanzlerberg, age-worthy 12 **13** 14 16 17. Young volume wines (esp Gewurz) well made. Fine new organic Evidence GEWURZ 16 17.

Lot SW Fr ★→★★ DYA. IGP of Lot département increasingly useful to CAHORS growers for rosé and white wines not allowed in AOP (eg. CLOS de Gamot, CH DU CÈDRE). Look outside for ★★DOMS Belmont, Sully, Tour de Belfort and esp ★★Clos d'Auxonne (nr Mercuq).

Loupiac B'x w sw ★★★ 13 14 15 **16** Minor SÉM-dominant *liquoreux*. Lighter, fresher than SAUT across River Garonne. Top CHX: CLOS Jean, Dauphiné-Rondillon, *de Ricaud*, Les Roques *Loupiac-Gaudiet*, Noble.

Luberon S Rh r p w ★★★ 16' 17' 18 Modish hilly annex to S Rh; terroir is arid, no more than okay. Too many technical wines. SYRAH has lead role. Whites improving. Bright bar: CH de la Canorgue. Also gd: CHX Clapier, Edem, Fontvert (bio, gd w), O Ravoire, Puy des Arts (w), St-Estève de Neri (improver), Tardieu-Laurent (rich, oak), DOMS de la Citadelle, Fontenille, Le Novi (terroir)and Marrenon, Val-Joanis and gd-value *La Vieille Ferme* (can be VIN DE FRANCE).

Lussac-St-Émilion B'x r ★★ 10' 14 15 **16** (18) Lightest of ST-ÉM satellites; 2nd to MONTAGNE in size. Top CHX: Barbe Blanche, Bel-Air, Bellevue, Courlat, DE LUSSAC, La Grenière, La Rose-Perrière, Le Rival, LYONNAT, Mayne-Blanc.

Macération carbonique Traditional fermentation technique: whole bunches of unbroken grapes in a closed vat. Fermentation inside each grape eventually bursts it, giving vivid, fruity, mild wine, not for ageing. Esp in BEAUJ, though not for best wines; now much used in the MIDI and elsewhere, even CHÂTEAUNEUF.

Macle, Dom Jura ★★★ Legendary producer of CH-CHALON VIN JAUNE for long ageing.

Mâcon Burg r (p) w DYA. Simple, juicy GAMAY reds and most basic rendition of Mâconnais whites from CHARD.

Mâcon-Villages Burg w ★★ 14' 15 17 18 Chief appellation for Mâconnais whites. Individual villages may also use their own names eg. Mâcon-Lugny. Co-ops at Lugny, Terres Secrètes, Viré for quality-price ratio, plus *brilliant grower wines* from Guffens-Heynen, Guillot, Guillot-Broux, LAFON, LEFLAIVE, Maillet, Merlin. Also major NÉGOCIANTS, DROUHIN, LATOUR, etc.

Macvin Jura From France, not Scotland. Grape juice is fortified by local marc to make a sweet apér tf between 16–22% alc. Most Jura producers make one.

Madiran SW Fr r ★★→★★ 00' **05** 10 12 15' 16 (18) Gascon AOP. France's home to TANNAT grape (this is bullfighting and rugby). Dark, traditional oaked style represented by ★★★CHX BOUSCASSÉ and MONTUS (owner BRUMONT has 15% of entire AOP), Laffitte-Teston, *Laplace*. Fruitier, sometimes easier examples from ★★★DOMS Berhoumieu, Capmartin, CLOS Basté, Damiens, Dou Bernés, Labranche-Laffont Laffont, Pichard and CH de Gayon. ★★Barréjat, ★★Crampilh, Maouries not far behind.

Madura, Dom la L'doc r w ★★★ Ex-*régisseur* of B'x CH FIEUZAL created own estate in ST-CHINIAN. Stylish Classique and Grand Vin. White an original blend of SAUV BL/PICPOUL.

Mailly Grand Cru Champ Top co-op, all GC grapes. Prestige CUVÉE des *Echansons* 08 12 for long ageing. Sumptuous Echansons Rosé 09, refined, classy L'Intemporelle 06. Sébastien Moncuit, cellarmaster since 14, a rising star.

Maire, Henri Jura r w sw ★ Former legend, creator of Vin Fou, still a huge producer, mostly from own v'yds, sometimes using DOM names eg. Sobief, Bregand, or supermarket brand Auguste Pirou. Part of BOISSET empire.

Maison Ventenac L'doc r (p) w ★★★ Cabardès producer; range of B'X, L'DOC varieties. Fresh acidity from Atlantic air gives elegance, freshness. Paul (CAB FR fermented in *jarres*), Le Pariah (GRENACHE) has outstanding fruit and vibrancy, Idiote (MERLOT), Candide (oak-fermented CHENIN), Prejugé (oaked CHARD) all excellent.

Mann, Albert Al r w ★★→★★★ Top grower at Wettolsheim: rich, elegant. V.gd AUXERROIS, ace range of GCS: HENGST, SCHLOSSBERG, Steingrubler. Great red PINOT N Les Stes Claires in 15. Immaculate bio v'yds.

Maranges C d'Or (w) ★★ 12 15' 16' 17 18' Name to watch. Robust well-priced reds from s end of CÔTE DE BEAUNE. Try PCS Boutière, Croix Moines, Fussière. Best: BACHELET-Monnot, Chevrot, Contat-Grangé, Giroud, MOREAU.

Marcillac SW Fr r p ★★ AVEYRON AOP known for love-or-hate curranty reds, almost all from Mansois (aka FER SERVADOU). Best at 3 yrs. Try with with strawberries as well as charcuterie or Toulouse sausages. ★★DOM du Cros largest independent grower (gd w IGPS too) also Doms Costes, Vieux Porche. Excellent co-op whose president owns Dom de Ladrecht. Local rosés as gd as reds.

Margaux H-Méd r ★★→★★★★ 05' 09' 10' 14 15 16' (18) Largest MÉD communal AC. Famous for elegant, fragrant wines; reality more diverse. Top CHX: BOYD-CANTENAC, BRANE-CANTENAC, DAUZAC, DU TERTRE, FERRIÈRE, GISCOURS, ISSAN, KIRWAN, LASCOMBES, MALESCOT-ST-EXUPÉRY, MARGAUX, PALMER, RAUZAN-SÉGLA. Gd-value chx: ANGLUDET, Haut Breton Larigaudière, LABÉGORCE, LA TOUR DE MONS, Paveil de Luze, SIRAN.

Marionnet, Henry Lo r w ★★→★★★ 16 17 18' Adventurous, far-e TOURAINE, 60-ha DOM incl ungrafted v'yds, run by son Jean-Sebastién. SAUV BL (top CUVÉE L'Origine), GAMAY, Provignage (v. old Romorantin), La Pucelle de Romorantin, Renaissance. Managing historic v'yd at CH de Chambord – 1st vintage 18 – incl Romorantin, Menu Pineau. Originality, character.

Marmande SW Fr r r p (w) ★→★★ 15' 16 18 Improving Gascon AOP. You won't find Abouriou grape anywhere else. ★★★cult winemaker Elian da Ros features it at his eponymous DOM. ★★Doms Beyssac, Bonnet, Cavenac and CH Lassolle blend it with usual B'X grapes. ★★CH de Beaulieu SYRAH-based. Co-ops (95% total production) still dull.

Marsannay C d'Or r p (w) ★★→★★★ (r) 12' 14 15' 17 18' Most n AOC of CÔTE DE NUITS, hoping to get PCS (eg. CLOS du Roy, Longeroies, Champ Salomon). Accessible, crunchy, fruit-laden reds, eg. Audoin, Bart, Bouvier, Charlopin, CLAIR, Fournier, *Pataille*, TRAPET. V.gd *rosé* needs 1–2 yrs; whites less exciting.

Mas, Doms Paul L'doc r p w ★★ Highly ambitious big player; 650 ha of own estates, controls 1312 ha from Grès de Montpellier to ROUSS. Based nr Pézenas. Mainly IGP. Innovative marketing. Esp known for Arrogant Frog range; also La Forge, Les Tannes, Les VIGNES de Nicole and DOMS Ferrandière, Crès Ricards in TERRASSES DU LARZAC, Martinolles in LIMOUX and CH Lauriga in ROUSS, Côté Mas brand from Pézenas. Working on organics and low sulphur.

Mas Bruguière L'doc ★★★ Successful family estate in PIC ST-LOUP; Xavier talented 7th generation. L'Arbouse, La Grenadière and Le Septième.

Mas de Daumas Gassac L'doc r p w ★★★ Set new standards in 80s in MIDI when Aimé Guibert created B'X-influenced CAB-based age-worthy reds from apparently unique soil. Now run by 2nd-generation Samuel G, who has introduced horse-powered viticulture. Also *perfumed white* from CHENIN; super-*cuvée Émile Peynaud* (r): delicious rosé Frizant. V.gd sweet Vin de Laurence (MUSCAT/SERCIAL).

Mas Jullien L'doc ★★★ Owned by early TERRASSES DU LARZAC leader Olivier Julllien. Typical Larzac freshness. Focus on Carignan Bl and Gris, CHENIN BL for white. MOURVÈDRE, CARIGNAN focus in red: Autour de Jonquières, Carlan, États d'Âme, Lous Rougeos from L'DOC varieties.

Massif d'Uchaux S Rh r ★★ 16' 17' 18' Gd Rh village, brightly fruited, spiced reds, not easy to sell, but best true, stylish. NB: CH St-Estève (incl gd VIOGNIER), DOMS *Cros de la Mûre* (character, gd value), de la Guicharde, La Cabotte (bio, on top form), Renjarde (seek fruit).

Maury Rouss r sw ★★→★★★ Reputation est on sweet VDN GRENACHES BL, Gris, Noir grown on island of schist. Now characterful dry red, AC Maury SEC prompted by recent improvements, led by *Mas Amiel*. New estates incl *Dom of the Bee*; Jones. Sound co-op. *Venerable old Rancios* v. rewarding, esp with chocolate.

Mazis- (or Mazy-) Chambertin C d'Or ★★★★ 90' 93 96' 99' 05' 09' 10' 12' 15' 16' 17 18' GC of GEVREY-CHAMBERTIN, top class in upper part; intense, *heavenly wines*. Best: Bernstein, DUGAT-Py, FAIVELEY, HOSPICES DE BEAUNE, LEROY, Maume-Tawse, MORTET, ROUSSEAU.

Mazoyères-Chambertin C d'O ★★★★ Can be sold as CHARMES-CHAMBERTIN, but more growers now labelling M as such. Style is different: less succulence, more stony structure. Try DUGAT-Py, LEROUX, Mortet, Perrot-Minot, Taupenot-Merme.

"Meursault" derives from *muris saltus* – mouse leap. There's a small stream there.

Médoc B'x r ★★ 10' 14 15 16 (18) AC for reds in nr-flat n part of Méd peninsula (aka Bas-Méd). Often more guts than grace. Many growers, so be selective. Top CHX: Bournac, CLOS Manou, Fleur La Mothe, Fontis, *Goulée*, GREYSAC, *La Tour-de-By*, LES ORMES-SORBET Lousteauneuf, *Patache d'Aux*, POITEVIN, *Potensac*, PREUILLAC, Ramafort, *Rollan-de-By* (HAUT-CONDISSAS), TOUR HAUT-CAUSSAN, TOUR ST-BONNET, Vieux Robin.

Meffre, Gabriel S Rh r w ★★→★★★ Consistent S Rh merchant, owns gd GIGONDAS DOM Longue Toque. Fruit quality rising, less oak. Also CHÂTEAUNEUF (gd St-Théodoric, also small doms), VACQUEYRAS St-Barthélemy. Reliable-to-gd S/N Rh Laurus (new oak, gd 15s) range, esp CONDRIEU, HERMITAGE (w), ST-JOSEPH.

Mellot, Alphonse Lo r p w ★★→★★★★ 14' 15' 16' 17 18 Top SANCERRE (r w), bio, incl La Moussière (r w), CUVÉE Edmond, Génération XIX (r w); gd single-v'yds incl *Satellite* (r): Demoiselle, En Champs; Les Pénitents (Côtes de La Charité IGP) CHARD, PINOT N. Run by Alphonse Jnr. Alphonse Snr comparing 18 with 47.

Menetou-Salon Lo r p v w ★★→★★★ 15' 17' 18' AOP 561 ha (376 w, 185 r). Nr SANCERRE; similar SAUV BL. Excellent, generous 18. Increasingly fine reds (PINOT N). Best: Bourgeois, *Clement* (Chatenoy), Gilbert (bio, gd r w), *Henry Pellé* (gd r w), Jacolin, Jean-Max Roger, Teiller, Tour St-Martin.

Méo-Camuzet C d'O r w ★★★★ Noted DOM in VOSNE-ROMANÉE: icons Brûlées, Cros Parantoux, RICHEBOURG. Value from M-C Frère et Soeur (NÉGOCIANT branch) and plenty of choice in between. Sturdy, oaky wines that age well.

Merande, Ch de Sav r ★★ Top producer delivers lasting MONDEUSE red 12': violets, spices, black fruits, saline finish of a great v'yd. Value.

Mercurey Burg r (w) ★★→★★★ 15' 16 17 18' Leading village of CÔTE CHALONNAISE, firmly muscled reds, aromatic whites. Try BICHOT, CH *de Chamirey*, de Suremain, FAIVELEY, *Juillot-Theulot*, Lorenzon, M Juillot, Raquillet.

Mesnil-sur-Oger, Le Champ Top Côte des Blancs village, v. long-lived CHARD. Best: André Jacquart-Doyard, Pierre Péters, JL Vergnon (till 17), KRUG CLOS du Mesnil. Needs 10 yrs+ ageing.

Méthode Champenoise Champ Traditional method of putting bubbles into CHAMP by refermenting wine in its bottle. Outside Champ region, makers must use terms "classic method" or *méthode traditionelle*.

Meursault C d'O (r) w ★★★→★★★★★ 09' 10' 11 12 14' 15 17' 18 Potentially great full-bodied whites from PCS: Charmes, Genevrières, Perrières, more nervy from hillside v'yds *Narvaux*, Tesson, *Tillets*. Producers: Boisson-Vadot, M BOUZEREAU, V Bouzereau, Boyer-Martenot, CH DE MEURSAULT, COCHE-DURY, Ente, Fichet, GIRARDIN, *Javillier*, JOBARD, *Lafon*, Latour (V), LEROUX, Matrot, Mikulski, *P Morey*, Potinet-Ampeau, PRIEUR, *Roulot*. Try de Cherisey for M-BLAGNY.

Meursault, Ch de C d'O r w ★★★ Huge strides lately at this 61-ha estate of big-biz Halley family: decent red from BEAUNE, POMMARD, VOLNAY. Now world-class white, mostly MEURSAULT, also v.gd BOURGOGNE BLANC, PULIGNY PC.

Minervois L'doc r (p) (w) ★★ 10 11 12 13 14 15 16 17 Hilly AC region, one of L'DOC's best. CRU La Livinière (potential AC) has stricter selection, lower yield, longer ageing. Characterful, savoury reds, esp CHX Coupe-Roses, *de Gourgazaud*, La Grave, La Tour Boisée, Oupia, *Ste Eulalie*, St-Jacques d'Albas, Villerembert-Julien; DOMS CLOS Centeilles, Combe Blanche, l'Ostal Cazes; *Abbaye de Tholomiès*, Borie-de-Maurel, Laville-Bertrou, Maris. *Gros and Tollot* (from Burg) raising bar. Potential new crus Cazelles, Laure.

Miquel, Laurent L'doc ★★★ 200 ha v'yds in CORBIÈRES (Les Auzines) and ST-CHINIAN (Cazal Viel). Unusual in specializing in aromatic whites, IGP VIOGNIER. ALBARIÑO impressive, claiming historic tradition through pilgrimage route to Santiago, linking Spain with MIDI. Own v'yds plus NÉGOCIANT activity, with Solas, VENDANGES Nocturnes, Nord Sud.

Mis en bouteille au château / domaine Bottled at CH, property, or estate. NB: *dans nos caves* (in our cellars) or *dans la région de production* (in the area of production) often used but mean little.

Moët & Chandon Champ By far largest CHAMP house, impressive quality for such a giant. Fresher, less sweet BRUT Imperial NV continues to improve. New rare prestige CUVÉE MCIII "solera" concept aimed at rich technophiles, addicts of exclusiveness. Better value in run of Grand Vintages Collection, long lees-aged; new sumptuous, elegant 09 08 a little sweeter. Branches across Europe and New World. *See also* DOM PÉRIGNON.

Monbazillac SW Fr sw sw ★★→★★★ 12 14' 15' 17 18 BERGERAC sub-AOP: ★★★★*Tirecul-la-Gravière* worthy challenge to best SAUTERNES. ★★★CLOS des Verdots, L'Ancienne Cure, Les Hauts de Caillavel, co-op's *Ch de Monbazillac*. ★★CHX de Belingard-Chayne, Grande Maison, Haut-Theulet, Pécoula, de Rayre, Theulet.

Mondeuse Sav r w ★★ SAVOIE grape and wine. Both white and red varieties. Red in ARBIN, BUGEY, CHIGNIN, etc. Best can age.

Monopole A v'yd that is under single ownership.

Montagne-St-Émilion B'x r ★★ 10' 14 15 16 (18) Largest satellite of ST-ÉM. Solid reputation. Top CHX: Beauséjour, CLOS de Boüard, Croix Beauséjour, Faizeau, La Couronne, Maison Blanche, Messile Aubert, Montaiguillon, Roudier, Teyssier, Vieux Bonneau, *Vieux Ch St-André*.

Montagny Burg w ★★ 14' 15 16 17 18 CÔTE CHALONNAISE village with crisp whites, mostly in hands of CAVE de BUXY but gd NÉGOCIANTS too, incl LOUIS LATOUR, JM PILLOT, O LEFLAIVE. Reference local grower is *S Aladame* but try also Berthenet, Cognard, *Feuillat-Juillot*.

Montcalmès, Dom L'doc ★★★ Talented brother-and-sister team in TERRASSES DU LARZAC. Organic. Cool Cévennes winds give fresh elegance. White AC from MARSANNE/ROUSSANNE, plus pure CHARD and intriguing blend VIN DE FRANCE. Stylish SYRAH/GRENACHE/MOURVÈDRE, varietal Grenache, AC L'DOC Le Geai based on Grenache.

Monthélie C d'O r (w) ★★→★★★ 09' 10' 12 15' 16 17 18 Pretty reds, grown uphill from VOLNAY, but a touch more rustic. Les Duresses best PC. Try BOUCHARD PÈRE & FILS, *Ch de Monthélie* (Suremain), *Coche-Dury*, Darviot-Perrin, Florent Garaudet, LAFON.

Montille, de C d'O r w ★★★ Dense, spicy, whole-bunch reds from BEAUNE, VOLNAY (esp Taillepieds), POMMARD (Rugiens), CÔTE DE NUITS (Malconsorts) and exceptional whites from MEURSAULT, plus outstanding PULIGNY-MONTRACHET Caillerets. From 2017 CH de Puligny wines to be incl under de Montille.

Montlouis sur Loire L w dr sw sp ★★ →★★★ 14′ 15′ 16 17 18′ Dynamic sister AC (450 ha) to VOUVRAY, s side of Lo. Top CHENIN BL; 55% sparkling incl Pétillant Originel. 16, 17 frost, 18 v.gd but some mildew. Top: Berger, BLOT, CHANSON, CHIDAINE, Delecheneau, Jousset, Merias, Moyer, Saumon, *Taille-aux-Loups*, Vallée Moray, Weisskopf.

Montpeyroux L'doc ★★→★★★ Lively village within TERRASSES DU LARZAC with growing number of talented growers. Aspiring to cru status. Try: Chabanon, DOM d'Aupilhac, Villa Dondona. Newcomers: Joncas, Mas d'Amile. Serious co-op.

Montrachet (or Le Montrachet) C d'O w ★★★★ 92′ 02′ 04 05′ 08 09′ 10 12 14′ 15 17 18 GC v'yd lent name to both PULIGNY and CHASSAGNE. Should be greatest white burg for intensity, richness of fruit and perfumed persistence. Top: BOUCHARD, COLIN, DRC, LAFON, LAGUICHE (DROUHIN), LEFLAIVE, Ramonet.

Montravel SW Fr r p w dr ★★ (r) 12 15 16 (p w) DYA. Sub-AOP of BERGERAC. Oaked MERLOT obligatory for modern-style reds. ★★★DOMS de Bloy, de Krevel. ★★CHX Jonc Blanc, Laulerie, Masburel (new owner), Masmontet, Moulin-Caresse. ★★dry white and red from same and other growers. See CÔTES DE MONTRAVEL, HAUT-MONTRAVEL for stickies.

Montus, Ch SW Fr r w ★★★ 00′ 05 09 10 12′ 14 15′ Long-lived all-TANNAT, much-oaked reds from ALAIN BRUMONT's top property require patience from lovers of old-fashioned MADIRAN. Classy sweet and dry white barrel-raised PACHERENCS DU VIC-BILH (drink at 4 yrs+) on same level.

Moreau Burg r w ★★→★★★ Widespread family in CHAB esp *Dom Christian M* (try CLCS des Hospices) and DOM M-Naudet. Other Moreau families in CÔTE DE BEAUNE, esp Bernard M for vigorous CHASSAGNE and David M in SANTENAY.

Morey, Doms C d'O r w ★★★ VIGNERON family in CHASSAGNE-MONTRACHET. Current generation features Caroline M and husband Pierre-Yves Colin-M, Sylvain, Thomas (fine Baudines), Vincent (Embrazées, plumper) and Thibault M-Coffinet (LA ROMANÉE). Also Pierre M in MEURSAULT for Perrières and BÂTARD-MONTRACHET.

Morey-St-Denis C d'O r (w) ★★★ →★★★★ 99′ 02′ 05′ 09′ 10′ 12′ 15′ 16′ 17 18′ Terrific source of top-grade red burg, to rival neighbours GEVREY-CHAMBERTIN, CHAMBOLLE-MUSIGNY. GCS CLOS DE LA ROCHE, CLOS DE LAMBRAYS, CLOS DE TART, CLOS ST-DENIS. Many gd producers: Amiot, ARLAUD, Castagnier, Coquard-Loison-Fleurot, CLOS DE TART,

---

Muscadet grows old gracefully

Everyone looks for the latest vintage of MUSCADET, but top Muscadets (top producers, gd vintages, esp with long lees-ageing) can last and improve for 20 yrs+, ending up not unlike old CHAB. Look for newly coined Cru Communaux: Clisson, Gorges, Le Pallet, with Goulaine, CH-Thébaud, Monnières-St-Fiacre, Mouzillon-Tillières waiting in wings (long lees-ageing and greater complexity). Look for: Bonnet-Huteau, Bruno Cormerais, CH de la Gravelle (Gunther Chereau), Daniel Rineau, DOM DE L'ECU (Frédéric Niger van Herck/Guy Bossard), Dom Michel Brégeon, Jérémie Huchet, Jérémie Mourat, Jo Landron, Les VIGNERONS du Pallet, Luneau-Papin, Marc Ollivier (Dom de la Pépière), Vincent Caillé (Le Faye d'Homme). That'll see you through a few oysters.

Clos des Lambrays, *Dujac*, Jeanniard, H LIGNIER, LIGNIER-Michelot, Perrot-Minot, PONSOT, Remy, *Roumier*, Taupenot-Merme, Tremblay.

Morgon Beauj r ★★★ 14 15' 17 18' Powerful BEAUJ cru, volcanic slate of Côte du Py makes meaty, age-worthy wine, clay of Les Charmes for earlier, smoother drinking. Grands Crus, Javernières of interest too. Try Burgaud, CH de Pizay, **Ch des Lumières** (JADOT), Chemarin, CLOS de Mez, Desvignes, Foillard, Gaget, Godard, Grange-Cochard, LAPIERRE, Piron, Sunier A, Sunier J.

Mortet, Denis C d'O r ★★★ →★★★★ Arnaud Mortet on song with powerful yet refined reds from BOURGOGNE Rouge to CHAMBERTIN. Key wines GEVREY-CHAMBERTIN Mes Cinq Terroirs, PCS Lavaut St-Jacques, Champeaux. From 2016 separate Arnaud M label, incl CHARMES- and MAZOYÈRES-CHAMBERTIN.

Moueix, J-P et Cie B'x Libourne-based NÉGOCIANT and proprietor named after legendary founder Jean-Pierre. Son Christian runs company with his son Edouard. CHX: BELAIR-MONANGE, HOSANNA, LA FLEUR-PÉTRUS, *La Grave à Pomerol*, LATOUR-À-POMEROL, TROTANOY. Distributes PETRUS. In California (see DOMINUS ESTATE).

Moulin-à-Vent Beauj r ★★★ 09' 11' 14 15' 18' Grandest BEAUJ cru, transcending GAMAY grape. Weight, spiciness of Rh but matures towards rich, gamey PINOT flavours. Increasing interest in single-v'yd bottlings from eg. CH du Moulin-à-Vent, DOM La Bruyère, JADOT's Ch *des Jacques*, Janin, Janodet, LIGER-BELAIR (Les Rouchaux), L BOILLOT (Brussellions), Merlin (La Rochelle).

Moulis H-Méd r ★★ →★★★ 05' 09' 10' 15 16 (18) Tiny inland AC w of MARGAUX. Honest, gd-value wines. Best have ageing potential. Top CHX: Anthonic, Biston-Brillette, BRANAS GRAND POUJEAUX, BRILLETTE, *Chasse-Spleen*, Dutruch Grand Poujeaux, Garricq, *Gressier Grand Poujeaux*, MAUCAILLOU, Mauvesin Barton, *Poujeaux*.

Moutard Champ Original champion of local Arbanne grape. Also eaux de vie. Geatly improved quality, esp CHARD Persin and CUVÉE des 6 CÉPAGES 11 15.

Mugneret C d'O r w ★★★ →★★★★ VIGNERON family in VOSNE-ROMANÉE. Sublime, stylish wines from Georges M-Gibourg (esp ÉCHÉZEAUX), almost matched by rapidly improving Gérard M. Try also Dominique M and DOM Mongeard-M.

Mugnier, J-F C d'O r w ★★★★ Outstanding grower of CHAMBOLLE-MUSIGNY *Les Amoureuses* and *Musigny*. Finesse, not muscle. Equally at home with MONOPOLE NUITS-ST-GEORGES CLOS de la Maréchale. Courageous decision to take young vintages of MUSIGNY off the market to avoid infanticide.

Mumm, GH & Cie Champ Abrupt departure for Australia of chef de CAVE Didier Mariotti, who led renaissance of Mumm in C21, raises questions of future direction. NB Mumm de Verzenay BLANC DE NOIRS 08 12, RSVR BLANC DE BLANCS 12. Mumm de Cramant, renamed Blanc de Blancs, still elegantly subtle. Cordon Rouge both NV and Vintage much improved.

Muscadet Lo w ★★ →★★★ 16 17 18' Popular, bone-dry wine from nr Nantes. 8200 ha in total. Ideal with fish, seafood. Best SUR LIE. Choose great value. Best SUR LIE. Choose ACS: see following entries. Frost in 16, 17 but v.gd 18: quality, quantity. Must try age-worthy MUSCADET CRUS COMMUNAUX. 10% CHARD allowed in generic Muscadet.

Muscadet-Coteaux de la Loire Lo w ★ →★★ 16 17 18' Small (150 ha, 40 growers), e of Nantes both sides Loire. Esp Carroget, Guindon, Landron-Chartier, La Pléiade, Ponceau, Quarteron, VIGNERONS de la Noëlle.

Muscadet Côtes de Grand Lieu Lo ★ →★★★ 16 17 18' MUSCADET zonal AOP (300 ha, 40 growers) by Atlantic. Best SUR LIE: Eric Chevalier, Herbauges (107 ha), Haut-Bourg, Malidain. 16, 17 frost, 18 exceptional.

Muscadet Crus Communaux Lo ★★ →★★★ MUSCADET's new top category. Long lees-ageing from specified sites, startlingly gd, complex wines. 1st three communes (2011): Clisson, Gorges, Le Pallet. Goulaine, La Haye Fouassière, Monnières-St Fiacre, Mouzillon-Tillières await ratification. Champtoceaux, Vallet in process.

Muscadet-Sèvre-et-Maine Lo w ↦→★★★ 15′ 16 17 18′ Largest (5890 ha) and best MUSCADET zone. Increasingly gd and great value. Top: Bonnet-Huteau, CH Briacé, Caillé, *Chereau Carré*, Cormerais, Delhommeau, DOM DE L'ECU, Dom de la Haute Fevrie, Douillard, *Gadais*, Gunther-Chereau, Huchet, Landron, Lieubeau, Luneau-Papin, Métaireau, Olivier, *Sauvion*. Can age a decade+. Try CRUS COMMUNAUX. Exceptional 18: quality, volume.

Muscat de Frontignan L'doc sw ★★ NV Small coastal AC outside Sète for Muscat Vin Doux Naturel. Also late-harvest, unfortified, oak-aged IGP wines. Leader remains CH la Peyrade. English elderflower wine also often called Frontignan – flavour is reminiscent. Nearby Muscat de Lunel (DOM du CLOS de Bellevue) and Muscat de Mireval (DOM de la Rencontre) v. similar.

Muscat de Rivesaltes Rouss w sw ★★ Sweet grapey fortified MUSCAT VDN AC from large area centred on town of Rivesaltes. Muscat SEC IGP increasing as demand for sweet VDN declines. Look Corneilla for DOM CAZES, Treloar; Baixas co-op.

Muscat de St-Jean de Minervois L'doc w sw ★★ Tiny AC for fresh, honeyed Muscat Vin Doux Naturel. Try DOM de Barroubio, CLOS du Gravillas, Clos Bagatelle. Village co-op prefers dry Muscat.

Musigny (Le Musigny) C d'O r (w) ★★★★ 90′ 93 96′ 99′ 02′ 05′ 09′ 10′ 12′ 15′ 17 18 GC in CHAMBOLLE-MUSIGNY. Can be most fragrantly beautiful, if not most powerful, of all red burgs. Best: DE VOGÜÉ, DROUHIN, FAIVELEY, JADOT, LEROY, MUGNIER, PRIEUR, ROUMIER, VOUGERAIE.

Nature Unsweetened esp for CHAMP: no dosage. Fine if v. ripe grapes, raw otherwise.

Négociant-éleveur Merchant who "brings up" (ie. matures) the wine.

Noëllat C d'O r ★★★ Noted VOSNE-ROMANÉE family. Georges N making waves since 2010 and expanding fast, Michel N offers sound range. *See also* v. stylish HUDELOT-N in VOUGEOT.

Notre Dames des Anges Prov r p ★★ Subzone of CÔTES DE PROV. Newest zone, hot central valley. Try Rimauresq.

Nuits-St-Georges C d'O r ★★→★★★★ 99′ 02′ 03 05′ 09′ 10′ 12′ 15′ 16 17 18′ Three parts to this major AC: Premeaux v'yds for elegance (various CLOS: de la Maréchale, des Corvées, des Forêts, St-Marc), centre for dense dark plummy wines (Cailles, Les St-Georges, Vaucrains) and n side for the headiest (Boudots, Cras, Murgers). Many fine growers: Ambroise, ARLOT, ARNOUX-LACHAUX, CATHIARD, Confuron, *Faiveley*, Gavignet, GOUGES, GRIVOT, J Chauvenet, Lechéneaut, LEROY, *Liger-Belair*, Machard de Gramont, Michelot, *Mugnier*, R CHEVILLON, *Rion*.

Ollier-Taillefer, Dom L'doc r p w ★★★ Dynamic FAUGÈRES family estate. Steep terraced v'yds. Delicious Allegro from VERMENTINO/ROUSSANNE (w); Collines (r p); Grand Rés (r) from old vines, and oak-aged Castel Fossibus (r). CUVÉE (r) Le Rêve de Noé, SYRAH/MOURVÈDRE blend.

Orléans Lo r p w ★ DYA. Small AC (69 ha) for white (chiefly CHARD), VIN GRIS, rosé, reds (PINOT N, esp PINOT M) around Orléans (13 communes). Formerly famous for vinegar. Try: Deneufbourg, CLOS St Fiacre, Chante d'Oiseaux. V. promising 18.

Orléans-Clery Lo r ★ DYA. Lo Micro-AOP (25 ha); sw of Orléans at n limit for for CAB FR, sandy soil. Try: Chante d'Oiseaux, CLOS St Fiacre, Deneufbourg.

Ostertag, Dom Al ≡ w ★★★ More interested in nuances of terroir than varietal expression. Bio-certified. Great RIES, esp Muenchberg 10 barrique-fermented, intense Muenchberg PINOT GR 15. Lovely PINOT N Fronholtz 12 15 17.

Pacherenc du Vic-Bilh SW Fr w dr sw ★★→★★★ AOP for wines from MADIRAN area. GROS, PETIT MANSENG, sometimes Petit Courbu and local Aruffiac produce dry and sweet styles. Mostly same growers as Madiran but note too ★★CH Mascaaras. Dry DYA, but sweet, esp if oaked, can be kept.

Paillard, Bruno Champ ★★★→★★★★ Youngest GRANDE MARQUE. BRUT Première CUVÉE NV, Rosé Première Cuvée; refined style, esp in long-aged BLANC DE BLANCS 04,

NPU 02. Brut Nature has clever use of PINOT M. Bruno heads LANSON-BCC; daughter Alice taking over reins at Paillard.

Palette Prov r p w ★★★ Tiny AC nr Aix-en-Prov. Characterful reds, mainly from MOURVÈDRE, GRENACHE; fragrant rosés, intriguing forest-scented whites. Traditional, serious **Ch Simone** and Crémade.

Patrimonio Cors r p w ★★→★★★ AC. Some of island's finest, from dramatic limestone hills in n. Individual reds from NIELLUCCIO, intriguing whites, even **late-harvest Vermentino**. Top: Antoine Arena, CLOS de Bernardi, **Gentile**, Montemagni, Pastricciola, Yves Leccia at E Croce. Worth the journey.

Pauillac H-Méd r ★★★→★★★★ 90' 96' 00' 05' 09' 10' 15 16' Communal AC in n MÉD with 18 Classed Growths, incl LAFITE, LATOUR, MOUTON. Famous for long-lived wines, the acme of CAB SAUV. Other top CHX: CLERC MILON, GRAND-PUY-LACOSTE, LYNCH-BAGES, PICHON-BARON, PICHON-LALANDE, PONTET-CANET. Gd-value CHX: FONBADET, La Fleur Peyrabon, PIBRAN.

Pays d'Oc, IGP L'doc r p w ★→★★★ Largest IGP, covering whole of L'DOC-ROUSS. Focus on varietal wines; 58 different grapes allowed. ALBARIÑO latest addition, CARIGNAN, esp old vines increasingly popular. Technical advances continue apace. Main producers: Jeanjean, DOMS PAUL MAS, GÉRARD BERTRAND, village co-ops. Extremes of quality; best are innovative, exciting.

Péchardant SW Fr r ★★ 12 14 15' (17) (18) Biggest wines (keepers) from BERGERAC (inner AOP) benefit from iron and manganese in soil. Veteran ★★★**Ch de Tiregand**, DOM du Haut-Péchardant, Les Chemins d'Orient; ★★CLOS des Côtes, La Métairie, CHX Beauportail, Champarel, Corbiac, de Biran, du Rooy, Hugon, Terre Vieille; Dom des Bertranoux.

Pélican, Dom du Jura Retired legend Jacques Puffeney's v'yds now run by VOLNAY's MARQUIS D'ANGERVILLE to make fine fresh styles. More to come...

Pernand-Vergelesses C d'O r w ★★★ (r) 05' 09' 10' 12 14 15' 17 18' Village next to ALOXE-CORTON incl part of CORTON-CHARLEMAGNE, CORTON. Île des Vergelesses v'yd 1st-rate for reds, elsewhere chiselled, precise whites. DOMS Rapet and Rollin lead the way but try also from CHANDON DE BRIAILLES, CHANSON, Dubreuil-Fontaine, JADOT.

Perret, André N Rh r w ★★★ 16' 17' 18' High-quality CONDRIEU, three wines, two plot-specific: Chanson (full, mineral in cool yrs), Chéry (rich, ripe, sustained); improving, gd St-Joseph (r), esp old-vine Grisières (peppery, dark-fruited, serious). Gd VIN DE PAYS (r w) too.

Perrier-Jouët Champ BRUT NV; Blason de France NV; Blason de France Rosé NV; Brut 02 04 06 08. Fine new BLANC DE BLANCS. 1st (in C19) to make dry CHAMP for English market; strong in GC CHARD, best for gd vintage and de luxe Belle Epoque 95 04 06 07 08' 12 15, Rosé 04 06, in painted bottle.

Jura jewels

What other region has so many styles? They seem to like confusing customers – sommeliers love the game. **Dry whites** from CHARD, many single-v'yd versions now. Also tangy blends with SAVAGNIN. Fresh or deliberately **oxidative** pure Savagnin exciting too; many made in natural style can be pretty gamey. *See* CÔTES DU JURA, ARBOIS, L'ETOILE. *Vin typé* on labels means heading towards Sherry. *Vin ouillé* means "ullaged": the barrel has been topped-up to avoid oxidation. **Light reds** from PINOT N, Poulsard, Trousseau, or blends. Some more rosé than red. Côtes du Jura, Arbois. Aged **sherrified whites** known as VIN JAUNE. *See* CH-CHALON. Intensely sweet *vin de paille* made fom red and white grapes. Fortified **Macvin**, local version of ratafia. Classic producers: Bourdy, MACLE, Overnoy, Puffeney. Avant garde: A&M TISSOT, GANEVAT, PIGNIER. Volume/value: co-ops (known here as CAVES Fruitières), Boilley, J Tissot, LABET, HENRI MAIRE.

Pessac-Léognan B'x r w ★★★ →★★★★ 00' 05' 09' 10' 15 16 AC created in 1987 for best part of n GRAV, incl all Crus Classés (1959): HAUT-BAILLY, HAUT-BRION, LA MISSION-HAUT-BRION, PAPE-CLÉMENT, etc. Firm, full-bodied, earthy reds; B'x's finest dry whites. Value from Brown, DE ROCHEMORIN, Haut-Vigneau, Lafont-Menaut, Le Sartre, Lespault-Martillac, Rouillac.

Petit Chablis Chab w ★ DYA. Fresh, easy, would-be CHAB from outlying v'yds mostly not on kimmeridgian clay. Priced too close to full Chablis. Best wines from Billaud, BROCARD, Defaix, DAUVISSAT, RAVENEAU and LA CHABLISIENNE co-op.

Pfersigberg Al GC in two parcels; v. aromatic wines. GEWURZ does v. well. RIES from BRUNO SORG, LÉON BEYER (Comtes d'Eguisheim), Paul Ginglinger.

Philipponnat Champ small house, intense, esp in pure Mareuil sur Ay CUVÉE under careful oak. Now owned by LANSON-BCC group. NV, Rosé NV, BRUT, CUVÉE 1522 04, remarkable single-v'yd *Clos des Goisses* 04, CHARD-led 08; exceptional 09 late-disgorged vintage 90.

Picpoul de Pinet L'd/c w ★→★★ DYA. "MUSCADET of MIDI". AC since 2013, from PICPOUL grown around Pinet. Best producers experimenting to find greater depth: reduced yields, harvest dates, ageing on lees. Use of oak not encouraged. Best: Félines-Jourdan, La Croix Gratiot, St Martin de la Garrigue; co-ops Pinet, Pomérols. Fresh, salty, so perfect *with oysters*. Best have sappy tang, sometimes almond, *garrigue* notes.

Pic St-Loup L'doc r (p) ★★→★★★ Coolest, wettest part of L'DOC. Dramatic scenery with some v'yds at altitude. AC reflects proximity to Rhône with high proportion of SYRAH, plus GRENACHE, MOURVÈDRE. Reds for ageing; white potential considerable but still AC L'doc or IGP Val de Montferrand. Growers: Bergerie du Capucin, Cazeneuve, CLOS de la Matane, Clos Marie, de Lancyre, *Dom de l'Hortus*, Gourdou, Lascaux, MAS BRUGUIÈRE, Mas Peyrolle, Valflaunès.

Pierre-Bise, Ch Lo r p w ★★ →★★★★ 10' 11 14' 15 16 17 18' Impeccable DOM in COTEAUX DU LAYON, incl Chaume, QUARTS DE CHAUME, SAVENNIÈRES (*Clos de Grand Beaupréau*, ROCHE-AUX-MOINES). V.gd ANJOU-GAMAY, ANJOU-VILLAGES (both CUVÉE Schist, Spilite), ANJOU Blanc Haut de la Garde. Patriarch Claude, architect of Quarts de Chaume GC, now semi-retired, son René in charge.

Pierrefeu Prov r p ★★ Subzone of CÔTES DE PROV: warmer maritime zone n of La Londe. Try ch la Gordonne.

Pinon, François Lo w sw sp ★★★ 09 10' 11 14' 15' 16 17 18' V.gd organic (from 2003) wines La Cousse Valley, Vernou, VOUVRAY. François and son Julien. Wines age.

Piper-Heidsieck Champ Historic house on surging wave of quality. Dynamic Brut Essentiel with more age, less sugar, floral yet vigorous; great with sushi, sashimi. Prestige Rare, now made as separate brand in-house, is a jewel, precise, pure, refined 98 02 06; 1st release of Rare Rosé 07.

Plageoles, Dom SW Fr r w sp Family of mentor growers defending true Gaillac style. Fans of rare grapes eg. Ondenc (base of v.gd sweet ★★★★Vin d'Autan), ★★Prunelard (n deep fruity), Verdanel (dr w, oak-aged) and countless sub-varieties of Mauzac. More reds from Duras and Braucol (local name for FER SERVADOU). ★★★ *Brilliant dry sparkler* Mauzac Natur another original.

Plan de Dieu S Rh r ★ →★★ 15' 16' 17' 18 Rh village nr CAIRANNE with stony, windswept plain. Heady, robust, peppery, mainly GRENACHE, grass-roots wines; drink with game, stews. Gd choice. Best: CH la Courançonne, CLOS St Antonin, LE PLAISIR; DOMS Aphillanthes (character), Arnesque, Bastide St Vincent, Durieu (full), Espiguette, Longue Togue, Martin (traditional), Pasquiers, St-Pierre.

Pol Roger Champ Family-owned Épernay house. BRUT Rés NV excels, dosage lowered since 2012; ★★Brut 02' 04 06 08, lovely 09 12'; Rosé 09; BLANC DE BLANCS 09. Fine *Pure* (no dosage). Sumptuous CUVÉE Sir Winston Churchill 88 02 always a blue-chip choice for long ageing, best value of prestige cuvées.

Pomerol B'x r ★★★→★★★★ 98' 00' 01' **05' 09' 10'** 15 16 Tiny, pricey AC bordering ST-ÉM; MERLOT-led, rich, voluptuous style, but long life. Top CHX on clay, gravel plateau: CLINET, HOSANNA, L'ÉGLISE-CLINET, L'ÉVANGILE, LA CONSEILLANTE, LAFLEUR, LA FLEUR-PÉTRUS, LE PIN, PETRUS, TROTANOY, VIEUX-CH-CERTAN. Occasional value (BOURGNEUF, CLOS du Clocher, LA POINTE, MAZEYRES).

Pommard C d'O r ★★★★→★) 90' **96'** 99' 03 05' 09' 10' 12 15' 16' 17 18' Antithesis of neighbour VOLNAY; potent, tannic wines to age 10 yrs+. Best v'yds: Rugiens for power, Epenots for grace. Growers: CH de Pommard, Clerget, COMTE ARMAND, COURCEL, DE MONTILLE, HOSPICES DE BEAUNE, Huber-Vedereau, J-M BOILLOT, Lejeune, Parent, Pothier-Rieusset, Rebourgeon, Violot-Guillemard.

Pommery Champ Historic house with spectacular cellars; brand now owned by VRANKEN. BRUT NV steady bet; Rosé NV; Brut **04 08** 09 12'. Once outstanding CUVÉE Louise 02 **04** less striking recently. Planting in England.

Ponsot C d'O r w ★★→★★★★★ Idiosyncratic, top-quality MOREY-ST-DENIS DOM. Rose-Marie P now in charge. Key wines: **Clos de la Roche**, unique white PC Monts Luisants (ALIGOTÉ). Laurent P now set up as NÉGOCIANT; outstanding from 2016.

Pouilly-Fuissé Burg w ★★→★★★ 14' 15 **17** 18 Top AC of MÂCON; potent, rounded but intense whites from around Fuissé, more mineral style by Vergisson. Enjoy young or with age. PCS about to happen soon, surely. Top: Barraud, Bouchacourt, Bret, CH de Beauregard, CH DE FUISSÉ, Ch des Quarts, Ch des Rontets, Cordier, Cornin, Drouin, Ferret, Forest, Merlin, Paquet, Robert-Denogent, Rollet, Saumaize, Saumaize-Michelin, VERGET.

Pouilly-Fumé Lo w ★→★★★★★ 14' 15 **17** 18' E-bank neighbour of SANCERRE. 1352 ha SAUV BL. Frost, esp 16, 17, but v.gd 18. Best improve at least 8–10 yrs+. Growers: Bain, Belair, BOURGEOIS, Cailbourdin, Champeau, CH de Favray, Ch de Tracy, Chatelain, DIDIER DAGUENEAU, Edmond and André Figeat, Jean Pabiot, Jonathan Pabiot, LADOUCETTE, Masson-Blondelet, Redde, Saget, Serge Dagueneau & Filles, Tabordet, Treuillet.

Pouilly-Loché Burg w ★★ 14' 15 **17** 18 Least known of Mâconnais' Pouilly family. Reference: CLOS des Rocs. Try also Bret Bros, Tripoz and local co-op.

Pouilly-sur-Loire Lo w ★★ DYA. In C19, Pouilly supplied Paris with CHASSELAS table grapes. Same area as POUILLY-FUMÉ. Just 27 ha remain, but Gitton, Jonathan Pabiot, Landrat-Guyollot, Masson-Blondelet, Redde, Serge Dagueneau & Filles determined to uphold tradition.

Pouilly-Vinzelles Burg w ★★ 14' 15 **17** 18 Between POUILLY-LOCHÉ and POUILLY-FUISSÉ geographically and in quality. Outstanding v'yd: Les Quarts. Best: Bret Bros, DROUHIN, Valette. Volume from CAVE des GCS Blancs.

Premier Cru (PC) First Growth in B'x; 2nd rank of v'yds (after GC) in Burg; 2nd rank in Lo: one so far, COTEAUX DU LAYON Chaume.

Premières Côtes de Bordeaux B'x w sw ★→★★★ **10'** 15' 16 (18) Same zone as CADILLAC-CÔTES de B'x but for sweet whites only. SÉM-dominated *moelleux*. Generally early drinking. Best CHX: Crabitan-Bellevue, du Juge, Fayau, **Suau**.

Prieur, Dom Jacques C d'O ★★★ Major MEURSAULT estate with range of underplayed GCS from MONTRACHET to MUSIGNY. Style aims at weight from late-picking and oak more than finesse. Owners Famille Labruyère also have CHAMP and MOULIN-À-VENT projects plus CH ROUGET, POM.

Prieuré de St-Jean de Bébian L'doc ★★★ Pézenas estate, CHÂTEAUNEUF varieties. Russian owned; Aussie winemaker Karen Turner. Complex soils: gravel, volcanic, clay, limestone. Three levels: La Chapelle, La Croix, Prieuré (r w); old-vines red 1152.

Primeur "Early" wine for refreshment and uplift; esp from BEAUJ; VDP too. Wine sold en primeur is still in barrel, for delivery when bottled.

Producteurs Plaimont SW Fr France's most dynamic co-op, injecting grapes not traditional to the SW, and reviving forgotten ones that are. Expanding into n

MADIRAN (acquiring independent DOMS), SAINT MONT (opening hotel in old abbey). All colours, styles mostly ★★, all tastes, purses.

Propriétaire récoltant Champ Owner-operator, literally owner-harvester.

Puisseguin St-Émilion B'x r ★★ 10' 14 15 **16** (18) Most e of four ST-ÉM satellites wines firm, solid. Potential 10 yrs. Top CHX incl: Beauséjour, Branda, Clarisse DES LAURETS, de Môle, Durand-Laplagne, Fongaban, Guibot la Fourvieille, Haut Bernat, La Mauriane, Le Bernat, Soleil.

Puligny-Montrachet C d'O (r) w ★★★ →★★★★ 09' 10' 12 14' 15 17 18 Floral, fine-boned, tingling white Burg. Decent at village level, outstanding PCS, esp: Caillerets, Champ Canet, Combettes, Folatières, Pucelles, plus amazing MONTRACHET GCS. Producers: _Bouchard Père & Fils_, CARILLON, Chartron, CH de Puligny, **Dom Leflaive**, Drouhin, Ente, JADOT, **J-M Boillot**, **O Leflaive**, Pernot, **Sauzet**.

Puyméras S Rh r w ★ 16' 17' **18** Sound, secluded village, high v'yds, supple plum-fruited reds centred on GRENACHE, fair whites, decent co-op. Try CAVE la Comtadine, DOM du Faucon Doré (bio), Puy du Maupas.

Pyrénées-Atlantiques SW Fr Mostly DYA. IGP in far SW for wines not qualifying for local AOPS. Thus ★★★CH Cabidos (superb dr and sw w PETIT MANSENG varietal that will age), ★★DOM Moncaut (nr Pau), ★BRUMONT non-AOP varietals and blends. Otherwise pot luck.

Quarts de Chaume Lo w SW ★★★ →★★★★ 07' 10' 11' 14' 15' **16** 17 18' 40 ha, slope close to Layon, CHENIN BL. Admirably strict rules should be enforced for GC and price. Some parcels still overcropped. Best richly textured. Best: Baudouin, Bellerive, Branchereau, CH PIERRE-BISE, FL, Guegniard, Ogereau, Pithon-Paillé, Suronde (same ownership Minière, BOURGUEIL).

Quincy Lo w ★→★★ 16 17 18' Revived AOP (303 ha, was 60 ha in 1990) SAUV B from low-lying sand/gravel banks – Cher Valley se of Vierzon; 1st Lo AC 1936. Growers: Mardon, Portier, Rouzé, Siret-Courtaud, Tatin-Wilk – DOMS Ballandors, Tremblay, Villain.

Rancio Rouss Most original, lingering, delicious style of VDN, reminiscent of Tawny Port, or old Oloroso Sherry in BANYULS, MAURY, RASTEAU, RIVESALTES, wood-aged and exposed to oxygen, heat. Not to be missed. Same flavour (pungent, tangy) a fault in table wine.

Rangen Al Most s GC of AL at Thann. Extremely steep (average 90%) slopes, volcanic soils. Top: majestic RIES ZIND-HUMBRECHT (CLOS St Urbain 05' 08' 10' 17'), SCHOFFIT (St-Théobald 08' 10 17'). Extra finesse in 15.

Rasteau S Rh r (p) (w) br (dr) sw ★★ 10' 12' 15' 16' **17'** 18 Full-strength reds from clay soils, mainly GRENACHE. Best in hot yrs. NB: Beaurenard (serious, age well), **Cave Ortas** (g̱l), CH La Gardine, **Ch du Trignon**, Famille Perrin; DOMS Beau Mistral, Collière, Combe Julière, Coteaux des Travers (bio), Didier Charavin, Elodie Balme, Escaravailles, Girasols, Gourt de Mautens (talented, IGP wine from 2010), Grand Nicolet (character), Grange Blanche, Rabasse-Charavin, M Boutin, Soumade (polished), St Gayan, Trapadis. Grenache dessert VDN quality on the up (Doms Banquettes, Combe Julière, Coteaux des Travers, Escaravailles, Trapadis). Rasteau doms also gd source CÔTES DU RHÔNE (r).

Raveneau Chab w ★★★★ Along with DAUVISSAT cousins, greatest CHAB producers using classic methods for **_extraordinary long-lived wines_**. Excellent value (except in secondary market). Look for Blanchots, Les CLOS, Vaillons.

Rayas, Ch S Rh r w ★★★★ 98' **99** 05' **06' 07'** 09' 10' 11' 15' 16' 17' Fascinating, lost in time 13-ha CHÂTEAUNEUF estate, tiny yields. Pale, subtle, aromatic, sensuous reds (100% GRENACHE) whisper quality, offer delight, age superbly. White Rayas (GRENACHE BL, CLAIRETTE) v.gd over 18 yrs+. Gd-value, stylish second wine: _Pignan_ Supreme CH Fonsalette CÔTES DU RH, incl marvellous SYRAH. Decant them all; each is an occasion. Also gd CH des Tours VACQUEYRAS (peppery), VDP.

Regnié Beauj r ★★ 15′ **16 17 18**′ Most recent BEAUJ cru, lighter wines on sandy soil, meatier nr MORGON. Try Burgaud, de la Plaigne, Dupré, Rochette, Sunier.

Reuilly Lo r p w ★→★★★ 15′ 16 17 18′ Revived AC (259 ha, was 30 ha in 1990) neighbour of QUINCY s of Vierzon. SAUV BL (127 ha), rosés and *Vin Gris* PINOT N (75 ha) and/or PINOT GR (50 ha). Some gd Pinot N reds. Best: Claude Lafond (run by daughter Natalie), *Jamain*, Mardon, Renaudat, Rouze, Sorbe. 18 potentially v.gd.

Riceys, Les Champ p DYA. Key AC in AUBE for a notable PINOT N rosé. Producers: *A Bonnet*, Jacques Defrance, Morize. Great 09; v. promising **14** after lean period 11–13; 15′ excels.

Richebourg C d'O r ★★★★ 90′ 93′ **96**′ 99′ 02′ **03** 05′ 09′ 10′ 12′ 15′ 16 17 18 VOSNE-ROMANÉE GC. Supreme burg with great depth of flavour; vastly expensive. Growers: DRC, GRIVOT, GROS, HUDELOT-NOËLLAT, LEROY, LIGER-BELAIR, MÉO-CAMUZET.

Rimage Rouss A growing mode: vintage VDN, super-fruity for drinking young. Think gd Ruby Port. Grenat is MAURY version.

Rion C d'O r (w) ★★→★★★ Related DOMS in NUITS-ST-GEORGES, VOSNE-ROMANÉE. Patrice R for excellent Nuits CLOS St-Marc, Clos des Argillières and CHAMBOLLE-MUSIGNY. Daniel R for Nuits and Vosne PCS; Bernard R more Vosne-based. All fairly priced.

Rivesaltes Rouss r w b dr sw ★★ NV or solera, also vintage, young and old VDN from large area in n ROUSS. Grossly underappreciated; deserves revival. Long-lasting wines, esp RANCIOS. Look for: Boucabeille, des Chênes, des Schistes, DOM CAZES, Rancy, Roc des Anges, Sarda-Malet, Vaquer. You won't be disappointed.

Egg-shaped wine tank; *coque au vin...* or *vin à la coque?*

Rives-Blanques, Ch L'doc sp w ★★★ LIMOUX. Irish-Dutch couple, now joined by son, make BLANQUETTE, CRÉMANT. Limoux white, incl unusual 100% MAUZAC, Occitania, blend Trilogie and age-worthy CHENIN BL Dédicace. Dessert Lagremas d'Aur.

Roche-aux-Moines, La Lo w sw ★★→★★★ 10′ 11 12 **14**′ **15**′ 16 33 ha cru of SAVENNIÈRES, ANJOU. Strict rules, age-worthy CHENIN BL. Try: aux Moines, *Ch Pierre-Bise*, CLOS de la Bergerie (Joly), FL, Forges, Laureau. Minimal crop 17, v. promising 18.

Roederer, Louis Champ Peerless family-owned house/DOM. Enviable v'yds: 240 ha, much organic/bio. ★★★BRUT Premier NV all finesse, flavour; Brut 08 **12**, BLANC DE BLANCS 12 **13** 15, Brut Saignée Rosé 09. Magnificent *Cristal* bio since 2012; 08. Superb Cristal Vinothèque Blanc 96 and Rosé 95. Brut Nature Philippe Starck (all Cumières 09,**12**,15). Also owns DEUTZ, PICHON-LALANDE. *See also* California.

Rolland, Michel B'x Veteran French consultant winemaker and MERLOT specialist (B'x and worldwide). Owner of FONTENIL in FRON. *See* Argentina (Clos de los Siete).

Rolly Gassmann Al w sw ★★★ Revered DOM, esp Moenchreben v'yd. Off-dry, rich, sensuous GEWURZ CUVÉE Yves **08** 09 12 15. Now into bio, more finesse. Mineral zesty RIES 13. Fine PINOT N 15 intense, gentle tannins. Small but exceptional 17.

Romanée, La C d'O r ★★★★ 09′ 10′ 12′ 15′ 16′ 17 18 Tiniest GC in VOSNE-ROMANÉE, MONOPOLE of COMTE LIGER-BELAIR. Exceptionally fine, perfumed, intense: now on peak form and understandably expensive.

Romanée-Conti, La C d'O r ★★★★ 85′ 89′ 90′ 93′ **96**′ **99**′ 00 02′ **03** 05′ 09′ 10′ 12′ **14**′ 15′ 16′ 17 18′ GC in VOSNE-ROMANÉE, MONOPOLE of DRC. Most celebrated GC in Burg, gold dust. On fabulous form. But beware Geeks bringing fake gifts.

Romanée-St-Vivant C d'O r ★★★★ 90′ 90′ 02′ 05′ 09′ 10′ 12′ 15′ 16′ 17 18′ GC in VOSNE-ROMANÉE. Downslope from LA ROMANÉE-CONTI, haunting perfume, delicate but intense. Ready a little earlier than famous neighbours. Growers: if you can't afford DRC or LEROY, or CATHIARD now, try ARLOT, ARNOUX-LACHAUX, Follin-Arbelet, HUDELOT-NÖELLAT, JJ Confuron, LATOUR, Poisot.

Rosacker Al GC at Hunawihr. Limestone/clay makes some of longest-lived RIES in AL (CLOS STE-HUNE).

Rosé d'Anjou Lo p ★→★★ DYA. Rosé – off-dry to sweet (mainly Grolleau). Big rosé

AOP, 2084 ha, 28c producers. V. popular, increasingly well made. Try: Bougrier, Clau de Nell, DOMs Le la Bergerie, Grandes VIGNES, Mark Angeli (VIN DE FRANCE).

Rosé de Loire Lo p ★ ★★ DYA. Dry rosé: six grapes incl Grolleau, CAB FR, GAMAY; AC (1044 ha) Best Bablut, Bois Brinçon, Branchereau, Cady, CAVE de SAUMUR, CH PIERRE-BISE, Ogereau, Passavant, Richou, Soucherie. Zone covers ANJOU to TOURAINE incl essentially Anjou.

Rosette SW Fr w s/rw ★★ Tiny AOP DYA. Birthplace of BERGERAC, now home to delicious off-dry apéritif whites. Gd too with foie gras or mushrooms. Avoid oaked versions that deny the style. Try CLOS Romain, CHX Combrillac, de Peyrel, Monplaisir, Puypezat-Rosette, Spingulèbre; DOMs de Coutancie, de la Cardinolle, du Grand-Jaure.

Rossignol-Trapet C d'O r ★★★ Equally bio cousins of DOM TRAPET, with healthy holdings of GC v'nes, esp CHAMBERTIN. Gd value across range from GEVREY VIEILLES VIGNES up. Also some BEAUNE v'yds from Rossignol side.

Rostaing, Dom N Rh w ★★★ 99' 01' 05' 09' 10' 12' 13' 15' 16' 17' 18' High-quality CÔTE-RÔTIE DOM: the tightly bound wines all v. fine, pure, clear, discreet oak, wait 6 yrs, decant. Son Pierre took over 2015. Complex, enticing, top-class Côte Blonde (5% VIOGNIER), Côte Brune (iron), also La Landonne (dark fruits, 15–20 yrs). Tangy, firm *Condrieu*, also L'DOC Puech Noble (r w).

Rouget, Emmanuel C d'O r ★★★★ Next generation refreshing DOM famed for Henri Jayer connection and CROS PARANTOUX v'yd. Fine NUITS-ST-GEORGES, VOSNE-ROMANÉE, as well as GCs.

Rosé Champ must choose between consistency of colour or of flavour. Can't have both.

Roulot, Dom C d'O w ★★★ →★★★★ Jean-Marc R leads outstanding MEURSAULT DOM, now cult status so beware secondary market prices. Great PCs, esp CLOS des Bouchères, Perrières; value from top village sites Luchets, Meix Chavaux, esp Clos du Haut Tesson.

Roumier, Georges C d'O r ★★★★ Reference DOM for BONNES-MARES and other *brilliant Chambolle* wines from Christophe R. Long-lived wines but still attractive early. Cult status means hard to find now at sensible prices. Best value is MOREY CLOS de la Bussière.

Rousseau, Dom Armand C d'O r ★★★★ Unmatchable GEVREY-CHAMBERTIN DOM thrilling with balanced, fragrant, refined, age-worthy wines from village to GC, esp CLOS ST-JACQUES. No changes expected anytime soon.

Roussette de Savoie Sav w ★★ S of Lake Geneva. 100% ROUSSETTE. 150 ha, 10% of SAV wines. Can age. Try: Curtet, de la Mar, Grisard, Maillet, Mérande, Quénard.

Roussillon Rouss Often linked with L'DOC, and incl in AC L'doc. Strong Spanish influence. GRENACHE key variety. Original, traditional VDN (eg. BANYULS, MAURY, RIVESALTES). Younger vintage RIMAGE/Grenat now competing with aged RANCIO. Also serious age-worthy table wines (r w). See COLLIOURE, CÔTES DU ROUSS-VILLAGES, MAURY SEC and CAP CÔTES CATALANES.

Ruchottes-Chambertin C d'O r ★★★★ 99' 02' 05' 09' 10' 12' 15' 16 17' 18' Tiny GC neighbour of CHAMBERTIN. Less weighty but ethereal, intricate, lasting wine of great finesse. Top growers: MUGNERET-Gibourg, ROUMIER, ROUSSEAU. Try also CH de MARSANNAY, H Magnien.

Ruinart Champ Oldest house (1729). High standards going higher still. Rich, elegant wine: "R" de Ruinart BRUT NV; Ruinart Rosé NV; "R" de Ruinart Brut 08. Prestige CUVÉE *Dom Ruinart* is one of two best vintage BLANC DE BLANCS in CHAMP (viz 9 esp in magnum, 02 04 07 09). DR Rosé also v. special 98'. NV Blanc de Blancs much improved. High hopes for 13, classic cool lateish vintage. Dom R 06 great structure in delicate yr.

Rully Burg r w ★★ (r) 15' 16 17 18' (w) 14' 16' 17' 18 CÔTE CHALONNAISE village. *Light fresh, tasty, gd-value whites*. Reds all about the fruit, not structure. Try *C Jobard*, Devevey, DROUHIN, *Dureuil-Janthial*, FAIVELEY, Jacqueson, Jaeger-Defaix, Ninot, *Olivier Leflaive*, Rodet.

Sablet S Rh r (p) w ★★ 16' 17' CÔTES DU RH-VILLAGE on plain below GIGONDAS. Easy wines, some serious. Sandy soils, neat red-berry reds, esp CAVE CO-OP Gravillas, CH Cohola (organic), *du Trignon*; DOMS de Boissan (organic, full), Les Goubert (r w), Pasquiers (full), Piaugier (r w). *Gd full whites* for apéritifs, food, NB: Boissan, St Gayan.

St-Amour Beauj r ★★ 15' 17 18' Most n BEAUJ cru: mixed soils, so variable character. Try: DOM de Fa, Janin, *Patissier*, Pirolette, Revillon.

St-Aubin C d'O r w ★★★ (w) 10' 12 14' 15 17 18 Fine source for *lively, refreshing whites*, challenging PULIGNY and CHASSAGNE, esp on price. Also pretty reds mostly for early drinking. Best v'yds: Chatenière, *En Remilly*, Murgers Dents de Chien. Best growers: COLIN-MOREY, JC BACHELET, Joseph Colin, *Lamy*, Marc COLIN. Also Prudhon for value.

St-Bris Burg w ★ DYA. Unique AC for SAUV BL in n BURG. Fresh, lively, but also worth keeping from GOISOT or de Moor. Try also Bersan, Davenne, Simonnet-Febvre.

St-Chinian L'doc r p ★ →★★★ 11 12 13 14 15 16 17 Large hilly area nr Béziers. Sound reputation. Incl CRUS of *Berlou* (mostly CARIGNAN) Roquebrun (mostly SYRAH) on schist. Warm, spicy reds, based on Syrah, GRENACHE, Carignan, MOURVÈDRE. Whites from ROUSSANNE, MARSANNE, VERMENTINO, GRENACHE BL. Gd co-op Roquebrun; CH Viranella Madura, DOMS Borie la Vitarèle, des Jougla, la Dournie, *la Madura*, Navarre, Rimbert; CLOS Bagatelle, Mas Champart. Several new estates.

Ste-Croix-du-Mont B'x w sw ★★ 07 09' 10' 11' 15 16 AC making sweet, white *liquoreux*. Faces SAUTERNES across River Garonne. Best: rich, creamy, can age. Top CHX: Crabitan-Bellevue, du Mont, la Rame, *Loubens*, Pavillon.

St-Émilion B'x r ★★→★★★★ 98' 00 01' 05' 09' 10' 15' 16 Big MERLOT-led district on B'x's Right Bank, currently on a roll. CAB FR also strong. UNESCO World Heritage site. ACS St-Ém and (lots of) St-Ém GC. Top designation St-Ém PREMIER GRAND CRU CLASSÉ. Warm, full, rounded style but much variation due to terroir and winemaking. Best firm, v. long-lived. Top CHX: ANGÉLUS, AUSONE, CANON, CHEVAL BLANC, FIGEAC, PAVIE. Many attractive value wines.

St-Estèphe H-Méd r ★★ →★★★★ 95 00' 05' 09' 10' 15 16' Most n communal AC in the MÉD. Solid, structured wines for ageing; happy hunting ground for value. Five Classed Growths: CALON-SÉGUR, COS D'ESTOURNEL, COS-LABORY, LAFON-ROCHET, MONTROSE. Top unclassified estates: HAUT-MARBUZET, LE BOSCQ, LE CROCK, LILIAN LADOUYS, MEYNEY, ORMES-DE-PEZ, PHÉLAN-SÉGUR.

Ste-Victoire Prov r p ★★ Subzone of CÔTES DE PROV from s limestone slopes, v'yds rising to 400m (1312ft) on Montagne Ste-Victoire. Broad creamy acidity. DOMS de St Ser, Gassier both benefit from high altitude. *Dom Richeaume*, v.gd, is IGP.

St-Gall Champ Brand of Union-CHAMP, top growers' co-op at AVIZE. BRUT NV; Extra Brut NV; Brut BLANC DE BLANCS NV; Brut Rosé NV; Brut Blanc de Blancs 08; CUVÉE Orpale Blanc de Blancs 02' 08' 17'. Fine-value PINOT-led *Pierre Vaudon NV*. Makes top *vins clairs* for some great houses.

St-Georges d'Orques L'doc r p ★★→★★★ Most individual and historic part of sprawling Grès de Montpellier, aspiring to individual cru status. Try Belles Pierres, CH l'Engarran, DOMS Henry, La Marfée, La Prose.

St-Georges-St-Émilion B'x r ★★ 10' 14 15 16 (18) Tiny ST-ÉM satellite. Sturdy, structured. Best CHX: Calon, CLOS Albertus, Macquin-St-Georges, St-André Corbin, ST-GEORGES, TOUR DU PAS-ST-GEORGES.

St-Gervais S Rh r (p) (w) r →★★★ 16' 17' 18 W-bank Rh village; gd soils but v. limited range. Co-op low-key; best is long-lived (10 yrs+) DOM Ste-Anne red (fresh, firm, MOURVÈDRE liquorice flavours); gd VIOGNIER. Also Dom Clavel (Regulus r).

St-Jacques d'Albas, Ch L'doc r p w ★★ Dynamic MINERVOIS estate since 2001. English-owner Graham Nutter and son Andrew, Oz winemaker, fruit-forward wines: Le Petit St-Jacques, Le DOM, Le CH and SYRAH-dominant La Chapelle (all r). Coteaux de Peyriac from VIOGNIER/VERMENTINO/ROUSSANNE.

St-Joseph N Rh r w ★★ →★★★ 99' 05' 09' 10' 12' 15' 16' **17**' 18' 64 km (40 miles) of mainly granite v'yds, some high, along w bank of N Rh. SYRAH reds. Best, oldest v'yds nr Tournon: rounded, stylish, red-fruited wines; further n darker, live, peppery, more oak. More complete, detailed than CROZES-HERMITAGE, esp CHAPOUTIER (Les Granits), DOM GONON (top class), *Gripa*, GUIGAL (VIGNES de l'Hospice), *J-L Chave* (gd style); also Alexandrins, Amphores (bio), A PERRET (Grisières), Chèze, Courbis (modern), Coursodon (racy, modern), Cuilleron, *Delas*, E Darnaud, Faury, Ferraton, F Villard, Gaillard, J&E Durand (fruit), Marsanne (traditional), Monier-Perréol (organic), P-J Villa, P Marthouret (traditional), Vallet, Vins de Vienne. Gd food-friendly white *(mainly Marsanne)*, esp A Perret, Barge, *Chapoutier* (Les Granits), Cuilleron, Dom Gonon (fab), Faury, Gouye (traditional), Gripa, J Pilon.

St-Julien H-Méd r ★★★ →★★★★ 90' 96' 05' 09' 10' 15 16' Super-stylish mid-MÉD communal AC. 11 classified (1855) estates own 95% v'yds so hardly any CRUS BOURGEOIS. Incl three LÉOVILLES, BEYCHEVELLE, DUCRU-BEAUCAILLOU, GRUAUD-LAROSE, LAGRANGE. Epitome of harmonious, fragrant, savoury red.

Saint Mont SW Fr r p w ★★ (r) 15' **15** 16 17 18 (p w) DYA AOP from Gascon heartlands. Huge PRODUCTEURS PLAIMONT would like to take over appellation as a brand, but Saxophonist J-L Garoussia (★DOM de Turet), CH de Bergalasse and ★★Dom des Maouries are the resistance.

St-Nicolas-de-Bourgueil Lo r p ★ →★★★ 15' 16 **17**' 18' Similar to BOURGUEIL: CAB FR but more popular. Largely sand/gravel, light wines; more structured from limestone slopes. Wind machines against frost. Try: DOM Amirault, David, Delanoue, Frédéric Mabileau, Laurent Mabileau, Lorieux, Mabileau-Rezé, Mortier, Taluau-Foltzenlogel, Vallée, *Yannick Amirault*. V.gd 18.

St-Péray N Rh w sp ★★ 16' **17**' 18' On-the-up white (MARSANNE/ROUSSANNE) from hilly granite, some lime v'yds opposite Valence, lots of new planting. Once *famous for fizz*; classic-method bubbles well worth trying (A Voge, TAIN co-op, J-L Thiers, R Nodin). Still white should have grip, be smoky, flinty. Best: A Voge (oak), CHAPOUTIER, *Clape* (pure), *Colombo* (stylish), Cuilleron, Durand, *du Tunnel* (v. elegant), Gripa (v.gd), J-L Thiers, R Nodin, Vins de Vienne; Tain co-op.

St-Pourçain Mass C r p w ★★ AC (557 ha upper Loire [Allier].) Mainly light red, rosé (GAMAY, PINOT N; AOP stupidly bans pure PINOT N), white from local Tressalier and/or CHARD, SAUV BL. Growers: Bérioles (rising star), DOM de Bellevue, Grosbot-Barbara, Laurent, Nebout, Pétillat, Ray; gd co-op (VIGNERONS de St-Pourçain).

St-Romain C d'O r w ★★ (w) 14' 15 **17** 18' *Crisp whites* from side valley of CÔTE DE BEAUNE. Excellent value by Burg standards. Best v'yds Sous le CH, Sous la Roche,

---

Sancerre: taste the chalk

Sancerre is proud of its three types of soil: caillottes (pure limestone), terres blanches (clay-limestone) and silex (flint). Caillottes and terres blanches each make up 40% of the appellation and silex 20%. The flavours? Caillottes: aromatic, early-drinking. Terres blanches: need time, gd potential to age. Some of appellation's most famous sites – Les Monts Damnés, Le Cul de Beaujeu (both Chavignol) and CLOS de la Poussie (Bué) are terres blanches. Silex: mineral, sometimes with a smoky character. Also age-worthy. Try: **Caillottes** Claude Riffault (Les Chasseignes) François Crochet (Le Chêne Marchand). **Silex** Pascal Jolivet (Le Roc), Dom Vacheron (Les Romains). **Terres blanches** Gérard Boulay (Clos de Beujeu); HENRI BOURGEOIS (La Côte des Monts Damnés).

Combe Bazin. Specialists Alain Gras, de Chassorney, H & G Buisson, but most NÉGOCIANTS have a gd one. Some fresh reds too.

St-Véran Burg w ★★ **14' 15** 17 18' S Burg AC either side of POUILLY-FUISSÉ. Try Chagnoleau, Corsin, Deux Roches, Litaud, Merlin for single-v'yd CUVÉES. Gd-value DUBOEUF, Poncetys, TERRES SECRETES CO-OP.

Salon Champ ★★★★ Original BLANC DE BLANCS, from LE MESNIL in Côte des Blancs. Tiny quantities. Awesome reputation for long-lived luxury-priced wines: in truth, inconsistent. On song recently, viz 83' **90** 97', but 99 disappoints, where is 02 going? Opinions differ. But 06 looks v.gd. *See also* DELAMOTTE.

Sancerre Lo r (p) w ★ ★★★★★ 14' 15' 16' **17'** 18' Touchstone SAUV BL (2987 ha), many fine light reds (PINOT N 600 ha). Exciting new generation in charge. Series of gd/v.gd vintages since 14. 62% exported. Best: ALPHONSE MELLOT, Boulay, *Bourgeois*, Claude Riffault, Cotat (variable), Dezat, Fouassier, François Crochet, Jean-Max Roger, *Joseph Mellot*, Lucien Crochet, Mollet, Natter, Neveu, Paul Prieur, Pierre Martin, Pinard, *P & N Reverdy*, Raimbault, Roblin, Thomas, Thomas Laballe, *Vacheron*, Vatan, Vattan, Vincent Delaporte.

Santenay C d'O r (w) ★★ ★★★★ 05' 09' 12 14 15' 16 17 18' S end of CÔTE DE BEAUNE, potential for fine reds; don't overlook. Best v'yds: CLOS de Tavannes, Clos Rousseau, Gravières (r *w*). Producers: Belland, Camille Giroud, Chevrot, LAMY, MOREAU, Muzard, Vincent. Some gd whites too, eg. CHARMES.

Saumur Lo r p w sp ★ ★★★★ 15' 16 17 **18'** Large AC. Whites: light to v. serious age-worthy; mainly easy reds except SAUMUR-CHAMPIGNY; Saumur Rosé – formerly Cabernet de Saumur. Centre of Lo fizz production: CRÉMANT most important, Saumur Mousseux. Saumur-Le-Puy-Notre-Dame AOP for CAB FR. Best: Antoine Foucault, BOUVET-LADUBAY, CHAMPS FLEURIS, CH de Brézé, CLOS Mélaric, CLOS ROUGEARD, Ditterie, Guiberteau, Nerleux, Paleine, Parnay, René-Hugues Gay, ROBERT ET MARCEL, Rocheville, St-Just, Targé, VILLENEUVE, Yvonne.

Saumur-Champigny Lo r ★★ ★★★★ 14' 15' 16' 17 **18'** V.gd CAB FR from nine-commune AC, gd vintages age 15–20 yrs+. Best: Bonnelière (value), Bruno Dubois, CH de VILLENEUVE, Ch Yvonne, CLOS Cristal, CLOS ROUGEARD (cult), de la Cune, Ditterie, DOM Antoine Sanzay, Dom des Champs Fleuris, *Filliatreau*, Hureau, Nerleux, Petit St-Vincent, P Vadé, Robert et Marcel (co-op), Roches Neuves, Rocheville, St Just, St-Vincent, Seigneurie, *Targé*, Val Brun. Biodiversity project.

Saussignac SW Fr w sw ★★ **15** 16' 17 18' BERGERAC sub-AOP, dessert wines with a shade more acidity than adjoining MONBAZILLAC. Best: ★★★DOMS de Richard, La Maurigne, Les Miaudoux, Lestevénie; ★★CHX Le Chabrier, Le Payral, Le Tap.

Sauternes B'x w sw ★★ ★★★★ **90'** 01' 05' 07' **09'** 11' 15' 16 AC making France's best *liquoreux* from "noble rotted" grapes. Luscious, golden and age-worthy. Hail in parts in 2018. Classified (1855) CHX: CLOS HAUT-PEYRAGUEY, GUIRAUD, *Lafaurie-Peyraguey*, LA TOUR BLANCHE, RIEUSSEC, SIGALAS-RABAUD, SUDUIRAUT, D'YQUEM. Gd-value from DOM de l'Alliance, *Fargues*, HAUT-BERGERON, Les Justices, *Raymond-Lafon*.

Sauzet, Etienne C d'O w ★★★★ Leading bio DOM in PULIGNY with superb range of PCS (Combettes, Champ Canet best), MONTRACHET and BÂTARD-M. Concentrated, lively wines, once again capable of ageing.

Savennières Lo w dr (sw) ★★ ★★★★★ 12 14' **15' 16** 18' Small ANJOU AC, high reputation, variable style and quality; v. long-lived whites (CHENIN BL) with marked acidity – a few DEMI-SEC. Baudouin, *Baumard*, Bergerie, Boudignon, *Ch d'Epiré*, *Ch Pierre-Bise*, CH Soucherie, Closel, DOM FL, Laureau, Mahé, Mathieu-Tijou, Morgat, Ogereau, Pithon-Paillé (Massonnat). Top sites: CLOS du Papillon, COULÉE DE SERRANT, ROCHE-AUX-MOINES. Almost no 17; fine 18.

Savigny-lès-Beaune C d'O r (w) ★★★ 05' 09' 10' 12 **14** 15' 18' Important village next to BEAUNE; similar mid-weight wines, savoury touch (but can be rustic). Top v'yds: Dominode, Guettes, Lavières, Marconnets, Vergelesses. Growers: *Bize*,

Camus, *Chandon de Briailles*, Chenu, CLAIR, DROUHIN, Girard, Guillemot (w), Guyon, LEROY, Pavelot, *Tollot-Beaut*.

Savoie r w sp ★★→★→★ Alps. Vin de Sav AC (2100 ha) three ACs – 20 "crus", incl AFRÉMONT, CHIGNIN, CRÉPY, Jongieux, Ripaille. Separate ACs: ROUSSETTE DE SAV (Altesse), SEYSSEL. Reds mainly GAMAY, MONDEUSE; w: Altesse, CHASSELAS, Jacquère, Mondeuse Bl, ROUSSANNE.

Schlossberg Al GC at Kientzheim famed since C15. Glorious compelling RIES from FALLER 10 and new TRIMBACH; 15 should be great Ries yr here.

Schlumberger, Doms Al w sw ★→★★★ Vast, top-quality AL DOM at Guebwiller owning approx 1% of all Al v'yds. Holdings in GCS Kitterlé and racy Saering 13 15 16 exceptional 17, Spiegel. Rich wines. Rare RIES, signature CUVÉE Ernest and now GC Kessler GEWURZ lovely in 14; great PINOT GR.

Schoenenberg Al V. rich, successful Riquewihr GC: PINOT GR, RIES, v. fine VENDANGE TARDIVE, SÉLECTION DES GRAINS NOBLES, esp DOPFF AU MOULIN. Also v.gd MUSCAT. HUGEL Schoelhammer from here. 17 small crop, but could be exquisite quality.

Schoffit, Dom Al w ★★★★ Exceptional Colmar grower, superb late-harvest GEWURZ, PINOT GR VENDANGE TARDIVE GC RANGEN CLOS St-Théobald 10' 15 on volcanic soil. Contrast with RIES GC Sonnenberg 13 15 16 17' on limestone. Delicious Harth C-HASSELAS. No oak= super elegant wines, esp drier styles.

Sec Literally means dry, though CHAMP so called is medium-sweet (and welcome at breakfast, teatime, weddings).

Séguret S Rh r p w ★★ 15' 16' 17' 18 Hillside village nr GIGONDAS in Rh-Villages top three. V'yds on both plain and heights. Mainly GRENACHE, peppery, quite deep reds, some full-on; crisp-fruited whites. Esp CH la Courançonne (gd w), DOMS Amandine de Cabasse (elegant), *de l'Amauve* (fine), Fontaine des Fées, Garancière, J David (organic), Maison Plantevin, Malmont (stylish), *Mourchon* (robust), Pourra (intense, time), Soleil Romain.

La Clape is Occitan for "The Heap of Stones". Not what you think.

Sélection des Grains Nobles Al Term coined by HUGEL for AL equivalent to German Beerenauslese, subject to ever-stricter rules. *Grains nobles* are grapes with "noble rot" for v. sweet wines.

Selosse, Anselme Champ ★★★★ Leading grower, an icon for many. "Winey", oxidative style, oak-fermented; Version Originale still vibrant after 7 yrs on lees. From named sites, top wine probably Mesnil Les Carelles, saline, complex, akin to MEURSAULT Perrières with bubbles. 99 v. stylish; 02 still a baby.

Sérafin, Dom C d'Or ★★★ Deep colour, intense flavours, new wood: Serafin wines need to age. Try GEVREY-CHAMBERTIN VIEILLES VIGNES, Cazetiers, CHARMES-CHAMBERTIN.

Serres Mazard L'do r p w Family estate in CORBIÈRES. Wide range of local varieties incl MACABEU, Terret and old CARIGNAN. Oak for long-ageing red (Joseph Mazard, Annie), also acacia (Jules w).

Seyssel Sav w sp ★★ AC 72 ha (55 ha w, 17 ha sp). Grapes: Altesse, CHASSELAS (sp only), Molette. Try: Lambert de Seyssel (organic), Mollex, Vens-le-Haut.

Sichel & Co B'x r w Respected B'x merchant est in 1883 (Sirius a top brand). Family-run: 6th generation at helm. Interests in CHX ANGLUDET, Argadens, PALMER and in CORBIÈRES (Ch Trillol).

Signargues S Rh ★→★★ 16' 17' 18 Modest CÔTES DU RH village, dry soils between Avignon and Nîmes (w bank). Spiced, robust reds to drink inside 4–5 yrs. NB: CAVE Estézargues (punchy), CH Terre Forte (bio), CLOS d'Alzan, Haut-Musiel, La Font du Vent (fruit); DOMS des Romarins (deep), Valériane.

Simone, Ch Prov r p w ★★★ Historic estate outside Aix-en-Prov, where Churchill painted Mont STE-VICTOIRE. Rougier family for nearly two centuries. Virtually synonymous with AC PALETTE. Age-worthy whites well worth seeking out;

characterful white and rosé, elegant reds from GRENACHE and MOURVÈDRE, with rare grape varieties Castet, Manosquin (r).

Sipp, Louis Al w sw ★★→★★★ Trades in big volumes of young wines, but also two GCS: fine RIES GC Kirchberg 13, luscious GEWURZ GC Osterberg VT 09. Gd classic dry wines too.

Sipp-Mack Al w sw ★★→★★★ Fine trad DOM in Hunawihr, great ALS village for peerless dry mineral wines (CLOS STE HUNE). Similar quality here but cheaper. Also RIES GC ROSACKER 13 and expansive PINOT GR. Magical holiday lets.

Sorg, Bruno Al w ★★★ 1st-class small grower at Eguisheim for GCS Florimont (RIES 13 14 16' great 17) and PFERSIGBERG (MUSCAT). Immaculate eco-friendly v'yds.

Sur lie "On the lees". Most MUSCADET is bottled straight from the vat, for max zest, body, character.

Tâche, La C d'O r ★★★★ 90' 93' 96' 99' 02' 03 05' 09' 10' 12' 14 15' 16' 17 18 GC of VOSNE-ROMANÉE, MONOPOLE of DRC. Firm in its youth, but how glorious with age. Headily perfumed, luxurious.

Taille-aux-Loups, Dom de la Lo w sw sp ★★★ 14' 15' 16r 17 18' Jacky Blot, top producer, with son Jean-Philippe. Barrel-fermented MONTLOUIS, VIN DE FRANCE (aka VOUVRAY) majority dry (**Remus**), esp single v'yds: CLOS Mosny, Michet (Montlouis), Venise (Vouvray); **Triple Zéro** Montlouis *pétillant* (p w); v.gd BOURGUEIL, DOM de la Butte. V. promising 18. V. age-worthy.

Tain, Cave de N Rh ★★→★★★ Top N Rh co-op, many mature v'yds, incl 25% HERMITAGE. Sound to v.gd red Hermitage, esp Epsilon (oak), Gambert de Loche, bountiful white Hermitage Au Coeur des Siècles, offer value. Gd ST-JOSEPH (r w), interesting Bio (organic) range (CROZES, St-Joseph), other wines modern, mainstream. Gd recent CROZES reds, eg. Saviaux. Distinguished VIN DE PAILLE.

Taittinger Champ BRUT NV, Rosé NV, Brut 06 08 09, Collection Brut 89 90 95' jewels of this again-family-run Reims house. Epitome of apéritif style, exquisite weightlessness. Ace luxury **Comtes de Champagne** 95' 99 02' 06 08'; Comtes Rosé also shines in 06 12. Excellent single-v'yd La Marquetterie. New English bubbly project in Kent, DOM Evremond. (*See also* Dom Carneros, California.) New cellarmaster fills Loec Dupont's big shoes.

Tavel S Rh p ★★ DYA. Celebrated GRENACHE rosé, aided by white grapes, should be bright red, robust, for vivid Med dishes. Now many lighter Prov-styles, often for apéritif; a pity. Top: DOM de l'Anglore (no sulphur), **Dom de la Mordorée** (full), Corne-Loup, GUIGAL (gd), Lafond Roc-Epine, Maby, Moulin-la-Viguerie (organic, traditional), Prieuré de Montézargues (fine), Rocalière (v. fine), Tardieu-Laurent, VIDAL-FLEURY, CHX Aquéria, de Manissy, Ségriès, **Trinquevedel** (fine).

Tempier, Dom Prov r p w ★★★★ Estate where in 30s Lucien Peyraud revived AC BANDOL with traditional MOURVÈDRE. Wines combine elegance, concentration, longevity. Maintains excellent quality; now rivalled by several others.

Terrasses du Larzac L'doc r ★★→★★★ Most n part of AC L'DOC. Wild and hilly region from Lac du Salagou to Aniane, incl MONTPEYROUX, St-Saturnin; wide day/night temperature variation, coolth makes fresher wines. AC since 2014; 25 new growers in recent yrs, plus est names: CAL DEMOURA, CLOS des Serres, Jonquières, Mas Conscience, Mas de l'Ecriture, **Mas Jullien**, MONTCALMÈS, Pas de l'Escalette. LA PEIRA. Over half organic/bio. **Definitely to watch**. White, rosé AC L'doc or IGP.

Thénard, Dom Burg r w ★★→★★★★ Historic producer with large holding of MONTRACHET, mostly sold on to NÉGOCIANTS. Should be better known for v.gd reds from home base in GIVRY.

Thévenet, Jean Burg r w sw ★★★ Top MÂCONNAIS purveyor of rich, some semi-botrytized CHARD, eg. CUVÉE Levroutée at **Dom de la Bongran**. Also DOMS de Roally and Emilian Gillet.

Thézac-Perricard SW Fr r p w ★★ 16 18 IGP adjoining CAHORS (reds from MALBEC MERLOT). Sandrine Annibal's ★★DOM de Lancement, esp exciting off-dry white from both MANSENC grapes. Reds lighter but otherwise an extension of Cahors. Lively co-op nearly as gd.

Thiénot, Alain Champ New generation now at helm. Ever-improving quality fairly priced ★★★BRUT NV; Rosé NV Brut; vintage Stanislas 02 04 06 08' 09 12 13 15. Voluminous VIGNE aux Gamins (single-v'yd AVIZE 02 04 08). CUVÉE Garance CHARD 07 sings, classic 08 for long haul. Also owns CHAMP CANARD-DUCHÊNE, CH Ricaud in LOUPIAC.

Thomas, André & fils Al w ★★★ Bijou DOM, 6 ha in Ammerschwihr. PINOT BL from 50-yr-old vines. Excellent RIES Kaefferkopf 10 13 16 17. Superb GEWURZ VIEILLES VIGNES 05 09 15 17. Organic precepts.

Tissot Jura Dominant family around ARBOIS. ★★Jacques T offers volume, value. ★★★Stephane T (also as André & Mireille Tissot), cult pioneer of single-v'yd CHARD, VIN JAUNE using bio/natural methods; top CRÉMANT du Jura, Indigène.

Tollot-Beaut C d'O r w ★★★ Consistent CÔTE DE BEAUNE grower with 20 ha in BEAUNE (Grèves, CLOS du Roi), CORTON (Bressandes), SAVIGNY and at CHOREY-LÈS-BEAUNE base (NB: Pièce du Chapitre). Easy to love the fruit-and-oak combo.

Cd'O's sweet spot for ripeness is now 50m higher up slope: warmer summers.

Touraine Lo r p w sw sp ★→★★★ 16 17 18' Big region, many ACS (eg. VOUVRAY, CHINON, BOURGUEIL plus umbrella AC of variable quality: fruity reds (CAB FR, CÔT, GAMAY, PINOT N), whites (SAUV BL), rosés, sparkling. Touraine Village ACs, see below: Azay-le-Rideau, Chenonceaux, Mesland, Noble-Joué, Oisly. Stocks down frost 16/17 but 18 generous, excellent. Producers: Biet, Bois-Vaudons, Corbillières, Joël Delaunay, Echardières, Garrelière, Gosseaume, Jacky Marteau, La Chapinière, Lacour, Mandard, *Marionnet*, Morantin, *Presle*, Prieuré, Puzelat, Ricard, Rousseby, Tue-Boeuf, Villebois.

Touraine-Amboise Lo r p (w) ★→★★★ TOURAINE Village-AC 60/30/10% r/p/w. François 1er post blend (GAMAY/CÔT/CAB FR); Côt/Cab Fr top reds; CHENIN BL top white. Best: Bessons, Closerie de Chanteloup, Dutertre, Frissant, Gabillière, Grange Tiphaine Mesliard, Truet. Working towards cru for Chenin, Côt.

Touraine-Azay-le-Rideau Lo p w (sw) ★→★★ TOURAINE sub-AC (60 ha). Rosé (60% of AC; Grolleau 60% min); white, dry and off-dry from CHENIN BL. Best: Aulée, Bourse, de la Roche, Grosbois, Nicolas Paget. Frost-prone, but fine 18.

Touraine-Mesland Lo r p w ★→★★ 15 16 17 18' Small TOURAINE villages AC (110 ha) w of Blois (mainly r p). Best: Grandes Espérances, Girault (bio) sold to DOM Cocteaux.

Touraine-Noble Joué Lo p ★→★★ DYA. V.gd rosé from three PINOTS (N, M, GR). AOP mainly Indre Valley s of Tours. Best: Astraly, Cosson, Rousseau, Sard-Pierru. Fine 18. Also Malvoisie (Pinot Gr) VIN DE FRANCE.

Trapet C d'O r ★★★ Long-est GEVREY-CHAMBERTIN DOM making sensual bio wines from village up to GC CHAMBERTIN plus AL whites by marriage. See also cousins ROSSIGNOL-TRAPET.

Treloar, Dom Rouss r p w Anglo-NZ ownership. Emphasis on old vines, traditional varieties and organic. Terre Promise IGP COTES CATALANES wild ferment in barrel MACABEU/GRENACHE Gris/CARIGNAN Blanc (w) and One Block Grenache (old-vine Grenache/Lledoner Pelut r) of special interest.

Trévallon, Dom de Prov r w ★★★ Top Prov dom at LES BAUX, created by Eloi Dürrbach; joined by daughter Ostiane. No GRENACHE, so must be IGP Alpilles. Huge reputation fully justified. Intense, age-worthy CAB SAUV/SYRAH. *Barrique-aged white* from MARSANNE/ROUSSANNE, drop of CHARD and now GRENACHE BL.

Trimbach, FE Al w ★★★★ Matchless grower of AL RIES on limestone soils at Ribeauvillé, esp austere CLOS STE-HUNE 71 89 still great. 10' 13 16 17 classically cool; almost-as-gd (and much cheaper) *Frédéric Emile 10* 12 13 14 16 17. Dry, elegant wines for great cuisine. Look out for 1st GC label: from v'yds of Couvent de Ribeauville, cultivated by Trimbach.

Tursan SW Fr r p w ★★ Mostly DYA. AOP in Landes. Super-chef Michel Guérard makes lovely wines in his chapel-like cellar at CH de Bachen. Less authentic than ★★DOM de Perchade. Lovely dry white from ★★DOM de Cazalet (two MANSENGS plus rare Baroque). Worthy co-op rather outclassed.

Vacqueyras S Rh r (p) w ★★ 07' 09' 10' 15' **16' 17'** 18 Hearty, peppery, GRENACHE-centred neighbour of GIGONDAS, hot v'yds; for game, big flavours. Lives 10 yrs+. NB: JABOULET; CHX de Montmirail, *des Tours* (v. fine); *Clos des Cazaux* (gd value); DOMS Amouriers, Archimbaud-Vache, Charbonnière, Couroulu (v.gd, traditional), Famille Perrin, Font de Papier (organic), Fourmone (gd form), Garrigue (traditional), Grapillon d'Or, Monardière (v.gd), Montirius (bio), Montvac (elegant), Roucas Toumba (organic), Sang des Cailloux (v.gd, esp Lopy), Semelles de Vent, Verde. *Full whites* (CH des Roques, CLOS des Cazaux, Sang des Cailloux).

Val de Loire Lo r p w mainly DYA. One of France's four regional IGPS, formerly Jardin de la France.

Valençay N Lo r (p) w ★→★★ AOP (170 ha), TOURAINE; SAUV BL, (CHARD); reds CÔT, GAMAY, PINOT N. BEST: Delorme, Lafond, Preys, Sébastien Vaillant, Sinson, VIGNERONS de Valençay. Fine 18.

Valréas S Rh r (p) (w) ★★ 15' 16' 17' 18' CÔTES DU RH-VILLAGE in n Vaucluse truffle area, quality on up; large co-op. Grainy, peppery, breezy, sometimes heady, red-fruited mostly GRENACHE red, improving white. Esp CH la Décelle, CLOS Bellane (gd white), Mas de Ste-Croix, DOMS Gramenon (bio, stylish), des Grands Devers, du Séminaire (organic), Prévôse (organic), du Val des Rois (best, organic).

VDN (Vin Doux Naturel) Rouss Sweet wine fortified with wine alc, so sweetness natural, not strength. Speciality of ROUSS based on GRENACHE, Noir, Blanc or Gris, or MUSCAT. Top wines esp aged RANCIOS can finish a meal on a sublime note.

VDP (Vin de Pays) *See* IGP.

VDQS (Vins Délimite de Qualité Supérieure) Now phased out.

VDT (Vin de Table) Category of standard everyday table wine now VIN DE FRANCE.

Vendange Harvest. **Vendange Tardive:** late-harvest; AL equivalent to German Auslese but usually higher alc.

Venoge, de Champ Venerable house, precise and more elegant under LANSON-BCC ownership. Gd niche blends: Cordon Bleu Extra-BRUT, Vintage BLANC DE BLANCS 00 04 06 08 12 13 14 16 17. Excellent Vintage Rosé 09 CUVÉE 20 Ans, Prestige Cuvée Louis XV 10-yr-old BLANC DE NOIRS.

Ventoux S Rh r p w ★★ 16' 17' **18** Straggling AC loops around Mont Ventoux between Rh, Prov. A few front-running DOMS v.gd value. Juicy, tangy red (GRENACHE SYRAH, café-style to deeper, peppery, rising quality), rosé, gd white (more oak). Best: CH Unang (gd w), Ch Valcombe, CLOS des Patris, Gonnet, La Ferme St Pierre (p w), *La Vieille Ferme* (r, can be VIN DE FRANCE), St-Marc, Terra Ventoux, VIGNERONS Mont Ventoux; DOMS Allois (organic), Anges, Berane, Brusset, Cascavel, Champ-Long, Croix de Pins (gd w), *Fondrèche*, Grand Jacquet, Martinelle, Murmurium, Olivier B, PAUL JABOULET, *Pesquié*, Pigeade, St-Jean du Barroux (organic), Terres de Solence, du Tix, Verrière, VIDAL-FLEURY, Vieux Lazaret; co-op Bédoin.

Vernay, Dom Georges N Rh r w ★★★★ 14' 15' 16' 17' 18' Top CONDRIEU name; three wines, cool, elegant; Terrasses de l'Empire *apéritif de luxe*; Chaillées d'Enfer, richness; Coteau de Vernon, mysterious, intricate, supreme style, lives 20 yrs+. CÔTE-RÔTIE, ST-JOSEPH (r) pure fruit, restrained. V.gd VIN DE PAYS (r w).

Véronique & Thomas Muré, Clos St-Landelin Al r w ★★→★★★ One of AL's great names; esp fine, full-bodied GC *Vorbourg Ries* and PINOT GR 13 14. *Pinot N Cuvée "V"* ripe, vinous, is region's best, exceptional in 15'.

Veuve Clicquot Champ Historic house of highest standing. Improved Yellow Label NV. a soupçon of oak. Best DEMI-SEC NV, new CUVÉE Extra BRUT Extra Age based on res wines only. 2010–1990. Vintage Rés 04 06 08 12', Rosé Rés 08 12'. Luxury La Grande Dame 06 12 almost BLANC DE NOIRS; La Grande Dame Rosé 06. CAVE Privée re-release of older vintages, esp **89 95** (magnums).

Veuve Devaux Champ Premium brand of powerful Union Auboise co-op. Excellent aged Grande Rés NV, and Œil de Perdrix Rosé, Prestige CUVÉE D 09 12, BRUT Vintage 09 11 12 15 17.

Vézelay Burg r w ★→★★ Age 1–2 yrs. Lovely location (with abbey) in nw Burg. Promoted to full AC for tasty whites from CHARD. Also try revived MELON (COTEAUX BOURGUIGNON) and light PINOT (generic BOURGOGNE). Best: DOM de la Cadette, des Faverelles, Elise Villiers, La Croix Montjoie.

Vidal-Fleury, J N Rh r w sw ★★→★★★ GUIGAL-owned Rh merchant/grower of CÔTE-RÔTIE. Top grade, tight, v. stylish *La Chatillonne* (12% VIOGNIER; much oak, wait min 7 yrs). Range wide, on the up. Gd CAIRANNE, CHÂTEAUNEUF (r), CÔTES DU RH (r p), MUSCAT DE BEAUMES-DE-VENISE, ST-JOSEPH (r w), TAVEL, VENTOUX.

Vieille Ferme, La S Rh r w ★→★★ Reliable gd-value brand from Famille Perrin of CH DE BEAUCASTEL; much has become VIN DE FRANCE, with VENTOUX (r), LUBÉRON (w) in some countries (France, Japan). Back on form from 2015, incl rosé.

Vieilles Vignes Old vines, which should make the best wine. Eg. DE VOGÜÉ, MUSIGNY, Vieilles Vignes. But no rules about age and can be a tourist trap.

Vieux Télégraphe, Dom du S Rh r w ★★★ 01' 05' 07' 09' 10' 12' 15' 16' 17' 18 Big, high-quality estate; classic stony soils, intricate, slow burn robust red CHÂTEAUNEUF; top two wines La Crau (crunchy, packed), since 2011 Pied Long et Pignan (v. pure, elegant). Also rich whites *La Crau* (v.gd 15 16), CLOS La Roquète (great with food, note 15 16). Owns fine, slow-to-evolve, complex *Gigondas Dom Les Pallières* with US importer Kermit Lynch.

Vigne or vignoble Vineyard (v'yd), vineyards (v'yds).

Vigneron Vine-grower.

Villeneuve, Ch de Lo r w ★★★ 10' 11 12 14' 15' 16' 17' 18' Model estate with impressive winery in old caves. Great SAUMUR Blanc (age-worthy Les Cormiers), SAUMUR-CHAMPIGNY (esp VIEILLES VIGNES, Grand CLOS). Organic. 18 promising, some mildew.

Vin de France Replaces VDT. At last rules allow mention of grape variety and vintage. Often blends of regions with brand name. Can be source of unexpected delights if talented winemaker uses this category to avoid bureaucractic hassle. Eg. Yves Cuilleron VIOGNIER (N Rh). ANJOU a hotbed of Vin de France.

Vin de paille Wine from grapes dried on straw mats, so v. sweet, like Italian passito. Esp in Jura. *See also* CHAVE, VIN PAILLÉ DE CORRÈZE.

Vin gris "Grey" wine is v. pale pink, made of red grapes pressed before fermentation begins; unlike rosé that ferments briefly before pressing. Or from eg. PINOT GR, not-quite-white grapes. "Œil de Perdrix" means much the same; so does "blush".

Vin jaune Jura w ★★★ Speciality of Jura; inimitable yellow wine. SAVAGNIN, 6 yrs+ in barrel without topping up, develops flor, like Sherry but no added alc. Expensive to make. Separate AC for top spot, CH-CHALON. Sold in unique 62cl Clavelin bottles.

Vin paillé de Corrèze SW Fr r w 25 small growers and a tiny co-op once more laying out grapes on straw in old way to make pungent wine once recommended to breast-feeding mothers. Wines will keep as long as you. If you're brave try ★Christian Tronche.

Vinsobres S Rh r (p) (w) ★★ 15' 16' 17' 18' Low-profile AC notable for SYRAH. Best reds can be heady, show decisive red fruit, punch, to drink with red meats. Leaders: CAVE la Vinsobraise; CH Rouanne; DOMS Chaume-Arnaud (organic), Constant-Duquesnoy, Coriançon, Famille Perrin (Hauts de Julien top, Cornuds value), Jaume (modern), Moulin (traditional, gd r w), Péquélette (bio), Peysson (organic).

Viré-Clessé Burg w ★★ 14' 15 16 17 18 AC based around two of best white villages of MÂCON. Known for exuberant rich style, sometimes late-harvest. Try Bonhomme, Bret Bros, Chaland, DOM de la Verpaille, Gandines, Gondard-Perrin, Guillemot, J-P Michel, LAFON, **Thévenet**.

Visan S Rh r (p) (w) ★★ 16' 17' 18' Progressive RH VILLAGE: peppery reds have sound filling, clear fruit; some more soft, plenty organic. Whites okay. Best: DOMS Art Mas (organic), Coste Chaude (organic, gd fruit), Dieulefit (bio, low sulphur), Florana, Fourmente (bio esp Nature), Guintrandy (organic), Montmartel (organic), Philippe Plantevin, Roche-Audran (organic), VIGNOBLE Art Mas.

Vogüé, Comte Georges de C d'O r w ★★★★ Aristo CHAMBOLLE estate with lion's share of LE MUSIGNY. Great from barrel, but takes many yrs in bottle to reveal glories. Unique white Musigny.

Volnay C d'O r ★★★→★★★★ 90' 99' 02' 05' 09' 10' 15' 16 17 18 Top CÔTE DE BEAUNE reds, except when it hails. Can be structured, should be silky, astonishing with age. Best v'yds: Caillerets, Champans, CLOS des Chênes, Clos des Ducs, Santenots, Taillepieds. Best growers: Bitouzet-Prieur, Bouley, Buffet, Clerget, D'ANGERVILLE, de MONTILLE, H BOILLOT, HOSPICES DE BEAUNE, LAFARGE, LAFON, N Rossignol, Pousse d'Or.

Vosne-Romanée C d'O r ★★★→★★★★ 90' 93' 96' 99' 02' 05' 09' 10' 12 15' 16' 17 18' Village with Burg's grandest crus (eg. ROMANÉE-CONTI, LA TÂCHE) and outstanding PCS Malconsorts, Beaumonts, Brûlées, etc. There are (or should be) no common wines in Vosne. There's just the question of price... Top names: ARNOUX-LACHAUX, CATHIARD, Clavelier, DRC, EUGÉNIE, Forey, GRIVOT, GROS, Guyon, Lamarche, LEROY, LIGER-BELAIR, MÉO-CAMUZET, MUGNERET, NOËLLAT, ROUGET, Tardy.

Vougeot C d'O r w ★★★ 99' 02' 05' 09' 10' 12' 15' 16 17 18 Mostly GC as CLOS DE VOUGEOT but also village and PC, Cras, Petits Vougeots, and outstanding white MONOPOLE, **Clos Blanc de V.** Clerget, HUDELOT-NOËLLAT, **Vougeraie** best.

Vougeraie, Dom de la C d'O r w ★★★→★★★★ Bio DOM uniting all BOISSET's v'yd holdings. Fine-boned, perfumed wines, most noted for sensual GCS, esp BONNES-MARES, CHARMES-CHAMBERTIN, MUSIGNY. Fine whites too, with unique **Clos Blanc de Vougeot** and four GCS incl CHARLEMAGNE.

Vouvray Lo w dr sw sp ★★→★★★★ (dr) 10 12 14 15' 16 17 18' (sw) 08 09' 10 11 15' 16 18' AC e of Tours, on n bank of Loire. Top v'yds on premier côte above Loire. Top producers reliably gd. DEMI-SEC is classic style, but in best yrs *moelleux* richly sweet balanced by acidity, almost immortal. Fizz variable (60% production): *pétillant* – local speciality. Best: Aubuisières, Autran, Bonneau, Brunet, Carême, **Champalou**, CLOS Baudoin, Florent Cosme, Fontainerie, Foreau, F PINON, Gaudrelle, **Huet**, Mathieu Cosme, Meslerie (Hahn), Perrault-Jadaud, **Taille-aux-Loups**, Vigneau-Chevreau. Old vintages: 19 21 24 37 47 59 70 71 76 89 90, 96, 97 03 05 must-try. 18 exceptional.

Zind Humbrecht, Dom Al w sw ★★★★ One of greats. Vyds incl GC Brand, HENGST and volcanic RANGEN at Thann. All expensive. For easier prices, MUSCAT GC Goldert 16 from ancient v'yd, dry, floral, structured and great with asparagus.

Strike a light

Burg flavours go through fashions – but what are these struck-match, or gunflint, aromas doing in my CHARD? They have been more and more trendy in recent yrs, in Burg and elsewhere. They are deliberate, and come from reductive winemaking, which creates a sulphur compound, much valued in the fight against premature oxidation. But don't let's take it too far. Leading proponents: COCHE-DURY, Pierre-Yves COLIN-MOREY, ROULOT in Burg. GIACONDA in Australia.

Châteaux of Bordeaux

Abbreviations used in the text:

B'x	Bordeaux
Bar	Barsac
Cas	Castillon-Côtes de Bordeaux
E-2-M	Entre-Deux-Mers
Fron	Fronsac
Grav	Graves
H-Méd	Haut-Médoc
List	Listrac
L de P	Lalande de Pomerol
Mar	Margaux
Méd	Médoc
Mou	Moulis
Pau	Pauillac
Pe-Lé	Pessac-Léognan
Pom	Pomerol
Saut	Sauternes
St-Ém	St-Émilion
St-Est	St-Estèphe
St-Jul	St-Julien

AC	appellation contrôlée
ch(x)	château(x)
dom(s)	domaine(s)

A remarkable number of the Bordeaux properties listed below are designated (in red) as good value. Remarkable because the word on the street is that the world's biggest fine wine region is overpriced. It often looks that way on restaurant lists that don't hesitate to mark up cast-iron reputations. It's true that the top growths – sometimes big, sometimes very small – attract collectors, who are often in reality just investors looking for a return. Compare the prices of mid-to-lower-ranking Bordeaux to similar wines from California or Italy and you find that Bordeaux is highly competitive – and more predictable. Perhaps it lacks novelty – hence less sommelier excitement. The growing Chinese

Châteaux of Bordeaux entries also cross-reference to France.

market is certainly helping Bordeaux. Fine; we all benefit from its continuing success. Hint: restaurants are not the most economical places to drink famous wines. 2018 was a year of two halves in Bordeaux – non-stop rain through the winter, then heat and semi-drought in the summer months all the way through to the harvest. Anyway, the recipe worked as the wines are rich, intense and pure with clear ageing potential. The only dampener was the disparity in yields, the result of localized hail and one of the worst attacks of mildew ever seen by this generation of winemakers. So it's another vintage for the cellar to add to 15 and 16. Luckily, there is a reserve of good red vintages for drinking. The luscious 09s are tempting at whatever level (but don't open them too soon). The 08s have come into their own. The 10s are just opening (as are the "classic" 14s), although the Grands Crus need longer. For early drinking try the often-charming 12s or often-underrated 11s; austere at first but improving with bottle age.

For all sorts of reasons St-Émilion is on a roll just now as the place to look for substantial, satisfying, modern-tasting wines at fair prices that are drinkable within two or three years. They may not be classic claret, with the freshness and cut of the Médoc, but they suit our crossover cooking, and those who drink red wine without food. Among the Grands Crus the mature vintages to look for are 98 (particularly Right Bank), 00, 01 (Right Bank again), 02 (top-end Médoc) and 04. The 06s are beginning to open, as are some of the splendid 05s, although patience is still a virtue here.

Dry white Bordeaux remains consistent in quality and value with another good vintage in 18. Remember that fine white Graves ages as well as white burgundy – sometimes better. And Sauternes continues to offer an array of remarkable years, to which 18 can be added. The problem here is being spoilt for choice. Even moderate years like 02 and 06 offer approachability and a fresher touch while the great years (01, 09, 11, 15) have the concentration and hedonistic charm that makes them indestructible.

A, Dom de L' Cas r ★★ 09' 10' 12 **14 15** 16 MERLOT-led CAS property owned by STÉPHANE DERENONCOURT and his wife. Created 1999. Consistent quality.

Agassac, D' H-Méd r ★★ 09' 10' 12 **14 15 16'** Consistent CH in S H-MÉD. Modern, accessible wine. CAB SAUV-led. Sustainable practices.

Aiguilhe, D' Cas r ★★ 10' 11 12 **14 15** 16 18 Large estate in CAS on high plateau. Same owner as CANON LA GAFFELIÈRE and LA MONDOTTE. MERLOT-led wine with **power and finesse**. Gd ageing potential.

Andron-Blanquet St-Est r ★★ 09' 10' 11 **14 15** 16' Sister CH to COS-LABORY. Often value.

Angélus St-Ém r ★★★★ 98' 00' 04 **05 10'** 15' 16' 18 PREMIER GRAND CRU CLASSÉ (A) since 2012 so prices high. Imposing cellars with wrought-iron bell tower. Pioneer of modern ST-ÉM; dark, rich, sumptuous. Lots of CAB FR (min 40%). Organic conversion. Second label: Le Carillon d'Angélus (production up).

Angludet Marg r (w) ★★ 08 09' **10' 14** 15' 16' Owned, run by NÉGOCIANT SICHEL family since 1961. CAB SAUV, MERLOT, 13% PETIT VERDOT. Fragrant, stylish. No 17 (frost).

Archambeau Grav r w dr (sw) (r) 10 15 **16** (w) **15** 16 17 Owned by Dubourdieu family; v'yd in single block on hill at Illats. Gd **fruity dry white**; fragrant barrel-aged reds. Also rosé.

Arche, D' Saut w sw ★★ 05' 10' **11 13** 15 17' Gd-value Second Growth on edge of SAUT. Also luxury hotel with spa in planning.

Armailhac, D' Pau r ★★★ 00 02 05' **09' 10'** 15' 16' 18 Substantial Fifth Growth in n PAUILLAC. (MOUTON) ROTHSCHILD owned since 1934. On top form, fair value. Supple and expressive earlier.

Aurelius St-Ém r ★★ 09 10 12 14 15 16 Top CUVÉE from the go-ahead ST-ÉM co-op. Grapes from eight terroirs. Modern, MERLOT-led, new oak, concentrated.

Ausone St-Ém r ★★★★ 89' 90 98' 00' 05' 09' 10' 15' 16' 17 18 Tiny, illustrious ST-ÉM First Growth (c.1500 cases) named after Roman poet. V'yd s and se facing, sheltered from winds. Lots of CAB FR (55%). Long-lived wines with volume, texture, finesse. At a price. Second label: Chapelle d'Ausone (500 cases). *La Clotte*, FONBEL, MOULIN-ST-GEORGES, Simard sister estates.

Balestard la Tonnelle St-Ém r ★★ 09 10 12 14 15 16 Historic DOM on limestone plateau, owned by Capdemoulin family. Now modern in style.

Barde-Haut St-Ém r ★★→★★★ 05' 08 09 10 15' 16 GRAND CRU CLASSÉ at St-Christophe-des-Bardes. Sister property of CLOS L'ÉGLISE, HAUT-BERGEY, Branon in Léognan. Rich, modern, opulent.

Bastor-Lamontagne Saut w sw ★★ 10 13 14 15 16 17 Large unclassified Preignac estate. Owned by Grands Chais de France since 2018. Earlier-drinking style. Organic certification from 2016. Second label: Les Remparts de Bastor.

Batailley Pau r ★★★ 05' 08 09' 10' 12 15 16 18 Gd-value Fifth Growth PAU estate owned by BORIE-MANOUX connections. On a gd run. Second label: Lions de Batailley.

Beaumont H-Méd r ★★ 10' 12 14 15 16 Large n H-MÉD estate (around 42,000 cases). Owned by Castel and Suntory; early-maturing, ***easily enjoyable wines***.

Beauregard Pom r ★★★ 05' 09' 10' 14 15 16' Environmentally friendly, mid-weight POM. More depth since 2015. Owned by SMITH-HAUT-LAFITTE and Galeries Lafayette family. Second label: Benjamin de Beauregard. Also Pavillon Beauregard (L DE P).

Beau-Séjour-Bécot St-Ém r ★★★ 08 09' 10' 14 15 16 18 Distinguished PREMIER GRAND CRU CLASSÉ (B) on limestone plateau. Family-owned and -run. Old quarried cellars. Lighter touch these days but still gd ageing potential.

Beauséjour-Duffau St-Ém r ★★★ 01 05' 09' 10' 15 16 18 Tiny PREMIER GRAND CRU CLASSÉ estate on côtes. Owned by Duffau-Lagarrosse family since 1847. Rich, intense and cellar-worthy. Second label: Croix de Beauséjour.

Beau-Site St-Est r ★★ 05 09 10 11 15 16 Gd-value CRU BOURGEOIS property owned by BORIE-MANOUX. 70% CAB SAUV. Supple, fresh, accessible.

Belair-Monange St-Ém r ★★★ 08 09' 10' 15 16' 17 18 PREMIER GRAND CRU CLASSÉ on limestone plateau and côtes. Owned by J-P MOUEIX since 2008. Loads of investment in v'yd. New cellar planned. Fine, fragrant but riper and more intense these days. Second label: Annonce de Belair-Monange.

Belgrave H-Méd r ★★ 08 09' 10' 14 15 16 Consistent n H-MÉD Fifth Growth. LAGRANGE in ST-JUL immediate neighbour. CAB SAUV dominant. Modern-classic in style. Second label: Diane de Belgrave.

Bellefont-Belcier St-Ém r ★★ 09' 10' 12 15' 16 17 18 ST-ÉM GRAND CRU CLASSÉ owned by Hong Kong businessman Peter Kwok (VIGNOBLES K). Suave, full, fresh.

Belle-Vue H-Méd r ★★ 10 11 14 15' 16 17 Consistent, gd-value s H-MÉD. Dark, dense but firm, fresh, aromatic. 15–25% PETIT VERDOT in blend.

Berliquet St-Ém r ★★ 05 09 10 14 15' 16' Tiny GRAND CRU CLASSÉ on côtes. Same

---

Cru Bourgeois hierarchy – again

A three-tier classification for CRU BOURGEOIS will be reintroduced from 2020. This will see the return of three quality levels: Crus Bourgeois, Cru Bourgeois Supérieur, Cru Bourgeois Exceptionnel. The classification will be based on a quality assessment conducted by an independent organization with technical and environmental factors considered. It will be renewable every 5 yrs. Applicants must also submit five vintages for tasting selected from 2008–16. Think of the paperwork.

ownership as CANON (since 2017). Fresh, elegant, ages well. Second label: Les Ailes de Berliquet.

Bernadotte H-Méd r ★★→★★★ 05' 09' 10' 15' 16' Environmentally friendly n H-MÉD CH. Owned by a Hong Kong-based group. Hubert de Boüard (ANGÉLUS) consults. Savoury style, lately with more finesse.

Beychevelle St-Jul r ★★★ 09' 10' 14 15' 16' 17 18 Fourth Growth with memorable label: ship with a griffin-shaped prow. Wines of consistent *elegance* rather than power. State-of-the-art, glass-walled winery. Second label: Amiral de Beychevelle.

Annual turnover of B'x wines is around €3.8 billion.

Biston-Brillette Mou r ★★ 09 10' 12 14 15 16' CRU BOURGEOIS owned by Barbarin family. 50/50 MERLOT, CAB SAUV. Gd-value, attractive, early-drinking wines.

Bonalgue Pom r ★★ 08 09 10 14 15 16 Dark, rich, meaty. 90% MERLOT from sand, gravel, clay soils. As gd value as it gets. Owned by Libourne NÉGOCIANT JB Audy. Sister estates CLOS du Clocher, CH du Courlat in LUSSAC-ST-ÉM.

Bonnet B'x r w ★★ (r) 14 15 16 (w) DYA. Owned by veteran (now 94) André Lurton. Big producer of some of best E-2-M and red (Rés) B'x. LA LOUVIÈRE, *Couhins-Lurton*, ROCHEMORIN and Cruzeau in PE-LÉ same stable.

Bon Pasteur, Le Pom r ★★★ 08 09' 10' 15 16 17 18 Tiny property on ST-ÉM border. Former owner, MICHEL ROLLAND, makes the wine. Ripe, opulent, seductive wines guaranteed. Second label: L'Étoile de Bon Pasteur.

Boscq, Le St-Est r ★★ 09' 10 14 15' 16' 17 Quality-driven CRU BOURGEOIS managed by DOURTHE since 1995. Consistently great value.

Bourgneuf Pom r ★★ 05' 09 10 14 15' 16' 18 V'yd situated to w of POM plateau. Subtle, savoury wines. 2015, 16 best yet (racy, balanced). As gd value as it gets.

Bouscaut Pe-Lé r w ★★★ (r) 08 10' 15 16' (w) 13 15 16 17 GRAV Classed Growth. MERLOT-based reds with 10% MALBEC. Sappy, age-worthy *whites*. Tourist-friendly.

Boyd-Cantenac Marg r ★★★ 05' 09' 10' 14 15 16 Tiny Cantenac-based Third Growth. Owned and run by Lucien Guillemet since 1996. CAB SAUV-dominated. Gd value. POUGET same stable. Second label: Jacques Boyd.

Branaire-Ducru St-Jul r ★★★ 08 09' 10' 15 16' 17 18 Consistent Fourth Growth; regularly gd value; ageing potential. Owner François-Xavier Maroteaux at helm since 2017. Second label: *Duluc*.

Branas Grand Poujeaux Mou r ★★ 05' 09 10 15 16' Tiny neighbour of CHASSE-SPLEEN and POUJEAUX. 50% MERLOT. Rich, modern style. Hubert de Boüard (ANGÉLUS) consults. Sister to Villemaurine in ST-ÉM. Second label: Les Eclats de Branas.

Brane-Cantenac Marg r ★★★→★★★★ 08 09' 10' 14 15' 16' 18 CAB SAUV-led Second Growth on Cantenac plateau. Classic, fragrant MARG with structure to age. Second label: Baron de Brane offers value and consistency.

Brillette Mou r ★★ 09 10 12 14 15 16 Reputable MOULIS CRU BOURGEOIS with v'yd on gravelly soils. Gd depth, fruit. Second label: Haut Brillette.

Cabanne, La Pom r ★★ 05 09 10 15' 16 17 18 MERLOT-dominant (94%) POM w of plateau. Firm when young; needs bottle-age. Second label: DOM de Compostelle.

Caillou Saut w sw ★★ 05 06 10' 13 15' 16 Discreet Second Growth BAR for pure, fruity *liquoreux*. 90% SÉM. Second label: Les Erables. Third label: Les Tourelles.

Calon-Ségur St-Est r ★★★★ 08 10' 14 15' 16' 17' 18 Third Growth with great historic reputation. 5 yrs of major renovation, now on flying form. More CAB SAUV these days. Firm but fine and complex. Second label: Le Marquis de Calon.

Cambon la Pelouse H-Méd r ★★ 09 10' 12 14 15 16' Big, reliable, fruit-forward s H-MÉD CRU BOURGEOIS. Environmental certification in 2018.

Camensac, De H-Méd r ★★ 05 09 10' 14 15 16 Fifth Growth in n H-MÉD. Owned by Merlaut family (GRUAUD-LAROSE, CHASSE-SPLEEN) since 2005. Steady improvement. Usually benefits from bottle-age. Second label: Second de Camensac.

Canon St-Ém r ★★★→★★★★ 08' 09' 10' 11 14 15' 16' 17 Esteemed PREMIER GRAND CRU CLASSÉ (B) with walled v'yd on limestone plateau. Wertheimer-owned, like BEELIQUET, RAUZAN-SÉGLA, ST-SUPÉRY. Now flying; elegant, long-lived wines. 2015 and 2016 superb. Managed by Nicolas Audebert (ex-LVMH). Second label: Croix Canon (until 2011 CLOS CANON).

Canon la Gaffelière St-Ém r ★★★ 08 09' 10' 14 15' 16 18 PREMIER GRAND CRU CLASSÉ (B) on s foot slope. Same ownership as AIGUILHE, CLOS DE L'ORATOIRE, LA MONDOTTE. Lots of CABS FR (40%) and SAUV (10%). Stylish, impressive wines. Organic certification.

Cantemerle H-Méd r ★★★ 05' 09' 10' 14 15 16 Large Fifth Growth in s H-MÉD with beautiful wooded park. CAB SAUV-dominant wines. On gd form and gd value too. Second label: Les Allées de Cantemerle.

An Impériale (6l) of Petrus 1989 sold for €47,450 at auction (2018). €7900 a glass.

Cantenac-Brown Marg r ★★→★★★ 05' 08 10' 14 15 16 18 Third Growth owned by Simon Halabi family. Sustainable approach. 65% CAB SAUV. More voluptuous, refined these days. Dry white AltO (90% SAUV BL). Second label: BriO de Cantenac-Brown.

Capbern St-Est r ★★ 09' 10' 14' 15 16' 17 18 Capbern-Gasqueton until 2013. Same ownership, management as sister CALON-SÉGUR. Gd form. Gd value.

Cap de Mourlin St-Ém r ★★→★★★ 08 09 10 11 15 16 GRAND CRU CLASSÉ on n slopes. Owning family gave name to estate. MERLOT-led (65%). MICHEL ROLLAND consults. More power, concentration than in past.

Carbonnieux Pe-Lé r ★★★ 09' 11 15' 16 GRAV Classed Growth making sterling red and white, large volumes of both. *Whites*, 65% SAUV BL, eg. 15 16 17, have ageing potential. Red can age as well. Tourist-friendly. Second label: La Croix de Carbonnieux.

Carles, De B'x r ★★★ 09 10 12 14 15 16 FRON property. Haut-Carles is prestige CUVÉE partly vinified in 500l oak barrels. Opulent, modern style.

Carmes Haut-Brion, Les Pe-Lé r ★★★ 08 09' 10' 14 15 16' Tiny walled-in v'yd in heart of B'x city. 42% MERLOT, 58% CAB FR and SAUV: structured but suave. Philippe Starck-designed winery from 2016. Second label: Le C des Carmes Haut-Brion from grapes grown in Martillac.

Caronne-Ste-Gemme H-Méd r ★★ 10' 11 14 15 16 17 Sizeable n H-MÉD estate. Same family ownership since 1900. Wines fresh, structured; more depth recently.

Carruades de Lafite Pau ★★★ Second label of CH LAFITE. 20,000 cases/yr. Second Growth (1855) prices. Refined, smooth, savoury; a junior Lafite, in fact. Accessible earlier. 09 should be about ready.

Carteau Côtes-Daugay St-Ém r ★★ 09 10' 14 15 16' 18 Gd-value ST-ÉM GRAND CRU; full-flavoured, supple wines. Owned by Bertrand family since 1850.

Certan-de-May Pom r ★★★ 10' 11 12' 14 15' 16' 18 Tiny v'yd on the POM plateau. Former PETRUS winemaker consults since 2013. Powerful, tannic wines.

Chantegrive, De Grav r w ★★→★★★ 12 14 15 16 Leading GRAV estate. V.gd quality, value. Rich, finely oaked reds but no 2017 (frost). CUVÉE Caroline is top, *fragrant white* 15 16 17.

Chasse-Spleen Mou (w) ★★★ 05' 08 09' 10' 15 16 Big (100 ha), well-known MOU estate run by Céline Villars. Produces gd, often outstanding, long-maturing wine; classical structure, fragrance. Environmental certification. Makes a little Blanc de C-S.

Chauvin St-Ém r ★★ 09 10' 12 14 15 16' GRAND CRU CLASSÉ acquired by Sylvie Cazes of LYNCH-BAGES in 2014. 2016 best yet. New Cupid label.

Cheval Blanc St-Ém r ★★★★ 98' 01' 04 05' 09' 10' 14 15' 16' 17 18 PREMIER GRAND CRU CLASSÉ (A) superstar of ST-ÉM, easy to love. High percentage of CAB FR (60%). Firm, fragrant wines verging on POM. Press wine never used. Delicious young;

lasts a generation, or two. RIP co-owner Albert Frère 2018. Second label: Le Petit Cheval. New Le Petit Cheval Blanc from 2014.

Chevalier, Dom de Pe-Lé r w ★★★★ 08 **09'** 14 15' 16' 17 An oasis in Léognan pine woods, tripled in size from when Bernard family bought in 1983. Pure, dense, finely textured red. Impressive, complex, long-ageing white has remarkable consistency; wait for rich flavours 02 08 14 **15'** 16' 17'. Second label: Esprit de Chevalier. CLOS des Lunes, DOM de la Solitude, Lespault-Martillac same stable.

Cissac H-Méd r ★★ 09 **10 14 15** 16' 17 N H-MÉD CRU BOURGEOIS. Same family ownership since 1895. Classic CAB SAUV-led wines; used to be austere, now purer fruit. Second label: Reflets du CH Cissac.

Citran H-Méd r ★★ **10' 14 15** 16 17 Sizeable s H-MÉD estate. CH a historical monument. Medium-weight, ageing up to 10 yrs. Second label: Moulins de Citran.

Clarence de Haut-Brion, Le Pe-Lé r ★★ 08 **09' 10'** 15 16' 17 18 Recent second label of CH HAUT-BRION, previously known as Bahans Haut-Brion. Blend changes considerably with each vintage (usually MERLOT-led) but same suave texture and elegance as *grand vin*. New white is called La Clarté.

Clarke List r (p) (w) ★★ **09'** 12 14 15 16 17 Leading LIST acquired by Edmund de Rothschild in 1973; now owned by son Benjamin. V.gd MERLOT-based (70%) red. Dark fruit, fine tannins. Eric Boissenot consults. Also dry white: Le Merle Blanc du CH Clarke. Ch Malmaison in MOU same stable.

Clauzet St-Est r ★★ 09 10 11 **14 15** 16' Gd-value CRU BOURGEOIS. CAB SAUV-led, consistent quality. Property sold in 2018; vines acquired by CH LILIAN LADOUYS, brand and buildings by CH La Haye.

Clerc Milon Pau r ★★★ 04 06 10' 15 16' 17 18 V'yd tripled in size since (MOUTON) Rothschilds purchased in 1970. Broader and weightier than sister D'ARMAILHAC. 1% CARMENÈRE in blend. Consistent quality but prices up. Second label: Pastourelle de Clerc Milon.

Climens Saut w sw ★★★★ 96 05 08 **11'** 14 15 16' BAR Classed Growth managed with aplomb by Bérénice Lurton. Concentrated wines with vibrant acidity; ageing potential guaranteed. Certified bio. No *grand vin* in 2017 due to frost. Second label: Les Cyprès (gd value).

Clinet Pom r ★★★ 05' **09' 10** 11 15' 16 Family-owned and -run (Ronan Laborde) estate on POM plateau. 90% MERLOT, 10% CABS SAUV/FR. Sumptuous, modern style. Second label: Fleur de Clinet.

Clos de l'Oratoire St-Ém r ★★ 05' 09 **10' 14** 15 16 Gd-value GRAND CRU CLASSÉ on ne slopes of ST-ÉM. Part of von Neipperg stable (CANON-LA-GAFFELIÈRE, etc.).

Clos des Jacobins St-Ém r ★★→★★★ 08 09 **10'** 12 15 16 Côtes GRAND CRU CLASSÉ at top of game. Renovated, modernized, now showing great consistency; powerful, modern style. CH de Candale, Atelier de Candale restaurant (ST-ÉM) same stable.

Clos du Marquis St-Jul r ★★ 06 **09' 10'** 15' 16' 17' 18 More typically ST-JUL than lofty stablemate LÉOVILLE-LAS-CASES; v'yd surrounded by St-Jul Second Growths. Second label: La Petite Marquise.

Clos Floridène Grav r w ★★ (r) 14 **15'** 16 18 (w) 15' **16** 17' 18 Creation of late Denis Dubourdieu, now run by his sons, Fabrice and Jean Jacques. SAUV BL/SÉM from limestone provides *fine modern white* GRAV, able to age; much-improved, CAB SAUV-led red. CHX DOISY-DAËNE, REYNON in same stable.

Clos Fourtet St-Ém r ★★★ 06 **09' 10'** 12 15' 16 18 PREMIER GRAND CRU CLASSÉ (B)

When it rains it pours
Spare a thought for some luckless growers in B'X. In 17 they had the worst bout of frost since 91, followed by a virulent attack of downy mildew in 18. For some in BLAYE, CÔTES DE BOURG, CAS, GRAV, SAUT, s H-MÉD there was the added blow of hail in May and July. Such are the risks.

on limestone plateau. 12 ha of quarried cellars below. Classic, stylish ST-ÉM. Consistently gd form. STÉPHANE DERENONCOURT consults. POUJEAUX in MOULIS same stable. Second label: La Closerie de Fourtet.

Clos Haut-Peyraguey Saut w sw ★★★ 08 11′ 13 15 16 17 First Growth SAUTERNES in the hands of magnate Bernard Magrez (FOMBRAUGE, LA TOUR-CARNET, PAPE-CLÉMENT same ownership). Elegant, harmonious wines with ageing potential. Second label: Symphonie.

Clos l'Église Pom r ★★★ 05′ 07 09′ 14 15′ 16 Top-flight, consistent POM on edge of plateau. Elegant wine that will age. Same ownership as BARDE-HAUT, Branon, HAUT-BERGEY). Second label: Esprit de l'Église.

White B'x accounts for 12% of B'x production; 70 yrs ago it was 45.

Clos Puy Arnaud Cas r ★★ 10 11 12 14 15 16′ 18 Leading CAS estate run with passion by Thierry Valette. Certified bio. Wines of depth, bright acidity. Earlier-drinking CUVÉE Pervenche.

Clos René Pom r ★★ 09 10 11 14 15′ 16 Family-owned for generations. MERLOT-led with a little spicy MALBEC. Less sensuous, celebrated than top POM; gd value, can age.

Clotte, La St-Ém r ★★ 10′ 12 14 15′ 16′ 17 18 AUSONE ownership since 2014. Steady improvement. Second label: L de La Clotte.

Conseillante, La Pom r ★★★★ 01 04 05′ 08 09′ 10′ 15′ 16′ 18 Owned by Nicolas family since 1871. Some of noblest, most fragrant POM with structure to age. 80% MERLOT on clay, gravel soils. Organic leaning. Second label: Duo de Conseillante.

Corbin St-Ém r ★★ 10′ 11 12 14 15′ 16 Consistent, gd-value GRAND CRU CLASSÉ. Power, finesse. No 2017 due to frost.

Cos d'Estournel St-Est r ★★★★ 90′ 95 98 05′ 09′ 10′ 14 15′ 16′ 17 18 Big Second Growth on PAU border with eccentric pagoda chai. Refined, suave, high-scoring ST-EST. Rare COS 100 MERLOT CUVÉE in 2015; only bottled in double magnums (3l) and Balthazars (12l). Cutting-edge cellars. Too-pricey SAUV BL-dominated white; now more refined. Second label: Les Pagodes de Cos.

Cos-Labory St-Est r ★★ 08 09′ 10′ 15 16′ 17 18 Small Fifth-Growth neighbour of COS D'ESTOURNEL owned by Audoy family; gd value. More depth, structure recently. Second label: Charme de Cos Labory.

Coufran H-Méd r ★★ 09′ 10 12 15 16 17 18 Atypical n HAUT-MÉD estate with 85% MERLOT. Owned by Miailhe family since 1924. Supple wine, but can age. Neighbouring CH Verdignan sister property.

Couhins-Lurton Pe-Lé r ★★ →★★★ (r) 09 10′ 14 15 16 17 (w) 05 06 09′ 14 15′ 16 *Fine*, tense, long-lived Classed Growth *white* from SAUV BL (100%). Much-improved (1st vintage 2002), MERLOT-led red.

Couspaude, La St-Ém r ★★★ 10′ 11 14 15 16 17 18 GRAND CRU CLASSÉ on limestone plateau. Rich creamy, lashings spicy oak. CH Jean de Gué (L DE P) sister property.

Coutet Saut w sw ★★★ 89′ 10′ 14′ 15′ 16 17 Large BAR property owned and run by Baly family since 1977. Consistently v. fine. CUVÉE Madame: v. rich, old-vine selection 01 03 09. Second label: La Chartreuse de Coutet. V.gd dry white, Opalie.

Couvent des Jacobins St-Ém r ★★ 09 10 12 14 15 16 GRAND CRU CLASSÉ vinified within walls of town. Same family ownership since 1902. MERLOT-led with CAB FR and PETIT VERDOT. Lighter style but can age.

Crabitey Grav r v ★★ (r) 15 16 17 18 (w) 15 16 17 Former orphanage at Portets. V'yd in one block. Owner Arnaud de Butler now making harmonious MERLOT/CAB SAUV, small volume of lively SAUV BL (70%)/SÉM.

Crock, Le St-Est r ★★ 08 09′ 10 15 16′ 17 Gd-value CRU BOURGEOIS, going for Exceptionnel status in new hierarchy (2020). Solid, fruit-packed, can age.

Croix, La Pom r ★★ 09 10 12 14 15 16 Owned by NÉGOCIANT Janoueix. Organically run. MERLOT-led (60%). La Croix St-Georges, HAUT-SARPE same stable.

Croix-de-Gay, La Pom r ★★★ 09' 10' 12 14 15 16 18 Tiny MERLOT-dominant (95%) v'yd on POM plateau. Owned by Chantal Raynaud-Lebreton. Racy, elegant style. La Fleur-de-Gay from distinct parcels.

Croix du Casse, La Pom r ★★ 09 10 12 14 15' 16 MERLOT-based (90%+) POM on sandy/gravel soils. Steady progress. Medium-body; gd value. Owned by BORIE-MANOUX.

Croizet-Bages Pau r ★★→★★★ 05 09 10' 14 15 16 18 Striving Fifth Growth; still work to be done. Lately, more consistency but fails to excite. Same owner as RAUZAN-GASSIES.

Cru Bourgeois Méd Certificate awarded annually. 270 CHX in 2016. Quality variable.

Cruzelles, Les L de P r ★★ 09 10 14 15' 16' 17 18 Consistent, gd-value wine. Ageing potential in top yrs. La Chenade sister L DE P. L'ÉGLISE-CLINET same owner.

Dalem Fron r ★★ 09' 10' 12 15 16 17 18 MERLOT-dominated (90%) property. Smooth, ripe, fresh. Second label: Tentation de Dalem.

Dassault St-Ém r ★★ 09 10 12 14 15 16 Consistent, modern, juicy GRAND CRU CLASSÉ in n of AC on sand, clay soils. 70% MERLOT, 30% CABS FR/SAUV. Bought by Marcel Dassault in 1955. Second label: D de Dassault.

Dauphine, de la Fron r ★★→★★★ 09' 12 14 15 16 17 18 Substantial FRON estate. Sweeping change from 2000. Renovation of CH, v'yds plus new winery, additional land acquired, organic certification, bio practices. Now more substance, finesse. Owned by Labrune family since 2015. Second label: Delphis. Also rosé.

Dauzac Marg r ★★→★★★ 08' 09' 10' 14 15 16' Fifth Growth at Labarde; now dense, rich, dark wines. Large format, Primat bottles (27l) by reservation from 2016. New owner 2019. Second label: La Bastide Dauzac. Also fruity Aurore de Dauzac. D de Dauzac is AC B'X.

Desmirail Marg r ★★→★★★ 06 09' 10' 14 15 16' Third Growth owned by Denis Lurton. CAB SAUV-led (70%). Fine, delicate style. Second label: Initial de Desmirail. Visitor friendly.

Destieux St-Ém r ★★ 08 09' 14 15 16 17 18 GRAND CRU CLASSÉ located at St-Hippolyte. Solid, powerful, needs time in bottle; consistent. MICHEL ROLLAND consults.

Doisy-Daëne Bar (r) w dr sw ★★★ 01 08 11' 15' 16 17 Second Growth owned by Dubourdieu family (Clos Floridéne). Age of vines 40 yrs+. Produces *fine, sweet Barsac*. L'Extravagant 06 16 17 an intensely rich, expensive CUVÉE. Also dry white Doisy-Daëne SEC.

Doisy-Védrines Saut w sw ★★★ 01' 04 05' 13 15' 16' BAR estate with v'yd in one block (82% SÉM). Richer style than DOISY-DAËNE. *Long-term fave*; delicious, gd value. Second label: Petit Védrines.

Dôme, Le St-Ém r ★★★ 05 09 10' 15 16 17 Microwine; rich, modern, powerful. Two-thirds old-vine CAB FR, nr ANGÉLUS. NB string of other gd ST-ÉMS in same stable: CH Teyssier (value), Laforge, Le Carré, Le Pontet, Les Astéries, Vieux-Ch-Mazerat.

Dominique, La St-Ém r ★★★ 08 09' 11 15 16' 17 18 GRAND CRU CLASSÉ owned by the Fayat family. Rich, powerful, juicy style. MERLOT-led (81%). Jean Nouvel-designed winery with rooftop restaurant (La Terrasse Rouge) and shop. Next to CHEVAL BLANC. Environmental certification. Second label: Relais de la Dominique.

Ducru-Beaucaillou St-Jul r ★★★★ 95 01 05' 06 08 09' 14 15' 16 17 Outstanding Second Growth in astute hands of Bruno Borie. Majors in CAB SAUV (85%+). Excellent form; classic cedar-scented claret, suited to long ageing. Croix de Beaucaillou, Lalande-Borie sister estates.

Duhart-Milon Rothschild Pau r ★★★ 00' 09' 10' 14 15 16' 18 Fourth Growth owned by

---

B&B&B'x

Visiting B'X and want a night of comfort in the v'yds? These are some of the CHX offering a B&B experience: BEAUREGARD (POM), FOMBRAUGE (ST-ÉM), ORMES-DE-PEZ (ST-EST), Le Pape (PE-LÉ), LA RIVIÈRE (FRON), TERTRE (MARG).

LAFITE ROTHSCHILDS since 1962. CAB SAUV-dominated (65–80%). V. fine quality, esp in last 10 yrs. Second label: Moulin de Duhart.

Durfort-Vivens Marg r ★★★ 05 08 **09' 15' 16' 17** Much-improved MARG Second Growth; now lively and consistent. CAB SAUV-dominated (70%). Certified bio from 2016 (responsible for the change?). Second labels: Vivens and Relais de Durfort-Vivens.

Eglise, Dom de l' Pom r ★★ 08 **09 10' 15 16 17** Oldest v'yd in POM (1589). Part of BORIE-MANOUX stable. Clay/gravel soils of plateau. Consistent, fleshy wines of late.

Église-Clinet, L' Pom r ★★★ →★★★★ 95 98' 01' 05' **09' 10' 14 15 16' 17 18** Tiny but high-flying POM estate. Owner Denis Durantou a driving force. Great consistency; full, concentrated, fleshy but expensive. Second label: La Petite Église.

Evangile, L' Pom r ★★★★ 98' 01 05' 08 **09' 10' 12 14 15' 16' 18** Rothschild (LAFITE)-owned property since 1990. Early ripening site. Lots of investment. MERLOT-dominated (80%) with CAB FR. Consistently rich and opulent. Second label: Blason de L'Evangile.

Fargues, De Saut w sw ★★★ 04 08 **14 15' 16' 17** Unclassified but top-quality SAUT owned by Lur-Saluces. Classic SAUT: rich, unctuous but refined. Badly hit by hail in 2018.

Faugères St-Ém r ★★ →★★★ 08 09' **12 14 15 16** Sizeable GRAND CRU CLASSÉ in e of ST-ÉM owned by Silvio Denz. Rich, modern wines. Sister CH Péby Faugères (100% MERLOT) also classified. Cap de Faugères (CAS), LAFAURIE-PEYRAGUEY in same stable.

Ferrand, De St-Ém r ★★ →★★★ 09' **10' 12 14** 15 16 Big St-Hippolyte GRAND CRU CLASSÉ owned by Pauline Bich Chandon-Moët. Historic Grottes de Ferrand CAVES. Fresh, firm, expressive. Visitor-friendly.

Ferrande Grav r (w) ★★ 09 **10 14 15 16' 17** Substantial GRAVES property at Castres-sur-Gironde. Owned by NÉGOCIANT Castel. Much-improved; easy, enjoyable red; clean, fresh white.

Ferrière Marg r ★★★ 09 **10' 14 15 16' 17** Tiny Third Growth in MARG village. Organically certified; now in conversion to bio. Dark, firm, perfumed wines; gaining in finesse.

Feytit-Clinet Pom r ★★ →★★★ 08 **09' 10' 14 15 16' 18** Tiny 6-ha former MOUEIX property run by Jérémy Chasseuil. 90% MERLOT on clay-gravel soils. Top, consistent form. Rich, seductive. Relatively gd value for a POM.

Fieuzal Pe-Lé r (w) ★★★ (r) 08 **15 16** (w) **14 15 16** Classified PE-LÉ estate owned by Irish Quinn family. Rich, ageable white (oak, acacia barrels); generous red. No 17 (r w, frost). Second label: L'Abeille de Fieuzal (r w).

Figeac St-Ém r ★★★★ 90 95 **98' 00' 01' 05' 14 15' 16' 17' 18** Large PREMIER GRAND CRU CLASSÉ (B) currently on roll (magnificent 17 16 15). Classical CH, gravelly v'yd with unusual 70% CABS FR/SAUV. Now richer but always elegant wines; need long ageing. New winery under construction. Second label: Petit-Figeac.

Filhot Saut w dr sw ★★ 09' **11' 12 15 16 17'** Second Growth with 62-ha v'yd. 60% SÉM, 36% SAUV BL, 4% MUSCADELLE. Richer, purer style from 2009. Extensive hail damage in 2018.

Only markets to age top Grav white: UK, Japan. Others missing out.

Fleur Cardinale St-Ém r ★★ 08 **09' 10' 14 15 16** GRAND CRU CLASSÉ at St-Étienne-de-Lisse. In overdrive for last 15 yrs. Tiny quantity of 2017 (frost); bottled uniquely in magnum. Ripe, unctuous, modern style.

Fleur de Boüard, La B'x r ★★ →★★★ 09 **10 11 14** 15 16' 18 Leading estate in L DE P. Owned by de Boüard family (ANGÉLUS). Tiny crop in 2017 due to frost (22hl instead of 2000). Dark, dense, modern. Special CUVÉE, Le Plus: 100% MERLOT; more extreme. Second label: Le Lion.

Fleur-Pétrus, La Pom r ★★★★ 98' **05' 06 09' 10' 15 16 17' 18** Top-of-the-range

Wanting it all

Production of dry white in b'x may have fallen to around 8% but it seems that more and more top estates want to produce a drop. In the MÉD, LYNCH-BAGES, MARGAUX, MOUTON-ROTHSCHILD have been doing it for some time and are joined by CANTENAC-BROWN, COS D'ESTOURNEL, LAGRANGE, PALMER, TALBOT, DU TERTRE. In ST-ÉM, CHEVAL BLANC and VALANDRAUD both produce dry whites and the rumour is PAVIE will soon follow.

BORDEAUX

J-P MOUEIX property; now grown to 18.7 ha. 91% MERLOT, 6% CAB FR, 3% PETIT VERDOT. Finer style than PETRUS or TROTANOY. Needs time.

Fombrauge St-Ém r ★★→★★★ 05' 10 12 14 15 16' 18 A Bernard Magrez (PAPE-CLÉMENT) estate. C16 origins. GRAND CRU CLASSÉ from 2012. Rich, dark, creamy, opulent. Magrez-Fombrauge is special red CUVÉE; also name for dry white B'X. Second label: Prélude de Fombrauge.

Fonbadet Pau r ★★ 10' 12 14 15 16' 17 18 Small non-classified estate; parcels neighbour top growths. CAB SAUV-led (60%). Less long-lived but reliable.

Fonbel, De St-Ém r ★★ 10 11 12 14 15 16 Consistent source of juicy, fresh, gd-value ST-ÉM. Same stable as AUSONE. Tiny volume in 2017 (frost).

Fonplégade St-Ém r ★★ 08 09 12 14 15 16' American-owned GRAND CRU CLASSÉ. Previously concentrated, modern; now more fruit, balance. Certified organic. Visitor-friendly. Second label: Fleur de Fonplégade.

Fonréaud List r ★★ 09' 10' 11 15 16' 17 One of bigger, better LIST for satisfying, savoury wines. CAB SAUV-led (53%). Some ageing potential. Small volume of v.gd dry white: Le Cygne.

Fonroque St-Ém r ★★★ 09 10' 12 14 15 16 18 Côtes GRAND CRU CLASSÉ owned by insurance agent. Organic and bio certification. Firm but fresh and juicy.

Fontenil Fron r ★★ 09' 10' 12 14 15' 16 18 Leading FRON, owned by MICHEL ROLLAND since 1986. Ripe, opulent, balanced.

Forts de Latour, Les Pau r ★★★★ 90' 95' 07 15 16' 17 Second label of CH LATOUR (about 40% of production); authentic flavour in slightly lighter format; high price. No more en PRIMEUR sales; only released when deemed ready to drink – 2012 in 2018 – but still requires lots more time.

Fourcas-Dupré List r ★★ 09 10' 12 14 15' 16' Well-run property making fairly consistent wine. V'yd in one block. A little SAUV BL (67%), SÉM (33%) white too.

Fourcas-Hosten List r ★★→★★★ 09 10' 12 14 15 16 Large LIST estate. Environmentally friendly. Considerable investment since 2006; now more precision, finesse. Also SAUV BL-led dry white.

France, De Pe-Lé r w ★★ (r) 09 15 16 (w) 15 16 17 Unclassified Léognan estate run by Arnaud Thomassin; ripe, modern, consistent wines. White fresh and balanced.

Franc-Mayne St-Ém r ★★ 09 10' 11 14 15' 16 Tiny GRAND CRU CLASSÉ on côtes. New ownership from 2018. Same management as CH Paloumey in H-MÉD. Fresh, fruity, round but structured.

Gaby, Du Fron r ★★ 09 10 12 15 16 17 18 Splendid s-facing slopes in CANON-FRON. MERLOT-dominated wines age well. Sister CHX du Parc (ST-ÉM) and Moya (CAS). Organic certification.

Gaffelière, La St-Ém r ★★★ 08 10' 11 14 15' 16' 18 First Growth at foot of côtes. Gallo-Roman origins. Investment, improvement; part of v'yd replanted. Elegant, long-ageing wines. 75% MERLOT, 25% CAB FR. Second label: CLOS la Gaffelière.

Garde, La Pe-Lé r w ★★ (r) 05 15 16' (w) 15 16 17 Owned by DOURTHE; supple, CAB SAUV/MERLOT reds. Tiny production of SAUV BL (90%)/SÉM white. Second label: La Terrasse de La Garde.

Gay, Le Pom r ★★★ 08 09' 10' 14 15' 16 Fine v'yd on n edge of POM. Owned by Vignobles Péré-Vergé. Major investment, MICHEL ROLLAND consults. Racy and suave with ageing potential. CH Montviel, La Violette same stable. Second label: Manoir de Gay.

Gazin Pom r ★★★ 05' 06 10' 14 15' 16 18 Large MERLOT-led (90%) estate. Same family ownership since 1917. On v.gd form; generous, long ageing. Second label: L'Hospitalet de Gazin.

Gilette Saut w sw ★★★★ 88 89 90 96 97 99 Extraordinary small Preignac CH. Family-owned since C18. Vintages back to 1953. Stores its sumptuous wines in concrete vats for 16–20 yrs. CH Les Justices (SAUTERNES) is sister estate.

Giscours Marg r ★★★★ 08 09' 10' 15 16' 17 18 Substantial Third Growth at Labarde. V'yd composed of three gravelly hillocks. Full-bodied, long-ageing MARG capable of greatness (eg. 1970). RIP owner Eric Albada Jelgersma; oversaw improvements here and at CH DU TERTRE over last 20 yrs. Second label: La Sirène de Giscours. Little rb'x rosé.

Glana, Du St-Jul r ★★ 08 09 10' 15 16' 17 Big, unclassified CAB SAUV-led (65%) estate. Undemanding; robust; value. Considerable renovation over last 20 yrs. Second label: Pavillon du Glana.

Gloria St-Jul r ★★ ★★★ 08 09' 10' 15' 16 17 18 V'yd located in three zones of ST-JUL, average age 40 yrs. CAB SAUV-dominant (65%). Unclassified, like GLANA, but sells at Fourth-Growth prices. Superb form recently.

Grand Corbin-Despagne St-Ém r ★★ ★★★ 08 09' 10' 14 15 16' Gd-value, family-owned GRAND CRU CLASSÉ in n ST-ÉM. 7th generation at the helm. Aromatic wines now with riper, fuller edge. No *grand vin* in 2017 due to frost. CH Ampélia (CAS) sister estate. Second label: Petit Corbin-Despagne.

Grand Cru Classé St-Ém 2012: 64 classified; reviewed every 10 yrs.

Grand-Mayne St-Ém r ★★★ 09' 10' 12 14 15 16' Impressive GRAND CRU CLASSÉ. Louis Mitjavile (TERTRE-RÔTEBOEUF) consults. Consistent, full-bodied, structured wines. Second label: Les Plantes du Mayne.

Grand-Puy-Ducasse Pau r ★★ 05' 08 10' 14 15' 16' 18 Fifth Growth showing a steady rise in quality in recent yrs. 62% CAB SAUV, 38% MERLOT. Reasonable value. Hubert de Boüard (ANGÉLUS) consults. Second label: Prélude à Grand-Puy-Ducasse.

Grand-Puy-Lacoste Pau r ★★★ 96' 02 06' 09' 10' 14' 15' 16' 18 Fifth Growth famous for gd-value CAB SAUV-driven (75%+) PAU to lay down. Prices up though. Owned and astutely managed by François-Xavier Borie. Eric Boissenot consults. Second label: Lacoste-Borie.

Grave à Pomerol, La Pom r ★★★ 08 09' 10 15 16' 17 18 Small J-P MOUEIX property on w slope of EM plateau. Mainly gravel soils. MERLOT-dominant (85%). Gd value. Can age.

Greysac Méd r ★ 09 10' 12 15 16' 17 Same stable as HAUT CONDISSAS. Clay-gravel soils. MERLOT-ed (65%), fine, fresh, consistent quality.

Gruaud-Larose St-Jul r ★★★★ 95' 00' 05' 09' 10' 14 15' 16' 18 One of biggest, best-loved Second Growths. Owned by the Merlaut family (CITRAN). Smooth, rich, vigorous claret to age. Visitor-friendly. Second label: *Sarget de Gruaud-Larose.*

Guadet St-Ém ★★ 08 09 10 14 15 16' Tiny, family-run (7th generation) GRAND CRU CLASSÉ. Better form in last 10 yrs. DERENONCOURT consults. Organic/bio certification.

Guiraud Saut (r) w (dr) sw ★★★ 98 02 05' 11' 14 15' 16' 17' Substantial organically certified neighbour of YQUEM. Owners incl long-time manager Xavier Planty. Recommended on-site restaurant La Chapelle. Visitor friendly. No *grand vin* in 2018 (hail). Dry white G de Guiraud. Second label: Petit Guiraud.

Gurgue, La Marg r ★★ 08 09' 10 14 15 16' Neighbour of CH MARGAUX. Same management as FERRIÈRE, HAUT-BAGES-LIBÉRAL. Organic certification. Fine, gd value.

Hanteillan Méd r ★★ 09 10 12 14 15 16 Large CRU BOURGEOIS. Almost 50/50 CAB SAUV/MERLOT. Round, balanced, early drinking. DERENONCOURT consults. Second label: CH Laborde.

Haut-Bages-Libéral Pau r ★★★ 05′ 09′ 10′ 14 15′ 16 Medium-bodied Fifth Growth (next to LATOUR). CAB SAUV-led (70%). Eric Boissenot consults. Reasonable value. Second label: La Fleur de Haut-Bages-Libéral.

Haut-Bailly Pe-Lé r ★★★★ 98′ 00′ 05′ 06 09′ 10′ 14 15′ 16′ 17 18 Top-quality PE-LÉ Classed Growth. RIP owner Bob Wilmers; son Chris now in charge. Refined, elegant, CAB SAUV-led red (parcel of v.-old, 100-yr+ vines). Second label: La Parde de H-B. MERLOT-dominant CH Le Pape (Pe-Lé) in same ownership.

Haut-Batailley Pau r ★★★ 96 06 14 15 16′ 17′ Fifth Growth owned by Cazes family of CH LYNCH-BAGES. A sure thing. New label from 2017 vintage. Steady progression in last 10 yrs. Second label: La Tour-l'Aspic.

Haut-Beauséjour St-Est r ★★ 09 10 11 14 15 16 Property created and improved by CHAMPAGNE ROEDERER; sold in 2017. MERLOT-led (60%+). Juicy but structured.

Haut-Bergeron Saut w sw ★★ 05 10 11 15′ 16 17′ Consistent non-classified SAUT. V. old vines (average 50 yrs). Mainly SÉM (90%). Rich, opulent, gd value. Also L'Ilot from parcel on island in Ciron River.

Haut-Bergey Pe-Lé r (w) ★★→★★★ (r) 09 15 16 (w) 14 16 17 Non-classified property with Classed Growth pretentions. Rich, bold red. Fresh, concentrated dry white. No *grand vin* in 2017 due to frost. CLOS L'ÉGLISE in POM sister estate.

Haut-Brion Pe-Lé r ★★★★ 86′ 95′ 07 15′ 16′ 17′ 18 Only non-MÉD First Growth in list of 1855, owned by American Dillon family since 1935. Documented evidence of wine from 1521. Deeply harmonious, wonderful texture, for many no.1 or 2 choice of all clarets. Constant renovation: next project the *cuvier*. Can be tasted at restaurant Le Clarence (two-star Michelin) in Paris. A little *sumptuous dry white* (SAUV BL/SÉM) for tycoons: 13 15′ 16′ 17 18. Also new La Clarté white from both H-B and La Mission H-B. *See* LA MISSION HAUT-BRION, LE CLARENCE DE HAUT-BRION, QUINTUS.

Haut Condissas Méd r ★★★ 09′ 10′ 14 15 16 17 18 Top wine from the Jean Guyon stable; created 1995. Annual production 5000 cases. Sister to CH Rollan-de-By. Rich, concentrated, consistent. MERLOT-LED plus 20% PETIT VERDOT.

Haut-Marbuzet St-Est r ★★ →★★★ 05′ 09′ 10′ 14 15 16 Started in 1952 with 7 ha; now 70; owned by Duboscq family. Opulent, easy to love, but unclassified. 60%+ sold directly by CH. Scented, unctuous wines matured in new oak BARRIQUES. CAB SAUV-led with MERLOT, CAB FR and PETIT VERDOT. Second label: MacCarthy.

Haut-Sarpe St-Ém r ★★ 05 10 12 14 15 16 GRAND CRU CLASSÉ owned by Janoueix family. Hubert de Boüard (ANGÉLUS) consults. Rich, dark, modern with lashings of oak.

Hosanna Pom r ★★★★ 01 05′ 08 15 16′ 17 18 Tiny 4.5 ha v'yd in heart of POM plateau. 70% MERLOT, 30% CAB FR. Created by J-P MOUEIX in 1999 from parcels of former CH Certan Guiraud. Wines have power, purity, balance and need time.

Issan, D' Marg r ★★★ 00′ 05′ 08 14 15′ 16′ Third Growth with fine moated CH. Fragrant wines; at top of game. Cruse family owners since 1945. Yearly harvesting team from Denmark. Second label: Blason d'Issan.

Jean Faure St-Ém r ★★ 09 10 12 14 15 16 GRAND CRU CLASSÉ on clay, sand, gravel soils. 18C origins. Organic certification (2017). Horses for ploughing. 50% CAB FR gives fresh, elegant style. Hubert de Boüard (ANGÉLUS) consults.

Kirwan Marg r ★★★ 05′ 09 10′ 15′ 16′ 17 18 Third Growth on Cantenac plateau. New

---

Keep that mud on your boots
It has been confirmed that the MOUEIX family has sold a 20% stake in PETRUS to Alejandro Santo Domingo, a Colombian-American businessman. Rumour has it that Petrus was valued at €1 billion and that Santo Domingo therefore paid €200 million for his shares. Further calculations hypothetically show the 11.4-ha estate valued at €87 million/ha, which has to be a record for any piece of earth, anywhere. The mud on v'yd workers' boots could be worth more than their annual wages.

> Organic blue blo▪▪
> Only 8% of the B'x v'yd is cultivated organically or biodynamically
> but this incl an increasing number of prestigious crus. CHX from the
> 1855 classification now officially certified organic or bio incl: CLIMENS,
> DURFORT-VIVENS, FERRIÈRE, GUIRAUD, LA LAGUNE, LATOUR, PALMER, PONTET-CANET.
> Gives organics a noble air. But mildew-hit 2018 had some questioning
> whether organics are really sustainable in B'x.

Stolnikoff-designed winery in 2017. CAB SAUV-dominant (60%). Dense, fleshy in 90s; now more finesse. Visitor friendly. Second label: Charmes de Kirwan.

Labégorce Marg r ★★ ★★★ 09 10' 12 14 15 16' Substantial unclassified MARG owned by the Perodo family. Former CH Labégorce Zédé integrated in 2009. Considerable investment and progression. Fine, modern style. CH MARQUIS-D'ALESME same stable.

Lafaurie-Peyraguey S▪nt w sw ★★★ 01' 05' 08 **09' 11'** 15' 16' 17' 18 Leading Classed Growth owned by Lalique crystal owner Silvio Denz (*see* FAUGÈRES). Rich, harmonious, sweet 90% SÉM. Relais & Châteaux hotel with gastronomic restaurant (2018) Second label: La Chapelle de Lafaurie-Peyraguey. Also SÉM-led dry white B'x.

Lafite-Rothschild P▪▪ r ★★★★ 89' **95'** 99' 02 **05'** 09' 10' 14' 15' 16' 18 Big (112 ha) First Growth of famously elusive perfume and style, never great weight, although more dense and sleek these days. Great vintages need keeping for decades. Saskia de Rothschild now at helm with Eric Kohler as winemaker. Joint ventures in the ▪DI, Argentina, California, Chile, China, Italy, Portugal. Second label: CARRUADES DE LAFITE. Also owns CHX DUHART-MILON, L'EVANGILE, RIEUSSEC.

Lafleur Pom r ★★★★ 95' 00' 01' **05' 09'** 15' 16' 17' Superb but tiny family-owned/-managed property cultivated like a garden. Elegant, intense wine for maturing. Expensive. Second label: *Pensées de Lafleur*. Also Les Champs Libres 100% SAUV BL.

Lafleur-Gazin Pom ▪ r ★★ 09 10 11 14 15 16' Small, gd-value J-P MOUEIX estate. 85% MERLOT, 15% CA▪ R. Fine, fragrant, accessible.

Lafon-Rochet St-Es▪ r ★★★ 04 06 **09'** 14 15' 16' 18 Fourth Growth neighbour of COS LABORY run ▪y Michel and Basile Tesseron. On gd form. Former PETRUS winemaker consults. Eye-catching canary-yellow buildings and label. Organic trials halted – ▪oo much copper added to soils. Second label: Les Pélerins de Lafon-Rochet.

Lagrange St-Jul r ★★★ 01 05' **08'** 15' 16' 17 18 Substantial (118 ha) Third Growth owned since 1983 by Suntory. Classic MÉD style. Much investment in v'yd and cellars. Eric Bessenot consults. Dry white Les Arums de Lagrange. Second label: Les Fiefs de Lagrange (gd value).

Lagrange Pom r ★★ 09 10 14 15' 16' 17 18 Tiny POM v'yd; clay, gravel soils. Owned by J-P MOUEIX (195▪. 95% MERLOT. Supple and accessible early.

Lagune, La H-Mé▪r ★★★ 06 08 10' 15' 16' 17 Third Growth in v. s of MÉD. Dipped in 90s; now on form. Fine-edged with more structure, depth. Organic certification. Considerable mail damage in 2018. Second label: Moulin de La Lagune. Also CUVÉE Mademoiselle L from v'yd in Cussac-Fort-Méd.

Lamarque, De H-▪éd r ★★ **08** 09' 10' **14** 15 16 H-MÉD estate with medieval fortress. CAB SAUV-led ▪▪ with an increased percentage of PETIT VERDOT. Competent, mid-term wines, c▪arm, value. Second label: D de Lamarque.

Lanessan H-Mé▪ r ★★ **09** 10' 12 **14** 15' 16' Gd-value MÉD-style claret. Property located just s ▪▪ ST-JUL. Improvement under manager Paz Espejo over last 10 yrs. Visitor friendly.

Langoa-Barton St▪ul r ★★★ 05' **08'** 10' 15' 16' 17 18 Small Third-Growth sister CH to

LÉOVILLE-BARTON. CAB SAUV-led (57%); charm and elegance. C17 ch in Barton hands since 1821. Consistent value.

Larcis Ducasse St-Ém r ★★★ 05′ 08 10′ 14 15′ 16 18 PREMIER GRAND CRU CLASSÉ managed by Nicolas Thienpont. S-facing terraced v'yd. MERLOT-led (85%). On top form today. Second label: Murmure de Larcis Ducasse.

Larmande St-Ém r ★★ 08 10 12 14 15 16 18 GRAND CRU CLASSÉ owned by La Mondiale insurance (as is SOUTARD). V'yd planted to MERLOT (65%), CAB FR (30%), CAB SAUV (5%). Sound but lighter weight.

Laroque St-Ém r ★★→★★★ 08 09′ 10′ 15 16 17 Large GRAND CRU CLASSÉ at one of highest points in ST-ÉM. Terroir-driven wines. Second label: Les Tours de Laroque.

Larose-Trintaudon H-Méd r ★★ 09′ 10 12 14 15 16 Largest v'yd in MÉD (165 ha). 75,000 cases/yr. Sustainable viticulture. Almost 50/50 MERLOT, CAB SAUV with 7% PETIT VERDOT. Generally for early drinking. Second label: Les Hauts de Trintaudon. Also CHX Arnauld, Larose Perganson.

Laroze St-Ém r ★★ 09′ 10′ 12 14 15 16′ GRAND CRU CLASSÉ run by Guy Meslin since 1990. Environmental certification. Lighter-framed wines from sandy soils; more depth of late. Second label: La Fleur Laroze.

Larrivet-Haut-Brion Pe-Lé r w ★★★ (r) 08 15 16 Unclassified PE-LÉ property owned by Gervoson Family since 1987; v'yd expanded from 17 to 75 ha. Bruno Lemoine (ex-MONTROSE) winemaker since 2007. Visitor-friendly. Rich, modern red. Voluptuous, aromatic, SAUV BL/SÉM *white* 15 16 17.

Lascombes Marg r (p) ★★★ 05′ 06 08 14 15′ 16 18 Large (112-ha v'yd) Second Growth with chequered history now owned by insurance group. Wines rich, dark, concentrated, modern with a touch of MARG perfume. Lots of MERLOT (50%+). Second label: Chevalier de Lascombes.

Latour Pau r ★★★★ 90′ 96′ 00′ 05′ 08 09′ 10′ 15′ 16′ 17 First Growth considered the grandest statement of B'X. Profound, intense, almost immortal wines in great yrs; even weaker vintages have the unique taste and run for many yrs. 1st First Growth to be certified organic (2018); part of historical "Enclos" section is bio. Ceased en PRIMEUR sales in 2012; wines now only released when considered ready to drink (2006 in 2018: still too soon). New cellars for more storage. Owned by Pinault family; vines also in Burgundy, Rhône, Napa. Second label: LES FORTS DE LATOUR; *third label: Pauillac*; even this can age 20 yrs.

Latour-à-Pomerol Pom r ★★★ 01 09′ 10′ 15′ 16′ 17′ 18 Managed by J-P MOUEIX (1962). Extremely consistent, well-structured wines that age. Relatively gd value.

Latour-Martillac Pe-Lé r w ★★ (r) 05′ 15′ 16 GRAV Cru Classé owned by Kressmann family (1930). Regular quality; gd value at this level; (w) 15 16 17. Second label: Lagrave-Martillac (r w).

China is now B'x's top export market in volume and value.

Laurets, Des St-Ém r ★★ 09 10 12 14 15 16 Substantial property owned by Benjamin de Rothschild. Hearty, MERLOT-led wine. Les Laurets is 100% Merlot special CUVÉE. Also CH de Malengin.

Laville Saut w sw ★★ 09′ 11′ 13 14 15 16 Non-classified Preignac estate run by Jean-Christophe Barbe; also lectures at B'x University (speciality noble rot). SÉM-dominated (85%) with a little SAUV BL, MUSCADELLE. Lush, gd-value, botrytized wine.

Léoville-Barton St-Jul r ★★★★ 90′ 96′ 00′ 05′ 08′ 09′ 10′ 14′ 15′ 16′ 18 Second Growth with longest-standing family ownership; in Anglo-Irish hands of Bartons since 1826. Lilian Barton Sartorius 9th generation to run property; assisted by her children, Mélanie and Damien. Harmonious, classic claret; CAB SAUV-dominant (86%). Second label: La Rés de Léoville Barton.

Léoville Las Cases St-Jul r ★★★★ 90′ 96′ 00′ 01 09′ 10′ 15′ 16′ 17′ 18 Largest Léoville and original "Super Second"; *grand vin* from Grand Enclos v'yd. CAB SAUV dominant. Elegant, complex wines built for long ageing. Second label: Le Petit Lion; CLOS DU MARQUIS separate wine in ST-JUL. NÉNIN, PCTENSAC same ownership.

Léoville-Poyferré St-Jul r ★★★★ 90' 96' 01 05' 08 09' 10' 14 15' 16' Owned by Cuvelier family since 1920. Now at "Super Second" level with dark, rich, spicy, long-ageing wines. MICHEL ROLLAND consults. *Ch Moulin-Riche* is a separate 21-ha parcel. Second label: Pavillon de Léoville-Poyferré.

Lestage List r ★★ 09 10 12 14 15 16 Same Chanfreau-family ownership as FONRÉAUD. MERLOT-led. Firm, slightly austere. Also dry white La Mouette.

Lilian Ladouys St-Est r ★★ 09' 10' 12 14 15 16 Now 80 ha with additional parcels from CLAUZET and Tour de Pez. Environmental certification. More finesse in recent vintages. Same stable as PÉDESCLAUX. Second label: La Devise de Lilian.

Liversan H-Méd r ★★ 10 12 14 15 16 CRU BOURGEOIS in n H-MÉD. V'yd in single block. PATACHE D'AUX sister. Round, savoury, early drinking.

Loudenne Méd r ★★ 09 10 12 14 15 16 Large CRU BOURGEOIS, once Gilbeys, then Lafragette family, now Chinese-owned and labelled Loudenne Le CH. Landmark C17 pink-washed *chartreuse* by river. Visitor-friendly. 50/50 MERLOT/CAB SAUV reds. Oak-scented SAUV BL.

Louvière, La Pe-Lé r w ★★★ (r) 09' 15' 16' (w) 14 15 16 André Lurton property since 1965. Excellent *white* (100% SAUV BL), red of Classed Growth standard (60/40 CAB SAUV/MERLOT). *See also* BONNET, COUHINS-LURTON.

Lussac, De St-Ém r ★★ 09 10 12 14 15 16 Top estate in LUSSAC-ST-ÉM. Plenty of investment. Supple red and rosé, Le Libertin dry white.

Lynch-Bages Pau r (w) ★★★★ 95' 01 05' 08 09' 10' 14 15 16' 17 Always popular, now a star, far higher than its Fifth-Growth rank. CAZES family owners. Rich, dense CAB SAUV-led wine. Second label: Echo de Lynch-Bages. Gd white, *Blanc de Lynch-Bages*, now fresher style. New winery under construction designed by Chinese architect Chien Chung Pei. HAUT-BATAILLEY same stable (2017).

Lynch-Moussas Pau r ★★ 09 10' 14 15' 16 Fifth Growth owned by Castéja family. Lighter-style Pau (75% CAB SAUV) but much improved in recent yrs.

Lyonnat St-Ém r ★★ 10 12 14 15 16 Leading LUSSAC-ST-ÉM owned by Milhade family. MERLOT-led; more precision lately. Also special CUVÉE Emotion.

Malartic-Lagravière Pe-Lé (w) ★★★ (r) 01 15' 16' (w) 15 16 17 GRAV Classed Growth. Owned by Bonnie family since 1997. Loads of investment and expansion. Rich, modern, CAB SAUV-led (65%) red; a little lush white (majority SAUV BL). CH Gazin Rocquencourt (PE-LÉ) same stable.

Malescasse H-Méd r ★★ 10 12 14 15' 16' 17 18 CRU BOURGEOIS nr MOULIS. Recent investment, upgrade. DERENONCOURT consults. Supple, value; now more depth.

Malescot-St-Exupéry Marg r ★★★ 08 09' 10' 14 15' 16 On-form MARG Third Growth owned by the Zuger family. Ripe, fragrant, finely structured wines. Second label: Dame de Malescot.

Malle, De Saut r w dr sw ★★★ (w sw) 05 06 09 15' 16' 17' Preignac Second Growth

---

Prince on the go
Prince Robert of Luxembourg's tenure as CEO and president of DOM Clarence Dillon (his mother's family business), owner of HAUT-BRION, has been anything but somnolent. In the last 15 yrs he has created a new NÉGOCIANT house and B'X brand, Clarendelle, overseen the renovation of LA MISSION HAUT-BRION, developed a new property in ST-ÉM (QUINTUS) and launched a restaurant in Paris, Le Clarence (two-star Michelin). A renovation of the cellars at HAUT-BRION is now underway as are new promotional activities with Primum Familiae Vini, a group of family owner/producers.

(1855) with classical CH owned by de Bournazel family. Fine, medium-bodied SAUT; also M de Malle dry white GRAV.

Margaux, Ch Marg r (w) ★★★★ 95' 96' 01' 05' 09' 10' 14 15' 16 17 18 First Growth; most seductive, fabulously perfumed, consistent wines. Owned by Mentzelopoulos family (1977). Winemaker Paul Pontallier RIP an inspiration for 33 yrs. Recent addition: Norman Foster-designed cellars. Second label: Pavillon Rouge 04' 08' 15' 18. Third label: Margaux du CH Margaux from 2009. *Pavillon Blanc* (100% SAUV BL): best white of MÉD, recent vintages fresher 13' 15' 16' 18.

2.6% of the B'x v'yd changed hands in 2017.

Marojallia Marg r ★★★ 10 11 12 15 16 17' Micro-CH looking for big prices for big, rich, un-MARG-like wines. Recent vintages touch more fragrant. Second label: CLOS Margalaine.

Marquis-d'Alesme Marg r ★★→★★★ 09' 10' 12 15 16' 17 Third Growth in MARG village. Investment and steady progress; now more consistency. CAB SAUV-led (63%). Same Perrodo family ownership as LABÉGORCE.

Marquis-de-Terme Marg r ★★→★★★ 10' 11 12 14 15' 16 18 Fourth Growth with v'yd dispersed around MARG. Sénéclauze family owners since 1935. Recent investment, renovation; previously solid wine, now more seductive.

Maucaillou Mou r ★★ 09 10 12 15' 16 17 Large, consistent MOU estate. Güntzian gravel soils. Clean, fresh, value wines. Second label: N°2 de Maucaillou.

Mayne Lalande List r ★★ 09 10 12 14 15 16 Leading LIST estate. ANGÉLUS owner consults. Full, finely textured. B&B too.

Mazeyres Pom r ★★ 09 10 12 14 15 16' 17 18 Lighter but consistent POM. Supple, earlier-drinking. Unusual 2–3% PETIT VERDOT. Converting to bio. Second label: Le Seuil.

Meyney St-Est r ★★→★★★ 06 09' 10' 14 15 16' Big river-slope v'yd, superb site next to MONTROSE. Structured, age-worthy; improvement under winemaker Anne Le Naour. Same stable as GRAND-PUY-DUCASSE, LA TOUR DE MONS (2004). ANGÉLUS owner consults. Second label: Prieur de Meyney.

Mission Haut-Brion, La Pe-Lé r ★★★★ 89' 96' 01 05' 09' 10' 15' 16' 17' 18 Owned by Dillon family of neighbouring HAUT-BRION since 1983. Consistently grand-scale, full-blooded, long-maturing wine. Second label: La Chapelle de la Mission. Magnificent SÉM-dominated white: previously Laville-Haut-Brion; renamed La Mission-Haut-Brion Blanc (2009) 15 16 17' 18. Second label: La Clarté (fruit from both H-Bs).

Monbousquet St-Ém r (w) ★★★ 08 09' 10' 14 15 16' GRAND CRU CLASSÉ on sand/gravel soils. Transformed by Gerard Pérse (*see* PAVIE). Concentrated, oaky, voluptuous. 50% of crop lost in 2017 (frost). Rare *v.gd Sauv Bl/Sauvignon Gris* (AC B'x). Second label: Angélique de Monbousquet.

Monbrison Marg r ★★→★★★ 09' 12 14 15 16 17 18 Tiny (13.2 ha), family-owned property at Arsac. CAB SAUV-led (60%). Delicate, fragrant MARG.

Mondotte, La St-Ém r ★★★★ 01 08 09' 15 16 17' 18 Tiny (4.5 ha) PREMIER GRAND CRU CLASSÉ on limestone-clay plateau. Old vines (60 yrs). Intense, firm, virile wines. Organic certification. Same stable as AIGUILHE, CANON-LA-GAFFELIÈRE, CLOS DE L'ORATOIRE.

Montrose St-Est r ★★★★ 90 96' 00' 05' 08 09' 10' 14 15' 16' 18 Second Growth with riverside v'yd. Famed for forceful, long-ageing claret. Vintages 1979–85 were lighter. Bouyges brothers owners. Ongoing environmental programme. Second label: *La Dame de Montrose*. CLOS ROUGEARD (Loire) and 51% of DOM Henri Rebourseau (Burgundy) same stable.

Moulin du Cadet St-Ém r p ★★ 10' 12 14 15 16 17' Tiny (2.85 ha) GRAND CRU CLASSÉ; 100% MERLOT. Same owner as SANSONNET. Formerly robust, now more finesse.

Moulinet Pom r ★★ ▭ 11 12 15 Large CH for POM: 25 ha. MERLOT-led. Lighter style. Chinese-owned (2016).

Moulin-Haut-Laroque Fron r ★★ 09' 10' 12 14 15' 16 18 Leading FRON property run by Thomas Hervé. MERLOT-led (65%) with 5% MALBEC. Consistent quality. Structured wines, can age.

B'x wines account for 1% of all French wines and 1.8% of the world's.

Moulin Pey-Labrie Fron r ★★ 09' 10' 12 15 16 17 18 Same family ownership (1988). Limestone-clay soils. Sturdy, well-structured wines that can age.

Moulin-St-Georges St-Ém r ★★★ 09' 10' 12 15' 16' 17 18 Same stable as AUSONE, LA CLOTTE. 80% MERLOT, 20% CAB FR. Dense, polished wines.

Mouton Rothschild Pau r (w) ★★★★ 89' 95' 01' 05' 06' 09' 15' 16' 17' 18 Rothschild-owned (1853); current generation Camille, Philippe, Julien. Most exotic, voluptuous of Pau First Growths, now at top of game. 2016 label by S African artist William Kentridge. White Aile d'Argent (SAUV BL/SÉM) more graceful these days. Second label: Le Petit Mouton. *See also* D'ARMAILHAC, CLERC MILON.

Nairac Saut w sw ★★ 01' 05' 11 13 14 15 BAR Second Growth run by brother and sister, Nicolas and Eloïse Heeter Tari. C17 origins. Rich but fresh. Second label: Esquisse de Nairac.

Nénin Pom r ★★★ 05 06 09' 15' 16' 17 Large POM estate. Same owners as LÉOVILLE-LAS-CASES since 1997. Investment, evolution clearly paid off since 2015. Restrained style but generous, precise, built to age. Gd-value second label: Fugue de Nénin.

Olivier Pe-Lé r w ★★ (r) 05' 08 10' 14 15 16' (w) 15 16 17 Beautiful classified property owned by Bethmann family since C19. Significant investment in last 15 yrs. Now structured red (65% CAB SAUV) and juicy SAUV BL-led (75%) white.

Ormes-de-Pez St-Est r ★★ 01 05 08' 15' 16' 17 18 CAZES family of LYNCH-BAGES own (1940). Consistent, full, age-worthy.

Ormes-Sorbet, L Méd r ★★ 09 10 12 14 15 16' 17 Reliably consistent CRU BOURGEOIS. Same family owners since 1764. CAB SAUV (65%), MERLOT (30%), PETIT VERDOT (5%). Elegant, gently oaked wines.

Palmer Marg r ★★★★ 95 00 06' 08' 09' 10' 14 15' 16' 17 18 Third Growth on a par with "Super Seconds" (occasionally Firsts). Voluptuous wine of power, complexity and much MERLOT (40%). Dutch (Mähler-Besse) and British (SICHEL) owners. Identification code on bottles to guarantee authenticity. Second label: *Alter Ego de Palmer*. Original Vin Blanc de Palmer (Loset/ MUSCADELLE/Sauvignon Gris).

Pape-Clément Pe-Lé r (w) ★★★★ (r) 05 09' 10' 15' 16' 17 (w) 15 16 17' Historic estate in B'x suburbs (wine shop and tastings too). Owned by magnate Bernard Magrez. Dense, long-ageing reds. Tiny production of rich, oaky white; fresher in 2017. Second label (r w): Clémentin.

Patache d'Aux Méd r ★★ 09 10 12 14 15 16' Sizeable CRU BOURGEOIS at Bégadan. Reliable, largely CAB SAUV (60%). DERENONCOURT consults. Part of Advini group.

Pavie St-Ém r ★★★ 98 06 07 09' 10' 15' 16' 17 18 PREMIER GRAND CRU CLASSÉ (A), splendidly sited on plateau and s côtes. Intense, oaky, strong wines; recent vintages less extreme. MERLOT-led but now more CABS FR/SAUV. Impressive, state-of-the-art winery. Second label: Arômes de Pavie.

Pavie-Decesse St-Ém r ★★★ 08 09' 10' 14 15' 16 18 Tiny (3.5 ha) Classed Growth. 90% MERLOT. Powerful, muscular like sister PAVIE.

Pavie-Macquin St-Ém r ★★★ 05' 06 09' 15 16' 17 18 PREMIER GRAND CRU CLASSÉ (B) with v'yd on limestone plateau. 80% MERLOT, 20% CABS FR/SAUV. Winemakers Nicolas and son Cyrille Thienpont. Sturdy, full-bodied wines need time. Second label: Les Chênes de Macquin.

Pédesclaux Pau r ★★ 05 09 10' 14' 15 16' Underachieving Fifth Growth

BORDEAUX

revolutionized by owner Jacky Lorenzetti. Extensive investment since 2014; cellars, more v'yds. More fruit/flavour. Second label: Fleur de Pédesclaux.

Petit-Village Pom r ★★★ 01 05 09' 15' 16 17 18 Much-improved POM opposite VIEUX-CH-CERTAN. Owned by AXA Insurance. Diana Berrouet Garcia the winemaker. Suave, dense, increasingly finer tannins. Second label: Le Jardin de Petit-Village.

Petrus Pom r ★★★★ 88' 98' 01 05' 07 09 10' 15' 16' 17' 18 (Unofficial) First Growth of POM: MERLOT solo *in excelsis*. 11.5 ha v'yd on blue clay gives 2500 cases of massively rich, concentrated wine for long ageing. One of 50 most expensive wines in world. 20% stake sold to Colombian-American investor in 2018 for rumoured €200 million. No second label.

Pey La Tour B'x r ★★ 14 15 16 Large (176 ha) DOURTHE property. Quality-driven B'x SUPÉRIEUR. Three red CUVÉES: Rés du CH top selection. Also rosé, dry white.

Peyrabon H-Méd r ★★ 09' 10 11 12 15 16 Savoury CRU BOURGEOIS owned by NÉGOCIANT Millésima. Also La Fleur-Peyrabon in PAU.

Pez, De St-Est r ★★★ 05' 08 09' 15' 16' 17 18 Consistent cru owned by ROEDERER (as is PICHON COMTESSE). MERLOT/CAB SAUV with a little CAB FR, PETIT VERDOT. Dense, reliable.

Phélan-Ségur St-Est r ★★★ 05' 06 08 15' 16' 17' 18 Reliable, top-notch, unclassified CH with Irish origins; long, supple style. Belgian shipper acquired the property in 2017. Second label: Frank Phélan.

Pibran Pau r ★★ 09' 10' 11 15 16' 17 18 Earlier-drinking PAU allied to PICHON-BARON. Classy, MERLOT-led wine.

Pichon-Baron Pau r ★★★★ 96 04 05' 07 08 09' 10' 15' 16' 17 18 Owned by AXA; formerly CH Pichon-Longueville (until 2012). Revitalized Second Growth; reverted to original, core v'yd. Powerful, long-ageing PAU at a price. Second labels: Les Tourelles de Longueville (approachable: more MERLOT); Les Griffons de Pichon Baron (CAB SAUV dominant).

Pichon-Longueville Comtesse de Lalande (Pichon Lalande) Pau r ★★★★ 95 96 01 05' 08 09' 10' 15' 16' 17 18 ROEDERER-owned Second Growth, neighbour of LATOUR. Always among top performers; long-lived wine of famous breed. MERLOT-marked in 80s, 90s; more CAB SAUV in recent yrs (70% in 2017). New high-tech, gravity-fed winery and buildings. Second label: Rés de la Comtesse.

Pin, Le Pom r ★★★★ 01' 05' 06' 07 08' 09' 10' 15 16' 17' The original B'x cult wine (2018 is 40th vintage). Only 2.8 ha. Tiny cellar now given way to modern winery. 100% MERLOT; almost as rich as its drinkers, but prices are out of sight. Ageing potential. L'If (ST-ÉM), L'Hêtre (CAS) new stablemates.

Plince Pom r ★★ 09 10 11 12 14 15 16 Neighbour of NÉNIN and LA POINTE. J-P MOUEIX exclusivity. Lighter style of POM.

Pointe, La Pom r ★★ 09' 11 12 14 15 16 18 Large (for POM), well-managed estate. Investment, progress in last 10 yrs. Second label: Ballade de La Pointe.

Status symbol in B'x nowadays, a crane: new cellars on way in another building boom.

Poitevin Méd r ★★ 11 12 14 15 16 17 Supple, elegant CRU BOURGEOIS. Guillaume Poitevin driving force. Consistent quality.

Pontet-Canet Pau r ★★★★ 05' 07 08 09' 10' 14 15 16' Fashionable, bio-certified, Tesseron-family-owned Fifth Growth. Radical improvement has seen prices soar. New *cuvier* with 32 amphora-shaped vats. Big crop loss in 2018 due to mildew. Second label: Les Hauts de Pontet-Canet.

Potensac Méd r ★★ 05' 08 09' 15 16' 17' 18 Same stable as LÉOVILLE LAS CASES. Firm, long-ageing wines; gd value. MERLOT-led (45%) but lots of old-vine CAB FR. Second label: Chapelle de Potensac.

Pouget Marg r ★★ 09' 10' 12 14 15 16 Obscure Fourth Growth sister of BOYD-CANTENAC. 66% CAB SAUV. Sturdy; needs time.

Poujeaux Mou r ★★ 05 08 09 14 15' 16' Same stable as CLOS FOURTET. CAB SAUV-led (50%). Full, robust wines with ageing potential. Second label: La Salle de Poujeaux.

Premier Grand Cru Classé St-Ém 2012: 18 classified; ranked into A (4) and B (14).

Pressac, De St-Ém r →★ 09 10 12 15 16 17 18 GRAND CRU CLASSÉ at St-Étienne-de-Lisse. MERLOT-LED but CABS FR/SAUV, MALBEC, CARMENÈRE. Value.

Value of a ha of vines in Pau is around €2 million.

Preuillac Méd r ★★ 09 10 11 14 15 16 Savoury, structured CRU BOURGEOIS. Chinese-owned. MERLOT-led (53%). Second label: Esprit de Preuillac.

Prieuré-Lichine Marg r ★★★ 05 08 09' 15' 16' 17 18 Fourth Growth owned by a NÉGOCIANT; put on map in 60s by Alexis Lichine. Parcels in all five MARG communes. Fragrant Marg currently on gd form. Second label: Confidences du Prieuré-Lichine. Gd SAUV BL/SÉM.

Puygueraud B'x r ★★ 10 11 12 15' 16' 17' Leading CH of this tiny FRANCS-CÔTES DE B'X AC. Nicolas Thienpont and son Cyrille winemakers (see PAVIE-MACQUIN). MERLOT-led. Oak-aged wines of surprising class. Two-thirds lost to frost in 2017; higher proportion of CAB FR. A little white (SAUV BL/Sauvignon Gris).

Quinault L'Enclos St-Ém r ★★ →★★★ 09 10 11 15 16 17 18 GRAND CRU CLASSÉ located in Libourne. Same team and owners as CHEVAL BLANC. New *cuverie* in 2017; 22% CAB SAUV; more freshness, finesse. Aged in 500l casks.

Quintus St-Ém r →★★ 11 12 14 15 16' 17' Created by the Dillons of HAUT-BRION from former Tertre Daugay and L'Arrosée v'yds. Gaining in stature; more CAB FR in 2017 (45.6%) adds length and fragrance. Price has soared. Second label: Le Dragon de Quintus.

Rabaud-Promis Saut w sw ★★ →★★★ 09' 11 12 14 15 16 17' First Growth owned by Déjean family. Quality, gd value. Second label: Promesse.

Rahoul Grav r w ★★ (r) 10 12 14 15 16 Owned by DOURTHE; reliable, MERLOT-led red. SÉM-dominated white 15 16 17. Gd value.

Ramage-la-Batisse H-Méd r ★★ 10 11 12 14 15 16 Reasonably consistent, widely distributed, classic, CRU BOURGEOIS. CAB SAUV-led with MERLOT, PETIT VERDOT, CAB FR.

Rauzan-Gassies Marg r ★★★ 09' 10 12 15 16' 17 Second Growth owned by Quié family; part of huge Rauzan estate in C18. Improvement over last 10 yrs. Second label: Gassies.

Rauzan-Ségla Marg r ★★★★ 96 04 05' 06 09' 10' 14 15' 16' Leading MARG Second Growth long famous for its fragrance; owned by Wertheimers of Chanel (1994). CAB SAUV-led (60%). Always seeking to improve. Second label: Ségla (value).

Raymond-Lafon Saut w sw ★★★ 05' 09' 11' 15' 16 17' 18 Unclassified SAUT owned by Meslier family producing First-Growth quality. Majority SÉM (80%). Rich, complex wines that age.

Rayne Vigneau Saut w sw ★★★ 01' 04 10' 15 16' 17 Substantial First Growth owned by Trésor du Patrimoine group. Wines rich, suave, age-worthy. Visitor-friendly. Second label: Madame de Rayne. Also dry white Le Sec.

Respide Médeville Grav r w ★★ (r) 14 15 16 (w) 14 15 16 Top GRAV property for elegant red and complex *white*. Gonet-Médeville owners (CHAMP as well).

Reynon B'x r w ★★ Leading CADILLAC-CÔTES DE B'X estate. Owned by Dubourdieu family (see DOISY-DAËNE). Serious MERLOT-led red 15' 16' 17. Fragrant SAUV BL (DYA).

Reysson H-Méd r ★★ 10' 12 14 15 16 17 CRU BOURGEOIS owned by NÉGOCIANT DOURTHE. Mainly MERLOT (88%); unusually no CAB SAUV. Rich, modern style.

Rieussec Saut w sw ★★★★ 01' 05' 08 09' 10' 14 15' 16 First Growth with substantial v'yd in Fargues, owned by (LAFITE) Rothschilds (1984). Regularly powerful, opulent, SÉM-dominant (90%); a bargain. Second label: Carmes de Rieussec. Dry wine "R" de Rieussec.

Rivière, De la Fron r ★★ 10 12 14 15 16' 17 18 Largest (65 ha), most impressive FRON property with 25 km of quarried galleries. Chinese-owned. Formerly big, tannic; now more refined. Claude Gros consults. Second label: Les Sources.

Roc de Cambes B'x r ★★★ 07 10 12 15' 16 17 18 Undisputed leader in CÔTES DE BOURG; MERLOT (80%) and v. old (50 yrs) CAB SAUV. Savoury, opulent but pricey. Sister to TERTRE-RÔTEBOEUF.

Rochemorin, De Pe-Lé r w ★★ →★★★ (r) 10' 12 14 15 16 17 (w) 15 16 17 Large property at Martillac owned by André Lurton of COUHINS-LURTON. Fleshy, MERLOT-led (55%) red; aromatic white (100% SAUV BL). Fairly consistent quality. CH Coucheroy (r w) also produced.

Rol Valentin St-Ém r ★★★ 09' 11 12 15 16' 17' 18 Once garage-sized; now bigger v'yd with clay-limestone soils. MERLOT-led (90%). Rich, modern wines but balanced.

Rouget Pom r ★★ 10' 11 12 14 15 16' Go-ahead estate on n edge of POM. Owned by Burgundian Labruyère family since 1992. Michel Rolland consults. Rich, unctuous wines. Second label: Le Carillon de Rouget.

St-Georges St-Ém r ★★ 09 10 12 14 15 16 V'yd represents 25% of ST-GEORGES AC. Jean-Philippe Janoueix co-owner and manager. MERLOT-led with CABS FR/SAUV. Gd wine sold direct to public. Second label: Puy St-Georges.

St-Pierre St-Jul r ★★★ 08 09' 10' 14 15' 16' 17 18 Tiny Fourth Growth to follow, owned by Triaud family. Stylish, consistent, classic ST-JUL. Second label: Esprit de St-Pierre.

Sales, De Pom r ★★ 09 10' 12 15 16 17 Biggest v'yd of POM (10,000 cases). Younger generation at helm. Ex-PETRUS winemaker consults. Honest, drinkable; can age. Second label: CH Chantalouette (5000 cases).

Sansonnet St-Ém r ★★★ 10' 12 14 15 16' 17' 18 Ambitious GRAND CRU CLASSÉ; neighbour of TROTTEVIEILLE. Modern but refreshing. Second label: Envol de Sansonnet.

Saransot-Dupré List r (w) ★★ 09' 10' 11 12 15 16 Small property owned by Yves Raymond. Firm, fleshy, MERLOT-led with 2% CARMENÈRE. Also dry white B'x.

Sénéjac H-Méd r (w) ★★ 09 10' 12 14 15 16' S H-MÉD (Pian). Consistent, well-balanced wines. Drink young or age. Sister to TALBOT.

Serre, La St-Ém r ★★ 10 12 14 15 16' 17 Small GRAND CRU CLASSÉ on limestone plateau. MERLOT-led (80%). Fresh, stylish wines with fruit.

Sigalas-Rabaud Saut w sw ★★★ 05 10' 13 15' 16 17' Tiny First Growth owned by Laure de Lambert. *V. fragrant and lovely.* Second label: Le Lieutenant de Sigalas. Also La Sémillante dry white.

Siran Marg r ★★→★★★ 09' 10' 12 14 15' 16' 18 Surprisingly unclassified MARG estate in Labarde. Recent investment and change. Visitor friendly. Wines have substance, fragrance. Owner president of AC Marg. Second label: S de Siran.

Smith-Haut-Lafitte Pe-Lé r (p) (w) ★★★★ (r) 01 08 10' 15' 16' 17 (w) 15 16 17 Celebrated Classed Growth with spa hotel (Caudalie), regularly one of PE-LÉ stars. White is full, ripe, sappy; red precise/generous. Second label: Les Hauts de Smith. Also CAB SAUV-based Le Petit Haut Lafitte. Winner of 2019 International Best of Wine Tourism award, and new spa hotel nr Fontainebleu.

Sociando-Mallet H-Méd r ★★★ 96' 00' 05' 15' 16' 17 Substantial H-MÉD estate in St-Seurin-de-Cadourne built from scratch by former NÉGOCIANT. 54% MERLOT, 46% CABS SAUV/FR. Classed-Growth quality. Big-boned wines to lay down for yrs. Second label: La Demoiselle de Sociando-Mallet. Special CUVÉE Jean Gautreau.

You'd like your own?

ST-ÉM remains a desirable region for investing in a v'yd. Demand is high and price of land continues to rise (little under €250,000/ha) and top sites on plateau going for €3 million/ha+. Among the classified estates (2012) the following have changed hands recently: BELLEFONT BELCIER, BERLIQUET, CLOS La Madeleine, FONROQUE, FRANC MAYNE, TROPLONG MONDOT.

Sours, **De** B'x r p w ★★ Valid reputation for popular B'x rosé (DYA). Gd white; improving B'x red. Owned by Jack Ma of Alibaba fame since 2016.

Soutard St-Ém r ★★★ 10 11 12 15 16' 17 18 *Potentially excellent* GRAND CRU CLASSÉ on limestone plateau. Massive investment, still room for improvement; 16 best yet. Visitor-friendly. Second label: Petit Soutard from 2016 (previously Les Jardins de Soutard).

Suduiraut Saut w sw ★★★★ 99' 06 09' 10' 13 15' 16' 17 18 One of v. best SAUT. SÉM-dominant (90%+. Greater consistency, luscious quality. Big crop loss in 2018 due to mildew. Second labels: Castelnau de Suduiraut; Lions de Suduiraut (fruitier). Dry wines "S" and entry level Le Blanc Sec.

Taillefer Pom r ★★ 10 11 12 14 15 16 Family-owned property. MERLOT-led (75%). Sandier soils. Lighter weight but polished and refined. Can age.

Talbot St-Jul r (w) ★★★ 06 05' 08 09' 14 15 16 18 Huge (110 ha) Fourth Growth in heart of AC ST-JUL. Wine rich, *consummately charming*, *reliable*. 66% CAB SAUV. Jean-Michel Laporte new winemaker/manager from 2018 (EX-LA CONSEILLANTE). Second label: Connétable de Talbot. Approachable SAUV BL-based Caillou Blanc.

Tertre, **Du** Marg r ★★★ 05' 09' 10' 15' 16' 17 Fifth Growth isolated s of MARG, sister-ch to GISCOURS. Fragrant (20% CAB FR) fresh, fruity but structured (CAB SAUV-led) wines. Visitor-friendly; B&B also available. Second label: Les Hauts du Tertre. Also Tertre Blanc VIN DE FRANCE dry white CHARD/VIOGNIER/GROS MANSENG/SAUV BL.

Tertre-Rôteboeuf St-Ém r ★★★★ 95 00' 05' 08 09' 10' 14' 15' 16' 17 Tiny, unclassified, family-owned, ST-ÉM star; concentrated, exotic, MERLOT-based. Hugely consistent; can age. Frightening prices. V.gd ROC DE CAMBES, DOM DE CAMBES.

Thieuley B'x r p w ★★ E-2-M supplier of consistent quality AC B'x (r w); oak-aged CUVÉE Francis Courselle (r w). Run by sisters Marie and Sylvie Courselle.

Tour-Blanche, **La** Saut (r) w sw ★★★ 05' 08 09' 11' 13 15 16 17' Excellent First Growth SAUT; rich, bold, powerful wines on sweeter end of scale. SÉM-dominant (83%), some MUSCADELLE (5%). Second label: Les Charmilles de La Tour-Blanche. Also dry white B'x Duo de La Tour Blanche.

Tour-Carnet, **La** H-Méd r ★★★ 08 09' 10' 14 15 16' N H-MÉD Classed Growth owned by Bernard Magrez (*see* FOMBRAUGE, PAPE-CLÉMENT). MICHEL ROLLAND consults. Concentrated, opulent wines. Second label: Les Pensées de La Tour Carnet. Also dry white B'x Blanc de La Tour Carnet.

Tour-de-By, **La** Méd r ★★ 09 10 11 14 15' 16 Extensive family-run estate in n MÉD. Popular, sturdy, reliable, CAB SAUV-led (60%) wines with 5% PETIT VERDOT. Also rosé and special CUVÉE Héritage Marc Pagès.

Tour de Mons, La Marg r ★★ 05' 09' 10 14 15' 16' MARG CRU BOURGEOIS. Same winemaker (Anne Le Naour) as MEYNEY. MERLOT-led (55%). Steady improvement.

Tour-du-Haut-Moulin H-Méd r ★★ 05' 09 14 15' 16' 17 5th-generation, family-owned n H-MÉD CRU BOURGEOIS. Intense, structured wines to age.

Tour-du-Pas-St-Georges St-Ém r ★★ 10 12 14 15 16 ST-GEORGES-ST-ÉM estate run by Delbeck family. MERLOT-led (60%) with 2% CARMENÈRE. Classic style.

Tour Figeac, **La** St-Ém r ★★ 05' 09' 10' 12 14 15' 16' 18 GRAND CRU CLASSÉ in "graves" sector of ST-ÉM. Gd proportion of CAB FR (35%). Fine, floral, harmonious. 17 frost.

Tour Haut-Caussan Méd r ★★ 10' 12 14 15 16 17 Consistent, Courrian family-run CRU BOURGEOIS. 50/50 CAB SAUV, MERLOT. Value.

Tournefeuille L de P r ★★ 10' 12 14 15 16 Reliable L DE P on clay and gravel soils. Owned by Petit family. 70% MERLOT, 30% CAB FR. Round, fleshy wine.

Tour-St-Bonnet Méd r ★★ 10' 11 12 14 15 16 CRU BOURGEOIS at St-Christoly. 45/45 MERLOT/CAB SAUV, FR. Reliable. Value.

Trois Croix, Les Fron r ★★ 10 12 14 15 16 17 Fine and balanced wines from consistent producer. Clay-limestone soils. 80% MERLOT. Gd value. RIP owner Patrick Léon, former MOUTON ROTHSCHILD winemaker.

Tronquoy-Lalande St-Est r ★★★ 10' 12 14 15' 16' 17 18 Same owners as MONTROSE; plenty of investment. MERLOT-led wines; consistent, dark, satisfying. Second label: Tronquoy de Ste-Anne. A little SÉM/Sauvignon Gris B'X white.

Troplong-Mondot St-Ém r ★★★ 07 12 14 15' 16 17 18 PREMIER GRAND CRU CLASSÉ (B) on limestone plateau. New owner in 2017; plenty of investment; new winery under construction. *Wines of power, depth* with increasing elegance (and price) these days (earlier picking, less new oak). Second label: Mondot.

Trotanoy Pom r ★★★★ 90 01 05' 09' 10' 15' 16' 17 18 One of jewels in J-P MOUEIX crown. 90% MERLOT, 10% CAB FR. Power, elegance, long ageing. Second label: Espérance de Trotanoy.

Trottevieille St-Ém r ★★★ 05' 09' 11 14 15' 16' PREMIER GRAND CRU CLASSÉ (B) owned by BORIE-MANOUX. Much improved in last 10 yrs; wines long, fresh, structured. Lots of CAB FR (40–50%) incl some pre-phylloxera vines. Second label: La Vieille Dame de Trottevieille.

Valandraud St-Ém r ★★★★ 98 01 05' 09' 14 15 16' 17' 18 PREMIER GRAND CRU CLASSÉ (B) in e ST-ÉM. Garage wonder turned First Growth. Formerly super-concentrated; now rich, costly, dense but balanced. Also Virginie de Valandraud from unclassified land and Valandraud Blanc (SAUV BL/Sauvignon Gris).

Vieille Cure, La Fron r ★★ 06 10' 12 15 16 17 18 Leading FRON estate; new owner in 2018. Fruity, appetizing. Jean-Luc Thunevin (VALANDRAUD) consults. Value.

Vieux-Ch-Certan Pom r ★★★★ 90' 01' 05' 06 09' 10' 14' 15' 16' 17' 18 Rated close to PETRUS in quality; different in style; *elegance, harmony, fragrance*. Plenty of CAB FR/SAUV (30%) one of reasons. Alexandre Thienpont and son Guillaume at helm. Second label: La Gravette de Certan.

Vieux Ch St-André St-Ém r ★★ 10 11 12 14 15' 16 Small MERLOT-based v'yd in MONTAGNE-ST-ÉM. Owned by former PETRUS winemaker and son. *Gd value.*

Villegeorge, De H-Méd r ★★ 10 12 14 15 16 Tiny s H-MÉD. CAB SAUV-led (63%). Light but elegant wines. Eric Boissenot consults.

Vray Croix de Gay Pom r ★★★ 05' 09' 14 15 16' 17 Tiny v'yd in best part of POM. More finesse of late. 2018. LATOUR owner a shareholder. Bio certification from 2018. LATOUR owner a shareholder. CHX Siaurac (L DE P), Le Prieuré (ST-ÉM) same stable.

Yquem Saut w sw (dr) ★★★★ 89' 96 01' 09' 11' 13' 14 15' 16' 17' King of sweet, *liquoreux* wines. Strong, intense and luscious; kept 3 yrs in barrel. Most vintages improve for 15 yrs+, some live 100 yrs+ in transcendent splendour. 100 ha in production (75% SÉM/25% SAUV BL). No Yquem made in 51, 52, 64, 72, 74, 92, 2012. No second label (rejected wine sold to NÉGOCIANTS). Makes a small amount (800 cases/yr) of off-dry, SAUV BL (75%), SÉM (25%) "Y" (pronounced "ygrec").

St-Émilion classification – current version

The latest classification (2012) incl a total of 82 CHX: 18 PREMIERS GRANDS CRUS CLASSÉS and 64 GRANDS CRUS CLASSÉS. The new classification, now legally considered an exam rather than a competition, was conducted by a commission of seven, nominated by INAO, none from B'X. CHX ANGÉLUS and PAVIE were upgraded to Premier Grand Cru Classé (A) while added to the rank of Premier Grand Cru Classé (B) were CANON LA GAFFELIÈRE, LA MONDOTTE, LARCIS DUCASSE and VALANDRAUD. New to status of Grand Cru Classé were Chx BARDE-HAUT, CLOS de Sarpe, Clos la Madeleine, Côte de Baleau, DE FERRAND, de Pressac, FAUGÈRES, FOMBRAUGE, JEAN FAURE, La Commanderie, La Fleur Morange, Le Chatelet, Péby Faugères, QUINAULT L'ENCLOS, Rochebelle and SANSONNET. Although a motivating force for producers, the classification (which is reviewed every 10 yrs, since 1955) is still an unwieldy guide for consumers.

Italy

VALLE
D'AOSTA

L Cor

L Maggiore

Mila

LOMBAR

Turin O
PIEDMONT

Genoa O

LIGURIA

Ligurian Sea

More heavily shaded areas are
the wine-growing regions.

Abbreviations used in
the text:

Ab	Abruzzo	Mol	Molise
Bas	Basilicata	Pie	Piedmont
Cal	Calabria	Pu	Puglia
Cam	Campania	Sar	Sardinia
E-R	Emilia-Romagna	Si	Sicily
F-VG	Friuli-Venezia Giulia	T-AA	Trentino-Alto Adige
Lat	Latium	Tus	Tuscany
Lig	Liguria	Umb	Umbria
Lom	Lombardy	VdA	Valle d'Aosta
Mar	Marches	Ven	Veneto

Consistency is not Italy's great quailty. In fact it's not Italy's quality
at all. But who wouldn't sacrifice consistency for variety, style,
originality and frequent flashes of brilliance? Italy has many wines to
avoid; usually either incompetent or cynical takes on the best-known
names. "Prosecco", "Chianti", "Amarone" are no more guarantees of
anything than the plain name "Bordeaux". But down the length of the
country's tortuously bumpy geography the number of plantable places is
enormous, and enormously varied. Over 2000 years most of them have
been exploited, usefully or not. Hundreds have given rise to their own
varieties of grapes. Some 30% of all the world's wine-grape varieties are
Italian. And it's fair to say that noone has kept track of them all.
Which is why, year after year, alongside wines as famous and esteemed
(ie. expensive) as any in the world we are offered names we've never seen
before. So a pocket guide is at full stretch to list all, or most of, the place
names and their best producers you are likely to meet. As everywhere,
"best producers" is the crux. In case you hadn't noticed, Italy is a land
of motivated, opinionated people with, on top of a shrewd sense of
business, a lot of style. The wines we want are the ones that express
the style, rather than the sense of business.

You can't count on the official DOC/DOCG system. And that, of
course, is a crying shame, because the good examples of those wines
are among the world's most enjoyable, best and often least expensive,
given the quality in the bottle. Remember that Italian wine is always
part of a whole ecosystem of the table. Glass goes beside plate. Why
are Italian restaurants universally popular? Even the Chinese are smitten
with them. Because bright people, as soon as they can afford it, get busy
pleasing their palates. Joining them is worth a little study.

ITALY

Recent vintages

Amarone, Veneto & Friuli

2018 Optimal weather conditions. Gd for quantity and quality, esp fresh whites.

2017 V. difficult vintage (non-stop rain); weedy Amarones a risk, green reds in general.

2016 V. hot summer; round but low-acid, big reds, chunky whites.

2015 Quantity gd, quality better; v.gd Friuli reds. Fresher than initially thought.

2014 Not memorable for Amarone, better Soave, Friuli whites, v.gd Valpolicellas.

2013 Gd whites. Reds, esp passito, suffered October/November rain/hail.

2012 Prolonged heat, drought = showy but tough tannic reds, blowsy whites.

2011 "Greatest year" for Amarone an exaggeration; some too tannic, high alc. V.gd whites.

Campania & Basilicata

2018 Rainy, but whites fresh, lively; sleek reds (Aglianico best).

2017 Low-volume yr, reds plagued by gritty tannins. Whites often flat; Greco best.

2016 Cold spring delayed flowering, hot summer allowed catch-up. Fiano best.

2015 Hot, dry early summer means ripe but at times tough reds, broad whites; drink up.

2014 Lots of rain; spotty quality. Avoid green Aglianicos, Piedirossos. Whites pretty gd.

2013 Classic perfumed fresh whites, thinner late-picked Aglianicos.

2012 Too hot; September rains saved whites. Indian summer made memorable Aglianicos.

2011 Wines concentrated, but reds mostly too high alc, tannins. Whites better.

Marches & Abruzzo

2018 Patchy spring. More balanced than 17. V. high volume, gd quality (r w).

2017 Best to forget: hot, droughty. Reds gritty, whites overripe. Low volume.

2016 Rain, cold, lack of sun = difficult yr. Lemony, figgy Pecorino probably best.

2015 Hot summer, whites fresher than expected (esp Trebbiano), reds ripe, not cooked

2014 Marches: sleek reds, classic whites. Abruzzo: best for Pecorino.

2013 Whites classically mineral and age-worthy; reds refined, classic, not lean.

2012 Too hot: tough reds, blowsy whites.

Piedmont

2018 Despite difficult spring, potentially classic Barolo/Barbaresco.

2017 Among earliest harvests in living memory. Usually showy, can lack depth.

2016 Potentially top vintage; classic, perfumed, age-worthy Barolo/Barbaresco.

2015 Outstanding Barolo/Barbaresco. Should be long-lived. Barbera/Dolcetto gd; Grignolino less so.

2014 Because of rains, later-picked grapes thrived, early ones (eg. Dolcetto) didn't. Barbaresco (not Barolo) best.

2013 Bright, crisp wines (r w) improving with time; classic vintage of steely, deep wines.

2012 Overrated Barolo/Barbaresco with unfailingly green, gritty tannins. Beware hype.

2011 Forward, early-drinking, scented reds despite highish alc levels, big tannins.

Fine vintages: 10 08 06 04 01 00 99 98 97 96 95 90 89 88. Vintages to keep: 01 99 96. Vintages to drink up: 03 00 97 90 88.

Tuscany

2018 Gd-quality reds of steely personality, age-worthiness.

2017 V. difficult hot vintage. Better in Chianti Classico than coast.

2016 Hot summer, fresher September; success from Chianti to Montalcino to Maremma. Small crop.

2015 Grapes healthy but small: rich flavourful reds of gd ripeness; some soft.

2014 Cool, wet summer, fine late season. Quantity up, quality patchy, buyer beware.

2013 Uneven ripening. Not a great year, but some peaks.

2012 Drought and protracted heat; overrated wines, mostly.

2011 Some fruity but high-alcohol reds. Whites can be unbalanced. Drink soon.

Fine vintages: 08 07 06 04 01 99 97 95 90. Vintages to keep: 01 99. Vintages to drink up: 03 00 97 95 90.

Abrigo Orlando Pie ★★★ BARBARESCO crus Montersino, Meruzzano little known, but high quality, and Abrigo's clean, precise interpretations allow terroir to sing.

Accornero Pie ★★★★ Italy's best GRIGNOLINO producer. V.gd: Bricco del Bosco (steel vat) and Vigne Vecchie (oak-aged, v.gd 13). Also gd: BARBERA del Monferrato (Bricco Battista, Cima) and Brigantino sweet (MALVASIA di Casorzo).

Adriano, Marco e Vittorio Pie ★★★ High quality, low prices, BARBARESCO full of early appeal. One of great buys in Italian wine.

Aglianico del Taburno Cam DOCG r dr ★→★★★ Around Benevento. Spicier notes (leather, tobacco) and herbs, higher acidity than other AGLIANICOS. Gd: CANTINA del Taburno, Fontanavecchia, La Rivolta.

Aglianico del Vulture Bas DOC(G) r dr ★→★★★ 11 12 13 15 16 DOC after 1 yr, SUPERIORE after 3 yrs, RISERVA after 5. From slopes of extinct volcano Monte Vulture. More floral (violet), dark fruits (plum), smoke, spice than other AGLIANICOS. V.gd: ELENA FUCCI, GRIFALCO. Also gd: Armando Martino, Basilisco, CANTINA di Venosa, CANTINE DEL NOTAIO, D'Angelo, Eubea, Madonna delle Grazie, Mastrodomenico, PATERNOSTER, Re Manfredi, Terre dei Re.

Alba Pie Major wine city of PIE, se of Turin in LANGHE hills; truffles, hazelnuts and Pie's, if not Italy's, most prestigious wines: BARBARESCO, BARBERA D'ALBA, BAROLO, DOGLIANI (DOLCETTO), Langhe, NEBBIOLO D'ALBA, ROERO.

Albana di Romagna E-R DOCG w dr sw s/sw (sp) ★→★★★ DYA. Italy's 1st white DOCG, justified only by sweet PASSITO; dry and sparkling often unremarkable. Best: FATTORIA ZERBINA (esp AR Passito RISERVA), Giovanna Madonia, PODERE Morini (Cuore Matto Riserva Passito), Tre Monti.

Allegrini Ven ★★ Popular VALPOLICELLA producer. Best wine is refined, not-over-the-top AMARONE. Owner of POGGIO al Tesoro in BOLGHERI, Poggio San Polo in MONTALCINO, TUS.

Alta Langa Pie DOCG (p) w sp ★★→★★★ PIE's major zone for quality vintage METODO CLASSICO (sp), produced only from PINOT N and CHARD. Best: BANFI, Cocchi, Enrico Serafino, ETTORE GERMANO, FONTANAFREDDA, GANCIA, RIZZI.

Altare, Elio Pie ★★★ Past leader of modernist BAROLO. Now run by Silvia, Elio's daughter. Try Barolos: Arborina, Cannubi, Cerretta VIGNA Bricco, Unoperuno (selection from Arborina); also Giarborina (LANGHE NEBBIOLO), Larigi (BARBERA D'ALBA), Langhe Rosso La Villa (BARBERA/NEBBIOLO).

Alto Adige (Sudtirol) T-AA DOC r p w dr sw sp Mountainous province of Bolzano (Austrian until 1919); among best Italian whites today. Germanic varieties dominate. GEWURZ, KERNER, SYLVANER, but PINOT GRIGIO too; probably world's best PINOT BIANCO. PINOT N can be excellent (but often overoaked); *Lagrein* in gd yrs.

Alto Piemonte Pie Microclimate and soils of ne ideal for NEBBIOLO (here called Spanna); wines rarely 100%, with additions of other local grapes (Croatina, Uva Rara, Vespolina). Home of DOC(G): BOCA, BRAMATERRA, Colline Novaresi, Coste della Sesia, FARA, GATTINARA, GHEMME, LESSONA, Sizzano, Valli Ossolane. Many outstanding wines.

What do the initials mean?

DOC (Denominazione di Origine Controllata) Controlled Denomination of Origin, cf. AOC in France.

DOCG (Denominazione di Origine Controllata e Garantita) "G" = "Guaranteed". Italy's highest quality designation. Guarantee? It's still *caveat emptor*.

IGT (Indicazione Geografica Tipica) "Geographic Indication of Type". Broader and more vague than DOC, cf. Vin de Pays in France.

DOP/IGP (Denominazione di Origine Protetta/Indicazione Geografica Protetta) "P" = "Protected". The EU's DOP/IGP trump Italy's DOC/IGT.

Ama, Castello di Tus ★★★★ Top CHIANTI CLASSICO estate of Gaiole. Plain *Chianti Classico is one of best* and most expensive. Worth seeking: TUS/B'x blend Haiku and MERLOT L'Apparita, despite the high price. Outstanding Chianti Classico Gran Selezione VIGNETO Bellavista and La Casuccia.

Amarone della Valpolicella Ven DOCG r ★★ ★★★★ 10 11' 13 15 (16) Intense, strong red from winery-raisined VALPOLICELLA grapes; relatively dry version of more ancient RECIOTO DELLA VALPOLICELLA; CLASSICO if from historic zone. (*See also* Valpolicella, and box p.152.) Older vintages are rare, as 1st created in 50s.

Angelini, Paolo Pie ★ ★★★ Small family-run MONFERRATO estate: v.gd GRIGNOLINO del Monferrato Casalese Arbian (steel vat) and Golden Dream (oak-aged).

Angelini, Tenimenti Tus *See* BERTANI DOMAINS (TOSCANA).

Antinori, Marchesi L&P Tus ★★ ★★★★ Historic Florentine house of ancient Antinori family, led by Piero and three daughters. Leader of Italy's wine renaissance. Famous for CHIANTI CLASSICO (Tenute Marchese Antinori and *Badia a Passignano*, latter now elevated to Gran Selezione), also polished but oaky white Cervaro (Umb *Castello della Sala*), PIE (PRUNOTTO) wines. Pioneer TIGNANELLO and SOLAIA among few world-class SUPER TUSCANS. Also estates in BOLGHERI (Guado al Tasso), FRANCIACORTA (*Montenisa*), MONTALCINO (Pian delle Vigne), MONTEPULCIANO (La Braccesca), PUG (Tormaresca), TUS MAREMMA (Fattoria Aldobrandesca). LIES-based white from estate of Monteloro n of Florence. Interests in Calfornia, Romania, etc.

Antoniolo Pie ★★★ Age-worthy benchmark GATTINARA. Outstanding Osso San Grato and San Francesco.

Argiano, Castello di Tus ★★★ Beautiful property, next to and distinct from estate called "Argiano", transformed by Sesti family into one of MONTALCINO's finest sources of BRUNELLO. Best is Brunello RISERVA Phenomena.

Argiolas, Antonio Sar ★★ ★★★★ Top producer using native island grapes. Outstanding crus *Turriga* (★★★), Iselis MONICA, Iselis Nasco, *Vermentino* di Sardegna and top sweet Angialis (mainly local Nasco grape). V.gd CANNONAU RISERVA Senes.

Asti Pie DOCG sw sp ★★★ NV PIE sparkler from MOSCATO Bianco grapes, inferior to MOSCATO D'ASTI, not really worth its DOCG. Sells like mad in Russia. Try Bera, Cascina Fonda, Caudrina, Vignaioli di Santo Stefano. Now dry version, Asti Secco.

Barbaresco subzones

There are substantial differences between BARBARESCO's four main communes – **Barbaresco**: most complete, balanced. Asili (BRUNO GIACOSA, CERETTO, Ca' del Baio, PRODUTTORI DEL BARBARESCO), Martinenga (Marchesi di Gresy), Montefico (Produttori del Barbaresco, Roagna), Montestefano (Produttori del Barbaresco, Rivella Serafino, Giordano Luigi), Ovello (CANTINA del Pino, ROCCA ALBINO), Pora (Ca' del Baio, Produttori del Barbaresco), Rabaja (CASTELLO DI VERDUNO, Giuseppe Cortese, BRUNO GIACOSA, Produttori del Barbaresco, Rocca Bruno), Rio Sordo (Cascina Bruciata, Cascina delle Rose, Produttori del Barbaresco), Roncaglie (Poderi Colla) **Neive**: most powerful, fleshiest. Albesani (Castello di Neive, Cantina del Pino), Basarin (Marco e Vittorio Adriano, Giacosa Fratelli, Negro Angelo, Sottimano), Bordini (La Spinetta), Currà (Rocca Bruno, Sottimano), Gallina (Castello di Neive, ODDERO, Lequio Ugo), Serraboella (Cigliuti). **San Rocco Seno d'Elvio**: readiest to drink, soft. Sanadaive (Marco e Vittorio Adriano). **Treiso**: freshest, most refined. Bernardot (CERETTO), Bricco di Treiso (PIO CESARE), Marcarini (Ca' del Baio), Montesino (Abrigo Orlando, Rocca Albino), Nervo (RIZZI), Pajoré (Rizzi, Sottimano).

Avignonesi Tus ★★★ Large bio estate, Belgian-owned since 2007. 200 ha in MONTEPULCIANO, Cortona. *Italy's best Vin Santo*. VINO NOBILE has returned to 1st division after period in wilderness. Top: VN Grandi Annate but MERLOT Desiderio, 50&50 (Merlot/SANGIOVESE), CHARD Il Marzocco creditable internationals.

Azienda agricola / agraria Estate (large or small) making wine from its own grapes.

Badia a Coltibuono Tus ★★★ Historic CHIANTI CLASSICO. Organic certified. 100% SANGIOVESE barrique-aged Sangioveto and entry-level Chianti Classico one of best too. Age-worthy. No RISERVAS in 2014.

Banfi (Castello or Villa) Tus ★→★★★ Giant of MONTALCINO, 100s of ha, though not in ideal situations, at extreme s of zone; but top, limited-production wine POGGIO all'Oro is a great BRUNELLO. V.gd Moscadello.

Barbaresco Pie DOCG r ★★→★★★★ 10 11 12 13 14 15 (16) Wrongly looked down upon as BAROLO's poor cousin: both 100% NEBBIOLO, similar complexity, but plenty of differences. Barbaresco has warmer microclimate, more fertile soils, lower slopes, so less austere, "muscular" than Barolo. Min 26 mths ageing, 9 mths in wood; at 4 yrs becomes RISERVA. Like Barolo, most these days sold under a cru name or *menzione geografica*. (For top producers *see* box, left.)

Barbera d'Alba DOC r Richest, most velvety of BARBERAS. Gd: CAVALLOTTO (VIGNA del Cucculo), GIACOMO CONTERNO (Cascina Francia and Ceretta), GIUSEPPE RINALDI, VIETTI (Scarrone).

Barbera d'Asti DOCG r Fruity, high-acid version of BARBERA grape. Higher quality is Barbera d'Asti SUPERIORE Nizza (or simply, Nizza). Gd: BERSANO (Nizza La Generala), BRAIDA (Bricco dell'Uccellone, Bricco della Bigotta, Ai Suma), Cascina Castlet, ***Chiarlo Michele*** (Nizza La Court), Dacapo (Nizza), TENUTA Olim Bauda (Nizza), *Vietti* (La Crena).

Barbera del Monferrato Superiore Pie DOCG r Relatively light, fruity BARBERA with sharpish tannins, gd acidity. Gd: Accornero (Cima RISERVA della Casa), Iuli (Barabba).

Barberani ★★→★★★ Brothers Bernardo and Niccolò run organic estate on slopes of Lago di Corbara, make gd to excellent ORVIETO. Cru Luigi e Giovanna is star, Orvieto Castagneto and (noble rot) Calcaia also excellent. Reds gd too.

Bardolino Ven DOC(G) r p DYA Light summery red from Lake Garda. Bardolino SUPERIORE DOCG has much lower yield than Bardolino DOC; its pale-pink CHIARETTO one of Italy's best rosés, gd value. Reds mostly nondescript, boring. Gd producers: Albino Piona, Cavalchina, ***Guerrieri Rizzardi***, Le Fraghe (top: Bol Grande), ZENATO, Zeni.

Barolo Pie DOCG r 06 07 08 09 10' 11 12 13 15 (16) (17) Italy's greatest red? 100% NEBBIOLO, from 11 communes incl Barolo itself. Traditionally a blend of v'yds or communes, but these days most is single-v'yd (like Burgundian crus), called Menzione Geografica Aggiuntiva. Best are age-worthy wines of power, elegance, with alluring floral scent and sour red-cherry flavour. Must age 38 mths before release (5 yrs for RISERVA), of which 18 mths in wood. (For top producers *see* box, p.129.) Division between traditionalists (long maceration, large oak barrels) and modernists (shorter maceration, often barriques) is less helpful these days as producers use techniques of both schools.

Bastianich ★★→★★★ American Joe Bastianich oversees 35 ha from his US base, with star consultant Maurizio Castelli. Knockout Vespa Bianco, typically Friulian blend of CHARD/SAUV BL with a *pizzico* of native Picolit, outstanding FRIULANO Plus.

Belisario Mar ★★→★★★ Largest producer of VERDICCHIO DI MATELICA. Many different bottlings; gd quality/price. Top: RISERVA Cambrugiano e Del Cerro. V.gd Meridia and Vigneti B (organic).

Bellavista Lom r w sp ★★★ Owned by Francesca Moretti, one of best FRANCIACORTA producers. Alma Gran Cuvée is flagship. Top: Vittorio Moretti.

Barolo subzones

The concept of "crus" gaining acceptance although it is not allowed on the label. It is replaced (in BAROLO and BARBARESCO at least) by "geographic mentions" (Menzioni Geografiche Aggiuntive), known unofficially as subzones. Currently Barolo has 11 village mentions and 170 additional geographic mentions. Some of best incl (by commune) – **Barolo:** Bricco delle Viole, Brunate, Bussia, Cannubi, Cannubi Boschis, Cannubi San Lorenzo, Cannubi Muscatel, Cerequio, Le Coste, Sarmassa; **Castiglione Falletto:** Bricco Boschis, Bricco Rocche, Fiasco, Monprivato, Rocche di Castiglione, Vignolo, Villero; **Cherasco:** Mantoetto; **Diano d'Alba:** La VIGNA, Sorano (partly shared with Serralunga); **Grinzane Cavour:** Canova, Castello; **La Morra:** Annunziata, Arborina, Bricco Manzoni, Bricco San Biagio, Brunate, Cerequio, Fossati, La Serra, Rocche dell'Annunziata, Rocchettevino, Roggeri; **Monforte d'Alba:** Bussia, Ginestra Gramolere, Mosconi, Perno; **Novello:** Bergera, Ravera; **Roddi:** Bricco Ambrogio; **Serralunga d'Alba:** Baudana, Boscareto, Cerretta, Falletto, Francia, Gabutti, Lazzarito, Marenca, Ornato, Parafada, Prapò, Vignarionda; **Verduno:** Massara, Monvigliero.

Benanti Si r w ★★★ Benanti family turned world on to ETNA. Bianco SUPERIORE *Pietramarina* one of Italy's best whites. V.gd: ETNA Rosso Rovittello mono-variety Nerello Cappuccio and NERELLO MASCALESE.

Berlucchi, Guido Lom sp ★★ Italy's largest producer of METODO CLASSICO fizz; five million+ bottles from 100 ha v'yd. FRANCIACORTA Brut Cuvée Imperiale is flagship. New Cuvée J.R.E. N°4 Extra Brut RISERVA.

Bersano Pie ★★★ Large volume but gd quality. V.gd: BARBERA D'ASTI, Freisa, GRIGNOLINO and Ruchè, all inexpensive, delightful.

Bertani Ven ★★ →★★★ Long-est producer of VALPOLICELLA and SOAVE; v'yds in various parts of Verona province. Basic Veronese/Valpantena lines plus restoration of abandoned techniques, eg. white using skin maceration, red (Secco Bertani Original Vintage Edition). *See also* BERTANI DOMAINS (TOSCANA).

Bertani Domains (Toscana) Tus ★★–★★★ Previously Tenimenti Angelini. Angelini group has taken over name, using it for all operations incl TUS. Three major wineries: San Leonino, CHIANTI CLASSICO; Trerose, MONTEPULCIANO; Val di Suga, MONTALCINO (esp BRUNELLO Spuntali).

Biondi-Santi Tus ★★★★ Classic wines from traditional MONTALCINO estate that 1st created BRUNELLO, recently sold to Epi group (Piper-Heidsieck): Brunellos and esp RISERVAS high in acid, tannin requiring decades to develop fully. Recently trying more user-friendly style.

Bisol Ven ★★★ Top brand of PROSECCO; now owned by Lunelli family (FERRARI). Outstanding CARTIZZE. Try new labels: Prosecco SUPERIORE Rive di Campea e Rive di Guia Relio. V. interesting white from rare Dorona grape (from estate in Venissa island retreat in Venice lagoon; not part of deal with Lunelli).

Boca Pie DOC r *See* ALTO PIEMONTE. Potentially among greatest reds. NEBBIOLO (70–90%), int up to 30% Uva Rara and/or Vespolina. Volcanic soil. Needs long ageing. Best: *Le Piane.* Gd: Carlone Davide, Castello Conti.

Bolgheri Tus DOC r p w (sw) Arty walled village on w coast giving name to stylish, expensive SUPER TUSCANS, mainly French varieties. Big names: ALLEGRINI (POGGIO al Tesoro, ANTINORI (Guado al Tasso), FRESCOBALDI (ORNELLAIA), FOLONARI (Campo al Mare), GAJA (CÀ MARCANDA), Grattamacco. Outstanding Le Macchiole, MICHELE SATTA, SAN GUIDO (SASSICAIA, the original SUPER TUSCAN).

Bolla Ven ★★ Historic Verona firm for AMARONE, RECIOTO DELLA VALPOLICELLA, RECIOTO DI SOAVE, SOAVE, VALPOLICELLA. Today owned by powerful GRUPPO ITALIANO VINI.

ITALY

Borgo del Tiglio F-VG ★★★→★★★★ Nicola Manferrari is one of Italy's top white winemakers. COLLIO FRIULANO RONCO della Chiesa, MALVASIA Selezione, Studio di Bianco esp impressive.

Boscarelli, Poderi Tus ★★★ Small estate of Genovese de Ferrari family with reliably high-standard VINO NOBILE DI MONTEPULCIANO, cru Nocio dei Boscarelli, RISERVA Sotto Casa. New Costa Grande (100% SANGIOVESE).

Botte Big barrel, anything from 6–250 hl, usually between 20–50, traditionally of Slavonian but increasingly of French oak. To traditionalists, the ideal vessel for ageing wines without adding too much oak smell/taste.

Brachetto d'Acqui / Acqui Pie DOCG r sw (sp) DYA. Pink version of ASTI made with Brachetto grape; similarly undeserving for most part of its DOCG status.

Braida Pie ★★★ Giacomo Bologna's children, Giuseppe and Raffaella, continue in his footsteps: BARBERA D'ASTI Bricco dell'Uccellone remains top, backed by Bricco della Bigotta and Ai Suma. V.gd GRIGNOLINO d'Asti Limonte. Gd MOSCATO D'ASTI.

Bramaterra Pie DOC r *See* ALTO PIEMONTE. Gd: Antoniotti Odilio.

Brezza Pie ★★→★★★ Organic certified. Brezza family run Hotel BAROLO in village while Enzo B makes some of Barolo's best-value crus, incl Cannubi, Castellero, Sarmassa. Range incl BARBERA, DOLCETTO, Freisa, plus surprisingly gd CHARD and LANGHE NEBBIOLO.

Brigaldara Ven ★★★ Elegant but powerful benchmark AMARONE from estate of Stefano Cesari. Top: Case Vecie. Try charming Dindarella Rosato, when made.

Brolio, Castello di Tus ★★→★★★ Historic estate, CHIANTI CLASSICO's largest, oldest, now thriving under Francesco RICASOLI with SANGIOVESE getting chance to shine again. V.gd Chianti Classico and CC Collidelà Gran Selezione (*see* Chianti Classico box, p.132).

Brunelli, Gianni Tus ★★★ Lovely refined user-friendly BRUNELLOS (top RISERVA) and Rossos from two sites: Le Chiuse di Sotto n of MONTALCINO and Podernovone to s, with views of Monte Amiata.

Brunello di Montalcino Tus DOCG r ★★★→★★★★ 07 09 10' 12 13 (15') (16) (17) Top

---

Top Barolos

Here are a few top crus and their best producers: **Bricco Boschis** (Castiglione Falletto) CAVALLOTTO (RISERVA VIGNA San Giuseppe; **Bricco delle Viole** (BAROLO) GD VAJRA; **Bricco Rocche** (Castiglione Falletto) CERETTO; **Brunate** (La Morra, Barolo) Ceretto, GIUSEPPE RINALDI, ODDERO, VIETTI; **Bussia** (Monforte) ALDO CONTERNO (Gran Bussia e Romirasco), Poderi Colla (Dardi Le Rose), Oddero (Bussia Vigna Mondoca); **Cannubi** (Barolo) BREZZA, LUCIANO SANDRONE (Cannubi Boschis), E. Pira e Figli – Chiara Boschis; **Cerequio** (La Morra, Barolo) Boroli, Chiarlo Michele, ROBERTO VOERZIO; **Falletto** (Serralunga) BRUNO GIACOSA (Riserva Vigna Le Rocche); **Francia** (Serralunga) GIACOMO CONTERNO (Barolo Cascina Francia and Monfortino); **Ginestra** (Monforte) CONTERNO FANTINO (Sorì Ginestra and Vigna del Gris), Domenico Clerico (Ciabot Mentin); **Lazzarito** (Serralunga) ETTORE GERMANO (Riserva), VIETTI; **Monprivato** (Castiglione Falletto) GIUSEPPE MASCARELLO (Mauro); **Monvigliero** (VERDUNO) CASTELLO DI VERDUNO, COMM. GB BURLOTTO, PAOLO SCAVINO; **Ornato** (Serralunga) PIO CESARE; **Ravera** (Novello) Elvio Cogno (Bricco Pernice), GD Vajra, Vietti; **Rocche dell'Annunziata** (La Morra) Paolo Scavino (Riserva), Roberto Voerzio, Rocche Costamagna, Trediberri; **Rocche di Castiglione** (Castiglione Falletto) Brovia, Oddero, Vietti; **Vigna Rionda** (Serralunga) Massolino, Oddero; **Villero** (Castiglione Falletto) Boroli, Brovia, Giacomo Fenocchio. And the Barolo of Bartolo MASCARELLO blends together Cannubi San Lorenzo, Ruè and Rocche dell'Annunziata.

The best of Brunello

Any of the below provide a satisfying BRUNELLO DI MONTALCINO, but we have put a star next to the ones we think are best: Altesino, CASTELLO DI ARGIANO, Baricci★, BIONDI-SANTI★, GIANNI BRUNELLI★, Campogiovanni, Canalicchio di Sopra, Canalicchio di Sotto, Caparzo, CASE BASSE★, Castelgiocondo, CASTIGLION DEL BOSCO, Ciacci Piccolomini, COL D'ORCIA, Collemattoni, Colombini, Costanti, Cupano, Donatella Cinelli, Eredi, Fossacolle, Franco Pacenti, FULIGNI, Il Colle, Il Marroneto★, Il Paradiso di Manfredi, La Gerla, La Magia, La Poderina, Le Potazzine, Le Ragnaie★ LISINI★, Mastrojanni★, PIAN DELL'ORINO★, Pieri Agostina, Pieve di Santa Restituta, POGGIO ANTICO, POGGIO DI SOTTO★, San Filippo, Salvioni★, Siro Pacenti, Stella di Campalto★, TENUTA IL POGGIONE★, Tenuta di Sesta, Uccelliera, Val di Suga.

wine of TUS, dense but elegant with scent, structure; potentially v. long-lived. Min 4 yrs ageing, 5 for RISERVA. Moves to incl other grapes eg. MERLOT in this 100% SANGIOVESE have been fought off, but those producers saddled with bad v'yds keep trying to change law. (For top producers *see* box, above.)

Bucci Mar ★★★ →★★★★ Quasi-Burgundian VERDICCHIOS, slow to mature but complex with age, esp RISERVA. Red Pongelli is user-friendly, fruity. Gd ROSSO PICENO. Seek out Vintage Collection

Burlotto, Commendatore GB Pie ★★★ →★★★★ Commander GB Burlotto was one of 1st to make/bottle top BAROLO in 1880. Descendant Fabio Alessandria's best: crus Cannubi, Monvigliero and traditional Barolo Acclivi. V.gd VERDUNO Pelaverga.

Bussola, Tommaso Ven ★★★★ Self-taught maker of some of the great AMARONES, RECIOTOS, RIPASSOS of our time. The great Bepi QUINTARELLI steered him; he steers his two sons. Top TB selection.

Ca' dei Frati Lom ★ →★★ Foremost quality estate of revitalized DOC LUGANA, I Frati a fine example at entry level; *Brolettino* a superior cru.

Ca' del Baio Pie ★★→★★ Small family; best-value producer in BARBARESCO. Outstanding Asili (RISERVA too) and Pora. V.gd Vallegrande, Autinbej and LANGHE RIES.

Ca' del Bosco Lom →★★★ No 1 FRANCIACORTA estate owned by giant PINOT GR producer Santa Margherita, still run by exuberant founder Maurizio Zanella. **Outstanding classico-method fizz**, esp Annamaria Clementi (rosé too); Krug-like. Great Dosage Zero, Dosage Zero Noir Vintage Collection; top B'x-style Maurizio Zanella (r).

Ca' del Prete Pie ★★→★★★ Small estate produces great Freisa d'ASTI, MALVASIA di Castelnuovo Don Bosco.

Caiarossa Tus ★★★ Dutch-owned (Ch Giscours; *see* B'x) estate, n of BOLGHERI. Excellent Caiarossa Rosso plus reds Aria, Pergolaia.

Calcagno Si r w →★★ Outstanding family estate at top of ETNA's quality hierarchy. Outstanding Feudo di Mezzo and Rosso Arcuria. V.gd Ginestra (w) and Pomice delle Sciare (p).

Calì, Paolo Si r w ★★→★★★ Paolo C's wines express best of Vittoria area. Top: CERASUOLO DI VITTORIA Forfice, Frappato. V.gd Manene (r), GRILLO Blues (w), Osa (p).

Caluso / Erbaluce di Caluso Pie DOCG w ★ →★★★ Wines can be still, sparkling (dry) and sweet (CALUSO PASSITO). V.gd: Bruno Giacometto, Cieck (Misobolo, Brut San Giorgio). Gd: Favaro, Ferrando, Orsolani (La Rustia), Salvetti (Brut).

Ca' Marcanda Tus ★★★★ BOLGHERI estate of GAJA. Three wines in order of price (high, higher, highest): Promis, Magari, Ca' Marcanda. Grapes mainly international.

Campania The region of Naples and Vesuvius, Capri and Ischia, Amalfi and Ravello: the former "country" (*campania*) retreat of the Romans. But best wines from mtns inland. Outstanding red grape AGLIANICO; at least three fascinating whites: FALANGHINA, GRECO, FIANO all capable of freshness, complexity, character.

Prices not high. Classic DOCS: FIANO D'AVELLINO, GRECO DI TUFO, TAURASI, with newer areas emerging eg. Sannio, Benevento. Gd producers: Benito Ferrara, Caggiano, CANTINA del Taburno, Caputo, Cantine Lonardo, COLLI DI LAPIO, D'AMBRA, De Angelis, *Feudi di San Gregorio*, GALARDI, Guastaferro, LA GUARDIENSE, Luigi Tecce, Marisa Cuomo, *Mastroberardino*, Molettieri, MONTEVETRANO, Mustilli, Pietracupa, QUINTODECIMO, Terredora, Traerte, VILLA MATILDE.

Canalicchio di Sopra Tus ★★★ Dynamic Ripaccioli family make beautifully balanced, complex BRUNELLO (and RISERVA), ROSSO DI MONTALCINO. Look for new Brunello cru, Casaccia v'yd (15); outstanding Brunello (13).

Cantina A cellar, winery or even a wine bar.

Cantine del Notaio Bas ★★→★★★ Organic and bio estate specializing in AGLIANICO, incl white, rosé, sparkling and PASSITO. Star is La Firma, but super-ripe, AMARONE-like Il Sigillo almost as gd.

Capezzana, Tenuta di Tus ★★★ Noble TUS family estate, certified organic, of late legend Count Ugo Contini Bonacossi, now run by his children. Excellent CARMIGNANO (Villa di Capezzana and Selezione, Trefiano RISERVA) and exceptional VIN SANTO, one of Italy's five best.

Capichera Sar ★★★ Ragnedda family make some of SAR's best whites, noteworthy reds (Assajè CARIGNANO 100%). Outstanding Isola dei Nuraghi Bianco Santigaìni, Vendemmia Tardiva and VIGNA'ngena.

Cappellano Pie ★★★ The late Teobaldo Cappellano, a BAROLO hero, devoted part of his cru Gabutti to ungrafted NEBBIOLO (Pie Franco). Son Augusto keeps highly traditional style; also "tonic" Barolo Chinato, invented by an ancestor.

Caprai Umb ★★★→★★★★ Marco Caprai and consultant Attilio Pagli have turned large estate (nearly 200 ha) into MONTEFALCO leader. Many outstanding wines eg. 25 Anni. Non-cru Collepiano is better for less oak, while ROSSO DI MONTEFALCO is smooth, elegant. GRECHETTO Grecante is reasonably priced.

Carema Pie DOC r ★★→★★★ 07 08 09 10 11 13 15 (16) Little-known, light, intense, outstanding NEBBIOLO from steep lower Alpine slopes nr Aosta. Best: Luigi Ferrando (esp Etichetta Nera), Produttori Nebbiolo di Carema.

Carignano del Sulcis Sar DOC r p ★★→★★★ 08 09 10 12 13 14 15 (16) Mellow but intense red from SAR's sw. Best: Rocca Rubia from CS di SANTADI, Mesa, *Terre Brune*.

Carmignano Tus DOCG r ★★★ 08 09 10 11 12 13 15 Fine SANGIOVESE/B'x-grape blend invented in C20 by late Count Bonacossi of CAPEZZANA. Best: Ambra (Montalbiolo), CAPEZZANA, Farnete, Piaggia (Il Sasso), Le Poggiarelle, Pratesi (Il Circo Rosso).

Carpenè-Malvolti Ven ★★ Perhaps 1st to specialize in PROSECCO. Founded 1868 by Antonio Carpene. Range incl Brut, Dry and Extra Dry, though none is all that dry (probably a gd thing).

Carpineti, Marco Lat w sw ★★ Phenomenal bio whites from little-known Bellone and GRECO Moro, Greco Giallo varieties. Benchmark Caro and Ludum, one of Italy's best stickies.

Barolo fever: €2million+ paid for 0.5 ha of prestigious cru Cerequio (2018).

Cartizze Ven ★★ DOCG PROSECCO from hilly, steep 106 ha in heart of VALDOBBIADENE. Usually on sweet side. Best: Col Vetoraz, NINO FRANCO; gd: BISOL, Bortolomiol, Le Colture, Ruggeri.

Case Basse Tus ★★★★ Gianfranco Soldera makes mostly bio, long-oak-aged, definitive-quality BRUNELLO-style (if not DOCG) wines as before. Rare, precious.

Castel del Monte Pug DOC r p w ★→★★ (r) 10 11 13 14 (15) (p w) DYA. Dry, fresh, increasingly serious wines of mid-PUG DOC. Esp *Bocca di Lupo* from Tormaresca (ANTINORI). Il Falcone RISERVA (Rivera) is iconic.

Castel Juval, Unterortl T-AA ★★★ Owned by mountaineer Reinhold Messner. Distinctive, crystalline wines. Difficult to contact, unfortunately. Best: RIES Windbichel, WEISSBURGUNDER. V.gd PINOT N.

Castellare Tus ★★★ Classy Castellina-in-CHIANTI producer of long standing. First-rate SANGIOVESE/MALVASIA Nera I Sodi di San Niccoló and updated CHIANTI CLASSICO, esp RISERVA Il Poggiale Also POGGIO ai Merli (MERLOT), Coniale (CAB SAUV).

Castell' in Villa Tus ★★★★ Individual, traditionalist CHIANTI CLASSICO estate in extreme sw of zone. Wines of class, excellence by self-taught Princess Coralia Pignatelli. Very age-worthy. Top RISERVA.

Castelluccio E-R ★★─★★★ Quality SANGIOVESE from E-R estate of famous oenologoist Vittorio Fiore, run by son Claudio. IGT RONCO dei Ciliegi and Ronco delle Ginestre are stars. Le More is tasty, relatively inexpensive Romagna DOC.

Castiglion del Bosco Tus ★★★ Ferragamo-owned up-and-coming BRUNELLO producer.

Cataldi Madonna Ab ★★★ Organic certified. Top is PECORINO Frontone, from oldest Pecorino vines in Ab. V.gd: CERASUOLO D'ABRUZZO Piè delle Vigne, Malandrino, MONTEPULCIANO d'Ab Toni.

Cavallotto Pie ★★★ Leading BAROLO traditionalist of Castiglione Falletto, v'yds in heart of zone. Outstanding RISERVA Bricco Boschis VIGNA San Giuseppe, Riserva Vignolo, v.gd LANGHE NEBBIOLO. Surprisingly gd GRIGNOLINO, Freisa too.

Cave Mont Blanc VdA Quality co-op at foot of Mont Blanc, with ungrafted indigenous 60–100-yr-old Prie Blanc vines. Organic certified. Outstanding sparkling. Top Blanc de Morgex et de la Salle Rayon and Brut MC Extreme. V.gd Cuvée du Prince

Cerasuolo d'Abruzzo Ab DOC p ★ DYA ROSATO version of MONTEPULCIANO D'ABRUZZO, don't confuse with red CERASUOLO di VITTORIA from SI. Can be brilliant; best (by far): CATALDI MADONNA (Pie delle Vigne), EMIDIO PEPE, Praesidium, TIBERIO, VALENTINI.

Cerasuolo di Vittoria Si DOCG r ★★ 11 13 15 16 17 Potentially charming fresh red from Frappato/NERO D'AVOLA in se of island. To date, absurdly, the only SI DOCG. Try Arianna Occhipinti, COS, Gulfi, Paolo Calì, PLANETA, Valle dell'Acate.

Ceretto Pie ★★★ Leading producer of BARBARESCO (Asili, Bernradot), BAROLO (Bricco Rocche, Brunate, Prapò, Cannubi San Lorenzo), plus LANGHE Bianco Blange (ARNEIS). Older generation handing over. Organic certified and bio (60%+, from 2015). Wines recently more classic.

Cerro, Fattoria del Tus ★★★ Estate owned by insurance giant UNIPOL-SAI, making v.gd DOCG VINO NOBILE DI MONTEPULCIANO (esp cru Antica Chiusina); also owns Colpetrone (MONTEFALCO SAGRANTINO), La Poderina (BRUNELLO DI MONTALCINO), Monterufoli (MAREMMA).

Cerruti, Ezio Pie ★★─★★★ Small estate in gd area for MOSCATO: best sweet Sol, naturally dried Moscato. New Sol 10 (06 after 10 yrs of ageing). V.gd Fol (dr).

Who makes really good Chianti Classico?

CHIANTI CLASSICO is a large zone with hundreds of producers, so picking out the best is tricky. The top get a ★: AMA★, ANTINORI, BADIA A COLTIBUONO★, Bibbiano, BROLIO, Cacchiano, Cafaggio, Capannelle, Casaloste, Casa Sola, CASTELLARE, CASTELL' IN VILLA, CASTELO DI VOLPAIA★, FELSINA★, FONTERUTOLI, FONTODI★, I Fabbri★, Il Molino di Grace, ISOLE E OLENA★, Le Boncie, Le Cinciole★, Le Corti, Le Filigare, Lilliano, Mannucci Droandi, MONSANTO★, Monte Bernardi, Monteraponi★, NITTARDI, NOZZOLE, Palazzino, Paneretta, Poggerino, POGGIOPIANO, QUERCIABELLA★, Rampolla, RIECINE, Rocca di Castagnoli, Rocca di Montegrossi★, RUFFINO, San Fabiano Calcinaia, SAN FELICE, SAN GIUSTO A RENTENNANO★, Paolina Savignola, Selvole, Vecchie Terre di Montefili, Verrazzano, Vicchiomaggio, VIGNAMAGGIO, Villa Calcinaia★, Villa La Rosa★, Viticcio.

Cesanese del Piglio or Piglio Lat DOCG r ★→★★★ Medium-bodied red, gd for moderate ageing. Best: Petrucca e Vela, Terre del Cesanese. Cesanese di Olevano Romano, Cesanese di Affile are similar.

Chianti Tus DOCG r ★→★★★ Ancient region between Florence and Siena and its light red. Chianti has come a long way from the raffia-bottle-as-lamp days when it was laced with white grapes and beefed up with imports from the s. Now should be typical TUS wine at reasonable price.

Cannubi cru already famous in C18, long before delimitation of Barolo.

Chianti Classico Tus DOCG r ★★→★★★ 11 12 13 15 16 Historic CHIANTI zone became "CLASSICO" when the Chianti area was extended to most of central TUS in early C20. Covering all or part of nine communes, the land is hilly (altitude 250–500m/820–1640ft) and rocky. The "Black Rooster" wine is traditionally blended: the debate continues over whether the support grapes should be French (eg. CAB SAUV) or native. Gran Selezione is new top level, above RISERVA. *See also*, box, left.

Chiaretto Ven Pale, light-blush-hued rosé (the word means "claret"), produced esp around Lake Garda. *See* BARDOLINO.

Ciabot Berton Pie ★★★ Marco and Paola Oberto, following their father, have turned this La Morra estate into one of the best-value producers. V.gd blended BAROLO ("1961" and BAROLO del Comune di La Morra); crus Roggeri, Rocchettevino have distinctive single-v'yd characters.

Cinque Terre Lig DOC w dr sw ★★ Dry VERMENTINO-based whites from vertiginous LIG coast. Sweet version: Sciacchetrà. Try Arrigoni, Bisson, Buranco, De Battè.

Ciolli, Damiano Lat ★★★ r One of most interesting wineries in central Italy. Best is Cirsium, 100% Cesanese d'Affile, 80-yr-old vines. V.gd Silene (Cesanese d'Affile/Comune).

Cirò Cal DOC r (p) (w) ★→★★★ Brisk strong red from Cal's main grape, Gaglioppo, or light, fruity white from GRECO (DYA). Best: Caparra & Siciliani, IPPOLITO 1845, *Librandi* (Duca San Felice ★★★), San Francesco (Donna Madda, RONCO dei Quattroventi), Santa Venere.

Classico Term for wines from a restricted, usually historic and superior-quality area within limits of a commercially expanded DOC. *See* CHIANTI CLASSICO, VALPOLICELLA, VERDICCHIO, SOAVE, numerous others.

Clerico, Domenico Pie ★★★ RIP 2017, one of greatest innovators of Italian wine, modernist BAROLO producer of Monforte d'ALBA, esp crus Ginestra (Ciabot Mentin and Pajana) and Mosconi (Percristina only in best vintages). Mercifully, winemaking change towards much less oak.

Coffele Ven ★★★ Sensitive winemaker in up-and-coming SOAVE-land. Gd Soave CLASSICO, cru Ca' Visco, Alzari (100% GARGANEGA), Recioto Le Sponde.

Cogno, Elvio Pie ★★★ Top estate; super-classy, austere, elegant BAROLOS. Best: RISERVA VIGNA Elena (NEBBIOLO Rosè variety), Bricco Pernice, Ravera. V.gd Anas-Cëtta (100% Nascetta) and BARBERA D'ALBA Pre-Phylloxera (100-yr-old vines).

Col d'Orcia Tus ★★★ Top-quality MONTALCINO estate (3rd-largest) owned by Francesco Marone Cinzano. Best wine: BRUNELLO RISERVA POGGIO al Vento, new Brunello Nastagio. Col d'Orcia is valley between Montalcino and Monte Amiata.

Colla, Poderi Pie ★★★ Tino, Federica and Pietro now run this winery based on experience of Beppe Colla. Classic, traditional, age-worthy. Top: BARBARESCO Roncaglie, BAROLO Bussia Dardi Le Rose, LANGHE Bricco del Drago. V.gd Langhe NEBBIOLO and Pietro Colla Extra Brut.

Colli = hills; singular: Colle. **Colline** (singular Collina) = smaller hills. *See also* COLLIO, POGGIO.

Colli di Catone Lat ★→★★★ Top producer of FRASCATI and IGT. Outstanding aged whites from MALVASIA del Lazio (aka Malvasia Puntinata) and GRECHETTO. Look for Colle Gaio or Casa Pilozzo labels.

Colli di Lapio Cam ★★★ Clelia Romano's estate is Italy's **best Fiano** producer.

Colli di Luni Lig, Tus DOC r w ★★→★★★ Nr Spezia. VERMENTINO and Albarola whites; SANGIOVESE-based reds easy to drink, charming. Gd: Ottaviano Lambruschi (Costa Marina); Giacomelli (Boboli), La Baia del Sole (Oro d'Isèe); Bisson (VIGNA Erta).

Collio F-VG DOC r w ★★→★★★ Hilly zone on border with Slovenia. Recently in vogue for complex, sometimes deliberately oxidized whites, some vinified on skins in earthenware vessels/amphorae in ground. Some excellent, some shocking blends from various French, German, Slavic grapes. Numerous gd-to-excellent producers: Aldo Polencic, BORGO DEL TIGLIO, Castello di Spessa, LA CASTELLADA, Fiegl, GRAVNER, MARCO FELLUGA, Livon, Podversic, Primosic, Princic, *Radikon*, Renato Keber, RUSSIZ SUPERIORE, *Schiopetto*, Tercic, Terpin, Venica & Venica, VILLA RUSSIZ.

Colli Piacentini E-R DOC r p w ★→★★ DYA Light gulping wines, often fizzy, from eg. BARBERA, BONARDA (r), MALVASIA di Candia Aromatica, Pignoletto (w).

Colterenzio CS / Schreckbichl T-AA ★★→★★★ Cornaiano-based main player among ALTO ADIGE co-ops. Whites (SAUV Lafoa, CHARD Altkirch, PINOT BIANCO Weisshaus Praedium) tend to be better than reds, despite renown of CAB SAUV Lafoa.

Conegliano Valdobbiadene Ven DOCG w sp ★→★★ DYA. Name for top PROSECCO, tricky to say: may be used separately or together.

Conero DOCG r ★★→★★★ 15 17 Aka ROSSO CONERO. Small zone making powerful, at times too oaky MONTEPULCIANO. Try: GAROFOLI (Grosso Agontano), Le Terrazze (Praeludium), Marchetti (RISERVA Villa Bonomi), Moncaro, Monteschiavo (Adeodato), Moroder (Riserva Dorico), UMANI RONCHI (Riserva Campo San Giorgio).

Conterno, Aldo Pie ★★★★ Top estate of Monforte d'ALBA, was considered a traditionalist, esp concerning top BAROLOS Granbussia (outstanding 09), Cicala, Colonello and esp Romirasco.

Conterno, Giacomo Pie ★★★★ For many, top wine, Monfortino, is best wine of Italy. Roberto C sticks religiously to formula of forebears. Recently acquired Nervi estate in GATTINARA. Outstanding BARBERAS. Top BAROLO Cascina Francia, Cerretta. Waiting for Barolo Airone 15.

Conterno, Paolo Pie ★★→★★★ A family of NEBBIOLO and BARBERA growers since 1886, current *titolare* Giorgio continues with textbook cru BAROLOS Ginestra and Riva del Bric, plus particularly fine LANGHE *Nebbiolo Bric Ginestra*.

Conterno Fantino Pie ★★★ Organic certified. Two families joined to produce excellent modern-style BAROLO crus at Monforte: Ginestra (VIGNA Sorì Ginestra and Vigna del Gris), Mosconi (Vigna Ped) and Castelletto (Vigna Pressenda). Also NEBBIOLO/BARBERA blend Monprà.

Contini Sar ★★★ Benchmark VERNACCIA DI ORISTANO, oxidative-styled whites not unlike v.gd Amontillado or Oloroso. Antico Gregori one of Italy's best whites. Amazing Flor 22. V.gd Nieddera Maluentu.

Conti Zecca Pug ★★→★★★ SALENTO estate. Donna Marzia line of Salento IGT wines is gd value, as is SALICE SALENTINO Cantalupi. Best-known is Nero (NEGROAMARO/ CAB SAUV blend)

Cornelissen, Frank ★★★ From Belgium to ETNA to produce some of Italy's most interesting reds. Outstanding: NERELLO MASCALESE Magma. V.gd VA and CS (r).

Correggia, Matteo Pie r ★★★ Organic certified. Leading producer of ROERO (RISERVA Rochè d'Ampsej, Val dei Preti), Roero ARNEIS, plus BARBERA D'ALBA (Marun). Waiting for 6-y-aged Roero Arneis Val dei Preti 12.

CS (Cantina Sociale) Cooperative winery.

Cuomo, Marisa Cam ★★★ Fiorduva is one of Italy's greatest whites. V.gd Furore Bianco and Rosso (Costa d'Amalfi).

Cusumano Si ★★ →★★★ Recent major player with 500 ha in various parts of SI. Reds from NERO D'AVOLA, CAB SAUV, SYRAH; whites from CHARD, INSOLIA. Gd quality, value. Best from ETNA (Alta Mora).

Dal Forno, Romano Ven ★★★★ V.-high-quality VALPOLICELLA, AMARONE, RECIOTO (latter not identified as such any more); v'yds outside CLASSICO zone but wines great.

D'Ambra Cam r w ★★ →★★★ On ISCHIA; fosters rare local native grapes. Best: single-v'yd Frassitelli (w, 100% Biancolella). V.gd Forastera (w) and AGLIANICO-based La VIGNA dei Mille Anni (r).

De Bartoli, Marco Si ★★★ The late great Marco de Bartoli fought all his life for "real" MARSALA and against cooking or flavoured Marsala. His dry Vecchio Samperi couldn't be called "Marsala" because it wasn't fortified. Top is 20-yr-old Ventennale, a blend of old and recent wines. Delicious table wines (eg. GRILLO Vignaverde, ZIBIBBO Pietranera and Pignatello), outstanding sweet Zibibbo di PANTELLERIA *Bukkuram*.

Dei Pie ★★ →★★★ Pianist Caterina Dei runs this aristocratic estate in MONTEPULCIANO, making VINO NOBILES with artistry and passion. Her *chef d'oeuvre* is Bossona.

Derthona Pie w ★ →★★★ Timorasso grapes grown in COLLI Tortonesi. One of Italy's unique whites (like v. dry RIES from Rheinhessen). Gd: POGGIO Paolo, Mariotto, La Colombera, Mutti, VIGNETI MASSA.

Di Majo Norante Mol ★★ →★★★ Best-known of Mol with decent Biferno Rosso Ramitello, Don Luigi Molise Rosso RISERVA, Mol AGLIANICO Contado. Whites uninteresting; MOSCATO PASSITO Apianae quite gd.

DOC / DOCG Quality wine designation: *see box, p.125.*

Dogliani Pie DOCG r ★ →★★★ 12 13 15 16 (17) DOLCETTO monovariety wine. Some to drink young, some for moderate ageing. Gd: Chionetti, Clavesana, EINAUDI, Francesco Boschis, Marziano Abbona, Pecchenino.

Donnafugata Si r w ★★ →★★★ Classy range. Reds Mille e Una Notte, Tancredi; whites Chiaranda, Lighea. Also v. fine MOSCATO PASSITO di PANTELLERIA Ben Ryé.

Duca di Salaparuta Si ★★ Its Corvo more listed in every Italian restaurant abroad. Now owned by Ilva of Saronno. More upscale wines incl, w Kados from GRILLO grapes and INSOLIA (Colomba Platino), r NERELLO MASCALESE Làvico and NERO D'AVOLA Suormarchesa. Plus old favourite Duca Enrico.

Einaudi, Luigi Pie ★★★ 52-ha estate founded late C19 by ex-president of Italy, in DOGLIANI. Solid BAROLOS from Cannubi and Terlo Costa Grimaldi v'yds. Top Dogliani (DOLCETTO) from VIGNA Tecc. Now also in Bussia, Monviglieri.

Elba Tus r w (sp) ★ →★★★ DYA. Island's white, TREBBIANO/ANSONICA, can be v. drinkable with fish. Dry reds are based on SANGIOVESE. Gd sweet white (MOSCATO) and red (*Aleatico Passito DOCG*). Gd: Acquabona, La Mola, Ripalte, Sapereta.

Enoteca Wine library; also shop or restaurant with ambitious wine list. There is a national enoteca at the *fortezza* in Siena.

Est! Est!! Est!!! Lat DOC w dr s/sw ★ DYA. Unextraordinary white from Montefiascone, n of Rome.

Etna Si DOC r p w ★★ →★★★ (r) 12 13 14 15 16 (17) Wine from high-altitude, volcanic, n slopes, currently right on trend. New money brings flurry of planting and some excellent (and some overrated) wines. Burgundy-styled, but based on NERELLO MASCALESE (r) and CARRICANTE (w). For red try: Benanti, Calcagno (Arcuria), Cottanera, Girolamo Russo, Graci (Quota 600), I Vigneri (Vinupetra), Franchetti (formerly Passopisciaro), TASCA D'ALMERITA, TENUTA delle TERRE NERE. For white try: Barone di Villagrande (EBS), BENANTI (EBS – Pietramarina), Femina (Patria), Fessina (EB – Bianco A' Puddara), Girolamo Russo, I Vigneri (EB – Aurora), TERRE NERE.

Falchini Tus ★★ →★★★ Producer of gd DOCG VERNACCIA DI SAN GIMIGNANO.

Falerno del Massico Cam ★★ →★★★ DOC r w ★★ (r) 13 15 Falernum was the Yquem of ancient Rome. Today only so-so. Best are elegant AGLIANICO reds, fruity dry FALANGHINA whites. Try: Masseria Felicia, VILLA MATILDE.

Fara Pie *See* ALTO PIEMONTE.

Faro Si DOC r ★★★ 12 13 14 15 16 (17) Intense, harmonious red from NERELLO MASCALESE, NERO D'AVOLA and Nocera in hills behind Messina. Palari most famous, but Bonavita, Le Casematte and Cuppari just as gd if not better.

Felluga, Livio F-VG ★★★ Consistently fine FRIULI COLLI ORIENTALI wines, esp blends Terre Alte and Abbazia di Rosazzo; *Pinot Gr*, PICOLIT (Italy's best?), MERLOT/ REFOSCO blend Sossó.

Felluga, Marco F-VG *See* RUSSIZ SUPERIORE.

Felsina Tus ★★★ CHIANTI CLASSICO estate of distinction in se corner of zone: classic RISERVA Rancia, IGT Fontalloro, both 100% SANGIOVESE. V.gd Maestro Raro (CAB SAUV).

Fenocchio Giacomo Pie ★★★ Small but outstanding Monforte d'ALBA-based BAROLO cellar. Traditional style. Crus: Bussia, Cannubi, Villero. Top: Bussia 90 Dì RISERVA.

Ferrara, Benito Cam ★★★ Maybe Italy's best GRECO DI TUFO producer (VIGNA Cicogna and Terra d'Uva). Talent shows in excellent TAURASI too.

Ferrari T-AA sp ★★★★★★ Trento maker of one of two best Italian METODO CLASSICO wines. Giulio Ferrari is top. New outstanding Giulio Ferrari Rosè. Also gd: CHARD-based Brut RISERVA Lunelli, new Perlè Bianco (gd value), PINOT N-based Extra Brut Perlè Nero.

Ferraris, Luca Pie r ★★★★ Top producer of Ruchè di Castagnole MONFERRATO. Top Opera Prima and VIGNA del Parroco. V.gd Clàsic.

Feudi di San Gregorio Cam ★★★★★★ Much-hyped CAM producer, with DOCGS FIANO DI AVELLINO Pietracalda, GRECO DI TUFO Cutizzi, TAURASI Piano di Montevergine. Also gd: Serpico (AGLIANICO); whites *Campanaro* (Fiano/Greco), FALANGHINA.

What to drink with *bollito alla Piemontese*? Barbera, Freisa or Alta Langa sparkler.

Feudo di San Maurizio VdA ★★★★ Outstanding wines from rare native grapes CORNALIN, Mayolet and Vuillermin; last two rank among Italy's greatest reds. V.gd Petite ARVINE.

Feudo Montoni Si r w ★★★★ Exceptional estate in upland e Sicily. Best: NERO D'AVOLA Lagnusa and Vrucara. V.gd GRILLO della Timpa (w) and Perricone del Core (r).

Fiano di Avellino Cam DOCG w ★★★★★★ 10 12 15 16 Can be either steely (most typical) or lush. Volcanic soils best. Gd: Ciro Picariello, COLLI di Lapio-Romana Clelio, MASTROBERARDINO, Pietracupa, QUINTODECIMO, Vadiaperti, Villa Diamante.

Fino, Gianfranco Pug ★★★★ Greatest PRIMITIVO, from old, low-yielding bush vines. Outstanding Es among Italy's top 20 reds. V.gd Jo (NEGROAMARO).

Florio Si Historic quality maker of MARSALA. Specialist in Marsala Vergine Secco. For some reason Terre Arse (= burnt lands), its best wine, doesn't do well in the UK.

Folonari Tus ★★★★★★ Ambrogio Folonari and son Giovanni, ex-RUFFINO, have v'yds in TUS and elsewhere. Estates/wines incl *Cabreo* (CHARD and SANGIOVESE, CAB SAUV), Gracciano Svetoni (VINO NOBILE DI MONTEPULCIANO), La Fuga (BRUNELLO DI MONTALCINO), NOZZOLE (incl top Cab Sauv Pareto). Also wines from BOLGHERI, FRIULI COLLI ORIENTALI, MONTECUCCO.

Fongaro Ven ★★★★ Classic-method fizz Lessini Durello (Durello = grape). High quality, even higher acidity, age-worthy.

Fontana Candida Lat ★★ Biggest producer of once-fashionable FRASCATI. Single-v'yd Santa Teresa much lauded, and that's Frascati's big problem in a nutshell. Part of huge GIV.

Fontanafredda Pie ★★ Large producer of PIE wines on former royal estates, incl BAROLOs. V.gd Barolo La Rosa, Alta Langa Brut Nature VIGNA Gatinera and LANGHE Freisa.

Fonterutoli Tus ★★★ Historic CHIANTI CLASSICO estate of Mazzei family at Castellina

Notable: Castellodi Fonterutoli (once v. dark, oaky, now more drinkable), IGT Mix 36 (SANGIOVESE), Siepi (Sangiovese/MERLOT). Also owns TENUTA di Belguardo in MAREMMA (gd MORELLINO DI SCANSANO) and Zisola in SI.

Fontodi Tus ★★★★ One of v. best CHIANTI CLASSICOS, also Gran Selezione VIGNA del Sorbo and memorable all-SANGIOVESE Flaccianello. IGTS PINOT N, SYRAH Case Via among best of these varieties in TUS. Experimental fermentation in ceramic; resultant wine called Dino (v. limited production).

Foradori T-AA ★★★ Elizabeth F pioneer for 30 yrs, mainly via great red grape of TRENTINO, **Teroldego**. Now she ferments in *anfore*, with reds like Morei, Sgarzon and whites like Nosiola Fontanasanta. Top wine remains TEROLDEGO-based Granato.

Franciacorta Lom DOCG w (p) sp ★★→★★★★ Italy's zone for top-quality METODO CLASSICO fizz. Best: Barone Pizzini, Bellavista, **Ca' del Bosco**, Cavalleri, Uberti, Villa. Also v.gd: Bersi Serlini, Contadi Castaldi, Gatti, Monte Rossa, Mosnel, Ricci Curbastro.

Frascati Lat DOC w dr sw s/sw (sp) ★→★★ DYA. Best-known wine of Roman hills. MALVASIA di Candia and/or TREBBIANO Toscano. Most is disappointingly neutral. Gd stuff is Malvasia del Lazio (aka M Puntinata), low crop makes it uncompetitive. Look for Castel de Paolis, Conte Zandotti, Santa Teresa, Villa Simone, from FONTANA CANDIDA or Colle Gaio from COLLI DI CATONE, 100% Malvasia del Lazio though IGT.

Frascole Tus ★★ →★★★★ Most n winery of most n CHIANTI RÚFINA zone, small estate run organically by Enrico Lippi, with an eye for typicity. Chianti Rúfina is main driver, but VIN SANTO is to die for.

Frescobaldi Tus ★★ →★★★★ Ancient noble family, leading CHIANTI RÚFINA pioneer at NIPOZZANO estate (look for ★★★**Montesodi**), also BRUNELLO from Castelgiocondo estate in MONTALCINO. Sole owners of LUCE estate (MONTALCINO), ORNELLAIA (BOLGHERI), new TENUTA Perano (CHIANTI CLASSICO). V'yds also in COLLIO, MAREMMA, Montespertoli, Gorgona Island.

Friuli Colli Orientali F-VG DOC r w dr sw (p) (Was COLLI Orientali del Friuli.) The e hills of F-VG, on Slovenian border. Zone similar to COLLIO but less experimental, making more reds and stickies. Top: Aquila del Torre, Ermacora, Gigante, Grillo Iole, La Busa dal Lôf, La Sclusa, LIVIO FELLUGA, Meroi, Miani, Moschioni, Petrussa, Rodaro, Ronchi di Cialla, RONCO del Gnemiz, VIGNA Petrussa. Sweet from VERDUZZO grapes (called Ramandolo if from specific DOCG zone: Anna Berra best) or PICOLIT grapes (Aquila del Torre, Livio Felluga, Marco Sara, Ronchi di Cialla, Vigna Petrussa) can be amazing.

Friuli Grave F-VG DOC r w ★→★★ (r) **12** 15 16 Previously Grave del Friuli. Largest DOC of F-VG, mostly on plains. Big volumes of underwhelming wines. Exceptions from Borgo Magredo, Di Lenardo, RONCO Cliona, San Simone, Villa Chiopris.

Friuli Isonzo F-VG DOC r w ★★★ Used to be just Isonzo. Gravelly, well-aired river plain with many varietals and blends. Stars mostly white, scented, structured: JERMANN'S Vintage Tunina; LIS NERIS' Gris, Tal Luc and Lis; RONCO del Gelso's MALVASIA, PINOT GRIGIO (Sot lis rivis) and FRIULANO (Toc Bas); VIE DI ROMANS' Flors di Uis and Dessimis. Gd: Borgo Conventi, Pierpaolo Pecorari.

Friuli-Venezia Giulia F-VG Ne region of Italy. Wine-wise best in hills on Slovenian border rather than alluvial plains to w. DOCS like ISONZO, COLLI ORIENTALI, Latisana, Aquileia all now preceded on label by "Friuli". Only COLLIO, theoretically best, keeps old name. Some gd reds, but home to Italy's best whites, along with ALTO ADIGE.

Frizzante Semi-sparkling, up to 2.5 atmospheres, eg. MOSCATO D'ASTI, much PROSECCO, LAMBRUSCO and the like.

Fucci, Elena Bas ★★★★ AGLIANICO DEL VULTURE Titolo from 55–70-yr-old vines in

Mt Vulture's Grand Cru; one of Italy's 20 best. Organic. Seek out 08 11 and outstanding 13 15 (also SUPERIORE RISERVA).

Fuligni Tus ★★★★ Outstanding BRUNELLO producer (also RISERVA), ROSSO DI MONTALCINO.

Gaja Pie ★★★★ Old family firm at BARBARESCO led by eloquent Angelo Gaja; daughter Gaia G following. High quality, higher prices. Top: Barbaresco (Costa Russi, Sorì San Lorenzo, Sorì Tildìn), BAROLO (Conteisa, Sperss). Splendid CHARD (Gaia e Rey). Also owns CA' MARCANDA in BOLGHERI, Pieve di Santa Restituta in MONTALCINO.

Galardi Cam ★★★ Producer of Terra di Lavoro, much-awarded AGLIANICO/Piedirosso blend, in n CAM. Makes only one wine.

Gancia Pie Famous old brand of MUSCAT fizz, also ALTA LANGA; still gd.

Garda Ven DOC r p w ★ →★★ (r) 13 15 16 (p w) DYA. Catch-all DOC for early-drinking wines of various colours from provinces of Verona in Ven, Brescia and Mantua in Lom. Gd: Cavalchina, Zeni.

Garofoli Mar ★★ →★★★ Quality leader in the Mar, specialist in VERDICCHIO (Podium, Serra Fiorese and sparkling Brut Riserva), CONERO (Grosso Agontano).

Gattinara Pie DOCG r 11 12 13 15 Best-known of a cluster of ALTO PIE DOC(G)s based on NEBBIOLO. Volcanic soil. Suitable for long ageing. Best: Antoniolo (Osso San Grato, San Francesco), Iarretti Paride, Nervi, Torraccia del Piantavigna, Travaglini (RISERVA and Tre Vigne). *See also* ALTO PIEMONTE.

Gavi / Cortese di Gavi Pie DOCG w ★ →★★★ DYA. At best, subtle dry white of Cortese grapes, though much is dull, simple or sharp. Most comes from commune of Gavi, now known as Gavi del Comune di Gavi. Best: *Bruno Broglia*/La Meirana, Castellari Bergaglio (Rovereto Vignavecchia and Rolona, Fornaci v.gd Gavi di Tassarolo), Franco Martinetti, La Raia, TENUTA San Pietro, Villa Sparina.

When in Rome: beware clip joints in Trastevere; just follow the local lunchers.

Germano, Ettore Pie ★★★ Small family Serralunga estate run by Sergio and wife Elena. Top BAROLOS: RISERVA Lazzarito and Cerretta. Look for 1st cru VIGNA Rionda. V.gd: LANGHE RIE. Herzù and ALTA LANGA.

Ghemme Pie DOCG r NEBBIOLO (at least 85%), incl up to 15% Uva Rara and/or Vespolina. Top: *Antichi Vigneti di Cantalupo* (Collis Braclemae and Collis Carellae), Ioppa (Balsina). V.gd Torraccia del Piantavigna (VIGNA Pelizzane). *See also* ALTO PIEMONTE.

Giacosa, Bruno Pie ★★★★ RIP 2018. Italy's greatest winemaker? Splendid traditional-style BARBARESCOS (Asili, Rabajà), BAROLOS (Falletto, Falletto VIGNA Rocche). Top wines (ie. RISERVAS) get famous red label. Range of fine reds (BARBERA, DOLCETTO, NEBBIOLO), amazing METODO CLASSICO Brut and ROERO ARNEIS (w)

GIV (Gruppo Italiano Vini) Complex of co-ops and wineries, biggest v'yd holders in Italy: Bigi, BOLLA, Ca'Bianca, Conti Serristori, FONTANA CANDIDA, Lamberti Macchiavelli, MELINI, Negri, Santi, Vignaioli di San Floriano. Also in s: SI, Bas.

Grappa Pungent spirit made from grape pomace (skins, etc., after pressing), can be anything from disgusting to inspirational. What the French call "marc".

Grasso, Elio Pie ★★★ →★★★★ Tiptop BAROLO producer (crus Gavarini VIGNA Chiniera Ginestra Casa Maté and RISERVA Rüncot); v.gd BARBERA D'ALBA Vigna Martina DOLCETTO d'Alba.

Gravner, Josko F-VG ★★★ →★★★★ Controversial but talented COLLIO producer (unlike some who copy him), vinifies on skins (r w) in buried amphorae without temperature control; long ageing, bottling without filtration. Wines either loved for complexity or loathed for oxidation and phenolic components. Look out for Breg (white blend) and RIBOLLA GIALLA 2006 for something different.

Greco di Tufo Cam DOCG w (sp) DYA. Better versions are among Italy's best whites. V.gd examples from Bambinuto (Picoli), Caggiano (Devon), COLLI di Lapio (Alexandros) Donnachiara, Ferrara Benito (VIGNA Cicogna), FEUDI DI SAN GREGORIO

(Cutizzi), Macchialupa, **Mastroberardino** (Nova Serra, Vignadangelo), Pietracupa, QUINTODECIMO, Vadiaperti (Tornante).

Grifalco Bas ★★★ Small estate in high-quality Ginestra and Maschito subzone. Best: AGLIANICO DEL VULTURE Daginestra, Damaschito (SUPERIORE DOCG from 15).

Grignolino Pie DOC r DYA. Two DOCS: Grignolino d'ASTI, Grignolino del MONFERRATO Casalese. At best, light, perfumed, crisp, high in acidity, tannin. D'Asti: try BRAIDA, Cascina Tavijin, Crivelli, Incisa della Rocchetta, Spertino. MONFERRATO C: try Accornero (Bricco del Bosco and Bricco del Bosco Vigne Vecchie – vinified like BAROLO), Bricco Mondalino, Canato (Celio), Il Mongetto, PIO CESARE.

Grosjean VdA r ★★★ Top quality; best CORNALIN, Premetta. Vigne Rovettaz one of Valle's oldest, largest.

Guardiense, La Cam ★★→★★★ Dynamic co-op, decent-value whites (FALANGHINA Senete, FIANO COLLI di Tilio, GRECO Pietralata) and reds (esp I Mille per l'AGLIANICO); World's largest producer of Falanghina, but that in itself means little.

Guerrieri Rizzardi Ven ★★→★★★ Long-est aristocratic producers of wines of Verona, esp of Veronese GARDA. Gd BARDOLINO CLASSICO Tacchetto, elegant AMARONE Villa Rizzardi and cru Calcarole, and ROSATO Rosa Rosae. V.gd SOAVE Classico Costeggiola. Historic garden.

Gulfi Si ★★★ SI's best producer of NERO D'AVOLA, 1st to bottle single-*contrada* (cru) wines. Organic certified. Outstanding: Nerobufaleffj and Nerosanlorè. V.gd: CERASUOLO DI VITTORIA CLASSICO, Nerobaronj, Nerojbleo. Interesting Pinò (PINOT N).

Gutturnio dei Colli Piacentini E-R DOC r dr ★→★★ DYA. BARBERA/BONARDA blend from COLLI PIACENTINI; sometimes frothing.

Haas, Franz T-AA ★★★ ALTO ADIGE producer of excellence and occasional inspiration; v.gd PINOT N, LAGREIN (Schweizer), IGT blends, esp Manna (w). Best: MOSCATO Rosa.

Hofstätter T-AA ★★★ Top quality; gd PINOT N. Look for Barthenau VIGNA Sant'Urbano. Also whites, mainly GEWURZ (esp *Kolbehof*, one of Italy's two best). Now owner of Mosel's Dr. Fischer.

IGT (Indicazione Geografica Tipica) Increasingly known as Indicazione Geografica Protetta (IGP). *See* box, p.125.

Ippolito 1845 Cal ★→★★ This CIRÒ Marina-based winery claims to be oldest in Cal. Run quasi-organically, international and indigenous grapes. Top: Cirò RISERVA COLLI del Mancuso, Pecorello Bianco and GRECO Bianco (Gemma del Sole).

Ischia Cam DOC (r) w ★→★★ DYA. Island off Naples, own grape varieties (w: Biancolella, Forastera; r: Piedirosso, also found in Cam). Frassitelli v'yd best for Biancolella. Best: Cenatiempo (Kalimera), D'Ambra (Biancolella Frassitelli, Forastera), Antonio Mazzella (VIGNA del Lume).

Isole e Olena Tus ★★★★ Top CHIANTI CLASSICO estate run by astute Paolo de Marchi, with superb red IGT Cepparello. Outstanding VIN SANTO; v.gd CHIANTI CLASSICO, CAB SAUV, CHARD, SYRAH. Also owns fantastic Proprietà Sperino in LESSONA.

Jermann, Silvio F-VG ★★→★★★ Famous estate with v'yds in COLLIO and ISONZO: top white blend Vintage Tunina and Capo Martino. V.gd Vinnae (mainly RIBOLLA GIALLA) and "Where Dreams …" (CHARD).

Köfererhof T-AA ★★→★★★ Great whites: KERNER, SYLVANER; MÜLLER-T excellent too.

Lacrima di Morro d'Alba Mar DYA. Curiously named aromatic medium-bodied red from small commune in the Mar, no connection with ALBA or La Morra (PIE). Gd: Mario Lucchetti (SUPERIORE Guardengo), Marotti Campi (SUPERIORE Orgiolo and Rubico), Stefano Mancinelli (Superiore, Sensazioni di Frutto) and Vicari. For PASSITO: Lucchetti, Stefano Mancinelli (Re Sole).

Lacryma (or Lacrima) Christi del Vesuvio Cam r p w dr (sw) (sp) ★→★★ DOC Vesuvio wines based on Coda di Volpe (w), Piedirosso (r). Despite romantic name Vesuvius comes nowhere nr ETNA in quality stakes. Sorrentino and De Angelis best; Caputo, MASTROBERARDINO, Terredora less inspired.

Lageder, Alois T-AA ★★→★★★ Famous ALTO ADIGE producer. Most exciting are single-v'yd varietals: *Sauv Bl Lehenhof*, PINOT GR Benefizium Porer, CHARD Löwengang, GEWURZ Am Sand, PINOT N Krafuss, LAGREIN Lindenberg, CAB SAUV Cor Römigberg. Also owns Cason Hirschprunn for v.gd IGT blends.

Lagrein Alto Adige T-AA DOC r p ★★→★★★ 11 12 13 15 (16) Alpine red with deep colour, rich palate (plus a bitter hit at back); refreshing pink *Kretzer rosé* made with LAGREIN. Top ALTO ADIGE: CS Andriano, C Bolzano, C Santa Maddalena, LAGEDER, MURI GRIES (cru Abtei), Niedermayr, Niedrist Ignaz, Plattner, Elena Walch. From TRENTINO try Francesco Moser's Deamater.

Lambrusco E-R DOC (or not) r p w dr s/sw ★→★★★ DYA. "Lambrusco" does not exist: rather there are 17 different LAMBRUSCO varieties (all giving distinct wines) and a plethora of different denominations. Once v. popular fizzy red from nr Modena, mainly in industrial, semi-sweet, non-DOC version. Should be fresh, lively, *combine magically with rich* E-R fare. DOCs: L Grasparossa di Castelvetro, L Salamino di Santa Croce, L di Sorbara. Best: [Sorbara] Cavicchioli (VIGNA del Cristo Secco and Vigna del Cristo Rose), Cleto Chiarli (Antica Modena Premium), Paltrinieri. Grasparossa: Cleto Chiarli (VIGNETO Enrico Cialdini), Moretto (Monovitigno and Vigna Canova), Pederzana (Canto Libero Semi Secco), Vittorio Graziano (Fontana dei Boschi). Maestri: Ceci (Nero di Lambrusco Otello), Dall'Asta (Mefistofele). Salamino: Cavicchioli (Tre Medaglie Semi Secco), Luciano Saetti (Vigneto Saetti), Medici Ermete (Concerto Grancomcerto).

Langhe Pie The hills of central PIE, home of BAROLO, BARBARESCO, etc. DOC name for several Pie varietals plus Bianco and Rosso blends. Those wishing to blend other grapes with NEBBIOLO can at up to 15% as "Langhe Nebbiolo" – a label to follow.

Langhe Nebbiolo Pie ★★ Like NEBBIOLO D'ALBA (Nebbiolo > 85%) but from a wider area: LANGHE hills. Unlike N d'Alba may be used as a downgrade from BAROLO or BARBARESCO. Gd: BURLOTTO, GIUSEPPE RINALDI, PIO CESARE, *Vajra*.

Le Piane Pie ★★★ BOCA DOC has resurfaced thanks to Christoph Kunzli. Gd: Maggiorina, Piane (Croatina) and Mimmo (NEBBIOLO/Croatina).

Les Cretes VdA ★★★ Costantino Charrère is father of modern VALLE D'AOSTA viticulture and saved many forgotten varieties. *Outstanding Petite Arvine*, two of Italy's best CHARDS; v.gd Fumin, NEBBIOLO Sommet and Neige d'Or (w blend).

Lessona Pie DOCG r *See* ALTO PIEMONTE. NEBBIOLO (at least 85%). Elegant, age-worthy, fine bouquet, long savoury taste. Best: Proprietà SPERINO. Gd: Cassina, Colombera & Garella, La Prevostura, TENUTE Sella.

Librandi Cal ★★★ Top producer pioneering research into Cal varieties. V.gd red CIRÒ (*Riserva Duca San Felice* is ★★★), IGT Gravello (CAB SAUV/Gaglioppo blend), Magno Megonio (r) from Magliocco grape, IGT Efeso (w) from Mantonico.

Liguria Lig r w sw ★→★★ Steep, rocky Italian riviera: most wines sell to sun-struck tourists at fat profits, so don't travel much. Main white grapes: VERMENTINO (best are Lambruschi, Giacomelli, La Baia del Sole); Pigato (best are Bio Vio and Lupi). Don't miss CINQUE TERRE's Sciacchetrà (sw); Ormeasco di Pornassio and ROSSESE DI DOLCEACQUA (r).

Lisini Tus ★★★→★★★★ Historic estate for some of finest, longest-lasting BRUNELLO esp RISERVA Ugolaia.

Lis Neris F-VG ★★★ Top ISONZO estate for whites esp PINOT GR (Gris), SAUV BL (Picol), FRIULANO (Fiore di Campo), plus outstanding blends Confini and Lis. V.gd Lis Neris Rosso (MERLOT/CAB SAUV), sweet white Tal Luc (VERDUZZO/RIES).

Lo Triolet VdA r w ★★★ Top PINOT GR, v.gd Fumin, Coteau Barrage (SYRAH/Fumin), MUSCAT, Mistigri (sw).

Luce Tus ★★★ FRESCOBALDI now sole owner (formerly shared with Mondavi). Luce (SANGIOVESE/MERLOT blend for oligarchs), but lovely Luce BRUNELLO DI MONTALCINO too. From 15 Lux Vitis (blend CAB SAUV/Sangiovese).

Lugana DOC w (sp) ★★→★★★ DYA. Much-improved white of s Lake Garda, rivals gd SOAVE next door. Main grape Turbiana (Formerly TREBBIANO di Lugana). Best: CA DEI FRATI (I Frati esp Brolettino), Fratelli Zeni, Le Morette (owned by Valerio ZENATO), Ottella (Brut, Le Crete), Zenato (oaked).

Lungarotti Umb ★★ →★★★ Leading producer of TORGIANO. Star wines DOC Rubesco, DOCG RISERVA *Monticchio*. Gd VIGNA Il Pino, Sangiorgio (SANGIOVESE/CAB SAUV), Giubilante, MONTEFALCO SAGRANTINO.

Macchiole, Le Tus ★★★★ Organic. One of few native-owned wineries of BOLGHERI; one of 1st to emerge after SASSICAIA. Cinzia Merli, with oenologist Luca Rettondini, makes *Italy's best Cab Fr* (Paleo Rosso), one of best MERLOTS (Messorio), SYRAHS (Scrio). V.gd Bolgheri Rosso.

Maculan Ven ★★★ Quality pioneer of Ven, Fausto Maculan continues to make excellent CAB SAUV (Fratta, Palazzotto). Perhaps best-known for sweet TORCOLATO (esp RISERVA Acininobili).

Malvasia delle Lipari Si DOC w sw ★★★ Luscious sweet wine, made with one of the many MALVASIA varieties. Best: Capofaro, Caravaglio, Fenech, Lantieri, Marchetta. Gd: Hauner.

Manduria (Primitivo di) Pug DOC r s/sw ★★→★★★ Manduria is the spiritual home of PRIMITIVO, alias ZIN, so expect wines that are gutsy, alcoholic, sometimes porty, to go with full-flavoured fare. Best: GIANFRANCO FINO, Gd producers, located in Manduria or not: Cantele, CS Manduria, de Castris, Morella, Polvanera, Racemi.

Manni Nössing T-AA ★★★ Outstanding KERNER, MÜLLER-T Sass Rigais, SYLVANER. Benchmark wines.

White truffles are tough on wine: drink Barbera rather than Barolo.

Marcato Ven New owner Gianni Tessari likely to improve already v.gd Lessini Durello sparklers and Durella PASSITO stickie.

Marchesi di Barolo Pie ★→★★ Large, historic BAROLO producer, making crus Cannubi, Coste di Rose and Sarmassa, plus other ALBA wines.

Maremma Tus Fashionable coastal area of s TUS, largely recovered from grazing and malarial marshland in early C20. DOC(G)s: MONTEREGIO, MORELLINO DI SCANSANO, PARRINA, Pitigliano, SOVANA (Grosseto) Maremma Toscana IGT, more recently Maremma Toscana DOC.

Marrone, Agricola Pie ★★★ Small estate, low price but gd-quality BAROLO. Top: Bussia. Gd: ARNEIS, BARBERA D'ALBA, BAROLO Pichemej.

Marsala Si DOC w sw SI's once-famous fortified (★→★★★★), created by Woodhouse Bros of Liverpool in 1773. Downgraded in C20 to cooking wine (no longer qualifies for DOC). Can be dry to v. sweet; best is bone-dry Marsala Vergine. *See also* DE BARTOLI.

Marzemino Trentino T-AA DOC r ★→★★ Pleasant everyday red. Isera and Ziresi are subzones. Best: Bruno Grigoletti, Conti Bossi Fredrigotti, Eugenio Rosi (Poiema), Riccardo Battistotti. Gd: De Tarczal, Enrico Spagnolli, Letrari, Longariva, Vallarom, VallisAgri (VIGNA Fornas).

Mascarello Pie The name of two top producers of BAROLO: the late Bartolo M, of Barolo, whose daughter Maria Teresa continues her father's highly traditional path (v.gd Freisa); and Giuseppe M, of Monchiero, whose son Mauro makes v. fine, traditional-style Barolo from the great *Monprivato* v'yd in Castiglione Falletto. Both deservedly iconic.

Masi Ven ★★→★★★★ Archetypal yet innovative producer of the wines of Verona, led by inspirational Sandro Boscaini. V.gd Rosso Veronese *Campo Fiorin* and Osar (Oseleta). Top AMARONES Costasera, Mazzon, Campolongo di Torbe. New F-VG Moxxé fizz from PINOT GRIGIO/partly dried VERDUZZO.

Massa, Vigneti Pie ★★★ Walter Massa brought the Timorasso (w) grape back from nr-extinction. Top: Coste del Vento, Montecitorio, Sterpi. Gd: BARBERA Bigolla, Monleale.

Massolino Vigna Rionda Pie ★★★ One of finest BAROLO estates, in Serralunga. Excellent Parafada, Margheria have firm structure, fruity drinkability; long-ageing VIGNA RIONDA best. V.gd Parussi. New LANGHE RIES from 19.

Mastroberardino Cam ★★★ Historic top-quality producer of mountainous Avellino province in CAM. Top *Taurasi* (look for Historia Naturalis, Radici), also FIANO DI AVELLINO (More Maiorum and new Stilèma), GRECO DI TUFO Nova Serra. Antonio M essentially saved Fiano (if not Greco too) from extinction.

Melini Tus ★★ Major producer of CHIANTI CLASSICO at Poggibonsi, part of GIV. Gd quality/price, esp Chianti Classico Selvanella.

Meroi F-VG ★★★ Dynamic estate. Top FRIULANO, MALVASIA Zittelle Durì, RIBOLLA GIALLA, SAUV BL Zitelle Barchetta.

Metodo classico or tradizionale Italian for "Champagne method".

Mezzacorona T-AA ★ ★★ Massive TRENTINO co-op in commune of Mezzocorona (sic) with wide range of gd technical wines, esp TEROLDEGO ROTALIANO Nos and METODO CLASSICO Rotari.

Miani F-VG ★★★ Enzo Pontoni is Italy's best white winemaker. Top: FRIULANO (Buri and Filip), RIBOLLA GIALLA Pettarin, SAUV BL Zitelle. V.gd: SAUV BL Saurint, CHARD Zitelle, MERLOT, REFOSCO Buri.

Mogoro, Cantina di Sar ★★→★★★ 450 ha+ and 900,000 bottles/yr of high-quality wine from co-op. Rare producer of Semidano (w) variety. Best: Monica San Bernardino and Semidano SUPERIORE Puistéris. V.gd NURAGUS Ajò.

Mollettieri, Salvatore Cam ★★★ Outstanding: TAURASI, RISERVA VIGNA Cinque Querce. Gd FIANO DI AVELLINO Apianum.

Monaci Pug r p ★★→★★★ Part of GIV. Characterful NEGROAMARO Kreos (p), PRIMITIVO Artas and SALICE SALENTINO Aiace (r).

Monferrato Pie DOC r p w sw ★→★★ Hills between River Po and Apennines. Some of Italy's most delicious and fairly priced wines from typical local grapes BARBERA, Freisa, GRIGNOLINO, MALVASIA di Casorzo and Malvasia di Schierano, Ruché di Castagnole Monferrato.

Monica di Sardegna Sar DOC r ★→★★★ DYA. Delightfully perfumed, medium-weight wines. Same grape also DOC in Cagliari. Best: ARGIOLAS (Iselis), CANTINA DI MOGORO, CANTINA SANTADI (Antigua), CONTINI, Dettori (Chimbanta), Ferruccio Deiana (Karel), Josto Puddu (Torremora).

Monsanto Tus ★★★ Esteemed CHIANTI CLASSICO estate, esp for Il POGGIO RISERVA (1st single-v'yd Chianti Classico), Chianti Classico (RISERVA and Fabrizio Bianchi), Nemo (CAB SAUV).

Montagnetta, La Pie ★★→★★★ Arguably Italy's best producer of many different Freisas. V.gd: Freisa d'ASTI SUPERIORE Bugianen.

Montalcino Tus Hilltop town in province of Siena, fashionable and famous for concentrated, expensive BRUNELLO and more approachable, better-value ROSSO DI MONTALCINO, both still 100% SANGIOVESE. (Purists resent occasional efforts by big players to squeeze a bit of MERLOT into the Rosso.)

Drink with vitello tonnato or bagna cauda: Grignolino d'Asti/Monferrato Casalese.

Montecarlo Tus DOC r w ★★ (w) DYA. White (increasingly red) wine area nr Lucca.

Monte Carrubo Si r ★★★ Pioneer Peter Vinding-Diers planted SYRAH on a former volcano s of ETNA. Exciting, complex results.

Montecucco Tus SANGIOVESE-based TUS DOC between Monte Amiata and Grosseto. As Montecucco Sangiovese it is DOCG. Don't confuse with MONTALCINO.

Montefalco Sagrantino Umb DOCG r dr (sw) ★★★→★★★★ Super-tannic, powerful, long-lasting, potentially great but difficult to tame without losing the point.

Traditional bittersweet PASSITO version may be better suited to grape, though harder to sell. Gd: Adanti, Antano Milziade, Antonelli, CAPRAI, Colpetrone, LUNGAROTTI, Paolo Bea, Scacciadiavoli, Tabarrini.

Montepulciano d'Abruzzo Ab DOC r p ★★→★★★ (r) **12 13** 14 15 1st all-region DOC of Italy. Subdenomination: Colline Teramane (now DOCG), wines often tough, charmless despite hype, and Controguerra (DOC), usually more balanced. Reds can be either light, easy-going or structured, rich. Look for Cataldi Madonna (Toni, lighter Malandrino), EMIDIO PEPE, Marina Cvetic (S Martino Rosso), TIBERIO (Colle Vota and regular), Torre dei Beati (Cocciapazza, Mazzamurello), *Valentini* (best, age-worthy), Zaccagnini.

Old Venetian term for a glass of white is *un ombra*: a shade.

Montevertine Tus ★★★★ Organic certified estate in Radda. Outstanding IGT Le Pergole Torte, world-class, pure, long-ageing SANGIOVESE. V.gd Montevertine.

Montevetrano Cam ★★★ Iconic CAM AZIENDA, owned by Silvia Imparato, consultant Riccardo Cotarella. Superb IGT Montevetrano (AGLIANICO, CAB SAUV, MERLOT). V.gd Core Rosso (Aglianico).

Morella Pug ★★★→★★★★ Gaetano Morella and wife Lisa Gilbee make outstanding PRIMITIVO (Old Vines, La Signora, new Mondo Nuovo) from c.90-yr-old vines.

Morellino di Scansano Tus DOCG r ★→★★★ **11** 13 15 16 SANGIOVESE red from MAREMMA. Used to be a gd simple swallow. Now, sometimes regrettably, gaining weight, substance, perhaps to justify its lofty DOCG status. Best: *Le Pupille*, Mantellasi, Moris Farms, PODERE 414, POGGIO Argentiera, Terre di Talamo, *Vignaioli* (co-op).

Moris Farms Tus ★★★ One of 1st new-age producers of TUS's MAREMMA; Monteregio and *Morellino di Scansano* DOCS, plus VERMENTINO IGT. Top cru is now iconic IGT Avvoltore, rich SANGIOVESE/CAB SAUV/SYRAH blend. But *try basic Morellino*.

Moscato d'Asti Pie DOCG w sw sp ★★→★★★ DYA Similar to DOCG ASTI, but usually better grapes; lower alc, lower pressure, sweeter, fruitier, often from small producers. Best DOCG MOSCATO: L'Armangia, Bera, *Braida*, Ca' d'Gal, Cascina Fonda, Caudrina, Elio Perrone, Forteto della Luja, Il Falchetto, Icardi, Isolabella, La Morandina, Marchesi di Grésy, Marco Negri, Marino, RIZZI, RIVETTI, SARACCO, Scagliola, *Vajra*, VIETTI, Vignaioli di Sante Stefano.

Muri Gries T-AA ★★→★★★ This monastery, in Bolzano suburb of Gries, is a traditional and still top producer of LAGREIN ALTO ADIGE DOC. Esp cru Abtei-Muri.

Nals Margreid T-AA ★★→★★★ Small quality co-op making mtn-fresh whites (esp PINOT BIANCO Sirmian), from two communes of ALTO ADIGE. Harald Schraffl is an inspired winemaker.

Nebbiolo d'Alba Pie DOC r dr ★★→★★★ **11 12** 13 14 15 16 (100% NEBBIOLO) Sometimes a worthy replacement for BAROLO/BARBARESCO, though it comes from a distinct area between the two and may not be used as a declassification from top DOCGS. Gd: BREZZA (VIGNA Santa Rosalia), BRUNO GIACOSA (Valmaggiore), Fratelli Giacosa, PAITIN, LUCIANO SANDRONE (Valmaggiore).

Negrar, Cantina Ven ★★ Aka CS VALPOLICELLA. Major producer of high-quality Valpolicella, RIPASSO, AMARONE; grapes from various parts of CLASSICO zone. Look for brand name Domini Veneti. So-so quality but affordable.

Niedrist, Ignaz r w ★★★ LAGREIN Berger Gei is reference. So are RIES, WEISSBURGUNDER (Limes). V.gd BLAUBURGUNDER, SAUV BL, Trias (w blend).

Nino Franco Ven ★★★→★★★★ Winery of Primo Franco, named after his grandfather. Among v. finest PROSECCOS: Primo Franco Dry, Riva di San Floriano Brut. Excellent CARTIZZE, *delicious basic Prosecco di Valdobbiadene Brut*.

Nipozzano, Castello di Tus ★★★ FRESCOBALDI estate in RÚFINA, e of Florence, making excellent CHIANTI Rúfina. Top Nipozzano RISERVA (esp Vecchie Viti) and IGT *Montesodi*. Gd Mormoreto (B'x blend).

Nittardi Tus ★★→★★★ Reliable source of quality modern CHIANTI CLASSICO. German owned; oenologist Carlo Ferrini.

Nozzole Tus ★★ Famous estate in heart of CHIANTI CLASSICO, n of Greve, owned by Ambrogio and Giovanni FOLONARI. V.gd Chianti Classico RISERVA, excellent CAB SAUV Pareto.

Nuragus di Cagliari Sar DOC w ★ DYA. Lively, uncomplicated SAR wine from Nuragus grape, finally gaining visibility. Best: ARGIOLAS (S'Elegas), MOGORO (Ajò), Pala (I Fiori).

Occhio di Pernice Tus "Partridge's eye". A type of VIN SANTO made predominantly from black grapes, mainly SANGIOVESE. *Avignonesi's is definitive.* Also an obscure black variety found in RÚFINA and elsewhere.

Occhipinti, Arianna Si ★★★ Cult producer, deservedly so. Organic certified. Happily, wines now less oxidized and more about finesse than power. Top: Il Frappato. V.gd NERO D'AVOLA Siccagno, Nero d'Avola Frappato SP68 and Bianco SP68.

Oddero Pie ★★★ Traditionalist La Morra estate for excellent BAROLO (Brunate, Villero, VIGNA Rionda RISERVA now 10 yrs), BARBARESCO (Gallina) crus, plus other serious PIE wines. V.gd value Barolo. New acquisition in Monvigliero.

Oltrepò Pavese Lom DOC r w dr sw sp ★→★★★ Multi-DOC, incl numerous varietal and blended wine from Pavia province; best is SPUMANTE. Gd growers: Anteo, Barbacarlo, cs Casteggio, Frecciarossa, Le Fracce, Mazzolino, Monsupello, Ruiz de Cardenas, Travaglino; La Versa co-op.

Ornellaia Tus ★★★★ 10 11 12 13 15 (16) Fashionable, indeed cult, estate nr BOLGHERI founded by Lodovico ANTINORI, now owned by FRESCOBALDI. Top wines of B'x grapes/method: Bolgheri DOC Ornellaia, IGT Masseto (MERLOT), Ornellaia Bianco (SAUV BL/VIOGNIER), gd: Bolgheri DOC Le Serre Nuove and POGGIO alle Gazze (w).

Orvieto Umb DOC w dr sw s/sw ★→★★★ DYA Classic Umb white, blend of mainly Procanico (TREBBIANO)/GRECHETTO. *Secco* most popular today. Top: BARBERANI (Luigi e Giovanna); *amabile* more traditional. Sweet versions from noble-rot (*muffa nobile*) grapes can be superb, eg. Barberani Calcaia. Other gd: Bigi, Cardeto, Castello della Sala, Decugnano dei Barbi, Palazzone; Sergio Mottura (Lat).

Pacenti, Siro Tus →★ Modern-style BRUNELLO, ROSSO DI MONTALCINO from small, caring producer

Paitin Pie ★★→★★★ Pasquero-Elia family have been bottling BARBARESCO since C19. Used to be intensely authentic, had a flutter with modernism (new barriques); today back on track making "real" Barbaresco in large barrels. Sorì Paitin is star.

Palrinieri ★★→★★★ One of top three LAMBRUSCO producers. Among 1st to produce 100% Lambrusco di Sorbara. Best: Secco Radice; v.gd Leclisse.

Pantelleria Si ★★★ Windswept, black-(volcanic) earth SI island off Tunisian coast, famous for superb MOSCATO d'Alessandria stickies. PASSITO versions particularly dense/intense. By DE BARTOLI (Bukkuram), DONNAFUGATA (Ben Ryé), Ferrandes.

Parrina, La Tus ★★ Popular estate and *agriturismo* on TUS coast dominates DOC Parrina; solid rather than inspired wines.

Passito Tus, Ven One of Italy's most ancient and most characteristic wine styles, from grapes hung up, or spread on trays to dry, briefly under harvest sun (in s) or over a period of weeks or mths in airy attics of winery – a process called *appassimento.* Best-known versions: VIN SANTO (TUS); AMARONE/RECIOTO (Ven), VALPOLICELLA/SOAVE. *See also* MONTEFALCO, ORVIETO, TORCOLATO, VALLONE. Never cheap.

Paternoster Bas ★★★ Old estate now owned by TOMMASI family. 25 ha organically farmed. Top: Don Anselmo. V.gd AGLIANICO DEL VULTURE Rotondo.

Pepe, Emidio Ab →★★ Artisanal winery, 15 ha, bio and organic certified. Top MONTEPULCIANO D'ABRUZZO. Gd: TREBBIANO D'ABRUZZO (Vecchie Vigne Selezione).

Pian dell'Orino ★★★ Small MONTALCINO estate, committed to bio. BRUNELLO seductive, technically perfect, Rosso nearly as gd. Many epic wines.

Piave Ven DOC r w ★→★★ (r) 12 13 15 (w) DYA. Volume DOC on plains of e Ven for budget varietals. CAB SAUV, MERLOT, Raboso reds can all age moderately. Above average from Loredan Gasparini, Molon, Villa Sandi.

Picolit F-VG DOCG w sw s/sw ★★→★★★ 10 12 13 15 (16) Quasi-mythical but inconsistent sweet white from FRIULI COLLI ORIENTALI, might disappoint those who can a) find it and b) afford it. Most from air-dried grapes. Ranges from light/sweet (rare) to super-thick. Gd: Aquila del Torre, Ermacora, Girolamo Dorigo, I Comelli, LIVIO FELLUGA, Marco Sara, Paolo Rodaro, Ronchi di Cialla, VIGNA PETRUSSA.

Piedmont / Piemonte Pie Alpine foothill region; with TUS, Italy's most important for quality. TURIN is capital, MONFERRATO (ASTI) and LANGHE (ALBA) important centres. No IGTS allowed; Pie DOC is lowest denomination, for basic reds, whites, SPUMANTE, FRIZZANTE. Grapes incl: BARBERA, Brachetto, Cortese, DOLCETTO, Freisa, GRIGNOLINO, MALVASIA di Casorzo, Malvasia di Schierano, MOSCATO, NEBBIOLO, Ruché, Timorasso. *See also* ALTO PIEMONTE, BARBARESCO, BAROLO, ROERO.

Pieropan Ven ★★★★ RIP 2018. Leonildo Pieropan led renaissance of SOAVE, which brought this noble wine back to credibility. Cru *La Rocca* is still ultimate oaked Soave; Calvarino best of all. V.gd AMARONE.

Pio Cesare Pie ★★→★★★ Veteran ALBA producer, offers BAROLO, BARBARESCO in modern (barrique) and traditional (large-cask-aged) versions. Particularly gd NEBBIOLO D'ALBA, *a little Barolo at half the price.*

What to drink with sushi, wasabi? Ruchè di Castagnole Monferrato, served cool. Hard to find in Japan.

Planeta Si ★★★ Leading SI estate with six v'yd holdings in various parts of island, incl Vittoria (CERASUOLO Dorilli), Noto (NERO D'AVOLA Santa Cecilia), most recently on ETNA (Carricante, NERELLO MASCALESE Eruzione 1614). Also gd: La Segreta (r w), Cometa (FIANO).

Podere Tus Small TUS farm, once part of a big estate.

Poggio Tus Means "hill" in TUS dialect. "**Poggione**" means "big hill".

Poggio Antico Tus ★★★ Paola Gloder looks after this 32-ha estate, one of highest in MONTALCINO at c.500m (1640ft). Restrained, consistent, at times too herbal.

Poggio di Sotto Tus ★★★★ Small MONTALCINO estate with a big reputation recently. Has purchased adjacent v'yds. Top BRUNELLO, RISERVA and Rosso of traditional character with idiosyncratic twist.

Poggione, Tenuta Il Tus ★★★ S MONTALCINO estate; consistently excellent BRUNELLO, ROSSO. Top Brunello RISERVA VIGNA Paganelli.

Poggiopiano Tus ★★ Opulent CHIANTI CLASSICO from Bartoli family. Chiantis are pure SANGIOVESE, but SUPER TUSCAN Rosso di Sera incl up to 15% Colorino. V.gd Colorino Taffe Ta'.

Poggio Scalette Tus ★★ Vittorio Fiore and son Jury run CHIANTI organic estate at Greve. Top: Il Carbonaione (100% SANGIOVESE); needs several yrs bottle age. Above-average Chianti CLASSICO and B'x-blend Capogatto.

Poliziano Tus ★★★ MONTEPULCIANO organic estate of Federico Carletti. Superior if often v. dark, herbal VINO NOBILE (esp cru Asinone); gd IGT Le Stanze (CAB SAUV/ MERLOT), Cortona In Violas (Merlot).

Pomino Tus DOC r w ★★★ (r) 12 13 15 16 Appendage of RÚFINA, with fine red and white blends (esp Il Benefizio). Virtually a FRESCOBALDI exclusivity.

Potazzine, Le Tus ★★★★ Organic estate of Gorelli family just s of MONTALCINO. V'yd is quite high. Outstanding BRUNELLOS (also RISERVA) and Rossos, serious and v. drinkable. Try them at family's restaurant in town.

Prà Ven ★★★ Leading SOAVE CLASSICO producer, esp crus Monte Grande, Staforte (latter 6 mths in tanks on lees with mechanical *bâtonnage*) v. tasty. Excellent VALPOLICELLA La Morandina, AMARONE.

ITALY

The best of Prosecco

PROSECCO is the wine, GLERA the grape variety with which it is made (meant to ward off copycats). Most is plain ordinary. Quality is higher in the Valdobbiadene. Look for: Adami, Biancavigna, BISOL, Bortolin, Canevel, CARPENÈ-MALVOLTI, Case Bianche, Col Salice, Col Vetoraz, Le Colture, Gregoletto, La Riva dei Frati, Mionetto, NINO FRANCO, Ruggeri, Silvano Follador, Zardetto.

Produttori del Barbaresco Pie ★★★ One of Italy's earliest co-ops, perhaps best in the world. Aldo Vacca and team make excellent traditional straight BARBARESCO plus crus Asili, Montefico, Montestefano, Ovello, Pora, Rio Sordo. Super values.

Proprietà Sperino Pie ★★★→★★★★ Top estate of LESSONA. One of best of ALTO PIEMONTE run by Luca De Marchi (*see* ISOLE E OLENA). Outstanding: LESSONA; V.gd L Franc (one of best Italian CAB FR), Rosa del Rosa (p, NEBBIOLO/Vespolina).

Prosecco Ven DOC(G) w sp ★→★★ DYA. World has gone mad for Italy's favourite fizz. Why is not clear. For details plus selection of producers *see* box, above.

Prunotto, Alfredo Pie ★★★→★★★★ Traditional ALBA firm modernized by ANTINORI in 90s. V.gd BARBARESCO (Bric Turot), BAROLO (Bussia and VIGNA Colonnello), NEBBIOLO (Occhetti), BARBERA D'ALBA (Pian Romualdo).

Puglia The heel of the Italian boot. Generally gd-value, simple wines (mainly red) from various grapes like NEGROAMARO, PRIMITIVO and Uva di Troia, but dubious winemaking talent and old equipment a real problem. Most interesting wines from SALENTO peninsula incl DOCS BRINDISI, COPERTINO, SALICE SALENTINO.

Querciabella Tus ★★★ Top CHIANTI CLASSICO estate, bio since 2000. Top IGT Camartina (CAB SAUV/SANGIOVESE), Batàr (CHARD/PINOT BL) and the new single-commune wines (Greve in Chianti, Radda in Chianti, Gaiole). V.gd Chianti Classico (and RISERVA).

Quintarelli, Giuseppe Ven ★★★★ Arch-traditionalist artisan producer of sublime VALPOLICELLA, RECIOTO, AMARONE; plus a fine Bianco Secco, a blend of various grapes. Daughter Fiorenza and sons now in charge, altering nothing, incl the old man's ban on spitting when tasting.

Quintodecimo Cam ★★★ Oenology professor/winemaker Luigi Moio's beautiful estate. Outstanding: TAURASI VIGNA Grande Cerzito; great AGLIANICO (Terra d'Eclano) and GRECO DI TUFO (Giallo d'Arles).

Ratti, Renato ★★→★★★ Iconic BAROLO estate. Son Pietro now in charge. Modern wines; short maceration but plenty of substance, esp Barolos Rocche dell'Annunziata and Conca.

Recioto della Valpolicella Ven DOCG r sw (sp) ★★★→★★★★ Historic, made from PASSITO grapes along lines est before C6; unique, potentially stunning, with sumptuous cherry-chocolate-sweet fruitiness.

Recioto di Soave Ven DOCG w sw (sp) ★★★→★★★★ SOAVE from half-dried grapes: sweet, fruity, slightly almondy; sweetness is cut by high acidity. *Drink with cheese.* Best: Anselmi, COFFELE, Gini, PIEROPAN, Tamellini; often v.gd from Ca' Rugate, Pasqua, PRÀ, Suavia, Trabuchi.

Refosco (dal Peduncolo Rosso) F-VG ★★ 12 13 15 (16) Gutsy red of appetizing rustic style. Best: FRIULI COLLI ORIENTALI DOC, *Volpi Pasini*; gd: Ca' Bolani, Denis Montanara, Dorigo, LIVIO FELLUGA, MIANI, Ronchi di Manzano, Venica in Aquileia DOC.

Ricasoli Tus Historic Tuscan family. First Italian Prime Minister Bettino R devised the classic CHIANTI blend. Main branch occupies medieval Castello di BROLIO.

Riecine Tus ★★★→★★★★ Since the 70s a SANGIOVESE specialist estate at Gaiole. Riecine di Riecine and La Gioia (100% Sangiovese) potentially outstanding.

Rinaldi, Giuseppe Pie ★★★ RIP 2018. Beppe R's daughters Marta and Carlotta continue their father's highly traditional path. Outstanding: Brunate, Tre Tine. Don't miss v.gd Freisa, LANGHE NEBBIOLO.

ITALY

Ripasso Ven *See* VALPOLICELLA RIPASSO.

Riserva Wine aged for a statutory period, usually in casks or barrels.

Rivetti, Giorgio (La Spinetta) Pie ★★★ Fine MOSCATO D'ASTI, excellent BARBERA, series of super-concentrated, oaky BARBARESCOS. Also owns v'yds in BAROLO, CHIANTI COLLI Pisane DOCGS, and traditional SPUMANTE house Contratto.

Rizzi Pie ★★★ Sub-area of Treiso, commune of BARBARESCO, where Dellapiana family look after 35-ha v'yd. Organic. Top cru is Barbaresco Pajore and Rizzi RISERVA Boito. V.gd: Nervo, Rizzi, also gd METODO CLASSICO Pas Dosè, MOSCATO D'ASTI.

Rocca, Bruno Pie ★★★★ Outstanding modern-style BARBARESCO (Rabajà, Coparossa, Maria Adelaide) and other ALBA wines, also v. fine BARBERA d'Asti.

Rocca Albino Pie ★★★ A foremost producer of elegant, sophisticated BARBARESCO: top crus Ovello VIGNA Loreto, Ronchi, new Cottà.

Rocca delle Macìe Tus ★★ Large estate in Castellina-in-CHIANTI run by Sergio Zingarelli. Gd quaffing Chianti, plus top wines incl Gran Selezione Sergio Zingarelli and Fizzano. Also Campo Macìone estate in Scansano zone.

Roero Pie DOCG r w ★★→★★★ 10 11 13 15 16 (17) Serious, occasionally BAROLO-level NEBBIOLOS from LANGHE hills. Also gd ARNEIS (w ★★→★★★). Best: Almondo, BRUNO GIACOSA, Ca' Rossa, Cascina Chicco, Cornarea, Correggia, Malvirà (Trinità, Renesio), Morra, Negro (Perdaudin), Rosso, Taliano, Val di Prete, Valfaccenda.

Romagna Sangiovese Mar DOC r ★★→★★★ At times too herbal and oaky, but often well-made, even classy SANGIOVESE red. Gd: Cesari, Drei Donà, Nicolucci, Papiano, Paradiso, Tre Monti, Trere (E-R DOC), Villa Venti (Primo Segno), FATTORIA ZERBINA. Seek also IGT RONCO delle Ginestre, Ronco dei Ciliegi from CASTELLUCCIO.

Ronco Term for a hillside v'yd in ne Italy, esp F-VG.

Ronco del Gelso F-VG ★★★ Tight, pure ISONZO: PINOT GR Sot lis Rivis, FRIULANO Toc Bas and MALVASIA VIGNA della Permuta are regional benchmarks.

Rosato General Italian name for rosé. Other rosé wine names incl CHIARETTO from Lake Garda; CERASUOLO from Ab; Kretzer from ALTO ADIGE.

Rossese di Dolceacqua o Dolceacqua Lig DOC r ★★→★★★ Interesting reds. Intense, salty, spicy; greater depth of fruit than most. Gd: Ka Mancine, MACCARIO-DRINGBERG, TENUTA Anfosso, Terre Bianche, Poggi dell'Elmo. ***Rosso Conero*** Mar *See* CONERO.

Rosso di Montalcino Tus DOC r ★★→★★★ 11 12 13 15 16 DOC for earlier-maturing wines from BRUNELLO grapes, usually from younger or lesser v'yd sites, but bargains exist.

Rosso di Montefalco Umb DOC r ★★ 12 13 15 16 SANGIOVESE/SAGRANTINO blend, often with a splash of softening MERLOT. *See* MONTEFALCO SAGRANTINO.

Rosso di Montepulciano Tus DOC r ★ 13 15 16 Junior version of VINO NOBILE DI MONTEPULCIANO, growers similar.

Rosso Piceno / Piceno Mar DOC r ★ 13 15 (17) Generally easy-drinking blend of MONTEPULCIANO/SANGIOVESE now often sold as plain Piceno to help distinguish it from all other Rossos of Italy. SUPERIORE means it comes from far s of region. Gd: Boccadigabbia, BUCCI, GAROFOLI, Moncaro, Monte Schiavo, Saladini Pilastri, Santa Barbara, TENUTA di Tavignano, Velenosi.

Ruffino Tus ★→★★★ Venerable CHIANTI firm, in hands of FOLONARI family for 100 yrs, split apart a few yrs ago. This part, at Pontassieve nr Florence, then bought by US giant Constellation Brands, produces reliable wines such as CHIANTI CLASSICO RISERVA Ducale and Ducale Oro, Greppone Mazzi in MONTALCINO, Lodola Nuova in MONTEPULCIANO, not to mention Borgo Conventi in F-VG.

Rúfina Tus ★★→★★★ Most n sub-zone of CHIANTI, e of Florence in s-facing foothills of Apennines, known for tight, refined wines capable of long ageing. Gd-to-outstanding: CASTELLO DI NIPOZZANO (FRESCOBALDI), Castello del Trebbio, Colognole, Frascole, Grati/Villa di Vetrice, I Veroni, Lavacchio, ***Selvapiana***, TENUTA Bossi, Travignoli. Don't confuse with RUFFINO, which happens to have HQ in Pontassieve.

Russiz Superiore F-VG ★★→★★★ LIVIO FELLUGA's brother, Marco, est v'yds in various parts of F-VG. Now run by Marco's son Roberto. Wide range; best is PINOT GRIGIO, COLLIO Bianco blend Col Disôre. V.gd PINOT BIANCO RISERVA.

Salento Pug Flat peninsula at tip of Italy's heel; seems unlikely for quality, but deep soils, old *alberello* vines and sea breezes combine to produce remarkable red and rosé from NEGROAMARO, PRIMITIVO, with a bit of help from MALVASIA Nera, MONTEPULCIANO, local Sussumaniello. *See also* PUG, SALICE SALENTINO.

Salice Salentino Pug DOC r ★★→★★★ 11 13 15 16 Best-known of Salento's too many NEGROAMARO-based DOCs. RISERVA after 2 yrs. Gd: Agricole Vallone (Vereto RISERVA), Cantele, Due Palme, Leone de Castris (Riserva), Mocavero.

Salvioni Tus ★★★★ Aka La Cerbaiola; small, high-quality MONTALCINO operation of irrepressible Giulio Salvioni and ditto daughter. BRUNELLO, ROSSO DI MONTALCINO among v. best available, worth not inconsiderable price.

Sandrone, Luciano Pie ★★★★ Modern-style ALBA wines. Deep BAROLOS: Aleste (formerly Cannubi Boschis), Le Vigne, new Vite Talin. Also gd NEBBIOLO D'ALBA.

San Felice Tus ★★→★★★ Important historic TUS grower, owned by Gruppo Allianz, run by Leonardo Bellaccini. Fine CHIANTI CLASSICO and RISERVA POGGIO Rosso from estate in Castelnuovo Berardenga. Gd too: IGT *Vigorello* (1st SUPER TUSCAN, from 1968), BRUNELLO DI MONTALCINO Campogiovanni.

San Gimignano Tus Tourist-overrun TUS town famous for its towers and dry white VERNACCIA DI SAN GIMIGNANO DOCG. Forgettable reds. Producers: Cesani, FALCHINI, Guicciardini Strozza, Il Palagione, Montenidoli, Mormoraia, Panizzi, Pietrafitta, Pietrasereno, Podera del Paradiso.

San Giusto a Rentennano Tus ★★★★ Top CHIANTI CLASSICO estate. Outstanding SANGIOVESE IGT Percarlo, sublime VIN SANTO (Vin San Giusto), MERLOT (La Ricolma); v.gd Chianti Classico, RISERVA Le Baroncole.

Smallest DOCG in Italy? Moscato di Scanzo, 31 ha. With Gorgonzola, dark chocolate.

San Guido, Tenuta Tus *See* SASSICAIA.

San Leonardo T-AA ★★★★ Top TRENTINO estate of Marchesi Guerrieri Gonzaga. Main wine is B'x blend, *San Leonardo*, Italy's most claret-like wine, with consistent style of a top ch.

San Michele Appiano T-AA ★★★ Historic co-op. *Mtn-fresh whites*, brimming with varietal typicity, drinkability, are speciality. Seek out wines of The Wine Collection (selected by Hans Terzer). Top PINOT BL Schulthauser and Sanct Valentin line.

Santadi Sar ★★★ SAR's, and one of Italy's, best co-ops, esp for CARIGNANO-based reds *Terre Brune*, Grotta Rossa, Rocca Rubia RISERVA (all DOC CARIGNANO DEL SULCIS). V.gd MONICA DI SARDEGNA Antigua.

Santa Maddalena / St-Magdalener T-AA DOC r ★→★★★ DYA. Teutonic-style red from SCHIAVA grapes from v. steep slopes behind ALTO ADIGE capital Bolzano. Notable: CS St-Magdalena (Huck am Bach), Gojer, Hans Rottensteiner (Premstallerhof), Untermoserhof, Waldgries.

Sant'Antimo Tus DOC r w sw ★★ Lovely little Romanesque abbey gives its name to this catch-all DOC for (almost) everything in MONTALCINO zone that isn't BRUNELLO DOCG or Rosso DOC.

Saracco, Paolo Pie ★★★★ Top MOSCATO D'ASTI. V.gd: LANGHE RIES, PINOT N.

Sardinia / Sardegna The Med's 2nd-largest island produces much decent and some outstanding wines, incl *Vermentino di Gallura* DOCG, VERMENTINO DI SARDEGNA (little less alc, little less character), Sherry-like VERNACCIA DI ORISTANO, and NURAGUS among whites, late-harvest sweet Nasco; CANNONAU (GRENACHE) and CARIGNANO among reds. Outstanding wines: Terre Brune and Rocca Rubia from SANTADI, *Turriga* (r) from ARGIOLAS, VERMENTINO from Capichera. SELLA & MOSCA is great standby.

Sassicaia Tus DOC r ★★★★ 04' 05 06 07' 08 09 10 13 15' Italy's sole single-v'yd DOC

(BOLGHERI), a CAB (SAUV/FR) made on First Growth lines by Marchese Incisa della Rocchetta at TENUTA San Guido. More elegant than lush, made for age – often bought for investment, but hugely influential in giving Italy a top-quality image. 15 may be one to remember.

Satta, Michele Tus ★★★ Virtually only BOLGHERI grower to succeed with 100% SANGIOVESE (Cavaliere). Also Bolgheri DOC red blends Piastraia, SUPERIORE I Castagni.

Scavino, Paolo Pie ★★★ Modernist BAROLO producer of Castiglione Falletto, esp crus Rocche dell'Annunziata, Bric del Fiasc, Cannubi, Monvigliero. Less oaky now. Not to be missed new BAROLO RISERVA Novantesimo.

Schiava Alto Adige T-AA DOC r ★ DYA. Schiava (VERNATSCH in German) gives practically tannin-free, easy-glugging red from most s territory of German-speaking world. Sadly disappearing from Tyrolean v'yds.

Schiopetto, Mario F-VG ★★★ Legendary late COLLIO pioneering estate now owned by Rotolo family. V.gd DOC SAUV BL, *Pinot Bl*, RIBOLLA GIALLA, FRIULANO, IGT blend Blanc des Rosis, etc.

Sella & Mosca Sar ★★★ Major SAR grower and merchant with v. pleasant white Torbato (esp Terre Bianche) and light, fruity VERMENTINO Cala Viola (DYA). Gd Alghero DOC Marchese di Villamarina (CAB SAUV) and Tanca Farrà (CANNONAU/Cab Sauv). Also interesting Port-like Anghelu Ruju.

Selvapiana Tus ★★★★ CHIANTI RÚFINA estate among Italian greats. Best: RISERVA Bucerchiale, IGT Fornace; but even *basic Chianti Rúfina is a treat*. Also fine red POMINO, Petrognano.

Settesoli, CS Si ★→★★ Co-op with some 6000 ha, giving SI gd name with reliable, gd-value wines.

Sforzato / Sfursat Lom ★★★ AMARONE-like dried-grape NEBBIOLO from VALTELLINA in extreme n of Lom on Swiss border. Ages beautifully.

Sicily Si The Med's largest island, modern source of exciting original wines and value. Native grapes (r. Frappato, NERO D'AVOLA, NERELLO MASCALESE; w. CATARRATTO, Grecanico, GRILLO, INZOLIA), plus internationals. V'yds on flatlands in w, hills in centre, volcanic altitudes on Mt Etna.

Soave Ven DOC w (sw) ★→★★★ Famous, hitherto underrated, Veronese white. CHARD, GARGANEGA, TREBBIANO di Soave. Wines from volcanic soils of CLASSICO zone can be intense, saline, v. fine, quite long-lived.

Solaia Tus r ★★★★ 04 06 07 08 09 10 11 12 13 15 Occasionally magnificent CAB SAUV/SANGIOVESE blend by ANTINORI, made to highest B'x specs; needs yrs of laying down.

Sottimano Pie ★★★→★★★★ Family estate. One of most inspired in BARBARESCO (crus: Basarin, Cottà, Currà, Fausoni, Pajorè). V.gd DOLCETTO D'ALBA, BARBERA D'ALBA.

Speri Ven ★★★ VALPOLICELLA family estate, organic certified since 2015, with sites such as outstanding Monte Sant'Urbano. Traditional style. Top: AMARONE VIGNETO Monte Sant'Urbano.

Spumante Sparkling. What used to be called ASTI Spumante is now just Asti. **Südtirol** T-AA The local name of German-speaking South Tyrol ALTO ADIGE.

Superiore Wine with more ageing than normal DOC and 0.5–1% more alc. May indicate a restricted production zone, eg. ROSSO PICENO Superiore.

Super Tuscan Tus Wines of high quality and price developed in 70s/80s to get round silly laws then prevailing. Now, esp with Gran Selezione on up, scarcely relevant. Wines still generally considered in Super Tuscan category, strictly unofficially: CA' MARCANDA, Flaccianello, Guado al Tasso, Messorio, ORNELLAIA, Redigaffi, SASSICAIA, SOLAIA, TIGNANELLO.

Sylla Sebaste Pie ★★★ Illustrates merits of rare NEBBIOLO Rosé variety: lighter, v. perfumed BAROLO. A beauty.

Tasca d'Almerita Si ★★★ New generation of Tasca d'Almeritas runs historic, still prestigious estate High-altitude v'yds; balanced IGTS under its old Regaleali label. Top: NERO D'AVOLA-based ***Rosso del Conte***. V.gd MALVASIA delle Lipari Capofaro CRILLO Mozia TENUTA Whitaker.

Taurasi Cam DOCG r ★★★ 09 10 11 12 13 15 (16) S's answer to the n's BAROLO and the centre's BRUNELLO needs careful handling and long ageing. There are friendlier versions of AGLIANICO but none so potentially ***complex, demanding, ultimately rewarding***. Made famous by MASTROBERARDINO, other outstanding: Caggiano Caputo, FEUDI DI SAN GREGORIO, Luigi Tecce, Molettieri, QUINTODECIMO, Terredora.

Europe's highest v'yds in Alto Adige: 1340m/4396ft high.

Tedeschi Ven ★★★ Bevy of v. fine AMARONE, VALPOLICELLA. Amarone Capitel Monte Olmi and RECIOTO Capitel Monte Fiontana best.

Tedeschi, Fratelli Ven ★★★★ One of original quality growers of VALPOLICELLA when zone was still ruled by mediocrities.

Tenuta An agricultural holding (*see* under name – eg. SAN GUIDO, TENUTA).

Terlano T-AA w ★★→★★★ DYA. ALTO ADIGE Terlano DOC applies to one white blend and eight white varietals, esp PINOT BL, SAUV BL. Can be v. fresh, zesty or serious and surprisingly long-lasting. Best: CS Terlano (esp Pinot Bl Vorberg), LAGEDER, Niedermayr, Niederst.

Teroldego Rotaliano T-AA DOC r p ★★→★★★ TRENTINO's best local variety makes seriously tasty wine on flat Campo Rotaliano. ***Foradori*** is tops. Gd: Dorigati, Endrizzi, MEZZACORONA's RISERVA Nos, Zeni.

Terre del Barolo Pie r ★★★ Co-op in Castiglione Falletto; millions of bottles of BAROLO and other LANGHE wines; remarkably consistent quality. Look for new Aldo Rivera, dedicated to the founder.

Terre Nere, Tenuta delle Si ★★★★ Marc de Grazia shows great wine can be made from NERELLO and CARRICANTE grapes, on coveted n side of Mt Etna. Top: Guardiola, Vigne Niche and pre-phylloxera La VIGNA di Don Peppino. V.gd Le Vigne di Eli.

Terriccio, Castello del Tus ★★★ Large estate s of Livorno: excellent, v. expensive B'x-style IGT Lupicaia, Lgd IGT Tassinaia. Impressive IGT Terriccio, unusual blend of mainly Rhône grapes.

Tiberio ★★★★ Outstanding TREBBIANO D'ABRUZZO Fonte Canale (60-yr-old vines) one of Italy's best whites and new MONTEPULCIANO D'ABRUZZO Colle Vota; CERASUOLO D'ABRUZZO, PECORINO also exceptional.

Tiefenbrunner T-AA ★★★→★★★★ Grower-merchant in Teutonic castle (*Turmhof*) in s ALTO ADIGE. Wide range of mtn-fresh white and well-defined red varietals: French, Germanic and local, esp 1000m-high MÜLLER-T ***Feldmarschall***, one of Italy's best whites.

Tignanello Tus r ★★★★ 07' 08 09 10 11 12 13 15 SANGIOVESE/CAB SAUV blend, barrique-aged, wine that put SUPER TUSCANS on map, created by ANTINORI's great oenologist Giacomo Tachis in early 70s. Today one of greatest cash cows of world wine.

Tommasi Ven ★★★ 4th generation now in charge. Top: AMARONE (RISERVA Ca' Florian, new RISERVA De Buris), VALPOLICELLA Rafael. Other estates in Bas (PATERNOSTER), OLTREPÒ PAVESE (TENUTA Caseo), PUG (Masseria Surani), Ven (Filodora).

Torcolato Ven Sweet wine from BREGANZE in Ven; Vespaiolo grapes laid on mats or hung up to dry for mths, as nearby RECIOTO DI SOAVE. Best: CS Beato Bartolomeo da Breganze, MACULAN.

Torgiano Umb DOC r p w (sp) ★★ and **Torgiano, Rosso Riserva** DOCG r ★★→★★★ 08 09 10 11 12 13 15. Gd-to-excellent red from Umb, virtually an exclusivity of LUNGAROTTI. Top: ***Vigna Monticchio*** Rubesco RISERVA. Keeps many yrs.

Torrette VdA DOC r ★→★★★ Blend based on Petit Rouge and other local varieties. Best: Torrette SUPERIEUR. Gd: Anselmet, D&D, Didier Gerbelle, GROSJEAN, FEUDO DI SAN MAURIZIO, LES CRÊTES, Elio Ottin.

Travaglini Pie ★★★ Along with Antoniolo, solid producer of n PIE NEBBIOLO, with v.gd GATTINARA RISERVA, Gattinara Tre Vigne, pretty-gd MC Nebolè (sp, 100% Nebbiolo). Seek out Riserva 60° Anniversario.

Trebbiano d'Abruzzo Ab DOC w ★→★★★★ DYA. Generally crisp, simple wine, but VALENTINI's and Tiberio's Fonte Canale are *two of Italy's greatest* whites.

Trediberri Pie ★★★ Dynamic estate, top BAROLO Rocche dell'Annunziata (best value); v.gd BAROLO, LANGHE NEBBIOLO, BARBERA D'ALBA.

Trentino T-AA DOC r w dr sw ★→★★★ DOC for 20-odd wines, mostly varietally named. Best: CHARD, PINOT BL, MARZEMINO, TEROLDEGO. Provincial capital is Trento, which is DOC name for potentially high-quality METODO CLASSICO wines.

Trinoro, Tenuta di Tus ★★★★ Individualist TUS red wine estate, pioneer in DOC Val d'Orcia between MONTEPULCIANO and MONTALCINO. Heavy accent on B'x grapes in flagship TENUTA di Trinoro, also in Palazzi, Le Cupole, Magnacosta. See also FRANCHETTI VINI (ETNA).

Tua Rita Tus ★★★★ 1st producer to est Suvereto, some 20-km down coast, as new BOLGHERI in 90s. Producer of possibly Italy's greatest MERLOT in Redigaffi, also outstanding B'x blend *Giusto di Notri*, SYRAH Per Sempre. See VAL DI CORNIA.

Tuscany / Toscana Tus Focal point of Italian wine's late-C20 renaissance, 1st with experimental SUPER TUSCANS, then modernized classics, CHIANTI, VINO NOBILE, BRUNELLO. Development of coastal zones like BOLGHERI, MAREMMA, has been a major feature of Tus wine over last half-century.

Uberti Lom ★★★ →★★★★ Historical estate, excellent interpreter of FRANCIACORTA's terroir. Outstanding Quinque (blend of 5 yrs) and Comarì del Salem. V.gd Dosaggio Zero Sublimis. Seek out DeQuinque (blend of 10 yrs).

Umani Ronchi Mar ★★ →★★★ Leading Mar producer, esp for VERDICCHIO (Casal di Serra, Plenio), CONERO Cumaro, IGTS Le Busche (w), Pelago (r).

Vajra, GD Pie ★★★ Leading quality BAROLO producer in Vergne. Outstanding Bricco delle Viole and LANGHE Freisa Kyè. Gd: Langhe RIES Petracine, Barolo Albe, DOLCETTO Coste & Fossati and Serralunga's Luigi Baudana Barolos.

Valdadige T-AA DOC r w dr s/sw ★ Name (in German: *Etschtaler*) for simple wines of valley of Adige, from ALTO ADIGE through TRENTINO to n Ven.

Val di Cornia Tus DOC r p w ★★→★★★ 10 11 12 13 15 16 Quality zone s of BOLGHERI. CAB SAUV, MERLOT, MONTEPULCIANO, SYRAH. Look for: Ambrosini, Bulichella, Gualdo del Re, Incontri, Jacopo Banti, Montepeloso, Petra, Russo, San Michele, TENUTA Casa Dei, Terricciola, TUA RITA.

Valentini, Edoardo Ab r w ★★★→★★★★★ Collectors seek out his MONTEPULCIANO D'ABRUZZO, TREBBIANO D'ABRUZZO, among Italy's v. best wines. Traditional, age-worthy; 70s wines esp memorable.

Want to see a 350 yrs+ old vine covering 350m²+? At Castel Katzenzungen, Alto Adige.

Valle d'Aosta VdA DOC r p w ★★→★★★ Regional DOC for some 25 Alpine wines, geographically or varietally named, incl Arnad Montjovet, Blanc de Morgex, Chambave, Donnas, Enfer d'Arvier, Fumin, Nus MALVOISIE, Premetta, Torrette. Tiny production, wines rarely seen abroad but potentially worth finding.

Valle Isarco T-AA DOC w ★★ DYA. ALTO ADIGE DOC for seven Germanic varietal whites made along the Isarco (Eisack) River ne of Bolzano. Gd GEWURZ, MÜLLER-T, RIES, SILVANER. Top: Abbazia di Novacella, Eisacktaler, KOFERERHOF, Kuenhof, Manni Nossing.

Valpolicella Ven DOC(G) r ★ →★★★★ Complex denomination, running from light quaffers with a certain fruity warmth through stronger SUPERIORES (that may or may not be RIPASSO) to AMARONES and RECIOTOS. Today straight Valpol is getting hard to find: a shame, as all best grapes going into trendy, profitable Amarone, which often disappoints (*see box, p.152*).

> **Valpolicella: the best**
>
> VALPOLICELLA has never been better than today. AMARONE DELLA VALPOLICELLA and RECIOTO DELLA VALPOLICELLA have now been elevated to DOCG status, while Valpolicella RIPASSO has at last been recognized as a historic wine in its own right. The following producers make gd to great wine: ALLEGRINI★, Begali, BERTANI, BOLLA, Boscaini, Brigaldara★, BRUNELLI, BUSSOLA★, Ca' la Bianca, Ca' Rugate, Campagnola, CANTINA Valpolicella, Castellani, Corte Forte, Corte Sant'Alda, CS Valpantena, DAL FORNO★, GUERRIERI-RIZZARDI★, Le Ragose, Le Salette, MASI★, Mazzi★, Nicolis, FRÀ, QUINTARELLI★, Roccolo Grassi★, Serego Alighieri★, SPERI★, Stefano Accordini★, TEDESCHI★, TOMMASI★, Valentina Cubi, Venturini, Viviani★, ZENATO, Zeni.

Valpolicella Ripasso Ven DOC r ★★→★★★ 09 10 11 12 13 15 In huge demand, some changes from 2015. Used to be only from VALPOLICELLA SUPERIORE re-fermented (only once) on RECIOTO or AMARONE grape-skins to make a more age-worthy wine. Now can blend ten per cent Amarone with standard Valpolicella and call it Ripasso. Best: BUSSOLA, Castellani, DAL FORNO, QUINTARELLI, ZENATO.

Valtellina Lom DOC DOCG r ★★→★★★ Long e to w valley on Swiss border. Steep terraces have for millennia grown NEBBIOLO (here called CHIAVENNASCA) and related grapes. DOCG Valtellina SUPERIORE has five zones: Grumello, Inferno, Sassella, Maroggia, Valgella. Best today: Ar.Pe.Pe., Fay, Mamete Prevostini, Nera, Nino Negri, Plozza, Rainoldi, Triacca. DOC Valtellina has less stringent requirements. *Sforzato* is its AMARONE.

Vecchio Samperi Si See DE BARTOLI.

Verdicchio dei Castelli di Jesi Mar DOC w (sp) ★★→★★★ DYA. Versatile white from nr Ancona on Adriatic; light and quaffable or sparkling or structured, complex long-lived (esp RISERVA DOCG, min 2 yrs old). Also CLASSICO. Best: Andrea Felici, *Bucci* (Riserva), Ca'alfarneto, Colognola, Coroncino (Gaiospino e Stracacio), Fazi Battaglia (Riserva San Sisto), GAROFOLI (Podium), La Staffa, Marotti Campi (Salmariano), MONTE SCHIAVO (Le Giuncare), Montecappone (Federico II), Santa Barbara, Sartarelli (Balciana, a rare late-harvest, and Tralivio), TENUTA di Tavignano (Misco and Riserva), UMANI RONCHI (Plenio and Casal di Serra).

Verdicchio di Matelica Mar DOC w (sp) ★★→★★★ DYA. Similar to last, smaller, more inland, higher, so more acidic, so longer lasting though less easy drinking young. RISERVA is likewise DOCG. Esp Belisario, Bisci, Borgo Paglianetto, Collestefano, La Monacesca (Mirum), Pagliano Tre, San Biagio.

Verduno Pie DOC r ★→★ DYA. Berry and herbal flavours. Top: CASTELLO DI VERDUNO (Basadone), Fratelli Alessandria, GB BURLOTTO. Gd: Ascheri (Do ut Des), Bel Colle (Le Masche), Reverdito.

Verduno, Castello di Pie ★★★ Husband/wife team, v.gd BARBARESCO Rabaja, BAROLO Monvigliero, VERDUNE Basadone.

Verduzzo F-VG DOC Friuli Colli Orientali) w dr sw s/sw ★★→★★★ Full-bodied white from local variety. Ramandolo (DOCG) is well-regarded subzone for sweet wine. Top: Anna Berra, Dorigo, Meroi.

Vermentino di Gallura Sar DOCG w ★★→★★★ DYA. VERMENTINO makes gd light wines in TUS, LIG and all over SAR, but best, most intense in ne corner of island, under this its DOCG name. Ty Capichera, CS del Vermentino/Monti, CS di Gallura, Depperu, Mura, Zanatta.

Vermentino di Sardegna Sar DOC w ★★ DYA. From anywhere on SAR; generally fails to measure up to VERMENTINO DI GALLURA for structure, intensity of flavour. Gd producers: ARGIOLAS, Santadi, *Sella & Mosca*.

Vernaccia di Oristano Sar DOC w dr ★→★★★★ SAR flor-affected wine, similar to light

Sherry, a touch bitter, full-bodied. SUPERIORE 15.5% alc, 3 yrs of age. Delicious with *bottarga* (dried, salted fish roe). Must try. Top: CONTINI. Gd: Serra, Silvio Carta.

Vernaccia di San Gimignano Tus *See* SAN GIMIGNANO.

Vie di Romans F-VG ★★★ →★★★★ Gianfranco Gallo has built up his father's ISONZO estate to top FV-G status. Outstanding Isonzo PINOT GR Dessimis, SAUV BL Piere and Vieris (oaked), Flors di Uis blend and MALVASIA. V.gd Pinot Gr Dessimis.

Vietti Pie ★★★★ Organic estate at Castiglione Falletto owned by Krause Group but still run by Luca Currdo and Mario Cordero. Characterful PIE wines at Castiglione Falletto. Textbook BAROLOS: Lazzarito, Ravera, Brunate, Rocche di Castiglione, Villero. V.gd BARBARESCO Masseria, BARBERA D'ALBA Scarrone, BARBERA D'ASTI la Crena.

Vignamaggio Tus ★★→★★★ Historic, beautiful CHIANTI CLASSICO estate, nr Greve. Leonardo da Vinci painted the *Mona Lisa* here. RISERVA is called – you guessed it.

Vigna (or vigneto) A single v'yd, generally indicating superior quality.

Vigna Petrussa F-VG ★★★ Small family estate: high-quality Schiopppettino, PICOLIT.

Villa Matilde Cam ★★★ Top CAM producer of FALERNO Rosso (VIGNA Camarato), Bianco (Carracci), PASSITO Eleusi.

Villa Russiz F-VG ★★★ Historic estate for DOC COLLIO. V.gd SAUV BL and MERLOT (esp "de la Tour" selections), PINOT BL, PINOT GR, CHARD, FRIULANO.

Vini Franchetti Si ★★★ ETNA estate (former Passopisciaro) run by Franchetti (*see* TENUTA DI TRINORO), contributor to fame of Etna. Outstanding NERELLO MASCALESE single-*contrada* wines. Best: Contrada G (Guardiola) and Contrada C (Chiappemacine). V.gd Contrada R (Rampante).

Vino Nobile di Montepulciano Tus DOCG r ★★→★★★ 08 09 10 11 12 13 15 (16) Historic Prugnole Gentile aka SANGIOVESE-based wine from TUS town (as distinct from grape) MONTEPULCIANO. Often tough with drying tannins, but complex and long-lasting from best: AVIGNONESI, Bindella, BOSCARELLI, Canneto, Contucci, Fattoria della Talosa, La Braccesca, DEI, Fattoria del Cerro, Montemercurio, POLIZIANO, Romeo, Salcheto, Valdipiatta, Villa Sant'Anna. RISERVA after 3 yrs.

Vin Santo / Vinsanto / Vin(o) Santo T-AA, Tus DOC w sw s/sw ★★→★★★★ Sweet PASSITO wine, usually TREBBIANO, MALVASIA and/or SANGIOVESE in TUS (Vin Santo), Nosiola in TRENTINO (Vino Santo). Tus versions extremely variable, anything from off-dry and Sherry-like to sweet and v. rich. May spend 3–10 unracked yrs in small barrels called *caratelli*. *Avignonesi's is legendary*; plus CAPEZZANA, Fattoria del Cerro, FELSINA, FRASCOLE, ISOLE E OLENA, Rocca di Montegrossi, SAN GIUSTO A RENTENNANO, SELVAPIANA, Villa Sant'Anna, Villa di Vetrice. *See also* OCCHIO DI PERNICE.

Voerzio, Roberto Pie ★★★★ BAROLO modernist: conc, tannic. More impressive/ expensive than delicious, usually aged in toasted barriques. Range incl Brunate, Cerequio, Rocche dell'Annunziata-Torriglione, Sarmassa, La Serra, Torriglione, Sarmassa, RISERVA 10 yrs Fossati Case Nere; excellent BARBERA D'ALBA. Two new Barolos from 16.

Volpaia, Castello di Tus ★★→★★★ V.gd CHIANTI CLASSICO estate at Radda. Organic certified. Top Chianti Classico RISERVA, Gran Selezione Coltassala (SANGIOVESE/ Mammolo), Balifico (Sangiovese/CAB SAUV).

Zenato Ven ★★★ V. reliable, sometimes inspired GARDA wines, also AMARONE, LUGANA, SOAVE, VALPOLICELLA. Look for labels RISERVA Sergio Zenato.

Zerbina, Fattoria E-R ★★★ Leader in Romagna; best sweet ALBANA DOCG (Scacco Matto and AR), v.gd SANGIOVESE (Pietramora); barrique-aged IGT Marzieno.

Zibibbo Si ★★★ dr sw Alluring SI table wine from the MUSCAT d'Alessandria grape, most associated with PANTELLERIA and extreme w Si. Dry version exemplified by DE BARTOLI.

Zonin Ven ★ →★★ One of Italy's biggest estate owners, based at Gambellara in Ven, but also big in F-VG, TUS, PUG, SI and elsewhere in world (eg. Virginia, US).

Germany

Abbreviations used in the text
Bad	Baden
Frank	Franken
M-M	Mittelmosel
M Rh	Mittelrhein
Mos	Mosel
Na	Nahe
Pfz	Pfalz
Rhg	Rheingau
Rhh	Rheinhessen
Sa-Un	Saale-Unstrut
Sachs	Sachsen
Würt	Württemberg

More heavily shaded areas are the wine-growing regions.

The vintage 2014 brought a smile to every German grower's face: so much wine, and such good quality! The provisos are all about climate change. Only 25 years ago, growers were trained to fight for ripeness: every extra degree of sugar in their grapes was a good thing. Today, they need to do the opposite. Ripeness needs to be slowed to avoid alcoholic, clumsy wines. Only 10 or 15 years ago, harvest started mid/end of September and lasted six weeks or longer. In 2018, many regions started picking in late August, and after a two- or three-week rush, everything was over. Most of this is good news: the acidity in those unripe wines could be punishing. Ripe Riesling is a lot nicer than unripe Riesling; and who would complain about yet another great year? But it does mean that growers have to work differently, and be reactive to changing conditions. And Kabinett, the lightest and most filigree of German wines, is becoming more difficult to make. Perhaps one day it will be the most expensive of all. At least it would no longer be underrated.

Recent vintages

Mosel

Mos (incl Saar and Ruwer wines) are so attractive young that their capabilities for developing are not often enough explored. But fine Kabinetts can gain from at least 5 yrs in bottle and often much more: Spätlese from 5–20, and Auslese and BA anything from 10–30 yrs. "Racy" is their watchword. Dry Mos used to be pretty mean; climate change is rounding them out. Saar and Ruwer make leaner wines than Mos, but surpass the whole world for elegance and thrilling, steely "breed".

2018 Powerful, at times really big wines, but balanced; better acidity than 2003.

2017 Low yield (frost) = high extract. Brilliant Kabinett, Spätlese with steely acidity.

2016 Balanced wines of textbook raciness.

2015 Warm yr, rich Trocken and Spätlesen, Auslesen to keep.

2014 Difficult yr, careful selection necessary.

2013 Top wines have freshness, elegance (but rare). M-M better than Saar, Ruwer.

2012 Classic, discreet wines, might turn out to be long-lived.

2011 Brilliant vintage, particularly Saar, Ruwer, sensational TBAs.

2010 High acidity identifying feature, some gd Spätlesen, Auslesen.

2009 Magnificent Spätlesen, Auslesen, gd balance. Keep.

2008 Kabinetts, Spätlesen can be fine, elegant. Now perfect to drink.

2007 Round, lovely wines, now approaching maturity.

Fine vintages: 05 04 03 01 99 97 95 94 93 90 89 88 76 71 69 64 59 53 49 45 37 34 21.

Rheinhessen, Nahe, Pfalz, Rheingau, Ahr

Apart from Mos, Rhg wines tend to be longest-lived of all German regions, improving for 15 yrs or more, but best wines from Rhh, Na and Pfz can last as long. Modern dry wines such as Grosses Gewächs (GG) are generally intended for drinking within 2–5 yrs, but the best undoubtedly have the potential to age. The same holds for Ahr Valley reds (and their peers from Bad and other regions of the s): their fruit makes them attractive young, but best wines can develop for 10 yrs and longer. Who will give them a chance?

2018 A record summer, with powerful wines. Growers were allowed to acidify.

2017 Southern regions and steep slopes best: rare combination of freshness and extract. Roter Hang and Mittelhaardt outstanding.

2016 Quality, quantity mixed, well-balanced Spätburgunder.

2015 Hot, dry summer. Rhg excellent, both dry and nobly sweet.

2014 Complicated, mixed results, now mostly mature.

2013 Much variation; best in s Rhh, Franken, Ahr Valley.

2012 Quantities below average, but v.gd, classical at every level.

2011 Fruity wines, harmonious acidity.

2010 Uneven quality, some v.gd Spätburgunder; dry whites should be drunk now.

2009 Excellent wines, esp dry. Some acidification needed.

2008 Ries of great raciness, ageing well.

2007 Dry wines now ready to drink.

Fine vintages: 05 03 02 01 99 98 97 96 93 90 83 76 71 69 67 64 59 53 49 45 37 34 21.

German vintage notation

The vintage notes after entries in the German section are mostly given in a different form from those elsewhere in the book. If the vintages of a single wine are rated, or are for red wine regions, the vintage notation is identical with the one used elsewhere (*see* front jacket flap). But for regions, villages & producers, two styles of vintage are indicated:

Bold type (eg. **15**) indicates classic, ripe vintages with a high proportion of SPÄTLESEN and AUSLESEN; or, in the case of red wines, gd phenolic ripeness and must weights.

Normal type (eg 17) indicates a successful but not outstanding vintage. Generally, German white wines, esp RIES, can be drunk young for their intense fruitiness or kept for a decade or two to develop more aromatic subtlety and finesse.

Adams, Weingut Rhh ★★ →★★★ Simone A proves why in C19 PINOT N from INGELHEIM was considered to be among Germany's best.

Adelmann, Weingut Graf Würt ★★ →★★★ Young Count Felix Adelmann now in charge at idyllic Schloss Schaubeck. V.gd Clevner 15 (FRÜHBURGUNDER), PINOT GR 16

Ahr Ahr ★★ →★★★★ cc' 15' 16 18 Small river valley s of Bonn, a sort of PINOT N canyon Slate gives fruit, minerality. Best: Adeneuer, Bertram, Brogsitter, Deutzerhof, Heiner-Kreuzberg, Kreuzberg, MEYER-NÄKEL, Nelles, Riske, Schumacher, STODDEN co-ops Mayschoss-altenahr and Dagernova.

Aldinger, Gerhard Würt ★★★ →★★★★ Family estate of great versatility. Whites and reds with density and tension, sensational Brut Nature SEKT (5 yrs lees-ageing 09' 10 11' 12').

Alte Reben Old vines. An obvious analogy to the French term vieilles vignes. Analogy is perfect 10 min age.

Alter Satz Frank Wine from old co-planted (different varieties all mixed up) v'yds esp in FRANK, many of them being more than 100 yrs old and ungrafted. Try (w) Otmar Zang, Schäuring, Scholtens – or Stritzinger (r).

Amtliche Prüfungsnummer (APNr) Official test number, on every label of a quality wine. Useful for discerning different lots of AUSLESE a producer has made from the same v'yd.

Assmannshausen RHG ★★ →★★★★ 05' 09 10 13 15' 16 The only RHG village with tradition for *Spätburgunder*. Wines from GROSSE LAGE v'yd Höllenberg (45 h on slate) age extremely well. Growers: BISCHÖFLICHES WEINGUT RÜDESHEIM, CHAT SAUVAGE, KESSELER, KÖNIG, KRONE, KÜNSTLER, Schloss Reinhartshausen.

Auslese Wines from selective picking of super-ripe bunches affected by noble rot (*Edelfäule*). Unctuous in flavour, but – traditionally – elegant rather than super concentrated. When fermented dry elegance is at risk.

Ayl Mos ★ →★★★ All v'yds known since 1971 by name of historically best site: Kupp. Such are German wine laws. Growers: BISCHÖFLICHE WEINGÜTER TRIER, **Lauer**, Vols

BA (Beerenauslese) Luscious sweet wine from exceptionally ripe, individually selected berries concentrated by noble rot. Rare, expensive.

Bacharach M Rh ★ →★★★ Small, idyllic town; centre of M RH RIES. Classified GROSS LAGE: Hahn, Posten Wolfshöhle. Growers: Bastian, JOST, KAUER, RATZENBERGER.

Baden Huge sw region and former Grand Duchy, 15,000 ha stretch over 230 km (143 miles), best-known for PINOT N, GRAU- and WEISSBURGUNDER and pockets of RIES, usually dry. Two-thirds of crop goes to co-ops.

Bassermann-Jordan Pfz ★★★ Famous DEIDESHEIM estate with stake in FORST's most acclaimed Kirchenstück and Jesuitengarten v'yds. *Majestic dry Ries*, but also a tradition for TBA. Stock of historic vintages: a bottle of 1811 Forster Ungeheuer showed perfectly in 2018.

ecker, Friedrich Pfz ★★→★★★★ Outstanding SPÄTBURGUNDER (Kammerberg, Sankt Paul, Res, Heydenreich) from most s part of PFZ; some v'yds actually lie across border in Alsace. Wines need 5–10 yrs cellaring. Gd whites (CHARD, RIES, PINOT GR) too.

ecker, JB Rhg ★★→★★★ Delightfully old-fashioned, cask-aged (and long-lived) dry RIES, SPÄTBURGUNDER at WALLUF and Martinsthal. Mature vintages, eg. 89 90 92, are outstanding value.

ercher Bad ★★★ KAISERSTUHL family estate, known for barrique-aged PINOTS from Burkheim (r w).

ergdolt Pfz ★★★ Organic estate at Duttweiler, known for culinary, age-worthy WEISSBURGUNDER GG Mandelberg 98' 01' 04'. Gd RIES, SPÄTBURGUNDER too.

ernkastel M-M ★★★ Senior wine town of the M-M, known for timbered houses and flowery, perfectly round RIES. GROSSE LAGE: DOCTOR, Lay. Top growers: Kerpen, JJ PRÜM, LOOSEN, Studert-Prüm, THANISCH, WEGELER. Kurfürstlay GROSSLAGE name is a deception: avoid.

iffar Pfz ★★→★★★ Old name of DEIDESHEIM, revived by Japanese oenologist Fumiko Tokuoka; prolonged lees contact gives RIES to age.

ischöfliche Weingüter Trier Mos ★★ 120 ha of mostly 1st-class v'yds uniting historical donations. Not v. reliable; do not buy without prior tasting.

ischöfliches Weingut Rüdesheim Rhg ★★★ 8 ha of best sites in RÜDESHEIM, ASSMANNSHAUSEN, JOHANNISBERG; vault cellar in Hildegard von Bingen's historic monastery. Peter Perabo (ex-KRONE) is *Pinot N specialist*, RIES also v.gd.

ocksbeutel Frank Belly-shaped bottle dating back to C18, today only permitted in FRANKEN and village of Neuweier, BAD. Now new modernized (and stackable) "Bocksbeutel PS".

odensee Bad Idyllic district of s BAD, on Lake Constance, at considerable altitude: 400–580m (1312–1903ft). Dry MÜLLER-T with elegance, light but delicate SPÄTBURGUNDER. Top villages: Hagnau, Meersburg, Reichenau. Lovely holiday wines.

oppard M Rh ★→★★★ Wine town of M RH with GROSSE LAGE Hamm – an amphitheatre of vines. Growers: Heilig Grab, Lorenz, M Müller, Perll, WEINGART. Unbeatable *value*.

rauneberg M-M ★★★→★★★★ Top village nr BERNKASTEL; excellent full-flavoured RIES of great raciness. GROSSE LAGE v'yds Juffer, Juffer-SONNENUHR. Growers: *F Haag*, *W Haag*, KESSELSTATT, Paulinshof, MF RICHTER, SCHLOSS LIESER, THANISCH.

remer Ratskeller Town-hall cellar in n Germany's commercial town of Bremen, founded in 1405, a UNESCO World Heritage Site. Oldest wine is a barrel of 1653 RÜDESHEIMER Apostelwein.

astest-growing markets for German wine: Israel (+65%), Czech Rep. (+61%), Poland (+54%).

reuer Rhg ★★★→★★★★ Exquisite RIES from RÜDESHEIM, RAUENTHAL. Berg Schlossberg has depth at 12% alc, Nonnenberg transforms austerity into age-worthiness. Theresa B set to take over, from relatives, 15-ha Altenkirch estate at LORCH.

uhl, Reichsrat von Pfz ★★★ Historic PFZ estate at DEIDESHEIM. Since ex-Bollinger cellarmaster Mathieu Kauffmann joined (2013), stunning SEKT, textbook "French-style" GGS, rich (in extract; generous) and bone-dry at the same time.

unn, Lisa Rhh ★★→★★★ Shooting star in NIERSTEIN, refined Hipping and Oelberg RIES, stylish Res CHARD,

ürgerspital zum Heiligen Geist Frank ★★★ Ancient charitable estate with great continuity: only six directors in past 180 yrs. Traditionally made whites (*Silvaner*, RIES) from best sites in/around WÜRZBURG. SILVANER GG from monopole Stein-Harfe 15' 16' 17' is a monument.

> **New EU terminology**
> Germany's part in the new EU classification involves, firstly, abolishing the term Tafelwein in favour of plain **Wein** and secondly changing Landwein to **geschützte geographische Angabe (ggA)**, or Protected Geographical Indication. QUALITÄTSWEIN and QUALITÄTSWEIN MIT PRÄDIKAT will be replaced by **geschützte Ursprungsbezeichnung (gU)**, or Protected Designation of Origin. The existing terms – SPÄTLESE, AUSLESE and so on (*see* box, p.165) – will be tacked on to gU where appropriate; the rules for these styles won't change.

Bürklin-Wolf, Dr. Pfz ★★→★★★★ 30 ha of best MITTELHAARDT v'yds incl important holdings of FORST's Kirchenstück, Jesuitengarten, Pechstein. Estate own classification since 1994, bio farming (incl horses). Wines made to age.

Busch, Clemens M-S ★★★→★★★★ Steep Pündericher Marienburg farmed by hand, bio, for a series of GGs from parcels Fahrlay, Falkenlay, Rothenpfad, Raffes. Now also RES line: 2 yrs barrel-ageing (monumental Rothenpfad Res 15).

Castell'sches Fürstliches Domänenamt Frank ★★→★★★ Superb dry SILVANER, RIES from monopoly v'yd *Casteller Schlossberg*, occasionally also TBA (outstanding Ries 06 GR BA (Silvaner 6~08).

Chat Sauvage Rhg ★★★→★★★★ Created out of nothing in 2000, Burgundian approach to RHG PINOT N. Sensational 15s (ASSMANNSHAUSEN Höllenberg, Clos d Schultz, LORCH Schlossberg). Some CHARD too, and delicate SEKT.

Christmann Pfz ★★★ VDP President Steffen Christmann, MITTELHAARDT bio pioneer now joined by daughter Sophie. Best known is RIES Königsbacher Idig 05' 08 but other GGs fine too, eg. Mandelgarten Meerspinne 17.

Clüsserath, Ansgar Mos ★★★ Tense RIES from TRITTENHEIMER Apotheke. KABINETTS are delicious, crystalline.

Corvers-Kauter Rhg ★★★ Organic estate at Mittelheim making a name for textbook mineral RÜDESHEIM RIES. Now taking over most of former LANGWERTH v'yds, doubling surface to 31 ha, adding eg. MARCOBRUNN and RAUENTHAL Baiken to portfolio.

Crusius, Dr. Na ★★→★★★ Family estate at TRAISEN, NA. Vivid, age-worthy RIES from sun-baked Bastei and Rotenfels of Traisen and SCHLOSSBÖCKELHEIM.

Deidesheim Pfz ★★→★★★★ Central MITTELHAARDT village and series of GROSSE LAGE v'yds: Grainhübel, Hohenmorgen, Kalkofen, Kieselberg, Langenmorgen Top growers: BASSERMANN-JORDAN, BIFFAR, BUHL, BÜRKLIN-WOLF, CHRISTMANN, Fusser JF Kimich, MOSBACHER, Seckinger, Siben, Stern, VON WINNING. Gd co-op.

Deinhard, Dr. Pfz ★→★★★ Since 2008, a brand of the VON WINNING estate, used for wines with no oak influence.

Diel, Schlossgut Na →★★→★★★★ Caroline Diel follows her father, with exquisite GG Ries (best usually Burgberg of Dorsheim). Magnificent SPÄTLESEN, serious Sekt (Cuvée Mo 6 yrs on lees, and exquisite single-v'yd Brut Nature from Dorsheimer Goldloch).

Doctor M-M Emblematic steep v'yd at BERNKASTEL, the place where TBA was invented (1921, THANISCH). Only 3.2 ha, and five owners: both Thanisch estates, WEGELER (1.1 ha, of which 0.06 ha is leased to KESSELSTATT), Patrick Lauerburg and local Heiligen Geist charity (0.26 ha, leased until 2024 to SCHLOSS LIESER, MARKUS MOLITOR). RIES of extraordinary richness, but pricey.

Dönnhoff Na ★★★→★★★★ Cornelius D continuing success of father Helmut with splendid series of GGs from Roxheim (*Höllenpfad* was ERSTE LAGE until 2016 now promoted to GG), NIEDERHAUSEN (Hermannshöhle), *Norheim (Dellchen)* an SCHLOSSBÖCKELHEIM (Felsenberg). Dazzling EISWEIN.

Durbach Bad ★★→★★★ ORTENAU village for full-bodied RIES, locally called

Klingelberger, granite soils. Growers: Graf Metternich, LAIBLE (both), Männle (both), MARKGRAF VON BADEN. Reliable co-op.

gon Müller zu Scharzhof Mos ★★★★ 59 71 83 90 03 15 16 17 18 Legendary SAAR estate at WILTINGEN with a treasury of old vines. Its racy SCHARZHOFBERGER RIES is among world's greatest wines: sublime, vibrant, immortal. *Kabinetts* feather-light and long-lived.

inzellage Individual v'yd site. Never to be confused with GROSSLAGE.

iswein Made from frozen grapes with the ice (ie. water content) discarded, thus v. concentrated: of BA ripeness or more. Outstanding Eiswein vintages: **98 02 04 08**. Less and less produced in past decade: climate change is Eiswein's enemy.

mrich-Schönleber Na ★★★ Werner Schönleber and son Frank make precise RIES from Monzingen's classified Frühlingsplätzchen and Halenberg (usually better).

rden M-M ★★★ →★★★★ Village on red slate soils; noble AUSLESEN and TROCKEN RIES with rare delicacy. GROSSE LAGE: Prälat, Treppchen. Growers: BREMER RATSKELLER, JJ Christoffel, LOOSEN, MERKELBACH, MARKUS MOLITOR, Mönchhof, Rebenhof, Schmitges.

rste Lage Classified v'yd, 2nd-from-top level, similar to Burgundy's Premier Cru, only in use with VDP members outside AHR, M RH, MOS, NA, RHH.

rstes Gewächs Rhg "First growth". Only for RHG v'yds, but VDP-members there changed to the GG designation after 2012. Pay attention.

rzeugerabfüllung Bottled by producer. Incl the guarantee that only own grapes have been processed. May be used by co-ops also. GUTSABFÜLLUNG is stricter, applies only to estates.

scherndorf Frank ★★★ Village with steep GROSSE LAGE Lump ("scrap" – as in tiny inherited parcels). Marvellous *Silvaner* and RIES, dry and sweet. Growers: Fröhlich, H SAUER, R SAUER, Schäffer, zur Schwane.

einherb Imprecisely defined traditional term for wines with around 10–25g sugar/litre, not necessarily tasting sweet. More flexible than HALBTROCKEN. I often choose Feinherbs.

orst Pfz ★★ →★★★★ Outstanding MITTELHAARDT village, 100% RIES, full-bodied and fine at the same time, long-lasting. Most-acclaimed GROSSE LAGE v'yds are Kirchenstück, Jesuitengarten, Pechstein, but Ungeheuer and Freundstück not far behind. ORTSWEIN usually excellent value. Top growers: Acham-Magin, BASSERMANN-JORDAN, BÜRKLIN-WOLF, H Spindler, MOSBACHER, VON BUHL, VON WINNING, WOLF. Gd co-op.

ranken / Franconia Region of distinctive dry wines, esp *Silvaner*, often bottled in round-bellied flasks (BOCKSBEUTEL). Centre is WÜRZBURG. Top villages: Bürgstadt, ESCHERNDORF, IPHOFEN, Klingenberg, Randersacker.

ranzen Mos ★★ →★★★ From Europe's steepest v'yd, Calmont at Bremm, young Kilian Franzen makes rich and "warm" but also mineral RIES.

ricke, Eva Rhg ★★ →★★★ Born nr Bremen without viticultural background, now rising star in RHG: expressive, taut RIES (10 ha, organic) from KIEDRICH, LORCH.

uder Traditional German cask, sizes 600–1800 litres depending on region, traditionally used for fermentation and (formerly long) ageing.

Germany has 17,000 growers, but more than half have less than 3 ha.

ürst, Weingut Frank ★★★ →★★★★ Successful father-son team at Bürgstadt with v'yds there and on steep terraces of Klingenberg. *Spätburgunders* 97' 05' 09 15' 16 of great finesse from red sandstone need 5–10 yrs to age, dense FRÜHBURGUNDER, excellent whites too. Pur Mineral [sic] is a reliable mid-price label.

allais, Le Mos 2nd estate of EGON MÜLLER ZU SCHARZHOF with 4-ha-monopoly Braune Kupp of WILTINGEN. Soil is schist with more clay than in SCHARZHOFBERG; AUSLESEN can be exceptional.

Grosse Lage / Grosslage: spot the difference
Bereich means district within an *Anbaugebiet* (region). *Bereich* on a label should be treated as a flashing red light; the wine is a blend from arbitrary sites within that district. Do not buy. The same holds for wines with a GROSSLAGE name, though these are more difficult to identify. Who could guess if "Forster Mariengarten" is an EINZELLAGE or a Grosslage? (It's Gross.) But now, from the 2012 vintage, it's even more tricky. Don't confuse Grosslage with GROSSE LAGE: the latter refers to best single v'yds, Germany's Grands Crus according to the classification set up by wine-grower's association VDP. They weren't thinking about you.

Geisenheim Rhg Town primarily known for Germany's top university of oenology and viticulture. One GROSSE LAGE too: Rothenberg.

GG (Grosses Gewächs) "Great/top growth". The top dry wine from a VDP-classified GROSSE LAGE (since 2012). *See also* ERSTES GEWÄCHS.

Goldkapsel / Gold Capsule Mos, Na, Rhg, Rhh Designation (and physical sealing) mainly for AUSLESE and higher. V. strict selection of grapes, which should add finesse and complexity, not primarily weight and sweetness. Lange Goldkapsel (Long Gold Capsule) is even better.

Graach M-M ★★★ →★★★★ Small village between BERNKASTEL and WEHLEN. GROSSE LAGE v'yds: Domprobst, Himmelreich, Josephshof. Top growers: Kees-Kieren, LOOSEN, MARKUS MOLITOR, *JJ Prüm*, SA PRÜM, SCHAEFER, *Selbach-Oster*, Studert-Prüm, KESSELSTATT, WEGELER.

Griesel & Compagnie Hess ★★★ SEKT startup at Bensheim, top Prestige series (Rosé Extra Brut, PINOT Brut Nature).

Grosse Lage The top level of the VDP's new classification, but only applies to VDP members. *NB* Not on any account to be confused with GROSSLAGE. The dry wine from a Grosse Lage site is called GG. Stay awake there.

Grosser Ring Mos Group of top (VDP) MOS estates, whose annual Sept auction at TRIER sets world-record prices.

Grosslage Term destined, maybe even intended, to confuse. Introduced by the disastrous 1971 wine law. A collection of secondary v'yds with supposedly similar character – but no indication of quality. Not on any account to be confused with GROSSE LAGE. Repeat after me.

Gunderloch Rhh ★★★ →★★★★ Historical NACKENHEIM estate known for nobly sweet RIES and culinary *Kabinett Jean-Baptiste*. Recently increasing emphasis on TROCKEN wines, eg. dense, terroir-driven Rothenberg GG 17.

Gut Hermannsberg Na ★★★ Former state domain at NIEDERHAUSEN, privatized in 2010. Some of densest RIES GGs of NA, eg. Kupfergrube, Felsberg from SCHLOSSBÖCKELHEIM and Hermannsberg at Niederhausen.

Gutsabfüllung Estate-bottled, and made from own grapes.

Gutswein Wine with no v'yd or village designation, but only the producer's name: entry-level category. Ideally, Gutswein should be an ERZEUGERABFÜLLUNG (from own grapes), but is not always the case.

Haag, Fritz Mos ★★★★ BRAUNEBERG's top estate; Oliver Haag follows footsteps of his father, Wilhelm, but wines more modern in style. *See also* SCHLOSS LIESER.

Haag, Willi Mos ★★ →★★★ BRAUNEBERG family estate, led by Marcus Haag. Old-style RIES, mainly sweet, rich but balanced, and inexpensive.

Haart, Julian Mos ★★ →★★★ Talented nephew of Theo Haart making a name for dense, spontaneously fermented RIES.

Haart, Reinhold M-M ★★★ →★★★★ Best estate in PIESPORT with important holding in famous Goldtröpfchen ("gold droplet") v'yd, RIES SPÄTLESEN, AUSLESEN and higher PRÄDIKAT wines are *racy, copybook Mosels* – with great ageing potential.

Haidle Würt ★★★ Family estate now led by young Moritz Haidle, using the cool climate of Remstal area for RIES, LEMBERGER of distinctive freshness.

Halbtrocken Medium-dry with 9–18g unfermented sugar/litre, inconsistently distinguished from FEINHERB (which sounds better).

Hattenheim Rhg ★★→★★★★ Town famous for classic RHG RIES from GROSSE LAGEN Nussbrunnen, Hassel, STEINBERG, Wisselbrunnen. Estates: Barth, HESSISCHE STAATSWEINGÜTER, Kaufmann (ex-Lang), Knyphausen, Ress, Schloss Reinhartshausen, SPREITZER. The *Brunnen* ("well") v'yds (eg. MARCOBRUNN) lie on a rocky basin that collects water, protection against drought.

Heger, Dr. Bad ★★★ KAISERSTUHL estate known for dry parcel selections from volcanic soils in Achkarren and IHRINGEN, esp Vorderer Berg (sensational SPÄTBURGUNDER 16') from steepest Winklerberg terraces.

Heitlinger / Burg Ravensburg Bad ★★→★★★ Two leading estates in Kraichgau, BAD, under same ownership: Heitlinger more modern, elegant in style, Burg Ravensburg full-bodied. Best usually Schellenbrunnen RIES, Königsbecher PINOT N.

Hessische Bergstrasse Hess ★→★★★ Germany's smallest wine region (only 440 ha), n of Heidelberg. Pleasant RIES from Bergsträßer Winzer co-op, GRIESEL (SEKT), HESSISCHE STAATSWEINGÜTER, Simon-Bürkle, Stadt Bensheim.

Hessische Staatsweingüter Hess, Rhg ★★→★★★★ State domain of big – and historical – dimensions, holding 220 ha in ASSMANNSHAUSEN, RÜDESHEIM, *Rauenthal*, HATTENHEIM (monopoly STEINBERG), HOCHHEIM and along HESSISCHE BERGSTRASSE. Superb C12 Cistercian abbey KLOSTER EBERBACH has vinotheque and 12 historical presses. New winemaker (2018).

Heyl zu Herrnsheim Rhh ★★→★★★ Historic NIERSTEIN estate, bio, part of the ST-ANTONY estate. GG from monopoly site Brudersberg can be excellent.

Heymann-Löwenstein Mos ★★★ Pacemaker downstream on Mosel at WINNINGEN nr Koblenz. Spontaneously fermented RIES from steep terraces, intense, individual.

Hochgewächs Designation for a MOS RIES that obeys stricter requirements than plain QbA, today rarely used. A worthy advocate is *Kallfelz* in Zell-Merl.

Hochheim Rhg ★★→★★★★ Town e of main RHG, on River Main. Rich, earthy RIES from GROSSE LAGE v'yds: Domdechaney, Hölle, Kirchenstück, KÖNIGIN VICTORIABERG, Reichestal. Growers: *Domdechant Werner*, Flick, HESSISCHE STAATSWEINGÜTER, Himmel, *Künstler*.

Hock Traditional English term for Rhine wine, derived from HOCHHEIM.

Hövel, Weingut von Mos ★★★ Fine SAAR estate, now bio, with v'yds at Oberemmel (Hütte is 4.8-ha monopoly), at KANZEM (Hörecker) and in SCHARZHOFBERG (delicate 17 Auslese No 48).

Mittelrhein's next-most-important fruit: cherries. Pliny the Elder praised them.

Huber, Bernhard Bad ★★★→★★★★★ Young Julian H has vision of BAD as Germany's burgundy: Wildenstein SPÄTBURGUNDER 16' ranks among best reds ever produced by this fine estate. Equally outstanding tight, demanding CHARDS (eg. Bienenberg 16').

Ihringen Bad ★→★★★ Village in KAISERSTUHL known for fine SPÄTBURGUNDER, GRAUBURGUNDER on steep volcanic Winklerberg. Top growers: DR. HEGER, Konstanzer, Michel, Stigler, von Gleichenstein.

Immich-Batterieberg M-M ★★→★★★ Revived historic estate named after slopes that were blasted into the slate rock in C19 ("battery" = bundle of dynamite). Deeply mineral TROCKEN and off-dry RIES, but no sweet wines.

Ingelheim Rhh ★★→★★★ RHH town with limestone beds under v'yds; historic fame for SPÄTBURGUNDER being reinvigorated by estates as ADAMS, Arndt F Werner, Bettenheimer, Dautermann, NEUS, Schloss Westerhaus, Wasem.

Iphofen Frank ★★ →★★★ STEIGERWALD village with famous GROSSE LAGE Julius Echter-Berg. Rich, aromatic, well-ageing SILVANER from gypsum soils. Growers Arnold, Emmerich, JULIUSSPITAL, RUCK, Seufert, VETTER, Weigand, WELTNER, **Wirsching**, Zehntkeller.

Jahrgang Year – as in "vintage".

Johannisberg Rhg ★★ →★★★★ RHG village best known for berry- and honey-scented RIES from SCHLOSS JOHANNISBERG. GROSSLAGE (avoid!): Erntebringer.

Johannishof (Eser) Rhg ★★ →★★★★ Family estate with v'yds at JOHANNISBERG, RÜDESHEIM. Johannes Eser makes RIES with perfect balance of ripeness and steely acidity.

Josephshöfer Mos ★★ →★★★★ GROSSE LAGE v'yd at GRAACH, the sole property of KESSELSTATT. Harmonious, berry-flavoured RIES.

Jost, Toni M Rh ★★★ Leading estate in BACHARACH with monopoly Hahn, now led by Cecilia J. Aromatic RIES with nerve, and recently remarkable PINOT N 15'. Family also run estate at WALLUF (RHG).

Juliusspital Frank ★★= Ancient WÜRZBURG charity with top v'yds all over FRANK known for **dry Silvaners** that age well. Recently less opulence and more structure – GGs now cellared 1 yr more before sale.

Kabinett See box, p.165. Germany's unique featherweight contribution, but with climate change ever more difficult to produce.

Kaiserstuhl Bad Outstanding district nr Rhine with notably warm climate and volcanic soil. Renowned above all for SPÄTBURGUNDER and GRAUBURGUNDER.

Kanzem Mos ★★★ SAAR village with steep GROSSE LAGE v'yd Altenberg (slate and weathered red rock). Growers: BISCHÖFLICHE WEINGÜTER TRIER, **Van Volxem**, VON OTHEGRAVEN.

Karthäuserhof Mos ★★★★ Outstanding RUWER estate with monopoly v'yd Karthäuserhofberg. Characteristic neck-only label stands for refreshing dry and sublime sweet wines.

Kauer ★★ →★★★ Family estate at BACHARACH. Fine, aromatic organic RIES. Randolf Kauer is professor of organic viticulture at GEISENHEIM.

Keller, Franz Bad See SCHWARZER ADLER.

Keller, Weingut Rhh →★★ →★★★★ Star of RHH, cultish for powerful RIES G-Max, and GGs Hubacker, Morstein. Also Ries from NIERSTEIN (Hipping, Pettenthal) and M-M (PIESPORT Schubertslay). Outstanding PINOT N.

Kesseler, August Rhg ★★★ →★★★★ Passionate August K is about to retire, but long-time employees keep level of SPÄTBURGUNDERS from ASSMANNSHAUSEN and RÜDESHEIM as high as ever. Also fine RIES, dry and sweet.

Kesselstatt, Reichsgraf von Mos ★★ →★★★★ In her 30 yrs+ hard work, Annegret Reh-Gartner (RIP 2016) made this estate splendid: 35 ha top v'yds on MOS and both tributaries, incl remarkable stake in SCHARZHOFBERG.

Kiedrich Rhg ★★ →★★★★ Top RHG village, almost a monopoly of the WEIL estate; other growers (e.g. FRICKE, Knyphausen, PRINZ VON HESSEN) own only small plots. Famous church and choir.

Landwein rebels

Official quality testing helps remove flawed wines from the market. But it has a downside too: it tends to punish experiments. Thirty-five yrs ago, Germany's barrique pioneers needed to declassify their wines to Tafelwein. Today, a dozen BAD growers have joined forces to promote LANDWEIN (GGA) instead of QUALITÄTSWEIN because their spontaneously fermented samples were rejected by the quality commission. The mastermind of these Landwein rebels is the ever-energetic Hanspeter ZIEREISEN. Some more estates to watch: Brenneisen, Enderle&Moll, Fendt, Forgeurac, Geitlinger, Nieger, Scherer, Wasenhaus.

Kloster Eberbach Rhg Glorious C12 Cistercian abbey in HATTENHEIM with iconic STEINBERG, domicile of HESSISCHE STAATSWEINGÜTER.

Klumpp, Weingut Bad ★★★ Rising star in Kraichgau. SPÄTBURGUNDER LEMBERGER of depth, elegance. Markus Klumpp is married to Meike Näkel of MEYER-NÄKEL.

Knewitz, Weingut Rhh ★★★ 20-ha family estate puts RHH village of Appenheim on map. Young brothers Tobias and Björn produce focused, skilful whites. Top: Hundertgulden RIES.

Third of VDP members certified organic: way more than Germany's average of 8%.

Knipser, Weingut Pfz ★★★→★★★★ N PFZ family estate, barrique-aged SPÄTBURGUNDER (iconic RdP 15') straightforward RIES (GG Steinbuckel), Cuvée X (B'x blend). Many specialities, incl historical bone-dry Gelber Orleans.

Königin Viktoriaberg Rhg ★★→★★★ Classified vyd at HOCHHEIM, 4.5 ha along shores of River Main, known for textbook RHG RIES, today run by Flick estate of Wicker. After 1845 visit, Queen Victoria granted owner right to rename v'yd as "Queen-Victoria-mountain".

Kraichgau Bad Small district se of Heidelberg. Top growers: HEITLINGER/BURG RAVENSBURG, Hoensbroech, Hummel, KLUMPP.

Krone, Weingut Rhg ★★★ Famous SPÄTBURGUNDER estate with old v'yds in ASSMANNSHAUSEN's steep Höllenberg (slate), run by WEGELER. Fine Rosé SEKT too.

Kühling-Gillot Rhh ★★★★ Top bio estate, run by Caroline Gillot and husband HO Spanier. Best in already outstanding range of ROTER HANG RIES: GG Rothenberg Wurzelecht from ungrafted, 70 yrs+ vines.

Kühn, Peter Jakob Rhg ★★★→★★★★ Excellent estate in OESTRICH led by PJ Kühn and son. Obsessive bio v'yd management and long macerations shape **nonconformist but exciting** RIES. Res RPJK Unikat aged 4 yrs in cask.

Kuhn, Philipp Pfz ★★★ Reliable estate of great versatility. Rich RIES (eg. SAUMAGEN, Schwarzer Herrgott), succulent barrel-aged SPÄTBURGUNDER, specialities (FRÜHBURGUNDER, SAUV BL, SEKT).

Künstler Rhg ★★★ Superb dry RIES at HOCHHEIM (Hölle), Kostheim (Weiß Erd), and other side of RHG at RÜDESHEIM (Schlossberg, Rottland).

Kuntz, Sybille Mos ★★★ Progressive individual organic 12-ha estate at Lieser, esp Niederberg-Helden v'yd. Intense wines, one of each ripeness category, intended for gastronomy, listed in many top restaurants.

Laible, Alexander Bad ★★→★★★ DURBACH estate of ANDREAS LAIBLE's (*see* next entry) younger son; aromatic dry RIES, SCHEUREBE, WEISSBURGUNDER.

Laible, Andreas Bad ★★★ Crystalline dry RIES from DURBACH's Plauelrain v'yd: 17 ERSTE LAGE Achat and GG Am Bühl GG exhibit typicity of Ries on granite soil at its v. best. Gd SCHEUREBE, GEWÜRZ too.

Landwein Now "ggA". *See* box, p.158. *See also* box, left.

Langwerth von Simmern Rhg Once famous, but now history: In 2018, von Langwerth family sold their manor house in Eltville and leased their v'yds to the CORVERS-KAUTER estate. Label will disappear.

Lanius-Knab M Rh ★★★ Often overlooked family estate at Oberwesel, M RH: crystalline, harmonious RIES at all levels.

Lauer Mos ★★★ Fine, precise SAAR RIES: tense, poised. Parcel selections from huge Ayler Kupp v'yd. Best: Kern, Schonfels, Stirn.

Leitz, Josef Rhg ★★★ RÜDESHEIM-based family estate known for rich but elegant single-v'yd RIES (sweet and dry) and inexpensive but reliable Eins-Zwei-Dry label.

Liebfrauenstift, Weingut Rhh Owner of best plots of historical LIEBFRAUENSTIFT-KIRCHENSTÜCK v'yd. Formerly linked to a merchant house, but now autonomous. Promising: Katharina Prüm (of JJ PRÜM) consults. *See* next entry.

Liebfrauenstift-Kirchenstück Rhh A walled v'yd in city of Worms producing flowery

RIES from gravelly soil. Producers: Gutzler, Schembs (01' almost youthful in 2017), WEINGUT LIEBFRAUENSTIFT. Not to be confused with Liebfraumilch, a cheap and tasteless imitation.

Loewen, Carl Mos ★★→★ RIES of elegance, tension, complexity. Best v'yd Longuicher Maximin Herrenberg (planted 1896, ungrafted). Entry-level Ries Varidor excellent *value*.

Loosen, Weingut Dr. M-M ★★→★★★ Charismatic Ernie Loosen produces traditional RIES from old vines in BERNKASTEL, ERDEN, GRAACH, ÜRZIG, WEHLEN. Erdener Prälat AUSLESE cultish for decades, dry Prälat Res (2 yrs cask-ageing, 1st vintage 2011) about to follow. Dr L Ries, from bought-in grapes, is reliable. *See also* WOLF (PFZ), Chateau Ste Michelle (Washington State), J. Christopher (Oregon).

Lorch Rhg ★→★★★ Village in extreme w of RHG, conditions more M RH-like than Rhg-like. Sharply crystalline wines, both RIES and PINOT N, now re-discovered. Best: EAT SAUVAGE, FRICKE, Johanninger, KESSELER, von Kanitz. Soon to come: BREUER.

Löwenstein, Fürst Frank, Rhg ★★★ Princely estate with holdings in RHG, FRANK. Classic Rhg RIES from HALLGARTEN, unique *Silvaner*, *Ries* from ultra-steep v'yd Homburger Kallmuth.

Lützkendorf, Weingut Sa-Un ★★→★★★ Quality leader in SA-UN. Outstanding 17 Hohe Gräte GGs (TRAMINER, WEISSBURGUNDER, RIES).

Marcobrunn Rhg Historic 7-ha v'yd in Erbach, GROSSE LAGE. Potential for rich, long-lasting RIES. Growers: HESSISCHE STAATSWEINGÜTER, Knyphausen, Schloss Reinhartshausen, von Oetinger.

Markgräflerland Bad District s of Freiburg, cool climate due to breezes from Black Forest. Typical GUTEDEL (try Lämmlin-Schindler Res 16') a pleasant companion for local cuisine. Climate change makes PINOT varieties successful.

Markgraf von Baden Bad ★★→★★★ Important noble estate (135 ha) at Salem castle (BODENSEE) and Staufenberg castle (ORTENAU), young Prince Bernhard being more involved than his father was. Rising quality.

Maximin Grünhaus Mos ★★★★ Supreme RUWER estate led by Carl von Schubert, who also presides over GROSSER RING (VDP MOS). V. traditional winemaking shapes herb-scented, *delicate*, *long-lived Ries*. Astonishing WEISSBURGUNDER, PINOT N.

Merkelbach, Weingut M-M ★★→★★★ Tiny Estate at ÜRZIG, 2 ha. Brothers Alfred and Rolf (both c.80) inexpensive MOS made not to sip, but to drink. Superb list of old vintages.

Meßmer, Weingut Pfz ★★→★★★ Brothers Gregor and Martin M keep an important stake in Burrweiler's Schäwer v'yd, one of few pockets of schist in PFZ. V. consistent in quality, many specialities eg. MUSKATELLER FEINHERB and barrel-fermented PINOT GR AUSLESE.

Meyer-Näkel Ahr ★★★→★★★★ Werner Näkel and daughters make the most fruit-driven, refined Ahr Valley SPÄTBURGUNDER. Freshness of wines obscures how hard it is to produce them: eg. Walporzheimer Kräuterberg has ten steep terraces on a surface equal to football penalty area. All must be done by hand. Also in S Africa (Zwalu, together with Neil Ellis) and Portugal (Quinta da Carvalhosa).

Mittelhaardt Pfz 04' 08' **09** 11 12 15 16 17' 18 N-central and best part of PFZ, incl DEIDESHEIM, FORST RUPPERTSBERG, WACHENHEIM; largely planted with RIES.

Mittelmosel Central and best part of MOS, a RIES Eldorado, incl BERNKASTEL, BRAUNEBERG, GRAACH, PIESPORT, WEHLEN, etc.

Mittelrhein ★★→★★★★ Dramatically scenic Rhine area nr tourist-magnet Loreley. Best villages: BACHARACH, BOPPARD. Delicate yet *steely Ries*, *underrated* and underpriced. As long-lived as neighbours in RHG and MOS.

Molitor, Markus M-M, Mos ★★★ Growing estate (now 100 ha in 170 parcels throughout M-M and SAAR) led by perfectionist Markus M. Styles, v'yds and

---

Germany's quality levels

The official range of qualities and styles in ascending order is (take a deep breath):

1 Wein: formerly known as Tafelwein. Light wine of no specified character, mostly sweetish.

2 ggA (geschützte geographische Angabe): or Protected Geographical Indication, formerly known as LANDWEIN. Dryish Wein with some regional style. Mostly a label to avoid, but some thoughtful estates use the Landwein, or ggA designation to bypass official constraints.

3 gU (geschützte Ursprungsbezeichnung): or protected Designation of Origin. Replacing QUALITÄTSWEIN. So far, only two: Bürgstadter Berg, and Uhlen of Winningen.

4 Qualitätswein: dry or sweetish wine with sugar added before fermentation to increase its strength, but tested for quality and with distinct local and grape character. Don't despair.

5 Kabinett: dry/dryish natural (unsugared) wine of distinct personality and distinguishing lightness. Can occasionally be sublime – esp with a few yrs' age.

6 Spätlese: stronger, sweeter than KABINETT. Full-bodied (but no botrytis). Dry SPÄTLESE (or what could be considered as such) is today mostly sold under Qualitätswein designation.

7 Auslese: sweeter, stronger than Spätlese, often with honey-like flavours, intense and long-lived. Occasionally dry and weighty. The lower the alc (read the label) the sweeter the wine.

8 Beerenauslese (BA): v. sweet, dense and intense, but seldom strong in terms of alc. Can be superb.

9 Eiswein: from naturally frozen grapes of BA/TBA quality: concentrated, sharpish and v. sweet. Some examples are extreme, unharmonious.

10 Trockenbeerenauslese (TBA): intensely sweet and aromatic; alc slight. Extraordinary and everlasting.

---

vintages in amazing depth. 1st vintage of Molitor's Doctor (16) fetched €1249/bottle at auction.

Mosbacher Pfz ★★★ Some of best GG RIES of FORST: rather refined than massive. Traditional ageing in big oak casks. Excellent SAUV BL too ("Fumé").

Mosel (Moselle in French) 90 01 05 09 11 15 16 17 18 Wine-growing area formerly known as Mosel-Saar-Ruwer. Conditions on the RUWER and SAAR tributaries are v. different from those along the Mosel. 60% RIES.

Moselland Mos Huge MOS CO-OP, at BERNKASTEL, after mergers with co-ops in NA, PFZ; 3290 members, 2400 ha. Little is above average.

Nackenheim Rhh ★→★★★★ NIERSTEIN neighbour with GROSSE LAGE Rothenberg on red shale, famous for *Rhh's richest Ries*, superb TBA. Top growers: *Gunderloch*, KÜHLING-GILLOT.

Nahe Tributary of the Rhine and dynamic region with dozens of lesser-known producers, excellent value. Great variety of soils; best RIES from slate has almost MOS-like raciness.

Naturrein "Naturally pure": designation on old labels (pre-1971), indicating as little technical intervention as possible, esp no chaptalizing (sugar added at fermentation). Should be brought back.

Neipperg, Graf von Würt ★★★ LEMBERGER and SPÄTBURGUNDER of grace and purity, and v. fine sweet TRAMINER. Count Karl-Eugen von Neipperg's younger brother Stephan makes wine at Canon la Gaffelière in St-Émilion and elsewhere.

Neus Rhh ★★★ Revived historic estate at INGELHEIM, excellent PINOT N (best: Pares).

Niederhausen Na ★★ →★★★★ Village of the middle NA Valley. Complex RIES from famous GROSSE LAGE Hermannshöhle and neighbouring steep slopes. Growers: CRUSIUS, *Dönnhoff*, GUT HERMANNSBERG, J Schneider, Mathern, von Racknitz.

Nierstein Rhh ★→★★→★ Important wine town (c.800 ha) with accordingly variable wines. Best are rich, tense, eg. GROSSE LAGE v'yds Brudersberg, Hipping, Oelberg, Orbel, Pettenthal Growers: BUNN, FE Huff, Gehring, GUNDERLOCH, Guntrum, HEYL ZU HERRNSHEIM, KELLER, KÜHLING-GILLOT, Manz, Schätzel, ST-ANTONY, Strub. But *beware Grosslage Gutes Domtal*: a supermarket deception.

Ockfen Mos ★★→★★★ Village with almost atypical powerful SAAR RIES from GROSSE LAGE v'yd Bockstein. Growers: OTHEGRAVEN, SANKT URBANS-HOF, WAGNER, *Zilliken*.

Odinstal, Weingut Pfz ★★→★★★ Highest v'yd of PFZ, 150m (492ft) above WACHENHEIM. Bio farming and low-tech vinification bring pure RIES, SILVANER, GEWURZ. Harvest often extends into Nov.

Oechsle Scale for sugar content of grape juice.

Oestrich Rhg ★★→★★★ Exemplary steely RIES, fine AUSLESEN from GROSSE LAGE v'yds: Doosberg, Lenchen. Top growers: A Eser, KÜHN, Querbach, SPREITZER, WEGELER.

Oppenheim Rhh ★→★★★ Town S of NIERSTEIN, GROSSE LAGE Kreuz, Sackträger. Growers: Guntrum, Kissinger, KÜHLING-GILLOT, Manz. Spectacular C13 church.

Ortenau Bad ★★→★★ District around and S of city of Baden-Baden. Mainly Klingelberger (RIES) and SPÄTBURGUNDER from granite soils. Top villages: DURBACH, Neuweier, Waldulm.

Ortswein Second rank up in VDP's pyramid of qualities: a village wine, often from single-v'yd grapes. Many bargains.

Othegraven, von Mos ★★★ Fine SAAR estate with superb GROSSE LAGE Altenberg of KANZEM, as well as parcels in OCKFEN (Bockstein) and Wawern (Herrenberg). Since 2010 owned by TV star Günther Jauch.

Palatinate Pfz English for PFALZ.

Pfalz 2nd-largest German region, balmy climate, Lucullian lifestyle. MITTELHAARDT RIES best; S Pfalz (SÜDLICHE WEINSTRASSE) is better suited to PINOT varieties. ZELLERTAL now fashionable cool climate.

Piesport M-M ★→★★★★ M-M village for rich, aromatic RIES. GROSSE LAGE v'yds Domherr, Goldtröpfchen. Growers: GRANS-FASSIAN, Joh Haart, JULIAN HAART, Hain, KESSELSTATT, *Reinhold Haart*, SANKT URBANS-HOF. Avoid GROSSLAGE Michelsberg.

Piwi ★→★★ Designation for crossings of European and American vines, for fungal resistance ("Pilz-Widerstandsfähigkeit"). Best known: Johanniter (w), Regent (r).

Prädikat Legally defined special attributes or qualities. See QMP.

Prinz von Hessen Rhg ★★★ Glorious wines from historic JOHANNISBERG estate, esp at SPÄTLESE and above, and mature vintages.

Prinz, Weingut Rhg ★★★ Organic grower Fred P made name for distinctly fresh, elegant RIES from Hallgarten's altitude v'yds, incl Jungfer GOLDKAPSEL KABINETT.

Prüm, JJ Mos ★★★★ 59 71 76 83 90 03 15 16 17 18 Legendary WEHLEN estate; also BERNKASTEL, GRAACH. Delicate but extraordinarily long-lived wines with finesse and distinctive character.

Prüm, SA Mos →★ Less traditional in style and less consistent than WEHLEN neighbour JJ PRÜM. Be v. selective.

QbA (Qualitätswein bestimmter Anbaugebiete) "Quality Wine", controlled as

---

The Bocksbeutel vending machine

WÜRZBURG is in uproar: a clever grocer set up a BOCKSBEUTEL vending-machine in front of his store, so that you may buy a well-chilled bottle of STEINWEIN 24/7 with your credit card. He argues that the payment method ensures youth protection. Neighbouring bars disagree. We say: can we have one?

to area, grape(s), vintage. May add sugar before fermentation (as in French chaptalization). Intended as middle category, but now VDP obliges its members to label their best dry wines (GGS) as QbA. New EU name gU is scarcely found on labels (*see* box, p.158).

QmP (Qualitätswein mit Prädikat) Top category, meant to replace the NATURREIN designation: no sugaring of must. Apart from that, less strict. Six levels according to ripeness of grapes: KABINETT to TBA.

Randersacker Frank ★★→★★★ Village s of WÜRZBURG with GROSSE LAGE: Pfülben. Top growers: BÜRGERSPITAL (remarkable RIES), JULIUSSPITAL, SCHMITT'S KINDER, STAATLICHER HOFKELLER, Störrlein & Krenig.

A lime plant growing wine? Kalkwerk Istein (s Baden) farms a recultivated ex-quarry.

Ratzenberger M Rh ★★→★★★ Family estate known for racy RIES from BACHARACH and gd SEKT too. Bought 10 ha steep slope Oberdiebacher Fürstenberg (2017), saving it from becoming fallow.

Rauenthal Rhg ★★→★★★★ Once RHG'S most expensive RIES. *Spicy, austere but complex* from inland slopes. Baiken, Gehrn and Rothenberg v'yds contain GROSSE LAGE and ERSTE LAGE parcels, while neighbouring Nonnenberg (monopole of BREUER) is unclassified, despite its equally outstanding quality. Top growers: A ESER, BREUER, CORVERS-KAUTER, Diefenhardt, HESSISCHE STAATSWEINGÜTER.

Raumland Rhh ★★★ SEKT expert with deep cellar and full range of fine and balanced cuvées. Best are usually: CHARD Brut Nature (disgorged after 10 yrs) and Cuvée Triumvirat.

Rebholz, Ökonomierat Pfz ★★★ Top SÜDLICHE WEINSTRASSE estate: bone-dry, zesty and reliable RIES GGS, best usually Kastanienbusch from red schist 07' 11' 15 16 17. Also gd CHARD, SPÄTBURGUNDER.

Restsüsse Unfermented grape sugar remaining in (or in cheap wines added to) wine to give it sweetness. Can range from 1g/l in a TROCKEN wine to 300g in a TBA.

Rheingau ★★→★★★★ 08 09 15 16 17 18 Birthplace of RIES. Historic s- and sw-facing slopes overlooking Rhine between Wiesbaden and RÜDESHEIM. Classic, substantial Ries, famous for steely backbone, and small amounts of delicate SPÄTBURGUNDER. Also centre of SEKT production.

Rheinhessen ★→★★★★ Germany's largest region by far (26,600 ha and rising), between Mainz and Worms. Much dross, but also treasure trove of well-priced wines from gifted young growers.

Richter, Max Ferd M-M ★★→★★★ Reliable estate, at Mülheim. Esp gd RIES KABINETT, SPÄTLESEN: full and aromatic. Round and pretty Brut (EISWEIN dosage). Thoughtful winemaking.

Riffel Rhh ★★★ Organic family estate with holdings in Bingen's once famous Scharlachberg (red soils). RIES Turm has class. Now also Pét-Nat (cloudy SEKT) and barrel-fermented SILVANER.

Rings, Weingut Pfz ★★★→★★★★ Brothers Steffen and Andreas have made a name for dry RIES (esp Kallstadt SAUMAGEN), and precise SPÄTBURGUNDER (Saumagen, Felsenberg im Berntal).

Roter Hang Rhh ★★→★★★★ 11 12 15 16 17' 18 Leading RIES area of RHH (NACKENHEIM, NIERSTEIN, OPPENHEIM). Name ("red slope") refers to red shale soil.

Ruck, Johann Frank ★★★ Spicy, age-worthy SILVANER, RIES, SCHEUREBE, TRAMINER from IPHOFEN.

Rüdesheim Rhg ★★→★★★★ Most famous RHG RIES on slate, best GROSSE LAGE v'yds (Kaisersteinfels, Roseneck, Rottland, Schlossberg) called Rüdesheimer Berg. Full-bodied but never clumsy wines, floral, gd even in off-yrs. Best growers: *Breuer*, CHAT SAUVAGE, CORVERS-KAUTER, HESSISCHE STAATSWEINGÜTER, *Johannishof*, KESSELER, KÜNSTLER, LEITZ, Ress.

GERMANY

Ruppertsberg Pfz ★★→★★★ MITTELHAARDT village known for elegant RIES. Growers: BASSERMANN-JORDAN, FFFAR, BUHL, BÜRKLIN-WOLF, CHRISTMANN, VON WINNING.

Ruwer Mos ★★→★★★ Tributary of MOS nr TRIER, higher in altitude than M-M. Quaffable light dry and intense sweet RIES. Best growers: Beulwitz, Karlsmühle, KARTHÄUSERHOF, KESSELSTATT, MAXIMIN GRÜNHAUS.

Saale-Unstrut ★→★★★ N-E region around confluence of these two rivers nr Leipzig. Terraced v'yds have Cistercian origins. Quality leaders: Böhme, Born, Gussek, Hey, Kloster Pforta LÜTZKENDORF (VDP member), Pawis (VDP).

Saar Mos ★★→★★★★ Tributary of Mosel, bordered by steep slopes. Most austere, steely, ***brilliant Ries*** of all, consistency favoured by climate change. Villages incl: AYL, KANZEM, OCKFEN, SAARBURG, Serrig, WILTINGEN (SCHARZHOFBERG).

Saarburg Mos Small town in the SAAR Valley. Growers incl: WAGNER and ZILLIKEN. GROSSE LAGE: Rausch.

Sachsen ★→★★★ Region in Elbe Valley around Meissen and Dresden. Characterful dry whites. Best growers: Aust, Richter, ***Schloss Proschwitz***, Schloss Wackerbarth, Schuh, Schwarz (try co-fermented RIES/TRAMINER), ZIMMERLING.

St-Antony Rhh ★★→★★★ NIERSTEIN estate with exceptional v'yds, known for sturdy ROTER HANG RIES, complex BLAUFRÄNKISCH. New winemaker (2018).

Salm, Prinz zu Na, Rhh ★★→★★★ Owner of Schloss Wallhausen in NA and v'yds there and at BINGEN (RHH); ex-president of VDP.

Salwey Bad ★★★ Leading KAISERSTUHL estate. Konrad S picks early for freshness. Best: GGS Henkenberg and Eichberg GRAUBURGUNDER, Kirchberg SPÄTBURGUNDER and WEISSBURGUNDER.

Sankt Urbans-Hof Mos ★★★ Large family estate based in Leiwen, v'yds along M-M and SAAR. Limpid RIES, impeccably pure, racy, age well.

Sauer, Horst Frank ★★★ Finest exponent of ESCHERNDORF's top v'yd Lump. Racy, straightforward dry Silvaner and RIES, sensational TBA.

Sauer, Rainer Frank ★★★ Top family estate producing seven different dry SILVANERS from ESCHERNDORF's steep slope Lump. Best: GG am Lumpen, ALTE REBEN and L 99' 03' 07'.

Saumagen Popular local dish of PFZ: stuffed pig's stomach. Also one of best v'yds of region: a calcareous site at Kallstadt producing excellent RIES, PINOT N.

Schaefer, Willi Mos ★★ Willi S and son Christoph finest in GRAACH (but only 4 ha). MOS RIES at its best: pure, crystalline, feather-light, rewarding at all levels.

Schäfer-Fröhlich Na ★★★ Ambitious NA family estate known for spontaneously fermented RIES of great intensity, ***GG*** incl Bockenau Felseneck and Stromberg.

Scharzhofberg Mos ★★→★★★★ Superlative SAAR v'yd: a rare coincidence of microclimate, soil and human intelligence to bring about the perfection of RIES. Top estates: BISCHÖFLICHE WEINGÜTER TRIER, EGON MÜLLER, KESSELSTATT, VAN VOLXEM, VON HÖVEL.

Schlossböckelheim Na ★★→★★★★ Village with GROSSE LAGE v'yds Felsenberg,

---

Pinot Meunier

PINOT M – Champagne's workhorse – is rarely vinified as a red wine. Its thin skins and bright colour usually work better when it's vinified as white. But in Germany, there is a tradition for reds made of Meunier, mostly under the misleading name of SCHWARZRIESLING ("Black RIES"). (It's a member of the Pinot family, with no connection to Ries.) Best known for delicate perfume und supple, fine-grained tannin are eg. Schwarzrieslings Fyerst and Res by Konrad Schlör (TAUBERTAL), R by Thomas SEEGER, Neipperger ORTSWEIN by GRAF NEIPPERG, Res versions by KRAICHGAU estates Heitlinger and Hummel, and Terrain Calcaire by Weingut Nett (PFZ).

Kupfergrube. Firm RIES that needs ageing. Top growers: C Bamberger, CRUSIUS, DÖNNHOFF, GUT HERMANNSBERG, KAUER, SCHÄFER-FRÖHLICH.

Schloss Johannisberg Rhg ★★ →★★★ Historic RHG estate and Metternich mansion, 100% RIES, owned by Henkell (Oetker group). Usually v.gd SPÄTLESE Grünlack ("green sealing-wax"), reliable GUTSWEIN (Gelblack). New (2017) is Bronzelack (ERSTE LAGE TROCKEN), a kind of 2nd wine beside GG Silberlack.

Top five Ries producers worldwide, in order: Germany, Romania (!), US, France and Australia.

Schloss Lieser M-M ★★★ →★★★★ Thomas Haag (elder son of FRITZ HAAG estate) produces painstakingly elaborate RIES both dry and sweet from Lieser (Niederberg Helden), BRAUNEBERG, WEHLEN, PIESPORT. Now also small (leased) plot in BERNKASTEL'S DOCTOR. Hotel Lieser Castle has no ties to wine estate.

Schloss Proschwitz Sachs ★★ Prince Lippe's resurrected estate at Meissen in SACHSEN; the beacon of E Germany, esp with *dry Weissburgunder*, GRAUBURGUNDER. 80 ha, S African winemaker.

Schloss Vaux Rhg ★★ →★★★ SEKT house known for single-v'yd RIES Sekt (eg. MARCOBRUNN, RÜDESHEIMER SCHLOSSBERG).

Schloss Vollrads Rhg ★★ →★★★ One of greatest historic RHG estates, now owned by a bank. Recent improvements (eg. fine SPÄTLESE 17).

Schmitt's Kinder Frank ★★ →★★★ Family estate in Randersacker s of WÜRZBURG, known for classical dry SILVANER, barrel-aged SPÄTBURGUNDER and nobly sweet RIESLANER.

Schnaitmann Würt ★★ →★★★★ Excellent barrel-aged reds from Fellbach (nr Stuttgart). Whites (eg. RIES, SAUV BL), Sekt (Evoé!), and wines from lesser grapes (SCHWARZRIESLING, TROLLINGER) tasty too.

Schneider, Cornelia and Reinhold Bad ★★★ Age-worthy SPÄTBURGUNDERS from Endingen, KAISERSTUHL, denoted by letters – R for volcanic soil, C for loess – and old-fashioned dry RULÄNDER.

Schneider, Markus Pfz ★★ Shooting star in Ellerstadt, PFZ. A full range of soundly produced, trendily labelled wines.

Schoppenwein Café (or bar) wine, ie. wine by the glass.

Schwarzer Adler Bad ★★★ →★★★★ French restaurant (Michelin star continuously since 1969) at Oberbergen, KAISERSTUHL, and top wine estate. Young Friedrich Keller Jr makes his PINOTS taste even more burgundian than father Fritz.

Schwegler, Albrecht Würt ★★★ →★★★★ 7 ha, now led by young Aaron S. Red blends Beryll, Saphir, Granat have ultra-pure fruit. Top selection Solitär only produced once in a decade 03' 11'. New: powerful yet balanced CHARD Res.

Seeger Bad ★★★ Best producer of the Badische Bergstrasse area s of Heidelberg, known for clever barrel-ageing. Reds and whites equally gd.

Sekt ★ →★★★★ German sparkling wine, v. variable in quality: bottle fermentation is not mandatory, nor is German origin of base wine(s). But serious Sekt producers are making spectacular progress, eg. ALDINGER, Bardong, Barth, BUHL, GRIESEL, Melsheimer, RAUMLAND, Schembs, SCHLOSS VAUX, Solter, S Steinmetz, Strauch, WAGECK, WEGELER, Wilhelmshof.

Selbach-Oster M-M ★★★ Scrupulous ZELTINGEN estate with excellent v'yd portfolio, known for classical style and focus on sweet PRÄDIKAT wines (magnificent ***Zeltingen Sonnenuhr AUSLESE 17).

Sonnenuhr M-M Sundial. Name of GROSSE LAGE sites at BRAUNEBERG, WEHLEN, ZELTINGEN.

Sorentberg M-M ★★ →★★★★ V'yd in a side valley of M-M nr Reil, fallow for 50 yrs (except a tiny plot of 1000 vines), now replanted by young Tobias Treis and partner from South Tyrol. Red slate, cool climate.

Spätlese Late-harvest. One level riper and potentially sweeter than KABINETT. Gd examples age at lea<u>s</u>t 7 yrs. Spätlese TROCKEN designation was abandoned by VDP members: a shame.

Spreitzer Rhg ★★★ Brothers Andreas and Bernd S produce deliciously *racy, harmonious* RIES from v'yds in HATTENHEIM, OESTRICH, Mittelheim. Mid-price range ALTE REBEN a bargain.

Staatlicher Hofkeller Frank ★★ Bavarian state domain; 120 ha of fine FRANK v'yds, spectacular cellars under great baroque Residenz at WÜRZBURG. Three directors in past 5 yrs: waiting for better times.

Staatsweingut / Staatliche Weinbaudomäne State wine estates or domains exist in BAD (IHRINGEN, Meersburg), WÜRT (Weinsberg), RHG (HESSISCHE STAATSWEINGÜTER), RHH (OPPENHEIM), EFF (Neustadt), MOS (TRIER). Some have been privatized in recent yrs, eg. Marienthal (AHR), NIEDERHAUSEN (NA).

Steigerwald Frank District in e FRANK. V'yds at considerable altitude, but soils allow powerful SILVANER, RIES. Best: Castell, Hillabrand, Roth, RUCK, VETTER, VELTNER, *Wirsching*

Steinberg Rhg ★★★ Completely walled-in v'yd above HATTENHEIM, est by Cistercian monks 700 yrs ago: a German Clos de Vougeot. Monopoly of HESSISCHE STAATSWEINGÜTER. Classified parcels (14 ha out of 37) have unique soil (clay with fragments of decomposed schist in various colours) and microclimate (altitude, walls). Berry-scented RIES, fascinating old vintages (eg. NATURREIN 43, TBA 59).

Steinwein Frank Wine from WÜRZBURG's best v'yd, Stein. Goethe's favourite. Only five producers: BÜRGERSPITAL, JULIUSSPITAL, L Knoll, Reiss, STAATLICHER HOFKELLER.

Stodden Ahr ★★★→★★★★ AHR SPÄTBURGUNDER with a Burgundian touch, delicately extracted and subtle. Best usually ALTE REBEN and Rech Herrenberg. Pricey – but production is tiny.

Südliche Weinstrasse Pfz District in s PFZ, famous esp for PINOT varieties. Best growers: BECKER, Leiner, Minges, Münzberg, REBHOLZ, Siegrist, WEHRHEIM.

Taubertal Bad, Frank, Würt ★→★★★ Cool-climate district along Tauber River divided by Napoleon into BAD, FRANK and WÜRT sections, SILVANER from limestone soils, local red Tauberschwarz. Frost a problem. Growers: Hofmann, Schlör, gd co-op at Beckstein.

TBA (Trockenbeerenauslese) Sweetest, most expensive category of German wine, extremely rare, viscous and concentrated with dried-fruit flavours. Made from selected dried-out grapes affected by noble rot (botrytis). Half bottles a gd idea.

Thanisch, Weingut Dr. M-M ★★★ BERNKASTEL estate, founded 1636, famous for its share of the DOCTOR v'yd. After family split-up in 1988 two homonymous estates with similar qualities: Erben (heirs) Müller-Burggraef and Erben Thanisch.

Trier Mos The n capital of ancient Rome, on MOS, between RUWER and SAAR. Big charitable estates have cellars here among awesome Roman remains.

Trittenheim M-M ★★→★★★ Racy, textbook M-M RIES if from gd plots within extended GROSSE LAGE v'yd Apotheke. Growers: A CLÜSSERATH, Clüsserath-Weiler, E Clüsserath, FJ Eifel, Grans-Fassian, Milz.

Trocken Dry. Used to be defined as max 9g/l unfermented sugar. Generally the further s in Germany, the more Trocken wines.

Salami shuttle to Wachenheim

When Nicola Libelli's parents come from Piacenza to see him at BÜRKLIN-WOLF, they stuff their car with dozens of salami and a couple of prosciutti – as many as will fit. Japanese Fumiko Tokuoka, winemaker at the BIFFAR estate, also runs a Japanese restaurant. The third MITTELHAARDT blow-in, Mathieu Lauffmann (at VON BUHL) is from Alsace. Show them how to make choucroute, Mathieu.

Ürzig M-M ★★★→★★★★ MOS village on red sandstone and red slate, famous for ungrafted old vines and *unique spicy Ries*. GROSSE LAGE v'yd: Würzgarten. Growers: Berres, Christoffel, Erbes, LOOSEN, MERKELBACH, MARKUS MOLITOR, Mönchhof, Rebenhof. New Autobahn bridge 160m (525ft) high overshadows v'yds.

Van Volxem Mos ★★★ Historical SAAR estate revived by obsessed Roman Niewodniczanski. Low yields from top sites (KANZEM Altenberg, OCKFEN Bockstein, SCHARZHOFBERG, WILTINGEN Gottesfuss). Up to now, mainly dry or off-dry, but in 2016 a brilliant Bockstein SPÄTLESE (and a new cellar).

Marsanne seems to have been trialled at Würzburg in C19: documents mention "Eremitage".

VDP (Verband Deutscher Prädikatsweingüter) Influential association of 200 premium growers setting highest standards. Look for its eagle insignia on wine labels, and for GROSSE LAGE logo on wines from classified v'yds. A VDP wine is usually a gd bet. President: Steffen CHRISTMANN.

Vetter, Stefan Frank ★★→★★★ Natural wine (*see* A Little Learning, back of book): SILVANER fermented on skins. To watch.

Vollenweider, Daniel Mos ★★★ A Swiss in M-M: excellent RIES in v. small quantities from Wolfer Goldgrube v'yd nr Traben-Trarbach.

Wachenheim Pfz ★★★ Celebrated village with, according to VDP, no GROSSE LAGE v'yds. See what you think. Top growers: BIFFAR, BÜRKLIN-WOLF, Karl Schäfer, ODINSTAL, WOLF, Zimmermann (bargain).

Wageck Pfz ★★→★★★ MITTELHAARDT estate for unaffected, brisk CHARD (still and sparkling) and PINOT N of great finesse.

Wagner, Dr. Mos ★★→★★★ Estate with v'yds in OCKFEN and Saarstein led by young Christiane W. SAAR RIES with purity, freshness.

Wagner-Stempel Rhh ★★★ Seriously crafted RHH wines from Siefersheim nr NA border. Best usually RIES GGS Heerkretz (porphyry soil).

Walluf Rhg ★★★ Underrated village, 1st with important v'yds as one leaves Wiesbaden, going w. GROSSE LAGE v'yd: Walkenberg. Growers: *JB Becker, Jost*.

Wegeler M-M, Rhg ★★→★★★★ Important family estates in OESTRICH and BERNKASTEL (both in top form) plus a stake in the famous KRONE estate of ASSMANNSHAUSEN. Geheimrat J blend maintains high standards, single-v'yd RIES usually outstanding value. Old vintages available.

Wehlen M-M ★★★→★★★★ Wine village with legendary steep SONNENUHR v'yd expressing RIES from slate at v. best: rich, fine, everlasting. Top growers: JJ PRÜM, Kerpen, KESSELSTATT, LOOSEN, MARKUS MOLITOR, RICHTER, SA PRÜM, SCHLOSS LIESER, SELBACH-OSTER, Studert-Prüm, THANISCH, WEGELER. Concern that just-built Autobahn above v'yds will affect water balance in subsoil.

Wehrheim, Weingut Dr. Pfz ★★★ Top organic estate of SÜDLICHE WEINSTRASSE. V. dry, culinary style, esp white PINOT varieties.

Weil, Robert Rhg ★★★→★★★★★ 17 37 59 90 01 05 09 11 12 15 16 17 18 Outstanding estate in KIEDRICH with classified v'yds Gräfenberg (steep slope on phyllite schist), Klosterberg, Turmberg. Superb sweet KABINETT to TBA (magnificent 17s) and EISWEIN, gd GG.

Weingart M Rh ★★★ Outstanding estate at Spay, v'yds in BOPPARD (esp Hamm Feuerlay). Refined, taut RIES, low-tech in style, superb value.

Weingut Wine estate.

Weins-Prüm, Dr. M-M 4 ha of prime v'yd holdings in ERDEN, GRAACH, ÜRZIG, WEHLEN. In 2016 bought by Katharina Prüm (of JJ PRÜM) and Wilhelm Steifensand (WEINGUT LIEBFRAUENSTIFT). Label will cease to exist.

Weissherbst Pale-pink wine, made from a single variety, often SPÄTBURGUNDER. V. variable quality.

Weltner, Paul Frank ★★☆ STEIGERWALD family estate. Densely structured, age-worthy SILVANER from und-rated Rödelseer Küchenmeister v'yd and neighbouring plots at IPHOFEN.

Wiltingen Mos ★★→★→★ Heartland of the SAAR. SCHARZHOFBERG crowns a series of GROSSE LAGE v'yds Braune Kupp, Braunfels, Gottesfuss, Kupp). Top growers: BISCHÖFLICHE WEING-TER TRIER, EGON MÜLLER, KESSELSTATT, Le Gallais, SANKT URBANS-HOF, VAN VOLXEM, V☐.

Winning, von Pfz ★→→★★★★ Estate in DEIDESHEIM, incl former DR. DEINHARD. *Ries of great purity* with terroir expression, slightly influenced by fermentation in new FUDER casks. Breathtaking Jesuitengarten 17. Also ambitious PINOT N and SAUV BL.

Winningen Mos ★★☆★★★ Lower MOS town nr Koblenz; powerful dry RIES. GROSSE LAGE v'yds: Röttg☐l, Uhlen. Top growers: HEYMANN-LÖWENSTEIN, Knebel, Kröber, Richard Richter.

Wirsching, Hans Fr☐k ★★★ Renowned estate in IPHOFEN known for classically structured dry r☐s and *Silvaner*. Andrea W extends range with spontaneously fermented Ries ☐ster Act and kosher SILVANER. Excellent SCHEUREBE (ALTE REBEN).

Wittmann Rhh ★★★ Philipp Wittmann has propelled this bio estate to the top ranks. Crystal-pure, zes☐ dry RIES GG (Morstein 05 07' 08 11 12' 15 16 17).

Wöhrle Bad ★★★ ☐rganic pioneer at Lahr (25 yrs+), son Markus a PINOT expert, excellent GGS.

Wöhrwag Würt ★★☐★★★ Source of elegant dry RIES – arguably best in all WÜRT. Now children Johan☐a, Philipp, Moritz involved too. Reds also gd.

Wolf JL Pfz ★★☆★→★ WACHENHEIM estate, leased by Ernst LOOSEN of BERNKASTEL. Dry PFZ RIES (esp F☐ter Pechstein), sound and consistent rather than dazzling.

Renovating a dry ☐one wall in a steep terraced v'yd costs up to €200/m² (= 1 vine).

Württemberg Fo☐erly mocked as "TROLLINGER republic", but today it is dynamic, with many ☐ung growers eager to experiment. Best usually LEMBERGER, SPÄTBURGUNDE☐. Only 30% white varieties. RIES needs altitude v'yds.

Würzburg Fran☐ ★★→★★★ Great baroque city on the Main, centre of FRANK wine. Classif☐d v'yds: Innere Leiste, Stein, Stein-Harfe. Growers: BÜRGERSPITAL, JULIUSSPITAL, R☐iss, STAATLICHER HOFKELLER, Weingut am Stein.

Zell Mos ★→→☐★ Best-known lower MOS village, notorious for GROSSLAGE Schwarze K☐z (Black Cat) – avoid! Gd v'yd is Merler Königslay-Terrassen. Top grower: Lallfelz.

Zellertal Pfz ★★→★★★★ Area in n PFZ, high, cool, recent gold-rush: Battenfeld-Spanier, Ku☐ have bought in Zellertal's best RIES v'yd Schwarzer Herrgott or neighbour☐g RHH plot Zellerweg am Schwarzen Herrgott. Gd local estates: Bremer, Ja☐ on Bernhard, Klosterhof Schwedhelm.

Zeltingen M-N ★★→★★★ Top but sometimes underrated MOS village nr WEHLEN. Rich thoug☐ crisp RIES. GROSSE LAGE v'yd: SONNENUHR. Top growers: JJ PRÜM, MARKUS MOLITOR, SE☐ACH-OSTER.

Ziereisen Ba☐ ★★→★★★★ Outstanding estate in MARKGRÄFLERLAND, mainly PINOTS and GUTE☐E. Best are SPÄTBURGUNDERS from small plots: Rhini, Schulen, Talrain. Jaspis = ☐c-vine selections. *See* box on LANDWEIN rebels, p.162.

Zilliken, Fors☐eister Geltz Mos ★★★→★★★★ 93 94 95 96 97 99 01 03 04 05 07 08 09 10 11 ☐ 14 15 16 17 SAAR family estate: intense racy/savoury *Ries from Saarburg Rausch* a☐d OCKFEN Bockstein, incl superb long-lasting AUSLESE, EISWEIN. V.gd SEKT too – and Ferdinand's gin.

Zimmerling, Klaus Sachs ★★★ Small, perfectionist estate, one of 1st to be est☐ after the ☐wall came down. Best v'yd is Königlicher Weinberg (King's v'yd) a☐ Pillnitz ☐ Dresden. RIES, sometimes off-dry, can be exquisite.

Luxembourg

The tiny Duchy of Luxembourg lies on the River Moselle/Mosel a short distance before it enters Germany. With a population of 600,000 it is one-quarter of the size of many cities, but it's a country nonetheless. If its wine is really of local interest only it is because Luxembourgers and international bureaucrats drink it all. The Mosel's genius for golden sweetness and fine acidity is in abeyance here; put it this way: no schist – no late harvest. The soil is limestone, and has more in common with Chablis or Champagne than Piesport. Only 11% is Riesling. The big ones are Müller-Thurgau (aka Rivaner), Koeppchen, Auxerrois and Pinots Blanc and Gris. Crémant fizz is a strong speciality. Climate change has been kind – 2018 brought the most powerful Pinots of Luxembourg's history – even if frost is still a danger (and hit in 2016 and 2017). Most whites have strong acidity and some sweetness – labels don't differentiate between dry and off-dry. A common term (but of little significance) is "Premier Grand Cru". More reliable are groups of winemakers who come together to promote their high standards: Domaine et Tradition (eight producers) has most credibility.

Alice Hartmann ★★★→★★★★ Star producer with parcel selections from Luxembourg's best RIES v'yd, Koeppchen (Les Terrasses from 70-yr-old vines, Au Coeur de la Koeppchen a culmination of limestone minerality). Best RIES, CHARD, PINOT N are called Sélection du Château. Mid-price Clos du Kreitzerberg is outstanding value for Chard, Pinot N 16'. Excellent Crémant too (Grande Cuvée, Rosé Brut). Also owns v'yds in Burgundy (St-Aubin), Mittelmosel (Trittenheim) and leases a plot in Scharzhofberg. Sells out fast.

Aly Duhr ★★→★★★ Brothers Ben and Max Duhr are known for reliable white Barrique (PINOT BL/AUXERROIS – top value) and refined RIES Ahn Palmberg. Gd Crémant too.

Bastian, Mathis ★★→★★★ Substantial whites (v.gd 17 Domaine et Tradition RIES Wellenstein Foulschette).

Bernard-Massard ★→★★★ Big producer, esp Crémant. Top labels: Ch de Schengen and Clos des Rocher. Makes Sekt in Germany too.

Château Pauqué ★★★→★★★★ Passionate Abi Duhr bridges gap between Burgundy and Germany (substantial RIES Paradaïs Vieilles Vignes, Botrytis Ries in exceptional sweet/sour Auslese style). From the 17 vintage, breathtaking Ries "15 hl/ha".

Duhr Frères/Clos Mon Vieux Moulin ★★→★★★ Classically built whites (mineral 17 RIES Ahn Palmberg and rich, but dry 17 PINOT GR Ahn Göllebur).

Gales ★★→★★★ Reliable producer at Remich. Best: Crémant (value Héritage Brut, Prestige Cuvée G Brut) and Domaine et Tradition labels. Old cellar labyrinth worth seeing.

Schumacher-Knepper ★★→★★★ Some v.gd wines under Ancien Propriété Constant Knepper label (esp Wintringer Felsberg RIES), excellent 15 PINOT GR Barrique.

Sunnen-Hoffmann ★★★ Corinne Sunnen and brother Yves (5th generation), once merchants, turned organic growers in 2001. A full range of textbook whites, best usually RIES Wintrange Felsberg VV Domaine et Tradition from a v'yd planted in 1943.

Other good estates: Cep d'Or, Fränk Kayl, L&R Kox, Paul Legill, Ruppert, Schmit-Fohl, Stronck-Pinnel. Domaines Vinsmoselle is a union of co-ops.

Spain

Abbreviations used in the text:

PORTUGAL		Jum	Jumilla
Alen	Alentejo	La M	La Mancha
Alg	Algarve	Mad	Madeira
Bair	Bairrada	Mall	Mallorca
Bei Int	Beira Interior	Man	Manchuela
Dou	Douro	Mén	Méntrida
Lis	Lisboa	Mont-M	Montilla-Moriles
Min	Minho	Mont	Montsant
Set	Setúbal	Mur	Murcia
Tej	Tejo	Nav	Navarra
Vin	Vinho Verde	Pen	Penedès
		Pri	Priorat
SPAIN		P Vas	País Vasco
Alel	Alella	Rib del D	Ribera
Alic	Alicante		del Duero
Ara	Aragón	Rio	Rioja
Bier	Bierzo		
Bul	Bullas		
Cád	Cádiz		
Can	Canary Islands		
C-La M	Castilla-	R Ala	Rioja Alavesa
	La Mancha	R Alt	Rioja Alta
C y L	Castilla y León	R Or	Rioja Oriental
Cat	Cataluña	Rue	Rueda
Cos del S	Costers del Segre	Som	Somontano
Emp	Empordà	U-R	Utiel-Requena
Ext	Extremadura	V'cia	Valencia
Gal	Galicia		

S pain doesn't let up in terms of interest, quality and diversity. It lacks big-name, high-production fine-wine brands, but what it has instead is a proliferation of small producers, each working their own plots of land, sharing ideas with their contemporaries, and rediscovering old vines. It's a bucolic dream, and in such small quantities the wines can be hard to track down. Persevere: from the heroic viticulture of Ribeira Sacra to the extraordinary *trenzado* vineyards of Tenerife and the Garnacha aficionados of the centre and the north, there are original flavours to enjoy. There are fascinating niche projects from Catalunya down the Mediterranean coast with winemakers who are returning to the old ways, using *lagares* and *tinajas* (amphoras), and using them expertly. In Catalonia, meanwhile, Cava continues to try to fight its way out of the cheap-as-chips category. Changes of ownership of the two leading producers of Cava in 2018 highlighted just how tough the fight is. Sherry, another wine that has been in long decline, is undergoing a surprising shake-up. A new generation is exploring different ways of working with the Palomino grape. Not all are successful, but the wine undoubtedly has a renewed sense of energy.

Portugal & Spain

SPAIN

Recent Rioja vintages

2018 Rain at right time meant super-abundant harvest, excellent quality to match.

2017 Much reduced harvest, but what was left is v.gd.

2016 Difficult spring, v. hot summer, rain at harvest. Pick your producer.

2015 Reliably back to form. Top wines may be as gd as 2010.

2014 After two small vintages, a return to quality, quantity.

2013 Cool yr, small harvest, with some gd wines.

2012 Gd. One of lowest yields for two decades.

2011 Officially *excelente*; not as gd as 2010, perhaps, but still v.gd.

2010 *Excelente*. Perfect yr. Wines to enjoy now, best have plenty of time ahead.

2009 Can drink now, but will develop further.

2008 Cool yr, wines fresh, aromatic, a little lower in alc. Ready to drink.

Aalto Rib del D r ★★★→★★★★ Big, polished, structured wines: Aalto; flagship PS (from 200 small plots). Mariano García, ex-VEGA SICILIA, builds wines for cellaring. García's family wineries: San Román (TORO), MAURO (C Y L), Garmón (RIB DEL D). Co-owner with Masaveu (owners of Enate, Fillaboa, Murúa). Co-founder Javier Zaccagnini left 2018 to focus on his Sei Solo, Preludio.

Abadal, Bodegas Cat Family business in Plà de Bages DO has popular wines plus CAT specialities under several brands: Abadal, La Fou (TERRA ALTA DO; w Mandó grape), Ramón Roqueta. Also makes wine in traditional stone tanks.

Abadía Retuerta C y L r ★★→★★★ Height of luxury, Michelin-starred restaurant, glam hotel – and winery. Just outside RIB DEL D. V.gd white blend DYA Le Domaine. Single-v'yd international reds, eg. Pago Garduña SYRAH.

Abel Mendoza R Ala ★★→★★★ For knowledge of RIO villages and varieties Abel and Maite Mendoza have few equals. Discover no less than five varietal whites. Grano a Grano are the every-berry-selected TEMPRANILLO and GRACIANO.

Alexander Jules Sherry ★★→★★★ US-based négociant bottling selected BUTTS of distinctive Sherries.

Algueira Gal r w ★★★ V. fine selection of elegant reds, from local varieties, incl Brancellao and MENCÍA. Outstanding is Merenzao (aka Jura's Trousseau), almost burgundian in style.

Alicante r w sw ★→★★★ Spiritual home of MONASTRELL; spicy reds, increasingly rare traditional fortified **Fondillón**. Heritage of old bush-vines on high plateau. Top: ARTADI, Bernabé Navarro (gd natural wines, uses clay *tinajas*), ENRIQUE MENDOZA.

Almacenista Sherry Man A Sherry stockholding cellar; provides wines for BODEGAS to increase or refresh stocks. Important in MANZANILLA production. Can be terrific. Few left; many now sell direct to consumers, eg. GUTIÉRREZ COLOSÍA, EL MAESTRO SIERRA. Often source for individual négociant bottlings.

Alonso, Bodegas Man ★★★→★★★★ Newish entrant to Sherry. Owners Asencio brothers also own Dominio de Urogallo (Asturias). Bought exceptional bankrupt stock of Pedro Romero, incl. v. fine SOLERAS of Gaspar Florido. From this comes an outstanding but super-pricey four-bottle collection. More accessibly priced is Velo FLOR, 9–10-yr-old MANZANILLA.

Alonso del Yerro Rib del D, Toro r ★★→★★★ Stéphane Derenoncourt (B'x consultant) enticing elegance from extreme continental climate of RIB DEL D. Transformation with 2016 wines, altogether more delicate. Family business, estate wines. Top wine: María, inky but not overblown. Paydos is its TORO.

Alta Alella Cat ★★→★★★ With toes in the Med and just up the coast from Barcelona, the BODEGA welcomes visitors warmly. Renowned for CAVAS. Delightful sweet red Dolç Mataró from MONASTRELL. Organic.

Álvaro Domecq Sherry, Man ★★→★★★ Relatively young BODEGA. SOLERAS drawn from former ALMACENISTA Pilar Aranda. Polished wines. Gd FINO La Janda. Excellent 1730 VORS series. Now part of Avanteselecta group.

Alvear Mont-M, Ext ★★→★★★★ Historic Alvear has superb array of PX wines in MONT-M. Gd, dry FINO CB and Capataz, lovely sweet SOLERA 1927, unctuous DULCE Viejo. V. fine vintage wines. Owns Palacio Quemado BODEGA in Ext. Promising new projects with ENVINATE, making table wines as well as special PX selections.

Añada Vintage.

Argüeso, Herederos de Man ★★→★★★ One of SANLÚCAR's top producers and proprietors. Now owned by Yuste. V.gd San León, dense and salty **San León Res** and youthful Las Medallas; also impressively lively VORS AMONTILLADO Viejo.

Arrayán, Bodegas Mén ★★ Founded 1999. Winemaker Maite Sánchez is restoring reputation of MÉN with her indigenous vines, esp fine GARNACHAS and Albillo Real (w).

Artadi Alic, Nav ★★→★★★★ Formed in 1985 from a growers' co-op around Laguardia in R Ala. Since then meticulous Juan Carlos López de Lacalle has led it to outstanding success (focus on single v'yd, French oak). Left RIO DO end 2015, believing it failed to defend quality. Former Rios now called Álava. Gd-value VIÑAS de Gain, luxuriant La Poza de Ballesteros, dark, stony El Carretil; outstanding single-v'yd El Pisón. Also in ALIC (v.gd r El Sequé), NAV (r Artazuri, p DYA).

Atlantic Wines Gal, Rio, P Vas r p w Unofficial collective term for bright, often unoaked style of wine, with firm acidity. Increasingly used to describe crisp, delicate reds. Specifically relates to wine grown close to the Atlantic – in RÍAS BAIXAS – or the Cantabrian Sea – the TXAKOLIS. Also used to describe cool climatic influences, eg. inland GAL DOS, and specific vintages in R Ala, R Alt.

Baigorri R Ala r w ★★→★★★ Wines as glamorous as BODEGA's glassy architecture. Gravity-fed, producing bold, modern RIO. Worth the detour: gd restaurant, tasting menus, v'yd views.

Barbadillo Man ★→★★★★ Cathedral-like grand cellars dominate SANLÚCAR's upper town. Montse Molina manages wines from supermarket to superb. Pioneer of MANZANILLA EN RAMA. Reliquía range unbeatable, esp AMONTILLADO, PALO CORTADO. Outstanding century-old Versos Amontillado. Sherry guru Armando Guerra advises on adventurous new releases (Nude is Beaujolais-style Tintilla de Rota) and returning to traditional practices, eg. Mirabras, unfortified PALOMINO. Worth following: this once slumbering giant is now wide awake. Also owns Vega Real (RIB DEL D), BODEGA Pirineos (SOM).

Báscula, La Alic, Rio, Jum r w sw ★★ Reliable gd-value portfolio from upcoming regions, plus classics. Run by S African wine guru Bruce Jack and British MW Ed Adams. Also TERRA ALTA.

Belondrade C y L, Rue r w ★★→★★★ Didier Belondrade was early (1994) exponent of finesse in VERDEJO in RUE, and lees-ageing. Also Quinta Apollonia (w) and light, summery, Quinta Clarisa TEMPRANILLO (r), both C y L.

Whisky loves Sherry. 1000 ex-Sherry casks are shipped to The Macallan every wk.

Bentomiz, Bodegas Mál ★★→★★★ Dutch by birth, Spanish by adoption, Clara and André est as growers in Axarquía, inland from MÁLAGA. Experts in sweet MOSCATEL, MERLOT, also in revival of rare Romé (p).

Beronia Rio r p w ★→★★★ Best-selling RIO BODEGA owned by GONZÁLEZ BYASS. RES v. reliable. Top: glossy but unpronounceable III a. C.

Bierzo r w ★→★★★★ MENCÍA grapes on slate soil make crunchy *Pinot-like red*. Best sites are high-altitude, made without much oak. Styles/quality are uneven. Best advice – follow the producer. Look for DESCENDIENTES DE J PALACIOS, RAÚL PÉREZ, plus Dominio de Tares, Losada, Luna Berberide, MENGOBA, Vino Valtuille. Also has fine GODELLO (w).

Bodega A cellar; a wine shop; a business making, blending and/or shipping wine.

Butt Sherry 600-litre barrel of long-matured American oak used for Sherry. Filled 5/6 full, allows space for FLOR to grow. Popular in Scotland, post-Sherry use: adds final polish to whisky. Trend for whites aged in ex-FINO butts – CVNE's Monopole Clasico, BARBADILLO Mirabras: revival of old style.

Calatayud Ara r p w ★→★★★ Old bush-vine GARNACHA grown at 700–900m (2297–2953ft) finally putting Calatayud on map, part of heritage of Ara, though still best known for cheap co-op wines. Best: Ateca, EL ESCOCÉS VOLANTE, San Alejandro.

Callejuela Sherry, Man ★★→★★★ Blanco brothers have v'yds in some of Sherry's most famous PAGOS. In 1915 launched Callejuela Sherries, and v.gd aged MANZANILLA, AMONTILLADO, OLOROSO; vintage releases of Manzanilla.

Campo de Borja Ara r p w ★→★★★★ Self-proclaimed "Empire of GARNACHA". Heritage of old vines, plus young v'yds = 1st choice for gd-value Garnacha, now starting to show serious quality: BODEGAS Alto Moncayo, Aragonesas, Borsao, Frontonio.

Campo Viejo Rio r p w sp ★→★★★ RIO's biggest brand. In addition to value RES, GRAN RES, has varietal GARNACHA, and adds TEMPRANILLO Blanco to white RIO. V.gd top Res Dominio. Part of Pernod Ricard (also owns much-improved Calatrava-designed Ysios winery in Rio).

Canary Islands r p w ★→★★★ Seven main islands, nine DOS. TENERIFE alone has five

DOs. Plenty of dull wine for tourists. Seek out unusual varieties, old vines, distinct microclimates, volcanic soils. Dry white LISTÁN (aka PALOMINO) and Marmajuelo, black Listán Negro, Negramoll (TINTA NEGRA), Vijariego offers *enjoyable original flavours*. Gd dessert MOSCATELS, MALVASÍAS, esp fortified El Grifo from Lanzarote. Top: Borja Pérez, ENVÍNATE, Matías i Torres, SUERTES DEL MARQUÉS.

Cañas, Luis R Ala r w ★→★★★ Reliable, polished wines. Classics eg. Selección de la Familia RES, youthful, enjoy-now GRAN RES, plus moderns eg. ultra-concentrated Hiru 3 Racimos, Amaren – need cellaring.

Cangas ★→★★ Isolated DO in wild Asturias beginning to export. Isolation has led to distinct vines, characters: Fresh (w) Albarín Blanco, firm red from Albarín Negro, Verdejo Negro, and most promising, Carrrasquín. Producers: Dominio de Urogallo (same owners as BODEGAS ALONSO), Monasterio de Corias, VidAs.

Capçanes, Celler de Mont r p w sw ★→★★ One of Spain's top co-ops. Great-value expressive wines from MONT. Kosher specialist, esp Peraj Ha'abib.

Cariñena Ara r p w ★→★★ The one DO that is also name of a grape variety. The vine can be outstanding in PRI. The DO, formerly co-op country, is not exciting, but gd value; promising 3 de Tres Mil from VINOS DE PAGO FINCA Aylés. Consultant Jorge Navascués also winemaker at CONTINO, makes own wines at Navascués Enología: Cutio, Mas de Mancuso.

New-wave Garnacha is poor man's Pinot: hits spot for flavour, delicacy.

Casa Castillo Jum ★★→★★★ Proves JUM can be tiptop. Family business high up in Jum *altiplano*. V. fine Las Gravas single-v'yd blend. Showcase for MONASTRELL, esp PIE FRANCO (plot escaped fairly recent phylloxera).

Castell d'Encús Co del S r w ★★→★★★ CAT wineries are searching for cool sites: Raül Bobet (also of PRI FERRER-BOBET) has all the cool climates he wants at 1000m (3281ft), for *superbly fresh, original wines*. Ancient meets modern: grapes fermented in stone *lagares*, winery is up to date. Ekam RIES, Thalarn SYRAH, Acusp PINOT have become classics. MERLOT rosado is recent.

Castilla y León r p w ★→★★★ Spain's largest wine region. Plenty to enjoy with many new projects. DOS: Arlanza, Arribes, BIERZO, CIGALES, RUE, Tierra de León, Tierra de Vino de Zamora, TORO, Sierra de Salamanca (one to watch), Valles de Benavente, Valtiendas. Red grapes: Juan García, MENCÍA and clones of TEMPRANILLO. White Doña Blanca. Gd, deeply coloured ROSADO from Prieto Picudo. Plus independent stars: ABADÍA RETUERTA, Dehesa La Granja, MAURO, Prieto Pariente.

Castillo de Cuzurrita R Alt Walled v'yd. C14 castle, excellent consultant Ana Martín. Great basis for v. fine RIO.

Castillo Perelada Emp, Nav, Pri r p w sp ★→★★★ Glamorous estate and tourist destination. Vivacious CAVAS, esp Gran Claustro; modern reds. Rare 12-yr-old SOLERA-aged GARNATXA de l'EMPORDÀ. V. fine Casa Gran del Siurana from PRI. Has purchased CHIVITE group, an old fave of mine.

Catalonia r p w sp Vast DO, covers whole of Cat: seashore, mtn, in-between. Top chefs and top BODEGAS (eg. TORRES), many v. creative. Yet actual DO is just umbrella, too large to have identity, an excuse for characterless cross-DO blends.

Cava Spain's traditional-method sparkling. Made same way as Champagne, often same grapes. Med ripeness of fruit means zero dosage/Brut Nature popular. Vast majority made in PEN – in or around San Sadurní d'Anoia – also RIO (esp M*ga Conde de Haro), V'CIA. Local grapes back in favour: MACABEO (VIURA of R*D), PARELLADA, XAREL·LO (best for ageing). Best can age 10 yrs, though 9 mths is legal min. Highest quality category is CAVA DE PARAJE CALIFICADO. Still too much low-quality fizz, so producers have left DO or avoid it, eg. TORRES sparkler not Cava, nor Corpinnat group. *See* CAVA DE PARAJE CALIFICADO, CLÀSSIC PENEDÈS, CONCA DEL RIU ANOIA.

Cava de Paraje Calificado Cava Launched 2017 as top category of single-v'yd CAVA with stringent rules. Min 36 mths age, most exceed that.

César Florido Sherry ★→★★★ Master of MOSCATEL, since 1887. Explore gloriously scented, succulent trio: Dorado, Especial, Pasas.

Chacolí *See* TXAKOLÍ.

Chipiona Sherry Sherry's MOSCATEL grapes come from this sandy coastal zone. César Florido is a classic. Best as floral delicacies, far less dense than PX.

Chivite Nav r p w sw ★★→★★★ Popular DYA range Gran Feudo. Colección 125, **top Chard** (the late Denis Doubordieu consulted). Gd late-harvest MOSCATEL. Historic name in NAV, more recently troubled times. Sold to CASTILLO PERELADA 2017. Expect changes and timely revamp.

Clàssic Penedès Pen Category of DO PEN for traditional-method fizz, more strict rules than Cava. Min 15 mths ageing. Since 2017, organically grown grapes. Members incl Albet i Noya, Colet, LOXAREL, Mas Bertran.

Clos Mogador Pri r w ★★★ René Barbier was one of PRI's founding quintet and mentor to many. Still commands respect. One of 1st wineries to gain a VI DE FINCA designation. Son René Jr in charge, also working with partner Sara Pérez of MAS MARTINET.

Codorníu Raventós Cos del S, Pen, Pri, Rio r p w sp ★→★★★★ Historic art nouveau CAVA winery worth a visit. Bruno Colomer has raised quality impressively across range. V. fine Ars Collecta Cavas: three single-v'yd, single-variety CAVAS DE PARAJE CALIFICADO; and 456, a blend of three v'yds and most expensive Cava ever produced. Elsewhere, Legaris in RIB DEL D and Raimat in COS DEL S continue to improve. Bodega Bilbaínas in RIO has bestseller VIÑA Pomal, Vinos Singulares, original Cava Blanc de Noirs (GARNACHA). *See also* outstanding PRI SCALA DEI. Now under new ownership. Choppy waters ahead?

Conca de Barberà Cat r p w Small CAT DO once purely a feeder of quality fruit to large enterprises, now some excellent wineries, incl bio Escoda-Sanahuja, TORRES.

Conca del Ríu Anoia Cat Small traditional-method sparkling DO created in 2013 by RAVENTÓS I BLANC as umbrella for tighter quality controls than CAVA. Bio, lower yields, min ageing 18 mths, only local grape varieties.

Consejo Regulador Organization that controls a DO – each DO has its own. Quality as inconsistent as wines they represent: some bureaucratic, others enterprising.

Contador Cat, R Alt r w ★★★ Benjamin Romeo (ex-ARTADI) at foot of San Vicente de la Sonsierra is scrupulously focused on his terroir. Flagship r Contador, "super-second" La Cueva del Contador. Rich, **top white Que Bonito Cacareaba.** Wines to lay down; Predicar (r w) are more approachable. Macizo is powerful, silky GARNACHA BLANCA/XAREL·LO blend (w) in CAT at Vins del Massis.

Contino R Ala r p w ★★→★★★★★ Estate incl one of RIO's great single v'yds. Winemaker Jorge Navascués took over from Jesús Madrazo 2017. He's a GARNACHA specialist: will we see a greater focus on this? Part of CVNE portfolio.

Corpinnat Cat sp New (2018) group of top-rank CAVA producers of traditional-method sparkling, incl Recaredo, Gramona. More stringent quality controls. Left Cava DO 2019.

Costers del Segre r p w sp ★→★★★ Geographically divided DO combines mountainous CASTELL D'ENCÙS and lower-lying Castell del Remei, Raimat within same boundary.

Cota 45, Bodegas Sherry ★→★★ From SANLÚCAR Sherry star Ramiro Ibáñez. Ube brand is PALOMINO from different famous PAGOS, eg. Carrascal, Miraflores. Unfortified but aged in Sherry BUTTS to give FINO character. Reveals strong terroir differences. *See* Sherry trends box, p.182.

Crianza Label term, indicates ageing of wine, not quality. New or unaged wine is Sin Crianza (without oak) or JOVEN. In general Crianzas must be at least 2 yrs old (with 6 mths to 1 yr in oak) and must not be released before 3rd yr. *See* RES.

Cusiné, Tomás Cos del S r w ★★→★★★ Innovative winemaker, now returned to CASTELL DEL REMEI; group incl Cara Nord, Cérvoles, FINCA Racons, Vilosell. Individual, modern; incl multi-variety Auzells (w).

CVNE R Ala, R Alt r p w ★★→★★★★ One of RIO's great names, based in Haro. Pronounced *"coo-nee"*, Compañía Vinícola del Norte de España, founded 1879. Four Rioja wineries: CONTINO, CVNE, Imperial, VIÑA Real. Most impressive at top end. Great wines long-lived 64 70. Recent purchases in RIB DEL DUERO, RÍAS BAIXAS.

Delgado Zuleta Man ★→★★★ Oldest (1744) SANLÚCAR firm. Flagship is 6/7-yr-old La Goya MANZANILLA PASADA, served at wedding of King Felipe VI of Spain; also 10-yr-old Goya XL EN RAMA. Impressively aged 40-yr-old Quo Vadis? AMONTILLADO.

Díez-Mérito Sherry ★→★★★ After various owners, now settled with Salvador Espinosa. Reliable Bertola range; plus fine aged VORS Sherries: AMONTILLADO *Fino Imperial*, Victoria Regina OLOROSO, Vieja SOLERA PX.

Dinastía Vivanco R Alt r p w sw ★→★★ Briones BODEGA with *Vivanco – outstanding wine museum*.

DO / DOP (Denominación de Origen / Protegida) Replaced former Denominación de Origen (DO) category.

Domaines Lupier Nav r ★★★ Old-vine GARNACHA is star of NAV. Lupier rescues scattered v'yds of old Garnacha: floral La Dama, bold El Terroir. Bio.

Dominio do Bibei Gal r w ★★ One of stars of RIBEIRA SACRA DO. Lapena is GODELLO grown on schist. Lalama is spicy MENCÍA blend.

Dulce Sweet. Seek out treasures incl Alta Alella, BENTOMIZ, GUTIÉRREZ DE LA VEGA, OCHOA, TELMO RODRÍGUEZ, TORRES. Also EMPORDÀ, MÁLAGA, Yecla.

Emilio Hidalgo Sherry ★★★→★★★★ Outstanding family BODEGA. All wines (except PX) start by spending time under FLOR. Excellent unfiltered 15-yr-old La Panesa FINO, thrilling 50-yr-old AMONTILLADO Tresillo 1874, rare Santa Ana PX 1861.

Albariño is Portugal's Alvarinho. Only River Mino/Minho in between.

Emilio Rojo Gal w ★★★ One man, one winery, one wine. His eponymous wine is Treixadura/LOUREIRO/ALBARIÑO/Lado/TORRONTÉS/GODELLO. Superb, with thrilling freshness. Star of RIBEIRO.

Empordà Cat r p w sw ★→★★ One of number of centres of creativity in CAT. Best CASTILLO PERELADA, Celler Martí Fabra, Pere Guardiola, Vinyes dels Aspres. Quirky young Espelt grows 17 varieties: try GARNACHA/CARIGNAN Sauló. Sumptuous natural sweet wine from Celler Espolla: SOLERA GRAN RES.

En rama Sherry bottled from butt without filtration, to capture max freshness.

Enrique Mendoza Alic r w sw ★→★★ Pepe, son of Enrique, serious winemaker and lively host, cheerleader for ALIC and its MONASTRELLS. Top wines from dry inland *altiplano*: vibrant Tremenda, single-v'yd Las Quebradas. New: Casa Agrícola.

Envínate Team of four winemakers consulting in Almansa, Ext, RIBEIRA SACRA, TENERIFE, making original wines. Working for ALVEAR at Palacio Quemado, and a MONT-M making amphora wines.

Epicure Wines Cat, Pri r w sp ★★ Sommelier Franck Massard building portfolio of characterful wines from DOS across Spain, incl CAVA, MONT, RIBEIRA SACRA, TERRA ALTA, VALDEORRAS. Lively ROSADO Mas Amor.

Equipo Navazos Sherry ★★★→★★★★ Jesús Barquín and Eduardo Ojeda pioneered négociant approach to Sherry, selecting outstanding BUTTS. Collaborations inc Dirk Niepoort, Colet-Navazos (sparkling; uses Sherry in *liqueur d'expédition*), Navazos-Palazzi (brandy), Pérez Barquero (MONT-M), RAFAEL PALACIOS. Early adopters of unfortified PALOMINO: *see* Sherry trends box.

Escocés Volante El Gal, Ara r w ★→★★★ Norrel Robertson MW was flying (Scots) winemaker across Spain. Settled in CALATAYUD in 2003 focusing on old-vine GARNACHA grown at altitude, often blending in local varieties. Individual characterful wines, part of movement transforming Ara. Makes ALBARIÑO in RÍAS BAIXAS, GODELLO in MONTERREI.

spumoso Sparkling, but not made according to traditional method, unlike CAVA.

Ferrer-Bobet Pri r ★★★ Fine wines from Sergi Ferrer-Salat (who owns Barcelona's Monvínic wine bar/shop) and Raül Bobet (CASTELL D'ENCÚS). Slate soils, old vines culminate in Selecció Especial Vinyes Velles, 100% CARIÑENA. Spectacular winery.

Finca Farm or estate (eg. FINCA ALLENDE).

Finca Allende R Alt r w ★★→★★★★ Top (in all senses) RIO BODEGA at BRIONES in merchant's house with tower looking over town to v'yds, run by irrepressible Miguel Ángel de Gregorio. Single-v'yd, mineral Calvario; pure, fine Aurus. Splendid aromatic Martires (w). FINCA Nueva is prêt-à-porter range.

Finca Sandoval Man r ★★→★★★ Winery of Victor de la Serna, leading wine writer/critic, in DO MANCHUELA. Campaigns for MAN's native varieties, esp BOBAL.

flor Sherry Spanish for "flower": refers to the layer of *Saccharomyces* yeasts that grow and live on top of FINO/MANZANILLA Sherry in a BUTT 5/6 full. Flor consumes oxygen and other compounds ("biological ageing") and protects wine from oxidation. Traditional AMONTILLADOS begin as Finos or Manzanillas before the flor dies naturally or with addition of fortifying spirit. It grows a thicker layer nearer the sea at EL PUERTO DE SANTA MARÍA and SANLÚCAR, hence finer character of Sherry there. Trend to market unfortified Palomino aged for a short time with flor. Growing interest in Spain and elsewhere in creating flor wines.

Fondillón Alic sw ★→★★★ Fabled unfortified *rancio* semi-sweet wine from overripe MONASTRELL grapes, made to survive sea voyages. Now matured in oak for min 10 yrs; some SOLERAS of great age. Sadly shrinking production: outstanding aged wines from Brotons, GUTIÉRREZ DE LA VEGA, Primitivo Quiles.

Freixenet Pen, Cava r p w sp ★→★★★ Biggest CAVA producer. Best-known for black-bottled Cordón Negro. Elyssia is step up. Casa Sala is CAVA DE PARAJE CALIFICADO. La Freixeneda (r) from family's C13 estate. Other Cava brands: Castellblanch, Conde de Caralt, Segura Viudas. Plus: Morlanda (PRI), Solar Viejo (RIO), Valdubón (RIB DEL D), Vionta (RÍAS BAIXAS). Also B'x négociant Yvon Mau, Henri Abelé (Champagne), Gloria Ferrer (US), Katnook (Australia), FINCA Ferrer (Argentina). Recently sold to sparkling giant Henkell; expect changes.

Frontonio Ara Youthful (2014) project from Fernando Mora MW and team, focus on GARNACHA, GARNACHA BLANCA, working in Valdejalón. Cuevas de Arom is 2nd project made in underground cellars in DO CAMPO DE BORJA.

Fundador Pedro Domecq Sherry Former Domecq BODEGAS were sliced up through Sherry's multiple mergers. VORS wines now owned by OSBORNE; *La Ina, Botaina, Rio Viejo*, VIÑA 25 by LUSTAU. Andrew Tan of Emperador, world's largest brandy company, bought remainder, focus on Fundador brandy. Group also incl Terry Centenario brandy, Harvey's, famed for Bristol Cream and v. fine VORS, and Garvey, known for *San Patricio* FINO.

Galicia r w (sp) Isolated nw corner of Spain, destination of pilgrims walking the Camino de Santiago; home to many of Spain's best whites (*see* MONTERREI, RÍAS BAIXAS, RIBEIRA SACRA, RIBEIRO, VALDEORRAS), and bright crunchy reds. Isolation ensures number of rare varieties.

Genéricos Rio If there's no category shown on the bottle – such as RES – then it's a *genérico*. *Genéricos* need not follow all DO winemaking, ageing rules. Gives flexibility to express terroir better, though some too showy.

Gómez Cruzado R Alt Historic RIO BODEGA tucked between MUGA and LA RIOJA ALTA. Wines being revived by dynamic duo.

González Byass Sherry, Cád ★★→★★★★ GB (founded 1845) remains a family business. Cellarmaster Antonio Flores is a debonair, poetic presence. From the *Tío Pepe* SOLERA Flores continues to develop *a fascinating portfolio: En Rama and* *the Palmas Finos.* Plus consistently polished viña AB amontillado, Matúsaler oloroso, Noë px and gd brandies. Historical cellar recently opened in jere boutique hotel scheduled 2019. Other wineries: beronia (rio), Pazos de Lusc (rías baixas), Vilarnau (cava), viñas del Vero (somontano); plus (not so gd, bu popular) Croft Original Pale Cream. finca Moncloa, close by to Jerez, produce still reds; also Tintilla de Rota (sweet red fortified).

Gramona Pen r w sw sp ★★→★★★★ Cousins make impressively long-age traditional-method sparkling wine, esp Enoteca, *III Lustros, Celler Batll* Inspiring hive of research, incl bio; sweet incl Icewines, experimental wine Member of corenat.

Grandes Pagos Network of mainly family-owned estates across Spain. Wor together for collective marketing. Easily confused with vino de pago. Some a Vinos de Pago but not all.

Gran Reserva In red Gran Res spends min 2 yrs in 225-litre barrique, 3 yrs in bottl Seek out super old Rio Gran Res, often great value. Many recent less exciting

Guímaro Gal r w ★★ Leading name in revival of ribeira sacra's reputation. Loc family returning to traditional techniques: wild yeasts, foot-treading, ol oak barrels, single v'yds. Cepas Viejas godello from oldest vines is intens structured. finca Pombeiras is old-vine mencía. Makes Ladredo with Di Niepoort (*see* Portugal).

Guita, La Man ★→★★★ Reliable *Manzanilla*. Grupo Estévez-owned (also valdespinc

Gutiérrez Colosía Sherry ★→★★★ Rare remaining riverside bodega in el puerto i santa maría. Former almacenista. Excellent old palo cortado.

Gutiérrez de la Vega Alic r w sw ★★→★★★ Remarkable bodega specializing in swe wine. In alic, but no longer in do, after disagreement over regulations. Love expression of moscatel esp Casta Diva.

Hacienda Monasterio Rib del D r ★★★ peter sisseck consults on 160-ha property. Mo accessible in price, palate than his pingus, wines becoming more approachabl

Haro R Alt City at heart of R Alt, reputation made when railway enabled exports i B'x during phylloxera. Top producers of rio are clustered around station: bodega Bilbaínas (codorníu), cvne, gómez cruzado, la rioja alta, lópez de heredía, mug roda. Annual open house day for public.

Harvey's Sherry ★→★★★ Once-great Sherry name, famed for Bristol Cream. No owned by Emperador, owners of fundador pedro domecq. V.gd vors Sherries.

Hidalgo-La Gitana Man ★★→★★★★ Historic (1792) sanlúcar firm. V. refine manzanilla La Gitana a classic. Finest Manzanilla is single-v'yd *Pastrana Pasad* verging on amontillado maturity. Outstanding vors, incl Napoleon Amontillad Triana px, Wellington *Palo Cortado*.

Jerez de la Frontera Sherry Capital of Sherry region, between Cádiz and Sevill "Sherry" is corruption of C8 "Sherish", Moorish name of city. Pronounce "hereth". In French, Xérès. Hence do is Jerez-Xérès-Sherry. manzanilla has ow DO: Manzanilla-sanlúcar de barrameda.

Jiménez-Landi, Dani Mén Leader in new generation of garnacha producers, esp i méntrida, and Gredos, n of Madrid.

Joven Young, unoaked wine. *See also* crianza.

Sherry trends
At last the world of Sherry has come alive again. Plenty is happening. Dull old blends are fading out; the equivalent of Burgundy's grower-bottling revolution is giving us far more individual wines. Novelties incl négociants (eg. equipo navazos), single v'yds, not fortifying palomino to min 15% for fino, raisining grapes in sun to increase alc, vintage Sherries (eg. gonzalez byass, williams & humbert). Even mention of winemakers.

Juan Carlos Sancha Rio r w ★★ University professor of oenology turned winemaker, Sancha understands soils and traditions of RIO. Works with lesser-known varieties – eg. TEMPRANILLO Blanco, Maturana Tinta, Maturana Blanca, Monastel – as well as with GARNACHA.

Juan Gil Family Estates Jum r w ★→★★★ Family BODEGA; has helped transform reputation of JUM. Gd young MONASTRELLS (eg. 4 Meses); long-lived top Clio, El Nido. Other wineries incl Ateca (CALATAYUD), Can Blau (MONT), Shaya (RUE).

Jumilla Mur r (p) (w) ★→★★★ Arid v'yds in mts n of Mur with heritage of old MONASTRELL vines. TEMPRANILLO, MERLOT, CAB, SYRAH, PETIT VERDOT too. Top: CASA CASTILLO, JUAN GIL. Also: Agapito Rico, Carchelo.

Bag-in-box Sherry? Sanlúcar bodegas want to do this... Permission refused.

Juvé & Camps Pen, Cava w sp ★★→★★★ Consistently gd family firm for quality CAVA. RES de la Familia is stalwart, CAVA DE PARAJE CALIFICADO La Capella.

La Mancha C-La M r p w ★→★★ Don Quixote country, but Spain's least impressive (except for its size) wine region, s of Madrid. Key sources of grapes for distillation to brandy. Too much bulk wine, yet excellence still possible: JUAN GIL Volver, MARTÍNEZ BUJANDA'S FINCA Antigua, PESQUERA'S El Vínculo.

León, Jean Pen r w ★★→★★★ Pioneer of CAB SAUV in Spain in 1950s, now part of TORRES family, run by Mireia Torres. Getting better all the time; showing modern approach with experimentation, packaging.

López de Heredia R Alt r p w ★★→★★★★ Haro's oldest (1877), tradition incarnate, family business with wines that have become a cult. Worth a visit just for Txoritoki tower, cobwebbed cellars and Zaha Hadid-designed shop. See how RIO was made (as it still is, here). Cubillo is younger range with GARNACHA; darker Bosconia; delicate, ripe *Tondonia*. Whites have seriously long barrel-and-bottle age; GRAN RES ROSADO is like no other.

Loxarel Pen r p w sp ★★ Josep Mitjans is passionately committed to his terroir and to XAREL·LO variety. (Loxarel is anagram). Range incl skin contact and amphora wines. Cora is fun, fresh (w). Cent Nou 109 Brut Nature RES is quirky treat: traditional-method fizz, but lees never disgorged. Complex, cloudy, unsulphured, v. youthful after 109 mths. Bio.

Lustau Sherry ★★★→★★★★★ Launched original ALMACENISTA collection. Sherries from JEREZ, SANLÚCAR, EL PUERTO. Only BODEGA to produce EN RAMA from three Sherry towns – fascinating contrasts. Emilín is superb MOSCATEL, VORS PX is outstanding, carrying age, sweetness lightly. One of few bodegas to release vintage Sherries.

Maestro Sierra, El Sherry ★★★ Discover how a JEREZ cellar used to be. Run by Mari-Carmen Borrego, following on from her mother, the redoubtable Pilar Plá. Fine AMONTILLADO 1830 VORS, FINO, OLOROSO 1/14 VORS. *Brilliant quality wines.*

Málaga Mál r w sw ★→★★★ MOSCATEL-lovers should explore hills of Málaga. TELMO RODRÍGUEZ revived ancient glories with subtle, sweet *Molino Real*. Barrel-aged No 3 Old Vines Moscatel from Jorge Ordóñez is gloriously succulent. BENTOMIZ has impressive portfolio. Sierras de Málaga DO for dry table wines; Ordóñez' Botani is delicately aromatic.

Mallorca r w ★→★★★ Constantly improving, if high-priced and hard to find off island. Incl 4 Kilos, Án Negra, Biniagual, Binigrau, Hereus de Ribas, Son Bordils. Reds blend traditional varieties (Callet, Fogoneu, Mantonegro) plus CAB, SYRAH, MERLOT. Whites (esp CHARD) improving fast. DOS: BINISSALEM, PLA I LLEVANT.

Manchuela r w sw ★→★★ Traditional region for bulk wine, showing promise with Bobal, MALBEC, PETIT VERDOT. Leaders: Alto Landón, FINCA SANDOVAL, Ponce (ungrafted vines).

Marqués de Cáceres R Alt r p w ★→★★ Important contributor to RIO in 70s, introducing French winemaking techniques. Fresh white, rosé. Gaudium is modern top wine GRAN RES traditional classic. Owns Deusa Nai in RÍAS BAIXAS.

Marqués de Murrieta R Alt r p w ★★★ →★★★★ Between them, the marqueses of RISCA and Murrieta launched RIO. Both still family businesses. At Murrieta, recent step change in quality. Two styles, classic and modern: Castillo Ygay GRAN RES is one of Rio's traditional greats. Latest release of Gran Res Blanco is **86** (!), and Gran Res Tinto 75. Best-value is ripe, classic RES. Dalmau is impressive contrast, modern Rio, v. well made. *Capellania* is fresh, taut, complex white, one of Rio's v. best ROSADO, v. pale Primer from MAZUELO; v.gd Pazo de Barrantes ALBARIÑO (RÍAS BAIXAS)

Marqués de Riscal R Ala, C y L, Rue r (p) w ★★ →★★★★ Riscal is living history of RIO, able to put on a tasting of every vintage going back to its 1st in 1862. Take your pick of styles: reliable RES, modern FINCA Torrea, balanced GRAN RES. Powerful *Barón de Chirel* Res. The marqués discovered and launched RUE (1972). Make vibrant DYA SAUVBL, VERDEJO, though chose to put v.gd Barón de Chirel Verdejo in C Y L not Rue. Eye-popping Frank Gehry hotel attached.

Martínez Bujanda, Familia C-La M, Rio r p w ★ →★★ Commercially astute business with several wineries. Most attractive are *Finca Valpiedra*, charming estate in RIO FINCA Antigua in La M.

Mas Doix Pri ★★ →★★★ Fine family business in Poboleda, blessed with 70–100-yr old GARNACHA and CARIÑENA grown on slate. Treasure is rare, superb Cariñena all blueberry and velvet, astonishingly pure, named after yr v'yd was planted *1902*. Latest release is tiny quantity of Garnacha, named after planting yr, 1903

Mas Martinet Pri ★★ →★★★★ Sara Pérez is daughter of one of original PRI quinte She's the most passionate of Pri's 2nd generation, fermenting freshly picked grapes in vats in v'yds, and in TINAJAS. Venus La Universal is MONT project with partner René Barbier Jr of CLOS MOGADOR. Also consults on projects across Spain

One-third of world's Garnacha Blanca is grown in tiny DO of Terra Alta.

Mauro Rib del D, C y L, Toro r w ★★ →★★★ Founded by Mariano García of AALTO and formerly VEGA SICILIA, godfather of RIB DEL D. Mauro wines are typically García full-bodied, built to age. Latest release is GODELLO. Joined by sons Eduardo and Alberto, also working at San Román (TORO), Garmón (Rib del D).

Mengoba Bier r p w ★ →★★★ Not all Grégory Pérez's wines are accepted within DO. Le Vigne de Sanchomartín co-ferments a field blend of MENCÍA/GARNACHA Tintorera/GODELLO. Las Tinajas is amphora-aged GODELLO; an orange wine. La Botas is Godello aged in MANZANILLA butts for 10 mths.

Méntrida C-La M r p ★ →★★ Former co-op country s of Madrid, now being put on map by ARRAYÁN, Canopy and JIMÉNEZ-LANDI with GARNACHA, Albillo grapes.

Monterrei Gal r w ★ →★★★ Small DO on Portuguese border, where once Roman made wine. Discovering its potential. Best: Quinta da Muradella: fascinating parcels of unusual vines.

Montilla-Moriles ★ →★★★ Andalucian DO nr Córdoba. Hidden treasure, unfairly regarded as JEREZ's poor relation. Makes dry to sweetest wines all with PX. Shop nr top end for superbly rich treats, some with long ageing in SOLERA. Top: ALVEAR, PÉREZ BARQUERO, TORO ALBALÁ. Important source of PX for use in Jerez DO.

Montsant Cat r p w ★ →★★★★ Tucked in around PRI, plenty to discover. Fine GARNACHA BLANCA, esp acústic. Dense reds: Alfredo Arribas, Can Blau, CAPÇANES, Domènech Espectacle, Can d'Anguera, Mas Perinet, Masroig, Venus La Universal.

Muga R Alt r p w (sp) ★★ →★★★★ The tall Muga brothers and cousin are the friendly giants of HARO, producing some of RIO's finest reds. New-wave pale ROSADO; lively CAVA; classic reds delicately crafted. Best: classical GRAN RES *Prado Enea;* modern powerful *Torre Muga;* expressive, complex Aro.

Mustiguillo V r w ★★ →★★★ Dynamic BODEGA has led renaissance of unloved Bobal grape, also reviving Merseguera variety. V.gd GARNACHA. FINCA El Terrerazo

VINO DE PAGO: top wine Quincha Corral. New project: Hacienda Solana (RIB DEL D).

Navarra r p (w) sw ★→★★★ Next door to RIO and always in its shadow. Early focus on international varieties confused its identity. Best: old-vine GARNACHA from eg. DOMAINES LUPIER. Also CHIVITE, Nekeas, OCHOA, Otazu, Tandem, VIÑA ZORZAL. Also sweet MOSCATELS.

Ochoa Nav r p w sw sp ★→★★ Ochoa *padre* led modern growth of NAV, daughters now carry the torch. Winemaker Adriana O calls her range 8a, incl Mil Gracias GRACIANO, fun, sweet, Asti-like sparkling MdO, classic MOSCATEL.

Osborne Sherry ★★→★★★★ Historic Sherry BODEGA, treasure trove of richer styles incl AOS AMONTILLADO, PDP PALO CORTADO. Owns former DOMECQ VORS incl 51–1a Amontillado. Based in EL PUERTO; its FINO Quinta and mature Coquinero Fino typical of town. Wineries in RIO, RUE, RIB DEL D and super-succulent 5 Jotas jamón.

Pago, Vinos de Officially, top category of DOP; actually, not always. Currently fewer than 20, typically in less famous zones. Obvious absentees incl RIO, PRI, RIB DEL D.

Pago de los Capellanes Rib del D ★★→★★★ V. fine estate, once belonging to church as name suggests, founded 1996. All TEMPRANILLO. El Nogal has plenty of yrs ahead; top El Picón reveals best of RIB DEL D.

Palacio de Fefiñanes Gal w ★★★ Standard DYA *Rías Baixas* one of finest ALBARIÑOS. Two superior styles: barrel-fermented 1583 (yr winery was founded, oldest winery of DO); super-fragrant, lees-aged, mandarin-scented "III". Visit historic palace/winery in main square at Cambados.

Palacios, Álvaro Bier, Pri, Rio r ★★★→★★★★ Pioneer who helped build global reputation of Spanish wine by obsession with quality, plus eloquence. One of quintet who revived PRI. Old-vine Les Terrasses, a polished, structured village wine; FINCA Dofí mainly GARNACHA, superbly aromatic; Les Aubaguetes, from Bellmunt, boosted by 20% CARIÑENA. L'Ermita is powerful, from low-yielding Garnacha. Also at PALACIOS REMONDO in RIO, restoring reputation of R Or and its Garnachas, and at DESCENDIENTES DE J. PALACIOS in BIER.

Palacios, Descendientes de J Bier r ★★★→★★★★ Superb wines, MENCÍA at its best. Ricardo Pérez Palacios, Álvaro's nephew, grows old vines on steep slate. Sadly not all BIER lives up to this promise. Gd-value, floral *Pétalos* and Villa de Corullón; Las Lamas and Moncerbal are v. different soil expressions, one more clay, the other rocky. Exceptional single-v'yd La Faraona (but only one barrel), grows on complex tectonic fault. New winery promises even better quality. Bio.

Palacios, Rafael Gal w ★★★→★★★★ Unstoppable, constantly questioning, Rafael Palacios can't put a foot wrong in VALDEORRAS. Singular focus on GODELLO across many tiny v'yds over more than a decade. Lovely Louro do Bolo; As Sortes, a step up; *Sorte O Soro*, surely Spain's best white.

Palacios Remondo R Or r w ★★→★★★ ÁLVARO PALACIOS has put deserved spotlight on R Or and its GARNACHAS. Complex Plácet (w) originally created by brother Rafael. Reds: organic, Garnacha-led, red-fruited La Montesa; big, mulberry-flavoured, old-vine Propriedad. Top wine is Quiñon de Valmira from slopes of Monte Yerga.

Pariente, José Rue w ★★→★★★ Victoria P makes VERDEJOS of shining clarity. Cuvée Especial is fermented in concrete eggs; silky late-harvest Apasionado. Daughter Martina also runs Prieto Pariente with brother Ignacio, working in C Y L and with GARNACHA in Sierra de Gredos.

Pazo de Señorans Gal w ★★★ Consistently excellent ALBARIÑOS from glorious RÍAS BAIXAS estate. Outstanding Selección de AÑADA, proof v. best Albariños age beautifully.

Penedès Cat r w sp ★→★★★★ Region w of Barcelona, with v. varied styles. Best: Agustí Torelló Mata, Alemany i Corrio, Can Rafols dels Caus, GRAMONA, JEAN LEÓN, Parés Baltà, TORRES.

Pérez, Raúl Bier One of Spain's stars. Family winery is Castro Ventosa, BIER. Works mainly in nw. Terroir-driven; always interesting wines. Provides house-room for new winemakers in his cellar. Magnet for visiting (eg. Spanish and Argentine) winemakers keen to share ideas.

Pérez Barquero Mont-M ★→★★★ Part of revival of MONT-M PX. GD Gran Barquero FINO, AMONTILLADO, OLOROSO; La Cañada PX. Supplier to EQUIPO NAVAZOS.

Pesquera, Grupo Rib Del D r ★★ Alejandro Fernández put RIB DEL D on the map with his simply named Tinto Pesquera. Also now at Condado de Haza, Dehesa La Granja (C Y L), El Vínculo (LA MANCHA), plus hotel, restaurant, farm.

Pie franco Ungrafted vine, on own roots. Typically on sandy soils where phylloxera could not penetrate. Some are well over a century old.

Pingus, Dominio de Rib del D r ★★★★ One of RIB DEL D's greats. Tiny bio winery of Pingus (PETER SISSECK's childhood name), made with old-vine TINTO FINO, shows refinement of variety in extreme climate. *Flor de Pingus* from younger vines; Amelia is single barrel named after his wife. PSI uses grapes from growers, long-term social project to encourage them to preserve vines and viticultural practices and stay on land.

Priorat r w ★→★★★★ Some of Spain's finest wines. Named after former monastery tucked under craggy cliffs. Rescued in 80s by quintet incl René Barbier of CLOS MOGADOR, ALVARO PALACIOS. Renowned for LLICORELLA slate soil. Best show remarkable purity, sense of place. Pri pioneered "village" crus and VI DE FINCA.

Puerto de Santa María, El Sherry One of three towns forming the "Sherry Triangle". Production in decline; few BODEGAS incl GUTIÉRREZ COLOSÍA, OSBORNE, Terry. Puerto FINOS are prized as less weighty than JEREZ, not as "salty" as SANLÚCAR. Taste Lustau's EN RAMA trio to understand differences of Sherries aged in the three towns.

Raventós i Blanc Cava w ★★→★★★ One of stars of traditional-method sparkling. Pepe R left CAVA to create higher-specification CONCA DEL RÍU ANOIA DO. V. fine ROSADO De Nit. Zero SO2 Extrem (no added sulphur) v. lively, textured. Textures de Pedra is ringingly pure Blanc de Noirs. Bio. Also Can Sumoi, natural wine project.

Recaredo Pen w sp ★★→★★★ Outstanding producer of traditional-method sparkling, small family concern. Few wines, all outstanding. Hand-disgorges all bottles. Tops is characterful, mineral *Turó d'en Mota*, from vines planted 1940, ages brilliantly. Bio. Member of CORPINNAT.

Remelluri, La Granja Nuestra Señora R Ala r w ★★→★★★ TELMO RODRÍGUEZ's family property. Makes his original multi-varietal white here. Renewed focus on exceptional old GARNACHA v'yds. Some ethereal wines.

Reserva (Res) Has actual meaning in RIO: aged min 3 yrs, of which 1 yr is in oak of 225 litres. Many producers now prefer to follow own rules. *See* GENÉRICOS.

Rey Fernando de Castilla Sherry ★★→★★★★ Gloriously consistent quality. Seek out Antique Sherries; all qualify as VOS or VORS, but label doesn't say so. Youngest of these, Antique FINO, is fascinating, complex, fortified to historically correct 17% alc. Also v. fine brandy, vinegar. Favoured suppplier to EQUIPO NAVAZOS.

Rías Baixas Gal (r) w ★★→★★★ Atlantic DO growing ALBARIÑO in five subzones, mostly DYA. Best: Forjas del Salnés, Gerardo Méndez, Martín Códax, PALACIO DE FEFIÑANES, Lazo de Barrantes, *Pazo de Señorans*, Terras Gauda, ZÁRATE. Many small producers to discover. Until recently Spain's premier DO for whites, now at risk of overproduction. Influential new generation of consultants, eg. Dominique Roujou de Boubée (ADEGA Pombal), RAÚL PÉREZ (Sketch).

Ribeira Sacra Gal r w ★★→★★★ Magical DO with v'yds running dizzyingly down to River Sil. Increasingly fashionable, esp for fresh reds. Top: ADEGAS Moure, ALGUEIRA, DOMINIO DO BIBEI, FINCA Viñoa, GUÍMARO.

Ribeiro Gal (r) w sw ★→★★★ Historic region, famed in Middle Ages for Tostado sweet wine. Deserving rediscovery, with textured whites made from GODELLO, LOUREIRO, Treixadura. Top: Casal de Armán, Coto de Gomariz, EMILIO ROJO, FINCA Viñoa.

Ribera del Duero r p (w) ★→★★★★ Ambitious DO with great appeal in Spain, created 1982. Anything that incl AALTO, HACIENDA MONASTERIO, PESQUERA, PINGUS, VEGA SICILIA has to be serious, but consistency hard to find. Too many v'yds planted in wrong places. Finally, elegance breaking through. Other top names: Alión, ALONSO DEL YERRO, Cillar de Silos, *Pago de los Capellanes*. Also of interest: Arzuaga, Bohórquez, Dominio de Atauta, Dominio del Aguila, Garmón, Hacienda Solano, O Fournier, Pérez Pascuas, Tomás Postigo. *See also* C Y L neighbours ABADÍA RETUERTA, MAURO.

Rioja r p w sp ★→★★★★ Spain's most famous wine region. Three sub-regions: R Ala, R Alt and R Or (meaning e-facing; formerly named R Baja). Much-debated new regulations allow producers to name villages and "singular" v'yds, and make sparkling RIO.

Rioja Alta, La R Ala, R Alt r ★★→★★★★ For lovers of classic RIO, a favourite choice. Vanilla-edged *Gran Res 904* and GRAN RES 890, aged 6 yrs in oak are stars. But rest of range from *Ardanza*, down to Arana, Alberdi each carry classic house style. Also owns R Ala modern-style Torre de Oña with new Martelo, RÍAS BAIXAS Lagar de Cervera, RIB DEL D Àster.

Rioja 'n' Roll Rio Something new for RIO. New generation of winemakers formed a network for fun and for marketing. All small production, with serious focus on v'yds. Seek them out: Alegre & Valgañón, Artuke, Barbarot, Exopto, Laventura, Olivier Rivière, Sierra de Toloño.

Jerez is celebrating its 1st Michelin star. The restaurant: Lu.

Roda Rib del D, R Alt r ★★→★★★ One of HARO's seven "station quarter" wineries. TEMPRANILLO specialists: Roda, Roda I, Cirsión, approachable Sela. Also RIB DEL D BODEGAS La Horra, Corimbo (w) and Corimbo I.

Rosado Rosé. NAV dark rosados were defeated by Provence pinks. Spain has fought back with pale hues, esp: SCALA DEI's Pla dels Àngels (PRI), MARQUÉS DE MURRIETA's Primer Rosé (RIO), Dominio del Águila Pícaro Clarete (RIB DEL D).

Rueda C Y L w ★→★★★ Spain's response to SAUV BL: zesty VERDEJO. Mostly DYA. "Rueda Verdejo" is 85%+ Verdejo. "Rueda" is blended with eg. Sauv Bl, VIURA. Too much poor quality. Best: *Belondrade*, JOSÉ PARIENTE, MARQUÉS DE RISCAL, Naia, Ossian. Revival of Dorado, dry RANCIO style.

Saca A withdrawal of Sherry from the SOLERA (oldest stage of ageing) for bottling. For EN RAMA wines most common *sacas* are in *primavera* (spring) and *otoño* (autumn), when FLOR is richest, most protective.

Sacramento, El Rio ★→★★★ Impressive new estate with a classic approach. Still early days, but gd pedigree.

Sánchez Romate Sherry ★★→★★★ Old (1781) BODEGA with wide range, also sourcing and bottling rare BUTTS for négociants and retailers. 8-yr-old *Fino Perdido*, nutty AMONTILLADO NPU, PALÓ CORTADO Regente, excellent VORS AMONTILLADO and OLOROSO La Sacristía de Romate, unctuous Sacristía PX.

Sandeman Sherry ★→★★ More famous for its Port than its Sherry. Interesting VOS wines: Royal Esmeralda AMONTILLADO, Royal Corregidor Rich Old OLOROSO.

Sanlúcar de Barrameda Sherry-triangle town (with JEREZ, EL PUERTO DE STA MARÍA) at mouth of River Guadalquivir. Port where Magellan, Columbus and admiral of the Armada set off. Humidity in low-lying cellars encourages FLOR. Sea air said to encourage "saltiness". Wines aged in Sanlúcar BODEGAS qualify for DO MANZANILLA-Sanlúcar de Barrameda.

Scala Dei Pri r p w ★★★ Tiny v'yds of "stairway to heaven" cling to craggy slopes. Managed by part-owner CODORNÍU. Winemaker Ricard Rofes returning to the old ways, eg. fermenting in stone *lagares*. Focus on local varieties, esp GARNACHA and now CARIÑENA. Single-v'yds Sant'Antoni and Mas Deu show terroir. At Monasterio de Poblet in COS DEL S, UNESCO World Heritage Site, Rofes works with Garnacha, Garrut, Trepat vars.

Sierra Cantabria R Al₂, Toro r w ★★★ RIO brand with persistent quiet excellence. Eguren family specialize in single-v'yd, minimal-intervention wines. Organza (w). Reds, all TEMPRANILLO. At Viñedos de Paganos, superb El Puntido; powerful, structured La Nieta. Other properties: Señorío de San Vicente in RIO and Teso la Monja in TORO.

Sisseck, Peter Rib del D Dane who attracted world interest to RIB DEL D with PINGUS. With 2018 purchase of JEREZ BODEGA, he should work same magic for Sherry. Also at Ch Rocheyron, B'x.

Solera System for blending Sherry and, less commonly, Madeira (*see* Portugal). Consists of topping up progressively more mature BUTTS with younger wines of same sort from previous stage, or *criadera*. Maintains vigour of FLOR, gives consistency, refreshes mature wines.

Somontano Som r p w ★→★★ DO in Pyrenean foothills still searching for an identity, growing international varieties. Opt for GEWURZ – rare for Spain. Try Enate, VIÑAS del Vero (owned by GONZÁLEZ BYASS) – its high-altitude Secastilla has gd old-vine GARNACHA, GARNACHA BLANCA.

Suertes del Marqués Can r w ★→★★ Rising star in TENERIFE. Works with LISTÁN Blanco, Listán Negro, Vijariego, Tintilla, making vibrant village and single-v'yd wines. Exceptional v'yds, with unique *trenzado* – plaited vines.

Telmo Rodríguez, Compañía de Vinos Rio, Mál, Toro r w sw ★★→★★★ Ground-breaking winemaker Rodríguez has returned to REMELLURI in RIO but continues his pioneering business: in MÁLAGA (*Molino Real* MOSCATEL), ALIC (Al-Murvedre), Rio (Lanzaga), RUEDA (Basa), TORO (Dehesa Gago), Cigales (Pegaso), *Valdeorras* (DYA Gaba do Xil GODELLO). Return to Rio has led to work on GARNACHA, incl exceptionally pure Las Beatas, tiny old-vine v'yd.

Tenerife Can Rising star of CAN. Top: Borja Pérez, ENVINATE, SUERTES DEL MARQUÉS.

Terra Alta Cat Up-and-coming inland DO neighbouring PRI. GARNACHA territory, esp Bárbara Forés, Celler Piñol, Edetària, Lafou. 90% of Catalan GARNACHA BLANCA v'yds, 75% of Spain's.

Tinaja Aka amphora. Clay pots used in revival of traditional winemaking. Found across Spain, incl ALVEAR, LOXAREL, MAS MARTINET.

Toro r ★→★★★ Small DO w of Valladolid famed for rustic reds from Tinta del Toro (TEMPRANILLO). Today best more restrained, but still firm tannic grip. Dense old-vine San Román. Glamour from VEGA SICILIA-owned Pintia, and LVMH property Numanthia. Also: Las Tierras de Javier Rodríguez, Paydos, Teso la Monja.

Toro Albalá Mont-M ★→★★★★ From young dry FINOS to glorious sweet wines, a triumph for MONT-M. Among them lively AMONTILLADO Viejísimo. Seek out remarkable, sumptuous Don PX Convento Selección 1931.

Torres Cat, Pri, Rio r p w sw ★★→★★★★★ Miguel Jr runs the business, sister Mireia is technical director and runs JEAN LEÓN, Miguel Sr is busy on many fronts. Top wines: outstanding, elegant B'x-blend *Res Real*, top PEN CAB *Mas la Plana*; CONCA DE BARBERÀ duo (burgundy-like *Milmanda*, one of Spain's finest CHARDS, *Grans Muralles*) blend of local varieties is stunning. Also gd-value portfolio; lovely MOSCATEL. New-er, improving wineries in RIB DEL D (Celeste), RIO (Ibéricos) and PRI (Salmos). Pioneer in Chile. Marimar T a star in Sonoma.

Tradición Sherry ★★→★★★★ BODEGA assembled by the great José Ignacio Domecq from exceptional selection of SOLERAS. Based on oldest-known Sherry house (1650). Glorious VOS, VORS Sherries, also a 12-yr-old FINO. Outstanding art collection, archives of Sherry history.

Txakolí / Chacolí P Vas (r) (p) w (sw) ★→★★ Wines from Basque country DOS in

Sherry styles

Manzanilla: fashionable pale, dry, low-strength (15% alc): supposedly green-appley. Serve cool with almost any food, esp crustaceans. Matured by the sea at SANLÚCAR where the FLOR grows thickly and the wine grows salty. Drink up; it fades when open like any top white. Eg. HEREDEROS DE ARGÜESO, San León RES.

Manzanilla Pasada: mature, where flor is fading; v. dry, complex. Eg. HIDALGO-LA GITANA's single-v'yd Manzanilla Pasada Pastrana.

Fino: pale, dry, biologically aged in JEREZ or EL PUERTO DE SANTA MARÍA; weightier than MANZANILLA; min age is 2 yrs (as Manzanilla) but don't drink so young. Try eg. GONZÁLEZ BYASS 4-yr-old Tío Pepe. Don't keep more than 1 wk once opened. Trend for mature Finos aged more than 8 yrs, eg. FERNANDO DE CASTILLA Antique, González Byass Palmas range.

Amontillado: FINO in which layer of protective yeast flor has died. Oxygen gives more complexity. Naturally dry. Eg. LUSTAU Los Arcos. Many brands are sweetened: look for "medium" on label.

Oloroso: not aged under flor. Heavier, less brilliant when young, matures to nutty intensity. Naturally ultra-dry, even fierce. May be sweetened and sold as CREAM. Eg. EMILIO HIDALGO Gobernador (dr), Old East India (sw). Keeps well.

Palo Cortado: v. fashionable. Traditionally wine that had lost flor – between AMONTILLADO and v. delicate OLOROSO. Difficult to identify with certainty, though some suggest it has a "lactic" or "bitter butter" note. Rich, complex: worth looking for. Eg. BARBADILLO Reliquía, Fernando de Castilla Antique. Drink with meat or cheese.

Cream: blend sweetened with grape must, PX and/or MOSCATEL for a commercial medium-sweet style. Few great Creams as old VORS: EQUIPO NAVAZOS La Bota No. 21 is outstanding exception.

En Rama: Manzanilla or Fino bottled from BUTT with little or no filtration or cold stabilization to reveal full character of Sherry. More flavoursome, said to be less stable. Seasonal bottlings, in small batches, sell out fast. *Saca* or withdrawal is typically when flor is most abundant. Keep in fridge, drink up quickly.

Pedro Ximénez (PX): raisined sweet, dark, from partly sun-dried PX grapes (grapes mainly from MONT-M; wine matured in Jerez DO). Unctuous, decadent, bargain. Sip with ice-cream. Tokaji Essencia apart, world's sweetest wine. Eg. Emilio Hidalgo Santa Ana 1861, LUSTAU VORS.

Moscatel: aromatic appeal, around half sugar of PX. Eg. Lustau Emilín, VALDESPINO Toneles. Now permitted to be called "Jerez".

VOS / VORS: age-dated Sherries: some of treasures of Jerez BODEGAS . A v. necessary move to raise the perceived value of Sherry. Wines assessed by carbon dating to be more than 20 yrs old are called VOS (Very Old Sherry/Vinum Optimum Signatum); those over 30 yrs old are VORS (Very Old Rare Sherry/Vinum Optimum Rare Signatum). Also 12-yr-old, 15-yr-old examples. Applies only to Amontillado, Oloroso, PALO CORTADO, PX. Eg. VOS Hidalgo Jerez Cortado Wellington. Some VORS wines are softened with PX: sadly producers can be overgenerous with PX. VORS with more than 5 g/l residual sugar are labelled Medium.

Añada "Vintage": Sherry with declared vintage. Runs counter to tradition of vintage blended SOLERA. Formerly private bottlings now winning public accolades. Eg. Lustau Sweet Oloroso Añada 1997.

Getaria, Bizkaya and Álava. Many v'yds face Atlantic winds and soaking rain, hence acidity of *petillant* whites, esp in Getaria where DYA Txakolí is poured into tumblers from a height to add to spritz. Bizkaya wines, with less exposed v'yds, can have depth and need not be DYA. Top: Ameztoi, Astobiza, Doniene Gorrondona, Txomin Etxaníz. Also Gorka Izagirre, with Michelin three-star restaurant Azurmendi, nr Bilbao airport.

Utiel-Requena U-R r p (w) ★→★★ Marriage of two towns, slowly forging identity with Bobal grape. Try: Bruno Murciano, Caprasia, Cerrogallina.

Valdeorras Gal r w ★→★★★ Warmest, most inland of GAL's DOS, named after gold Romans found in valleys. Exceptional GODELLO, potentially more interesting than ALBARIÑO. Best: Godeval, RAFAEL PALACIOS, TELMO RODRÍGUEZ, Valdesil.

Valdepeñas C-La M r (v) ★→★★ Large DO s of LA MANCHA. Historic favourite for cheap reds. ARA reds now offer best quality/value.

Valdespino Sherry ★★→★★★★ Home to Inocente FINO from top Macharnudo single-v'yd, rare oak-fermented Sherry (EN RAMA bottled by EQUIPO NAVAZOS). Terrific dry AMONTILLADO Tío Diego; outstanding 80-yr-old **Toneles** MOSCATEL, JEREZ's v. best. Winemaker Eduardo Ojeda also experimenting (*see* Sherry trends box). Owned by Grupo Estévez (owns LA GUITA).

Valencia r p w sw ★→★★ Known for bulk wine and cheap MOSCATEL, and still guilty. Higher-altitude old vines and min-intervention winemaking: eg. Aranleon, Celler del Roure, El Angosto, Los Frailes are changing things.

VDT (Vino de la Tierra) Table wine usually of superior quality made in a demarcated region without DO. Covers immense geographical possibilities; category incl many prestigious producers, non-DO by choice to be freer of inflexible regulation and use varieties they want. (*See* Super Tuscan, Italy).

Once you start drinking Fino with smoked salmon you'll forget Sauv Bl.

Vega Sicilia Rib del D r ★★★★ Spain's First Growth recently acquired a new winemaker. But these wines take yrs, so any change of style will be slow. Único, 6 yrs in oak; second wine **Valbuena** outstanding despite lesser status. Flagship: RES Especial, NV blend of three vintages, with up to 10 yrs in barrel; v. fine. Neighbouring Alión shows modern take on RIB DEL D. Owns Pintia (TORO), Oremus in Tokaji (Hungary), joint-venture project Macan (RIO) with Rothschild.

Vendimia Harvest.

Vi de Finca Pri Single-v'yd category: in PRI, wine made for 10 yrs from same single v'yd and commercially recognized as such. Pioneered by ÁLVARO PALACIOS and colleagues, following Burgundian model.

Viña Literally, a v'yd.

Viña Zorzal Nav Rio Entrepreneurial new generation making young gd-value wines, eg. GRACIANO. Restoring old-vine NAV GARNACHA eg. Malayeto.

Williams & Humbert Sherry ★→★★★★ Winemaker Paola Medina transforming historic BODEGA. Initially famed for eg. Dry Sack, Winter's Tale AMONTILLADO, **As You Like It** sweet OLOROSO. Now pioneering specialities such as organic Sherry, vintage Sherries, incl FINO. One of new leaders; *see* Sherry trends box, p.182.

Ximénez-Spínola Sherry V. fine small producer of PX. Grows PX in JEREZ, which is v. rare; most source from MONT-M. Intriguing rarity is Exceptional Harvest, from overripe PX, unfortified.

Yecla Mur Traditional bulk wine country, but is changing. Drivers are Castaño family with MONASTRELLS (eg. Hécula), blends (GSM). Castaño Dulce a modern classic.

Zárate Gal (r) w ★★→★★★★ BODEGA in Val do Salnés, RÍAS BAIXAS. Elegant ALBARIÑOS with long lees-ageing. El Palomar is from centenarian v'yd, one of DO's oldest, on own rootstock, aged in *foudre* for texture, complexity. Ethereal. Owner/winemaker Eulogio Pomares is one of key figures in GAL.

Portugal

Portugal's trump card is hard to pronounce, but it's all those baffling grapes you find nowhere else. Singly or in blends, they give the country something utterly different from Spain, or anywhere else. After 20 years of rapid advance, which included new cellars, new oenology degrees and a great many internships around the globe, Portuguese winemakers have built a strong reputation for good wines at good prices. Repeat after me: Antão Vaz (Alentejo), Alvarinho (Vinho Verde), Bical (Bairrada), Encruzado (Dão) and Rabigato (Douro) for whites and Bastardo (Douro), Baga (Bairrada), Jaen (Dão), Moreto and Tinta Grossa (Alentejo) for reds. They have good acidity, lovely brisk freshness and decisive fruit. Traditional amphora (or *talha*) winemaking is also having a comeback; these big clay jars give fresh, oak-free, elegant whites and reds that are a pleasure to drink. Just what we want now.

Recent Port vintages

A vintage is "declared" when a wine is outstanding by shippers' highest standards. In gd but not quite classic yrs (increasingly in top yrs too by single-estate producers) shippers use the names of their quintas (estates) for single-quinta wines of real character but needing less ageing in bottle. The vintages to drink now are 63 66 70 77 80 83 85 87 92 94 00 03 04 05 though v. young Vintage Port is an unconventional delight, esp with chocolate cake, a sort of dorm feast.

2018 Exceptionally late harvest after a extreme rainy winter. Gd quality for some.

2017 Warm yr. Expected to be widely declared.

2016 Classic yr, widely declared. Great structure and finesse after challenging harvest.

2015 V. dry, hot. Controversial yr. Declared by many (top-quality Niepoort, Noval), but not Fladgate, Symingtons or Sogrape.

2014 Excellent from v'yds that ducked September's rain; production low.

2013 Single-quinta yr; mid-harvest rain. Stars: Vesuvio, Fonseca Guimaraens.

2012 Single-quinta yr. V. low-yielding, drought-afflicted. Stars: Noval, Malvedos.

2011 Classic yr, widely declared. Considered by most on par with iconic 1963. Inky, outstanding concentration, structure. Stars: Dow, Noval Nacional, Vargellas Vinha Velha, Fonseca.

2010 Single-quinta yr. Hot, dry but higher yields than 2009. Stars: Vesuvio, Senhora da Ribeira.

2009 Controversial yr. Declared by Fladgate, but not Symingtons or Sogrape. Stars: Taylor, Niepoort, Fonseca, Warre.

2008 Single-quinta year. Low-yielding, powerful wines. Stars: Noval, Vesuvio.

2007 Classic year, widely declared. Deep-coloured, rich but well-balanced wines. Stars: Dow, Taylor, Vesuvio.

Fine vintages: 03 00 97 94 92 91 87 83 80 77 70 66 63.

Recent table wine vintages

2018 Exceptionally late harvest. Decline in production but gd quality overall.

2017 3rd consecutive fine vintage. V.gd quality all around. Keep.

2016 V.gd quality for those who had patience. Keep for yrs.

2015 Fine yr on quality, quantity. Aromatic, balanced reds drinking specially well. Keep.

See Portugal map p.174.

2014 Rainy winter, cool summer. Fresh whites, bright reds (picked before rain). Drink now.

2013 Great whites, balanced reds (picked before rain). Keep/drink.

2012 Forward, scented reds, elegant whites. For early drinking.

2011 Outstanding all round. Benchmark Douro, Alentejo reds. Keep for yrs.

Açores / Azores (r) w sw ★→★★★★ Mid-Atlantic archipelago of nine volcanic islands with DOCS Pico, Biscoitos and Graciosa for whites and traditional *licoroso* (late-harvest/fortified). Eco landscape, incl vine-protecting *currais* (pebble walls), is UNESCO World Heritage Site. New dynamic winemakers producing exciting volcanic-soil, sea-threatened wines from indigenous varieties Arinto dos Açores, Terrantez do Pico, VERDELHO. Watch: Azores Wine Company, Pico Wines Co-op, Biscoitos Co-op.

Adega A cellar or winery.

Alentejo r (w) ★→★★★★ Reliably warm popular central region, divided into subregional DOCS Borba, Redondo, Reguengos, PORTALEGRE, Évora, Granja-Amareleja, Vidigueira (known for quality white), Moura. Atlantic-influenced Costa Vicentina area making fresh white and red (watch: CORTES DE CIMA, Vicentino). Ancient clay amphora technique Vinho de Talha seeing a comeback. More liberal VR Alentejano preferred by many top estates. Rich, ripe reds, esp from ALICANTE BOUSCHET, SYRAH, TRINCADEIRA, TOURIGA N. Whites fast improving. CARTUXA, ESPORÃO, JÃO PORTUGAL RAMOS, JOSÉ DE SOUSA, Malhadinha Nova, MOUCHÃO, Mouro have potency, style. Watch: Dona Maria, do Peso, do Rocim, Fita Preta, MONTE DE RAVASQUEIRA, boutique SUSANA ESTEBAN, Terrenus.

Algarve r p w sp ★→★★ S coast producing mostly VINHO REGIONAL, national and international varieties. Wines progressing but still fall short of famous beaches, Michelin-starred gastronomy. Barranco Longo, QUINTA dos Vales honourable mentions.

Aliança Bair r p w sp ★→★★★ Large firm with gd reds and *sparkling*. Art and wines at Aliança Underground Museum. Interests in ALEN (da Terrugem, Alabastro), DÃO (da Garrida), DOU (dos Quatro Ventos). Owner of popular Casal Mendes brand.

Ameal, Quinta do Lan w sw sp ★★★ Superior, age-worthy, organic LOUREIRO incl oaked Escolha and, in top yrs (11 14) low-yield, low-intervention Solo. Gd to visit.

Andresen Port ★★→★★★ Portuguese-owned house with excellent wood-aged Ports, esp 20-yr-old TAWNY. Outstanding *Colheitas* 1900' 1910' (bottled on demand) 68' 80' 91' 03'. Pioneered age-dated WHITE PORTS 10-, 20-, v.gd 40-yr-old.

Aphros Vin r p w sp ★★★ Bio, natural pioneer in VIN. V.gd LOUREIRO and Vinhão (both sp and oak-aged Silenus) will age beautifully. New cellar frees up old "medieval" one for traditional no-electricity/amphoras/*lagares* winemaking. Secluded retreat for wine-lovers.

Aveleda, Quinta da Vin r p w ★→★★ DYA Home of Casal García, biggest VIN seller (1939). Regular range of estate-grown wines. Now owns DOU's QUINTA VALE DONA MARIA. New visitor centre.

Bacalhôa Vinhos Alen, Lis, Set r p w sw sp ★★→★★★ Principal brand and HQ of billionaire art-lover José Berardo's group. Also owns National Monument QUINTA da Bacalhôa (v.gd CAB SAUV 1st planted 1974 also used in iconic red Palácio da Bacalhôa), sparkling estate Quinta dos Loridos. Top MOSCATEL DE SETÚBAL barrels, incl rare Roxo. Owner of historic Quinta do Carmo ALEN brand making v.gd reds. Modern, well-made brands: Serras de Azeitão, Catarina, Cova da Ursa (SET), TINTO da Ânfora (ALEN). Visit his amazing garden in Funchal.

Baga Friends Bair Group of BAIR producers mad about BAGA grape. BÁGEIRAS, BUÇACO, Dirk NIEPOORT, FILIPA PATO, LUIS PATO, QUINTA da Vacariça, Sidonio de Sousa.

Bágeiras, Quinta das Bair r w sp ★★★→★★★★ Iconic BAIR producer. Remarkable,

v. age-worthy whites (esp Avô Fausto barrique-aged 100% MARIA GOMES), BAGA reds matured in old wooden vats (esp GARRAFEIRA – RES, Pai Abel and Avô Fausto blended with TOURIGA N), fizz and fortified Baga *Abafado*.

Bairrada Bair r p w sw sp ★★→★★★★ Atlantic-influenced DOC and Beira Atlântico VR also famous for roast suckling pig. Age-worthy, structured BAGA reds, v.gd sparklings (new Baga BAIR designation for best). Top Baga specialists: BÁGEIRAS, FILIPA PATO, LUÍS PATO, Casa de Saima, CAVES SÃO JOÃO, Sidónio de Sousa. Watch: ALIANÇA, CAMPOLARGO, Colinas de S. Lourenço, NIEPOORT's QUINTA de Baixo, Vadio, V Puro. *See* BAGA FRIENDS.

Barbeito Mad ★★→★★★★ Innovative MAD producer with striking labels. Unique, single-v'yd, single-cask COLHEITAS. Outstanding 20-, 30-, 40-yr-old MALVASIAS. New 40-yr-old Boal "Vinho do Embaixador". Excellent Ribeiro Real range with 20-yr-old BOAL, Malvasia, SERCIAL, VERDELHO, with dash of 50s TINTA NEGRA. 96 Colheita pioneered mention of Tinta Negra on front label. Historic Series: MAD most coveted wine in US in C18, C19. Also *Rainwater* and new Verdelho table wine.

Barca Velha Dou r ★★★★ 91' 95' **99 00** 04 08' Portugal's iconic red, created 1952 by FERREIRA, forging DOU's reputation for world-class table wine. Released in only 18 exceptional yrs. Aged several yrs pre-release. Second label, released in great yrs when Barca Velha not made, from CASA FERREIRINHA's best barrels, *Res Especial*, v.gd, esp 89' 94' 97' 01' 07 09. Both last decades. Arguably 89' 94' 97' 01' 09 could have been Barca Velha.

Barros Port ★★→★★★ Founded 1913, Sogevinus-owned since 2006, maintains substantial stocks of aged TAWNY and COLHEITA. V.gd Colheitas from the 30s on, and 63 66' 74' 78 80' 97'. V.gd 20-, 30-, 40-yr-old Tawny. VINTAGE PORT: 87 95 05 07 11 16.

Madeira is now being bottled in 50cl instead of 75cl bottles. Check price.

Barros e Sousa Mad ★★→★★★ Acquired by neighbour PEREIRA D'OLIVEIRA (2013), which will bottle remaining stock under its name. Old lodge to be new visitor centre. Look for rare Bastardo Old RES.

Beira Interior Bei Int r p w ★→★★ Distinctive DOC with some of highest mtns in Portugal, between DÃO and Spanish border. Huge potential from old, high (up to 750m/2461ft) v'yds, esp for white Siria, Fonte Cal. V.gd-value Beyra, do Cardo, dos Currais, dos Termos. Also ANSELMO MENDES (VIN).

Blandy Mad ★★★★★ Historic MAD family firm with young, dynamic CEO Chris Blandy. *Funchal lodges* showcase history, incl vast library of FRASQUEIRA (BUAL 1920' 1957' 1966', MALMSEY **1988'** 1977', SERCIAL 1968' 1975' 1988', VERDELHO **1979'**). V.gd 20-yr-old Terrantez and COLHEITAS (Bual 1996 **2008**, Malmsey 1999, Verdelho 2000, Sercial 2002). Superb 50-yr-old Malmsey, outstanding Terrantez 1980', TINTA NEGRA 95; Also RAINWATER, and Atlantis table wine: white Verdelho, rosé Tinta Negra.

Borges, HM Mad ★→★★★ Sisters Helena and Isabel Borges hold tiny amounts of fine Terrantez 1877 demi-john from founding yr. V.gd 30-yr-old MALVASIA incl wine from 1932. V.gd SERCIAL 1990.

Branco White.

Bual (or Boal) Mad Classic MAD grape: medium-rich (sweet), tangy, smoky wines; less rich than MALVASIA. Perfect with harder cheeses and lighter desserts. Tends to be darkest in colour.

Buçaco Bei At r w ★★★ Manueline-Gothic monument *Bussaco Palace hotel* lists its classic, austere, age-worthy wines back to 40s. Blends of two regions. R: BAGA (BAIR), TOURIGA N (DÃO). W: Encruzado (Dão), MARIA GOMES, Bical (Bair). Barriques, new oak since 2000 have slightly modernized style, esp whites, single-v'yd red Vinha da Mata (VM). Member of BAGA FRIENDS.

Bucelas Lis w sp ★★ Tiny DOC making dry, racy, ARINTO-based whites. Gd-value fizz. Widely popular in C19 England as "Lisbon Hock". Best: da Murta, DA ROMEIRA.

Burmester Port ★→★★★ Est 1730, Sogevinus-owned since 2005. Elegant, wood-aged, gd-value Ports esp 20-, 40-yr-old TAWNY. 1890 1900' 37' 52' 55' 57' COLHEITAS. Age-dated WHITE PORTS, incl fine 30-, 40-yr-old. Gd VINTAGE PORT.

Cálem Port ★→★★★ Est 1859, Sogevinus-owned since 1998. Popular entry-level fruity Velhotes. Best are COLHEITAS 61', 10-, 40-yr-old TAWNY. Lodge in Gaia gets over 100,000 visitors/yr.

Campolargo Bair r w sp ★→★★★ Large estate, idiosyncratic pioneer with B'x varieties. V.gd native ARINTO, Bical, CERCEAL (w), Alvarelhão, PINOT N, Rol de Coisas Antigas blend, B'x blend Calda Bordaleza (r).

Canteiro Mad Method of naturally cask-ageing finest MAD in warm, humid lodges for greater subtlety/complexity than ESTUFAGEM.

Carcavelos Lis br sw ★★★ Unique, mouthwatering, gripping, off-dry fortified. New Villa Oeiras breathed life into v. old, tiny, ailing 12.5 ha seaside DOC.

Cartuxa, Adega da Alen r w sp ★★→★★★★ C17 cellars, restaurant, modern art centre a tourist magnet, while flagship Pêra Manca red 03 05' 07 08' 10' 11' 13' and white draw connoisseurs. Gd-value volume Vinea and EA (organic version available) reds. Consistent best-buy Cartuxa RES. Scala Coeli, reputed single variety (changes every yr).

How do you plant a v'yd in the rocky Dou? With dynamite. Standing well back.

Carvalhais, Quinta dos Dão r p w sp ★→★★★ SOGRAPE-owned boutique DÃO estate. V.gd, consistent, age-worthy range, esp oak-aged Encruzado, RES (r w), Alfrocheiro, TOURIGA N, TINTA RORIZ and top wine Único. Unusual oxidative BRANCO Especial (w). Home of popular Duque de Viseu and Grão Vasco.

Castro, Álvaro de Dão ★★→★★★★ Emblematic producer, characterful wines mostly under QUINTA names, gd-value Saes and superior Pellada. Superb Primus (w). *Pape* (r). Carrocel (TOURIGA N) released in great yrs.

Cello, Casa de Dão, Vin ★★★ Family-run project. Unique QUINTA de San Joanne (VIN) age-worthy white, incl outstanding Superior (only in v.gd yrs). V.gd Escolha, gd-value Terroir Mineral. Distinctive classic Quinta da Vegia (DÃO) range (r), esp RES, Superior.

Chaves, Tapada do Alen ★★★ Historic property now owned by CARTUXA. Unique old high-altitude v'yds making gd white, v.gd age-worthy reds, esp VINHAS VELHAS.

Chocapalha, Quinta de Lis r p w ★★★ Family-run, Atlantic-influenced estate blending mostly native with some international varieties. Winemaker Sandra Tavares da Silva (WINE & SOUL). *Among Lisboa's best reds* esp QUINTA, CASTELÃO, CAB SAUV and flagship Vinha Mãe and TOURIGA N CH. Vibrant, fresh whites, esp great-value old-v'yd ARINTO.

Chryseia Dou r ★★→★★★ B'x's Bruno Prats and SYMINGTON FAMILY ESTATES partnership. Polished TOURIGA-driven (Nacional and Franca) red. Fresher, finer since sourced from QUINTA de Roriz. Second label: *Post Scriptum*. Prazo de Roriz gd value.

Churchill Dou, Port r p w sw ★★★ Port house est 1981 by John Graham, whose family founded GRAHAM. V.gd DRY WHITE PORT (10 yrs old), 20-, 30-yr-old (new) unfiltered LBV, VINTAGE PORT 82 85 91 94 97 00 03 07' 11'. QUINTA da Gricha is source of old vine, grippy Single-Quinta Vintage Port and v.gd single-v'yd DOU red. Gd Churchill's Estates label (esp TOURIGA N).

Cockburn's Port ★★→★★★ Part of SYMINGTON FAMILY ESTATES and back on form, esp drier, fresher style of VINTAGE PORT in 11' 15' 16' (esp lush, tense Bicentenary Vintage Port. Extraordinary 08' 27' 34 63 67 70'. Consistently gd Special RES aged longer in wood than others. Vibrant LBV aged 1 yr less. V.gd single-QUINTA dos Canais. New Gaia visitor centre incl Symington's cooperage tour.

Colares Lis r w ★★★ Unique, historic coastal DOC (1908). Windswept ungrafted vines on sand produce Ramisco *tannic reds*, MALVASIA fresh, salty whites. Fundação Oriente and revitalized Casal Santa Maria bring modern flair to traditional style of ADEGA Regional de Colares and Viúva Gomes.

Colheita Port, Mad Vintage-dated Port or MAD of a single yr. Cask-aged: min of 7 yrs for TAWNY Port (often 50 yrs+, some 100 yrs+); min 5 yrs for Mad. Bottling date shown on label. Serve chilled.

Cortes de Cima Alen r w ★★★ Built from scratch by Danish/Californian couple in 1988. Pioneer in ALEN SYRAH, sustainable farming, Atlantic-coastal v'yds. V.gd, now more elegant, top red Incógnito 11' 12' 14'. Consistent range, esp (r w) Cortes de Cima, RES, varietals (PINOT N, ARAGONEZ, Syrah, TRINCADEIRA). V.gd whites from new coastal v'yds incl ALVARINHO, SAUV BL. Leading amphora/*talha* producer.

Cossart Gordon Mad ★★★ MADEIRA WINE COMPANY-owned brand. Drier style than BLANDY eg. bracing BUAL 1962 is bottled electricity.

Côtto, Quinta do Dou r ★★★ Historic DOU 70s table-wine pioneer. Making auspicious comeback after yrs of inattention. V.gd iconic Grande Escolha 15' (made only in best yrs), single-old-v'yd Vinha do Dote, rare limited-production Bastardo. Gd-value red.

Covela, Quinta de Vin w ★★ Uplifting revival of impressive C16 property on VIN/DOU border. V.gd age-worthy Avesso, incl new RES. Single-variety Edição Nacional, Avesso/CHARD Escolha, Avesso/ARINTO/Chard/VIOGNIER oak-aged RES. Gd rosé.

Crasto, Quinta do Dou, Port r w ★★★ →★★★★ (r) One of DOU's most reputed estates. Striking hilltop location. Jewels in crown are two v. old, field-blend, single-v'yd reds Vinha da Ponte 03 04 07' 10' 12 14, Vinha Maria Teresa 03 05' 06 07 09' 11' 13, plus new star Honore, a "super-blend" of both (also name of exquisite 100-yr-old+ TAWNY). Great-value old-v'yd RES. Superb single-variety TINTA RORIZ. Great TOURIGA N. V'yds in Dou Superior give gd-value wines, incl attractive red, innovative acacia-aged white and SYRAH with VIOGNIER dash. Gd VINTAGE PORT and unfiltered LBV.

Croft Port ★★ →★★★★ Fladgate-owned historic shipper with visitor centre in glorious v'yds nr Pinhão. Sweet, fleshy VINTAGE PORT 75 77 82 85 91 94 00 03' 07 09' 11' 16'. *Quinta da Roêda* Vintage Port 07 08' 09 12' 15' v.gd value. Popular: Indulgence, Triple Crown, Distinction and Pink ROSÉ PORT.

Crusted (Port) Port An almost secret treat. Gd-value, fine, rare, traditional NV Port style. Blend of two or more vintage-quality yrs, aged up to 4 yrs in casks and 3 yrs in bottle. Unfiltered, forms deposit ("crust") so decant. Look for DOW, FONSECA, GRAHAM, NIEPOORT, NOVAL.

Dão r p w sp ★★ →★★★★ Historic mtn-fenced DOC undergoing a revival. Modern pioneers ÁLVARO DE CASTRO, CARVALHAIS, Cabriz, Casa de Santar, Falorca, Maias, Roques, Vegia make fine age-worthy reds, textured, tasty whites (Encruzado is reputed king). Second wave incl Caminhos Cruzados, CASA DA PASSARELLA, CASA DE MOURAZ, Julia Kemper. To watch: António Madeira, Conciso (NIEPOORT-owned), outstanding Druida, Lemos, MOB, Paço dos Cunhas, Ribeiro Santo. Top Dão Nobre ("noble") designation now used. Superb, v.gd-value GARRAFEIRAS. Often known as Portugal's burgundy.

DOC / DOP (Denominação de Origem Controlada / Protegida) Quality-oriented protected designation of origin controlled by a regional commission. Similar to France's AC. *See also* VINHO REGIONAL.

Doce (vinho) Sweet (wine).

Douro r p w sw ★ →★★★★ World's 1st demarcated and regulated wine region (1756), named after its river. Dramatic UNESCO World Heritage Site. Once inaccessible, now wine-tourism ready. Famous for Port, now produces just as much quality table wine (Dou DOC). Three subregions (Baixo Corgo, Cima

> **Douro's slippery (upwards) slopes**
> The DOU is the largest area of mtn v'yds on earth, and it faces unique
> challenges. No other major European wine region is entirely picked by
> hand, for example. Because of those steep slopes, there's v. little chance
> of mechanizing. And the tourism boom has been drawing people away
> from agriculture, making it hard to find pickers the exact moment the
> grapes are ready. Will this push Dou prices up? Most probably.

Corgo and fast-expanding Dou Superior); great diversity of terroir. Over 100
native varieties (often planted together, 80 yrs+) in terraces of unforgiving
schist. Powerful, increasingly elegant, age-worthy reds; fine, characterful whites.
Best: ALVES DE SOUSA, BARCA VELHA, CASA FERREIRINHA, CHRYSEIA, CRASTO, Da Boavista,
Das Carvalhas, DO VESÚVIO, Muxagat, *Niepoort*, POEIRA, QUINTA Nova, RAMOS PINTO,
Vale Dona Maria, Vale Meão, VALLADO, WINE & SOUL. To watch: Conceito, Costa
Boal, DO CÔTTO, DO NOVAL, do Pôpa, dos Murças, Maria Izabel, POÇAS, Quanta
Terra, REAL COMPANHIA VELHA, de S. José, Transdouro Express. VR is Duriense.

Dow Port ★★★→★★★★ Historic SYMINGTON-owned shipper. Drier VINTAGE PORT 85'
94' 00' 07' 11' 19'. Single-QUINTAS do Bomfim and Senhora da Ribeira (v.gd 15)
in non-declared vintage yrs. Beautiful riverside Bomfim winery visitor centre
in Pinhão.

Duorum Dou, Port r w ★★→★★★★ Consistent DOU Superior project of JOÃO PORTUGAL
RAMOS and ex-FERREIRA/BARCA VELHA José Maria Soares Franco. Gd-value, fruity,
entry-level *Tons* COLHEITA. Fine RES. V.gd dense, pure-fruited VINTAGE PORT 07 11'
12 15' from 100-yr-old vines. Fine second label Vinha de Castelo Melhor and
gd-value LBV.

Esporão, Herdade o Alen r w ★★→★★★★ Landmark estate, increasingly certified
organic. High-quality, fruit-focused, modern. Gd-value entry-level Monte Velho,
reputed RES (r w). V.gd single-v'yd/variety range. Sophisticated GARRAFEIRA-like
Private Selection and rare Torre do Esporão 07' 11. New *talhas* (clay amphorae)
red, white using centuries-old ALEN tradition. Auspicious DOU project (QUINTA dos
Murças) making elegant, organic, single-v'yd reds.

Espumante Sparkling. Generally gd value. Best from BAIR (esp BÁGEIRAS, Colinas
São Lourenço, Kompassus, São Domingos. Lookout for BAGA Bair designation),
DOU (esp Vértice), Távora-Varosa (esp MURGANHEIRA), VIN (esp SOALHEIRO, Valados
de Melgaço).

Esteban, Susana Alen r w ★★→★★★ ALEN rising star. Stunning flagship Procura
(r w), from PORTALEGRE's v. old low-yield v'yds (red adds ALICANTE BOUSCHET from
Évora). V.gd amphora/*talha* wine. Gd-value second label: Aventura. Innovative:
Sidecar (invites other winemakers), Sem Vergonha (elegant, fresh, single-variety
CASTELÃO made with Dirk NIEPOORT).

Estufagem Mad Tightly controlled "stove" process of heating MAD for min 3 mths
for faster ageing, characteristic scorched-earth tang. Used mostly on entry-level
wines. Finer results with external heating jackets and lower max temperature
(45°C/113°F).

Falua Tej r p w ★→★★ Now owned by French group Roullier. Well-made export-
focused Tagus Creek blends native and international grapes. Gd-value entry-
level Conde de Vimioso (RES a step up). New gd Falua RES (r w) range.

Ferreira Port ★★→★★★ SOGRAPE-owned historic Port house. Vintages 11' 16' stand
out. Winemaker Luis Sottomayor (BARCA VELHA) reckons *LBV* now as gd as last
decade's VINTAGE PORT; both categories on the up here. V.gd-value spicy TAWNY incl
Dona Antónia RES, 10-, 20-yr-old Tawny (QUINTA do Porto, *Duque de Bragança*).

Ferreirinha, Casa Dou r w ★★→★★★★★ SOGRAPE-owned. Remarkable range of age-
worthy DOU wines. Gd-value entry-level Callabriga, Esteva, Papa Figos, Vinha

Grande. Superb QUINTA da Lêda (r) and Antónia Adelaide Ferreira (r w). Rarely released RES Especial and (iconic) BARCA VELHA.

Fladgate Port Important independent family-owned partnership. Owns leading Port houses (TAYLOR, FONSECA, CROFT, KROHN) and luxury wine hotels: Infante Sagres (Porto), The Yeatman (VILA NOVA DE GAIA), Vintage House (Pinhão).

Fonseca Port ★★★ →★★★★ FLADGATE-owned Port house, founded 1815. Gd-value Bin 27. V.gd 20-,40-yr-old TAWNY. Excellence in VINTAGE PORT 85' 94' 00' 03' 11' 16'. Superb second label: Fonseca Guimaraens. Single-QUINTA Panascal.

Fonseca, José Maria da Alen, Set r p w sw sp ★→★★★★ 200-yr-old, 7th-generation producer; extensive v'yds (650 ha) and portfolio. LANCERS, PERIQUITA are bread-and-butter brands. Jewel in crown is fortified *Moscatel de Setúbal*, which mines aged stock to great effect (great-value 20-yr-old Alambre). Remarkable SUPERIOR 55' 66 71) and limited-release Roxo Superior 18'. Owner of historic, amphora-based, great-value ALEN JOSÉ DE SOUSA estate. Innovative wine bars in Lisbon, Azeitão.

Frasqueira Mad Top MAD category. Also called Vintage. Single-yr, single-noble-variety aged min 20 yrs in wood, usually much longer. Date of bottling required. Highly respected, sought-after and dear.

Garrafeira Label term for superior quality. Traditionally a merchant's "private RES". Must be aged for min 2 yrs in cask and 1 yr in bottle (often much longer). Whites need 6 mths in cask, 6 mths in bottle. Special use in Port by NIEPOORT.

Global Wines Bair, Dão r w sp ★★→★★★ Also known as Dão Sul. One of Portugal's biggest producers, DÃO-based, with estates in many other regions. Great-value popular brands Cabriz (esp RES) and Casa de Santar (esp RES, superb Nobre). Classy Paço dos Cunhas single-v'yd Vinha do Contador. Modern wines, striking architecture, visitor centre at BAIR's QUINTA do Encontro. Other brands: Grilos, Encostas do Douro (DOU), Monte da Cal (ALEN), Quinta de Lourosa (VIN).

Graham's Port ★★★ →★★★★ SYMINGTON-owned Port house. Highly reputed Ports from RES RUBY Six Grapes to VINTAGE PORT 85' 91' 94' 97 00' 03' 07' 11' 16', incl superb Stone Terraces 11' 15' 16', gd-value single-QUINTA dos Malvedos. V.gd-value, attractive 20-, 30-, 40-yrs-old TAWNY, LBV. Fine Single-Harvest (COLHEITAS), esp 52' 63' 69' 72'. Top Ne Oublie V. Stunning Old Tawny, one of three 1882 casks.

Gran Cruz Port ★→★★★ French group La Martiniquaise runs Port's largest brand (Porto Cruz), focused on volume and cocktails. VILA NOVA DE GAIA museum, popular rooftop terrace bar, new Porto hotel tourist attractions. Dalva brand has outstanding TAWNY stocks (esp COLHEITAS, white 52' 63' 73'), gd VINTAGE PORT. Gd Pinhão-based QUINTA de Ventozelo wines.

Henriques & Henriques Mad ★★→★★★★ MAD shipper owned by rum giant La Martiniquaise. Unique extra-dry apéritif Monte Seco. Best are 20-yr-old MALVASIA and Terrantez, 15-yr-old (NB *Sercial)*, Single Harvest (aged in old bourbon barrels, 1997' 1998', BUAL 2000'), Vintage (VERDELHO 1957, Terrantez 1954', SERCIAL 1971'). V.gd new TINTA NEGRA 50-yr-old.

Horácio Simões Set r w sw ★★ Innovative boutique producer. Dynamic range incl late-harvest and fortified MOSCATEL (esp single-cask Roxo and Excellent). Thrilling, rare fortified Bastardo. Table wines to watch: light, fruity Bastardo, BOAL (esp 100-yr-old vines Grande RES), CASTELÃO.

Justino Mad ★→★★★ Largest MAD shipper, owned by rum giant La Martiniquaise, makes Broadbent label. Fairly large entry-level range. Some jewels: Terrantez Old Res (NV, probably around 50-yrs-old), Terrantez 1978' (oldest in cask), MALVASIA 1964' 1968' 1988'.

Kopke Port ★→★★★★ Oldest Port house, est 1638, now Sogevinus owned. Well-known for v.gd spicy, structured COLHEITAS 35' 41' 57' 64' 65' 66 78 80' 84 87 from middle/upper slopes of QUINTA S. Luiz. Unique WHITE PORT range, esp now-rare 1935' and 30-, 40-yr-olds. Gd old-vines DOU red.

Krohn Port ★ →★★★ Now FLADGATE-owned. Exceptional stocks of aged TAWNY (rich IC-, 20-yr-old), COLHEITA 83' 87' 91 97 dating back to 1863 (source of TAYLOR 1863 Single Harvest). Gd VINTAGE PORT 16'.

Lancers p w sp ★ JOSÉ MARIA DA FONSECA's semi-sweet, semi-sparkling, ROSADO, now white, fizzy (p w) and alc-free versions.

Lavradores de Feitoria Dou r w ★★ →★★★ Well-run collaboration of 15 producers (19 v'yds). Gd whites, esp SAUV BL, Meruge (100% oak-aged old-vines Viosinho). Value reds, incl Três Bagos RES. V.gd Grande Escolha (esp long-aged Estágio Frolongado), QUINTA da Costa das Aguaneiras, elegant Meruge (mostly TINTA RORIZ from n-facing 400m/1312ft v'yd).

Destinations for best grilled fish: coastal Alen, Bair, Lis, Set, Vin.

LBV *(Late Bottled Vintage)* Port Accessible, affordable alternative to VINTAGE PORT. A single-yr wine, aged 4–6 yrs in cask (twice as long as VINTAGE PORT). V.gd, age-worthy, unfiltered versions eg. DE LA ROSA, FERREIRA, NIEPOORT, NOVAL, RAMOS PINTO, SANDEMAN, WARRE. Best to decant them.

Lisboa Lis r p w sp ★ →★★★ Large, hilly region n of capital; varied terroir, muddle of local and international grapes. Best-known DOCS: microclimatic Alenquer (age-worthy reds from boutique great-value DE CHOCAPALHA, SYRAH pioneer MONTE D'OIRO) and traditional BUCELAS, COLARES. Crisp whites growing in strength, esp from limestone coastal/elevated v'yds, eg. ADEGA Mãe (Viosinho), Casal Figueira (Vital), Casal Sta Maria (Colares), QUINTA de Sant'Ana (PINOT N, RIES), do Pinto (blends), da Serradinha (natural), Vale da Capucha (organic).

Madeira Mad r w →★★★★ Island and DOC, famous for fortifieds. Modest table wines. VERDELHO best. Look for Atlantis, Barbeito, Barbusano, Moledo, Palmeira, Primeira Paixão, Terras do Avô and innovative TINTA NEGRA-based Ilha.

Madeira Wine Company Mad Association of all 26 British MAD companies, est 1913. Owns BLANDY, COSSART GORDON, Leacock, Miles and accounts for over 50% of bottled Mad exports. Since BLANDY family gained control, almost exclusively focused on promoting Blandy brand.

Malvasia (Malmsey) Mad Sweetest and richest of traditional MAD noble grape varieties, yet with Mad's unique sharp tang. Delightful with rich fruit, chocolate puddings or just dreams.

Mateus Rosé p (w sp ★ World's bestselling, medium-dry, lightly carbonated rosé now in transparent bottles and available in white (drier, no spritz) or fully fizzy (p w). Expressions range: (MARIA GOMES/CHARD) and three rosé blends (BAGA/SHIRAZ, Baga/MUSCAT; ARAGONEZ/ZIN).

Mendes, Anselmo Vin r w sw sp ★★★ Acclaimed winemaker and consultant. Several benchmark, age-worthy ALVARINHOS, incl gd-value (aged on lees) Contacto, excellent oaked voluptous Curtimenta, superb single-v'yd Parcela Única, classy Muros de Melgaço and vibrant new Expressões. Gd LOUREIRO, silky, modern red Vin (Pardusco), surprising orange Vin Tempo. Watch out for new BEI INT, DÃO, DOU wines.

Minho Vin River (and province) between n Portugal and Spain, also VR covering same region as VIN. Some leading Vin producers prefer VR Minho label.

Monte de Ravasqueira Alen r p w ★★ →★★★ Estate with great terroir (high amphitheatre clay-limestone, granite), precision viticulture and experienced winemaker. Gd Premium range, esp ALICANTE BOUSCHET. Gd range incl single-v'yd Vinha das Romãs.

Monte d'Oiro, Quinta do Lis r p w ★★ →★★★ Family estate started with Hermitage vines from Chapoutier. Now makes savoury, creamy SYRAH, peculiar VIOGNIER (Madrigal), fine TINTA RORIZ (Têmpera), esp Ex-Aequo, Bento & Chapoutier Syrah/TOURIGA N blend.

Moscatel de Setúbal Set sw ★★★ Fortified sweet MOSCATEL with exotic scents incl rare Roxo and Superior label. Best: BACALHÔA VINHOS, HORÁCIO SIMÕES, JOSÉ MARIA DA FONSECA (owns oldest stocks incl famous 100-yr-old Torna-Viagem), QUINTA do Piloto. Value: ADEGA DE PEGÕES, Casa Ermelinda Freitas, SIVIPA.

Moscatel do Douro Dou The high Favaios region produces surprisingly fresh, fortified MOSCATEL Galego Branco (MUSCAT Blanc à Petits Grains). Look for: Adega de Favaios, POÇAS, Portal.

Mouchão, Herdade de Alen r w sw ★★★ Historic family-run estate focused on ALICANTE BOUSCHET. V.gd estate red, COLHEITAS Antigas (cellar releases) 02′ 03′, iconic *Tonel 3–4* 05′ 08 11′ 13′, fortified *licoroso*. Gd-value Ponte das Canas blend (incl SYRAH), Dom Rafael.

Mouraz, Casa da Dão r w ★★ Boutique organic pioneer. Modern but characterful (esp Elfa) wines from family-owned v'yds at 140–400m (459–1312ft). Lost cellar, some v'yds in forest fires. AIR label from bought-in ALEN, DOU, VIN organic grapes.

Murganheira, Caves sp ★★★ Reputed ESPUMANTE producer; owns Raposeira. Blends and single varietal (native, French grapes) fizz: Vintage, Grande RES, Czar rosé.

Niepoort Bair, Dão, Dou r p w ★★★→★★★★ Port shipper and DOU pioneer with many interests. Owned by Dirk Niepoort. Port highlights: VINTAGE PORT, CRUSTED, unique demijohn-aged GARRAFEIRA and single v'yd Bioma. V.gd TAWNY, esp elegant bottle-aged COLHEITAS. Lalique-bottled 1863 Port is world's most expensive Port sold at auction (€100K+). Fine Dou range, esp *Redoma* (r p w Res w), Coche (superb w), Batuta, iconic Charme and unique 130-yr-old single-v'yd Turris. Exciting Projectos cross-region/winemaker wines, incl BUÇACO, Vitor Claro (ALEN), Spanish partnerships Ladredo (RIBEIRA SACRA) and Navazos (Jerez). Dirk's vision now in BAIR (esp GARRAFEIRA, Gonçalves Faria, Poeirinho, VV), DÃO (esp Conciso) and VIN.

Noval, Quinta do Dou, Port r w ★★★→★★★★ Historic estate bought by AXA in 1993. Consistent, fine VINTAGE PORT 97′ 00′ 03′ 07′ 08′ 11′ 12′ 13′ 15′ 16′. Extraordinary *Nacional* 63′ 66′ 94′ 96′ 97′ 00′ 01′ 03′ 04′ 11′ 16′ from 2.5 ha ungrafted vines is pricey jewel in crown. Second vintage label: Silval. Superb COLHEITAS, 20-, 40-yrs-old, unfiltered LBV. Since 2004 making DOU incl gd-value Cedro (native/SYRAH blend), v.gd Noval, varietal TOURIGA N.

Offley Port ★→★★ Old house now owned by SOGRAPE. Gd recent fruit-driven VINTAGE PORT, unfiltered LBV, TAWNY. Apéritif/cocktail styles: Cachuca RES WHITE PORT and ROSÉ PORT.

Palmela Set r w ★→★★★ CASTELÃO-focused DOC. Best: Herdade Pegos Claros, HORÁCIO SIMÕES, QUINTA do Piloto. To watch.

Passarella, Casa da Dão r p w ★★→★★★ C19 estate leading DÃO revival. V.gd range, esp flagship Villa Oliveira: Encruzado, TOURIGA N (from old field-blend v'yd), single-v'yd Pedras Altas (r), Vinha do Província (w), 1ª Edição (five vintages ENCRUZADO blend), oustanding 125 Anos (r). V.gd boutique Fugitivo range esp Enólogo, Enxertia (Jaen), Vinhas Centenárias (red blend of 100-yr-old vines); new Curtimenta. Excellent (gd-value) GARRAFEIRA (w).

Pato, Filipa Bair r w sp sw ★★→★★★ Reference winemaker in old-vines-driven BAIR. Defends "wines with no make-up". 90-yr-old-vine Nossa Calcario is v.gd

---

Certified shopping list
Certified organic and bio wines still a small fraction of market in Portugal. Many Portuguese producers use sustainable practices but consider the certification to be burdensome. Best certified table wines: Aphros, CASA de MOURAZ, ESPORÃO, FILIPA PATO, Julia Kemper, QUINTA de Baixo (NIEPOORT), Quinta da Palmirinha, Quinta do Romeu, Vale da Capucha. Port: Bioma (Niepoort), Quinta do Infantado, Terra Prima (FONSECA).

flagship label: silky, perfumed BAGA (r), complex Bical (w). V.gd old-vine, oak-*lagares* fermented Territorio Vivo. Tests boundaries (like her father LUIS PATO), esp with thrilling amphora-aged Post Quer**s (r w).

Pato, Luís Bair r w sp sp ★★→★★★★ Justifiably self-assured BAIR grower. Made his "Mr BAGA" name with **seriously age-worthy, single-v'yd Baga** (Vinhas Barrio, Barrosa, Pan) and two Pé Franco wines from ungrafted vines (superb sandy-soil QUINTA do Ribeirinho, chalky-clay Valadas). Ready-to-drink, gd-value: VINHAS VELHAS (r w), Baga Rebel, wacky red FERNÃO PIRES (fermented on Baga skins). V.gd whites incl Vinha Velhas (single-v'yd Vinha Formal), fizzy MARIA GOMES Método Antigo, early-picked (Informal). Daughter FILIPA PATO is BAIR's rising star.

Pegões, Adega de Set r p w sw sp ★→★★★ Dynamic co-op. Stella label and low-alc Nico white offer gd clean fruit. COLHEITA Seleccionada (r w) gd value.

Península de Setúbal Set ★→★★★ Atlantic-facing region s of Lisbon. VR wines mostly from chalky or sandy banks of Sado and Tagus Rivers. Est: ADEGA DE PEGÕES, BACALHÔA VINHOS, Casa Ermelinda Freitas, JOSÉ MARIA FONSECA, SIVIPA. Watch: QUINTA do Piloto, Herdade do Portocarro.

Pereira d'Oliveira Vinhos Mad ★★→★★★★ Family-run producer with vast stocks (1.6 million litres) of bottled-on-demand old FRASQUEIRA, many available to taste at emblematic 1619 cellar door. Best incl stunning C19 vintages (MOSCATEL 1875, SERCIAL 1875, Terrantez 1880) and rare Bastardo 1927.

Periquita Grape also known as CASTELÃO. Also trademark of JOSÉ MARÍA DA FONSECA's successful brand.

Poças Dou, Port ★→★★★ Family-owned firm est 1918. Old stocks allow for fabulous +90-yr-old "1918 Very Old Tawny", outstanding 20-, 30-, 40-yr-old TAWNY, COLHEITAS 00 01 03 07. V.gd VINTAGE PORT 15' 16'. Expanding table wine range. V.gd Símbolo (partnership with B'x Angélus-owner Hubert de Bouard). Gd RES (r w), gd-value Vale de Cavalos.

Poeira, Quinta do Dou r w ★★★ Consultant Jorge Moreira's own project. Cool n-facing slopes make intense yet softly spoken wines, esp red. V.gd CAB SAUV blend, single-v'yd Ímpar. Taut, keen, oaked rare DOU ALVARINHO. Classy second label Pó de Poeira (r w).

Portalegre Alen r w w ★→★★★ Ongoing revival of most n subregion of ALEN. Acquisition of high-altitude v'yds (SYMINGTON, SOGRAPE) and historic estates (TAPADA DO CHAVES) signal strong comeback. Pioneers incl QUINTA do Centro, now owned by SOGRAPE and João Afonso (Cabeças do Reguengo), chef Vitor Claro, consultant RUI REGUINGA (Terrenus), winemaker SUSANA ESTEBAN, ESPORÃO. Elevation, granite and schist, old vines, gd rainfall account for fresher, deeper, more structured ALEN's wines. To watch.

Quinta Portuguese for "estate". "Single-quinta" denotes single-estate VINTAGE PORTS made in non-declared yrs (increasingly made in top yrs too by single-estate producers).

Rainwater Mad Light style of MADEIRA, popular in US, admirable as apéritif or with many foods.

Ramos, João Portugal Alen r w ★→★★★ One of ALEN's most respected winemakers, also in VIN and other brands (DUORUM, Foz de Arouce, QUINTA da Viçosa, Vila Santa). Success due to gd-value, true-to-region wines with commercial appeal, incl Marquês de Borba (r, RES r), new old vines (r w). Estremus is classy top wine.

Ramos Pinto Dou, Port ★★★ 1880 pioneering Port and DOU producer owned by Champagne Roederer. Consistent, esp Duas Quintas RES (r), Res Especial (mainly TOURIGA N from Bom Retiro). V.gd age-worthy VINTAGE PORT incl single-QUINTA Vintage (de Ervamoira). Complex single-quinta TAWNY 10-yr-old (de Ervamoira) and best-in-class 20-yr-old (Bom Retiro). Gd 30-yr-old incl a dash of centenarian Tawny. Winemaker Ana Rosas replaced retired João Nicolau de Almeida.

Raposeira Dou sp ★★ MURGANHEIRA-owned. Classic-method fizz. Flagship Velha RES, CHARD/PINOT N lees-aged 4 yrs.

Real Companhia Velha Dou, Port r p w sw ★→★★★ Est 1765, so pretty *velha*. Silva Reis family renewing Port (incl Royal Oporto and Delaforce) and DOU portfolio with precision viticulture (540 ha) and winemaking (led by POEIRA's Jorge Moreira). Grandjó is best late-harvest in Portugal. Unique 149-yr-old Carvalhas Memories VERY OLD TAWNY. V.gd old-vine flagship QUINTA das Carvalhas (r w), VINTAGE PORT, 20-yr-old TAWNY. Value brands Aciprestes, Evel. Quinta de Cidrô (v.gd CAB SAUV/TOURIGA N, Rufete). New, thrilling whites from Quinta do Síbio incl rare Samarrinho, v.gd ARINTO (born from experimental project Séries). To follow.

Reserve / Reserva (Res) Port Higher quality than basic or ages before being sold (or both). In Port, bottled without age indication (used in RUBY, TAWNY). In table wines, ageing rules vary between regions. A pinch of salt.

Romeira, Quinta da r p w sp ★→★★ Historic BUCELAS estate, now owned by Sogrape. Consolidating position under new owner Wine Ventures. Extended v'yd (75 ha, mostly ARINTO) now offers s and n aspects for slightly different styles. V.gd Arinto (Prova Régia RES, oaked Morgado Sta Catherina Res). Gd-value Prova Regia Arinto, Principium French/native grape blends (VR LISBOA).

Rosa, Quinta de la Dou, Port r p w ★★★ Lovely riverside Pinhão estate. Port and DOU range increasingly gd under winemaker Jorge Moreira (POEIRA). V.gd VINTAGE PORT, LBV, new 30-yr-old TAWNY. Rich but elegant wines, esp RES (r w). Remarkable new age-worthy white TIM. Generous gd-value Passagem label. DouROSA is entry level.

Rosado Rosé. Growing category. Best incl Colinas São Lourenço Tête de Cuvée, Cortes de Cima, Covela, Monte da Ravasqueira, QUINTA Nova, SOALHEIRO (sp), Vértice (sp).

Portugal is home to five restaurants with two Michelin stars; two in Lisbon.

Rosé Port Port Pioneered by Croft's Pink (2005) now made by other shippers (eg. POÇAS). Quality variable. Serve chilled, on ice, or, if you must, in a cocktail.

Rozès Port ★★★ Port shipper owned by Vranken-Pommery. VINTAGE PORT, incl LBV, sourced from DOU Superior QUINTAS (Grifo, Anibal, Canameira). Terras do Grifo Vintage is blend of all three; v.gd LBV (from Grifo).

Ruby Port Most simple, young, cheap sweet Port style. Can still be delicious. RES a step up.

Rui Reguinga Alen, Tej ★★★ Consultant winemaker with own projects. ALEN: v.gd old-vines Terrenus range, incl single-v'yd, 100-yr-old vines Vinha da Serra (w). TEJO: v.gd Rhône-inspired SYRAH/GRENACHE/VIOGNIER blend Tributo. Also in Argentina.

Sandeman Port ★★→★★★ Historic house, now owned by SOGRAPE. V.gd-value 20-, 30-, 40-yr-old TAWNY (with new attractive bottle), unfiltered LBV. Great VINTAGE PORT 07' 11' 16' bring back quality. Superb Very Old Tawny Cask 33.

São João, Caves Bair r w sp ★★→★★★ Traditional, family-owned firm known for gd old-fashioned red/white, esp *Frei João*, Poço do Lobo (BAIR), Porta dos Cavaleiros (DÃO). Regular gd-value museum releases from vast stock (back to 1963). Gd ARINTO/CHARD white, sparkling blends.

Sercial Mad White grape. Makes driest MAD. *Supreme apéritif;* gd with gravlax or sushi. *See* Grapes chapter.

Smith Woodhouse Port ★★★ SYMINGTON-owned small Port firm est 1784. Gd unfiltered LBV; some v.gd drier VINTAGE PORT 83 85 91 94 97 00' 03 07 11'. Single-QUINTA da Madelena.

Soalheiro, Quinta de Vin r p w sp ★★→★★★ Leading ALVARINHO specialist incl age-worthy organic range. V.gd subtly barrel-fermented old-vine Primeiras Vinhas, oak-aged RES, chestnut barrel/partial malolactic fermentation Terramatter,

> **Turning back the clock**
> Field blends are how vines used to be grown in Portugal, until the
> C20 took hold: multiple grape varieties were planted together. The
> few that have survived are now treasured and cosseted – and envied.
> Abandonado, ALVES DE SOUSA (DOU): red, 80-yr-old field blend, 20+
> varieties. Pintas, WINE & SOUL (Dou): red, 80-yr-old field blend, 30+
> varieties. Procura, SUSANA ESTEBAN (ALEN): white, 80-yr-old field blend.
> Turris, NIEPOORT (Dou): *fuder*-aged red, 130-yr-old field blend, one of
> oldest v'yds in Portugal. Vinha da Ponte, QUINTA DO CRASTO (Dou): red
> from a 90-yr-old field blend of 49 varieties.

unfiltered Pur Nature, mineral Granit. 1st red, Oppaco, is unique Vinhão/
Alvarinho blend. V.gd PINOT N/Alvarinho blend rosé. Great *fizz* (p w).

Sogrape Alen, Dou, Vin ★★→★★★★ Portugal's most successful firm with global
interests (Portugal, Argentina, NZ, Spain). MATEUS ROSÉ, BARCA VELHA jewels in
crown for contrasting reasons. Portuguese portfolio encompasses ALEN (gd range
Herdade do Peso), DÃO (boutique CARVALHAIS), DOU (popular CASA FERREIRINHA/
reputed Legado), Port (FERREIRA, SANDEMAN, OFFLEY), VIN (gd-value Azevedo).

Sousa, Alves de Dou, Port r w ★★→★★★ Family-run DOU pioneer. Characterful range
from various quintas esp *Quinta da Gaivosa*, unique late-released RES Pessoal.
V.gd old-vine field-blends Abandonado, Vinha de Lordelo. Expanding Port range
incl elegant VINTAGE PORT, v.gd 20-yr-old TAWNY.

Sousa, José de Alen r (w) ★→★★★ Historic prestigious C19 estate. Ancient Roman
tradition kept alive with use of 114 ceramic amphorae/*talhas* (Portugal's largest
collection). Superb J de José de Sousa. Great-value Mayor and José de Sousa
Puro Talha range is 100% fermented in *talha*.

Symington Family Estates Dou, Port r w ★★→★★★★ DOU's biggest landowner, clutch
of top Port houses (incl COCKBURN, DOW, GRAHAM, VESUVIO, WARRE). Classy Dou
range (CHRYSEIA, Vesúvio, well-made organic Altano). New project in upper ALEN.

Tawny Port Wood-aged Port, ready to please on release. RES, age-dated (10-, 20-,
30-, 40-yr-old) wines go up in complexity, price. Single-year COLHEITAS can cost
gd deal more than VINTAGE PORT. Luscious Very Old Tawny Ports (min 40 yrs
old, most much older) can be expensive, give v. different pleasure from Vintage.
Best: 1918 (EDÇAS), 5G (WINE & SOUL), Honore (QUINTA DO CRASTO), Ne Oublie
(GRAHAM), Scion (TAYLOR), Tributa (VALLADO), VV (NIEPOORT).

Taylor Port ★★→★★★★ Historic Port shipper, FLADGATE's jewel in the crown.
Imposing VINTAGE PORTS 92' 94 97 00' 03' 07' 09' 11' 16', incl single-quinta
(Terra Feita, Vargellas), rare Vargellas VINHA VELHA from 70-yr-old+ vines. Market
leader for TAWNY incl v.gd, age-dated, 50-yr-old COLHEITAS and luscious 1863 Scion
Very Old Tawny.

Tejo r w ★→★★ Region surrounding River Tagus (Tejo) n of Lisbon. Quantity-
to-quality shifting slowly. Solid: da Alorna, da Lagoalva, da Lapa, FALUA. More
ambitious: Casal Branco, RUI REGUINGA/Tributo show potential of top terroir. Old
vines produce gd results with stalwart Castelão, Fernão Pires.

Tinto Red.

Trás-os-Montes Tras Mountainous inland DOC, just n of DOU. Valle Pradinhos is well-
known reference. Watch: Encostas de Sonim, Sobreiró de Cima, Valle de Passos.

Vale Dona Maria, Quinta do Dou, Port r p w ★★→★★★ Reputed DOU table wine
pioneer now owned by AVELEDA. V.gd plush yet elegant reds incl two top single-
parcel reds Vinha do Rio, Vinha da Francisca. Smoky, oaky but brisk whites
made with bought-in fruit, incl single-parcel Vinha do Martim, flagship CV
mid-range Van Zellers, new VVV. Entry level Rufo. V.gd Port 16'.

Vale Meão, Quinta do Dou r w ★★★→★★★★ Leading DOU Superior estate; once source of BARCA VELHA. Fine, age-worthy, elegant top red. Gd-value second label Meandro (also w). Gd single-QUINTA VINTAGE PORT. Single-varietal Monte Meão range.

Vallado, Quinta da Dou r p w ★★→★★★ Family-owned Baixo Corgo estate with modern hotel/winery. DOU Superior QUINTA do Orgal (boutique Casa do Rio) with new, fresh organic red. Range of Dou (r w), incl RES field blend, worth following. Gd 10-, 20-, 30-, 40-yr-old TAWNY. Adelaide designates top Dou red, VINTAGE PORT, thrilling Tributa Very Old (pre-phylloxera) Tawny.

Vasques de Carvalho Dou, Port ★★★ New producer (2012) est by António Vasques de Carvalho (inherited family cellars, stock, v'yd) and business partner Luís Vale (injected capital). V.gd, stylish 10-, 20-, 30- and 40-yr-old TAWNY.

Verdelho Mad Style and grape of medium-dry MAD; pungent but without spine of SERCIAL. Gd apéritif or pair with pâté. Increasingly popular for table wines.

Vértice Dou sp ★★★ Reputed DOU fizz producer. V.gd-value Gouveio. Superb, high-altitude, 8-mth-aged PINOT N.

Vesuvio, Quinta do Dou, Port ★★★★ Magnificent QUINTA and Port on par with best VINTAGE PORT 07' 08' 11' 13' 15' 16'. Still foot-trodden by people (not robots). V.gd, age-worthy, old-vine Vesuvio (r), plus gd-value second label Pombal do Vesuvio (r).

Vila Nova de Gaia Dou Historic home of major Port shippers', across River Douro from Oporto. Hotels, restaurants, tour boats, classy lodges are tourist attractions (CÁLEM, COCKBURN'S, GRAHAM'S, SANDEMAN).

Vinhas Velhas Old vines; though what constitutes old is usually undefined.

Vinho Verde Vin r p w sp ★→★★★ Portugal's biggest region in cool, rainy, verdant nw. Adequate for decades, now signs of renaissance: fresh, better blends. Best: high-end ALVARINHO from Monção e Melgaço subregion (eg. ADEGA de Monção, ANSELMO MENDES, do Regueiro, Luis Seabra, QUINTA de Santiago, Reguengo de Melgaço, SOALHEIRO, Valados de Melgaço), LOUREIRO from Lima (eg. APHROS, QUINTA DO AMEAL), Avesso from Baião (QUINTA DE COVELA). Red Vinhão grape getting a makeover by leading players (eg. Anselmo Mendes, Aphros, Soalheiro). Large brands are spritzy; DYA. Watch: Quinta de San Joanne, Vale dos Ares.

Vintage Port Port Classic vintages are best wines declared in exceptional yrs by shippers. Bottled without filtration after 2 yrs in wood, mature v. slowly in bottle, throwing a deposit – always decant. Modern vintages broachable earlier (and hedonistically young) but best will last more than 50 yrs. Single-QUINTA Vintage Ports also drinking earlier; best can last 30 yrs+.

Drink Vintage Port either v. young or when mature. Adolescent Port best shut away.

VR / IGP (Vinho Regional / Indicação Geográfica Protegida) Same status as French Vin de Pays. More leeway for experimentation than DOC/DOP.

Warre Port ★★★→★★★★ Oldest of British Port shippers (1670), now owned by SYMINGTON FAMILY ESTATES. Rich, long-aging VINTAGE 83 85 91 94 97 00' 03 07' 09' 11' 16' and unfiltered LBV. Elegant Single-QUINTA and 10-, 20-yr-old TAWNY Otima reflect Quinta da Cavadinha's cool elevation.

White Port Port Port from white grapes. Ranges from dry to sweet (*lágrima*); mostly off-dry and blend of yrs. Apéritif straight or drink iced with tonic and fresh mint. Growing, high-quality, niche: age-dated (10-, 20-, 30-, or 40-yr-old), eg. ANDRESEN, KOPKE, QUINTA de Santa Eufemia; rare COLHEITAS eg. Cℜ. da Silva's Dalva.

Wine & Soul Dou, Port r w ★★★→★★★★ Boutique DOU project of Sandra Tavares and Jorge Serôdio Borges, making terroir-expressive wines, incl v.gd, oak-aged Guru (w), superb old-vine QUINTA da Manoella VINHAS VELHAS and complex, dense (80-yr-old vine) Pintas. V.gd Pintas Character and second-label Manoella (r w). V.gd Pintas VINTAGE PORT. Oustanding 5G (120-yr-old barrel kept from five generations) Very Old TAWNY.

Switzerland

Abbreviations used in the text:

Aar	Aargau
Ber	Bern
Gris	Grisons
Luc	Lucerne
Neu	Neuchâtel
Schaff	Schaffhausen
Thur	Thurgau
Tic	Ticino
Val	Valais
Vd	Vaud
Zür	Zürich

The Swiss are known as great buyers of fine and rare wine: private cellars in Geneva, Bern and Zurich are full of great burgundy and Bordeaux. And Swiss wine: the best are too precious to export. Chasselas can be trivial. But connoisseurs esteem Switzerland's most traditional grape as a sensitive vehicle for terroir expression. Buy it only from prime producers – this recommendation holds for almost every wine in the world, but for Chasselas it is indispensable if you wish to get the point of its delicacy and subtlety. And then rarities like Petite Arvine and Completer, Cornalin and Humagne Rouge. But for these you might have to go to Switzerland and fight for them in person.

Recent vintages

2018 Powerful, round wines all over the country.
2017 Frost; some cantons have only 20% of a normal crop. V.gd quality.
2016 Frost in April, rainy summer then sun: mostly mid-weight wines.
2015 Great vintage, maybe best in 50 yrs: ripe fruit, perfectly balanced acidity.
2014 Yr of mid-weight, classically structured wines.
2013 V. small crop; e Switzerland outstanding, great freshness, purity.
Fine vintages: 09 05 (all) 00 (esp Pinot N, Valais reds) 99 (Dézaley)
97 (Dézaley) 90 (all).

Aargau Wine-growing canton se of Basel, mainly PINOT N, MÜLLER-T. Gd growers inc
Döttingen co-op, Haefliger (bio), Hartmann, LITWAN, Meier (zum Sternen). Also
has medieval Habsburg fortress that gave its name to a certain noble family.

igle Vd ★★→★★★ Commune for CHASSELAS best known for BADOUX Les Murailles. Try Terroir du Crosex Grillé.

OC The equivalent of French Appellation Contrôlée, but unlike in France, not nationally defined and every canton has its own rules. 85 AOCs countrywide.

achtobel, Schlossgut Thur ★★★ Since 1784 owned by descendants of Kesselring family, known for refined PINOT N from slopes nr Weinfelden.

ad Osterfingen Schaff ★★★ Restaurant and wine estate in historical baths (est 1472). As grower, Michael Meyer is a PINOT specialist, as chef renowned as "Spätzlekönig" (noodle king). Co-producer of ZWAA.

adoux, Henri Vd ★★ Big producer; CHASSELAS AIGLE les Murailles (classic lizard label) is most popular Swiss brand. Ambitious Lettres de Noblesse series has gd barrel-aged YVORNE.

aumann, Ruedi Schaff ★★★ Leading estate at Oberhallau; berry-scented, age-able PINOT N, esp -R-, Ann Mee. ZWAA a collaboration with BAD OSTERFINGEN estate.

ern Capital and canton. Villages Ligerz, Schafis, Twann (Lake Biel) and Spiez (Lake Thun) produce mainly CHASSELAS, PINOT N. Top growers: Andrey, Johanniterkeller, Schlössli, Steiner.

esse, Gérald et Patricia Val ★★★ Leading VAL family estate; Gérard and Patricia B now joined by daughter Sarah. Mostly steep terraces up to 600m (1969ft); superb old-vines *Ermitage Les Serpentines* 10' 13' 15 16 bears its name: MARSANNE from granite soils, planted 1945.

lattner, Valentin Vine-breeder in the Jura canton, known for crossings like Cabertin and Pinotin, bringing together fungal resistance and high quality.

onvin Val ★★→★★★ An old player of VAL, recently much improved, esp local grapes: *Nobles Cépages* series (eg. HEIDA, PETITE ARVINE, SYRAH).

ovard, Louis Vd ★★→★★★★ Family estate (ten generations) famous for textbook DÉZALEY La Médinette 99' 05' 12' 15 16 17; old vintages available from domaine. Equally outstanding: CALAMIN Ilex.

indner Herrschaft Gris ★★→★★★★ 05' 09' 11 13' 15' 16 17 18 Switzerland's burgundy: PINOT N (BLAUBURGUNDER) with structure, fruit and great capacity to age, individualistic growers. But only four villages: FLÄSCH, Jenins, Maienfeld, MALANS. Climate balanced between mild s winds and cool climate from nearby mtns.

alamin Vd ★★★ GRAND CRU of LAVAUX, tarter CHASSELAS than neighbour DÉZALEY. Only 16 ha, growers incl BOVARD, Dizerens, DUBOUX.

astello di Morcote Tic ★★★ One of most scenic v'yds of TIC, tended by art historian Gaby Gianini, well-balanced, warm, supple MERLOT with small amounts of CAB FR.

hablais Vd ★★→★★★ Wine region at upper end of Lake Geneva, top villages: AIGLE, YVORNE. Name is derived from Latin *caput lacis*, head of the lake.

hangins Secondary wine town of LA CÔTE, home of Switzerland's centre for viticultural and oenological teaching and research.

hanton, Josef-Marie and Mario Val ★★★ *Terrific Valais spécialitiés*; v'yds up to 800m (2625ft): Eyholzer Roter, Gwäss, HEIDA, Himbertscha, Lafnetscha, Resi.

happaz, Marie-Thérèse Val ★★★→★★★★ Small bio estate at Fully, famous for magnificent sweet wines of local grape Petite ARVINE 04' 06' (430g/l residual sugar!) and Ermitage (MARSANNE). Hard to find.

ôte, La Vd ★→★★★ 2000 ha w of Lausanne on Lake Geneva, mainly CHASSELAS of v. light, commercial style. Best-known villages: FÉCHY, Mont-sur-Rolle, Morges.

ruchon, Henri Vd ★★→★★★ Bio producer of LA CÔTE, lots of SPÉCIALITÉS (VIOGNIER, Altesse, Servagnin, BLATTNER-breedings). Top growth: PINOT N Raissennaz.

ézaley Vd ★★★ Celebrated LAVAUX GRAND CRU on steep slopes of Lake Geneva, 50 ha; planted in C12 by Cistercian monks. Potent CHASSELAS develops with age (7 yrs+). Best: DUBOUX, *Fonjallaz*, *Louis Bovard*, Monachon, Ville de Lausanne. Tiny red production too, mostly blends.

SWITZERLAND

> **The Goethe ber■**
> The steep, s-fac■g Sternenhalde v'yd at Stäfa, canton ZURICH, offers a
> "Goethe bench ■o rest and contemplate vines and lake. Goethe (who
> loved fine wine ■pent a whole month at Stäfa (1797) on his 3rd voyage
> to Switzerland, ■isiting his friend, painter Johann Heinrich Meyer. Here
> Goethe wrote a ■etter to Schiller about the Wilhelm Tell saga, describing
> it as a possible ■erary subject; and Schiller, of course, wrote the play.
> Stäfner Clevne■ (BLAUBURGUNDER) x Goethe = Swiss national epic.

Dôle Val ★★★★ va■s answer to Burgundy's Passetoutgrains: PINOT N plus GAMA■
Lightly pink Dô■ Blanche pressed straight after harvest.

Donatsch, Thoma■ Gris ★★★ Barrique pioneer (1974) at MALANS, joined by so■
Martin; rich, su■ple PINOT N, crisp CHARD. Family restaurant, zum Ochsen.

Duboux, Blaise Vd■★★★ 5-ha family estate in LAVAUX. Outstanding DÉZALEY vieille■
vignes Haut de ■ierre (v. rich, mineral), CALAMIN Cuvée Vincent.

Epesses Vd ★→★★★★ Well-known LAVAUX AOC, 130 ha surrounding GRAND CRU CALAMI■
sturdy, full-bod■ed whites. Growers incl BOVARD, DUBOUX, Fonjallaz, Luc Massy.

Féchy Vd ★→★★★ ■amous though unreliable AOC of LA CÔTE, mainly CHASSELAS.

Federweisser / We■sherbst German-Swiss pale rosé or even Blanc de Noirs mad■
from BLAUBURG■■DER.

Fendant Val ★→★■★ Full-bodied VAL CHASSELAS, ideal for fondue or raclette. Try BESS■
Domaine Cor■■lus, GERMANIER, PROVINS, SIMON MAYE. Name derived from Frenc■
se fendre (to b■■st) because ripe berries of local Chasselas clone crack open
pressed betwe■■ fingertips.

Fläsch Gris ★★★ ■★★★★ Village of BÜNDNER HERRSCHAFT on schist and limeston■
producing mi■■ral, austere PINOT N. Lots of gd estates, esp members of Adan■
Hermann, M■■gg families. ***Gantenbein*** is outstanding.

Flétri / Mi-flétri L■e-harvested grapes for sweet/slightly sweet wine.

Fribourg 115 ha o■shores of Lake Murten (Mont Vully): powerful CHASSELAS, elega■
TRAMINER, rou■■ PINOT N. Try Ch de Praz, Chervet, Cru de l'Hôpital, Derron.

Fromm, Georg ■■is ★★★ 05' 09' 13' 15' 16 17 18 Top grower in MALANS, know■
for subtle si■■le-v'yd PINOT N (Fidler, Self/Selvenen, Spielmann, Schöpf■
Plans to cons■■ct new cellar with architect Peter Zumthor blocked by objection■

***Gantenbein, Dan■* ■ Martha** Gris ★★★★ 09' 10' 13' 15' 16 17 18 Star growers, base■
in FLÄSCH. To■ PINOT N from DRC clones (*see* France), RIES clones from Loose■
(*see* Germany■ exceptional CHARD in v. limited quantity.

Geneva City su■■ounded by 1400 ha of vines remote from homonymous la■■
(v'yds there ■■long mainly to neighbouring canton VD). A wide range ■
varieties, gro■■rs incl Balisiers, Grand'Cour, Les Hutins, Novelle.

Germanier, Jea■ René Val ★★→★★★ Important VAL estate, reliable FENDANT L■
Terrasses, ele■■nt syrah Cayas, AMIGNE from schist at Vétroz (Mitis dr and sw).

Glacier, Vin du (*Gletscherwein*) Val ★★★ Fabled oxidized (larch)-wooded whi■
from rare R■■e grape of Val d'Anniviers. Find it at the Rathaus of Grimen■
A sort of sha■■ Alpine Sherry.

Grain Noble Co■■iden Ciel Val Quality label for authentic sweet wines, eg. CHAPPA■
DOMAINE DU M■■T D'OR, Dorsaz (both estates), GERMANIER, Philippe Darioli, PROVIN■

Grand Cru Val, ■■ Inconsistent term, in use in VAL (commune Salgesch for PINOT ■
and in VD (a■ "Premier Grand Cru" for a wide range of single-estate wines■
Switzerland ■as only two Grands Crus in the sense of a classification of v'y■
sites: CALAMI■ DÉZALEY.

Grisons (Grau■■nden) Mtn canton, German-speaking. PINOT N king. *See* BÜNDN■
HERRSCHAFT. ■est growers in other areas: Manfred Meier, VON TSCHARNER.

Huber, Daniel ★★→★★★ Pioneer who reclaimed possibly historical sites fro■

fallow in 1981. Partly bio since 2003. Now joined by son Jonas. Premium label Montagna Magica (MERLOT/CAB FR) combines elegance, density.

ohannisberg Val VAL name for SILVANER, often off-dry or sweet; great with fondue. Excellent: *Domaine du Mont d'Or*.

oris, Didier Val ★★★→★★★★ Only 3 ha, but a dozen varieties bringing wines of depth and complexity, incl outstanding (and rare) MARSANNE. Now also to revive nearly extinct local white grape Diolle.

a Colombe, Domaine Vd ★★→★★★ Family estate of FÉCHY, LA CÔTE, 15 ha, bio. Best known for range of ageable CHASSELAS, eg. La Brez.

a Rodeline, Domaine Val ★★★ VAL family estate known for local varieties from prime terraced single v'yds at Fully and Leytron, eg. Les Claives MARSANNE.

avaux Vd ★★→★★★★ 30 km (19 miles) of steep s-facing terraces e of Lausanne; UNESCO World Heritage site. Uniquely rich, mineral CHASSELAS. GRANDS CRUS DÉZALEY, CALAMIN, several village AOCS.

itwan, Tom Aar ★★★ Passionate organic grower at Schinznach, 3 ha. Delicate, fine-grained PINOT N Auf der Mauer ("On Top of the Wall") and Chalofe ("Lime Kiln").

Malans Gris ★★→★★★★ Village in BÜNDNER HERRSCHAFT. Top PINOT N producers incl DONATSCH, FROMM, Liesch, Studach, Wegelin. Late-ripening local grape Completer gives a long-lasting phenolic white. Monks used to drink it with day's last prayer (Compline). Adolf Boner 01' 05' is keeper of the Grail.

Maye, Simon et Fils Val ★★★ Perfectionist estate at St-Pierre-de-Clages. Dense SYRAH vieilles vignes arguably the best in Switzerland; spicy, powerful Païen (HEIDA), FENDANT v.gd too.

Mémoire des Vins Suisses Union of 56 leading growers in effort to create stock of Swiss icon wines, to prove their ageing capacities. Oldest wines from 1999.

Mercier Val ★★★→★★★★ SIERRE family estate, Anne-Catherine and Denis M now joined by daughter Madeleine, meticulous v'yd management produces dense, aromatic reds, eg. archetypal (but rare) CORNALIN 05' 09' **10'** 15 16 and SYRAH.

Mont d'Or, Domaine du Val ★★→★★★★ Emblematic VAL estate for semi- and nobly sweet wines, esp JOHANNISBERG Saint-Martin.

Neuchâtel ★→★★★ 600 ha around city and lake on calcareous soil. Slightly sparkling CHASSELAS, exquisite PINOT N from local clone (Cortaillod). Best: Domaine de Chambleau, Ch d'Auvernier (also PINOT GR), La Maison Carrée, Porret, TATASCIORE.

Oeil de Perdrix Neu "Partridge's eye": PINOT N Rosé, originally from NEU, now found elsewhere.

Pircher, Urs Zür ★★★→★★★★ Top estate at Eglisau, steep s-facing slope overlooking Rhine. Outstanding PINOT N Stadtberger Barrique 05' 09' 15' 16 17 from old Swiss clones. Whites of great purity.

rovins Val ★→★★★ Co-op with 4000+ members, Switzerland's biggest producer, 1500 ha, 34 varieties. Sound entry level, v.gd oak-aged Maître de Chais range.

Conservatoire mondial du Chasselas" grows 19 clones of the grape, at Rivaz, Lavaux.

Rouvinez Vins Val ★→★★★ Famous producer at SIERRE, best known for cuvées La Trémaille (w) and Le Tourmentin (r). Controls also BONVIN, Caves Orsat, Imesch.

Ruch, Markus Schaff ★★★ Excellent PINOT N from Hallau, eg. Chölle from 60-yr-old vines, Haalde from steep slope. Amphora-fermented MÜLLER-T. Only 2.5 ha.

t. Jodern Kellerei Val ★★→★★★ VISPERTERMINEN co-op famous for *Heida Veritas* from ungrafted old vines: superb reflection of Alpine terroir.

t-Saphorin Vd ★→★★★ Neighbour AOC of DÉZALEY, lighter, but equally delicate. Try Monachon's Les Manchettes.

chaffhausen ★→★★★ Canton/town on Rhine with famous falls, BLAUBURGUNDER stronghold. Best-known village is Hallau, but be v. careful. Top growers: BAD OSTERFINGEN, BAUMANN, RUCH, Strasser.

> **Wine regions**
> Switzerland has six major wine regions: VAL, VD, GENEVA, TIC, Trois Lacs (NEU, Bienne/BER, Vully/FRIBOURG), German Switzerland, which comprises ZÜR, SCHAFF, GRIS, AAR, St Gallen, Thur, some smaller wine cantons.

Schenk SA Vd ★→★★★ Wine giant with worldwide activities, based in Rolle founded 1893. Classic wines (esp VD, VAL); substantial exports.

Schwarzenbach, Hermann Zür ★★★ Leading family estate on Lake ZÜRICH, crisp whites (local Räuschling, MÜLLER-T) match freshwater fish.

Sierre Val ★★→★★★ VAL town on six hills, home of rich, luscious wines. Best-known des Muses, Imesch, MERCIER, ROUVINEZ, Zufferey.

Sion Val ★★→★★★ Capital/wine centre of VAL, domicile of big producers: *Charles Bonvin* Fils, Gilliard, PROVINS, Varone.

Spécialités / Spezialitäten Quantitatively minor grapes producing some of best Swiss wines, eg. Räuschling, GEWURZ or PINOT GR in German Switzerland, or local varieties (and grapes like JOHANNISBERG, MARSANNE, SYRAH) in VAL.

Sprecher von Bernegg Gris ★★★ Historic estate at Jenins, BÜNDNER HERRSCHAFT revived by young Jan Luzi, esp PINOT N: Lindenwingert, vom Pfaffen/Calander.

Stucky, Werner Tic ★★★→★★★★ Pioneer of MERLOT del TIC now joined by son Simon. Three wines: Temenos (Completer/SAUV BL), Tracce di Sassi (Merlot), Conte di Luna (Merlot/CAB SAUV). Stucky's best v'yd is only accessible via a funicular.

Tatasciore, Jacques Neu ★★★★ Shooting star in NEU, refined PINOT N to show that isn't far away.

Ticino ★→★★★ Italian-speaking; deemed *Sonnenstube* (sunny parlour) though nearby mtns bring much rain. MERLOT (leading grape since 1948) in a taut style. Best: Agriloro, CASTELLO DI MORCOTE, Gialdi, HUBER, Klausener, Kopp von der Cron, Visini, STUCKY, Tamborini, Valsangiacomo, Vinattieri, ZÜNDEL.

Tscharner, Gian-Battista von ★★★ Family estate at Reichenau Castle, Graubünder tannin-laden PINOT N (Churer Gian-Battista, Jeninser aus dem Tscharnergut) to age. Substantial, old-fashioned Completer in v. limited quantity. Son Johann Baptista aiming at more elegance than father Gian-Battista.

Valais (Wallis) Largest wine canton, in dry, sunny upper Rhône Valley. Local varieties are outstanding, and best MARSANNE, SYRAH rival French legends downstream. Top: BESSE, CHANTON, CHAPPAZ, Cornulus, Darioli, des Muses, Dorsaz, GERMANIER, JORIS, MAYE, MERCIER, MONT D'OR, PROVINS, ROUVINEZ, ST. JODERN, Zufferey.

Vaud (Waadt) Wine canton known for conservative spirit. Important big producers: Bolle, Hammel, Obrist, SCHENK. CHASSELAS is main grape – but only gd terroir justify growers' loyalty.

Visperterminen Val ★→★★★ Upper VAL v'yds, esp for HEIDA. One of highest v'yds in Europe (at 1000m/3281ft+; called Riben). Try CHANTON, ST. JODERN KELLEREI.

Yvorne Vd ★★→★★★ CHABLAIS village with v'yds on detritus of 1584 avalanche, eg Badoux, Ch Maison Blanche, Commune d'Yvorne, Domaine de l'Ovaille.

Zündel, Christian Tic ★★★→★★★★ German Swiss geologist in TIC. Bio farming, wines of great purity and finesse, esp MERLOT/CAB SAUV Orizzonte and CHARD Velabona, Coč.

Zürich Largest wine-growing canton in German Switzerland, 610 ha. Mainly BLAUBURGUNDER, Räuschling a local SPECIALITY. Best growers: Gehring, Lüthi, PIRCHER, SCHWARZENBACH, Zahner.

Zur Metzg, Winzerei Zür ★★→★★★ Banker turned winemaker, refined PINOT N and barrel-fermented MÜLLER-T (bought-in grapes), vinified in old butcher's shop.

Zwaa Schaff ★★★ Collaboration of two leading SCHAFF estates (BAUMANN – calcareous deep soil; BAD OSTERFINGEN – light, gravelly). PINOT N 94' 09' 13' 15' 16, white counterpart (PINOT BL/CHARD) is equally long-lasting.

Austria

Abbreviations used in the text:

Burgen	Burgenland
Carn	Carnuntum
Kamp	Kamptal
Krems	Kremstal
Nied	Niederösterreich
S Stei	Südsteiermark
Therm	Thermenregion
Trais	Traisental
V Stei	Vulkanland Steiermark
Wach	Wachau
Wag	Wagram
Wein	Weinviertel
W Stei	Weststeiermark

Everything in Austrian wine is pristine, crisp and precise. Growers are fixated on terroir expression, exploring every detail of their vineyards with a rigour that makes some parts of the world look positively lazy. They are not hidebound, though, and as game as anyone to do the wacky things: edgy orange wines and lots of biodynamism. Visit many a winery and you'll see a cow's horn on a windowsill as a sort of totem: we are bio, it says. Indigenous yeasts for fermentation are almost commonplace now, giving flavours that are less obviously fruity, more winey and tense. The DAC system has been evolving since 2002: by 2018 there were 13 DACs, with Wachau due to join in 2019. It allows for regional, village and single-site wines in some regions; other DACs are for a single grape variety in a single region. Either way, it reflects a healthy focus on provenance, with a classification scheme brewing.

Recent vintages

2018 The heatwave yr: ripe wines. Gd and plentiful.

2017 Gd juicy, rounded wines.

2016 Lovely fruit expression, fine freshness, but choose growers carefully.

2015 V.gd quality. Full-bodied, ripe, with the stuffing to age.

2014 Difficult, cooler yr. Tread carefully; thrilling freshness where selection was stringent. Slender but charming reds.

2013 Slender, v. fresh but expressive whites. Taut, crunchy reds.

2012 Warm, ripe yr, mild and rounded, even opulent whites, reds full-bodied. Don't hesitate to try more mature vintages from gd producers.

Achs, Paul Burgen r (w) ★★★ 10 13 14 16 Specialist in BLAUFRÄNKISCH: Edelgrund and Heideboden.

Allram Kamp w ★★★ 10 13 14 Always reliable, expressive GRÜNER V (esp Renner, Gaisberg), RIES Heiligenstein.

Alphart Therm w ★★ Regional focus on ROTGIPFLER, ZIERFANDLER. HEURIGER destination.

Alzinger Wach w ★★★★ 06 08 09 10 13 14 Underrated but 1st class. Look out for RIES, GRÜNER V, Steinertal and Loibenberg.

Arndofer Kamp r w ★★★ Young, enterprising and gd. Esp ZWEIGELT, oaked RIES.

Ausbruch Quality/style designation for Prädikat wine; restricted to RUST and botrytized, dried grapes. Min must weight 27°KMW or 138.6°Oechsle.

Ausg'steckt ("Hung out") Fresh greenery posted outside is traditional sign of open HEURIGEN or Buschenschank. In fact the "bush" that no gd wine needs.

Bauer, Anton Wag r w ★★★→★★★★ Leading producer of intense GRÜNER V: single-v'yds Rosenberg Spiegel. Increasingly poetic PINOT N.

Braunstein, Birgit Burgen r w ★★★ 10 13 15 16 Bio leader and purveyor of elegant LEITHABERG reds. Try amphora-aged Magna Mater CHARD.

Bründlmayer, Willi Kamp r w sw sp ★★★★ 06 08 10 11' Iconic producer in Langenlois. GRÜNER V, RIES, esp Heiligenstein and Steinmassl. Francophile traditional-method Sekt and PINOT N.

Burgenland r (w) Federal state and wine region bordering Hungary. Warmer than NIED, hence reds like BLAUFRÄNKISCH, ST-LAURENT, ZWEIGELT prevalent. Shallow NEUSIEDLERSEE, eg at RUST, creates ideal botrytis conditions.

Carnuntum Nied r w Underrated, often below-radar region se of VIENNA specialized in reds, esp ZWEIGELT marketed as Rubin Carnuntum. Spitzerberg area developing rapidly. Best: G Markowitsch, MUHR-VAN DER NIEPOORT, NETZL, TRAPL.

Signpost in Austrian village: "Ferries to Rust". Ho ho.

Christ Vienna r w ★★★ VIENNA institution and HEURIGEN. Exquisite GEMISCHTER SATZ and unusual red blends.

DAC (Districtus Austriae Controllatus) Provenance- and quality-based appellation system denoting regionally typical wines and styles. Creation of 1st DAC 2002 Wein, prompted regional quality turnaround. Currently 13 DACs: EISENBERG KAMP, KREMS, LEITHABERG, MITTELBURGENLAND, NEUSIEDLERSEE, TRAIS, Wein, Wiener GEMISCHTER SATZ. Latest s STEI, W STEI, VULKANLAND STEI with hierarchy of regional village and single-site wines. WACH DAC in pipeline.

Domäne Wachau Wach w ★★★→★★★★ Austria's top co-op. Impressive site portfolio eg. Achleiten, Buck, Kellerberg. Outstanding across board, great value.

Ebner-Ebenauer Wein w sp ★★★ Young couple shaking up WEIN with single-v'yd GRÜNER V. Gorgeous Blanc de Blancs traditional method.

Eichinger, Birgit Kamp w ★★★→★★★★ World-class RIES, esp Heiligenstein, and exceptionally expressive GRÜNER V, esp Hasel.

Eisenberg Burgen Small DAC (since 2009) restricted to BLAUFRÄNKISCH from local slate soil. Powerful but elegant.

Erste Lage Premier Cru designation in KAMP, KREMS, TRAIS, WAG. 2018 expansion into VIENNA and CARN 62 Erste Lagen now with further sites to be classified.

Esterhazy Burgen r (w) ★★★ Historic schloss of Josef Haydn fame in Eisenstadt (BURGEN), solid reds, bright whites.

Federspiel Wach VINEA WACHAU middle category of ripeness, min 11.5%, max 12.5% alc. Understated, gastronomic wines as age-worthy as SMARAGD.

Feiler-Artinger Burgen r w sw ★★★→★★★★ Leading producer of exquisite AUSBRUCH in historic town centre of RUST.

Gemischter Satz Vienna Revived historic concept of co-planted and co-fermented field-blend of white varieties. Prevalent in WEIN and VIENNA: determined producers achieved DAC status in 2013 for Vienna. No variety to exceed 50% Look for CHRIST, GROISS, LENIKUS, WIENINGER.

Gesellmann, Albert & Silvia Burgen r w (sw) ★★★ Specializes in indigenous reds.

Geyerhof Krems r w ★★→★★★ Stellar bio-producer with top RIES, esp Sprinzenberg. Notable entry-level Stockwerk.

Gols Burgen r (w) Wine village on n shore of NEUSIEDLERSEE. Top: Beck, G HEINRICH, NITTNAUS, PITTNAUER, PREISINGER.

There's a v'yd in Wein called Tod den Hengst – death of the stallion. V. steep.

Gritsch Mauritiushof Wach w★★→★★★ High-altitude plantings on 1000-Eimberberg v'yd make thrilling RIES, GRÜNER V.

Groiss, Ingrid Wein w ★★→★★★ Exuberant, quality-focused youngster specializing in old v'yds. Peppery GRÜNER V, GEMISCHTER SATZ from unusual varieties.

Grosse Lage Stei Highest v'yd classification in STEI, work still in progress along Danube (see ERSTE LAGE).

Gruber-Röschitz Wein w ★★ Enterprising family making racy RIES from granite soils, fine GRÜNER V.

Gumpoldskirchen Therm Once famed, still popular HEURIGEN village s of VIENNA. Home to white rarities ZIERFANDLER, *Rotgipfler.*

Gut Oggau Burgen r w ★★→★★★ Unconventional, hip but solid bio estate.

Harkamp S Stei w sp ★★★ STEI's top sparkling producer, long-aged traditional-method Sekts.

Heinrich, Gernot Burgen r w dr sw ★★★ PANNOBILE member and BLAUFRÄNKISCH specialist, branching out into skin-fermented and natural whites.

Heinrich, J Burgen r w ★★★ 08 09 10 Big but elegant BLAUFRÄNKISCH, esp Goldberg.

Heuriger Wine of most recent harvest. **Heurigen** homely taverns where growers serve own wines with rustic, local food – integral to VIENNA life. *See* AUSG'STECKT.

Hiedler Kamp w sw ★★★ Precise RIES, savoury GRÜNER V Thal and Kittmannsberg.

Hirsch Kamp w ★★★ 10 13 Outstanding RIES, GRÜNER V from Heiligenstein, Lamm. Affordable, easy entry-level Grüner V Hirschvergnügen.

Hirtzberger, Franz Wach w ★★★★ 06 07 08 10 13 Iconic, powerful WACH style of RIES, GRÜNER V, esp Honivogl, Singerriedel.

Huber, Markus Trais w ★★★ Young producer defining delicacy of TRAIS: RIES, GRÜNER V.

Illmitz Burgen sw SEEWINKEL town on NEUSIEDLERSEE, famous for BA, TBA (*see* Germany). Best from *Kracher*, Opitz.

Jäger Wach w ★★★ Great GRÜNER V, RIES, esp Achleiten, Klaus.

Jalits Burgen ★★★ Leading EISENBERG estate, elegant if powerful BLAUFRÄNKISCH, esp RES Szapary and Diabas.

Jamek, Josef Wach w ★★★→★★★★ Danube-facing WACH icon and famed *restaurant* at Joching, now returned to top tier. RIES, GRÜNER V, esp Achleiten, Klaus.

Johanneshof Reinisch Therm r w ★★★→★★★★ Estate at Tattendorf. Three talented brothers, one clear focus. Justly famed for PINOT N, ROTGIPFLER, ST-LAURENT, ZIERFANDLER. Esp single-v'yds Frauenfeld, Holzspur, Satzing, Spiegel.

Jurtschitsch Kamp w sp ★★★→★★★★ Exemplary bio estate at Langenlois; impressive across board. Gd sparkling.

In 1681 Rust bought free-town status with already famous sweet Ausbruch wines.

Kamptal Nied (r) w Wine region along Danube tributary Kamp n of WACH; rounder style, lower hills. Top v'yds: Heiligenstein, Lamm. Best: BRÜNDLMAYER, EICHINGER, HIEDLER, HIRSCH, JURTSCHITSCH, LOIMER, SCHLOSS GOBELSBURG. Kamp is DAC for GRÜNER V, RIES.

Kerschbaum, Paul Burgen ★★★ 09 13 BLAUFRÄNKISCH specialist, with notable single-v'yd Hochäcker.

Klosterneuburg Wag r w Wine town in WAG, seat of 1860-founded viticultural college and research institute. *See* next entry.

AUSTRIA

KMW Abbreviation for KLOSTERNEUBURGER Mostwaage ("must level"), Austrian unit denoting must weight, ie. sugar content of grape juice. 1°KMW = 4.86°Oe (*see* Germany). 20°B = 83°Oe.

Knoll, Emmerich Wach w ★★★★ 05 06 07 08 10 Defining WACH producer of iintense, **long-lived Ries**, GRÜNER V at any level. Notable Auslese. Best when mature.

Kollwentz Burgen r w ★★★ 10 11 Andi K is a national champ, equally famous for CHARD, BLAUFRÄNK CH and CAB blends.

Kracher Burgen sw ★★★★ 03 04 05 06 07 08 10 15 Botrytis specialist in ILLMITZ famed for TBA (*see* Germany). Nouvelle Vague series is oak-matured. Stock up on stellar 15s.

Kremstal (r) w Wine region and DAC for GRÜNER V, RIES. Top: MALAT, MOSER, NIGL, SALOMON-UNDHOF, STIFT GÖTTWEIG, WEINGUT STADT KREMS.

Krutzler Burgen r ★★★ 08 09 11 13 Muscular BLAUFRÄNKISCH. Icon wine: Perwolff.

Lagler Wach w ★★★ Precise RIES, GRÜNER V, rare NEUBURGER SMARAGD.

Laurenz V Kamp ★★★ Tiered range of GRÜNER V styles sold mostly outside Austria.

Leithaberg Burgen important DAC on n shore of NEUSIEDLERSEE, limestone and schist soils. Red restricted to BLAUFRÄNKISCH, whites can be GRÜNER V, PINOT BL, CHARD or NEUBURGER.

Lenikus Vienna w ★★ More than just an entrepreneurial vanity project. Gd GEMISCHTER SATZ from Bisamberg.

Lesehof Stagård Krems w ★★★ Long-est KREMS estate with flair for thrilling RIES.

Loimer, Fred Kamp (r) w sp ★★★→★★★★ 10 11 13 Bio trailblazer. Outstanding whites, esp single-v'yds Heiligenstein, Steinmassl. Growing following for PINOT N, setting new standards with *lovely sparkling*.

Malat Krems w ★★★→★★★ Vivid, expressive RIES, GRÜNER V, esp single v'yds Gottschelle, Silbe bichl.

Mantlerhof Krems w ★★★ Bio grower of expressive GRÜNER V on loess soils.

Mayer am Pfarrplatz Vienna (r) w ★★ VIENNA institution, out at Heiligenstadt HEURIGER where Beethoven wrote his 3rd symphony, now tourist heaven. Wine, food both gd.

Mittelburgenland Burgen r DAC (since 2005) on Hungarian border: structured, age-worthy BLAUFRÄNKISCH. Producers: GESELLMANN, J HEINRICH, KERSCHBAUM, WENINGER.

Moric Burgen ★★★→★★★★ 06 08 10 11 12 13 15 Cult producer of supreme BLAUFRÄNKISCH; note single-v'yds Neckenmarkt, Lutzmannsburg.

Moser, Lenz Krems ★→★★ Austria's largest producer and négociant.

Muhr-van der Niepoort Carn r w ★★★ Unconventional, uncompromising BLAUFRÄNKISCH. Spitzerberg revivalist. Approachable Samt & Seide, age-worthy Spitzerberg and Lebeskind.

Netzl, Franz & Christine Carn ★★★ Father-daughter team specializing in top ZWEIGELT, esp Haidacker. Gd red blends and value Rubin CARN Zweigelt.

Neumayer Trais w ★★★ Est quality producer of intense GRÜNER V, RIES.

Field blends

GEMISCHTER SATZ are Austria's scintillating, unpredictable trump cards. Co-planted and co-fermented, these are (usually) white blends that shimmer with endless nuance. Expect complexity, richness, power. VIENNA's Gemischter Satz supremo FRITZ WIENINGER compares them to an orchestra. Some of the best: **Fritz Wieninger**, Vienna: Wiener Gemischter Satz Ried Ulm, from v'yd planted with nine varieties, and Wiener Gemischter Satz Ried Rosengartel, five varieties. **Ingrid Groiss**, WEIN: Braitenpuechtorff, 17 varieties. **Mehofer**, WAG: Iuventus, eight varieties. **Rainer Christ**, Vienna: Wiener Gemischter Satz, four varieties. **Zahel**, Vienna: Wiener Gemsichter Satz Ried Kaasgraben, nine varieties.

Neumeister V Stei ★★★ 09 11 SAUV BL specialist, esp single-v'yds Klausen, Moarfeitl. Look for Stradener Alte Reben. Also notable GEWURZ.

Neusiedlersee (Lake Neusiedl) Burgen Largest European steppe-lake and nature reserve on Hungarian border. Lake mesoclimate and humidity key to botrytis development. Eponymous DAC limited to ZWEIGELT.

Austria's entire v'yd amounts to only 41% of the B'x wine region.

Niederösterreich (Lower Austria) Ne region comprising three parts: Danube (KAMP, KREM, TRAIS, WACH, WAG); WEIN (ne); CARN, THERM (s). 59% of Austria's v'yds.

Nigl Krems w ★★★★ Stylish, juicy, taut RIES, GRÜNER V, esp Privat bottlings.

Nikolaihof Wach w ★★★→★★★★ 08 09 10 13 Distinguished bio producer with ancient origins at Mautern on Danube right bank. Purity rather than strength. Thrilling, world-class RIES, GRÜNER V, esp late Vinothek releases.

Nittnaus, Anita & Hans Burgen r w sw ★★★→★★★★ Leading bio producer of concentrated, elegant reds. Single-v'yd BLAUFRÄNKISCH from Tannenberg, Lange Ohn, Jungenberg. Note PANNOBILE blend and Comondor.

Nittnaus, Hans & Christine Burgen ★★★ Fine, elegant reds, esp ZWEIGELT Heideboden, BLAUFRÄNKISCH Edelgrund; red blend Nit'ana. Super TBA, Eiswein.

Ott, Bernhard Wag w ★★★→★★★★★ Leading, defining GRÜNER V producer, esp Rosenberg, Spiegel, Stein v'yds.

ÖTW (Österreichische Traditionsweingüter) Kamp, Krems, Trais, Wag Private association working on v'yd classification. 2018 expansion into CARN, VIENNA saw members swell from 33 to 62 estates. *See* ERSTE LAGE, GROSSE LAGE; excludes WACH.

Pannobile Burgen Union of nine NEUSIEDLERSEE quality growers centred on GOLS. Pannobile bottlings may only use indigenous reds (ZWEIGELT, BLAUFRÄNKISCH, ST-LAURENT), whites only PINOTS BL, GR, CHARD. Members: ACHS, BECK, G HEINRICH, NITTNAUS, PITTNAUER, PREISINGER.

Pfaffl Wein r w ★★→★★★ 13 14 15 16 Large, enterprising négociant and grower. Gd RES wines, but famed for ultra-successful brand The Dot Austrian Pepper, Austrian Cherry, etc.

Pichler, Franz X Wach w ★★★★ 06 07 08 09 Iconic producer of cystalline *Ries*, GRÜNER V, from top WACH sites. Cult RIES Unendlich.

Pichler, Rudi Wach w ★★★★ 09 10 13 Intense and incisive RIES, GRÜNER V from top sites Achleiten, Steinriegl.

Pichler-Krutzler Wach w ★★★ Outstanding whites from top WACH single v'yds, *thrilling Ries*, esp In der Wand, Kellerberg.

Pittnauer, Gerhard Burgen r ★★★→★★★★ Constantly evolving, cutting-edge talent for reds. World-class ST-LAURENT, MashPitt orange wine and fun pét-nat.

Polz, Erich & Walter S Stei ★★★ SAUV BL, CHARD specialist in s STEI, esp single-v'yd Hochgrassnitzberg. Some Sekt too.

Prager, Franz Wach w ★★★★ 07 08 10 Visionary and leading light of WACH. World-class RIES, GRÜNER V from a portfolio of top sites.

Preisinger, Claus Burgen r ★★★ Modern, talented, irreverent PANNOBILE member. Try fun, crown-capped red Puszta Libre.

Prieler Burgen r w ★★★→★★★★ Long-lived, muscular BLAUFRÄNKISCH, esp Marienthal and Goldberg v'yds and PINOT BL from Haidsatz and Seeberg. Give wines time.

Proidl, A&F Krems w ★★★ Clean, bright, consistent RIES, GRÜNER V, both from Ehrenfels. Some worthy late Ries releases.

Reserve (Res) Attribute for min 13% alc and prolonged (cask) ageing.

Ried V'yd. As of 2016 compulsory term for single-v'yd bottlings.

Rust Burgen r w dr sw Well-preserved fortified C17 town on NEUSIEDLERSEE. Watch for noisy, nesting storks. Famous for Ruster AUSBRUCH. Top: E TRIEBAUMER, FEILER-ARTINGER, SCHRÖCK.

Sabathi, Hannes S Stei w ★★★ Expressive, age-worthy SAUV BL. Notable single-v'yd Pössnitzberg.

Salomon-Undhof Krems w ★★★→★★★★ Effortlessly reliable GRÜNER V, RIES, always racy, expressive, taut. Single-v'yds Kögl, Pfaffenberg, Wachtberg. Fun pét-nat. Bert Salomon presides.

Sattlerhof S Stei w ★★★→★★★★ 10 12 World-class, long-lived, creamy SAUV BL, MORILLON, esp single-v'yds Kranachberg, Sernauberg.

Schiefer, Uwe Burgen r ★★★ Individualistic, elegant BLAUFRÄNKISCH in EISENBERG, esp Szapary.

Schilcher W St Racy, peppery rosé of local importance from indigenous Blauer Wildbacher grape; speciality of W STEI.

Schilfwein (Strohwein) Sweet wine made from grapes dried on reeds from NEUSIEDLERSEE. *Schilf* = reed, *Stroh* = straw.

Schloss Gobelsburg Kamp r w dr sp sw ★★★★ 09 10 13 14 15 Cistercian-founded winery, outstanding wines. Michael Moosbrugger directs. Single-v'yd RIES, GRÜNER V, esp Gaisberg, Heiligenstein, Lamm, Renner. Excellent RES reds.

Schlumberger sp C 9 Sekt pioneer. Today high-volume, value producer of traditional-method fizz.

Schmelz Wach w ★★★ Exquisite, authentic wines strangely below the radar.

Schröck, Heidi Burgen (r) w sw ★★★ World-class RUST producer of exquisitely concentrated AUSBRUCH, also notable dry FURMINT.

Seewinkel Burgen ("Lake corner") nature reserve and region e of NEUSIEDLERSEE; ideal conditions for botrytis.

Wachau's picturesque drystone v'yd walls date from C12.

Smaragd Wach Ripest category of VINEA WACHAU, min 12.5% alc but often exceeding 14%, dry, potent, age-worthy. Often botrytis-influenced but dry. Named after emerald (=Smaragd) lizard.

Spätrot-Rotgipfler Therm Blend of ROTGIPFLER/Spätrot = synonym for ZIERFANDLER. Aromatic, weighty, textured. Typical for GUMPOLDSKIRCHEN. See Grapes chapter.

Spitz an der Donau Wach w Picturesque Danube-fronting town at narrowest and coolest part of WACH. Famous v'yds Singerriedel and 1000-Eimerberg. GRITSCH MAURITIUSHOF, HIRTZBERGER, LAGLER.

Stadlmann Therm r w sw ★★→★★★ Exquisite ZIERFANDLER/ROTGIPFLER, esp single-v'yds Tagelsteiner, Mandelhöh. Tender, aromatic PINOT N.

Steiermark (Styria) Most s region of Austria, known for aromatic fresh dry whites, esp SAUV BL. See S STEIV STEI, W STEI.

Steinfeder Wach Lightest VINEA WACHAU category for dry wines of max 11.5% alc. Named after fragrant Steinfeder grass. Increasingly difficult/impossible to produce in warm yrs.

Stift Göttweig w ★★→★★★★ Prominent hilltop Benedictine abbey surrounded by v'yds; quality ethos, crystalline RIES, GRÜNER V from single-v'yds Gottschelle, Silberbichl.

Strobl, Clemens Wag r w New estate, quality ethos. Expressive PINOT N.

Südsteiermark (South Styria) STEI region close to Slovenian border, famed for light but highly aromatic MORILLON, MUSKATELLER, SAUV BL from steep slopes. DAC from 2018. Best growers: SABATHI, SATTLERHOF, TEMENT, WOHLMUTH.

Tegernseerhof Wach w ★★→★★★ Juicy, pristine RIES, GRÜNER V. Lovely FEDERSPIEL.

Tement, Manfred S Stei w ★★★→★★★★ 09 10 12 13 15 Benchmark, long-lived SAUV BL, MORILLON. Top sites Grassnitzberg, Zieregg.

Thermenregion Nied r w Spa region e of VIENNA. Famous for indigenous ZIERFANDLER, ROTGIPFLER; historic PINOT N hotspot. Look our for: ALPHART, JOHANNESHOF REINISCH and STADLMANN.

Tinhof, Erwin Burgen r w ★★★→★★★★ Top bio BLAUFRÄNKISCH, esp Gloriette;

ST-LAURENT, esp Feuersteig. Nutty, rounded whites from Golden Erd v'yd: PINOT BL, NEUBURGER.

Traisental Nied Tiny district s of Krems. Notable for prevalence of limestone soils lending finesse. Top: HUBER, NEUMAYER.

Trapl, Johannes Carn r ★★→★★★ Talented, ambitious newcomer; poised, floral BLAUFRÄNKISCH, esp Sitzerberg and Pinot-esque ZWEIGELT.

830-km (516 miles) Niederösterreich Wine Route connects all eight of its growing regions.

Triebaumer, Ernst Burgen r (w) (sw) ★★★★ 08 09 10 12 Iconic RUST producer, blazed trail for indigenous reds, esp BLAUFRÄNKISCH in 80s, notably Mariental. V.gd AUSBRUCH.

Umathum, Josef Burgen r w dr sw ★★★→★★★★ Outstanding, elegant, bio reds. ZWEIGELT Hallebühl, BLAUFRÄNKISCH Kirschgarten.

Velich w sw ★★★ SEEWINKEL producer of Austria's cult CHARD Tiglat. Great sweet too.

Veyder-Malberg Wach ★★★ Rigorous WACH boutique producer, pure RIES, GRÜNER V.

Vienna (Wien) (r) w Capital boasting 637 ha v'yds within city limits. Ancient tradition, reignited quality focus. Local field-blend tradition enshrined as DAC GEMISCHTER SATZ in 2013. *Heurigen visa a must.* Best: CHRIST, LENIKUS, WIENINGER, Zahel.

Vinea Wachau Wach Pioneering quality WACH growers' association founded 1983. Strict charter with three-tier ripeness scale for dry wine: FEDERSPIEL, SMARAGD, STEINFEDER.

Vulkanland Steiermark (Southeast Styria) (r) Formerly Süd-Oststeiermark, DAC since 2018, famous for GEWURZ. Best: NEUMEISTER, Winkler-Hermanden.

Wachau Nied Danube region of world repute for age-worthy RIES, GRÜNER V. Top: ALZINGER, DOMÄNE WACHAU, F PICHLER, HIRTZBERGER, JAMEK, KNOLL, NIKOLAIHOF, PICHLER-KRUTZLER, PRAGER, R PICHLER, TEGERNSEERHOF, VEYDER-MALBERG.

Wachter-Wiesler, Weingut Burgen r (w) ★★★ Top producer of EISENBERG BLAUFRÄNKISCH, also WELSCHRIESLING.

Wagentristl Burgen r (w) ★★ Inspiring youngster with feel for PINOT N, BLAUFRÄNKISCH.

Wagram Nied (r) w Region just w of VIENNA, incl KLOSTERNEUBURG. (And another win for Napoleon.) Deep loess soils ideal for GRÜNER V and increasingly also PINOT N. Best: BAUER, Leth, OTT, STROBL.

Weingut Stadt Krems Krems r w ★★→★★★ Krems town's own wine estate with 31 ha v'yds within city limits.

Weinviertel (r) w ("Wine Quarter") Austria's largest wine region, 13,886 ha between Danube/Czech border, eponymous DAC for GRÜNER V. Region once slaked VIENNA's thirst, now quality counts. Try: EBNER-EBENAUER, GROISS, GRUBER-RÖSCHITZ, PFAFFL.

Weninger, Franz Burgen r (w) ★★★★ 08 10 12 13 15 16 Long-lived BLAUFRÄNKISCH from single-v'yds Hochäcker, Kirchholz.

Weststeiermark (West Styria) Small wine region specializing in SCHILCHER. New DAC from 2018.

Stei, 30 yrs ago too cold for reds. Now making fine, ripe, complex ones, 12–13% alc.

Weszeli Kamp w Expressive, spicy GRÜNER V, esp Schenkenbichl. Fab RIES.

Wieninger, Fritz Vienna r w sp ★★★→★★★★ 13 14 VIENNA leading light; bio benchmark GEMISCHTER SATZ from Nussberg, Rosengartl. Great PINOT N. Viennese HEURIGER in the Nussberg vines an institution.

Winzer Krems Krems w ★★ Co-op of 962 growers covering 990 ha, producing gd-value RIES, GRÜNER V, ZWEIGELT.

Wohlmuth S Stei w ★★★→★★★★ Outstanding STEI producer of SAUV BL, CHARD, RIES, esp from single-v'yds Edelschuh, Gola, Hochsteinrigel.

England

Another year, another crop of brand-new names: and good ones too. Typical style is super-fresh, elegant, with notes of apple and sometimes white flowers. Dosage is no higher than in Champagne, however: a surprise to drinkers who assume producers might balance higher acidity with more dosage. Quality at the top sparkling producers is rocketing, and the key, apart from careful viticulture, good winemaking and warmer summers, is time on the lees to allow the wines to round out and deepen, followed by time in bottle. English fizz shouldn't be rushed. Not all the wines here have national distribution, though some are in good supermarkets and some in good restaurants from south to north. Try them if you can: they're something to be proud of. Abbreviations: Berkshire (Berks), Buckinghamshire (Bucks), Cornwall (Corn), East/West Sussex (E/W S'x), Hampshire (Hants), Herefordshire (Heref).

Black Chalk Hants New name making precise, elegant 2015 and esp gd Wild Rose rosé, delicate, firm, v. pale.

Bluebell Vineyard Estates E S'x ★★ Blanc de Blancs is best bet here: subtle, balanced. Classic Cuvée is richer. Barrel Aged Blanc de Blancs a bit heavy.

Bolney Estate W S'x ★ Classic Cuvée (fresh, no malolactic fermentation, elderflower notes, high acidity) is best bet at this long-est v'yd.

Breaky Bottom E S'x ★★★ Wonderful elegance and precision from a tiny, long-est v'yd. Best: SEYVAL BL-based Cuvée Koizumi Yakumo, Champagne-blend Cuvée Gerard Hoffnung.

Bride Valley Dorset ★★ Steven and Bella Spurrier's v'yd nr sea. Super-freshness is aim, not time on lees. Appley Brut, gd Bella rosé. Crémant a gd new departure. Gd still CHARD.

Camel Valley Corn ★★ Juicy, pretty rosé, and elegant Brut NV (w) that repays bottle age. 1st to hold a royal warrant.

Chapel Down Kent ★→★★★ Big producer making accessible style. Kit's Coty, single-v'yd Blanc de Blancs and Coeur de Cuvée more interesting but super-pricey.

Coates & Seely Hants ★★★ Lovely ripe, brisk Brut Res NV and savoury, spicy Rosé NV Rich, creamy Blanc de Blancs. Lots of expertise, v. assured. Uses name "Britagne" for fizz.

Cottonworth Hants Tense, characterful wines from the Test Valley.

Court Garden E S'x ★★ Gd rich style with bit of power. Subtle, taut Blanc de Blancs; elegant, biscuity Classic Cuvée; rich Blanc de Noirs. Rosé is red-fruited, crunchy.

Denbies Surrey ★ UK's largest single v'yd. Style is commercial, with marked toastiness. Gd still PINOT N. Well-organized tourism: new v'yd hotel.

Digby Hants, Kent, W S'x ★★★ Négociant buying grapes from several counties. Well-aged, assured wines made by Dermot SUGRUE under contract at WISTON. PINOT-led NV, stylish Res Brut, v.gd *Leander Pink* NV, by appointment to rowers.

Exton Park Hants ★★★ Mouthwatering, characterful wines, balanced at quite low dosage. Lovely tense Rosé NV; rich, energetic Blanc des Noirs. *Half-bottles* too.

Greyfriars Surrey ★★ Best are balanced Classic Cuvée 13 and Blanc de Blancs 13. NV from CHARD/PINOT N/PINOT M also worth a look.

Gusbourne Kent, W S'x ★★★ V'yds on clay in Kent and chalk in Sussex. V.gd Blanc de Blancs; also Brut Res, still wines CHARD, crunchy PINOT N. New Late Disgorged 2010 for release 2019.

Hambledon Vineyard Hants ★★★ Accomplished wines, lovely balance and richness. Hambledon label is v.gd, top level. Meonhill label cheaper, also gd.

Harrow & Hope Bucks ★★ Stony v'yd nr Marlow sounds like a pub; vines planted in 2010, 1st release 2016. Elegant Blanc de Blancs, balanced Brut Res NV, pale, spice, raspberry Brut Rosé.

Hart of Gold Her ★★ Complex, layered, serious wine, distinguished. Wacky label.

Hattingley Valley Hants ★★★ Serious class. Subtle, structured Classic Res; Rosé 14 has lovely poise. Tops is Blanc de Blancs 11 with 4 yrs on lees: savoury, creamy.

Henners E S'x ★★ Classic ripeness, balance in Brut 11, Brut Res 10 and cherry-spice Rosé.

Herbert Hall Kent ★★ Promising wines, often a bit young, Rosé is pretty.

Hoffmann & Rathbone ★★ S'x-based, using bought-in fruit for gd toasty, creamy Blanc de Blancs; try also Classic Cuvée.

Hush Heath Estate Kent ★★★ Best is Balfour Brut Rosé. New Skye Blanc de Blancs is ripe, elegant. Cider too, and owns local pubs.

Jenkyn Place Hants ★★ Fresh, floral, hedgerow style, confident and harmonious. V.gd Brut, characterful, rich Blanc de Noirs, fruity Classic Cuvée.

Leckford Estate Hants ★ From Waitrose's own estate, vinified by RIDGEVIEW. Fair balance, a bit short on oomph.

Nyetimber W S'x ★★★★ Assured, confident wines. NV incl 5 yrs of reserve wines, gives depth. Splendid Blanc de Blancs 10 (5 yrs lees, toasty). Single-v'yd Tillington rounder, elegant. New prestige *cuvée 1086* (yr of Domesday Book, which mentions Nyetimber) v. elegant, delicate.

Plumpton College E S'x ★★ UK's only wine college; own wines to gd standard incl excellent Rosé NV.

Pommery England Hants Champagne's 1st venture into England being made at HATTINGLEY VALLEY until its own vines come on stream; 1st release promisingly fresh, savoury, elegant.

Raimes Hants New. Fine lemon-shortbread Brut; elegant, weighty Blanc de Noirs. Both lovely, winey.

Rathfinny E S'x New. Vast investment paying off with precise, assured wines, esp Blanc de Blancs. Still PINOTS BL, GR tight, tense. Also experiments with vermouth and others.

Ridgeview E S'x ★★ Invariably well made, enjoyable, reliable, gd value. Now run by 2nd generation. Various cuvées: tops are Blanc de Blancs, Blanc de Noirs, Rosé de Noirs. Contract maker of several brands.

Simpsons Kent Promising newcomer. Ruth and Charles S make wine in Languedoc; now gd s-facing chalk slopes nr Canterbury. Gd still CHARD; 1st sparkling release is tight, lean, will benefit from time in bottle.

Stopham Estate W S'x ★ Nice still PINOT BL, all sappy nuts and spice. PINOT GR richly exotic.

Sugrue E S'x ★★★★ (formerly Sugrue Pierre) Dermot S is winemaker at WISTON, where he also makes Black Dog Hill, DIGBY, JENKYN PLACE under contract. He makes one (CHARD-dominant) wine a yr from his own vy'ds, and it's glorious. The Trouble with Dreams is all lemon shortbread, exuberant fruit, complex, tense, crystalline. Best of all: *Cuvée Dr Bernard O'Regan.*

Westwell Kent New. Elegant, precise fizz; gd, interesting still Ortega.

Windsor Great Park Berks ★ Tony Laithwaite, of Laithwaite's and *The Sunday Times* Wine Club, grows CHARD, PINOTS N, M on 4 ha of s-facing slope in, yes, the royal park itself. Vines (and wines) will mature.

Wiston W S'x ★★★★ Superb Blanc de Blancs. Proper lees-ageing shows in depth with tension across the range. Brut NV now has up to 40% Res wines: big plus. Cuvée Brut gets 100% old oak barriques, for creaminess, not oakiness.

Wyfold Oxon ★★ Tiny (1-ha) Champagne-variety v'yd at 120m (394ft) above sea level in Chilterns. Part-owned by hands-on Laithwaite family.

Central & Southeast Europe

More heavily shaded areas are the wine-growing regions.

Prague ○
CZECH REPUBLIC

SLOVAK REPUBLIC

Bratislava ○ *Danube*
○ Budapest

MOLDOVA

Ljubljana ○
HUNGARY
Zagreb
SLOVENIA
Drava
CROATIA
○ Timişoara

ROMANIA
Chişinău ○
Prut
Olt

BOSNIA HERZEGOVINA
Belgrade ○ *Danube*
Bucharest ○ *Danube*

SERBIA
Split ○
Adriatic Sea
Sarajevo ○
Varna ○

MONTENEGRO
Dubrovnik ○ ○ Podgorica
BULGARIA
Sofia ○
Black Sea

Plovdiv ○
Skopje ○

MACEDONIA

Tirana ○

ALBANIA

Abbreviations
used in the text:

Bal	Balaton
Cri & Mar	Crişana & Maramureş
Cro Up	Croatian Uplands
Dalm	Dalmatia
Dan P	Danubian Plain
Dob	Dobrogea
Is & Kv	Istria & Kvarner
Mold	Moldovan Hills
Mun	Muntenia & Oltenia Hills

N Hun	North Hungary
N/S Pann	North/South Pannonia
Pod	Podravje
Pos	Posavje
Prim	Primorje
Sl & CD	Slavonia & Croatian Danube
Thr L	Thracian Lowlands
Tok	Tokaj
Trnsyl	Transylvania

HUNGARY

Hungary has taken its time to join the list of market favourites. Its language, its style and its grapes take a bit of learning. Tokaji is its unique contribution: one of the world's greatest sweet wines – itself not a category everyone wants. Hungary is turning the corner more with dry wines and reds full of a subtly different character. Furmint, the main Tokaj grape, is establishing itself as the next big thing in white grapes – able to offer everything from fine fizz to whites with burgundian complexity, as well, of course, as its beautiful stickies. Lighter reds like Kékfrankos (aka Blaufränkisch) and Kadarka are appealing to sommeliers searching for elegance. And in Hungary fine-food culture is booming, and needs wines that enhance rather than dominate. As do we all.

Aszú Tok Literally, "cry", here meaning botrytis-shrivelled grapes and the resulting sweet wine from Tok. From 2014, legal minimum sweetness is 120g/l residual sugar, equivalent to 5 PUTTONYOS. Option to label as 5 or 6 Puttonyos. Gd Aszú in 99' 05 06 07 08 09 13' 16 17. V. wet in 10, 14 so limited Aszú with careful selection; not much botrytis in 11 12 15. 18 v. high quality but low quantities.

Aszú Essencia / Eszencia Tok Term for 2nd-sweetest TOK level (7 PUTTONYOS+), not permitted since 2010. Do not confuse with ESSENCIA/ESZENCIA.

Badacsony Bal ★★→★★★ Volcanic slopes n of Lake BAL; full, rich whites. Look for Gilvesy, Laposa (Bazalt Cuvée, KÉKNYELŰ, 4-Hegy OLASZRIZLING), *Szeremley* (age-worthy Kéknyelű, SZÜRKEBARÁT), Villa Sandahl (excellent RIES), Villa Tolnay.

Balassa Tok w dr sw ★★★ Excellent Mézes-Mály FURMINT, Villő ASZÚ from personal winery of GRAND TOKAJ's viticulturalist.

Balaton Region, and Central Europe's largest freshwater lake.

Balatonboglár Bal r w dr ★★→★★★ Wine district, also major winery of TÖRLEY, s of Lake BAL. Gd: Budjosó, GARAMVÁRI, IKON, KONYÁRI, Kristinus, Légli Géza, Légli Otto, Pócz, Varga.

Barta Tok w dr sw ★★→★★★ Highest v'yd in TOK, impressive dry whites, esp Öreg Király FURMINT, HÁRSLEVELŰ, v.gd sweet SZAMORODNI, ASZÚ.

Béres Tok w dr sw ★★→★★★ Handsome winery at Erdőbénye producing v.gd ASZÚ and dry wines esp Lőcse FURMINT, Diókút HÁRSLEVELŰ.

Bikavér r ★→★★★ Means "Bull's Blood". PDO only for EGER and SZEKSZÁRD. Always a blend, min three varieties. In Szekszárd, KADARKA is compulsory, max 7%, with min 45% KÉKFRANKOS with no new oak. Look for: Eszterbauer (esp Tüke), HEIMANN, Meszáros, Sebestyén, TAKLER, VIDA. Egri Bikavér is majority Kékfrankos and no grape more than 50%, oak-aged for min 6 mths. Superior is min five varieties, 12 mths in barrel, from restricted sites. Best for Egri Bikavér: BOLYKI, DEMETER, GÁL TIBOR, Grof Buttler, ST ANDREA, Thummerer.

Useful word to know: Egészségére. ("Eggeshegerry", more or less). Means "Cheers".

Bock, *József* S Pann r ★★→★★★ In VILLÁNY, making rich, full-bodied, oaked reds. Try: Bock CAB FR Fekete-Hegy, Bock & Roll, SYRAH, Capella Cuvée.

Bolyki N Hun r p w ★★ Notable winery in a quarry in EGER, great labels. V.gd EGRI CSILLAG, Meta Tema, rosé, Indián Nyár (lit, Indian Summer) and excellent BIKAVÉR, esp Bolyki & Bolyki.

Csányi S Pann r p ★→★★ Largest winery in VILLÁNY with ambitious plans. Look for: Ch Teleki CAB SAUV, Kővilla CAB FR, unoaked KÉKFRANKOS.

Csopak Bal N of Lake BAL. Protected status for top v'yd OLASZRIZLING. Look for: FIGULA, Homola (Sáfránykert), Jasdi (esp single v'yds), St Donát.

Degenfeld, *Gróf* Tok w dr sw ★★→★★★ Improved estate with luxury hotel. Sweet wines best: 6 PUTTONYOS, SZAMORODNI. Decent Zomborka FURMINT.

Demeter, *Zoltán* Tok w dr sw sp ★★★★ Benchmark cellar in TOKAJ for elegant, intense dry wines, esp Boda, Veres FURMINTS; excellent Szerelmi HÁRSLEVELŰ, lovely Oszhegy MUSCAT. V.gd PEZSGŐ (sp). Eszter late-harvest cuvée, superb ASZÚ.

Dereszla, Chateau Tok w dr sw ★★→★★★ Notable for excellent ASZÚ. Gd dry FURMINT, Kabar. Also gd PEZSGŐ. Rare flor-aged dry SZAMORODNI Experience.

DHC (Districtus Hungaricus Controllatus) Term for Protected Designation of Origin (PDO). Symbol is a local crocus and DHC on label.

Disznókő Tok w dr sw ★★★→★★★★ Prominent "First Growth" estate; restaurant and winery tours. Fine expressive ASZÚ, superb *Kapi* cru in top yrs. Also gd-value late-harvest and Édes (sw) SZAMORODNI.

Dobogó Tok (r) w dr sw ★★★ Impeccable small estate in TOK (named for "Clip Clop" sound). Benchmark ASZÚ and late-harvest Mylitta, excellent long-lived dry FURMINT and *pioneering Pinot N* Izabella Utca.

Dűlő Named single v'yd. Top names in TOK: Betsek, Király, Mézes-Mály, Nyúlászó, SZENT TAMÁS, Úrágya.

Duna Great Plain. Districts: Hajós-Baja (try Sümegi, Koch – also VinArt in VILLÁNY), Csongrád (Somodi), Kunság (Frittmann, Font).

Eger N Hun ★→★★★ Top red region of n producing more burgundian-style reds and noted for Egri BIKAVÉR. Try: BOLYKI, Gróf Buttler, Demeter, *Gál Tibor*, Kaló Imre (natural wines), KOVÁCS NIMRÓD, Pók Tamás, ST ANDREA, Thummerer.

Egri Csillag N Hun "Star of Eger". Dry white blend of Carpathian grapes.

Essencia / Eszencia Tok ★★★★ Legendary, luscious free-run juice from ASZÚ grapes, occasionally bottled, alc usually well below 5%, sugar off the charts. Reputed to have medicinal/aphrodisiac properties.

Etyek-Buda N Pann Dynamic region noted for expressive, crisp whites, gd sparklers and promising for PINOT N. Leading producers: ETYEKI KÚRIA (esp Pinot N, SAUV BL, KÉKFRANKOS), György-Villa (premium estate of TÖRLEY), HARASZTHY (Sauv Bl, Sir Irsai, Orëghegy), Nyakas (v.gd CHARD), Kertész, Rókusfalvy.

Etyeki Kúria N Pann r p w ★★ Leading winery in ETYEK, producing v.gd SAUV BL, elegant PINOT N and KÉKFRANKOS.

Figula Bal r p w ★★→★★★ Family winery nr BAL, focus on v'yd selections of OLASZRIZLING esp Sáfránkert, Szákas. Excellent Köves (w blend).

Gál Tibor N Hun r w ★★ Hugely improved with new cellar. Try appealing EGRI CSILLAG, fine KADARKA and vibrant, modern TiTi BIKAVÉR.

Garamvári Bal r p w dr sp ★→★★★ Leading producer of bottle-fermented fizz (was Ch Vincent). Try Optimum Brut, FURMINT Brut Natur, PINOT N Evolution Rosé. Gd Garamvári range: SAUV BL, IRSAI OLIVÉR. Lellei label is consistent, great-value varietals.

Gere, Attila S Pann r p ★★★→★★★★ Leading light in VILLÁNY making some of country's best reds, esp elegant Solus MERLOT, intense Kopar Cuvée, top Attila barrel selection. New Fekete-Járdovány is rare historic grape.

Gizella Tok w ★★★ Small family winery, making delicious dry whites.

Grand Tokaj Tok w dr sw ★→★★ Huge TOK state-owned co-op, was Crown Estates, relaunch 2013. New winery, winemaker (Karoly Áts, ex-ROYAL TOKAJI). Gd Arany Késői Late-Harvest; dry FURMINT Kővágó DŰLŐ; v.gd Szarvaz ASZÚ 6 PUTTONYOS.

Haraszthy N Hun r w →★ Beautiful estate at ETYEK, v.gd SAUV BL, zesty Sir Irsai (w).

Heimann S Pann r ★★→★★★ Impressive family winery in SZEKSZÁRD, esp intense Barbár and BIKAVÉR. Fine KADARKA, Alte Reben KÉKFRANKOS.

Hétszőlő Tok w dr sw ★★★ Historic cellar and stunning v'yd, owned by Michel Reybier of Cos d'Estournel (B'x). Noted for delicacy. 6 PUTTONYOS ASZÚ impresses.

Heumann S Pann r p w ★★→★★★ Small German/Swiss-owned estate in Siklós making great KÉKFRANKOS Res, CAB FR, appealing SYRAH and Lagona (r).

Hilltop Winery N Pann r p w ★★ In Neszmély. Meticulous, gd-value DYA varietals, Hilltop, Moonriver labels for export. V.gd Kamocsay Premium range (esp CHARD, Ihlet Cuvée).

Holdvölgy Tok w dr sw ★★→★★★ Super-modern winery in MÁD, noted for complex dry wines (esp Vision, Expression), plus v.gd sweet wines.

Ikon Bal r w ★★ Well-made wines from KONYÁRI and former Tihany abbey v'yds. Try Evanglista CAB FR.

Kikelet w dr sw ★★★ Beautifully balanced wines from a small family estate owned by a French winemaker and her Hungarian husband.

Királyudvar Tok w dr sw sp ★★★ Bio producer in old royal cellars at Tarcal.

Furmint's friends and relations

With programmes like FURMINT February and International ASZÚ day, the chances of Furmint appearing in a glass nr you are increasing. Its personality is a bit RIES-ish and a bit CHARD-ish: the Ries side comes through in vibrant, steely, crisp whites and amazing sweet wines, while its Chard side shows in its ability to make fine fizz and complex, layered whites – it's actually a half-sibling of both. It has a track record for expressing terrroir and age-ability in all its guises too.

Highly regarded for FURMINT Sec, Henye PEZSGŐ, Cuvée Ilona (late-harvest), flagship 6 PUTTONYOS Lapis ASZÚ.

Konyári Bal r p w ★★→★★★ Gd family estate nr BALATON. Try DYA rosé; Loliense (r w), lovely Szarhegy. Top reds: Jánoshegy KÉKFRANKOS, Páva.

Kovács Nimród Winery N Hun r p w ★★→★★★ EGER producer, jazz-inspired labels. Try Battonage CHARD, Blues KÉKFRANKOS, Monopole Rhapsody, 777 PINOT N, NJK.

Kreinbacher w dr sp ★★→★★★ Hungary's best fizz; Prestige Brut Sparkling is world class, also v.gd Classic Brut PEZSGŐ (both based on FURMINT). V.gd dry *Juhfark*, HÁRSLEVELŰ, Öreg Tőkék (old vines).

Never clink beer glasses in Hungary – it's bad luck. Best stick to wine (or *bor*).

Mád Tok Historic town in TOK with superb v'yds, cellars and Mád Circle of leading producers: Árvay, Áts, BARTA, Budaházy, Demetervin (gd dry FURMINT, sweet Elvezet), HOLDVÖLGY, Lenkey, Orosz Gabor, ROYAL TOKAJI, SZENT TAMÁS WINERY, SZEPSY, Tok Classic, Úri Borok.

Malatinszky S Pann r p w ★★★ Certified organic VILLÁNY cellar. Top long-lived Kúria *Cab Fr*, Kövesföld (r). Gd: Noblesse blends.

Mátra N Hun ★→★★ N hill region for decent-value, fresh whites, rosé and lighter reds. Better producers: Balint, Benedek, Gábor Karner, NAG, NAGYRÉDE, Szöke Mátyás, Naygombos (rosé).

Mór N Pann w ★→★★ Small region, famous for fiery local *Ezerjó*. Also promising for CHARD, RIES, TRAMINI. Try Czetvei Winery.

Nagyréde N Hun (r) p w ★ Gd-value, commercial DYA varietal wines under Nagyréde and MÁTRA Hill labels.

Oremus Tok w dr sw ★★→★★★★ Perfectionist Tolcsva winery owned by Spain's Vega Sicilia: top ASZÚ; v.gd late-harvest and dry FURMINT *Mandolás*.

Pajzos-Megyer Tok w dr sw ★★→★★★ Back-on-form, French-founded (1991) winery in Sarospatak. Megyer label for modern dry and late-harvest sweet varietals. Pajzos for premium, esp age-worthy ASZÚ and lovely late-harvest HÁRSLEVELŰ.

Pannonhalma N Pann r p w ★★→★★★ 800-yr-old abbey, focused, aromatic whites: RIES (esp Prior), SAUV BL, TRAMINI. Lovely *Hemina* (w), decent PINOT N.

Patricius Tok w dr sw ★★→★★★ Beautiful estate in Bodrogkisfalud. Consistent dry FURMINT esp Selection, gd late-harvest Katinka, ASZÚ.

Pendits Winery Tok w dr sw ★★ Demeter-certified bio estate in Abaujszanto. Luscious long-ageing ASZÚ, pretty, dry DYA MUSCAT.

Pezsgő Hungarian for sparkling – a new string to Hungary's bow. Since 2017 must be bottle-fermented if from TOK.

Puttonyos (putts) Traditional indication of sweetness in TOK ASZÚ. Optional since 2013 (*see* ASZÚ). Historically a *puttony* was a 25kg bucket or hod of Aszú grapes, sweetness determined by number of Puttonyos added to a 136-litre barrel (gönci) of base must or wine.

Royal Tokaji Wine Co Tok dr sw MÁD winery that led renaissance of TOK in 1990 (I am a co-founder). Mainly "First Growth" v'yds. 6-PUTTONYOS single-v'yd bottlings: esp Betsek, *Mézes-Mály*, Nyulászó plus 5 Putt, SZENT TAMÁS. Gold, Blue and Red Labels are 5-putt blends. Also v.gd dry FURMINT, The Oddity. "By Appointment" label for exclusive winemaker projects: No 4 is Szt Tamás late-harvest, No 5 is Betsek HÁRSLEVELŰ.

St Andrea N Hun r p w ★★★ Leading name in EGER for modern, high-quality BIKAVÉR (Áldás, Hangács, Merengő). Gd white blends: Napbor, Örökké and delicious Szeretettel rosé. Flagships: Mária (w) and Nagy-Eged-Hegy (r).

Sauska S Pann, Tok r p w ★★→★★★★ Immaculate winery in VILLÁNY. V.gd KADARKA, KÉKFRANKOS, CAB FR and impressive red blends, esp Cuvée 7 and Cuvée 5. Also

Sauska-TOK with focus on excellent dry whites, esp Medve and Birsalmás FURMINTS. V.gd PEZSGŐ Extra Brut fizz.

Somló Bal Dramatic extinct volcano famous for long-lived, austere white **Juhfark** ("sheep's tail"), FURMINT, HÁRSLEVELŰ, OLASZRIZLING. Region of small producers, esp Fekete, Györgykovács, Kolonics, Royal Somló, Somlói Apátsági, Somlói Vándor, Spiegelberg. Bigger TORNAI (Top Selection), **Kreinbacher** also v.gd PEZSGŐ.

Sopron N Pann Or Austrian border overlooking Lake Fertő. KÉKFRANKOS most important, plus CAB SAUV, PINOT N, SYRAH. Bio **Weninger** is excellent, maverick Ráspi for natural wines. Also Luka, Pfneiszl, Taschner.

Szamorodni Polish word meaning "as it comes" for TOK made from whole bunches, with botrytis or not. **Édes** or sweet style is min 45g/l sugar, 6 mths oak-ageing, becoming more popular since 3 and 4 PUTTONYOS ASZÚ banned. Try BARTA, Bott, HOLDVÖLGY, KIKELET, OREMUS, Pelle, SZENT TAMÁS, SZEPSY. Best dry (szaraz) versions are flor-aged like Sherry; try CH DERESZLA, Karádi-Berger, **Tinon**.

Szekszárd S Pann. Famous for ripe, rich reds. Increasing focus on BIKAVÉR, KÉKFRANKOS and reviving lighter KADARKA. Look for: Dúzsi (rosé), Eszterbauer (esp Nagyapám Kadarka, Tüke Bikavér), Sebestyén (Ivan-Volgyi Bikavér), Szent Gaal, TAKLER, Vesztergombi (Csaba's Cuvée, Turul), VIDA.

Szent Tamás Winery Tok w sw ★★★ Significant winery (with handy café) in MÁD. Gd dry FURMINTS: Dongó, Percze. Sweet focus now on SZAMORODNI; Nyulászó, Dongó superb. Popular village-level Mád label.

Hungary has 100s of extinct volcanoes and 1000+ hot springs.

Szepsy, István Tok v dr sw ★★★★ Brilliant, soil-obsessed, no-compromise 17th-generation TOK producer in MÁD. Now focusing on dry FURMINT (esp Urágya, Betsek and Nyulászó DŰLŐ) and reviving sweet SZAMORODNI. Superb ASZÚ (esp Dűlő Úrágya) and amazing rare ESZENCIA.

Szeremley Bal w dr sw ★★ Pioneer in BADACSONY. Intense, fine RIES, **Szürkebarát**, (aka PINOT GR), age-worthy KÉKNYELŰ, appealing sweet Zeus.

Takler S Pann r p ★★ Super-ripe, supple SZEKSZÁRD reds. Decent, gd-value, entry-point red, rosé. Best: Res selections of CAB FR, KÉKFRANKOS.

Tinon, Samuel Tok w dr sw ★★★ Bordelais in TOK since 1991. Exceptional v'yd-selection dry FURMINTS. Distinctive complex ASZÚ, v. long maceration, barrel-ageing. Excellent sweet and iconic dry flor-aged **Szamorodni**.

Tokaj Nobilis Tok w dr sw ★★★ Fine small producer in Bodrogkisfalud run by Sarolta Bárdos, one of TOK's inspirational women. Excellent dry Barakonyi HÁRSLEVELŰ, FURMINT, v.gd SZAMORODNI, rare Kövérszőlő Edes (sw).

Tokaj / Tokaji Tok ★★-★★★★★ Tokaj is the town and wine region; Tokaji the wine. Recommended producers without individual entries here: Árvay, Áts, Bardon, Basilicus, Bodrog Borműhely, Bott Pince, Carpinus, Demetervin, Erzsébet, Espák, Füleky, Hommona Atilla, Juliet Bravo, Karádi-Berger, Lenkey, Pelle, Orosz Gábor, Sanzon, Zombory, Zsadányi. 30 yrs ago there were none.

Törley r p w dr sp ★★-★★★ Chapel Hill is major brand name. Well-made, gd-value DYA international and local varieties IRSAI OLIVÉR, Zenit, Zefir. Major fizz producer (esp **Törley**, Gala, Hungaria labels), v.gd classic method, esp François President Rosé Brut, CHA.D Brut. György-Villa for top selections.

Tornai Bal w ★★ 2nd-largest SOMLÓ estate. Gd-value entry-level varietals, excellent Top Selection range FURMINT, Juhfark.

Tűzkő S Pann r w ★★ Antinori-owned estate in Tolna: TRAMINI, KÉKFRANKOS, MERLOT.

Vida S Pann r ★★ V.gd BIKAVÉR, old-vine KADARKA, Hidaspetre KÉKFRANKOS, La Vida.

Villány S Pann Most s wine region. Noted for serious ripe B'x varieties (esp CAB FR) and blends, juicy examples of **Kékfrankos**, PORTUGIESER. High quality: ATTILA GERE, Bock, CSÁNYI, Gere Tamás & Zsolt (Aureus Cuvée), HEUMANN, Hummel, Jackfall,

Janus, Kiss Gabor, Lelovits (CAB FR), *Malatinszky*, Polgar, Riczu (Symbol Cuvée), Stier (MERLOT, Villányi Cuvée), Ruppert, *Sauska*, Tiffán, *Vylyan*, WENINGER-GERE.

Villányi Franc S Pann New classification for CAB FR from VILLÁNY. Premium version has restricted yield, 1 yr in oak. Super-premium from 2015 is max 35 hl/ha.

Vylyan S Pann r p ★★→★★★ Red specialist making v.gd v'yd selections, esp Gombás PINOT N, Mandolás CAB FR, Montenuovo, Pillangó MERLOT. *Duennium Cuvée* is flagship red. Also delicious rare Csoka.

Weninger N Hun r w ★★★ Standard-setting bio winery in SOPRON run by Austrian Franz Weninger Jr. Single-v'yd *Steiner Kékfrankos* is superb. SYRAH, CAB FR and red Frettner blend also impressive. Intriguing Orange Zenit.

Weninger-Gere S Pann r p ★★→★★★ Joint-venture between Austrian Franz WENINGER Sr and ATILLA GERE. Excellent CAB FR, tasty Tinta (TEMPRANILLO), Cuvée Phoenix and DYA fresh rosé.

BULGARIA

New investment and freedom from prescriptive rules means that Bulgarian winemaking is going through a dynamic phase, experimenting with unusual blends, often with great success. Amphorae, pét-nat and orange wines are also appearing. Most wineries now own or control vineyards so expect increasing emphasis on regional identity, as well as authenticity, through indigenous grape varieties. Look out for Cabernet Franc too, which is proving exciting.

Alexandra Estate Thr L r p w ★★ 60-ha estate; gd VERMENTINO, rosé and smooth reds.

Angel's Estate Thr L r p w ★★ Ripe, oaky, polished reds and smooth whites under Stallion label, also impressive Deneb.

Bessa Valley Thr L r p ★★★ Pioneering estate winery nr Pazardjik. Smooth, rich reds; firm, fresh rosé. Try Enira, v.gd SYRAH and Enira Res, excellent Grande Cuvée.

Better Half Thr L r p w ★★ True garage winery using amphorae. V.gd red blends, CHARD, MARSANNE/ROUSSANNE, NEBBIOLO rosé.

Black Sea Gold Thr L r p w ★ Large Black Sea coast winery. Better labels: Pentagram, Golden Rhythm, Salty Hills, Villa Marvella micro-winery.

Borovitsa Dan P r w ★★★ Handcrafted parcels of terroir wines in far nw. Dux is long-lived flagship. V.gd: MRV (Rhône whites), Cuvée Bella Rada (RKATSITELI), GAMZA (Granny's, Black Pack), rare local grape Bouquet, Ogy's legacy (w).

Boyar, Domaine Thr L r p w ★→★★★ Pioneering large winery. DYA entry-level labels like Deer Point, Bolgare, via mid-range Platinum, Elements, Quantum, to premium Supreme and Solitaire. Owns boutique Korten winery for v.gd MERLOT, SYRAH, CAB FR, esp Single Barrel.

Bratanov Thr L r w ★★ Low-intervention family estate in Sakar using wild-yeast fermentations. V.gd Tamianka, CHARD *sur lie*, SYRAH and red blends.

Bulgaria has never changed its name since it was founded in 681 AD.

Burgozone Dan P r w ★★ Gd whites from family estate close to Danube, esp VIOGNIER, SAUV BL, Eva, Iris Creation.

Damianitza Thr L r p w ★★ Holistic producer in Struma Valley with some certified organic wines. Try Ormano (w), Volcano SYRAH, Uniqato and flagship Kometa.

Domain Menada Thr L r p w ★ 3rd-biggest producer; cheerful Tcherga blends.

Dragomir Thr L r p w ★★→★★★ V.gd garage winery, for intense full-bodied reds, esp Pitos, flagship RUBIN Res, plus fresh Sarva (r p w). New CAB FR impressive.

Eolis Thr L r w ★★ Tiny estate, biodynamic principles. V.gd VIOGNIER, MERLOT, CAB FR.

Katarzyna Thr L r p w ★→★★ Large modern winery in border zone nr Greece. Noted for ripe soft reds. Try La Vérité CAB FR, Harvest MERLOT, Encore MALBEC.

> **The rise of the small**
> Wine estates barely existed 15 yrs ago in Bulgaria, but now they're
> everywhere. Look for: Bendida (MISKET, RUBIN), Bononia (GAMZA, Ooh
> La La rosé), Ch Copsa (Zeyla Misket), Gulbanis (CAB FR), Ivo Varbanov
> (CHARD, VIOGNIER), Rousse Wine House (RIES, Vrachanski Misket, Chard),
> Staro Oryahovo (Vrachanski Misket, Varnenski Misket), Stefan Pirev
> Wines (Chard Kosara, Top Blend), Stratsin (SAUV BL, rosé, MERLOT), Uva
> Nestum, Varna Winery (fresh DYA w, fruity PINOT N), Via Vinera (DIMIAT,
> Red Misket, MAVRUD), Villa Yustina (4 Seasons range, Monogram Rubin/
> Mavrud), Yalovo Misket blend, Rubin, sparkllng).

Logodaj Thr L r p w sp ★★★ In STRUMA VALLEY with winemaking guidance from protégé of Riccardo Cotarella. V.gd bottle-fermented Satin, esp rosé. Rich CHARD and excellent Noŝile MELNIK, serious Incantesimo SYRAH.

Maryan Dan P r w → →★★ V.gd Res (r), Queen Elena (r), Sense of Tears DIMIAT.

Medi Valley Thr L r p w ★★ Highest commercial v'yd in Bulgaria, plus plot nr Vidin. Try Incanto Black, MELNIK 55, MAVRUD, eXentric VIOGNIER.

Midalidare Estate Thr L r w ★★★ Immaculate boutique winery. Precise whites, plus v.gd reds. New elegant Brut sparkling.

Minkov Brothers Thr L r p w ★→★★ Boutique arm of one of Bulgaria's largest producers: value Cuvée (r), Res CAB SAUV, Le Photografie CAB FR, flagship Oak Tree.

Miroglio, Edoardo Thr L r p w sp ★★→★★★ Italian-owned estate at Elenovo. Gd bottle-fermented sparkling. Gd PINOT N in all styles, incl age-worthy RES, v.gd flagship Soli Invicto, also Elenovo CAB FR, RUBIN.

Neragora Thr L r v ★★ Organic estate producing gd MAVRUD and blends.

Power Brands r p ★ Formerly Vinprom Peshtera. Owns Villa Yambol (try better Kabile range) and New Bloom for easy-drinking Pixels, Verano Azur labels, plus characterful FzF reds.

Preslav, Vinex Thr L r w ★→★★ Whites best here, esp long-lived Rubaiyat CHARD. Also try Novi Pazar PINOT GR, RIES.

Rossidi Thr L r p w ★★→★★★ Boutique winery nr Sliven. Fine, part concrete-egg fermented CHARD. V.gd RUBIN, elegant PINOT N. Intriguing orange GEWURZ.

Rumelia Thr L r w ★★ V.gd MAVRUD specialist, alone and in Erelia blends.

Salla Estate Dan F w ★★ Bright, precise whites, esp Vrachanski MISKET, RIES, CHARD. Elegant CAB FR.

Santa Sarah Thr L r w ★★★ Pioneering *garagiste*. Bin reds are v.gd; long-lived Privat is flagship. Also smooth Petite Sarah (r), appealing No Saints rosé.

Slavyantsi, Vinex Thr L r p w ★→★★ "Fair for Life" certified for work with local Roma community. Reliable budget varietals and blends, esp under Leva brand.

Chickens 1st domesticated in Bulgaria – early Neolithic, in Haskovo region.

Struma Valley Thr L Warmest region, cooperating with tourist routes and plans for new PDO. Focus on local grapes: Shiroka Melnik, Melnik 55, Sandanski MISKET. Names to watch: Abdyika, Augeo, DAMIANITZA, Kapatovo, LOGODAJ, Orbelia, Orbelus (organic), Rupel, Seewines, Via Verde, VILLA MELNIK, Zlaten Rozhen.

Svishtov Dan P r p w ★→★★ Much-improved large producer close to Danube with Italian consultancy. Try Gorchivka, Legio.

Terra Tangra r p w ★★ Large estate in Sakar, certified organic red v'yds. Gd MAVRUD (r p), MALBEC, serious Roto.

Tohun Dan P r p w ★→★★ Bright refreshing whites and rosé, esp Greus SAUV BL/SEM, SYRAH rosé. Also restrained cool-climate reds.

Tsarev Brod Dan P r w ★★ New estate with experimental approach, esp pét-nat RIES, rare local Gergana, Amber CHARD, complex SAUV BL Res. Decent young PINOT N.

Villa Melnik Thr L r p w ★★ Family winery, focus on local grapes esp MELNIK, MAVRUD. Gd orange SAUV BL, and serious Res and Hailstorm labels.

Yamantiev's Thr L r w ★→★★ Sound commercial wines, plus excellent top Marble Land selections from marble bedrock at 400m (1312ft).

Zagreus Thr L r p w ★★ MAVRUD in all styles from acacia-fermented rosé to complex Amarone-style Vinica from semi-dried grapes.

Zelanos Dan P r w ★★ Pristine new winery. Try fresh Red MISKET, PINOT GR, elegant PINOT N (esp Z series).

SLOVENIA

One of the jewels of Central Europe, for its gorgeous scenery, amazing food and great wines. Its western end (especially Brda and Vipava) has long been established as the quality leader, but increasingly other regions are gaining serious recognition too, from the pristine Alpine-influenced whites of inland Styria to the overlooked green hills of Dolenjska in the southeast, which is rediscovering its potential. Recent discoveries show that the much-admired Blaufränkisch grape originally came from today's Slovenia – grown here as Modra Frankinja.

Batič Prim r p w sw ★★ Bio/natural wines in VIPAVA. Top-selling rosé, also Pinela, Rebula, Angel blends, Valentino (sw).

Bjana Prim sp ★★→★★★ V.gd traditional-method PENINA from BRDA, esp fine Brut Rosé, NV, Brut Zero.

Blažič Prim w ★★→★★★ From BRDA. Long-ageing, complex Rebula, esp Robida, Selekcija. Blaž in top yrs.

Brda (Goriška) Prim Top-quality district in PRIM. Many leading wineries: BJANA, BLAŽIČ, Dobuje, DOLFO, EDI SIMČIČ, Erzetič, JAKONČIČ, KLET BRDA, KRISTANČIČ, MOVIA, Prinčič, Reya, ŠČUREK, Zanut. Orange wines from KABAJ and Klinec.

Burja Prim r w ★★★→★★★★ Organic VIPAVA estate, all local grapes plus PINOT N. Excellent Burja Bela, Burja Noir (Pinot N), Burja Reddo based on SCHIOPPETTINO. Superb Žorž single-v'yd Pinot N.

Čotar Prim r w ★★ Intriguing, long-lived organic/natural wines from KRAS, esp Vitovska (w), MALVAZIJA, SAUV BL, TERAN, Terra Rossa red blend.

Cviček Pos Traditional, sharp, light red blend of POS, based on Žametovka: Albiana.

Dolfo Prim r w ★★→★★★ V.gd Spirito PENINA, Gredic (w), CAB SAUV Res.

Dveri-Pax Pod r w sw ★★→★★★★ Historic Benedictine-owned estate nr Maribor. Crisp, bright, gd-value whites, esp FURMINT, PINOT GR, SAUV BL. V.gd old-vine selections: RIES, GEWURZ. Superb sweet wines.

Edi Simčič Prim r w ★★★★ Red-wine superstar in BRDA: Duet Lex, barrel-selection Kolos. Excellent whites: Rebula, SAUV BL, Triton Lex; superb Kozana CHARD.

Gašper Prim r w sp ★★★ Brand of Slovenia's top sommelier with KLET BRDA. V.gd MALVAZIJA, PENINA, Rebula, PINOT GR. Promising CAB FR.

Gross Pod w ★★★ Austrian-run family estate. Superb Gorca FURMINT, Colles SAUV BL, orange TRAMINEC (GEWURZ).

Guerila Prim r w ★★ Bio producer in VIPAVA. V.gd PINELA, Retro (w) blend, BARBERA.

Istenič Pos sp ★★ Gd fizz specialist. Try Prestige Extra Brut, Gourmet Rosé, N°1 Brut, BARBARA Sec.

Istria Coastal zone partly in Croatia; main grapes: REFOŠK, MALVAZIJA. Best: Bordon (E Vin rosé, Malvazija), Korenika & Moškon (PINOT GR, Refošk, Kortinca red), MonteMoro, Rodica (organic), Rojac (Renero, Stari d'Or), Pucer z Vrha (Malvazija), SANTOMAS, Steras (Refošk Saurih Hills), VINAKOPER.

Jakončič Prim r w sp ★★★ V.gd BRDA producer, esp Carolina Rebula, Bela (w), Rdeča (r). Also gd PENINA.

Joannes Pod r w ★★ RIES specialist nr Maribor. Also fresh light PINOT N.

Kabaj Prim r w ★★★ French-directed. Noted for long-aged Amfora, also skin-contact Rebula, Ravan (FRIULANO), Corpus, serious MERLOT.

Klet Brda Prim r w sp ★★→★★★ Slovenia's largest co-op, surprisingly gd and forward-thinking. Try Bagueri v'yd selections. Also v.gd Quercus varietal whites, unoaked Krasno Colliano for US. Excellent flagship A+ (r w).

Kobal Pod w ★★ Former PULLUS winemaker gone solo. V.gd FURMINT, SAUV BL.

Kogl Pod r p w ★★ Hilltop estate nr Ormož, dating from 1542. Vibrant, precise whites esp Mea Culpa AUXERROIS, Ranina (aka BOUVIER).

Slovenia has more tractors/head than anywhere else in world.

Kras Prim Renowned district on Terra Rossa soil in PRIM. Best-known for TERAN, MALVAZIJA. Try Vinakras (esp Teranton, Prestige TERAN, Vitovska).

Kristančič r w ★★→★★★ Family producer in BRDA (no relation to winemaker surname at MOVIA). Pavó wines from old vines recommended.

Kupljen Pod r w ★★ Dry wine pioneer nr Jeruzalem.

Marof Pod r w ★★→★★★ Pioneering winery in Prekmurje. All wines now oak-aged under Classic, Breg and cru ranges. Try Breg CHARD, Mačkovci Cru BLAUFRÄNKISCH.

Movia Prim r w sp ★★★→★★★★ High-profile bio winery led by charismatic Aleš Kristančič. Excellent v. long-lived Veliko Belo (w), Rdeče (r), showstopping Puro Rosé (sp). V.gd MODRI PINOT. Orange Lunar spends eight full moons on skins.

Pasji Rep Prim r w ★★ Organic VIPAVA estate, now run by son. Much-improved, refined wines, esp MALVAZIJA, Jebatschin blends, PINOT N.

Penina Name for quality sparkling wine (charmat or traditional method). V. trendy.

Podravje Largest wine region covering Štajerska and Prekmurje in e. Best for crisp dry whites, gd sweet wines, reds typically lighter styles from MODRA FRANKINJA (aka BLAUFRÄNKISCH), PINOT N.

Posavje Region in se. V.gd sweet wines, esp Mavretič, Prus, Šturm. Improving PENINA and dry wines, esp in Dolenjska, Bizeljsko-Sremič regions.

PRA-VinO Pod w sw 70s pioneer of private wine production. Best for ★★★★sweet, incl Icewine (ledeno vino), botrytis wines from LAŠKI RIZLING, RIES, ŠIPON.

Primorje Region in w covering Slovenian IS & KV, BRDA, VIPAVA, KRAS. Aka Primorska.

Puklavec Family Wines Pod w sp ★★→★★★ Large family winery offering *consistent crisp aromatic whites* in Puklavec & Friends and Jeruzalem Ormož ranges. Top selections under Seven Numbers label are superb, esp FURMINT, PINOT GR.

Pullus Pod p w ★★ Gd modern whites from Ptuj winery: Pullus SAUV BL, RIES. Excellent "G" wines; LAŠKI RIZLING (sw), Rumeni MUSCAT.

Radgonske Gorice Pod sp ★→★★ Producer of bestselling Slovenian sparkler Srebrna (silver) PENINA, classic-method Zlata (golden) Penina and popular demi-sec black label TRAMINEC.

Santomas Prim r p w ★★→★★★ Leading IS & KV estate. Some of country's best *Refošk* and REFOŠK/CAB SAUV blends, esp Antonius from 60-yr-old vines and Grande Cuvée blend.

Ščurek Prim r p w sw ★★→★★★ Family estate in BRDA, five sons. Gd CAB FR, Jakot,

---

Glowing amber

Slovenia and Croatia still lead in orange/amber wines, esp close to border with Collio, where skin-contact whites were first revived by Gravner, Radikon and Prinčič. Time on skins varies from just a few days to wks or even mths for a full orange style, often with min sulphites. Long-lived, complex food wines are (or can be) the result. Look for BATIČ, ČOTAR, GROSS, JNK, kabaj, Klinec, Mlecnik, MOVIA, Ražman, plus CLAI, KABOLA, KOZLOVIČ, ROXANICH, TOMAC over the Croatian border.

> **Dolenjska**
> Improving region, focusing on better quality as sales of traditional light red CVIČEK decline. Promising sparkling from local Žametovka (Domaine Slapšak) and Rumeni Plavec. Reds to watch: MODRA FRANKINJA from Kobal (esp superb Luna), Žaren's Albiana, Klet Krško, Kozinc, Dular Selekcija.

PINOT BL, Rebula. Best wines from local grapes: Kontra, Pikolit, Stara Brajda (r w).

Simčič, Marjan Prim r w sw ★★★★ Exciting whites, esp single-v'yd Opoka Rebula, SAUV BL, CHARD, MERLOT. Selekcija, SIVI PINOT, Teodor blends always v.gd. MODRI PINOT is elegant. Leonardo (sw) consistently great.

Štajerska Pod Large e wine region incl important districts of Ljutomer-Ormož, Maribor, Haloze. Crisp, refined whites and top sw. Best (without individual entries): Doppler, Frešer, Gaube, Heaps Good Wine, Krainz, Miro, M-vina (esp ExtremM SAUV BL), Oskar, Šumenjak, Valdhuber, Zlati Grič.

Steyer Pod w sw ★★ TRAMINER specialist in ŠTAJERSKA.

Sutor Prim r w ★★★ Excellent small producer from VIPAVA. Try Sutor White from Rebula/MALVAZIJA, also v.gd Malvazija, fine CHARD, elegant red.

Tilia Prim r w ★★→★★★ "House of Pinots" in VIPAVA since co-owner gained PhD studying PINOT N. V.gd PINOT GR, appetizing SAUV BL. Juicy Vipava Pinot N.

World-famous Lipizzaner horses come from Lipica stud; still going after 425 yrs.

Verus Pod r w ★★★ Fine, focused, vibrant whites, esp v.gd FURMINT, crisp SAUV BL, flavoursome PINOT GR, refined RIES. Promising PINOT N.

Vinakoper Prim r w ★→★★ Large producer in IS & KV. Look for Capris and young MALVAZIJA, REFOŠK under Rex Fuscus, Capris labels.

Vipava Prim Valley noted for cool breezes in PRIM. Recommended without own entry: Benčina (PINOT N), Fedora (Zelen, Goli Breg), Jangus (SAUV BL, MALVAZIJA), JNK (orange wines), Lepa Vida (Malvazija, oOo orange), Miška (PINELA), Mlečnik (orange/natural), Štokelj (Pinela),Vina Krapež (excellent Lapor Belo).

CROATIA

Croatia saw record numbers of tourists last year: 18.5 million in a country with just 4.2 million residents. Exports remain small because of high prices that visitors are prepared to pay, and also very little organized promotion abroad. It's still a very divided country in wine terms with 2600 registered producers, of which around 500 sell commercially. This results in almost endless opportunities for discovery, not least because the country has so many unique grapes, combined with increasingly self-assured winemaking.

Agrokor r p w ★→★★ Troubled conglomerate, undergoing restructuring. Owns Agrolaguna in IS & KV; v.gd Vina Laguna Festigia and Riserva (v.gd MALVAZIJA, esp Vižinada, MERLOT, Castello); Vina Belje nr Danube (esp Goldberg GRAŠEVINA, premium CHARD).

Ahearne r p w ★★ British Master of Wine Jo Ahearne makes elegant PLAVAC MALI, deep Rosina Darnekuša rosé, Wild Skins (w) on HVAR.

Arman, Franc Is & Kv r w ★★★ 6th-generation family winery. V.gd TERAN, DYA MALVAZIJA, skin-contact Malvazija Classic. Gd MERLOT, CAB FR.

Badel 1862 r w ★★ Group of wineries. Best: Korlat SYRAH, CAB SAUV, esp Supreme. Gd-value Duravar range, esp SAUV BL, GRAŠEVINA. Gd PLAVAC and DINGAC 50°.

Benvenuti Is & Kv r w ★★★ Impressive family winery at Motovun. V.gd reds, esp Caldierosso, TERAN. Benchmark fresh MALVAZIJA, complex Anno Domini (w), gorgeous San Salvatore MUŠKAT (sw).

BIBICh Dalm r w ★★→★★★ Focus on local grapes, esp Debit (w), plus SYRAH. Try Lučica single-v'yd and sweet Ambra. Also local rarity Lasin.

Bolfan Cro Up r p w ★→★★★ Bio/natural wine. Gd Primus RIES, SAUV BL, PINOT N.

Bura-Mrgudič Dalm r p ★★ In Peljesac; renowned for Bura, DINGAČ and Mare POSTUP.

Cattunar Is & Kv r w ★★ Hilltop estate with gd range of MALVAZIJA from four soils. Excellent late-harvest Collina.

Clai Is & Kv r w ★★ Admired orange wines: Sveti Jakov MALVAZIJA, Ottocento blends.

Coronica Is & Kv r w ★★ Influential IS & KV winery, esp barrel-aged Gran MALVAZIJA and benchmark Gran TERAN.

Dalmatia Rocky coastal region and lovely islands s of Zadar. Tourism hotspot – location for *Game of Thrones*. Many exciting wineries.

Damjanić Is & Kv r p w ★★ Up-and-coming family winery. IS & KV's best Borgonja (aka BLAUFRÄNKISCH). V.gd MALVAZIJA, Clemente red.

Dingač Dalm 10 11' 12 13 15 1st quality designation (1961), now PDO, on s DALM's Peljesac peninsula. Full reds from PLAVAC MALI. Try: BURA-MRGUDIČ, Kiridžija, Lučič, Madirazza, Matuško, Miličič, SAINTS HILLS, Skaramuča, Vinarija Dingač.

2nd-biggest white truffle ever found was from Is & Kv: 1.31kg. Finder gave feast.

Enjingi, Ivan Sl & CD w sw ★★ Influential natural winemaker in SLAVONIJA. Noted for GRAŠEVINA and long-lived Venje.

Fakin Is & Kv r w ★★★ Exciting young *garagiste* winemaker impressing with MALVAZIJA, esp La Prima, Il Primo TERAN.

Feravino Sl & CD r p w ★ Entry-level wines modern, decent value.

Galić Sl & CD r w ★★ V.gd GRAŠEVINA, red blend Crno 9.

Gerzinič Is & Kv r p w ★★ Brothers making v.gd TERAN (r p), MALVAZIJA, SYRAH, MUŠKAT Zuti (aka Yellow Muscat).

Gracin Dalm r p ★★→★★★ Small winery with rocky coastal v'yds nr Primošten owned by Prof Leo Gracin, making country's *best Babič*, Opol (p), Prošek (sw).

Grgič Dalm r w ★★→★★★ Napa Valley legend Mike Grgic, ex-Ch Montelena (*see* California), returned to Croatian roots to make PLAVAC MALI, rich POŠIP on Peljesac peninsula with daughter and nephew.

Hvar Beautiful island with world's oldest continuously cultivated v'yd and UNESCO protection. Noted for lavender and PLAVAC MALI, incl Ivan Dolac designation. Gd: Carič, PZ Svirče, TOMIČ, ZLATAN OTOK and new AHEARNE.

Iločki Podrumi Sl & CD r p w ★★→★★★ Historic winery revived; deep C15 cellars, ambitious plantings. Superb Premium GRAŠEVINA, TRAMINAC, Principovac range.

Kabola Is & Kv r p w ★★→★★★ Immaculate IS & KV estate. V.gd MALVAZIJA as fizz, young wine, cask-aged Unica, Amfora. Tasty DYA rosé; v.gd TERAN.

Katunar Is & Kv r w ★★ Leading producer of Žlahtina found only on island of Krk. Try Sv. Lucija. Also gd PLAVAC MALI.

Korta Katarina Dalm r p w ★★→★★★ Modern winemaking from Korcula. Excellent POŠIP, PLAVAC MALI, esp Reuben's Res.

Istria & Kvarner

N Adriatic peninsula and nearby islands. MALVAZIJA main grape. Gd CAB SAUV, MERLOT, TERAN. Look for: ARMAN FRANC, Arman Marijan, Banko Mario, BENVENUTI, Capo (Malvazija, Stellae range), CATTUNAR, CLAI, CORONICA, Cossetto, DAMJANIČ, Degrassi (VIOGNIER, CAB FR), Deklič, Domaine Koquelicot (Belaigra Grand Cru), FAKIN, Frankovič, GERZINIČ, KABOLA, KOZLOVIČ, MATOŠEVIČ, Medea, MENEGHETTI, Misal Peršurič (sparkling), Novacco, PILATO, Piquentum, Radovan (REFOŠK, Merlot), ROXANICH, SAINTS HILLS, Sitotic, Tomaz (Avantgarde, Sesto Senso), TRAPAN, Zigante. On islands, look for Boškinac (Cuvee), KATUNAR.

Kozlović Is & Kv r w ★★★ *Benchmark Malvazija* in all its forms, esp exciting, complex Santa Lucia, Po Mojem. Superb Santa Lucia Crna; MUŠKAT Momjanski.

Krajančić w ★★ Specialist in exciting white grape POŠIP: try Sur Lie, Intrada.

Krauthaker, Vlado Sl & CD r w sw ★★★ Top producer from KUTJEVO, esp GRAŠEVINA Mitrovac, Vidim, Izborna Berba. Also v.gd PINOT N, Incrocio Manzoni.

Kutjevo Cellars Sl & CD w dr sw ★★ 800-yr-old cellar in Kutjevo town; noted for gd GRAŠEVINA, esp De Gotho, Turkovič, lovely Icewine.

Vrhunsko vino: premium wine; *Kvalitetno Vino:* quality wine; *Stolno Vino:* table wine.

Matošević Is & Kv r w ★★ Benchmark MALVAZIJA, esp Alba, Alba Robinia (aged in acacia), Antiqua. V.gd Grimalda (r w).

Meneghetti Is & Kv r w ★★ Sleek, well-made blends (r w), fine precise MALVAZIJA.

Miloš, Frano Dalm r p ★★★ Much admired for legendary, long-lived Stagnum, also easier PLAVAC and rosé.

Pilato Is & Kv r w ★★ Consistent family winery; v.gd MALVAZIJA, PINOT BL, TERAN, MERLOT.

Postup Dalm Famous v'yd designation nw of DINGAČ. Full-bodied, rich red from PLAVAC MALI. Try: Donja Banda, Miličič, Mrgudič Marija, Vinarija Dingač.

Prošek Dalm Historic sweet made from sun-dried local grapes in DALM; 1st mention 1556. Gd versions: GRACIN, STINA, TOMIČ Hectorovich.

Roxanich Is & Kv r w ★★→★★★ Natural producer making powerful, intriguing orange wines (MALVAZIJA Antica, Ines U Bijelom); impressive complex reds, esp TERAN Ré, Superistrian Cuvée, MERLOT.

Saints Hills Dalm, Is & Kv r p w ★★→★★★ Two wineries, three locations, consultant Michel Rolland. V.gd Nevina (w) from IS & KV; richly fruity PLAVAC MALI St Roko, serious DINGAČ.

Slavonija Region in ne, famous for oak, and for whites, esp from GRAŠEVINA. Also gd reds now. Look for Adzič, Antunovič, Bartolovič, Belje, ENJINGI, FERAVINO, GALIČ, KRAUTHAKER, KUTJEVO, Orahovica, Zdjelarevič.

Dubrovnik one of 1st medieval cities in Europe to have sewage system: phew.

Stina Dalm r p w ★★→★★★ Dramatic steep v'yds on Brač island; v.gd POŠIP, PLAVAC MALI, esp Majstor label. Gd Tribidrag (AKA ZIN), Opol rosé, PROŠEK.

Tomac Cro Up r w sp ★★ Estate nr Zagreb with 200-yr history, famous for sparkling and pioneering amphora wines.

Tomić Dalm r p w ★★ Outspoken personality, bold wines on HVAR; organic PLAVAC MALI. Gd reds, esp Plavac Barrique, Hectorovich PROŠEK.

Trapan, Bruno Is & Kv r w ★★→★★★ Dynamic young producer. Try MALVAZIJA, incl natural Uroboros, orange Istrad2itional and DYA Ponente. Also sleek reds: Terra Mare TERAN, The One! (r).

Veralda Is & Kv r p w ★★ Smooth polished reds are hallmark, plus bright whites and orange amphora.

Zlatan Otok Dalm r p w ★★ Family winery from HVAR with v'yds also at Makarska, Šibenik. Famous for ripe reds, esp BABIČ, Crljenak, PLAVAC MALI. Gd DYA POŠIP.

BOSNIA & HERZEGOVINA, KOSOVO, MACEDONIA (FYROM), SERBIA, MONTENEGRO

The Balkans wine scene continues to develop rapidly. Rediscovering local grape varieties is the key. New small, quality-focused wineries continue to appear while large former state holdings evolve or die.

Bosnia & Herzegovina's 3500 ha are ever more exciting, helped by gd-quality local vines that dominate, esp aromatic white Žilavka, juicy gentle red Blatina and some v.gd Vranac in s█ Look for: Andrija, Carski, Čitluk, Crnjac & Zadro, Hercegovina Produkt, Keža, Đuić, Podrum Vilinka, Škegro, Tvrdos Monastery, Vukoje.

Kosovo has 3200 ░a, but is stuck between two sets of wine laws – its own and Serbia's – hasn'█ helped progress. Now up to 15 wineries: Stonecastle, Old Cellar (Bodrum i Vjet█r) biggest. Prokupac, Vranac, Smederevka most-planted grapes.

Republic of North█rn Macedonia, enabling progress towards EU candidacy. Now 25,000 ha and 74 commercial wineries, increasingly switching from bulk towards bottled wines, though some smaller investments have failed; domestic wine and food culture is limited. Unusually largest wineries are drivers in raising standards. Gia█t Tikveš has a French-trained winemaker, an intensive research and education programme and continues to impress with Barovo, Bela Voda single-v'yd win█s; gd Special Selection range and rich, oaked Domaine Lepovo, esp Grande Cu█ée. Stobi sources only from its own 600 ha of v'yds; try Vranec Veritas, Vrane█ classic, Aminta (r), Žilavka and refined PETIT VERDOT. Ch Kamnik leading boutique winery, with gd 10 Barrels, Temjanika Premium, Vranec Terroir, Cuvée Prestige. Other wineries to look for: Bovin (try A'gupka, Daron, Dissan), Dalv█na (Dionis range), Ezimit (Stardust range, Vranec Barrique), Lazar (Kratoši█a, Erigon r), Popov (gd w, Dom Vrshnik blends), Popova Kula (Stanušina in █hree styles), Puklavec & Friends (from Slovenia, make r here).

Montenegro has ░651 ha of v'yds and 500+ growers but 13 Jul Plantaže dominates with 2310 ha, ░ne of Europe's largest v'yds, but wines are pretty gd (try Vranac RES, Epoha, V█adika, Stari Podrumi, VRANAC Pro Corde). Also Lipovac (v.gd Amfora r w, V█anac Concept), though Vranac dominates (97%), though recent research sugg░sts here, not Croatia, is origin of Kratošija/ZIN.

Serbia has 25,00░ ha of registered v'yds and c.400 wineries, many new and tiny. Focus on rein█enting former workhorse grapes like Prokupac, obscurities like Bagrina, Sedu█a and trying newer local grapes like Probus, Morava, Neoplanta. Try: Aleksan█rović (Trijumf range, Regent, Rodoslav), Aleksić (Biser Brut, Amanet), Bot█njac (Sveti Grai), Budimir (Triada, Svb Rosa, Boje Lila), Cilić, Čokot (Rado█an, Experiment), Despotika (Morava, Dokaz), Deurić (Probus, PINOT N), Do░a (Prokupac), Dukay-Sagmeister, Ivanović (Prokupac, No.1/2), Janko (Vrtlog Zavet Stari, Zapis), Kovačević (CHARD, Aurelius), Matalj (Kremen Chard, Krem█n Kamen), Maurer, Pusula (CAB FR), Radovanović (C░b Res, Saga), Temet (Ergo░ Tri Morave), Tonković (KADARKA), Virtus (Prokupac, Marselan), Zivković, Zv█nko Bogdan (Cuvée No.1, Icon Campana Rubimus).

CZECHIA

Two wine regions cultivated by 18,300 growers, the tiny Bohemia (Boh) with 640 ha around and north of Prague and a much larger Moravia (Mor) with 17,100 ha in the southeast corner. Though hardly known to the outside world, their history goes back to Roman times. Money continues to flow into huge new wineries, some traditional village cellar settlements now resemble industrial estates. Wine tourism keeps these facilities busy, though boom may have peaked. Annual production of 600,000 h░ is less than half annual consumption which, given the patriotic instincts of consumers, keeps producers in an advantageous position, hence few bargains. Sauvignon Blanc can be good, and Pinot Noir surprisingly so. Exports are negligible, except for niche products.

Baloun, Rado█il Mor ★→★★★ Medium-sized producer, wide range of highly quaffable wines, all dry. Pinot N Blanc, Blaufränkisch Blanc curiosities.

Dobrá Vinice M█r ★★★ Authentist specializing in amphora-like *qvevri* from Georgia. Also Brut Nature.

Ova Duby Mor ★★★ Dedicated terroirist, bio principles. Granodiorite subsoil of Dolní Kounice is esp suited to BLAUFRÄNKISCH/ST LAURENT grapes. Flagship blends: Vox In Excelso, Rosa Inferni, Ex Monte Lapis.

Hartman, Jiří Mor ★★ Small producer of v.gd burgundy-style whites and reds in picturesque village cellar.

Lobkowicz, Bettina Boh ★★→★★★ Outstanding PINOT N and classic-method sparkling RIES, Pinot N Blanc de Noirs, Cuvée Pinot N/PINOT GR and CHARD Brut.

Mádl, František Mor ★★ Nicknamed "Malý vinař" (small vintner), family-run, top reds Mlask, Cuvée 1+1, also v.gd PINOT GR.

Spielberg Mor ★★ Modern operation nr site of Battle of the Three Emperors at Austerlitz. Souvignier Gris a speciality.

Stapleton & Springer Mor ★★★ Single-v'yd PINOT N Trkmanska, Čtvrtě, and Terasy's Craig's Res, Ben's Res, also Roučí blend Jaroslav Springer. Exports 20%, incl UK. NB excellent **Springer Family Reserve** Pinot N.

Stávek, Richard Mor ★→★★★ Specialist in "raw" and pét-nat. Orange wines a hit in some top restaurants/wine bars, esp in NYC.

Vinselekt Michlovský Mor ★→★★★ Innovator and technologist, wide range of grapes, incl some bred by himself. WELSCHRIESLING from Pálava Hills is a must.

Znovín-Znojmo r w ★→★★ Important wine centre in s, nr Austrian border. Useful SAUV BL, aromatic whites.

SLOVAKIA

Central European vines dominate, alongside international favourites. Slovakia's vineyard of 12,000 ha starts around Bratislava on the Danube, continues along the foothills of the Lesser Carpathians (L Car) to Nitra (Nit), Central Slovakia (C Slo) while in Southern Slovakia (S Slo) it follows the Hungarian border for 450-km (280-miles) east to the small Slovak Tokaj (Tok) region, adjacent to its larger Hungarian namesake, and further northeast to Eastern Slovakia (E Slo). Vinárske závody Topoľčianky and Sekt JE Hubert Sereď (both Nit) are country's largest wine and Sekt producers, respectively.

Château Belá S Slo ★★★ Fine RIES by Egon Müller (see Germany) and Miroslav Petrech joint venture.

Elesko L Car ★★★ Huge winery unrivalled in Central Europe (140 ha).

Fedor Malík & Sons L Car ★★ University professor of oenology planted 15 ha in Modra. Still and Modragne classic sparkling.

J&J Ostrožovič Tok ★★★ V.gd Slovak Tok, traditional and modern products.

Karpatská Perla L Car ★★★ V.gd wines from immaculately maintained v'yds (60 ha).

Movino C Slo ★★ Most important Central Slovakia producer, est in Veľký Krtíš 1973.

Víno Matyšák L Car ★→★★★ Large modern winery in Pezinok (2.5 million litres).

ROMANIA

Romania's strong domestic market is both a blessing and a curse. Many consumers are still happy with the sort of cheap semi-dry wines that have long been standard, but the culture is changing. The country has a history of fine wine, much influenced by France. Natural conditions could hardly be better and many native varieties should appeal in today's global search for authenticity. Romania's diverse climates, from cool but dramatic hillsides of Transylvania to the warm, sunny slopes of Dealu Mare, provide for a great diversity of styles. Just be patient.

Avincis Mun r w p ★★ Historic family estate and dramatic state-of-art winery in

DRĂGĂŞANI. Specialist in Negru de Drăgăşani (also in v.gd Cuvée Grandiflora) Crâmpoşie Selecţionată impresses and pretty Cuvée Amelie (sw).

Balla Géza Cri & Mar r p w ★→★★ Estate in Miniş. Best is Stone Wine range from v'yd at 500m (1640ft). V.gd Cadarca and fresh Mustoasă de Măderat.

Banat Wine region in w; incl DOC Recaş.

Bauer Winery Mun r p w ★★ Family winery of winemaker at PRINCE ŞTIRBEY. V.gd Crâmpoşie, FETEASCĂ NEAGRĂ, PETIT VERDOT. Orange wine pioneer.

Bears eat 50% of their own body weight each day. That's a lot of grapes.

Budureasca Mun r w ★→★★ Large DEALU MARE estate with British winemaker. Consistent Budureasca (esp FUMÉ, TĂMÂIOASĂ, Noble 5), top Origini range.

Catleya Mun r p w ★★ Personal project of CORCOVA's French winemaker; excellent Epopée top selection.

Corcova Mun r p w ★★ Stunning v'yds and renovated C19 royal cellar. Try FETEASCĂ NEAGRĂ, SYRAH; appealing SAUV BL, rosé.

Cotnari Mold DOC region in MOLD, only grows local varieties, esp FETEASCĂ ALBĂ, Frâncuşă, GRASĂ, TĂMÂIOASĂ.

Cotnari Wine House Mold p w ★→★★ Next-generation producer in COTNARI, 350 ha, dry wine focus. Colloquium label (esp GRASĂ de Cotnari), Busuioacă de Bohotin.

Cotnari Winery Mold w sw ★ Former collectivized winery with 1360 ha, replanted 2006/7. Mostly dry and semi-dry whites from local grapes. Aged sweet Collection wines *can be impressive*.

Crişana & Maramures Region in nw incl DOC Miniş. Carastelec (Carassia bottle-fermented sparkling and gd PINOT N) and renovated natural producer Nachbil (Grunspitz, Grandpa).

Davino Winery Mun r p w ★★★→★★★★ Excellent, consistent producer in DEALU MARE. Focus on blends for v.gd, age-worthy Dom Ceptura, Flamboyant, Revelatio. Local varieties feature in Monogram label.

Dealu Mare / Dealul Mare Mun Mun Means "The Big Hill". DOC on s-facing slopes. Location of several leading producers (*see* individual entries). Also Crama Basilescu (MERLOT, FETEASCĂ NEAGRĂ), tiny handcrafted Dagon Clan with Aussie Mark Haisma, organic Domeniile Franco-Române.

Dobrogea Dob Nr Black Sea. Incl DOC regions of Murfatlar, Badabag and Sarica Niculiţel (also improved winery of same name). Regarded for ripe reds today; sweet whites were historically famous.

DOC Romanian term for PDO. Sub-categories incl DOC-CMD: harvest at full maturity, DOC-CT: late-harvest and DOC-CIB: noble-harvest. PGI is Vin cu indicatie geografică or simply IG.

Domeniul Coroanei Segarcea Mun r p w ★→★★ Historic royal estate. Famous for TĂMÂIOASĂ Roze. Also try Minima Moralia CAB SAUV, Principesa Margareta Marselan, Simfonia red blend.

Drăgăşani Mun Dynamic region on River Olt for aromatic whites and intriguing reds. Leading producers: AVINCIS, BAUER, PRINCE ŞTIRBEY.

Girboiu, Crama Mold r w ★→★★ 200 ha in earthquake-prone Vrancea, hence Tectonic label (try Şarba) and Epicentrum blends, esp Plavaie/Şarba. Gd Bacanta FETEASCĂ NEAGRĂ, Cuartz (sp).

Halewood Romania Mun r p w sp ★→★★ Consistent gd-value commercial range, esp La Umbra, Colina Pietra, v'yd selections. Hyperion is top label: try FETEASCĂ NEAGRĂ, CAB SAUV. Also Rhein (sp).

Jidvei Trnsyl w ★→★★ Romania's largest single v'yd with 2460 ha. Stick to premium dry wines (with Marc Dworkin of Bulgaria's Bessa Valley), esp Owner's Choice.

LacertA Mun r w ★★ Quality estate in DEALU MARE, named after local lizards. Try Cuvée IX (r) and Cuvée X (w), SHIRAZ.

Licorna Wine House Mun r w ★★ In DEALUL MARE, opened 2013. impressing with Serafim for local grapes and Bon Viveur for international blends.

Liliac Trnsyl r p w sp ★★→★★★ Impeccable Austrian-owned estate; name means "bat". Crisp fine whites, delicious sweet Nectar and Icewine with Kracher (Austria). Pioneer of orange wine, gd PINOT N (r p). V.gd super-premium Titan.

Metamorfosis, Viile Mun r w ★★ Part-Antinori-owned (*see* Italy) estate in DEALUL MARE. Top: Cantvs Primvs in best yrs. V.gd Coltul Pietrei, esp Negru de Drăgăşani, PINOT N, fresh fruit-driven Metamorfosis range.

Moldovan Hills Mold Largest wine region ne of Carpathians. Crisp fresh whites and rosé incl Gramma, Hermeziu. Gd FETEASCĂ NEAGRĂ, Zghihara de Huşi under Nativus label from improving Crama Avereşti.

Muntenia & Oltenia Hills Major wine region in s covering the DOC areas of DEALU MARE, Dealurile Olteniei, DRĂGĂŞANI, Pietroasa, Sâmbureşti, Stefaneşti, Vanju Mare.

Oprişor, Crama Mun r p w ★★→★★★ La Cetate range consistently gd. Try Caloian Rosé, vibrant Rusalca Alba, Crama Oprişor CAB SAUV, excellent Smerenie red.

Petro Vaselo Ban r p w ★★ Italian investment in BANAT with organic v'yds. Gd Bendis (sp), Melgris FETEASCĂ NEAGRĂ, Ovas (r). V.gd entry-level Alb, Roşu and rosé.

Prince Ştirbey Mun r p w sp ★★→★★★ Pioneering estate in DRĂGĂŞANI. V.gd dry whites, esp local Crâmpoşie Selectionată (still and sparkling), SAUV BL, FETEASCĂ REGALĂ, TĂMÂIOASĂ Sec and local reds (Novac, Negru de Drăgăşani).

Recaş, Cramele Ban r p w ★★→★★★ Romania's most successful exporter, crushing over 20,000 tonnes. Progressive, consistent wines with longstanding Australian and Spanish winemakers. V.gd-value, bright varietal wines sold as Calusari, Dreambird, Frunza, I am, I heart, Paparuda, Werewolf. Mid-range: La Putere, Sole. Excellent premium wines, esp Cuvée Uberland, Selene reds, Solo Quinta.

S.E.R.V.E. Mun r p w ★★→★★★ 1st private winery in Romania, founded by late Corsican Count Guy de Poix. Reliable entry-point Vinul Cavalerului. V.gd Terra Romana esp PINOT N, rosé, Cuvée Amaury (w) and impressive Guy de Poix FETEASCĂ NEAGRĂ. *Cuvée Charlotte* quality red benchmark.

Transylvania Cool mtn plateau, central Romania. Mostly whites with gd acidity.

Valahorum Mun r w ★★ New premium winery in DEALU MARE from owners of Tohani and Mennini from DRĂGĂŞANI, with S African winemaker.

Villa Vinèa Trnsyl r w ★★ Italian-owned Târnave estate. Gd whites, esp GEWURZ, SAUV BL, DIAMANT and red blend Rubin (not from Bulgaria's grape).

Vinarte, Domaine Mun r w ★★ 20-yr est investment; v'yds in Sâmbureşti (Castel Bolovanu), Starmina (Mehedinţi). Best: Nedeea (r), Soare, Sirena Dunarii (sw)

Vişinescu, Aurelia Mun r w ★★ DEALU MARE estate. Try Artizan r w using local grapes. Anima is top label, esp Fete Negre 3, CHARD.

MALTA

A hot, humid climate makes for robust wines, with reds from Cabernet Sauvignon, Merlot and more Med varieties like Syrah and Grenache, with whites from Sauvignon Blanc, Chardonnay, Chenin Blanc and Moscato. Most growers sell their crop to the large wineries, including Delicata, Marsovin and Antinori-owned Meridiana. In addition wines are produced from imported Italian grapes. If you want something typically Maltese, look for local grapes Gellewza (light red, also makes acceptable fizz) and white Girgentina, which is often blended with Chardonnay. Malta's most celebrated wine is Marsovin's Grand Maître, Cabernets Sauvignon and Franc, costly but hardly good value. There are a handful of boutique wineries, some rustic, but others, such as San Niklaw, making high quality but in very limited quantities. San Niklaw's Vermentino, Sangiovese and Syrah are noteworthy.

Greece

The Greek quality revolution started in the mid-80s, with a cult of the winemaker. The wine producer was a magician, someone who could turn any grapes into great wine. Vineyards were almost a liability. In the last few years the pendulum has been swinging the other way. More and more growers have stopped selling their grapes and have built a cellar, and established wineries are planting more. Greece is moving towards the cult of the vineyard. Does Greece have a national style of wine? Clean, gutsy, with flavours just beyond the usual. Grape varieties are probably the best way to start. Abbreviations: Aegean Islands (Aeg), Attika (Att), Central Greece (C Gr), Ionian Islands (Aeg), Macedonia (Mac), Peloponnese (Pelop), Thessaloniki (Thess).

Alpha Estate Mac ★★★ Acclaimed KTIMA in AMYNTEO with outstanding v'yds. Classic MERLOT/SYRAH/XINOMAVRO blend, pioneering Ecosyste range, stunning Xinomavro Res from ungrafted vines.

Amynteo Mac (POP) Captivating XINOMAVRO reds, excellent rosés (and sp) from coolest Greek POP – and cold it is.

Argyros Aeg ★★★★ Top SANTORINI producer; several magnificent VINSANTOS (older the better). Top ASYRTIKOS to age for a decade.

Avantis C Gr ★★★ Boutique winery in Evia. Exquisite Aghios Chronos SYRAH/VIOGNIER and Rhône-like Collection Syrah. Plagies Gerakion range is equally gd. New winery in SANTORINI looks v. promising (try Afoura).

Biblia Chora Mac ★★★ Classic SAUV BL/ASSYRTIKO. Ovilos range (r w) could rival B'x at triple the price. Greek varieties takeover imminent; try Vidiano and AGIORGITIKO. Sister estate of GEROVASSILIOU.

Bosinakis ★★★ Relatively new in MANTINIA, powerful style but truly MOSCHOFILERO.

Boutari, J & Son ★-★★★ Historic brand across regions, initially from NAOUSSA. Excellent value, esp *Grande Res Naoussa* to age for 40 yrs+. Top wine: 1879 Legacy Naoussa, from v. old v'yd.

Carras, Dom Porto Mac ★★ Historic estate at Halkidiki. Chateau Carras is a classic; ambitious Grand Blanc and SYRAH, the original MALAGOUSIA; Limnio (r) is *best value*.

Cephalonia Ion Important Ionian island with three POPs: mineral ROBOLA (w), rare MUSCAT (w sw) and excellent MAVRODAPHNE (r sw). Dry Mavrodaphne is a trend here (as elsewhere in Greece) but cannot be POP.

Dalamaras ★★→★★★★ Young yet stellar producer in NAOUSSA. XINOMAVROS of great purity. Palaiokalias single v'yd is world class.

Dougos C Gr ★★★ Rich reds, increasing focus on RAPSANI, esp Old Vines. Try Mavrotragano (r) – best outside SANTORINI.

Economou Estate Crete ★★★ One of the great artisans of Greece, with brilliant, burgundian-like Sitia (r).

Gaia Aeg, Pelop ★★★ Top NEMEA and SANTORINI producer. Great Thalassitis Santorini (rare Submerged is aged underwater), modern VINSANTO and thought-provoking *wild-fermen. Assyrtiko*. Top wine: ever-evolving *Gaia Estate* from Nemea. Dazzling "S" red (AGIORGITIKO with touch of SYRAH).

Gentilini Ion →★-★★★ Leading CEPHALONIA name, incl *steely Robola*. Wild Paths

> ### Greek appellations
> Terms are changing in line with other EU countries. Quality appellations of OPAP and OPE now fused together into POP (or PDO) category. Regional wines, known as TO, will now be PGE (or PGI).

> **Hellenic taste**
> Having food with wine (and vice versa) in Greece is imperative. So, over the course of millennia, Greeks have preferred wines with edges rather than softness; high acid rather than high alc, complexity rather than intensity. While many wines still try too hard, Greek wines at their best are all about balance and drinkability.

redefines ROBOLA variety. Marvellous dry MAVRODAPHNE Eclipse (r) built to age.

Gerovassiliou Mac ★★★ Quality and trend leader. Original ASSYRTIKO/MALAGOUSIA and top Malagousia (he's the specialist). Top reds: Avaton (from indigenous varieties) and Evangelo. Linked with BIBLIA CHORA. Must-try.

Goumenissa Mac (POP) ★→★★★ Earthy, expressive XINOMAVRO/Negoska (r). Try Chatzyvaritis, natural-style Tatsis, Aidarinis (single v'yd), BOUTARI (Filiria).

Hatzidakis Aeg ★★★★ Top-class producer who tragically took his own life in 2017. All remaining bottles should be treated like national treasures. His children took up the baton.

Helios C Gr, Pelop ★★ Umbrella name for Semeli, Nassiakos and Orinos Helios, gd value across rapidly expanding range. Top MANTINIA.

Karydas Mac ★★★ Tiny family estate and amazing v'yd in NAOUSSA, crafting rare, classic, compact but always refined XINOMAVRO.

Katogi Averof Pelop, Epir ★★→★★★ Katogi was original cult Greek wine, now decent large-volume brand. Top: Rossiu di Munte range from plots at 1000m (3281ft)+.

Katsaros Thess ★★★ Tiny winery on Mt Olympus. KTIMA (CAB SAUV/MERLOT) is a Greek classic. XINOMAVRO Valos is getting there.

Ancient Greek festival game: trying to balance on a greased wineskin.

Kechris ★★→★★★ Maker of The Tear of the Pine, possibly *world's best Retsina*: fantastic wine. No kidding.

Kir-Yanni Mac ★★→★★★ V'yds across Macedonia. Age-worthy reds incl Ramnista Naoussa, Diaporos, Blue Fox. Akakies sparkling is notable, Tarsanas ASSYRTIKO is fab. Consistently excellent.

Ktima Estate. Should be used on export labels instead of "Estate".

Lazaridi, Nico Mac ★→★★★ Originally from Drama. Several large-volume, value ranges. Top: Magiko Vouno (CAB SAUV).

Lazaridi, Dom Costa Att, Mac ★★★ Wineries in Drama and Att (under Oenotria Land label). Popular Amethystos label. Top: Cava Amethystos CAB FR, then Oenotria Land CAB SAUV/AGIORGITIKO. New plantings in upper Drama v. promising.

Ligas Mac ★★★ Full-blown natural producer in Pella. Try Kydonitsa orange.

Lyrarakis Crete ★★→★★★ Heraklio-based, reviving old, almost extinct Cretan varieties like Plyto, Dafni and Melissaki. *Single-v'yd versions* extraordinary.

Malvasia Group of appellations created in the early 2010s, to recreate wine of Middle Ages. Not from MALVASIA grapes but a reflection of the local varieties. Four POPs: Monemvassia-Malvasia in Laconia (from Monemvassia/ASSYRTIKO/Kydonitsa), Malvasia of Paros (from Monemvassia/Assyrtiko), Malvasia Chandakas-Candia (from Assyrtiko/Vidiano/MUSCAT) and Malvasia of Sitia (ditto plus Thrapsathiri), both from Crete.

Manousakis (Nostos) Crete ★★★ Great estate, initially making Rhône-inspired blends, but Greek varieties here to stay: ASSYRTIKO, revealing MUSCAT of Spinas.

Mantinia Pelop (POP) w sp High-altitude, cool region. Fresh, crisp, low-alc, almost Germanic styles from MUSCAT-like *Moschofilero*. Excellent sparklers from TSELEPOS.

Mercouri Pelop ★★★ One of Greece's most beautiful estates, on w coast. V.gd KTIMA (r), delicious RODITIS (w), complex dry MAVRODAPHNE (r), REFOSCO (r).

Naoussa Mac ★★→★★★ (POP) Top-quality region for sophisticated, fragrant

> **The return of the Cretans**
> For many decades in the past, Crete has been widely considered as just a reliable source of cheap wine from undistinctive grape varieties. In the last 10 yrs, it is almost impossible to keep abreast of the developments in quality, together with the resurface of almost forgotten grapes like Vidiano, Dafni, Liatiko, Melissaki or Plyto.

XINOMAVRO. Best examples on par in quality and style (but not price) with Barolo. Top: DALAMARAS, KARYDAS, KIR-YIANNI, THIMIOPOULOS.

Nemea Pelop ★★→★★★ (POP) AGIORGITIKO reds. Can be stunning; styles from fresh to classic to exotic. Try Driopi from TSELEPOS, GAIA, HELIOS, Ieropoulos, Nemeion, PAPAÏOANNOU, SKOURAS. Single-v'yd bottlings on rise.

Palyvos Pelop ★★→★★★ Excellent producer in NEMEA making modern, big-framed reds. Fine single-v'yd selections. Try ultra-premium NV Nohma.

Papaïoannou Pelop ★★★ If NEMEA were Burgundy, Papaïoannou would be Jayer. Benchmark range: excellent value KTIMA, Palea Klimata (old vines), Microklima (micro-single-v'yd), top-end Terroir. Age everything.

Pavlidis Mac ★★★ Outstanding portfolio from Drama. Trendy Thema (w) ASSYRTIKO/ SAUV BL. Emphasis: expressive varietals incl AGIORGITIKO, TEMPRANILLO.

Rapsani Thess POP on Mt Olympus. Made famous in 90s by TSANTALIS (try Grande Res); now DOUGOS, THIMIOPOULOS add excitement. XINOMAVRO, Stavroto, Krasato.

Retsina New Retsinas (eg. GAIA, KECHRIS, natural-style Kamara), packed with freshness, great alternative to Fino Sherry. Yes, great, even age-worthy ones exist.

Samos Aeg ★★→★★★ (POP) Island famed for sweet MUSCAT Blanc. Esp fortified Anthemis, sun-dried Nectar. Rare old bottlings are steals at their price, eg. hard-to-find Nectar 75 or 80.

Santo Aeg ★★→★★★ Most successful SANTORINI co-op. Solid portfolio with dazzling Grande Res, dry Irini aged in VINSANTO barrels, rich yet crisp Vinsantos. Great-value ASSYRTIKO Nyhteri.

Santorini Aeg ★★★→★★★★ Dramatic volcanic island with POP white (dry and sweet) wines to match. Luscious VINSANTO, salty, *bone-dry Assyrtiko*. Top: ARGYROS, GAIA, HATZIDAKIS, SANTO, SIGALAS. Possibly cheapest ★★★★ dry whites around, able to age for 20 yrs. World class. MAVROTRAGANO reds (not incl in POP) can be sublime. Apex of Greek wine.

Sigalas Aeg ★★→★ Leading light of SANTORINI. Sublime Athiri, trail-blazing MAVROTRAGANO. Nyhteri and Cavalieros (dry w) out of this world; Seven Villages micro-cuvée is a thesis on the Santorinian terroir.

Skouras Pelop ★★★ V. consistent range. Lean, wild-yeast Salto MOSCHOFILERO. Top reds: high-altitude Grande Cuvée NEMEA, Megas Oenos. Solera-aged Labyrinth is weird but beautiful, while Peplo rosé is thought-provoking.

Tatsis Mac ★★★ Natural producer in GOUMENISSA. Top wine is Old Roots XINOMAVRO.

Thimiopoulos Mac ★★★★ New-age NAOUSSA with spectacular export success. New projects in RAPSANI (Terra Petra), SANTORINI. Popular, value Atma range.

Fancy making your own Santorini Assyrtiko? Grapes cost c.€7/kg = about 1 bottle.

Tsantalis Mac ★→★★★ Long-est producer. Huge range. Gd RAPSANI Res, Grande Res, gd-value wines from Thrace. Made monastery wines from *Mount Athos* famous, eg. excellent Avaton.

Tselepos Pelop ★★★ Leader in MANTINIA, NEMEA (as Driopi), SANTORINI (Canava Chrysou). Stunning, polished portfolio. Greece's best MERLOT (★★★★Kokkinomylos). Avlotopi CAB SAUV not far behind. Great Driopi Res.

Vinsanto Aeg ★★★★ Sun-dried, cask-aged luscious ASSYRTIKO and Aidani from SANTORINI can age forever. Insanely low yields. Essence of Santorini.

Eastern Mediterranean & North Africa

EASTERN MEDITERRANEAN

The Eastern Med has a wine history as old as wine culture itself. Imagining the vines Noah planted (where did he get the cuttings?), the wines Jesus and King David drank, or the ones described in Omar Khayyam's poetry, have become real pursuits as the region delves into its roots. Today high-altitude vineyards, rocky, stony and inhospitable soils, and plenty of sun make this a winemaker's paradise. It has become a fascinating wine region again.

Cyprus

The focus is on the island's legacy of almost-forgotten grapes, such as Promara, Morokanella and Yiannoudi, rescued from ancient v'yds never hit by phylloxera. It's now about "rewriting our own history, not just copy-pasting others", according to one producer. It's also encouraging to see a sense of pride in Cypriot wines at home; top restaurants are now switching to serving the best local wines, instead of imports. Unfortunately, cheap imports still remain a challenge as fodder for the all-inclusive tourist trade.

Cyprus has highest no. sunny days in Med. Best vines grow high – up to 1450m.

Aes Ambelis r p w br ★→★★ V.gd modern COMMANDARIA. Gd DYA XYNISTERI and rosé.

Anama Concept br ★★ Husband-and-wife handcrafting amazing rich COMMANDARIA from old-vine MAVRO only.

Argyrides Vineyards r w ★★ Immaculate pioneering estate winery with new visitor facility. Excellent MARATHEFTIKO, MOURVÈDRE. V.gd VIOGNIER.

Ayia Mavri w br sw ★→★★ Sweet wines recommended: MUSCAT, COMMANDARIA.

Commandaria Rich, sweet PDO wine from sun-dried XYNISTERI, MAVRO grapes. Probably most ancient named wine still in production, since 800 BC. New-generation producers: AES AMBELIS, ANAMA, AYIA MAVRI, KYPEROUNDA, TSIAKKAS. Traditional: St Barnabas (KAMANTERENA), St John (KEO), Alasia (Loel), Centurion (ETKO).

ETKO & Olympus r w br ★→★★ Former big producer, improved since move to Olympus winery. Best for COMMANDARIA (St Nicholas, Centurion labels).

Kamanterena (SODAP) r p w ★→★★ Large co-op in Pafos hills. Gd-value DYA whites and rosé, young unoaked MARATHEFTIKO.

KEO r p w br ★ Winemaking now at Mallia Estate in hills. Ktima Keo range is best.

Kyperounda r p w br ★★→★★★ Some of Europe's highest v'yds at 1450m (4757ft). Petritis remains standard-setting XYNISTERI. Flagship Epos CHARD and red from own-v'yd. V.gd: Skopos SHIRAZ, Andessitis blend. Excellent modern COMMANDARIA.

Makkas r p w ★→★★ Pafos region. Former economist with garage winery. Gd XYNISTERI, MARATHEFTIKO, SYRAH.

Phylloxera never made it to Cyprus. Ungrafted vines, believed to be centuries old.

Tsiakkas r p w br ★★→★★★ Banker turned winemaker. Expressive whites, esp SAUV BL, XYNISTERI, Promara. V.gd COMMANDARIA, Vamvakada (aka MARATHEFTIKO), Yiannoudi, organic Rodinos rosé.

Vasilikon Winery r p w ★★ Only female winemaker on Cyprus. V.gd whites, esp XYNISTERI, Morokanella. Appealing reds: Ayios Onoufrios, MARATHEFTIKO, Methy.

Constantinou r w ★→★★ Lemesos region. Gd CAB SAUV, SHIRAZ.

Vlassides r p w ★★☆★★★ UC Davis-trained Vlassides makes superb SHIRAZ, gd DYA Grifos, promising Yiannoudi, excellent long-ageing Opus Artis from dry sites.

Vouni Panayia r w ★★ Dynamic family winery with local grape focus. Try Alina XYNISTERI, MARATHEFTIKO, Promara, Spourtiko, Yiannoudi.

Zambartas r p w ★★☆★★★ Australia-trained winemaker making intense CAB FR/ LEFKADA rosé, excellent MARATHEFTIKO, zesty XYNISTERI. Fascinating old-vine Mavro from 1921 v'yd. Promising local Yiannoudi.

Israel

Israel is like an Eastern-Mediterranean California. That's part compliment, part criticism. Med varieties are becoming popular: S Rhône-style blends are in and some interestingly combine Med and B'x varieties. Experimentation goes on as Israel explores its wine identity. High-elevation regions are best. Abbreviations: Galilee (Gal), Upper Galilee (Up Gal), Golan Heights (Gol), Judean Hills (Jud), Negev (Neg), Samson (Sam), Shomron (Shom).

Local Israeli grapes incl Argaman, Baladi, Bittuni, Dabouki, Marawi/Hamdani, Jandali, Zeini.

Abaya Gal ★★ Terroirist. Organically farmed CARIGNAN, crisp COLOMBARD.

Agur Jud r w ★★☆★★ Ex-carpenter, great character, makes wines with individuality.

Amphorae ★☆★★ Beautiful winery, run by new broom. Real improvement (w p).

Ashkar Gal ★☆★★ Connects a people, land and their heritage. Unique SAUV BL.

Barkan-Segal Gal, Sam ★★ Israel's largest winery. Beta label of interest. Crisp COLOMBARD and flowery Marawi. Promising changes under new winemaker.

Bar-Maor Shom ★☆ Minimal-intervention winemaking. Lean CHARD, fresh rosé.

Carmel Up Gal ★☆★★ Historic winery focusing on basic wines. Private Collection gd value. 4 Vats fruity, easy drinking.

Château Golan Gol ★★★ Geshem (r w) v.gd Med blends. Excellent SYRAH, bold Eliad. Innovative winemaker.

Clos de Gat Jud ★★★ Estate exuding quality, style, individuality. Powerful Sycra SYRAH. Rare, concentrated MERLOT. Traditional, quality CHARD. Great-value Harel Syrah, fresh entry-level Chanson (w).

Cremisan Jud ★☆★★ Palestinian wines made in a monastery from indigenous grapes: Hamdani, Jandali, Dabouki, Baladi. Hamdani/Jandali (w blend) best.

Dalton Up Gal ★★☆★★ Family winery, creative winemaker. Refreshing PINOT GR, mineral CHENIN BL and spicy Alma (r).

Domaine du Castel Jud ★★★★ Pioneer of JUD, setting standards in Israel for style, quality. Beautiful winery. Latest Grand Vin may be best yet, with depth, complexity. Push Petit Castel. Exquisitely balanced CHARD back to its best. Characterful rosé. La Vie entry level.

Feldstein Jud, Gal ★★☆★★ Artisan. Superb rosés (GRENACHE, CARIGNAN), mineral SEM/SAUV BL, flowery Dabouki and dried-grape Argaman.

Flam Jud, Gal ★★☆★★★ Superb, elegant B'x blend Noble. Fruit-forward SYRAH, deep MERLOT. Classico great value. Excellent, fresh, fragrant white (SAUV BL/ CHARD), crisp rosé.

Galil Mountain Up Gal ★ Prestige blend Yiron always gd value.

Gush Etzion Jud r w ★☆★★ Central mtn v'yds. Gd GRENACHE/SYRAH/MOURVÈDRE.

Jezreel Valley Shom ★★ Best Israeli Argaman. Fun pét-nat Dabouki. Prestige Icon.

Kosher Necessary for religious Jews. Irrelevant to quality. Wines can be v.gd; 90%+ Israeli wine is kosher. Largest wineries only make kosher wine.

Lahat Gol, Jud ★★ Rhône specialist making precise wines; white has ageing ability.

Lewinsohn Gal ★★★ Quality *garagiste* in a garage. Gd CHARD. Red: chunky, spicy, yet elegant blend of PETITE SIRAH/MARSELAN.

Maia Shom ★→★★ Med-style. Greek consultants. Refreshing, drinkable wines.

Margalit Gal, Shom ★★★→★★★★★ Israel's 1st cult wine. Father and son. B'x blend Enigma. Complex CAB FR, fine CAB SAUV. Cellaring potential. Perfumed Paradigma, intriguing Optima (w), RIES.

Mia Luce Gal ★★→★★★ *Garagiste*. SYRAH with stems: N Rhône feel. Superb MARSELAN.

Nana Neg ★→★★ Desert pioneer making super CHENIN BL, crisp, citrus, refreshing.

Ortal Gol ★→★★ ROUSSANNE/VIOGNIER has richness with gd acidity. Crisp rosé.

Pelter-Matar Gol ★★ Gd whites: fresh Matar CHARD, crisp SAUV BL/SEM.

Psagot Jud ★★ Central mtn v'yds. Peak is succulent Med blend.

Recanati Gal ★★→★★★ Complex, wild CARIGNAN. Summer red from Bittuni (local variety). Spes Res, deep, velvety prestige red.

Sea Horse Jud ★★ Idiosyncratic winemaker with chewy Counoise.

Shvo Up Gal ★★★ Non-interventionist winemaker. Juicy, fresh, complex BARBERA, super-rustic red blend. Rare Gershon SAUV BL, racy CHENIN BL, characterful rosé.

Sphera Jud ★★★→★★★★★ Makes only white; cool-climate style. Racy, crisp White Concepts varietals (RIES, CHARD, SAUV BL) and crisp blend First Page. Outstanding, rare White Signature (SEM/Chard).

Tabor Gal ★★→★★★ V.gd whites, esp fantastic-value SAUV BL. Adama label v.gd value. Complex prestige Malkiya CAB SAUV. Bright single-v'yd TANNAT, fruity MARSELAN.

Teperberg Jud, Sam ★→★★ Israel's largest family winery; 5th generation. Excellent flavourful CAB FR; crisp PINOT GR.

Tulip Gal ★★→★★★ Innovative, progressive. Opulent Black Tulip, deep SHIRAZ, complex CAB FR/MERLOT. Works with adults with special needs.

Tzora Jud ★★★★ Terroir-led, precision winemaking. Talented winemaker (Israel's only MW). Wines show intensity, with balance and elegance. Crisp Shoresh SAUV BL; Jud Red excellent value. Complex, elegant prestige Misty Hills (CAB SAUV/SYRAH). Rare luscious Or dessert.

Vitkin Jud ★★→★★★ Quality CARIGNAN, complex GRENACHE BL. Gt-value entry level.

Vortman Shom ★→★★ One to watch. Gd COLOMBARD, FUMÉ, GRENACHE/CARIGNAN blend.

Yaacov Oryah Sam ★★→★★★ Creative artisan; bold approach; superb bottle-aged SEM.

Yarden Gol ★★→★★★★★ Pioneering winery farming sustainably. Rare, prestige Katzrin. Bold Bar'on CAB/SYRAH. Big-selling brand Mt Hermon (r). Cab Sauv shows quality, consistency, value. Particularly fine Blanc de Blancs. Delicious sweet HeightsWine. Second label: Gamla. SANGIOVESE of interest.

Yatir Jud ★★★ Desert winery with high-altitude forest v'yds. Velvety, concentrated Yatir Forest. Deep PETIT VERDOT.

Lebanon

French influence and powerful, spicy reds define the national character, but "lighter" blends (less oak, extraction) can give a sense of place, while whites, grown at over 1,000m (3281ft), show surprising freshness. Over 20 varieties planted, but Cab Sauv, Syrah, Cinsault, Chard, Sauv Bl, Clairette, Viognier are backbone, with increasing respect given to native Merwah, Obeideh, and red "heritage" varieties Grenache, Carignan.

Favourite Lebanese match with food? Arak, palate-cleansing aniseed eau de vie.

Atibaia r ★★★ *Garagiste*. Elegant red B'x style blend with soft tannins.

Chateau Belle-Vue r (w) ★★ Le Chateau, a plush blend of B'x grapes and SYRAH.

Château Ka r w ★→★★ Great-value, fruity cherry-berry Cadet de Ka. Souce Rouge and Source Blanche, more scrubbed-up.

Château Kefraya r w ★★→★★★★ Fine, ripe, concentrated, complex **Comte de M**. Full, fragrant, oaky Comtesse de M (CHARD/VIOGNIER). Les Breteches (CINSAULT-based).

Chateau Ksara r w ★★★ Founded 1857. Res du Couvent is fruity, easy-drinking, full of flavour. Blanc de Blancs (CHARD/SAUV BL/SEM) the outstanding white.

Château Marsyas r (w) ★★ Deep, powerful, fruity (mainly CAB/SYRAH). Owner of complex ★★★Bargylus (Syria), a miracle wine made in impossible conditions.

Château Musar r w ★★★ →★★★★ Icon wine of the e Med, CAB SAUV/CINSAULT/CARIGNAN 02 03 05' 07' 08-09 10. *Unique recognizable style.* Best after 15–20 yrs in bottle. Indigenous Obaideh and Merweh (w) age indefinitely. Second label: Hochar (r) now higher profile. Musar Jeune is softer, easy-drinking.

Locally, red wine is a winter drink; white and rosé for summer. And yes, arak...

Clos St. Thomas r w ★ →★★★ The Toumas are a famous Bekaa wine family. Fruity, elegant CINSAULT-based Les Gourmets. Aromatic Obaidy (sic).

Domaine de Baal r (w) ★★ Crisp CHARD/SAUV BL, and heady estate red from organic v'yd in Zahleh.

Domaine des Tourelles r w ★★ →★★★ Blockbuster SYRAH, gd Marquis des Beys. Outstanding new CINSAULT from 70-yr-old vines. Fast-improving winery.

Domaine Wardy r (w) ★★★ Les Terroirs (CAB SAUV/MERLOT/CINSAULT) and Clos Blanc (Obeideh/CHARD SAUV BL/VIOGNIER/MUSCAT) outstanding value.

IXSIR r w ★★ →★★★ Stony SYRAH-based blends, floral whites and prestige El. Altitudes range and Grande Res Rosé excellent.

Massaya r w ★★ Terraces de Baalbeck a refined, elegant GSM. Entry-level Les Colombiers v.gd value. Also Cap Est (r) from East Bekaa v'yds on the Anti-Lebanon Mtns.

Vertical 33 r w ★ →★★ Organic (and esoteric) CINSAULT, CARIGNAN, Obeideh varietals. Neo-Musar!

Turkey

Those investing in wine in Turkey today deserve praise and encouragement. It remains a fascinating country of enormous variety and all those interesting indigenous varieties that no one can pronounce.

Büyülübag ★★ One of new small, quality wineries. Gd CAB SAUV.

Corvus ★★★ Bozcaada island. Intense, concentrated Corpus, luscious Passito.

Doluca ★ →★★ DLC label showcases local varieties. Gd rounded OKÜZGÖZÜ.

Karaklidere ★ →★★★ Well-made, elegant. Pendore estate is best, esp OKÜZGÖZÜ, SYRAH. Cherry-berry Yakut. Stéphane Derenoncourt consults.

Kayra ★ →★★ Spicy SHIRAZ, fresh NARINCE. Ripe OKÜZGÖZÜ from E Anatolia.

Pasaeli ★ →★★ Fresh, vibrant B'x-style blends from single v'yd.

Sevilen ★ →★★ International variety specialist. Spicy SYRAH, aromatic SAUV BL.

Suvla ★ →★★ Full-bodied B'x blend Sur, and fruity SYRAH backed by oak.

Urla ★★ Tempus (r has complexity, depth. Expressive white NARINCE-Beyazkere.

Vinkara ★ Charming NARINCE and cherry-berry KALECIK KARASI.

NORTH AFRICA

Baccari Perhaps Mor's best red; Premiere de Baccari from Meknez region.

Bernard Magrez Mor ★★ Investment by B'x tycoon. Tannic, spicy SYRAH/GRENACHE.

Castel Frères Mor ★ Gd-value brands like Bonassia, Halana, Larroque, Sahari.

Celliers de Meknès, Les Mor ★ →★★ Virtual monopoly in Mor. Ch Roslane best.

Domaine Neferis Tun ★ →★★ Calastrasi joint venture. Selian CARIGNAN best.

Ouled Thaleb Mor ★★ Medaillon generous blend of CAB SAUV/MERLOT/SYRAH. Lively Syrah Tandem (Syrocco in US): Thalvin and Graillot (Rhône) joint venture.

Val d'Argan Mor ★ →★★ At Essaouira. Gd value: Mogador. Best: Orients.

Vignerons de Carthage Tun r p w ★ Best from UCCV co-op: Magon Magnus (r).

Vin Gris ★ Pale-pink resort of the thirsty. Castel Boulaouane brand best-known.

Volubilia Mor r p w ★ →★★ Best delicate pink *vin gris* in Morocco.

Asia & Old Russian Empire

ASIA

China China is still a big consumer of wine, though production fell by nearly 40% in 2018. Success in international tastings by Shanxi's Grace V'yd and Xinjiang's Ch Zhongfei have est MARSELAN (CAB SAUV x GRENACHE) as a key grape, and more is being planted. China's c.800,000 ha of vines are, however, still largely for table grapes; just 15% goes into wine. Xinjiang in the far-flung nw frontier and n-central Ningxia each have a quarter of plantings. Hebei and coastal Shandong share another 25%, with the rest in other provinces incl Shaanxi and Yunnan (bordering Laos and Myanmar) where Moët-Hennessy's Shangri-La Winery Ao Yun Cab/MERLOT in the Himalayan foothills is China's most expensive wine. Cab Sauv, at 60% of wine vyds, is the most planted, followed by Merlot, CHARD, Cab Gernischt (aka CARMENÈRE), Marselan, SYRAH, CAB FR and WELSCHRIESLING. Other varieties incl RIES, UGNI BL, SEM, PETIT MANSENG, PINOT N, GAMAY and PETIT VERDOT. Harsh winters in the n, where temperatures can fall to -20°C (-4°F), mean that vines have to be buried in autumn to survive. In coastal Shandong province, rain and typhoons in summer threaten rot. Best: Jia Bei Lan, Ch Zhongfei, Grace V'yd, Tiansai Skyline of Gobi (incl rosé), Silver Heights, Legacy Peak, Domaine Helan Mtn (Pernod Ricard), Ch Rongzi, Leirenshou, Silkroad, Domaine Fontaine Sable, Li's Family, Guofei and Shangri-La Winery. The most expensive offerings tend to be overoaked; mid-range whites and reds are often the best bet. Tiansai has v.gd mid-range Chard Selection, and Chinese Zodiac Chard/MUSCAT. Jade Valley outside Xi'an has gd Pinot N. Taila Winery, Shandong, has China's finest sweet wine, Petit Manseng. Changyu, the giant, puts out gd Icewine. The crown for sparkling belongs squarely to Domaine Chandon in Ningxia, owned by Moët-Hennessy.

India Headwinds incl religious sensitivities (both Muslim and Hindu), local indifference and a bureaucratic minefield of duties and taxes at state and national levels. India has about 115,000 ha of vines, of which a mere 2000 are for wine. Most are in Maharashtra, Karnataka and Andhra Pradesh. Moët-Hennessy's Domaine Chandon makes gd bubbles. Also gd: York Sparkling Cuvée (CHENIN BL), Sula SAUV BL, also Sauv Bl from Indus, Charosa and Grover (esp Zampa Art Collection). Englishman Steven Spurrier (*see* Bride Valley, England) is involved with Fratelli in Maharashtra. Grover now has 3rd generation involved: UC Davis-trained Karishma Grover.

Japan is now making more Koshu than all its reds put together.

Japan Japan's own wine-grape is white KOSHU, believed to have arrived 1000 yrs ago via the Silk Road. Total vine plantings are c.20,000 ha, of which 6% are for wine, from c.280 wineries. About 30% are in Yamanashi; Nagano has about 12%. Most grow table grapes as well. Big brewers Sapporo, Kirin and Suntory dominate wine, but the most ambitious are small, family-owned wineries, which use their own grapes. Floral, citrus and zesty, high-acid Koshu (best is unoaked) is the darling of writers and sommeliers seeking difference. The hybrid MUSCAT Bailey A is most planted red; you either like or hate its candy-floss aroma. Best: Domaine Hide. Best Koshu: Grace Wines' Cuvée Misawa Akeno; also gd sparkling CHARD. Other gd names: Ch Mercian, Haramo, Lumiere, Soryu, Marquis, L'Orient, Chitose Winery PINOT N.

Local legend says Buddhist monk Gyoki planted Japan's 1st grapes in 718 in Yamanashi.

THE OLD RUSSIAN EMPIRE

Of all the wine-growing areas around the Black Sea and the Caucasus, Georgia receives most international attention. Its practice of making wine in buried clay *qvevris* (amphorae), long considered archaic, now inspires winemakers around the globe. Armenia, Georgia's neighbour, is not short of real wine heritage, either. Both countries boast millennia of history and first-class local grapes. In Russia, quality winemaking is in vogue, a sign of new times and consumer moods. Moldova bets on tourism to get its rather splendid wines – and some unique wine cellars – known better. Off the beaten track are large-scale plantings, above 1000m (3281ft) for quality wines in Kazakhstan.

Armenia Vies with Georgia as a birthplace of winemaking (the most ancient winery dates back 6100 yrs). Its remote mountainous v'yds are phylloxera-free. Indigenous white Voskeat and Garandamak, red Areni, Hindogny and Kakhet can give good quality. Private investment and international consultants drive standards at ArmAs, Armenia Wines, Karas Wines, v.gd Zorah.

Georgia Prehistoric winemaking methods, using *qvevris*, its own unique grapes (around 500, though only a handful dominate), and 8000 yrs of unbroken viticultural history set Georgia apart from the rest of the world. Buried earthenware *qvevris*, protected by UNESCO, serve for long fermentations and ageing of both reds and whites. Whites are often skin-macerated, too, known as Kakheti method in Georgia and orange wines elsewhere. Signature varieties are red SAPERAVI, made in many styles from light semi-sweet to powerful, dry, tannic and needing age, and white RKATSITELI (vibrant). White Mtsvane and Kisi gain recognition. Leading producers incl Badagoni, Ch Mukhrani, Dakishvili, GWS, Jakeli Khashmi, Kindzmarauli Marani, Marani (TWC), *Pheasant's Tears*, Schuchmann, *Tsinandali* (a noble domaine restored), Tbilvino.

Moldova 6th in Europe by v'yd area, yet remains little known. With the Crimea, source of the tsar's best wines. Formerly a part of Romania, it inherited its grapes (w) FETEASCĂ ALBĂ, FETEASCĂ REGALĂ, (r) Rară Neagră, FETEASCĂ NEAGRĂ, but also cultivates anything from CHARD to PINOT GR to CAB SAUV to PINOT N. Wines can be excellent value. Not to be missed are red blends Roşu de Purcari (Cab Sauv/MERLOT/MALBEC) and *Negru de Purcari* (Cab Sauv/SAPERAVI/Rară Neagră), plus Icewine Vinăria Purcari is most acclaimed; other gd producers are Asconi, Carpe Diem, Ch Vartely, Cricova (sp), Et Cetera, Fautur, Gitana, Lion Gri, Salcuta, Vinăria Bostavan, Vinăria din Vale.

Russia A decade ago it was next to impossible to convince the Russians to drink their own wines. How things have changed. Russian wines are trendy in the home market; they have yet to make an impression elsewhere. Best conditions for production are by the Black Sea and the River Kuban. International grapes (incl RIES) lead. Harsh climate in the Don Valley, known for indigenous grapes (red Krasnostop, Tsimliansky), requires vines to be buried in winter. Ch le Grand Vostock and Lefkadia have consistent gd quality. Est large producers: Ch Tamagne, Fanagoria, Myskhako, Yubileinaya, Abrau Durso (sp); small: Burnier, Gai-Kodzor.

Ukraine Wine production is mainly spread around the Black Sea. The Crimea is buzzing, driven by small wineries (Uppa Winery, Oleg Repin) that make wines with a sense of place. International grapes are used, also some est local varieties (w Kokur, r Ekim Kara) and hybrids. Massandra, Solnechnaya Dolina, Koktebel continue strong Tsarist tradition of fortified styles. Wines modelled on Champagne are an important/popular heritage: try Artyomovsk Winery, Novy Svet, Zolotara Balka. Quality dry wines are made by Inkerman (Special Res), Guliev Wines, Prince Trubetskoy Winery, Satera (Esse, Kacha Valley), Veles.

United States

Abbreviations used in the text
(*see also* Principal Vineyard/
Viticultural Areas p.245, p.262, p.268):

CA	California
Clark	Clarksburg, CA
Coomb	Coombsville, CA
Mad	Madera, CA
Mend	Mendocino, CA
Mont	Monterey, CA
Oak Knoll	Oak K, CA
San LO	San Luis Obispo, CA
Santa B	Santa Barbera, CA
Santa Cz Mts	Santa Cruz Mountains, CA
Son	Sonoma, CA
ID	Idaho
NJ	New Jersey

OH	Ohio
OR	Oregon
PA	Pennsylvania
PNW	Pacific Northwest
TX	Texas
VA	Virginia
WA	Washington

UNITED STATES

California outweighs all other US wine by so much (the state makes 90% of the whole crop) that other states – and there are many building confident wine-profiles – hardly get a shout. But while they can't match up in volume, we are seeing definite stylistic differences. Oregon for elegant, fresh Pinot Noir; Washington for riper, rounder Merlot and Cabernet Sauvignon; Virginia for concentrated but fresh blends with Viognier, Petit Manseng, Tannat and Petit Verdot (not all at once); New York State for cool-climate Riesling; Texas for a surprising range, from Rhônish wines to good fizz. And that's before we look at the differences within California, which is not just one place. Napa is beginning to see the virtues of balance (at last); coastal Sonoma is taut and tight and there are many, many individual producers of talent and imagination taking risks and defying the luxury-goods image of the state. Sadly the luxury-goods category is too many winemakers' dream.

American Viticultural Areas

I'm not sure AVAs will ever catch on with the public as USPs. They're not exactly (or even approximately) like Appellations Contrôlées. One thing they do is stimulate local feelings and claims for specialness, which is, overall, a gd thing. Federal regulations on appellation of origin in the US were approved in 1977. Do you need to know? There are two categories: 1st is a straightforward political AVA, which can incl an entire state, ie. CA, WA, OR and so on. Individual counties can also be used, ie. Santa B or Son. When the county designation is used, all grapes must come from that county. The 2nd category is a geographical designation, such as Napa V or Will V, within the state. These AVAs are supposed to be based on similarity of soils, weather, etc. In practice, they tend to be inclusive rather than exclusive. Within these AVAs there can be further sub-appellations, eg. the Napa V AVA contains Ruth, Stags L and others. When these geographical designations are used, all grapes must come from that region. A producer who has met the regulatory standards can choose a purely political listing, such as Napa, or a geographical listing, such as Napa V. It will probably be many yrs before the public recognizes the differences, but there is no doubt that some AVAs already fetch hefty premiums.

Arizona

Under-the-radar hip-and-creative vibe drives the scene here. Soils and climate zones similar to Burgundian conditions. High-desert terroir of volcanic rock and limestone soils, gd ripening weather. Wineries incl **Arizona Stronghold** ★ flagship red Ehône blend Nachise and excellent white blend Tazi and VIDAL BLANC dessert wine. **Alcantara V'yds** elegant and earthy reds, esp red blends Confluence IV and Grand Rouge. **Burning Tree Cellars** artisanal, small batch, intense red blends. **Bodega Pierce** estate-grown grapes from family-run winery; gd SAUV BL. **Caduceus Cellars** ★★→★★★ ownership by Alt-rocker Maynard James Keenan gave winery early buzz and wines stepped up too; excellent white blend Dos Ladrones, top reds Sancha, Nagual del Marzo. **Callaghan V'yds** ★★ served at the White House, TANNAT, AGLIANICO and red blends are quality makers; top-rated Caitlin made by vintner's daughter. **Dos Cabezas WineWorks** on the radar for traditional-method sparklers, rosé. **Page Springs Cellars** GSM, other Rhône single-varietal white, esp Dragoon MARSANNE, and blends. **Pillsbury Wine Company** ★ Filmmaker Sam Pillsbury producing excellent dessert wine, PETITE

SIRAH Special Res, v.gd CHENIN BL; callouts to WildChild aromatic blend (w), MALVASIA, GRENACHE and Guns & Kisses SHIRAZ.

California

Destructive, deadly wildfires plagued both N and S CA late in the harvest seasons of 2017 and 2018, tainting the latest-picked grapes in some counties with smoke, incinerating neighbourhoods and taking a great toll. But natural disasters apart, we're in a wave of buyouts of mid-size wineries. In the last 2 yrs, Duckhorn has swallowed up Calera and Kosta Browne; Swanson and Napa legends HEITZ CELLAR, STONY HILL V'YD have also changed hands. GALLO collared The Prisoner, an outlaw brand that put high-end blends on the map. Growers and vintners continue to explore cool, elevated sites in Son Coast, Mend, and Lake County, scaling new heights literally, figuratively. Cab Sauv from P Rob (not just Napa) commands big bucks now, and Santa B continues to prove a prime incubator for visions and experiments. Guiding-star producers have emerged in the Sierras and Lodi. I just love "SoCal" and "NoCal". Like "Potus" and "Flotus". What a language!

Recent vintages

CA is too diverse for simple summaries. There can certainly be differences between the N, Central and S thirds of the state, but no "bad" vintages in over a decade. Some that have been challenging for winemakers have made drinkers happy. Here are some overviews of recent vintages in play, in stores, and what to expect.

2018 Bumper crop of great quality, but smoke tainted some grapes in Lake County, further n. Some Malibu v'yds burned in SoCal.

2017 Catastrophic wildfires in Napa, Son after most grapes picked; quality mostly v.gd.

2016 Gd quality: reds/whites show great freshness, charm.

2015 Dry yr, low yields, but quality surprisingly gd, concentrated.

2014 Despite 3rd year of drought, quality' high.

2013 Another large harvest with excellent quality prospects.

2012 Cab Sauv ounstanding. V. promising for most varieties.

2011 Difficult yr. Those who picked later reported gd Cab Sauv/Pinot N. Zin suffered.

2010 Cool, wet. But some outstanding bottlings, esp Rhône varieties, Zin.

Principal vineyard areas

There are well over 100 AVAs in CA. Below are the key players.

Alexander Valley (Alex V) Son. Warm region in upper Son. Best-known for gd Zin, Cab Sauv on hillsides.

Amador County (Am Co) Warm Sierra County with wealth of old-vine Zin; Rhône grapes also flourish.

Anderson Valley (And V) Mend. Pacific fog and winds follow Navarro River inland; superb Pinot N, Chard, sparkling, v.gd Ries, Gewurz, some stellar Syrah. Wild, stellar potential.

Arroyo Seco Mont. Warm AVA; gd Ries, Merlot, Chard.

Atlas Peak E Napa. Exceptional Cab Sauv, Merlot.

Calistoga (Cal) Warmer n end of Napa V. Red wine territory esp Cab Sauv.

Carneros (Car) Napa, Son. Cool AVA at n tip of SF Bay. Gd Pinot N, Chard; Merlot, Syrah, Cab Sauv on warmer sites. V.gd sparkling.

Coombsville (Coomb) Napa. Cool region nr SF Bay; top Cab Sauv in B'x pattern.

Diamond Mtn Napa. High-elevation vines, outstanding Cab Sauv.

Dry Creek Valley (Dry CV) Son. Outstanding Zin, gd Sauv Bl; gd hillside Cab Sauv and Zin.

Edna Valley (Edna V) San LO. Cool Pacific winds; v.gd Chard.

El Dorado County (El Dor Co) High-altitude inland area surrounding Placerville. Some real talent emerging with Rhône grapes, Zin, Cab and more.

Howell Mountain (Howell Mtn) Napa. Classic Napa Cab Sauv from steep hillside v'yds.

Livermore Valley (Liv V) Alameda. Historic gravelly white-wine district mostly swallowed by suburbs; regaining some standing with new-wave Cab Sauv, Chard.

Mendocino Ridge (Mend Rdg). Emerging region in Mendocino County, dictated by elevation over 365m. Cool, above fog, lean soils.

Mt Veeder Napa. High mtn v'yds for gd Chard, Cab Sauv.

Napa Valley (Napa V) Cab Sauv, Merlot, Cab Fr. Look to sub-AVAs for meaningful terroir-based wines, and mtn areas for most complex, age-worthy.

Oakville (Oak) Napa. Prime Cab Sauv territory on gravelly bench.

Paso Robles (P Rob) San LO. Popular with visitors; Rhône, B'x varieties, reds prominent.

Pritchard Hill (P Hill). E Napa. Elevated, rugged, prime terrritory for Cab Sauv.

Red Hills of Lake County (R Hills) N extension of Mayacama range, huge Cab Sauv potential.

Redwood Valley (Red V) Mend. Warmer inland region; gd Zin, Cab Sauv, Sauv Bl.

Russian River Valley (RRV) Son. Pacific fog lingers; Pinot N, Chard, gd Zin on benchland.

Rutherford (Ruth) Napa. Outstanding Cab Sauv, esp hillside v'yds.

Saint Helena (St H) Napa. Lovely balanced Cab Sauv.

Santa Lucia Highlands (Santa LH) Mont. Higher elevation, s-facing hillsides, great Pinot N, Syrah, Rhônes.

Santa Maria Valley (Santa MV) Santa B. Coastal cool; gd Pinot N, Chard, Viognier.

Sta Rita Hills (Sta RH) Santa B. Excellent Pinot N.

Santa Ynez (Santa Ynz) Santa B. Rhônes (r w), Chard, Sauv Bl best bet.

Sierra Foothills El Dor Co, Am Co, Calaveras County. All improving.

Sonoma Coast (Son Coast) V. cool climate; edgy Pinot N, Chard.

Sonoma Valley (Son V) Gd Chard, v.gd Zin; excellent Cab Sauv from Sonoma Mountain (Son Mtn) sub-AVA. Note Son V is area within Sonoma County.

Spring Mtn Napa. Elevated Cab Sauv, complex soil mixes and exposures.

Stags Leap (Stags L) Napa. Classic red, black fruited Cab Sauv; v.gd Merlot.

Abreu Vineyards Napa V ★★★→★★★★ Supple CAB SAUV-based wines from selected v'yds. Madrona v'yd leads the way with powerful, balanced opening, long, layered finish. V.gd cellar choice for 10–12 yrs.

Acaibo ★★★ B'x-like estate of Gonzague and Claire Lurton in Chalk Hill is called Trinité (CAB SAUV, MERLOT, CAB FR). Acaibo is top wine; a winner. Also seductive *G&C Lurton* blend.

Alban Vineyards Edna V ★★★→★★★★ John Alban, a SYRAH frontiersman, specialist and original Rhône Ranger, still making great wine in EDNA V sweet spot. Top VIOGNIER, GRENACHE too.

Albatross Ridge Mont ★★★ Bowlus family rules high-elevation roost 11km (7 miles) from Pacific nr Carmel. Early CHARDS, PINOT NS fresh and lively, warrant watching.

Alma Rosa Sta RH ★★★→★★★★ Dick Sanford's 2nd act after selling namesake winery. Continuing tradition of refined PINOT N, CHARD, also v.gd rosé.

Andrew Murray Santa B ★★★ Rhônes around the clock, hits keep coming. SYRAH leads pack, but VIOGNIER, ROUSSANNE, fresh GRENACHE BL hits too.

Antica Napa Valley Napa V ★★★ Piero Antinori's mtn SANGIOVESE venture initially flopped, but subsequent lessees improved v'yds, proving potential for fine CAB SAUV, CHARD. Antinori wisely reclaimed property.

A Tribute to Grace N Coast ★★★ Kiwi Angela Osborne's homage to GRENACHE. Fruit from exceptional v'yds, diverse terroirs all over state, none more exciting than 975m (3199ft), mtn-ringed Santa B Highlands.

Au Bon Climat Santa B ★★★ Jim Clendenen made PINOT N, crisp CHARD before it was hip, and advocated the balanced style now trending. Relevant as ever.

Banshee Wines Son Coast ★★★ Growing, scrappy PINOT N-driven label with no v'yds, but gd connections. New well-made single-v'yd wines.

Beaulieu Vineyard ("BV") Napa V ★–★★★ Iconic Georges de Latour Private Res CAB SAUV is back on track, as are other reds. Cheap Coastal Estate brand is fine in a pinch.

Beckmen Vineyards Santa B ★★★ Steve Beckmen's bio Purisma Mtn estate produces formidable SYRAH, GRENACHE and GRENACHE BL. Rhône blend Cuvée le Bec is rightly popular nationwide.

Bedrock Wine Co. Son V ★★–★★★ Morgan Peterson's label is a paean to historic ZIN v'yds, techniques. Great to see wisdom of ages through clear young eyes. Some reds rather wiry.

Zin becoming interesting again: cool vintages, trend toward elegance.

Beringer Napa ★★–★★★★ (Private Res) Big producer of average grocery-level, and exceptional top-rate wines. Private Res CAB SAUV and single-v'yd Cabs are serious, age-worthy. HOWELL MTN Cab Sauv strong, CHARDS now fresher, better. Winemaker Mark Beringer is direct descendant of founder.

Berryessa Gap Vineyards Central V ★★★ Upstart Yolo Co project nr Sacramento making fresh, lightly oaked, Iberian-inspired wines. TEMP dazzling, VERDEJO and DURIF also delicious. Popular in community, beyond.

Bokisch Lodi ★★–★★★ Markus B is CA leader when it comes to Spanish varieties. V.gd TEMPRANILLO leads list backed by superb GRACIANO, ALBARIÑO, flirty rosado.

Bonny Doon Mont ★★★ Randall Grahm's marketing is whimsical, but his wines are serious, more terroir-driven than ever. Vin gris is superb, juicy Clos de Gilroy GRENACHE, Le Cigare Volant Rhône blend always impressive; many tricks up his sleeve.

Bonterra See FETZER.

Brewer Clifton Santa B ★★★ Following recent sale to titan JACKSON FAMILY WINES, OG PINOT N brand back in game: bold, ripe Pinot; CHARD that never fails to impress with balance, verve.

Bronco Wine Company ★–★★ Provocateur, populist Fred Franzia's company, famous for Two-Buck Chuck and scores of other commercial labels.

CADE Napa V Superb wines, CAB SAUV, SAUV BL, from swanky, ultra-modern winery atop HOWELL MTN. Partnership between Getty family, CA Gov. Newsom, GM John Conover.

Cakebread Napa V ★★★ CAB SAUV still has massive cachet with baby boomers. SAUV BL popular, CHARD v.gd; management has diversified direct-to-consumer offerings.

Calera ★★★–★★★★ Josh Jensen, Central Coast PINOT N pioneer, sought property with limestone and altitude, struck gold. Sold to DUCKHORN in 2017, brand in gd hands. Selleck and Jensen v'yds always stylish.

Caymus Napa V ★★★ 12 14 15 One of Napa's foremost international status brands. Special Selection CAB SAUVS, esp iconic, but a bit sweet, sappy. High-quality, dense, doesn't hold forever.

Cedarville Sierra F'hills ★★★ Bootstrappers Jonathan Lachs and Susan Marks have built a powerhouse in the granite-rich Fairplay District of EL DOR CO. Superb wines across board, mostly red. GRENACHE and SYRAH, fine CAB SAUV, ZIN, VIOGNIER.

Chalone Mont ★★★ Historic property, been kicked around a bit, seeking rejuvenation under Foley Family umbrella. Known for subtle CHARD, PINOT N.

Chappellet Napa V ★★★★ P Hill original, great since 60s. Rugged terrain gives v. durable reds. Signature series CAB SAUV superb, affordable. CHARD v.gd; dry CHENIN BL a treat. Still family-owned, also owns SONOMA-LOEB.

Charles Krug Napa V ★★→★★★ Historically important winery made recent comeback, demanding recognition for role in modern Napa V. Late owner Peter Mondavi was Robert's estranged brother. Supple CAB SAUV, crisp, pure SAUV BL.

Chateau Montelena Napa V ★★★ Tons of history, great continuity of ownership and style. Serious, if slightly funky CAB SAUV is cellar-worthy; CHARD holds up well too. Grand stone winery worth a visit.

Chateau St Jean Son V ★★★ Rock of SON V, solid wines on all fronts, but consensus flagship wine for decades has been Cinq Cépages blend of five B'x varieties, reliable and age-worthy.

Chimney Rock Stags L ★★★ →★★★★ 10 12 14 15 Underrated name making best wines ever under steady stewardship of WM Elizabeth Vianna. Tomahawk V'yd CAB SAUV top-notch.

Cliff Lede Stags L ★★★ Excellent CAB SAUVS are big but balanced with tannin, gd acid. Small production Cabs from HOWELL MTN, DIAMOND MTN, OAK; leesy SAUV BL also notable. Owns Fel brand in AND V, SON V.

Clos du Val Napa V ★★★ Stags L classic. New owners slashed production, moved to upscale, estate-based model. Can estate v'yds make cut? CAB SAUV can improve, CAR PINOT N solid, jury still out.

Top Napa Cab Sauv grapes: $20,000/ton. Son: $5000/ton. Both old vines, mtn vyds.

Clos Pegase Napa V ★★★ Look-at-me winery, v.gd MERLOT from Car v'yd, gd CAB SAUV. Wine shares stage with paintings, sculpture.

Cobb Wines Son Coast ★★★ Ross Cobb is makes restrained, natural Son Coast PINOT N, CHARD from select v'yds. Pinots improve with few yrs. Emaline Ann, Coastlands top sites.

Constellation ★→★★★ Massive wine/beer/spirits company, publicly traded. Owns famed CA brands like Clos du Bois, Estancia, Franciscan, RAVENSWOOD, ROBERT MONDAVI, Simi, lately re-focusing on beer and cannabis products.

Continuum St H, Napa V ★★★★ Tim Mondavi broke with family tradition by leaving benchland for heights of P HILL, spared no expense developing extraordinary estate wine from B'x varieties. Among best of NAPA V. Super-expensive.

Copain Cellars And V ★★★ Old World-influenced, classically proportioned wines; recently sold to JACKSON FAMILY. PINOT N is strong suit, esp bright, spicy Kiser v'yd versions. Tous Ensemble line easy-going, balanced wines.

Corison Napa V ★★★★ While many in NAPA V follow $iren call of powerhouse wines for big scores, charming pleasure, Kathy Corison consistently makes elegant, fresh Cabernet, esp fresh, focused Kronos V'yd CAB SAUV.

Cuvaison Car ★★★ Quiet historic property, making great wine yr after yr. Top marks to PINOT N, CHARD from CAR estate; gd SYRAH, CAB SAUV from MT VEEDER. Single Block bottlings incl lovely rosé, v.gd SAUV BL.

Dalla Valle Oak ★★★ 1st-rate hillside estate transitioning to 2nd generation. Maya CAB SAUV is legendary, 2nd Cab Sauv a cult wine, Collina label affordable introduction to luxury Napa.

Daou P Rob ★★★ Elevated estate in Adelaida Dist is driving CABS SAUV in Paso to new heights literally, figuratively. Wines in high demand.

Dashe Cellars Dry CV, N Coast ★★★ RIDGE veteran Mike Dashe makes tasteful, balanced DRY C/ and ALEX V ZIN from urban winery in Oakland. Also terrific old-vine CARIGNANE zesty GRENACHE rosé.

Davis Bynum RRV ★★→★★★ Early RRV PINOT N pioneer still makes big, juicy single-v'yd RRV Pinot and rounded CHARD. Style evolving, more elegant than past.

Dehlinger RRV ★★★ PINOT N specialist still on par after more than four decades. Also v.gd CHARD, SYRAH and balanced CAB SAUV.

DeLoach Winery Son ★★★ Flamboyant maestro JC Boisset saw gd value in this progressive organic, bio-oriented winery making great PINOT N, CHARD, even great dry GEWURZ. Solid investment, if not his sexiest.

Diamond Creek Napa V ★★★★ 06 09 14 Napa Mtn jewel. Prices v. high for age-worthy, minerally CAB SAUV from famous hillside v'yds on DIAMOND MTN. Patience rewarded.

Domaine Carneros Car ★★★→★★★★ Taittinger outpost in Car offering consistently gd bubbly esp vintage Blanc de Blancs Le Rêve. V.gd NV Rosé. Vintage Brut impressive. The Famous Gate PINOT N formidable.

Domaine Chandon Napa V ★★→★★★ Moët outpost in Yountville, top bubbly is v.gd. NV Res Étoile Blanc and Rosé. Pairings and great nibbles on outdoor patio.

Domaine de la Côte Sta RH ★★★ Exacting, Burgundian-style estate PINOT N from coastal reaches of STA RH from former sommelier Rajat Parr and winemaker Sashi Moorman. *See also* SANDHI.

Dominus Estate Napa V ★★★★ Moueix-owned (*see* France) Brilliant winery is dazzling but not open to public. Wines from gravelly bench soils consistently elegant, impressive. Second wine: Napanook, v.gd. Important voice of S NAPA V.

Donum Estate N Coast ★★★→★★★★ Anne Moller-Racke has passionately worked CAR soils since 1981, her aim is true. PINOT N from four sites is focused, generous, complex. Among leaders of region.

Drew Family And V ★★★→★★★★ MEND RDG visionary making minimalist, savage PINOT N from AND V and higher up hills. Look for estate Field Selections Pinot N from Mend Rdg, SYRAH from coastal Valenti V'yd. Seek out.

Dry Creek Vineyard Dry CV ★★★ DRY CV standard-bearer back on A-game. Trustworthy, Loire-inspired, grassy FUMÉ BLANC and other SAUV BL always delicious, reds like CAB SAUV, MERLOT, ZIN all improved lately.

Duckhorn Vineyards ★★★→★★★★ Crowd-pleasing, super-consistent CAB SAUV, MERLOT, esp Three Palms v'yd, gd SAUV BL. Second label Decoy wines better than ever. Also owns Migration brand, Goldeneye in AND V, CALERA and Kosta Browne.

Dunn Vineyards Howell Mtn ★★★→★★★★ Mtn man Randy Dunn stubbornly resisted stampede to jammy, lush CAB SAUV styles, favouring restraint, age-ability. Wines aren't always spotless, but when great, they can last decades.

Dutton-Goldfield RRV ★★★ Steady-handed, classical cool-climate CA PINOT N, CHARD from RRV-based powerhouse grower, not super edgy or risky, maybe a gd thing.

Edna Valley Vineyard Edna V ★★★ Easy-drinking varietals from gentle Central Coast. Lovely, lilting SAUV BL, crisp but tropical CHARD. Impressive SYRAH, gd CAB SAUV from top v'yd.

Ernest Vineyards Son ★★★ Newcomer brings verve, acidity, style to a hip roster of excellent regional and single-v'yd wines with intriguing labels. Complex, racy, drinkable.

Etude Car ★★★→★★★★ Ever-trustworthy brand that always succeeded at making great CAB SAUV, PINOT N under same roof, using same attentive techniques. Now owned by Treasury Co, but legacy stays true. PINOT rosé to die for.

Failla Son Coast ★★★ One of savviest, most talented winemakers in CA, Ehren Jordan effortlessly tempers CA fruit to make savoury, compelling, complex PINOT N, SYRAH, CHARD from cool coastal sites.

Far Niente Napa V ★★★→★★★★ Pioneer of single-v'yd CAB SAUV, CHARD in big, generous, Napa style. Hedonism with soul. Dolce: celebrated dessert wine for sweet tooths.

Fetzer Vineyards N Coast ★★→★★★ Stalwart champion of organic/sustainable viticulture in Mend Co, still gd wines, now owned by Concha y Toro (Chile). Fetzer family members spun off to other sites.

Field Recordings P RO ★★★ Impressively subtle, perceptive wines from P ROB's Andrew Jones. Best are blends Neverland and Barter & Trade, but don't miss Alloy and Fiction, delicious in 500ml cans.

Firestone Santa Y ★★→★★★ Solid SANTA Y brand founded by tyre heirs sold to Foley Estates (2007), still relevant for value wines.

Flowers Vineyard & Winery Son Coast ★★★→★★★★ Extreme SON COAST pioneer (1st CHARD planted 1991 sold in 2009 to Huneeus Co, but wines remain great. Now organic, making pure PINOT N, Chard.

Foppiano Son ★★→★★★ Honest RRV wines loaded with sunny fruit and little pretence. PETITE SIRAH, SAUV BL notable.

Forman Vineyard Napa V ★★★ Ric F is dedicated veteran terroirist making elegant, age-worthy CAB SAUV-based wines from hillside v'yds. Also v.gd CHARD with nod to Chablis.

Fort Ross Vineyard Son Coast ★★★ Dazzling high-elevation estate a stone's-throw from Pacific mete out terrific, savoury PINOT N, zesty CHARD and surprisingly gd PINOTAGE (!).

Freeman RRV, Son Coast ★★★→★★★★ Restrained terroir-driven PINOT N, CHARD from cool-climate Son Coast and RRV, with nod to Burgundy. The Ryo-fu Chard ("cool breeze" in Japanese) is amazing, as is Akiko's Cuvée Pinot N.

Freemark Abbey Napa V ★★★ Classic name claimed by JACKSON FAMILY WINES in 2006, improved. Great values, incl classic single-v'yd bottlings Sycamore and Bosché CAB SAUV.

Freestone Son Coast ★★★ Fine expression of SON COAST. Intense, racy CHARD, PINOT N from vines only few miles from Pacific show gd structure, long finish, esp Chard. Investment by Napa's JOSEPH PHELPS.

Frog's Leap Ruth ★★★ John Williams, pioneer champion of organic and bio viticulture, coaxes best out of valley-floor estate. Supple CAB SAUV and MERLOT, elegant CHARD, popular SAUV BL and great ZIN.

Gallo of Sonoma Son ★★★ Formidable wines drawn from great Son v'yd sources and broader lands, un-fussy as founders would have wanted. Fruit quality speaks loudly.

Gallo Winery, E&J ★→★★★ Gigantic, privately held company, key to development of post-prohibition wine culture in US and beyond. Populist at core, also secretive. Barefoot, Ecco Domani, *Louis Martini*, Turning Leaf and more. *See also* GALLO OF SONOMA.

Gary Farrell RRV, Son Coast ★★★ Namesake vintner sold it yrs ago, but high performance continues. Excellent PINOT N, CHARD from cool-climate v'yds. Rocholi v'yd Chard superb.

Gloria Ferrer Car ★★★→★★★★ Exceptional CA bubbly. A toast to decades-long team of owners, growers and winemakers that made this Freixenet-owned venture extraordinary. All wines v.gd, vintage Royal Cuvée best of all.

Grace Family Vineyard Napa V ★★★★ 05 06 07 09 10 11 12 Stunning CAB SAUV shaped for long ageing. One of few cult wines that might actually be worth price.

Graziano Family Mend ★★★ Best-known for Italian varietals made under Enotria and Monte Volpe labels, namely BARBERA, MONTEPULCIANO, PINOT GRIGIO, SANGIOVESE. Savvy veteran, Champion of Mend Co.

Green and Red Napa V ★★★ Named for colours of its v'yd soils (iron red and green serpentine), Napa classic specializes in old-school, savoury, balanced ZIN. Exotic SAUV BL from new winemaker is a real head-turner.

Grgich Hills Cellars Napa V ★★★ Beret-wearing hall-of-famer Mike Grgich built

> **Wine in the city**
> Urban wineries are bringing tasting rooms to the city, blurring the
> lines between rural tasting rooms and urban wine bars. Be prepared to
> discuss what you're tasting, and don't worry about dirt on your shoes.

one of NAPA V's great early achievers, esp with CHARD, but CAB, delicious ZIN also blossomed. In latter days he adopted bio growing.

Gundlach Bundschu Son V ★★★ CA's oldest family-operated winery. Welcoming vibe makes it popular tasting destination with adventurous concerts for younger set. Best bets MERLOT, CAB SAUV, *Gewurz*.

Hahn Santa LH ★★★ Always overdelivers for $. B'x varieties combine Monterey/Paso fruit to great effect, Meritage often killer. Lucienne PINOT N releases also fantastic.

Hall Napa V ★★★→★★★★ Glitzy ST H winery makes great Napa CAB SAUV, but bewildering variety of selections. Signature offering best, velvety SAUV BL v.gd, MERLOT among best in CA. Also owns WALT coastal PINOT N, CHARD brand.

Hanzell Son V ★★★★ Pinot pioneer of 50s still making CHARD, PINOT N from estate vines. Both reward cellar time. Arguably among best of CA. Sebella Chard, from young vines, all bright, crisp fruit.

Harlan Estate Napa V ★★★★ Concentrated, robust CAB SAUV – one of original cult wines only available via mailing list at luxury prices. Still all those things today.

HdV Wines Car ★★★ Underrated Son gem makes fine complex *Chard* with a honed edge and v.gd PINOT N, from grower Larry Hyde in conjunction with Aubert de Villaine of DRC (*see* France). V.gd CAB SAUV, SYRAH.

Heitz Cellar Napa V ★★★ Once iconic, now steady source of gd CAB SAUV at fair price, sold in 2018. Gd *Sauv Bl*, even GRIGNOLINO.

Hendry Oak K ★★★ Classic, pure, minimalist wines. Est 1939, brambly, distinctive CAB SAUV, ZIN (try Block 28) from cool pocket of valley nr Napa town.

Hess Collection, The Napa V ★★★ Great mtn-top visit with world-class art gallery, also makes gd wine. CAB SAUV from MT VEEDER specialty, esp exceptional 19 Block Cuvée, blockbuster with gd manners.

Hirsch Son Coast ★★★ Pioneer of SON COAST, David Hirsch's v'yd won acclaim growing premium grapes; now family label gets cream of crop from towering Pacific ridge. Lithe PINOT N, breathtaking CHARD.

Honig Napa V ★★★→★★★★ Sustainably grown Napa CAB SAUV and SAUV BL are nationwide benchmarks thanks to consistent quality, hard-working family and team. Top Cab from Bartolucci v'yd in ST H.

Inglenook Oak ★★★★ FF Coppola's Rubicon reclaims original brand with classic central Napa CAB SAUV – balanced, elegant, historic. Also v.gd CHARD, MERLOT.

Iron Horse Vineyards Son ★★★ Amazing selection of 12 vintage bubblies, all wonderfully made. Ocean Res Blanc de Blancs is v.gd, Wedding Cuvée a winner. V.gd CHARD, PINOT N.

Jackson Family Wines ★★→★★★★ Visionary, massive v'yd owner in CA with prime elevated sites, owns hugely popular Kendall-Jackson brand, and high achievers like COPAIN, FREEMARK ABBEY, Lokoya, MATANZAS CREEK, Hartford Family, Verité. Jackson Estate series great for mtn CABS.

Jordan Alex V ★★★ Adjustments in grape sourcing led to brilliant revival of balanced, elegant wines from showcase ALEX V estate. CAB SAUV homage to B'x: and it lasts. Zesty, delicious CHARD.

Joseph Phelps Napa V ★★★→★★★★★ Expensive Napa "First Growth" Insignia, one of CA's 1st ambitious B'x blends, still dependably great, as is Napa CAB SAUV. Most offerings excellent quality, esp SYRAH. *See also* Son brand FREESTONE.

Joseph Swan Son ★★★ Long-time RRV producer of intense old-vine ZIN and single-v'yd PINOT N. Often overlooked Rhône varieties also v.gd, esp SYRAH, ROUSSANNE/MARSANNE blend.

Josh Cellars Napa ★★★ Fast-growing brand from sommelier and wine exececutive, Joseph Carr, culling grapes from Central, NoCal; boring labels, but palatable, resonates with consumers.

Keller Estate Son Coast ★★★ Lump it in with rest of new wave, but one more example of balanced, elegant CA wine coming off the cool coastal regions. PINOT N, CHARD thrilling.

Kenwood Vineyards Son V ★★→★★★ Landmark SON V producer steadily cranks out palatable reds and whites. CAB SAUV leads way, esp Jack London v'yd bottling.

Kistler Vineyards RRV ★★★★ Style of PINOT N and CHARD has adapted over yrs, wines have only improved. Still from a dozen designated v'yds in any given yr. Highly sought.

Kongsgaard Napa ★★★→★★★★ 5th-generation Napanista John Kongsgaard is valley fixture, influencer. *Remarkable Chard* from Judge v'yd in SON, and excellent CAB SAUV, SYRAH.

Korbel ★★ Cheap fizz sold in grocery stores, but all traditional method and remarkably decent for price. And a fun visit by Russian River.

Ladera Napa V ★★★→★★★★ Thesp Stotesbery clan sold their HOWELL MTN winery and set up shop in ST H. Hillside CAB SAUVS, MALBEC great; don't miss superb SAUV BL from NZ winemaker.

Lagier-Meredith Mt Veeder ★★★ Wine from renowned UC Davis vine researcher Carole Meredith and oenologist husband Steve Lagier. Handmade, tiny production of beautiful, pure SYRAH, MONDEUSE, MALBEC and ZIN (whose genetic ancestry in Croatia Meredith famously decoded).

Long & Reed Mend, Napa ★★★ No one in CA has flown CAB FR banner more passionately than L&R's John Skupny. Wines capture perfume, litheness with Napa generosity. Also delicious MEND CHENIN BL.

Larkmead Napa V ★★★★ Historic gravel-laced NAPA V estate revived; *outstanding Cab Sauv*, supple, balanced; bright, delicious SAUV BL. Rare Tocai FRIULANO a delight.

Laurel Glen Son ★★★ Brand has shrunk, but hillside CAB SAUV Counterpoint from SON MTN is high quality and has international clout.

Lewis Cellars Napa V ★★★★ CAB SAUV, CHARDS, SYRAH from former racing driver Randy Lewis can only be described as full-throttle. Unapologetic Napa hedonism at its best.

Lioco N Coast ★★★ Influential minimalist brand champions elegant, subtle PINOT N, CHARD, CARIGNAN. Wines are dependable, restrained, satisfying.

Littorai Son Coast ★★★★ Burgundy-trained Ted Lemon's N Coast P NOIRS, CHARDS are pure, inspiring wines with sense of place. Breathtaking, modern, worth seeking out.

Lohr, J ★★→★★★ Prolific producer of Central Coast makes CAB SAUV, PINOT N, CHARD for balance and gd value. Cuvée Pau and Cuvée St E pay homage to B'x. Don't miss floral red Wildflower VALDIGUIÉ.

Long Meadow Ranch Napa V ★★★→★★★★ Smart, holistic vision incl destination winery with restaurant, cattle on organic farm. Supple, age-worthy CAB SAUV has reached ★★★★ status; lively Graves-style SAUV BL.

Louis M Martini Napa ★★→★★★ Since buying the Martini brand and epic Monte

---

Lightweights

Canned wines are game-changers. They're practical, recyclable, light to transport. They keep white wines and rosés fresh. Catering to park loungers, hikers and campers, they're becoming popular in outdoorsy scenes like CA, OR, WA and CO.

Rosso v'yd, GALLO has restored latter to greatness. Martini brand is solid for workaday CABS, ZINS.

MacPhail Son Coast ★★★ Now owned by HESS COLLECTION, making mostly PINOT N from cool sites in Son and Mend, highlights are Gap's Crown, Sundawg Ridge and Toulouse v'yd bottlings.

MacRostie Son Coast ★★★→★★★★ New tasting room is a modern beauty; screwcapped wines steadily improving. Lovely PINOT N, SYRAH; SON MTN CHARD is absolute delight.

Marimar Torres Estate RRV ★★★ Great Catalan family's CA outpost issues several bottlings of CHARD, PINOT N. V'yds now all bio. Chards are excellent, long-lived, esp Acero (unoaked, *fresh, expressive*). Pinot N from Doña Margarita v'yd nr ocean is intense, rich.

CA winemakers are still absurdly resistant to bottling reds with screwcaps. Why?

Masút Mend ★★★ Newish elevated Eagle Peak property run by Ben and Jake FETZER shines brightly. Estate PINOT NS lithe, ethereal. Will inspire others to explore area.

Matanzas Creek Son ★★★ Exceptional JACKSON FAMILY WINES property in cool Bennett Valley focuses on exceptional MERLOT, SAUV BL from lavender-perfumed estate.

Matthiasson ★★★ Experimental wines have become cult hits. Racy CHARD, elegant CAB SAUV, epic white blend, plus esoterica like RIBOLLA GIALLA, SCHIOPPETINO.

Mayacamas Vineyards Mt Veeder ★★★★ Now owned by Charles Banks, former partner in SCREAMING EAGLE. CA classic has not changed classic big-boned style, only improved. Age-worthy CAB SAUV, CHARD recall great bottles of 70s, 80s.

Melville Sta RH ★★★ Family-run anchor of STA RH, with bold, v.gd CHARD, PINOT N, but estate SYRAH steals show. Worth tasting too is SamSara, Chad and Mary Melville's personal label.

Meritage Basically a B'x blend (r or w). Term invented for CA but has spread. It's a trademark, and users have to belong to The Meritage Alliance. Insider tip: not a French term – it rhymes with "heritage".

Merry Edwards RRV ★★★ One of great CA winemakers, and PINOT N pioneer. Single v'yds from Son always wildly popular. Ripe, rounded, layered, tad sweet by today's standards. Slightly sweet musqué SAUV BL also popular.

Miraflores Sierra F'hills Marco Cappelli left Napa to set up in Sierra Mtns, vinifies subtle, sublime, broad array of wines from an estate and region he rightly believes in.

Mount Eden Vineyards Santa Cz Mts ★★★ V'yd high up in Santa Cz Mts with gorgeous vistas, one of CA's 1st boutique wineries, taut, mineral CAB SAUV, PINOT N, stunning CHARD since 1945.

Mount Veeder Winery Mt Veeder ★★★ Classic CA mtn CAB SAUV, CAB FR grown at 500m (1640ft) on rugged, steep hillsides. Big, dense wines with ripe, integrated tannins.

Mumm Napa Valley Napa V ★★★ Quality bubbly, notably Blanc de Noirs and the pricier, complex DVX single-v'yd left on lees for a few yrs.

Nalle Dry CV ★★★ Family winery crafts elegant, lower alc, claret-style ZIN. Once quite fashionable, still excellent. Great stop nr Healdsburg.

Newton Vineyards Spring Mtn ★★→★★★★ Impressive estate at base of Spring Mtn, now LMVH-owned; wines have improved recently. Look for CAB SAUV and opulent unfiltered CHARD.

Niner Edna V, P Rob Young, ambitious family estate with excellent CAB SAUV from P ROB, great CHARD and ALBARIÑO from EDNA V. CA cuisine restaurant gd for lunch in P Rob countryside.

Obsidian Ridge Lake ★★★ Star of Lake County extension of Mayacamas mtn range. Super CAB SAUV, SYRAH from hillside v'yds at 780m (2559ft), volcanic soils scattered with glassy obsidian. Half Mile Cab 1st rate. Also owns Foseidon brand from CAR.

Ojai Santa B ★★★ In a change of style from big, super-ripe to leaner, finer, former AU BON CLIMAT partner Adam Tolmach making best wines of his career. V.gd PINOT N, CHARD, Rhône styles. SYRAH-based rosé is delicious.

Opus One Oak ★★★ B'x Rothschild family-controlled standard-bearer for fine Napa CAB SAUV in gd form; popular luxury export. Wines designed to cellar 10 yrs+.

Ovid St H ★★★★ Cult-styled, ultra-luxurious organic/Metamorphic estate on Pritchard Hill. Supple B'x blends star turn but SYRAH also fine.

Pahlmeyer Napa V ★★★→★★★★ Jammy, pricey, well-made Napa wines, B'x blend, MERLOT, lavish CHARD most notable. Gd-value second label: Jayson.

Palmina Santa B ★★★ Accurate Italian styles with CA flair, unusual vines. Sumptuous, meant for food. FRIULANO, VERMENTINO, LAGREIN, NEBBIOLO.

Patz & Hall N Coast ★★★★ James Hall is one of CA's most thoughtful winemakers culls fruit from top v'yds from Central Coast to Mend. Style is generous, tasteful, super-reliable. Rio Tony *Chard* v. special, lemony, electric, opulent.

Paul Hobbs N Coast ★★★→★★★★ Globe-trotting winemaker Paul Hobbs still a local hot shot. Bottlings of single-v'yd CAB SAUV, CHARD, PINOT N, SYRAH are top. V.gd-value second label: Crossbarn.

Peay Vineyards San Coast ★★★→★★★★ Standout brand from one of coast's coldest zones. Finesse-driven CHARD, PINOT N, SYRAH superb. Second label, Cep, also v.gd, esp rosé. Weightless, impeccably made wines.

Pedroncelli Son ★★ Old-school Dry CV winery updated v'yds, winery; still makes bright, elbow-bending CAB SAUV, ZIN, solid CHARD. Refreshingly unpretentious.

Smoke taint from forest fires only affects reds: whites get pressed off skins pre-fermentation.

Peter Michael Winery Mont, Son ★★★★ *Sir* Peter Michael to you. Brit in Knight's Valley, Napa. SON COAST sells mostly to restaurants, mailing list. Quality outstanding: rich, dense CHARD, B'x blend Les Pavots, hedonist's PINOT N.

Philip Togni Vineyards Spring Mtn ★★★★ 07 09 10 Living link to classic, early Napa, Togni, a student in B'x of Émile Peynaud, arrived in Napa in 1959. Outstanding estate mtn CAB SAUV-based red, powerful, age-worthy.

Pine Ridge Napa V ★★★ Outstanding CAB SAUV made from several Napa v'yds. Estate STAGS L bottling is silky and graceful. Lively CHENIN BL/VIOGNIER blend an innovative classic.

Pisoni Vineyards Santa LH ★★★ Family winery in SANTA LH became synonymous with PINOT N explosion and big, jammy wines. Still, Pinot N is and always was well made and remains popular.

Presqu'ile Sant, MV ★★★ New Central Coast winery, elegantly styled PINOT N, SYRAH. On watch list.

Quintessa Ruth ★★★★ Magnificent estate at heart of Napa V owned by Chilean international player Augustin Huneeus makes a single wine; superb, refined B'x blend justifies triple-digit price.

Qupé Santa B ★★★→★★★★ One of original SYRAH champions, brilliant range of Rhônes, esp X Block, from one of CA's oldest v'yds. Hillside Estate also epic; try impeccable MARSANNE, ROUSSANNE. Central Coast SYRAH unbeatable for $.

Ravenswood ★★ Owned by CONSTELLATION, but single-v'yd ZINS still come from remarkable sites like Teldeschi, Bedrock, Old Hill. "No wimpy wines" motto still applies.

Red Car Son Coast ★★★ Hip, artsy estate-based label making precise CHARD, lacy, fruit-forward PINOT N and killer rosé.

Ridge N Coast, Santa Cz Mts ★★★★ Saintly founder Paul Draper has retired, but his spirit lives on. Majestic, legendary, age-worthy estate Montebello CAB SAUV is always superb. Outstanding single-v'yd field-blend ZINS are special. Don't overlook sublime, minerally CHARD.

Robert Mondavi ★★→★★★ Owned by CONSTELLATION since 2004, many wines could be better; changing of winemaking guard appears at hand. Home To Kalon v'yd, still a great site; potential there.

Robert Sinskey Vineyards Car ★★★ Great, idiosyncratic Napa estate favouring balance, restraint. Great CAB SAUV and CAR PINOT N. Racy Abraxas white blend and Pinot rosé excellent.

Rodney Strong Son ★★★ Strong indeed, across the board, from 14 significant v'yds. Sinewy coastal PINOT N, CHARD, super ALEX V CAB SAUV from Alexander's Crown, Rockaway V'yds. Also owns DAVIS BYNUM.

Roederer Estate And V ★★★★ Adventurous Champagne Roederer venture brought glamour to AND V. Finesse, class off the charts, esp luxury cuvée L'Ermitage. Also makes Scharffenberger fizz. Domaine Anderson PINOT NS also excellent.

Saintsbury Car ★★★ Regional pioneer and benchmark still making v.gd, highly relevant PINOT N, CHARD, yummy Vincent Van Gris rosé.

St-Supéry Napa ★★★ Bought by owners of Chanel (and Ch Rausan-Ségla, B'x), but some continuity of talent. Tasteful, balanced Virtú (w) and Élu (r) B'x blends and SAUV BL, esp Dollarhide Ranch, thrilling.

Sandhi Sta RH ★★★ *See* DOMAINE DE LA CÔTE. Same winemaking team, grapes bought from top local v'yds. Must for lovers of white Burg: racy, intense CHARD, gd PINOT N.

Schramsberg Napa V ★★★★ Best bubbles in CA? Exacting quality in every cuvée esp luxurious J Schram and Blanc de Noirs. Great tours of historic caves.

Screaming Eagle Napa V, Oak ★★★★ Original "cult" CAB SAUV, famously ripe, rare, and four-figures *cher*. Highly collectible, and now edging towards freshness. Also limited production SAUV BL. Sister winery is Jonata.

Scribe Son ★★★ Hipster gentleman-farmer aesthetic a hit with younger set. Tasting room pours well-made esoterica like SYLVANER, ST-LAURENT and PINOT N rosé all day.

Sea Smoke Sta RH ★★★ Cultish, high-end PINOT N and CHARD estate-driven winery attempting a fine balance between opulence and freshness, mostly tipping in opulent direction.

Seghesio Son ★★★ Classic Sonoma ZINS. Rich, strong, but graceful. Old Vine bottling benchmark for price range. Rockpile Zin also dynamite.

Selene Napa V ★★★ Lovely B'x reds, whites from prominent consulting winemaker Mia Klein, incl great CAB FR, Hyde v'yd SAUV BL Musqué.

Sequoia Grove Napa V ★★★ Rutherford staple for more than 30 yrs, still v.gd. Flagship Cambium is stunning CAB BLEND, balanced, age-worthy. CHARD v.gd.

Shafer Vineyards Napa V ★★★→★★★★★ Prestigious, widely-respected brand. Hillside Select CAB SAUV a lavish CA classic, Relentless SYRAH/PETITE SIRAH blend powerful, clever. One Point Five a beaut. Fine MERLOT and CHARD sourced from nearby Car.

Shannon Ridge Lake ★★★ Ambitious, large, estate in elevated High Valley. Honest, well-made wines that over deliver for the $. Fast-growing brand, incl second label Vigilance.

Silverado Vineyards Stags L ★★★ V'yds owned by Walt Disney descendants since 1976, has kept up with times. Single-v'yd Solo CAB SAUV is powerful, smooth; new release of Geo B'x blend from COOMB AVA is dark, dense. *Cab Fr* v.gd.

Silver Oak Alex V, Napa V ★★★ So trendy in 90s that sommeliers in 2000s turned backs on it. NAPA V and ALEX V CABS still made in juicy, supple style.

Smith-Madrone Spring Mtn ★★★ Serious, purist producer, daring to dry farm in lean mtn soils. Superb RIES with brilliant floral briskness. Also powerful CAB SAUV from high-elevation v'yd.

> **Hold the chocolate milk**
> A lot of low-end wine has been plagued by the use of cheapo wood flavourings imitating the flavours of ageing in proper barrels, making wines taste like chocolate milk or vanilla latte. Signs are that the use of oak substitutes like sawdust and chips is waning.

Sonoma-Cutrer Vineyards Son ★★★ Flagship CHARD a classic, still by glass at restaurants all over country, rich but zesty and bright. Owsley PINOT N from RRV lush with black fruit.

Sonoma-Loeb Car, RRV ★★★ Precise, cool-climate PINOT N, CHARD. Made by CHAPPELLET's winemaker at its winery for 20 yrs, so 2011 sale to Napa brand made sense.

Spottswoode St H ★★★★ Crown jewel of ST H, sublime estate always chasing perfection. CAB SAUV pricey, not bulky; worth it. Value Lyndenhurst Cab Sauv, Spottswoode SAUV BL delightful.

Spring Mountain Vineyard Spring Mtn ★★★★ Top-notch estate delivers site-driven, age-worthy mtn wines. Signature Elivette B'x blend layered and sturdy, Estate CAB SAUV v.gd, estate SAUV BL is Rubenesque treat.

Staglin Family Vineyard Ruth ★★★★ Perennial 1st-class, potent CAB SAUV from family-owned estate. Also powerful, complex Salus CHARD.

Stag's Leap Wine Cellars Stags L ★★★ →★★★★ Gd to see quality maintained since founder Winiarski sold to large corp. Flagships still silky, seductive CABS (top-of-line Cask 23, Fay, SLV).

Sterling Napa V ★★ A fun visit; take aerial tram to tasting room with 90m (295ft)-high view of valley.

Stony Hill Vineyard Spring Mtn ★★★★ Revered NAPA V estate mostly famous for its whites, esp minerally, ageable CHARD, plus RIES, GEWURZ. Sold to LONG MEADOW RANCH in 2018. Expect to hold steady.

Sutter Home *See* TRINCHERO FAMILY ESTATES.

Tablas Creek P Rob ★★★ Joint venture between Beaucastel (*see* France) and importer Robert Haas with vine cuttings from Châteauneuf. Red and white blends the way to go: Patelin, Côtes de Tablas and Esprit lines all 1st rate.

Terre Rouge / Easton Sierra F'hills ★★★ Two-faced: traditional (old vine) ZIN (Easton) and Rhône variety (Terre Rouge). Mostly reds. Affordable Tete-a-tete blend.

Thomas Fogarty Santa Cz Mts ★★★ Spark and energy here, from focused PINOT N to zesty GEWURZ, CHARD. Do not overlook.

Trefethen Family Vineyards Oak K ★★★ Historic family winery in cool zone makes elegant CAB SAUV, MERLOT, crisp long-living CHARD and refreshing, food-friendly Napa Ries. A steady fave.

Trinchero Family Estates ★ →★★★ Foundational Napa producer with bewildering number of labels; ahead of pack is affordable, v. pleasing CAB SAUV under Napa Wine Company label.

Truchard Car ★★★ Look for zesty CHARD, focused MERLOT, and slightly rustic, earthy PINOT N from this storied CAR producer.

Turley Wine Cellars N Coast ★★★★ Selling mostly to mailing list, so rare in market. Known for big, brambly old-vine ZIN from century-old v'yds. True CA treasures.

Unti Dry CV ★ ★ Wines start in DRY CV v'yds; grower always refining range of luscious, tasty SYRAH, GRENACHE, ZIN, BARBERA.

Viader Estate Howell Mtn ★★★★ Ripe, powerful expression of HOWELL MTN still turns heads. "V" is marvellous B'x blend based on PETIT VERDOT, CAB FR.

Vineyard 29 Napa V ★★★ Top winemaker Philippe Melka's fingerprints all over gorgeous CABS at maturing estate venture. Gd but oaky SAUV BL.

Vino Noceto Sierra F'hills ★★★ Among best SANGIOVESE in state, star of Cal-Ital movement in Sierras and refreshingly homey stalwart.

Volker Eisele Family Estate Napa V ★★★ Special site tucked way back in Napa's Chiles Valley continues to overdeliver with CAB s and more. Looking for an adventure? Chiles V thousand-bend road trip.

Wente Vineyards ★★ ··★★★ Oldest continuing family winery in CA makes better whites than reds. Outstanding gravel-grown SAUV BL leads way.

Wind Gap Son Coast ★★★ ··★★★★ Pax Mahle one of CA's most talented winemakers, esp in cool climates. PINOT N, CHARD v.gd, in best vintages SON COAST SYRAH capable of genius.

Wine Group, The Central V ★ By volume, world's 2nd-largest wine producer; budget brands like Almaden, Big House, Concannon, Cupcake, Glen Ellen.

Colorado

Some of highest-altitude v'yds in nation and a climate similar to Rhône, Central Coast and Mendoza. CAB FR a rising star. AVAs incl Grand Valley and West Elks. Wineries on radar: **Bookcliff** ★★ excellent MALBEC, SYRAH, Res Cab Fr, CAB SAUV, VIOGNIER. **Boulder Creek** ★ Ensemble B'x blend, and Crescendo blend with Souzao. **Carlson** ★ unpretentious winery working with GEWURZ, RIES and LEMBERGER (r); well-made, value-priced wines, **Colterris** uses 100% locally grown grapes; B'x style. **Creekside** v.gd Robusto blend aged in Appalachian oak, gd PETIT VERDOT. **Grande River** focus on traditional B'x, Rhône styles, Lavande Vin Blanc is SEM/Viognier infused with lavender. **Guy Drew** ★★★ ambitious whites incl Viognier, dry Ries, unoaked CHARD; interesting Baco Noir. **Infinite Monkey Theorem** ★ hip, urban winery marching to its own beat. V.gd red blend, 100th Monkey, 1st traditional-method sparkling in CO with Grand Valley ALBARIÑO. **Jack Rabbit Hill** ★ only certified bio winery in state, notable Ries. **Snowy Peaks (Grande Valley)** v.high-altitude vines, Rhône varieties; Oso blends use hybrid grapes. **Sutcliffe** v.gd Cab Fr, Chard, MERLOT. **Turquoise Mesa** ★ award-winning Syrah, FUMÉ BLANC. **Two Rivers** ★ excellent Cab Sauv, v.gd Chard, Ries and Port-style. **Whitewater Hill V'yds** exceptional red blend Ethereal. **Winery at Holy Cross** ★ red-driven historic winery; award-winning Res Merlot, blend Sangre de Cristo Nouveau.

Georgia

Expanding region; 1st AVA Dahlonega Plateau approved 2018; wines shaping up, incl CHARD, CABS SAUV/FR; MERLOT, TANNAT, TOURIGA N, also native muscadine. Top estates: **Ch Élan**, **Crane Creek**, **Engelheim**, **Frogtown**, **Habersham**, **Sharp Mtn**, **Stonewall Creek**, **Three Sisters**, **Tiger Mtn**, **Wolf Mtn**, **Yonah Mtn**.

Idaho

Though there's long grape-growing history here, there are only 53 wineries and 1300 acres of v'yds. Early CHARDS were encouraging. Now results point to SYRAH as variety to keep eye on.

Cinder Wines Snake RV ★★ Former Ste Michelle (WA) assistant winemaker Melanie Krause shown knack for high-quality SYRAH, RIES. VIOGNIER also v.gd.

Coiled Snake RV ★★ One of state's top producers, making tasty dry RIES, SYRAH.

Ste Chapelle Snake RV ★ ID's 1st and largest winery, owned by WA-based Precept Wines. Dry and off-dry style reds and whites, incl quaffable RIES and SAUV BL.

Maryland (MD)

East Shore sandy soils, hills of Garrett and Allegheny mtns, blue-crab-rich Chesapeake Bay checks freezing winters, stifling summers. Gd sources for MD versions of B'x grapes like PETIT VERDOT, SAUV BL, MERLOT; ALBARIÑO; French hybrid VIDAL BLANC: 1st post-Prohibition winery **Boordy** (*Sun*-journalist founded), **Black Ankle**, **Bordeleau**, **Dodon**, **Linganore**, **Links Bridge**, **Elk Run** (PINOT N too), **Old Westminster** (natural wine style).

Michigan (MI)

Dubbed the "Third Coast" due to huge Lake Michigan. Five AVAs, two downstate, three up n; 3050 acres. Production up 47% over past few yrs; 148 wineries but many distracted by cider, fruit wine. Three PINOTS do well, also RIES, CHARD, CAB FR, MERLOT. Best: **2 Lads**, **Bel Lago** (incl AUXERROIS), **Hawthorne V'yds** (Old Mission Peninsula Pinot N, Cab Fr, Pinot Gr), **Left Foot Charley**, **Mari**, **Mawby** (all-sparkling, incl traditional-method Chard, spontaneous-fermentation blends), **Nathaniel Rose** (single-v'yd focus), **Rove Estate** (fresh whites).

Most MI v'yds within 40km (25 miles) of Lake Michigan; extends growing season up to 4 wks.

Missouri

The University of Missouri has a new experimental winery to test techniques and grape varieties in local conditions, which are warm and humid. Best so far: Chambourcin, SEYVAL BL, VIDAL, Vignoles (sweet and dry). **Stone Hill** in Hermann produces v.gd Chardonel (frost-hardy hybrid, Seyval Bl x CHARD), Norton and gd Seyval Bl, Vidal; **Hermannhof** is notable for Vignoles, Chardonel, Norton. Also: **Adam Puchta** for fortifieds and Norton, Vignoles, Vidal; **Augusta Winery** for Chambourcin, Chardonel, Icewine; **Les Bourgeois** for SYRAH, Norton, Chardonel, Montelle, v.gd Cynthiana, Chambourcin; **Mount Pleasant** in Augusta for rich fortified and Norton; **St James** for Vignoles, Seyval, Norton.

Nevada

Limited commercial wineries. **Churchill V'yds** in high-desert region producing gd SEM/CHARD; all Nevada-grown grapes. **Pahrump Valley** oldest winery here, v.gd PRIMITIVO, ZIN; Nevada Ridge signature label.

New Jersey

Much improvement; a few wineries among e US's best. Three AVAs: B'x varieties in S Jersey's flat gravelly Outer Coast Plain; limestone, granite hills in n's Warren Hills for elegant PINOT N, BLAUFRÄNKISCH, SYRAH, aromatic RIES, GRÜNER V, GEWURZ; Central Delaware Valley shared with PA. Gd fruit sometimes marred by heavy-handed makers. Quality ranks incl **Mount Salem** (all Austrian varieties, wild ferment, min sulphur), **Unionville V'yds**, **William Heritage** (v.gd sparkling), **White Horse**, **Working Dog**.

Chambourcin, French-US hybrid from Loire, is grown for herbal, juicy reds throughout NJ

Alba ★★★ 14 15 16 Exceptional CHARD, gd RIES, GEWURZ; one of largest PINOT N plantings on E Coast.

Beneduce Vineyards ★★★ Family estate winery founded by Cornell-trained terroir-focused wine-grower. Serious PINOT N, BLAUFRÄNKISCH, GEWURZ also made as orange wine, RIES in passito style too, CHARD.

New Mexico

High-altitude v'yds and diurnal variations give wines crisp character and lower alc. French-hybrid grape varieties; sparkling wines excellent. **Black Mesa ★★** red-driven winery, but has award-winning blend of Traminette, SEYVAL grapes.

Casa Abril family-owned, Spanish and Argentine varieties. **Gruet ★★★** still the regional standard for sparkling, blending Wash State and Lodi, CA fruit; esp Blanc de Noirs, Brut rosé, Sauvage; v.gd CHARD, PINOT N. **La Chiripada ★** oldest winery in state, 20+ varieties; top-notch Res CAB SAUV. **Noisy Water ★★** ambitious winery; gd Absolution CAB/MERLOT blend; new unfiltered Dirty brand. **Vivác ★★** excellent red blends Divino (Italian grapes), Diavolo (French), v.gd Port-style Amante.

New York (NY)

US's 3rd-largest producer. Ten AVAs, winter freeze and hybrids (some as serious, dry wine) throughout; lakes, rivers, ocean influence are crucial for vinifera relief. Climate like N Europe's. 113km (70 miles) from NYC: maritime Long Island (Long I) and colder Hudson Valley (Hudson V). Largest is remote Finger Lakes (Finger L). Farther n and w: Champlain Valley, Niagara Escarpment, Lake Erie.

21 Brix ★★ Exceptional estate on Lake Erie with 1st-rate RIES, CHARD, GEWURZ, GRÜNER V; aromatic BLAUFRÄNKISCH, CAB SAUV. Serious Noiret. VIDAL Blanc Icewine.

Anthony Road Finger L **★★★** Gold Standard dry and semi-dry RIES (some of best in US), also outstanding GEWURZ, GRÜNER V, PINOT GR, CAB FR, MERLOT, PINOT N. New styles, same quality: skin-contact CHARD, RIES, barrel-fermented Pinot Gr, Gewurz.

Bedell Long I **★★★** Leading LONG I estate since 1980. Uses native yeasts; maritime climate shows in powerful, saline wines: Musée (MERLOT/PETIT VERDOT/MALBEC) is top label; varietal bottlings of same, also SYRAH. VIOGNIER, SAUV BL, CHARD blended and varietal. Artist labels, eg. April Gornik, Chuck Close.

Cornell Uni has experimental lab where Long I splits into N Fork, Hamptons. Serious research.

Benmarl Winery Hudson V Pioneer overlooking Hudson River: New York Farm Winery license no.1. Serious, dry, estate Baco Noir, SEYVAL BL. Gd CAB FR, MERLOT, SAUV BL, Blanc de Blancs. New plantings: BLAUFRÄNKISCH, MUSCAT Ottonel, SAPERAVI.

Bloomer Creek Finger L **★★★** Min-intervention winemaking. Tanzen Dame RIES line in vintage-variance, late-harvest, or EDELZWICKER style; White Horse label is CAB FR/MERLOT blend.

Boundary Breaks Finger L **★★★** Top-notch dry to dessert RIES, lush and acid-driven. Serious GEWURZ and red B'x-style CAB-based blends.

Channing Daughters Long I **★★★** Deliciously experimental wines from South Fork producer, incl BLAUFRÄNKISCH, DORNFELDER, LAGREIN, MALVASIA, RIBOLLA GIALLA, and a range of *pétillants*, plus CAB FR, MERLOT, SYRAH. CHARD made masterfully and playfully, in styles from strong oak influence to hands-off, skin-macerated.

Element Winery Finger L **★★** Christopher Bates MS explores terroir-driven CHARD, RIES, CAB FR, LEMBERGER, PINOT N, SYRAH. Small production, cult status.

Fjord Hudson V **★★** 2nd-generation linked to BENMARL WINERY. V.gd, floral ALBARIÑO; gd CAB FR (some spontaneous fermentation), rosé, CHARD (still and Icewine).

Fox Run Finger L **★★★** Benchmark RIES. One of Seneca's top growers. CHARD, CAB FR, PINOT N, LEMBERGER, also for rosé. Café overlooking lake uses local ingredients incl from winery's veg garden.

Frank, Dr. Konstantin (Vinifera Wine Cellars) Finger L **★★★★** Vinifera pioneer in Finger L, still one of US's leading RIES producers. Also outstanding GEWURZ, GRÜNER V, PINOT GR, RKATSITELI, SAPERAVI, old-vine PINOT N, plus impeccable Ch Frank sparkling. Est 1961, 4th generation now involved.

Heart & Hands Finger L **★★★** Small production, excellent, and just two grapes: RIES, PINOT N in limestone (rare in Finger L), on shores of Cayuga Lake. Classic cool-climate white, rosé; delicate red.

The State (and regions) of New York
NY's heightened terroir focus and naturally low-alc, high-acid wines
are grabbing international attention. Quality is rising exponentially in
Finger L (sun hours equal to Napa's, squeezed into 190 days; RIES and
CAB FR rule; believers in PINOT N proven right when planting on banks of
deep Lake Seneca) and steadily in **Hudson V** (US's oldest wine region,
state's shortest season, most complex soils). On summer-destination
Long I (longest growing season, est producers, sandy-loam soil,
surrounded by ocean, bay, Long I Sound) payoffs for battling humidity,
high-priced land incl CHANNING DAUGHTERS' daring range in Hamptons;
SPARKLING POINT's Champagne methods and grapes in North F soils.
Both **Champlain Valley** (sparkling, Icewine) and **Niagara Escarpment**
(fast-growing area on NY-rare limestone) are ancient lake beds. In
Lake Erie region: a little CHARD, RIES in sea of grape-juice-bound Concord.

Hermann J Wiemer Finger L ★★★ Est 1979 by German winemaker. One of best RIE
producers in US; three main v'yds, incl bio original. Also fine CHARD, GEWURZ
CAB FR, PINOT N and superlative fizz. Owns fantastic Standing Stone (SAPERAVI) too

Keuka Lake Vineyards Finger L ★★★ Vivacious RIES incl Falling Man from steep
slopes on Keuka Lake. V.gd CAB FR. Hybrids incl Vignoles and old-vine Alsatian
Leon Millot (cult bottles).

Lakewood Finger L ★★★ Benchmark CAB FR. High-quality GEWURZ, RIES, PINOT N too.

Lamoreaux Landing Finger L ★★★ Excellent RIES, *Chard*, GEWURZ, Icewine, plu
CAB FR, MERLOT, PINOT N. Library wines available. Greek Revival building
overlooks Lake Seneca.

Liten Buffel ★★ Estate PINOT N, SYRAH, RIES planted on long slope from escarpment to
ancient lake ridge. Wild yeasts, no filtering, neutral oak. Noble rot in some yrs.

Macari Long I, North F ★★★ Cliff-top estate on Long I Sound. Top-notch SAUV B
Premium reds CAB FR, MERLOT, B'x-style blends, incl Alexandra label in best
vintages. Bio-minded growing incl estate cows, pigs, compost.

McCall Long I, North F ★★★ Top PINOT N, incl single-v'yd, Res. Gd CAB FR, CHARD
Fresh SAUV BL. Red blends incl MERLOT and other B'x varieties. Also home to
Charolais cattle.

McGregor Finger L ★★ On scenic Keuka Lake. Estate-grown Caucasus natives
Sereksiya Charni, SAPERAVI, RKATSITELI, Sereksiya Rosé. Gd RIES, PINOT N, B'x blend
Blanc de Blancs/Noir.

Martha Clara Long I, North F ★★★ Larger producer thriving on ex-potato farm. V.g
MERLOT, MALBEC, CHARD, PINOT GR, SAUV BL.

Millbrook Hudson V ★★★ Founded in 80s on old dairy farm; shale hills. 1st to grow
vinifera in Hudson V; estate RIES, CHARD, PINOT N. single-v'yd Tocai (FRIULANO)
CAB FR. Acidity lets reds age a few yrs.

Paumanok Long I ★★★ Succulent CHENIN BL, excellent red B'x-style blends
fine CHARD (barrel-ferm), RIES, MERLOT. Minimalist-label spontaneous ferm, littl
to no sulphur for some, incl CAB SAUV.

Beaujolais-style carbonic maceration is big in NY wineries: enhanced fruit
crunchy acidity.

Ravines Finger L ★★★ Seneca *inspired Ries*, GEWURZ, CAB FR, PINOT N, plus sparklin
CHARD/Pinot N blend. Sophisticated bistro.

Red Newt Finger L ★★★ Seneca estate; RIES-focused for top US quality. Elegan
GEWURZ, PINOT GR; gd CAB FR, MERLOT, PINOT N. Winery bistro.

Red Tail Ridge Finger L ★★★ Seneca. Superb CHARD, RIES, PINOT N, TEROLDEGO. Als
DORNFELDER, LEMBERGER and sparkling.

Sheldrake Point Finger L ★★ Exuberant cool-climate, fresh earthy B'x blends, gd RIES, GEWURZ, PINOT GR.

Shinn Estate Long I ★★★ Lively SAUV BL, earthy CAB FR, SEM, fine MERLOT, crisp Blanc de Blancs. Bio. Attractive farmhouse inn.

What is perfect for cold snowy winters, short hot summers? Georgian Saperavi, Rkatsiteli, obviously.

Sparkling Pointe Long I ★★★ Convincing *fizz*; French winemaker, trad Champagne grapes in Long I loam. Traditional-method, of course. Sparkling RIES, just as serious, in the works.

Stoutridge Vineyard Hudson V ★★ Serious about Hudson V terroir through hybrids, sourced within 2km (1.5 miles) of winery, vinified dry, sold after ageing min 6 yrs: earthy unfined/filtered Noiret, Niagara, SEYVAL BL. CAB FR (rosé) is lone vinifera.

Whitecliff Hudson V ★★ Site-and-soils-conscious, incl ex-cherry orchard, quartz-rich historic Olana slope for v.gd GAMAY (Res), CAB FR. Peachy, stony CHARD. PINOT N from limestone.

Wölffer Estate Long I ★★★ Premier S Fork estate and destination; German-born winemaker's classical approach results in quality CHARD, MERLOT, CAB SAUV. Gd rosé set off Hamptons vacationers' craze for the stuff.

North Carolina (NC)

Long hot summers; dry or rainy yrs. Mild winters can turn frigid. Three AVAs incl Yadkin Valley. Blue Ridge mtns offer High Country elevation or Piedmont hills for best quality; unremarkable v'yds clustered on flatlands where tobacco once grew. Lots of native muscadine grape Scuppernong (traditional se US wine). Gd CAB FR, MERLOT, CHARD, VIOGNIER: **Junius Lindsay** (also SYRAH), **McRitchie** (dry MUSCAT too), **RayLen**, **Shelton**. For Italian varieties like SANGIOVESE, MONTEPULCIANO: **Raffaldini**.

Historic NC Biltmore estate planted hybrids, vinifera in 70s: happy customers, more wineries.

Ohio

Lake Erie helps with freezing winters. Five AVAs. CHARD, RIES, PINOT N, PINOT GR, B'x varieties, MÜLLER-T, DOLCETTO. **Debonne**, family-run **Ferrante** (also GRÜNER V, GEWURZ), **Firelands** (Dolcetto rosé, MERLOT), **Harpersfield** (KERNER/RIES/MUSCAT OTTONEL blend), **Laurentia** (concrete-tank whites), **Markko** (late-harvest Chard), **M Cellars** (RKATSITELI, Meritage).

Mid-1800s OH made one-third of US wine, esp Sparkling Catawba, which CA tried, and failed, to copy.

Oklahoma

One AVA, Ozark Mtn. Mostly reds, esp CAB SAUV. **Clauren Ridge** gd Meritage, PETITE SIRAH, VIOGNIER. For better or worse, now on the canned wine trend: **Sand Hill** Norton and Cab Sauv; **Stable Ridge** v.gd Bedlam CHARD; **The Range Winery** 13 varieties of OK grapes; gd white blend Jackwagon.

Oregon

If you want warmth and dryness, OR can provide it, in the sw. If you want mtns, and desert too, they're in the e. If you want a maritime climate, there's plenty of that too: OR is not just one thing, though PINOT N from here gets better and better, in spite of wildfires in 2017 and 2018 that made everyone worry about potential smoke damage. Big companies as well as sommelier-led projects from CA continue to invest in v'yds and wineries; notably Foley Family Wines, Coppola Family Wines, Jackson Family Wines, Failla and Evening Land alums at Lingua Franca and Lavinea.

Principal viticultural areas

Southern Oregon (S OR) encompasses much of w OR, s of Will V, incl sub-AVAs Rogue (Rog V), Applegate (App V) and Umpqua (Um V) Valleys. Amid expansive experimentation, Albariño, Gewurz, Grüner V, Viognier, Cab Fr, Syrah and Tempranillo are standouts.

Willamette Valley (Will V) has sub-AVAs incl Dundee Hills (Dun H), Chehalem Mts, Ribbon Ridge (Rib R), Yamhill-Carlton (Y-Car), Eola-Amity Hills (E-A Hills) and McMinnville (McM); four more due soon. Chard, Pinot Bl/Gr and Ries also excel here. Four new AVAs in Will V are expected: Laurelwood District covers the n face of the existing Chehalem Mts AVA; the name refers to a particular soil type. Neighbouring Tualatin Hills is w of Portland, while Lower Long Tom is nw of Eugene and will be the most s AVA in the valley. Mount Pisgah, Polk County will incl Freedom Hill v'yd, a prestigious site with dozens of clients. And a fifth has only just been been approved – the Van Duzer Corridor, due w of the Eola-Amity Hills AVA. It is based upon the impact of ocean air rushing through a low spot in the coastal mtns.

Rocks District of Milton-Freewater (Walla Walla Valley [Walla]) entirely in OR produces cult wines from Cayuse and Syrah from others.

Abacela Um V ★★★ 14' 15 16 Planted 1st TEMPRANILLO in US; Barrel Select v.gd, Fiesta and NV Vintner's Blend for value. Deep, potent Res MALBEC, SYRAH, snappy ALBARIÑO.

Adelsheim Will V ★★★ 14' 15' 16 Founders retired, still making reliable PINOT N, CHARD. Brown Label single-v'yd Pinot N, Caitlin's Res CHARD best.

Alloro Chehalem Mts ★★★ 14' 15' 16 Beautiful site with elegant PINOT N, CHARD. Riservata, Justina age v. well.

Andrew Rich Will V ★★ 14' 15' 16 Fine value Prelude PINOT N and OR's best *Sauv Bl*.

Archery Summit Dun H ★★★★ 14' 15' 16 Winemaker change at this top-tier Dun H producer. Try CHARD, and Arcus, Red Hills, Looney and Summit for PINOT N, exotic Ab Ovo PINOT GR fermented in concrete egg.

Argyle Will V ★★ → ★★★ V.gd vintage *bubbly* and Brut Rosé; Master Series CHARD, RIES better than spotty PINOT NS.

A to Z Wineworks S OR ★★ 16' 17 Value-priced, soundly made and widely available CHARD, RIES, PINOT GR, PINOT N principally sourced from s OR.

Ayoub Dun H ★★★ → ★★★★ 14' 15 16 Brilliant handling of oak, superb v'yd sources for well-defined, cult-quality CHARD, PINOT N.

Beaux Frères Rib R ★★★ → ★★★★ Robert Parker co-founded this winery, recently sold to Maisons & Domaines Henriot. No expansion plans; winemaker Mike Etzel now focused on v.gd Sequitur label.

Bergström Rib R ★★★★ 14' 15' 16 Elegant, powerful PINOT N, CHARD. Sigrid Chard ethereal, Old Stones Chard v.gd value. Bergström, Shea, Temperance Hill best Pinot N.

Bethel Heights E-A Hills ★★★ → ★★★★ 14' 15' 16 Mid-priced Aeolian, Res Casteel PINOT N dense, dark, muscular. Old-vine CHARD, occasional PINOT BL v.gd.

Big Table Farm Will V ★★★ 14' 15' 16 Hand-drawn, letterpress labels; quirky, complex wines, esp Elusive Queen CHARD, Laughing Pig rosé and all single-v'yd PINOT N.

Brick House Rib R ★★★ 14' 15' 16 All bio; owned by ex-newsman Doug Tunnell.

Evelyn's, Les Dijonnais and Cuvée du Tonnelier PINOT N show gamey, earthy, textural strengths. Rare GAMAY Noir gd.

Brittan Vineyards McM ★★★★ 14' 15' 16 Veteran Robert Brittan makes this superb, focused portfolio of austere, age-worthy PINOT N; full-bodied CHARD.

Broadley Will V ★★★ 14' 15' 16' 17 Splendid estate also uses purchased grapes (esp for Zenith and Shea) yielding spicy, polished, medium-priced, exceptional-quality PINOT N.

Brooks E-A Hills ★★★ 15' 16 17 RIES specialist (up to 20 cuvées, all styles incl fizz). Also v.gd PINOT BL, PINOT N, Amycas (w blend).

Cowhorn App V ★★★★ 14' 15' 16' Bio, family-owned, makes dense, detailed VIOGNIER, GRENACHE, SYRAH; v.gd Rhône blends (r w).

Cristom Will V ★★★ 14 15' 16 Lightly herbal, long-lived PINOT N from Louise, Marjorie, Jessie and Eileen estate v'yds; new v'yds coming. V.gd VIOGNIER AND rare SYRAH.

DanCin S OR ★★★ 15' 16 17 Fine range of v.gd-value CHARDS (esp Chassé) and PINOT NS from throughout w OR. Winery to watch.

De Ponte Dun H ★★★ 14 15' 16 Dundee Hills site next to DOM DROUHIN OREGON, French-born winemaker Isabelle Dutartre crafts satiny, supple PINOT N, esp Baldwin Family Res.

Domaine Drouhin Oregon Dun H ★★★ 14' 15 16 1st Burgundy producer to invest in OR (1987). Édition Limitée, Lauren PINOT N, Arthur CHARD best. Drouhin Oregon Roserock wines from Eola-Amity Hills v'yd promising.

Domaine Serene Dun H ★★★★ 14' 15 16' Superb single-v'yd CHARD, PINOT N, esp Grace and Evanstad Res. Coeur Blanc is white Pinot N. New sparkling facility and vast visitor centre recently opened, becoming cultish. Also property in Burgundy.

Elk Cove Will V ★★★ 14' 15 16' 2nd-generation winemaker; reliable single-v'yd PINOT N, esp Clay Court, La Bohème, Res. New Pike Road label features non-estate wines.

Erath Will V ★★ 15 16 Widely available, unremarkable PINOT BL/GR/N. Founding OR winery now owned by WA's Ste Michelle Wine Estates.

Evening Land E-A Hills ★★★ 14' 15' 16 Sommelier-owned, exclusively Seven Springs estate v'yd CHARD, PINOT N. Pricey Summum is top drop; La Source best value.

Eyrie Vineyards, The Dun H ★★★★ 13' 14' 15 16' Founder David Lett planted first PINOT GR/N in WILL V; son Jason continues traditional, elegant, age-worthy style. Original Vines and Res CHARD and Pinot N are textural wonders; rare Trousseau, PINOT M.

Failla E-A Hills ★★★ →★★★★ 15 16' CA superstar Ehren Jordan builds OR portfolio with stunning GAMAY, PINOT N, esp Björnson, Eola Springs, Seven Springs v'yds.

Foris S OR ★★ 15' 16' 17 Reliable and inexpensive RIES, PINOT BL/GR/N. Exceptional dry Gewurz.

Hyland Estates McM ★★★ 14' 15' 16 Old-vine PINOT N with expressive minerality. Old-vine RIES and toasty CHARD v.gd.

Ken Wright Will V ★★★★ 13 14 15' 16' Superb v'yd knowledge informs deeply fruited PINOT N. Formerly high alc levels have come down, quality remains v. high.

King Estate Will V ★★→★★★ 15' 16 17 Now 100% bio and incl in expanded WILL V AVA. PINOT GR specialist with improving PINOT N. Domaine and Backbone are tops.

Lange Estate Will V ★★★ 15' 16' 17 Fine PINOT GR but CHARD tops here. Muscular, age-worthy PINOT N Res, Freedom Hill v'yd excel.

Lavinea Will V ★★★ →★★★★ 14' 15 16' EVENING LAND alum Isabelle Meunier makes vivid, AVA-specific CHARD, PINOT N from top v'yd sources.

Lingua Franca E-A Hills ★★★ 15' 16' EVENING LAND alum (another!) and top sommelier Larry Stone heads this new project, focused on dense, stylish CHARD, PINOT N, esp Avn.

Ovum OR ★★★ 15' 16' 17 Artisanal, impressive RIES, GEWURZ from both N and S OR.

Panther Creek Will V ★★→★★★ 14 15' 16' Long-time producer with strong PINOT N line-up. Lazy River, Carter, De Ponte selects best.

Patricia Green Will V ★★★★ 14 15' 16' Cult-calibre, impeccable single-v'yd PINOT N. Founder now deceased; still essential winery to watch. Etzel Block, Bonshaw Block sensational.

Ponzi Will V ★★★→★★★★ 14' 15' 16 2nd-generation Luisa P making outstanding wines across all price points. Aurora, Abetina PINOT N knockout; Avellana, Aurora CHARD also. Don't miss brilliant ARNEIS. Entry Tavola Pinot N v.gd value.

Purple Hands Will V ★★★ 14' 15' 16' Cody Wright (son of Ken) steps out with fine-tuned portfolio of single-v'yd PINOT N.

Quady North App V, S OR, Rog V ★★→★★★ 15' 16' 17 Winemaker Herb Quady deftly mixes Rhône and Loire influences, esp VIOGNIER, CAB FR, SYRAH, blends. Pistoleta white. Mae's is estate Res. V.gd rosés too.

Résonance Will V ★★★ 14' 15' 16 Jadot's OR project now in its own winery. Sleek PINOT N and CHARD from winemaker Guillaume Large incl less expensive WILL V cuvées.

Rex Hill Will V ★★★→★★★★ 14' 15' 16 Well-chosen v'yd selects incl Jacob-Hart, Antiquum Farm, La Colina and Shea among outstanding line of PINOT N.

Rose & Arrow Will V New venture from Mark Tarlov, with Louis Michel Liger-Belair making the wines and Pedro Parra consulting on terroir. Top quality, compelling PINOT N. First vintage 2016. To follow.

Pinot N Blancs white: made by pressing juice off (black) skins before fermentation

Scott Paul Will V ★★★ 14' 15' 16 Two winemaker changes in three vintages leave things a bit up in the air. 2015 PINOT N v.gd, esp Ribbon Ridge and Maresh.

Shea Wine Cellars Will V ★★★★ 14' 15' 16 Top-tier winemakers buy Shea grapes, in-house wines just as gd. Block 5, Block 23 and Homer Res PINOT N superb. Some excellent CHARD also.

Sineann Will V ★★★ 15' 16 17' Brightly fruity PINOT N from WILL V and Col Gorge v'yds; TFL, Wyeast and Yates-Conwill tops. Also v.gd old-vine ZIN.

Sokol Blosser Will V ★★→★★★★ 14 15' 16' 17 2nd-generation winemaker does best with value Evolution series. Standout PINOT NS: Big Tree, Goosepen, Orchard.

Soter Will V ★★★→ 14 15' 16 CA legend Tony Soter moved to OR to make PINOT N but his world class OR bubbly (all styles) is just as gd. Nothing but the finest all around.

Stoller Family Estate Dun H ★★★ 14' 15 16' Expansive Dun H v'yds with strong PINOT N, CHARD focus. Stoller Wine Group now owns Canned Oregon, Chehalem, History, plus Chemistry brands.

Trisaetum Will V, Rib R ★★★→★★★★ 14' 15' 16 Owner, artist, winemaker James Frey makes superior RIES, bone-dry to late-harvest, and Res from three estate v'yds. Ribbon Ridge is top drop. V.gd PINOT N, CHARD, sparkling under Pashey label.

WildAire Will V →★★ 14' 15' 16' Small production, complex, age-worthy, gd-value CHARD, PINOT BL N.

Willamette Valley Vineyards Will V ★★→★★★ 15 16 Hundreds of shareholder/owners; extensive v'yd holdings and diverse line-up, principally PINOT N and CHARD. Elton now its own label; new Pambrun v'yd in Walla. Recently acquired Walla's Maison Bleue.

Winderlea Will V ★★★ 14' 15' 16' Top bio producer with vibrant single-v'yd PINOT N, notably Shea, Weber, Winderlea. V.gd, age-worthy CHARD. Napa legend Robert Brittan makes wines.

Pennsylvania

Fifth-largest US producer, 200+ wineries. Three AVAs: from Lake Erie-softened nw to gentler temperatures, higher elevations in e. RIES, GRÜNER V, CHARD, PINOT N, CAB FR, MERLOT can fare well in this two-extremes continental climate. Many newer winemakers, still learning but smart. Leaders: **Allegro** since 1970s, reliable; **Briar Valley**, **Chaddsford**, **Fero V'yds**, **Galen Glen** (top aromatic whites), **Galer**, **Karamoor**, **Penns Woods** (Italian owner imports wines like Cantina Zaccagnini and Ruggeri too), **Setter Ridge**, **Va La** (CORVINA, BARBERA, FIANO, NEBBIOLO, both Michet and Lampia), **Vox Vineti**, **Waltz**. Promising newbies: **Wayvine** (BARBERA too), **1723 V'yds**.

Rhode Island

Although the smallest state in US, Rhode Island has a dozen wineries, and more to come. Leaders: **Greenvale**, **Newport**, **Nickle Creek**, **Sakonnet**.

Texas

First vines were planted by missionaries in 1650s. Quality has improved over past 10 (indeed, 400+) yrs, now led by Texas Fine Wine, a five-member association promoting Texas-appellation wines, and new generation of winemakers raising the bar. Also on rise, small collectives such as Dandy, Wine for the People and The Grower Project, dedicated to limited production, terroir-driven wines, demonstrating increasing understanding of TX territories. Dry conditions reduced yields for 2018 harvest, but many report high-quality, concentrated fruit. Med varieties, plus TANNAT and Portuguese Souzão. 1st harvests of CARIGNAN on rise. Pét-nat now a "thing." Stars among the whites: VERMENTINO, VIOGNIER and PICPOUL Blanc.

Becker Vineyards ★★★ 20-yr-old producer with B'x, Burgundian and Rhône-styled wines. Top picks: TEMPRANILLO Res, Prairie Rotie and MALBEC/PETIT VERDOT blend Raven. CAB SAUV Res Canada Family, Res Newsom V'yd Cab Sauv, Res Malbec, rosé Provencal.

Bending Branch ★★→★★★ Pioneering sustainable winery consistently awarded. Specializing in robust Med varieties; TANNAT a signature grape. V.gd Souzão, ROUSSANNE, Newsom V'yds TEMPRANILLO. Single Barrel PICPOUL Blanc is aged in used bourbon barrels.

Brennan Vineyards ★★→★★★ Known for dry VIOGNIER; white Rhône blend Lily is an award-winner; Res TEMPRANILLO; v.gd "Super Nero" NERO D'AVOLA.

Duchman Family Winery **★★★★** All TX grapes, specializes in Italian varieties, blends. Award-winning DOLCETTO, VERMENTINO. Gd TEMPRANILLO, refreshing Grape Growers (w) Blend, AGLIANICO rosé; v.gd Salt Lick Cellars GSM and BBQ White.

Fall Creek Vineyards **★★★** Pioneering winery in Hill Country released new single-v'yd reds under new ExTERRA label. Stunning Salt Lick TEMPRANILLO; rustic GSM that's perfect with burgers. Excellent B'x blend Meritus, old-vine whites, v.gd Res CHARD, delicious off-dry CHENIN BL.

Sharpshooters are the biggest problem in Texan v'yds. No jokes, now.

Haak Winery ★★ Gd dry and aromatic Blanc du Bois from coastal area; exceptional "Madeira" copies from a Spanish winemaker.

Inwood Estates ★★ Exceptional TEMPRANILLO and Mericana CAB SAUV, v.gd PALOMINO/CHARD blend and Dallas County Chard. Small but special producer worth checking out.

Kuhlman Cellars Young winery with proprietary red blends driven by PETITE SIRAH. Signature is Kankar (r). Estate CARIGNAN rosé and MARSANNE/ROUSSANNE blend.

Lewis Wines ★★ → ★★★ Quality grape-grower, focused on Spanish varieties; rosé specialist with four labels. Impressive reds: TEMPRANILLO (varietal and CAB SAUV blends), Portuguese Tinta Cão.

Llano Estacado ★ → ★★★ Historic winery, mix of outstanding and serviceable wines. Excellent MALBEC, 1836 (r w). V.gd Viviana (w), Viviano (r) that mimics a Supertuscan. THP TEMPRANILLO from all-TX fruit is outstanding.

Lost Draw Cellars ★ → ★★ Small-batch wines, Med varieties: CARIGNAN, PICPOUL Blanc, VIOGNIER. Signature is Gemütlich white blend GRENACHE BL/VIOGNIER/ROUSSANNE. V.gd TEMPRANILLO.

McPherson Cellars ★★★ Delicious Les Copains, excellent Res ROUSSANNE. Serviceable ALBARIÑO, MARSANNE. 40 yrs+ of winemaking; 1st to plant SANGIOVESE in TX.

Messina Hof Wine Cellars ★ → ★★★ Big range. Excellent RIES, esp late-harvest. V.gd Papa Paolo Port-style, Res CAB FR, unoaked CHARD.

Pedernales Cellars ★★★ → ★★★★ Spanish- and Rhône-style wines. Benchmark VIOGNIER Res, excellent TEMPRANILLO, GSM and TX Valhalla red blend.

Perissos Vineyard and Winery ★★ Family-run winery with compelling reds, esp excellent AGLIANICO, PETITE SIRAH, TEMPRANILLO. Strong in Italian blends.

Ron Yates ★ Up-and-coming sister winery to SPICEWOOD, opened 2016. Ten wines, with focus on Rhône, Spanish and Italian styles. Pét-nat SANGIOVESE is new addition.

Southold Farm and Cellar Ambitious new winery in Fredericksburg by artisanal winemaker Regan Meador, back to TX after successful run on Long I. Whimsically named wines belie serious intent: grapes trodden by foot and natural fermentations, lower levels of sulphur. Sparklings: LAGREIN, SANGIOVESE pét-nat.

Spicewood Vineyard ★★ → ★★★ Estate-grown; exceptional Sancerre-like SAUV BL, Gd TEMPRANILLO, powerful red blends. Pet-friendly grounds, tours, tastings.

Tatum Cellars Joshua Fritsche, winemaker at William Chris, named his new winery and a 100% MOURVÈDRE rosé for his 1st-born, Tatum. Fruit from Lost Draw and Salt Lick v'yds with focus on Mourvèdre, esp Hotspur brand.

William Chris Vineyards ★ In new wave of TX innovators. Pricey, but best buys: MALBEC rosé, PETIT VERDOT, red blend Enchante. Pét-nat making a splash, esp rosé.

Vermont

Mtns, harsh winters, brief if sunny summers, frost, hail, humidity: a few hardy souls plant v'yds anyway, rely on own-rooted hybrid grapes like Frontenac Noir, Marquette, La Crescent plus RIES and BLAUFRÄNKISCH to bring acclaim to these extreme n terroirs. **Lincoln Peak** planted in 2001, bio-farmed natural-wine-thinking **La Garagista**, same-minded fizz-focused **ZAFA Wines**, **Shelburne V'yds** are pioneers to look for.

Virginia

Continental climate, weather tied to East Coast. Ten AVAs; 281 producers, terroir-savvy plant sites from Eastern Shore to Blue Ridge slopes to beat humidity, winter freeze. Elegant world-class outcomes in classical (lots of rain on well-drained clay soils for CAB FR, PETIT VERDOT) and experimental (hardy, high-acid, Ju rançon-native PETIT MANSENG sings in sweet and still wines; noteworthy high-altitude PINOT N). VIOGNIER, TANNAT favoured too. Plenty of CAB SAUV, MERLOT. Vineyard is 79% vinifera (20% of which is CHARD, 16% CAB FR), 15% hybrids, <1% American incl Norton, US's oldest wine grape.

Ankida Ridge ★★★ Top, low-alc, ageable PINOT N, CHARD. Blanc de Blancs. Widely considered best Pinot N in VA, therefore among top in the e, drinkable by a lucky few since total production is under 1000 cases, from steep granite slopes, 518m (1700ft) up in Blue Ridge Mts.

Barboursville ★★★★ One of e US top estates, founded by Italy's Zonin family in Monticello where phylloxera-thwarted wine-lover Thomas Jefferson had tried a century earlier. Known for elegant B'x-style reds, led by Octagon, plus fine CAB SAUV, NEBBIOLO, PETIT VERDOT. Paxxito is luscious VIDAL/MUSCAT Ottonel blend. Onsite inn and restaurant showcase VA country elegance.

Boxwood ★★ 16 17 Founder of Middleburg AVA. All B'x grapes: blends based on CAB FR, MERLOT, plus CAB SAUV, PETIT VERDOT in both classic B'x style and fresher drink-now red; rosé of same grapes; one SAUV BL. Short drive from Washington DC.

Chrysalis ★★ Located in protected agricultural district, this is *the* advocate for Norton, VA's native grape and US's oldest winemaking one. Among 1st to grow VIOGNIER; also ALBARIÑO, PETIT VERDOT, TEMPRANILLO.

Early Mountain ★★★ Quality B'x-blends (heft, acidity) luxury-bottling Rise and flagship Eluvium; poised PETIT MANSENG; terroir-driven line-up of four CAB FR; pét-nats of SYRAH, MERLOT. Mission to support state's quality wines: tasting room pours other VA producers too; winemaker founding member of Research Exchange.

Gabriele Rausse ★★ Small estate nr Jefferson's Monticello. Owned by VA's 1st commercial grape-grower: the Italian viticulturalist who planted BARBOURSVILLE with Gianni Zonin. CHARD, CABS SAUV, FR, MERLOT, NEBBIOLO.

Grape root borer: v'yd pest in VA. Talks about rootstocks nonstop, bores vines to death.

Glen Manor Vineyards ★★ 5th-generation historic farm. Vines on steep rocky slopes in Blue Ridge Mts more than 305m (1000ft) up. Began with planting SAUV BL in 1995, now joined by rich CAB FR from 20–30-yr-old vines, off-dry PETIT MANSENG, PETIT VERDOT.

Keswick ★★ For those after quality opulent VA wines with oak-component: dense dark CAB FR and CAB SAUV; MERLOT, B'x blends, PINOT GR, VIOGNIER, CHARD, some Traminette. Often spontaneously fermented.

King Family Vineyards ★★★ French winemaker for dignified, age-worthy Meritage; outstanding, tiny-prod *vin de paille*-style PETIT MANSENG; and experimental Small Batch Series (he's a member of state's Winemaker Research Exchange) line-up that changes yearly and recently incl lively, quality no-sulphur CHARD, skin-contact VIOGNIER.

Linden ★★★ Leading estate in n VA with notable high-altitude wines from three distinct sites: rich CHARD, vivacious SAUV BL, savoury PETIT VERDOT, elegant, complex B'x-style red blends often require ageing. Delicious demi-sec PETIT MANSENG. Experimental soul Jim Law founded in 80s for taste of site over fruit; has been VA-wine mentor ever since.

Michael Shaps Wineworks ★★ Modern-minded classic VA producer with solid examples of VIOGNIER, CHARD, PETIT MANSENG on the luscious side; plus tasty TANNAT and PETIT VERDOT, Meritage and Raisin d'Etre in white (Petit Manseng) and red (blend) from grapes dried in old tobacco-drying barns.

Pollak ★★ On the international side of VA: heftier CABS SAUV, FR, MERLOT, Meritage, lush, spicy VIOGNIER, creamy PINOT GR.

RdV Vineyards ★★★★ 13' Top e US estate making only B'x-inspired red blends, from vines growing in granite-soil hillside. Elegant wines of complexity, power; Lost Mountain label is VA's 1st $100 wine.

Veritas ★★★ Founded 1995, incl steep 20-yr-old forest v'yds. Concentrated, floral CAB FR with plenty of acidity can age 10 yrs+. White-grape efforts on luscious, lifted VIOGNIER. Gd CHARD, MERLOT, PETIT VERDOT.

Washington

WA is the wild west with over 85 varieties planted and more on the way. CHARD, RIES, CAB SAUV, MERLOT and SYRAH make up 80%+ production, but many limited-production varieties make some of the state's best wines. In recent yrs, Cab Sauv plantings have increased dramatically and this and B'x blends are state's strength. Syrah, though, is the true star for insiders, making wines that are terroir-driven and compelling. The state's wines also offer v.gd value, though many come from small producers whose wines can be difficult to find.

Principal viticultural areas

Columbia Valley (Col V) Huge AVA in central and e WA with a touch in OR. High-quality Cab Sauv, Merlot, Ries, Chard, Syrah. Key sub-divisions incl Yakima Valley (Yak V), Red Mtn, Walla Walla AVAs.

Red Mountain (Red Mtn) Sub-AVA of Col V and Yak V. Hot region known for Cabs and B'x blends

Walla Walla Valley (Walla) Sub-AVA of Col V with own identity and vines in WA and OR. Home of important boutique brands and prestige labels focusing on quality. Cab Sauv, Merlot, Syrah.

Yakima Valley (Yak V) Sub-AVA of Col V. Focus on Merlot, Syrah, Ries.

Col V gets 17cm (7in) rain/year. B'x gets c.58cm (23in).

Abeja Walla ★★★ Producer of top COL V CAB SAUV, CHARD. SYRAH also v.gd.

Andrew Will Col V, Red Mtn ★★★→★★★★ 10' 12' 14' Celebrated 30th anniversary in 2019. Some of state's best, most age-worthy red blends. Sorella is flagship, no misses in line-up. 2nd-generation winemaker Will Camarda increasing role.

Avennia Yak V, Col V ★★★ 10 12' 14' Rising star focusing on old vines, top v'yds. Turning heads with cellar-worthy B'x, Rhône styles. Sestina B'x blend and Arnaut SYRAH tops. SAUV BL v.gd.

Betz Family Winery Col V ★★★→★★★★ 10 12' 14' Maker of high-quality Rhône, B'x styles with new winemaker Louis Skinner. Pére de Famille CAB SAUV and La Côte Patriarche SYRAH consistent standouts.

B Leighton Yak V ★★★ Side project for Brennon Leighton, formerly at CHATEAU STE MICHELLE and current winemaker for K VINTNERS. Rhône blend Gratitude, SYRAH, PETIT VERDOT v.gd.

Brian Carter Cellars Col V ★★★ Blend specialist, with wines aged additional time before release. Solesce B'x blend flagship wine.

Cadence Red Mtn ★★★ 10' 12' 14 Producer of some of the state's most age-worthy, compelling wines. Dedicated to B'x-style blends from RED MTN fruit. Coda from declassified barrels v.gd value.

Cayuse Walla ★★★★ 10 11 12' 14 Mailing list only, and yrs-long wait. All estate-v'yd wines from Walla; stratospheric scores. Earthy, savoury SYRAH (esp Cailloux and Bionic Frog) and God Only Knows GRENACHE worth seeking out. TEMPRANILLO also v.gd. Sister wineries No Girls, Horsepower, Hors Categorie also top-notch.

Charles Smith Wines Col V ★★ Sold to Constellation in 2016 for $120 million. Focus on value wines. Look for Kung Fu Girl RIES.

Chateau Ste Michelle Col V ★★ →★★★ Largest single producer of RIES in world; all prices/styles: v.gd quaffers (excellent COL V Ries) to TBA-style rarities (Eroica

---

Washington wizards

WA is adding about 40 wineries/yr, and some of them are making the state's best wines. Try: **Kerloo Cellars**, Walla; **Kevin White**, Woodinville; **Savage Grace**, Woodinville (tasting room); **WT Vintners**, Woodinville; **Two Vintners**, Woodinville; **Waters**, Walla.

Single Berry Select). Gd-value reds and whites from Col V as well as estate offerings from Cold Creek, Canoe Ridge.

Col Solare Red Mtn ★★★ →★★★★ 10 12' Partnership between Ste Michelle Wine Estates and Tuscany's Antinori. Focus on single CAB SAUV from RED MTN. Complex, long-lasting.

Columbia Crest Col V ★★ →★★★ WA's top-value producer and by far largest winery makes oodles of v.gd, affordable wines under Grand Estates, H3, Res labels. Res wines offer v.gd value esp CAB SAUV and Walter Clore (r).

WA's viticultural secret weapon? Soil brought in by massive floods 15,000 yrs ago.

Corliss Estates Col V ★★★ 08' 10 12' WALLA producer of cult B'x blend and CAB SAUV. All wines see substantial time in barrel and bottle before release. Sister winery Tranche offers v.gd value.

Côte Bonneville Yak V ★★★ 09' 10 12' Estate winery for highly regarded DuBrul v'yd making age-worthy wines in sophisticated style that see additional bottle age before release. *Carriage House* v.gd value. Don't overlook CHARD, RIES.

DeLille Cellars Col V, Red Mtn ★★★ 10' 12' 14' Long-time producer of B'x and Rhône styles. Chaleur Blanc one of state's best whites. Harrison Hill top B'x blend. D2 red v.gd value. No misses in line-up.

Doubleback Walla ★★★ 10' 12 Former footballer Drew Bledsoe makes one wine, CAB SAUV, a feminine expression of WALLA fruit with cellaring potential. Bledsoe Family sister winery making v.gd SYRAH.

Dusted Valley Vintners Walla ★★★ B'x and Rhône styles. Stoney Vine SYRAH from estate plantings worth seeking out. Boomtown label gd value.

Efeste Yak V, Col V, Red Mtn ★★★ Woodinville producer of zesty RIES, racy CHARD from cool Evergreen V'yd, also v.gd SYRAH, old-vine CAB SAUV. Final Final gd value.

Fidélitas Red Mtn ★★★ Producer of B'x style blends and CAB SAUV from RED MTN made in a bold, ripe style. Quintessence V'yd Cab Sauv top-notch.

Fielding Hills Col V ★★★ Small producer focusing on estate v'yd on Wahluke Slope. CAB SAUV, MERLOT outstanding as well as v.gd value.

Figgins Walla ★★★ 10 12 14 2nd-generation winemaker Chris F also winemaker at famed LEONETTI. Single-estate B'x blend, RIES from WALLA fruit. Toil OR PINOT N project.

Force Majeure Red Mtn ★★★ Producer of estate B'x and Rhône styles from RED MTN. VIOGNIER a standout. Recently moved to WALLA.

Gramercy Cellars Walla ★★★ 10 12' 13 Founder master sommelier Greg Harrington produces lower alc, higher acid wines. Speciality earthy SYRAHS (esp Lagniappe), herby CAB SAUV. John Lewis Res Syrah tops. Lower East value label.

Hedges Family Estate Red Mtn ★★★ Venerable family winery; polished, reliable wines, esp estate red blend and DLD SYRAH. CMS blend gd value.

Januik Col V ★★★ 10 12' Former CH STE MICHELLE winemaker Nike Januik makes v.gd-value B'x styles. Single-v'yds a step above. Champoux V'yd CAB SAUV stands out. Novelty Hill sister winery.

K Vintners Col V, Walla ★★★ Owner Charles Smith is an outsized personality focusing on single-v'yd SYRAH, plus Syrah/CAB SAUV blends. WALLA wines v.gd. Sixto CHARD-focused sister winery. Other brands CasaSmith, Substance, ViNo.

Latta Wines Col V ★★★ Former K VINTNERS winemaker Andrew Latta makes stunning GRENACHE, MOURVÈDRE, ROUSSANNE one of state's best whites. Latta Latta gd value.

L'Ecole No 41 Walla ★★★ 10 12' 14 One of WALLA's founding wineries; wide range of COL V and WALLA wines. Ferguson top B'x blend. CHENIN BL, SEM v.gd value.

Leonetti Cellar Walla ★★★★ 08 10' 12' 14 Founding WALLA winery celebrated 40th harvest in 2018. Has cult status, steep prices for collectable CAB SAUV, MERLOT, SANGIOVESE. AGLIANICO recently added. Res B'x blend flagship.

Long Shadows Walla ★★★→★★★★ Former Ste Michelle Wine Estates CEO Allen Shoup brings a group of globally famous winemakers to WA to make one wine each. All high quality, worth seeking out.

Maison Bleue Walla ★★★ Rhône-focused winery using WALLA fruit, turning heads with GRENACHE, SYRAH. Recently purchased by Willamette Valley V'yds (OR).

Mark Ryan Yak V, Red Mtn ★★★ Producer of big, bold B'x and Rhône styles. MERLOT-based Long Haul and Dead Horse CAB SAUV stand out. Crazy Mary MOURVÈDRE is swoonworthy. Board Track Racer second label.

Milbrandt Vineyards Col V ★★ Focus on value. The Estates are higher-tier, single-v'yd wines from Wahluke Slope and Ancient Lakes. Look for PINOT GR, RIES.

Northstar Walla ★★★ 10 MERLOT-focused winery. Premier Merlot (made to age) is gorgeous. Also v.gd CAB SAUV.

Pacific Rim Col V ★★ RIES specialist making oceans of tasty, inexpensive yet eloquent Dry to Sweet and Organic. For more depth *single-v'yd releases*.

Passing Time Col V ★★★ New project from former NFL quarterbacks Dan Marino and Damon Huard focusing on CAB SAUV. Wines made by Chris Peterson (AVENNIA).

Tax means WA state government now gets more money from cannabis than wine.

Pepper Bridge Walla ★★★ B'x styles from estate fruit. Pepper Bridge and Seven Hills v'yd blends among WA's best. Give time in cellar.

Quilceda Creek Col V ★★★★ 04' 07 10 12' 14' 15 Flagship producer of cult status CAB SAUV known for ageing potential. One of most lauded producers in US. Sold by allocation. Find it if you can.

Reynvaan Family Vineyards Walla ★★★→★★★★ 10' 11 12' 14 All fruit from estate v'yds in Rocks District and foothills of Blue Mtn. Dedicated to SYRAH, CAB SAUV, Rhône-style whites. Wait-list winery but worth it.

Rôtie Cellars Walla ★★★ Rhône-style wine specialist. Northern Blend from WALLA a consistent standout. Also v.gd GRENACHE BL.

Saviah Cellars Walla ★★★ Exquisite SYRAH, TEMPRANILLO, B'x blends. Funk V'yd Syrah is knee-buckler. Une Vallée top B'x blend. The Jack label gd value.

Seven Hills Winery Walla ★★★ 10 12' 14 One of WALLA's oldest, most respected wineries, known for age-worthy reds made in a reserved style. Recently bought by Crimson Wine Group but same winemaker.

Sleight of Hand Walla ★★★ Winemaker and audiophile Trey Busch makes dazzling B'x blends and Rhône styles. Psychedlic SYRAH from Rocks District worth seeking out. Also gd CHARD. Renegade value label.

Sparkman Cellars Yak V, Red Mtn ★★★ Woodinville producer makes a staggering 27 wines, focus on power. Stella Mae and Ruby Leigh B'x blends offer excellent quality and value. Evermore Old Vines CAB SAUV cellar-worthy.

Spring Valley Vineyard Walla ★★★ 10' 12' 14' All estate red wines. Uriah MERLOT blend consistent standout. Katherine Corkrum CAB FR also superb.

Syncline Cellars Col V ★★★ Rhône-dedicated producer making wines in distinct, fresh style. Subduction Red is v.gd value. NB MOURVÈDRE. Sparkling GRÜNER delicious. PICPOUL a consistent standout.

Woodward Canyon Walla ★★★★ 07 10 12' 14 One of oldest WALLA producers, focusing on B'x styles. *Old Vines Cab Sauv* is complex, age-worthy. CHARD one of best in state. Nelms Road value label.

Wisconsin

Wollersheim Winery (est 1840s) is one of best estates in midwest, with hybrid and Wisconsin-native American hybrid grapes. Look for Prairie Fumé (SEYVAL BL), Prairie Blush (Marechal Foch).

Mexico

Baja California in the northwest, and in particular the Guadalupe Valley, is the centre of action in Mexico: this is where you'll find modern, quality winemaking. Spearheaded by Hugo d'Acosta, who has trained some 300 winemakers in his wineries and oenology school, the region now attracts expat investment and some terrific cooking. Most of the roughly 150 wineries are small-scale and produce fewer than 100,000 cases annually. But enthusiasm for the mainly French, Spanish and Italian grapes that grow here is high, with new projects opening each year. Wineries leverage the high-altitude, cool-climate vineyards, and wines often have a saline character. The better wines are produced on hillsides where the water comes from mountain springs.

Adobe Guadalupe ★★→★★★ Hugo d'Acosta helped est this showcase winery. Wines incl B'x blends, named after angels. Serafiel blend of CAB SAUV and SYRAH is top. Fresh Jardín Romántico CHARD is the only varietal.

Alximia Founded by mathematician-turned-winemaker, featuring Italian, Spanish, French varieties grown organically. Vertical Libis Special Res (r) blend v.gd.

Bibayoff Vinos ★★→★★★ A nod to early Russian Molokan settlers. Outstanding ZIN and v.gd Zin/CAB SAUV blend. Zesty CHENIN BL from dry-farmed hillside old vines.

Casa de Piedra ★★→★★★ Modern winery in historic stone house, 1st project of Hugo d'Acosta. V.gd blend of CAB SAUV/TEMPRANILLO; San Antonio de las Minas CHARD.

Château Camou ★★→★★★ Pioneering, French-inspired winery with serious B'x credentials. Gran Vinos line long-aged with CAB SAUV-based blend Tinto is velvety with a supple, elegant finish.

Finca La Carrodilla 1st certified organic winery in Valle de Guadalupe. Focus on monovarietals; CAB SAUV, SHIRAZ among best. Small, careful production.

#vinochingon: popular # used by young winemakers, slang for "f'ing gd wine!"

Las Nubes Sustainable winery with French focus. Gd Res red blends, NEBBIOLO, and Kuiiy, fresh white blend.

Mogor Badan ★★ Small-production passion project; B'x-informed. Michelin-starred chef on same site.

Monte Xanic ★★→★★★ Spanish oenologist with excellent CAB SAUV, v.gd MERLOT. Awarded whites; look for SAUV BL, unoaked CHARD, fresh CHENIN BL. Interesting CAB FR Res Limitada. Now trying PINOT N in v'yd at 800m (2625ft).

Paralelo ★★ Eco-winery conceived by Hugo d'Acosta, ultra-modern presentation. Small production. Emblema SAUV BL, and two versions of red B'x style Ensamble.

Tres Mujeres ★★→★★★ Rustic co-op owned by women reflects new wave of artisan producers in Baja. Top TEMPRANILLO; v.gd GRENACHE/CAB SAUV, La Mezcla del Rancho; Isme MERLOT.

Tres Valles Powerful reds from Guadalupe, Santo Tomas, San Vincente Valleys. V.gd Kuwal blend driven by TEMPRANILLO. Top-rated single varieties: Maat from GRENACHE and Kojaa from PETITE SIRAH are cult quality.

Vena Cava ★★★ Possibly the hippest winery in Mex, founded by expats and constructed from reclaimed fishing boats. Well-priced, modern, organic wines. Focus on CAB SAUV and SAUV BL. V.gd, complex, oak-aged Cab Sauv and TEMPRANILLO. Nearby food truck serves top-notch tacos.

Viñas Pijoan Honest *garagista*-style wines named for the winemaker's family. Mostly French varieties. B'x blend Leonora is flagship wine. Approachable Coordinates line.

Canada

Canada's wine industry was founded on Icewine, and still makes lots; but the latest generation of growers is all about cool-climate, dry wine. What they seek is authentic, pristine flavours with a Canadian identity, or that most slippery of ideas, a sense of place. Sparkling in multiple styles joins Chardonnay and Riesling as white favourites, while Pinot Noir leads a shift in red style: acid balance and finesse are now more popular. Syrah and Cabernet Franc can also work well, as do Meritage red blends.

Ontario

Prime appellations of origin: Niagara Peninsula, Lake Erie North Shore (LENS) and Prince Edward County (P Ed). Within the Niagara Peninsula: two regional appellations – Niagara Escarpment (Niag E) and Niagara-on-the-Lake (Niag L) – and ten sub-appellations. New LENS sub-appellation South Islands.

Bachelder Niag r w ★★★ 13 15' 16' Pure, precise, elegant, age-worthy CHARD, PINOT N in Burgundy, Oregon and on the Dolomitic limestone and clay of Niag.

Cave Spring Niag r w sw (sp) ★★★ 16' 17 (18) Respected pioneer; CSV (old vines) esp RIES, CHARD. Elegant estate labels age gracefully: CAB FR, Chard and top late-harvest, Icewine.

Château des Charmes Niag r w sw (sp) ★★ 16' 17 (18) Pioneering Bosc family began winery in 1978 and now farm 114 ha. Sparkling, RIES (bone-dry to Icewine); unique upright GAMAY Droit clone, Equuleus flagship red blend.

Flat Rock Niag r w (sp) ★★★ 16' 17 (18) A two-tier line-up: Estate (varietal), Res (single block); juicy crisp RIES, PINOT N, CHARD. Top picks Nadja's Ries, Rusty Shed Chard. All screwcapped.

Henry of Pelham Niag r w sw (sp) ★★★ 16' 17 (18) Speck brothers, 6th-gen farmers, grow CHARD, RIES, gd Cuvée Catherine Brut fizz, Speck Family Res (SFR), unique Baco Noir, Ries Icewine.

Irritating bear habit: uprooting and taking away vines. Presumably not to replant.

Hidden Bench Niag r w ★★★★ 15 16' 17 (18) Lauded Beamsville Bench artisanal grower. RIES, PINOT N, CHARD; top Terroir Series Roman's Block Ries plus Nuit Blanche and La Brunate blends.

Huff Estates P Ed r w r sp ★★ 17 (18) 9-ha South Bay v'yd on clay/shale loam over limestone. Traditional-method sparkler, still CHARD, PINOT N, RIES.

Inniskillin Niag r w sw ★★★ 16' 17 (18) Icewine pioneer making juicy Res RIES, PINOT GR, PINOT N and super CAB FR; Single-v'yd series CHARD, Pinot N in best yrs.

Malivoire Niag, Ont r p w (sp) ★★★ 16' 17 (18) Malivoire success mantra is economic, social and environmental. Tasty GAMAY, CAB FR, CHARD, PINOT N, GEWURZ, trio of rosés.

Norman Hardie P Ed r w ★★★★ 15 16' 17 (18) Iconic P Ed pioneer hand-crafting CHARD, PINOT N, RIES, CAB FR on limestone-clay soils. Buy Cuvée L Chard, Pinot N in best yrs.

Pearl Morissette Niag r w ★★★ 16' 17 (18) Min-intervention, low-sulphur RIES aged in *foudre*, CHARD, CAB FR, PINOT N in concrete eggs and *foudres*.

Ravine Vineyard Niag r p w sp ★★★ 16' 17 (18) Organic 14-ha St David's Bench v'yd spans ancient riverbed. Top Res CHARD, CAB FR; drink-now: Sand and Gravel.

Stratus Niag r w ★★★★ 15 16' 17 (18) Winemakers JL Groux, v.gd CAB FR/GAMAY blends and Charles Baker RIES seek out somewhereness.

Tawse Niag r w (sp) p ★★★★ 15 16' 17' (18) Owner Moray Tawse also in Burgundy at Marchand-Tawse and Domaine Tawse making v.gd CHARD, RIES, gd PINOT N, CAB FR, MERLOT; v'yds certified organic and bio.

Two Sisters Niag r p w ★★★ 13 14 15 16' New to Niag scene, focused on aged, high-end estate reds of CAB FR, CAB SAUV, MERLOT; flagship Stone Eagle blend.

British Columbia

Geographical Indications for BC wines of distinction are BC, Fraser Valley, Gulf Islands, Kootenays, Lillooet, Okanagan Valley (Ok V), Golden Mile Bench and Okanagan Falls (subdivisions of Ok V), Shuswap, Similkameen Valley, Thompson Valley, Vancouver Island.

Blue Mountain Ok V r w sp ★★★ 16' 17 (18) 2nd generation makes traditional-method fizz incl smart RD versions; reliable age-worthy PINOT N, CHARD, PINOT GR, GAMAY. Outstanding Res Pinot N.

Burrowing Owl Ok V r w ★★★ 16' 17 (18) Pioneer 25-yr old estate; excellent CAB FR, v.gd PINOT GR, SYRAH on Black Sage Bench; boutique hotel/restaurant.

CedarCreek Ok V r w ★★★ 16' 17 (18) Rich array of aromatic RIES, GEWURZ; Ehrenfelder, Platinum single-v'yd blocks PINOT N, CHARD. New visitor facilities.

Haywire Ok V r p w sp ★★★ 16' 17 (18) Summerland growers use natural, pét-nat, organics, concrete ferments, amphora, for wines of precision and grace. CHARD, PINOT GR, PINOT N, GAMAY, sparkling.

BC boasts 80+ grape varieties, planted to 929 v'yds, across 10,260 acres.

Mission Hill Ok V r p w (sp) ★★★★ 14 15 16' 17 (18) Canadian benchmark, elite Legacy Series: Oculus, Perpetua, Quatrain, Compendium plus v.gd varietal Terroir Series. Experiential visitor centre/outdoor restaurant.

Nk'Mip Ok V r w ★★★ 16' 17 (18) Steady, fresh RIES, PINOT N; top-end Qwam Qwmt CHARD, SYRAH. Part of $25 million aboriginal resort/Desert Cultural Centre.

Osoyoos Larose Ok V r ★★★ 15' 16' (17) B'x-based Groupe Taillan owns this 33-ha single v'yd. Track record of age-worthy Le Grand Vin echoes B'x.

Painted Rock Ok V r w ★★★ 15 16' 17 (18) Skaha Bench, steep, 24-ha, 13-yr-old estate v'yd below 500-yr-old native pictographs; big, weighty SYRAH, CAB FR, CHARD, signature red blend Icon.

Quails' Gate Ok V r w ★★★ 16' 17 (18) Inspired style. Fresh, aromatic RIES, CHENIN BL; continued refinement of core PINOT N, CHARD, limited Collector Series.

Road 13 Ok V r (sp) ★★★★ 16' 17 (18) Excellent Golden Mile Bench producer of Rhône-style VIOGNIER, SYRAH and treasured old-vine CHENIN BL (w sp), plus premium Jackpot series, PINOT N, CAB FR.

Stag's Hollow Ok V ★★★ 16' 17 (18) Eclectic Ok Falls producer of ALBARIÑO, VIOGNIER, GRENACHE, PINOT N, SYRAH. In great yrs, one-off, top-lot Renaissance labels.

Tantalus Ok V r w sp ★★★ 16' 17 (18) Natural, terroir-driven RIES, PINOT N, CHARD, sparkling from oldest (1927) continuously producing Ok V v'yds.

Nova Scotia

Benjamin Bridge sp ★★★ 08' 11' 12 Gaspereau Valley; traditional-method fizz. Excellent age-worthy vintage and NV Brut from CHARD/PINOTS N/M blends.

It's all about water in Canada

These northerly latitudes may promise well with climate change, but it will have to change a lot to enable vines to survive the winters without the moderating effects of large bodies of water. You can't plant vines more than about 1km (0.6-miles) away from BC's Ok Lake, for example, because winters are just too cold. In Gaspereau Valley mesoclimate is marked by twice-daily air movements caused by 15.24m (50ft)-high Bay of Fundy tides. In Niag and P Ed, the cool Lake Ontario breezes are said to retard spring flowering and stave off early autumn frosts in the v'yds.

South America

Abbreviations used in the text:

CHILE

Aco	Aconcagua
Bío	Bío-Bío
Cach	Cachapoal
Casa	Casablanca
Cho	Choapa
Col	Colchagua
Coq	Coquimbo
Cur	Curicó
Elq	Elqui
Ita	Itata
Ley	Leyda
Lim	Limarí
Mai	Maipo
Mal	Malleco
Mau	Maule
Rap	Rapel
San A	San Antonio

ARGENTINA

Cata	Catamarca
La R	La Rioja
Luján	Luján de Cuyo
Men	Mendoza
Neu	Neuquén
Pat	Patagonia
Río N	Río Negro
Sal	Salta
San J	San Juan
Uco V	Uco Valley

CHILE

It used to be just Chilean Merlot – even if it was Carmenère; then it was coastal Sauvignon Blanc or mountain Cabernet Sauvignon. Now this 500-year-old wine country is offering so much more. Old vines in the south boast characterful País, Muscat, Cinsault, Carignan, Malbec and Semillon, while new vineyards look to Chardonnay, Syrah, Pinot Noir and Riesling. There are plantations in the Atacama Desert and coastal vineyards shrouded in fog; vineyards on Patagonian lakes overlooking volcanoes and gravity-defying Andes vineyards at over 2000m (6562ft).

Recent vintages

Vintage variation is becoming more marked as wine regions spread further up and down the country and climate change kicks in. While the past couple of vintages have been more challenging, with too much and too little rain, 2018 is one of the best in the last decade, with a relative return to normal. Expect rich and full-bodied red wines with complexity and depth.

Aconcagua N of Santiago; region spans from Andes to coastal hills. Andes is best for reds, coast for CHARD, SYRAH, PINOT N.

Almaviva Mai ★★★★ Franco-Chilean adventure between Rothschild family

(Mouton) and CONCHA Y TORO. Making rich, complex B'x blends in Puente Alto, MAI, since 1996. Collectable.

Altaïr Wines Rap ★★★ Top end of SAN PEDRO and one of Cachapoal's best reds. Rich, concentrated CAB SAUV blend. Second label: Sideral.

Antiyal Mai ★★★ Family winery of top bio consultant in Chile, Alvaro Espinoza. Heartfelt, earth-conscious, elegant reds from MAI.

Apaltagua ★★ Col winery with v'yds across Central Valley. Large, often gd-value portfolio incl Pacifico Sur brand.

Aquitania, Viña Mai ★★★ Classy producer in MAI with stellar CAB SAUV (Lazuli is the top ticket). Pioneer in Mal with v.gd CHARD, PINOT N, SAUV BL.

Arboleda, Viña Aco ★★→★★★ Baby sister of ERRÁZURIZ. ACO but coastal, so cool. Fresh, bright, modern. V.gd SAUV BL, CHARD, PINOT N.

Aristos Cach ★★★→★★★★ CAB SAUV, CHARD from top terroirs. Boutique adventure with Louis-Michel Liger-Belair of Burgundy.

Bío-Bío One of Chile's oldest, far s wine valleys being rediscovered. Treasure trove of old vines (PAIS, MUSCAT), promising new vines (RIES, SAUV BL, PINOT N).

Bouchon Mau ★★→★★★ Historic family producer with fresh vision. Champion of PAIS and juicy MAU reds. Top SEM too.

Caliboro Mau ★★→★★★ Boutique, organic project of a count (Cinzano) in MAU. Juicy red blends (Erasmo) and sweet old-vine Torontel (MUSCAT family).

Caliterra Casa, Col, Cur, Ley ★★→★★★ Col winery owned by ERRÁZURIZ. V.gd MALBEC; Cenit is top blend. DSTNTO is jovial, juicy.

Calyptra Cach ★★★ One of top names in Cach. Altitude adds intensity, perfume to CAB SAUV. Textural CHARD, barrel-aged SAUV BL.

Carmen, Viña Casa, Col, Mai ★★→★★★ Chile's oldest winery (1850); modern wines. V.gd CARMENÈRE, CAB SAUV (top is Gold Res). Exciting DO range.

Casablanca Casa Pioneering cool coastal region in 80s and now Chile's largest coastal GI. Hills offer wide range of temperatures, soils. V.gd for CHARD, SAUV BL, PINOT N, SYRAH.

Casa Marín San A ★★★ Trailblazing family affair in SAN A, just 4km (2.5 miles) from sea. Chilly climate makes v.gd RIES, SAUV BL, SYRAH and Chile's top Sauv Gris.

Casas del Bosque Casa, Mai ★★→★★★ Top CASA wines since late 90s. Cool site for Casa making noteworthy SAUV BL, SYRAH, CHARD among others.

Casa Silva Col, S Regions ★★→★★★ 5th-generation, still family-run. Diverse portfolio, mainly in Col (top CARMENÈRE) but also in Lago Ranco, Pat (PINOT N, SAUV BL).

Clos des Fous Cach, Casa, S Regions ★★→★★★ Terroir-hunting project by soil specialist Pedro Parra and winemaker François Massoc. Juicy red blends, PINOT N, CHARD.

Clos Ouvert Mau ★★ Chile's leading natural wine producer is Frenchman Louis Antoine Luyt. Champion of old-vine PAIS, plus CARIGNAN, CINSAULT from MAU.

Concha y Toro Cent V ★→★★★★ Few producers come as big as CyT and few manage to produce such volume at such value, quality. Wines from all major regions; you'll be hard-pushed to find something that CyT doesn't have in its portfolio. Highlights incl Terrunyo SAUV BL, CAB SAUV; Maycas de Limarí range; Gravas SYRAH from MAI and top Cab Sauv in Marques and Don Melchor. Casillero del Diablo is everyday brand. *See also* ALMAVIVA, TRIVENTO (Argentina).

Cono Sur Casa, Col, Bio ★★→★★★ One of New World's top-value PINOT NS (Bicicleta) and largest Pinot producer too. Also look for RIES, SAUV BL, CAB SAUV (v.gd Silencio).

Cousiño Macul Mai ★★→★★★ Traditional family winery in MAI, founded 1810. Consistently gd CAB SAUV, esp Lota.

De Martino Cach, Casa, Elq, Mai, Mau, Ita ★★→★★★★ A leader in fresher, leaner wines. Diverse portfolio from all over Chile, incl 2000m (6562ft) ELQ SYRAH, old-vine MALBEC, CARIGNAN. Viejas Tinajas from ITA is amphora-aged.

> **Mountains to coast**
> When you think Chile, forget North to South – think East to West.
> Chile's wine regions and appellation system are divided into Andes
> (East), Entre Valles (Central Valleys) and Costa (West, Coastal).

Elqui Distinctive n wine valley. Altitude wines with extreme temperatures and intense sunlight. V.gd SYRAH, SAUV BL, PX. Big for Pisco too.

Emiliana Casa, Rap, Bio ★★→★★★ Consistently gd, organic. Alvaro Espinoza (*see* ANTIYAL) is consultant. Complex reds, refreshing whites, gd fizz. Adobe and Novas offer value, G and Coyam for special occasions.

Errázuriz Aco, Casa →★ ★★★★★ One of Chile's top names. Dedicated to ACO valley from coast to Andes. Excellent Pizzaras CHARD and PINOT N; Don Maximiliano is renowned CAB SAUV blend; V.gd SAUV BL, SYRAH from Costa (*see* box). *See also* CALITERRA, SEÑA, VIÑA ARBOLEDA, VIÑEDO CHADWICK.

Falernia, Viña Elq ★★→★★★ Notable ELQ producer. Excellent Rhône-like SYRAH, herbaceous SAUV BL, uncommon PX. Labels incl Alta Tierra, Mayu.

Garcés Silva, Viña San A ★★→★★★ Big grower in Leyda (SAUV BL, CHARD, PINOT N, SYRAH) and own wines Amayna (voluptuous, complex) and Boya (fresh, fruity).

Haras de Pirque Mai ★★→★★★ V.gd rich CAB SAUV, SYRAH, CAB FR, flinty SAUV BL.

Itata Old vines with new vibes. Historical s valley reinvented by new generation of winemakers. Top CINSAULT, PAÍS, MUSCAT.

Koyle Col, Ita ★★→★★★ New vision of 5th-generation winemaker Toti Undurraga (family owned UNDURRAGA) makes vibrant, juicy bio wines in Col and ITA.

Lapostolle Cach, Casa, Col ★★→★★★ Landmark bio producer in Apalta famous for rich reds (CARMENÈRE, SYRAH, CAB SAUV). Collection range is wilder side with single-site, natural wines.

Leyda, Viña Col, Mai, San A ★★→★★★ Pioneering producer in Ley, SAN A. Cool coastal wines pack a punch (CHARD, SAUV BL, Sauv Gris, SYRAH, PINOT N). Often v.gd value.

Limarí Cool coast in n with limestone soils. Excellent CHARD, SAUV BL, SYRAH, PINOT N, but drought yrs often fatal for v'yds and investors' wallets.

Loma Larga Casa ★★ Penchant for reds on steep slopes: MALBEC, CAB FR, herbal SAUV BL.

Maipo Mai Most sought-after CAB SAUV region in Chile. Alluvial, gravel soils and sunny, mtn climate. Sub-regions Pirque, Puente Alto, Alto Jahuel best.

Matetic Casa, San A ★★★ One of Chile's top bio estates, between CASA and SAN A. V.gd SYRAH, *Sauv Bl*, PINOT N. Classy, understated.

Maule Mau Major valley, but more than just workhorse wines. Old-vine CARIGNAN (*see* VIGNO) and PAÍS v.gd indeed.

Maycas del Limarí Lim ★★→★★★ Prolific LIM winery making v.gd *Sauv Bl*, CHARD, PINOT N, SYRAH. Part of CONCHA Y TORO family.

Montes Casa, Col, Cur, Ley ★★→★★★★ Modern wine dynasty. Rich, complex reds inland (Alpha CAB SAUV, *Folly Syrah*, Purple Angel CARMENÈRE) and fresh wines from coast (v.gd Outer Limits SAUV BL, PINOT N).

MontGras Col, Ley, Mai ★★ Gd-value reds and range of varieties (try TEMP, CAB FR). Also produce Intriga CAB SAUV (MAI), excellent Amaral SAUV BL (Ley).

Montsecano Casa ★★★ Bio, boutique and no oak. PINOT N, just two labels but worth seeking. *Top stuff.*

Morandé Casa, Mai, Mau ★★→★★★ Innovation has always been a pillar of this large producer, best seen in Limited Edition range. Brut Nature NV (CHARD, PINOT N) is top Chilean *bubbly*.

Neyen Col ★★★ Single-label bio wine from VERAMONTE. Old-vine CARMENÈRE/CAB SAUV in Apalta. Complex, age-worthy.

Odfjell Cur, Mai, Mau ★ →★★★ MAI winery but v'yds in Cur, MAU too. Bio, sustainable, organic. Rich reds (v.gd MALBEC, CARIGNAN, CAB SAUV).

Pérez Cruz, Viña Mai ★★→★★★★ Top CAB SAUV, PETIT VERDOT, CAB FR, v.gd SYRAH, GRENACHE. Style, substance.

Pisco Traditional grape spirit, famous in "sours", back in fashion.

Polkura Col ★★→★★★ Indy producer in Marchigüe, Col. Med varieties, v.gd SYRAH. Some dry farmed.

Quebrada de Macul, Viña Mai ★★→★★★ Iconic CAB SAUV Domus Aurea one of MAI's best. Peñalolén is entry line.

Rapel Umbrella denomination used for big blends from Central Valley. Covers mtn to coast in Cach and Col.

RE, Bodegas Casa ★★★ Pablo Morande 2.0, this time with talented son, Pablo Jr. Experimental, often excellent wines from CASA, MAU.

Ribera del Lago Mau ★★→★★★ One of Chile's most distinctive SAUV BL (and v.gd PINOT N) from Rafael Tirado's labyrinthine v'yds in MAU.

San Antonio San A Similar to CASA but cooler. Coastal valley best for SAUV BL, CHARD, SYRAH, PINOT N. Ley subregion.

San Pedro Cur ★→★★★ Major player. Main winery in CUR, but brands, vines all over Chile. Ranges from supermarket brands (35 Sur, Castillo de Molina) to top table Cabo de Hornos CAB SAUV. Gd mid-point in single-v'yd 1865 Limited Edition line. (Also owns ALTAÏR, Missiones de Rengo, Santa Helena, TARAPACÁ, Viña Mar).

Santa Carolina, Viña ★★→★★★★ Large producer with v'yds all over Chile. Historic but not old fashioned. V.gd CAB SAUV, CARMENÈRE across ranges. Luis Pereira Cab Sauv is superb; Herencia (Carmenère) one of best.

Santa Rita Mai ★★→★★★★ Key player since 1880 and still on top of game. Large, diverse range. Starts at everyday wines (Tres Medallas, 120, Medalla Real), consistently gd-value CAB SAUV, CARMENÈRE. V.gd Floresta, Triple C, Bougainville. ***Casa Real Cab Sauv*** is jewel in crown.

Seña Aco ★★★★ This wine puts ACO valley in running for top Chilean terroir. Complex CAB SAUV-based B'x blend by Chadwick/ERRÁZURIZ.

Tabalí Lim ★★→★★★ Top LIM producer championing cool coast and limestone with v.gd CHARD, SAUV BL, PINOT N, SYRAH.

Tarapacá, Viña Casa, Ley, Mai ★★ Reliable line-up from Isla de MAI (600 ha+). V.gd CAB SAUV, esp Etiqueta Negra. Owned by VSPT.

Torres, Miguel Cur ★★→★★★★ Top producer in Cur with v'yds in MAU, ITA and now Pat. Diverse portfolio incl v.gd CAB SAUV (esp ***Manso de Velasco***), delightful sparkling PAÍS, complex Escaleras de Empedrado PINOT N. Miguel Torres (*see* Spain) has been innovating in Chile since 1979.

Undurraga Casa, Ley, Lim, Mai ★→★★★ Major producer in Chile, esp for sparkling. V.gd Altazor, Vigno CARIGNAN, TH (Terroir Hunter) series is ***superb value*** for single-v'yd wines.

Valdivieso Cur, San A ★→★★★ Big brand in Chile (esp for sp), covers all major valleys. Highlights single-v'yd range (esp CAB FR, MALBEC, ***Ley Chard***), Caballo Loco and CARIGNAN-based Éclat.

Deep s (Bío, Ita) has over 120 different ancient vine varieties, incl over 20 unknowns.

Vascos, Los Rap ★→★★★ Classic line-up of B'x varieties in Col from slightly disappointing Lafite-Rothschild venture in Chile. Top: Le Dix, Grande Res.

Ventisquero, Viña Casa, Col, Mai ★→★★★ Notable producer ranging valleys and styles. Fruit-forward reds (top Enclave CAB SAUV, Pangea SYRAH), fresh whites (Kalfu), innovative Tara (PINOT N, CHARD) from Atacama.

Veramonte Casa, Col ★★→★★★★ Now bio and greatly improved. V.gd PINOT N, SYRAH, SAUV BL (esp Ritual) from CASA. Owned by González Byass (*see* Spain).

Vigno Mau Old-vine CARIGNAN association in MAU. Several producers but all making wines of min 70% Carignan, 30-yr-old+ v'yds, 2 yrs+ in bottle, dry-farmed.

> **Going bio**
> As each vintage passes there are new recruits to the bio movement in
> Chile. A naturally healthy environment for grapes (dry, sunny, warm)
> makes bio and organic production relatively easy. Top bio producers:
> MATETIC, KOYLE, LAPOSTOLLE, VERAMONTE, EMILIANA.

Villard Casa, Mai ★★ Family producer of French-descent, based in CASA. Classy MAI reds, v.gd PINOT N. MERLOT, Equis CAB SAUV, fresh whites.

Viñedo Chadwick Mai ★★★→★★★★ One of Chile's top pours. 100% CAB SAUV from Puente Alto by Chadwick/ERRÁZURIZ.

Viu Manent Casa, Col ★★ Focused on MALBEC but lots to taste on the side (fresh coastal SAUV BL, rich CARMENÈRE). Col based.

Von Siebenthal Aco ★★→★★★ Indy producer in ACO. Full-bodied, rich reds (B'x varieties) and VIOGNIER. Parcela 7 blend v.gd value.

ARGENTINA

"**V**ast" is an understatement for Argentina. Mendoza province alone is more than 50% bigger than Portugal. And it still has unexplored potential wine lands. The latest movement of producers towards the Atlantic coast, up the hills of Cordoba and into the crevices of Patagonia show the potential outside the traditional Andean corridor. As for the 99% of production that remains in the Andean corridor, there is plenty of exploration there too: higher altitudes, lower latitudes and a constant search for poor soils and high water supply. Malbec accounts for over a third of Argentina's production, but there's also world-class Chardonnay, distinctive Cabernet Franc, promising Garnacha and even pockets of Fiano. Torrontés, Criolla and Bonarda are also coming on strong. Despite the shaky economy, Argentine wine has never been more exciting.

Achaval Ferrer Men ★★→★★★★ Focused on single-v'yd MALBEC since 1995 but today producing much more. Owned by Stolichnaya spirits group.

Aleanna Men ★★→★★★★ Rebel El Enemigo brand is brainchild of CATENA ZAPATA winemaker Alejandro Vigil and CZ heiress Adrianna Catena. Excellent CHARD, CAB FR, MALBEC.

Alicia, Viña Men ★★★ Old vines, complex wines in personal project of LUIGI BOSCA family. Interesting varieties incl Tiara (RIES/ALBARIÑO/SAVAGNIN) and NEBBIOLO.

Alta Vista Men ★→★★★ French investment, Mendoza terroir. MALBEC focus (v.gd single-v'yd line) with gd TORRONTES and sparkling.

Altocedro Men ★★→★★★ Karim Mussi is top winemaker in La Consulta. V.gd TEMPRANILLO, MALBEC. Some vines 100 yrs+.

Altos las Hormigas Men ★★★ Top MALBEC producer with excellent single-v'yd range from Lujan to Uco V. Tinto is new all-Argentine blend of BONARDA/SEM/Malbec. Headed by Alberto Antonini, Attilio Pagli, Pedro Parra, Leo Erazo. Also gd Bonarda under Colonia Las Liebres.

Atamisque Men ★→★★★ Impressive estate at entrance to Tupungato in Uco V. V.gd Catalpa CHARD, PINOT N. Top-value Serbal CAB FR, SAUV BL.

Benegas Men ★★→★★★ Traditional wine family, founded TRAPICHE in 1883, now with own project. Complex CAB FR, B'x blends.

Bianchi, Bodegas Men ★→★★★ Leading San Rafael producer now in Uco V too (Bodega Enzo Bianchi). Lots of bubbles and wide range of still wines too.

Bressia Men ★★→★★★ Family winery under guidance of Walter Bressia. Excellent, age-worthy red blends (Profundo, Conjuro, Ultima Hoja) and v.gd Monteagrelo SYRAH, CAB FR, Lagrima Canela CHARD.

Caelum Men ★★ Young, energetic family winery run by brother and sister in Luján. Gd MALBEC, CHARD and one of few FIANOS in S America.

Callia San J ★→★★ Top-value from SAN J. Calling card is spicy, fruit-forward SYRAH.

Canale, Bodegas Humberto Río N ★→★★★ Old vines and history in RÍO N. Highlights incl RIES, MALBEC, PINOT N.

Caro Men ★★★→★★★★ CATENA and Rothschild (*see* France) families together make rich B'x-style blends in MEN.

Casarena Men ★★ →★★★ Modern producer focused on single-v'yd reds from Luján. V.gd MALBEC, CAB FR, CAB SAUV. Ramanegra easier drinking, 505 entry-level.

Catena Zapata, Bodega Men ★★ →★★★★ Leading wine dynasty, now a large group with many projects. Top pours incl Adrianna Gualtallary MALBEC, CHARD, CAB FR. Alamos (distributed by Gallo) is worthy workhorse.

Chacra Río N ★★★ →★★★★ PINOT N producer, sophisticated bio wines from old vines. Piero Incisa della Rocchetta of Sassicaia (*see* Italy) took a gamble in the New World and it paid off. Superb.

Clos de los Siete Men ★★ One blend made by Michel Rolland using grapes from his estate (BODEGA ROLLAND) and three other B'x families in Vista Flores (*see* DIAMANDES, MONTEVIEJO, Cuvelier los Andes).

Cobos, Viña Men ★★★→★★★★ Paul Hobbs started Cobos, now owned by same group as NIETO SENETINER. Top CAB SAUV (Volturno, Bramare), v.gd MALBEC, CHARD.

Colomé, Bodega Sal ★★→★★★ Dizzying heights with vines reaching 3100m (10,171ft). Extreme wines too – complex, dark, intense MALBEC and bright TORRONTÉS.

Cuvelier los Andes Men ★★ →★★★ B'x family (Léoville-Poyferré); sophisticated red blends. Part of CLOS DE LOS 7.

Decero, Finca Men ★★→★★★ Slick operation in Luján with Swiss owners. Precise reds, v.gd PETIT VERDOT.

DiamAndes Men ★★★ Bonnie family (B'x's Malartic-Lagravière) making B'x blends in CLOS DE LOS SIETE neighbourhood. Age-worthy, classy reds, crisp whites.

Doña Paula Men ★★ →★★★★ Chilean-owned (SANTA RITA), Argentine-managed. Consistent quality across large portfolio. Known for steely SAUV BL, plush MALBEC (v.gd Parcel range), complex blends.

Cafayate, Chacayes, Vistalba, Gualtallary: trademarks and regions. Complicated.

El Esteco Sal ★★→★★★ V.gd producer in Cafayate. Gd-value Don David, Ciclos, El Esteco has top CAB SAUV, MALBEC.

Etchart Sal ★→★★ Long-standing Cafayate producer, founded 1850. Consistently gd-value TORRONTÉS; intense, high-altitude reds.

Fabre Montmayou Men, Río N ★★ →★★★ Sophisticated wines from old vines. V.gd CAB SAUV, MALBEC, MERLOT and B'x blends.

Fin del Mundo, Bodega Del Neu ★→★★ Pioneer in NEU and biggest today. Bold reds (v.gd CAB FR). Postales is entry level, also gd-value Ventus, Newen.

Flichman, Finca Men ★★→★★★ Large producer, diverse range covering complex reds (v.gd Dedicado, Paisaje) to easy-drinking, gd-value (Caballero de la Cepa). Owned by Sogrape (*see* Portugal).

Fournier, O Men ★★→★★★ Uco V, best-known for top TEMPRANILLO. V.gd SAUV BL, MALBEC.

Kaikén Men ★★ →★★★ MONTES family (*see* Chile). Rich, ripe reds do best in Vistalba location. V.gd CAB SAUV.

La Anita, Finca Men ★★ →★★★ Old-World style with patient bottle-ageing – a rarity in MEN. V.gd CAB SAUV, SYRAH, PETIT VERDOT.

La Riojana La R ★→★★ Lone ranger co-op (Argentina's largest) in Fatamina Valley, pooling grapes of 500 growers. Gd value. Fairtrade and organic.

Las Moras, Finca San J ★→★★ Top value from TRAPICHE'S SAN J outpost. Juicy, bright SYRAH, BONARDA.

> **Criolla comeback?**
> Much like the país revival in Chile, old Criolla vines are making a
> comeback in Argentina (and with 75,000 ha planted, there's plenty to
> go around). Look for: Cara Sur, Cadus, Ernesto Catena, PASSIONATE WINE.

Luca / Tikal / Tahuan / Alma Negra / Animal Men ★★→★★★ Projects of CATENA kids
who flew the nest. Laura (Luca) focuses on plush and premium, Ernesto (T/T/
A/A) tends towards natural wines.

Luigi Bosca Men ★★→★★★ Historic family producer in Luján with smart collection
of old-vine reds (Finca Las Nobles range), modern whites (v.gd RIES) and La Linda
for everyday.

Manos Negras / Tinto Negro / TeHo / ZaHa Men ★★→★★★ Excellent single-v'yd
wines from MEN and beyond. Top MALBEC, CAB FR.

Marcelo Pelleriti Men ★★→★★★ Eponymous label by MONTEVIEJO winemaker
who has a penchant for rock music. Portfolio incl several labels made with
Argentina's top musicians.

Masi Tupungato Men ★★→★★★ CORVINA in Argentina! No surprise that it comes
from Veneto family. V.gd *ripasso*-style MALBEC/CORVINA/MERLOT and Amarone-style
Corbec (Corvina/Malbec).

Matias Riccitelli Men ★★→★★★ Riccitelli Jr making name in family winery. Exciting
MALBEC, SEM at top end; Hey Malbec! is young brand for millennials.

Mendel Men ★★★ Classy wines from Roberto de la Motta. Old vines in Maipú, new
terroirs in Uco V. V.gd SEM, MALBEC. Lunta is great value.

Mendoza Heartland of MALBEC; Argentina's major wine region producing over two-
thirds of national total. Sub-regions: historic Maipú for old vines; Luján, cradle
of Malbec and home to large wineries; Uco V furthest, coolest, highest altitude.

Michel Torino Sal ★★ Large producer in Cafayate. Gd-value TORRONTÉS.

Moët-Hennessy Argentina Men ★→★★★ Making bubbles in MEN since 50s. Chandon
(charmat, party fizz) is workhorse, Baron B (traditional method) is complex
counterpart. *See* TERRAZAS DE LOS ANDES.

Monteviejo Men ★★→★★★★ Top Vista Flores winery. Festivo for everyday, v.gd-value
Petite Fleur (esp MALBEC), Lindaflor age-worthy, La Violeta superb. Owned by B'x
family behind Ch Le Gay.

Neuquén Pat S region 1st planted commercially in 2000s. Now home of rich reds
(MALBEC, CAB FR) and aromatic PINOT N. Old dinosaur haunt.

Nieto Senetiner, Bodegas Men ★→★★★ Large, historical producer in Luján with
modern outlook. Ranges from value lines (Benjamin, Emilia) to single-v'yd Don
Nicanor. Gd MALBEC, fresh SEM. Big in bubbles.

Noemia Pat ★★→★★★★ Elegant, complex MALBEC blends from RÍO N under Hans
Vinding-Diers.

Norton, Bodega Men ★→★★★ Popular locally and abroad, Norton is known for value
at friendly prices. Try Lot MALBEC range for special occasions. Founded by a
British train engineer in 1895, now owned by Gernot Langes Swarovski.

Passionate Wine Men ★★→★★★ Rule-bending winemaker Matias Michelini
pioneers new styles in Uco V. Don't miss mouthwatering Agua de Roca SAUV BL,
complex CAB FR/MALBEC Demente.

Peñaflor Men ★→★★★ Argentina's largest. Owns FINCA LAS MORAS, EL ESTECO, Santa
Ana, Navarro Correas, Suter, Mascota, TRAPICHE among others.

Piatelli Sal ★★ V.gd reds (MALBEC, CAB SAUV, TANNAT) and perfumed TORRONTÉS. V'yds,
wineries in SAL, MEN.

Piedra Negra Men ★→★★★ Best-known as François Lurton's winery. Champion of
Chacayes subregion in Uco V; rich MALBEC, great white blends (PINOT GR base).

Porvenir de Cafayate, El Sal ★★→★★★ Historical winery in Cafayate with precision focus. Bright TORRONTÉS, deep TANNAT, MALBEC, CAB SAUV. Gd-value Amauta blends.

Pulenta Estate Men ★★ →★★★ Pulenta bros focus on fast cars, slow wines. Excellent single-v'yd CAB FR, MALBEC, CAB SAUV. La Flor is v.gd everyday range.

Renacer Men ★★ →★★★ 2nd-generation Chilean growers in charge. Full MALBEC, rich CAB FR, fresh SAUV BL from CASA in Chile, and Amarone-style Enamore.

Riglos Men ★★ →★★★ Smart Uco V wines from Gualtallary. V.gd CAB FR, CAB SAUV, and MALBEC.

Río Negro Río N Historic s wine region being reappreciated for older vines and milder climes. V.gd PINOT N, SEM, MALBEC.

Rolland, Bodega Men ★★★ Michel Rolland's baby in CLOS DE LOS SIETE neighbourhood. Concentrated, perfumed reds (Val de Flores, Mariflor, Camille), intense SAUV BL.

Ruca Malén Men ★★ Consistent producer of gd reds in Luján. Look for PETIT VERDOT.

Salentein, Bodegas Men ★★ →★★★ Impressive estate in Los Arboles. Everyday El Portillo; sophisticated single-v'yd and Primus. Dutch owners; superb art gallery.

Salta Heartland of TORRONTÉS and intense reds (TANNAT, MALBEC) from high-altitude v'yds. Wine regions outside city in the Andes, planted at over 2300m (7546ft).

San Juan Just n of MEN and a little warmer. Home to gd-value SYRAH, BONARDA, MALBEC. Exciting new developments in hills.

San Pedro de Yacochuya Sal ★★★ ETCHART family's altitude project with Michel Rolland (*see* France). Intense MALBEC and fragrant TORRONTÉS.

Schroeder, Familia Neu ★★ PINOT N focus (incl bubbles) at this NEU winery. Visit cellar for dinosaur fossils.

Sophenia, Finca Men ★★ →★★★ Precise wines from Gualtallary. One of Uco V's top SAUV BL (esp Synthesis range), v.gd MALBEC, BONARDA.

Susana Balbo Wines Men ★★ →★★★★ Argentina's 1st female winemaker is known as the Queen of TORRONTÉS; now her son is moving towards throne. Also complex red blends (try Ben Marco, Nosotros), v.gd whites.

Tapiz Men ★★ →★★★ Luján-based but v'yds in Maipú, Uco V and now Pat too. Gd-value entry line; rich, top-end Black Tears MALBEC.

Terrazas de los Andes Men ★★ →★★★★ Rich reds, voluptuous whites. V.gd single-v'yd MALBEC series, superb **Cheval des Andes** blend made with Cheval Blanc (*see* B'x).

Toso, Pascual Men ★★ →★★★ Italian roots planted in MEN for over 120 yrs. Mainly MALBEC focus; top Magdalena Toso is superb.

Trapiche Men ★ →★★★ One of Argentina's biggest brands, Trapiche reaches far and wide – as do its v'yds, with ambitious Costa & Pampa project on Atlantic coast. Highlights incl *Medalla* CAB SAUV; Iscay MALBEC/CAB FR blend; single-v'yd Finca range. Part of PEÑAFLOR.

Trivento Men ★ →★★ Outpost of Chile's CONCHA Y TORO making gd-value reds. Eolo MALBEC is pricey flagship.

Vines of Mendoza / Winemaker's Village Men ★★ Small neighbourhood of mini-bodegas in Uco V owned by renowned winemakers and wealthy hobbyists. Look for Abremundos (*see* MARCELO PELLERITI), Corazon del Sol, Recuerdo, Super Uco.

Zorzal Men ★★★ V.gd-value, wide range, stylish wines from Gualtallary. Min oak, max texture. Excellent CAB FR, SAUV BL, PINOT N (esp Eggo).

Zuccardi Men ★★ →★★★★ Leading wine family in MEN, now led by 3rd generation. Modern, stylish wines from Uco V, incl v.gd Alluvional MALBEC, Emma BONARDA, Fossil CHARD. Preference for concrete vs. oak. Santa Julia in Maipú is everyday brand, gd-value, easy-drinking.

BRAZIL

B razil's fun-loving nature is reflected in its penchant for making bubbles. But there's more to Brazil than fun-fuelled fizz. Its cooler, southern regions are getting serious about Syrah, Merlot, Chardonnay,

Cabernet Sauvignon and – unsurprisingly – Malbec. Wine regions extend from the border with Uruguay, around the metropolitan hubbub of São Paolo and all the way up to Vale São Francisco in Bahia. The majority, however, are in Rio Grande do Sul – Brazil's answer to Piedmont, with hillside vineyards and cooler temperatures.

Aurora ★→★★ Big name with bigger numbers: 1000+ growers contribute to Brazil's largest co-op. Diverse portfolio from Serra Gaucha.

Casa Valduga ★→★★★ Known for gd bubbles, but also gd MERLOT and red blends.

Cave Geisse ★★★ One of country's top fizz producers. All traditional-method, complex, age-worthy. Nature is top pour.

Lidio Carraro ★→★★ V.gd producer with vines in Vale dos Vinhedos and Serra do Sudeste. Juicy easy-drinking. Quorum blend more complex.

Miolo ★→★★★ Large producer with premium focus (v.gd MERLOT, CHARD, TOURIGA N). Diverse portfolio from Brazil's major regions incl sparkling.

Pizzato ★→★★★ Personality and passion in Flavio P's wines. V.gd CHARD, MERLOT, fizz. Fausto is young range.

Salton ★→★★★ Brazil's oldest winery and one of biggest with wide range. Gd party fizz, v.gd Salton Gerações blend.

URUGUAY

Don't underestimate this small country. It consumes more wine per capita than the rest of the continent, and more beef per capita than anywhere else in the world. The natural pairing for all that steak is Uruguay's emblematic red variety – Tannat. Here the tannins are tamed, the acidity is bright and wines can be elegant rather than fierce. The Atlantic influence also gives excellent conditions for fresh whites.

Alto de la Ballena ★→★★ Family producer with pioneering spirit. Excellent SYRAH, CAB FR and juicy TANNAT/VIOGNIER blend from coast.

Bouza ★★→★★★ One of Uruguay's top producers. Family winery in Montevideo, v'yds in Pan de Azucar too. Pioneer of Uruguayan ALBARIÑO, top TANNAT, RIES, MER.

Garzón, Bodega ★→★★★ Argentine billionaire Bulgheroni puts his money where his mouth is with oustanding investment nr Punta del Este. Energetic, vibrant wines wth Alberto Antonini (Italy) as consultant.

Juanico Establecimiento ★→★★★ Uruguay's biggest. Entry-level brands (Pueblo del Sol, Don Pascual) important on domestic market, premium labels (Familia Deicas, Preludio) can wow for export. V.gd single-v'yd TANNAT series in Deicas.

Marichal ★→★★ 3rd gen growers now making wines. Gd TANNAT, PINOT N (and blends).

Pisano ★→★★★ Energetic family winery. V.gd TANNAT, TORRONTÉS, VIOGNIER.

Viñedo de los Vientos ★★→★★★ Interesting coastal range. Blending Italian ancestry (NEBBIOLO, ARNEIS, BARBERA) with Uruguayan terroir.

OTHER SOUTH AMERICAN WINES

Bolivia Landlocked in mtns, Bolivia is all about altitude. Vines start at 1800m (5900ft) and run to 3000m (9843ft)+. Expect reds with deep colour and laser-sharp acidity (SYRAH, CAB SAUV) and fragrant whites (v.gd dry MUSCAT). Although finding Bolivian wine outside Bolivia is rare, keep an eye out for Campos de Solana, Kohlberg, Kuhlmann, La Concepción, Sausini.

Peru is wine country in S America (since 1500s), Peru suffered several centuries of oppression by jealous Spanish producers. Today wine is making a comeback with producers Intipalka, Quebrada de Ihuanco, Mimo, Tacama, Vista Alegre in particular. Range of international varieties and also Pisco grapes used for wine.

Australia

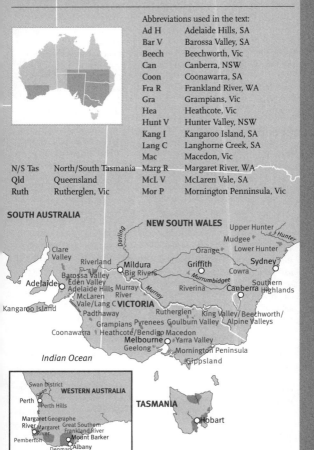

Abbreviations used in the text:

Ad H	Adelaide Hills, SA
Bar V	Barossa Valley, SA
Beech	Beechworth, Vic
Can	Canberra, NSW
Coon	Coonawarra, SA
Fra R	Frankland River, WA
Gra	Grampians, Vic
Hea	Heathcote, Vic
Hunt V	Hunter Valley, NSW
Kang I	Kangaroo Island, SA
Lang C	Langhorne Creek, SA
Mac	Macedon, Vic
N/S Tas	North/South Tasmania	Marg R	Margaret River, WA
Qld	Queensland	McL V	McLaren Vale, SA
Ruth	Rutherglen, Vic	Mor P	Mornington Penninsula, Vic

SOUTH AUSTRALIA

NEW SOUTH WALES

Upper Hunter
Mudgee
Orange — Lower Hunter
Clare Valley
Riverland — Mildura — Griffith — Sydney
Barossa Valley — Big Rivers — Cowra
Adelaide — Eden Valley — Murray — Riverina — Southern Highlands
Adelaide Hills — River — Canberra
McLaren Vale/Lang C
Kangaroo Island — Padthaway — **VICTORIA** — Rutherglen — King Valley/Beechworth/
Grampians Pyrenees Goulburn Valley — Alpine Valleys
Coonawarra — Heathcote/Bendigo Macedon
Melbourne — Yarra Valley
Geelong — Mornington Peninsula
Gippsland

Indian Ocean

Swan District
Perth — Swan
Perth Hills — **WESTERN AUSTRALIA**
Margaret River — Geographe
Margaret — Great Southern
River — Frankland River
Pemberton — **Mount Barker**
Denmark — Albany

TASMANIA

Hobart

Australian winemakers don't see Australia as one vast country, and nor should we. Its national trend of the moment is to fresher, less potent wines, so cooler climates are in high demand. The south coast, whether in the west, around Adelaide, south of Melbourne or in Tasmania, is doing better than inland irrigated areas where global warming is seen as a threat. But everywhere the soils and microclimates of much more specific areas are now in focus, and their wines better than ever.

Barossa Shiraz, Margaret River Cabernets, Yarra Pinot Noirs are all refining their game. Tense, complex Chardonnays with no perceptible oak; aromatic, pale Pinots; floral, almost delicate Grenaches; pungent, lime-scented Rieslings are today's prize-winners, and Italian Spanish and

Portuguese grapes are finding niches. But the biggest change is coming in the market. China is now the largest market for Australian wine by value. When you factor in that a significant number of Australian wineries have been sold to Chinese buyers over the past decade, a clear theme emerges. Busman's holidays to China among Australian winemakers are becoming the rage. Australian styles and prices haven't yet been skewed by this change, but they surely will. When Chinese drinkers discover en masse just how well suited perky young Australian Pinot Noir is to Peking Duck, indeed a wide range of classic Chinese cuisine, then look out. Australian Pinot has come a long way over the past 20 years but it remains comparatively cheap. When Chinese demand for Australian Pinot starts to burn holes in supply, let's just say that they'll be interesting times.

Recent vintages

New South Wales (NSW)
2018 Big ripe reds for long haul. Hot/tough yr for whites.
2017 Hot summer followed a wet spring; whites lapped up; reds too, in general.
2016 Be wary of Hun V reds (drink early); gd mid-ageing red/white elsewhere.
2015 Difficult in most parts, but Orange and Can excellent; Hilltops v.gd.
2014 Hun V Shiraz will be exceptional. Can Ries, Shiraz right up there.
2013 Rich reds, whites. Hun V Sem, Can Ries esp gd.

Victoria (Vic)
2018 Overshadowed by yr before. Slow-evolving.
2017 Excellent yr. Red/white looked gd young and will stay.
2016 Warm, dry season produced many overripe reds. Tread carefully.
2015 Strong yr across board.
2014 Frost damage galore but v.gd red vintage for most.
2013 Wines look surprisingly age-worthy given hot, dry, tough nature of season.

South Australia (SA)
2018 Expect gutsy reds with yrs up their sleeve. Whites gd, not in same class.
2017 High yield, high quality, highly drinkable young.
2016 Hopes are high for a special vintage for red/white.
2015 Warm regions coped well with summer of wild temperature swings.
2014 Hot, low-yield yr produced generous white/red.
2013 Water a problem so yields generally well down. Streaky vintage.

Western Australia (WA)
2018 Reds will outlive most of us; whites will do medium-term in a canter.
2017 Tricky vintage. Medium-term wines.
2016 Humid, sultry vintage. Nothing wrong with wines; mid-termers.
2015 Challenging, mixed results; be selective.
2014 Luck continued; almost getting monotonous. Another tip-top yr.
2013 Cab Sauv, Chard v. strong. Some rain but, again, gods were kind.

Accolade Wines r w Name for wines/wineries previously under the once-mighty Constellation, HARDYS groups. The master of the false dawn, though wine quality is generally v.gd.

Adelaide Hills SA Cool 450m (1476ft) sites in Mt Lofty ranges. CHARD, SAUV BL, SHIRAZ outgun PINOT N. ASHTON HILLS, HAHNDORF HILL, HENSCHKE, JERICHO, MIKE PRESS, MURDOCH HILL, SHAW & SMITH, TAPANAPPA all in excellent form.

Adelina Clare V, SA r w ★★ Reds (SHIRAZ, GRENACHE, MATARO, NEBBIOLO) the stars here. Imposing, intense, but polished. Excellent producer. Label designs quite something too.

Alkoomi Mt Barker, WA r w (RIES) 05′ 10′ 17 (CAB SAUV) 10′ 12′ 16 Veteran maker of fine Ries; rustic reds; more accessible young than they were.

All Saints Estate Ruth, Vic r w ★★ Great fortifieds, past/present. Hearty table wines.

Alpine Valleys Vic In valleys of Victorian Alps. Best: BILLY BUTTON, MAYFORD, Ringer Reef. TEMPRANILLO the star, though aromatic whites have come out swinging.

Andevine Hun V, NSW r w ★ Shot from blocks with initial SHIRAZ, SEM, CHARD releases from mature HUN v v′yds; 2nd-album blues since, now back on form.

Andrew Thomas Hun V, NSW r w ★ Old-vine SEM; silken SHIRAZ. Reds particularly gutsy in HUN v context.

Angove's SA r (br) ★★ MURRAY v family business. Cheapies (r w) often standouts of a broad range, Mainstream face of organic grape-growing, both value and premium ends.

Annie's Lane Clare V, SA r w Part of TWE. Boldly flavoured wines. Flagship Copper Trail (can be) excellent, esp RIES, SHIRAZ. Lower-tier wines serviceable.

Arenberg, d' McL V, SA r w (br) (sw) (sp) ★★ Sumptuous SHIRAZ, GRENACHE. Many varieties, wacky labels (incl The Cenosilicaphobic Cat SAGRANTINO). The Elton John of Oz wineries, fancy shirts and all. Often at best at value end.

A. Rodda Beech, Vic r w ★★ Bright CHARD from est v′yds; whole-bunch-fermented *Tempranillo* grown at high altitude is routinely a beauty.

Ashton Hills Ad H, SA r w (sp) ★★★ (PINOT N) 05′ 10′ 15′ 17 Totemic AD HILLS producer. Compelling Pinot N from 30-yr-old+ v′yds. Bought in 2015 by WIRRA WIRRA.

Bailey's NE Vic r w br ★★ Rich SHIRAZ, magnificent dessert MUSCAT (★★★★) and TOPAQUE. V′yds all organic. Sold by TWE to CASELLA in 2017.

Balgownie Estate Bendigo, Vic, Yarra V, Vic r ★★ Capable of medium-bodied, well-balanced, minty CAB of elegance, finesse, character from its BENDIGO heartland. Separate YARRA v arm.

Balnaves of Coonawarra SA r w ★★★ Family-owned COON champion. Lusty CHARD; v.gd spicy SHIRAZ, full-bodied Tally CAB SAUV flagship. "Joven-style" Cab gd.

Bannockburn Vic r w ★ ★ (CHARD) 14′ 15′ 17 (PINOT N) 10′ 12′ 17 Intense, complex Chard, spice-shot Pinot N. Put GEELONG region on map, but star not as bright as once was.

Barossa Valley SA Ground zero of Aussie red. V.-old-vine SHIRAZ, MOURVÈDRE, CAB SAUV, GRENACHE. Can produce bold, black, beautiful reds with its eyes closed, and has done for just about ever. New guard chasing fresher, (slightly) lighter styles, but richness never far off.

Same Shiraz, but different

Australia grows a lot of SHIRAZ, and if you think it all tastes rich, inky and sweet you've some catching up to do. Working w to e across Australia you can broadly say there is more earthy mid-to-upper-weight Shiraz out of MARG R and GREAT SOUTHERN (CAPE MENTELLE, Cherubino, HOWARD PARK); richer, warmer, more chocolatey wines out of BAR/EDEN VS and MCL V (CHAPEL HILL, D'ARENBERG, HENSCHKE, LANGMEIL, PENFOLDS, ST HALLETT, WIRRA WIRRA, YALUMBA), more peppery, cooler wines out of several regions within Vic (BY FARR, CRAIGLEE, GIANT STEPS, MOUNT LANGI, SEVILLE ESTATE, YABBY LAKE) and then again into more earthy, leathery, savoury-fruited wines out of HUN V (TYRRELL'S, MOUNT PLEASANT, MEEREA PARK). There are over 60 distinct wine regions across Australia; we've only scratched the surface with this summary. The Australian Shiraz tapestry has more panels than a car junkyard.

Bass Phillip Gippsland Vic r ★★★★ (PINOT N) 10′ 14′ 15′ 16 Ultimate soloist. Tiny amounts of variable but mostly exceptional Pinot N. In top form.

Bay of Fires N Tas r w sp ★★★ Home of Arras: Australia's most prestigious (and best) sparkling house. PINOT N shouldn't be passed over but *super-cuvee sparklings* rightly dominate. Owned by ACCOLADE.

Beechworth Vic The rock-strewn highlands of ne Vic. Tough country. CHARD, SHIRAZ best-performing varieties, but NEBBIOLO fast rising from (winter) fog. CASTAGNA, DOMENICA, FIGHTING GULLY ROAD, GIACONDA, SAVATERRE, SCHMÖLZER & BROWN, SORRENBERG essential producers.

Bendigo Vic Hot central Vic region. BALGOWNIE ESTATE the stalwart. Home of rich SHIRAZ, CAB SAUV.

Best's Great Western Gra, Vic r w ★★★ (SHIRAZ) 05′ 10′ 15′ 17 Shiraz master; *v.gd mid-weight reds.* Thomson Family Shiraz from 120-yr-old vines superb. Wines generally sit on plush side of elegant.

Billy Button Vic r w ★ So many wines, such small quantities. Everything from SHIRAZ and CHARD to Verduzzo, VERMENTINO, SCHIOPPETTINO, SAPERAVI and more.

Bindi Mac, Vic r w ★★★ (PINOT N) 04′ 10′ 15′ 17 Ultra-fastidious maker of outstanding, long-lived PinotN (esp), CHARD. Tiny production.

Bortoli, De Griffith, NSW, Yarra V, Vic r w (br) dr sw ★★ (Noble SEM) Both irrigation-area winery and leading YARRA V producer. Excellent cool-climate PINOT N, SHIRAZ, CHARD, SAUV BL and gd sweet, botrytized, Sauternes-style Noble Sem. Yarra V arm is where interest lies. Expanding in Vic.

Brash Higgins McL V, SA r ★★ Brad Hickey is a smart cookie. He has degrees in English and botany, but has also worked as a brewer, baker, sommelier and now makes radical expressions of MCL V (r w). Yeast is his thing. Modern face of McL V.

Bremerton Lang C, SA r w ★★ Silken CAB, SHIRAZ with mounds of flavour. Never a bad wine.

Brokenwood Hun V, NSW r w ★★ (ILR Res SEM) 07′ 09′ 11 (Graveyard SHIRAZ) 00′ 06′ 14 HUN V classic. Outside of the *Cricket Pitch* Sem/SAUV BL can be hard to find value, but quality generally gd.

Brown Brothers King V, Vic r w br dr sw sp ★ Wide range of crowd-pleasing styles, varieties. General emphasis on sweetness. Innocent Bystander (YARRA V) and Devil's Corner/Tamar Ridge (TAS) recent and savvy) acquisitions.

By Farr / Farr Rising Vic r w ★★★★ 10′ 14 15′ 17 (PINOT N) Superb producer, at Bannockburn. CHARD, Pinot N can be minor masterpieces.

Campbells Ruth. Vic r (w) br ★ Smooth ripe reds (esp Bobbie Burns SHIRAZ); extraordinary Merchant Prince Rare *Muscat*, Isabella Rare TOPAQUE (★★★★).

Canberra District NSW Both quality, quantity rising; site selection important; cool climate. CLONAKILLA best known. New guns: EDEN ROAD, GUNDOG ESTATE, Mount Majura, RAVENSWORTH.

Cape Mentelle Marg R, WA r w ★★★ (CAB SAUV) 01′ 10′ 14′ 15′ 16 MR pioneer on great form. Robust Cab has become more elegant (with lower alc), CHARD v.gd; also ZIN, v. popular SAUV BL/SEM. Owned by LVMH Veuve Clicquot.

Casella Riverina, NSW r w ★ Casella's Yellow Tail range of budget reds/whites have helped build an Australian wine empire. Now owner of BAILEY'S, Brand's of Coonawarra, MORRIS, PETER LEHMANN.

Castagna Beech, Vic r w ★★ (SYRAH) 06′ 10′ 12′ 14′ Julian C leads Oz bio brigade. Estate-grown SHIRAZ/VIOGNIER, SANGIOVESE/Shiraz excellent.

Chambers Rosewood NE Vic (r) (w) br Viewed with MORRIS as greatest maker of sticky TOPAQUE (★★★★), *Muscat*.

Chapel Hill McL V, SA r (w) ★★ Leading MCL V producer. SHIRAZ, CAB the bread and butter, but TEMPRANILLO and esp GRENACHE on rise.

Charles Melton Bar V, SA r w (sp) ★ Low-profile winery with bold, ripe, traditional reds, esp Nine Popes, an old-vine GRENACHE/SHIRAZ blend.

Chatto Tas r ★★★★ Young v'yd, but already among Australia's best PINOT N producers. Fruit, spice and all things nice. Smoky savouriness abounds. Open a bottle and enter its world.

Clarendon Hills McL V, SA r ★★ Full-Monty reds (high alc, intense fruit) from grapes grown on hills above MCL V. Cigar wines.

Clare Valley SA Small, pretty, high-quality area 160-km (100-miles) n of Adelaide. Best toured by bike, some say. Australia's most prominent RIES region. Gumleaf-scented SHIRAZ; earthen, tannic CAB SAUV. ADELINA, GROSSET, KILIKANOON, KIRRIHILL, MOUNT HORROCKS, TIM ADAMS, Wendouree lead way.

Clonakilla Can, NSW r w ★★★★ (SHIRAZ) 05' 07' 09' 10' 14' 15' 17 CAN region superstar. RIES, VIOGNIER excellent, Shiraz/Viognier blend famous.

Clos du Tertre Fra R, WA ★★ Stunning RIES. Textural, intense, long. Ries fanatics.

Clyde Park Vic r w ★★★ Broody single-v'yd CHARD, PINOT N in stellar form. SHIRAZ turning heads.

Coldstream Hills Yarra V, Vic r w (sp) ★★★★ (CHARD) 10' 12' 15' 17 (PINOT N) 06' 10' 15' 17 Est 1985 by critic James Halliday. Delicious PINOT N to drink young, *Res to age*. Excellent Chard (esp Res). Head-turning *single-v'yd releases*. Part of TWE.

Coonawarra SA Almost in Vic: home to some of Australia's best (value, quality) CAB SAUV; land of richest red soil (on limestone). WYNNS is senior, and champion, resident. BALNAVES, KATNOOK, LINDEMANS, MAJELLA, RYMILL, YALUMBA all key.

Coriole McL V, SA r w ★★★ (Lloyd Res SHIRAZ) 04' 10' 14' 16 Renowned producer: SANGIOVESE, old-vine SHIRAZ Lloyd Res. Interesting Italians, esp FIANO, NERO D'AVOLA.

Craiglee Mac, Vic r w ★★★ (SHIRAZ) 10' 12' 14' 15 Salt-of-the-earth producer. N Rhône inspired. Fragrant, peppery Shiraz, age-worthy CHARD.

Crawford River Hea, Vic w ★★★ Outstanding RIES producer. Cool, cold, scintillatingly (dry) style, great for seafood, highly age-worthy.

Cullen Marg R, WA r w ★★★★ (CHARD) 10' 13' 14' 15' 16' 17 (CAB SAUV/MERLOT) 05' 09' 12' 13' 14' 15' 16 2nd-generation star Vanya Cullen makes substantial but subtle SEM/SAUV BL, outstanding Chard, elegant, sinewy Cab/Merlot. Bio in all she does. Forever reaching for quality extremes.

Curly Flat Mac, Vic r w ★★★ (PINOT N) 10' 12' 13' 14' 15' 16 Robust but perfumed Pinot N on two price/quality levels. Full-flavoured CHARD. Both age-worthy. In safe hands with new winemaker Matt Harrop.

David Franz Bar V, SA r w SEM from 100-yr-old+ vines, a rosé made with 108 different varieties (yes 108), old-vine CAB suave, experimental VERMENTINO, pristine CHARD. You name it, they're playing with it here.

Deakin Estate Vic r w ★ V.-low-alc MOSCATO. Spicy SHIRAZ, CAB SAUV. Keeps delivering.

Deep Woods Estate Marg R, WA r w ★★★ Compelling CHARD, CAB SAUV. Powerhouse wines, built to impress/last.

Devil's Lair Marg R, WA r w ★ Opulent CHARD, CAB SAUV/MERLOT. Fifth Leg gd second label. Owned by TWE.

Domaine A S Tas r w ★★ V.gd oak-matured SAUV BL. Polarizing cool-climate CAB SAUV. Charismatic, to say the least. Recently acquired by MOORILLA.

Domaine Chandon Yarra V, Vic r w (w) sp ★★ Cool-climate sparkling and table wine. Owned by Moët & Chandon. Known in UK as Green Point. NV cuvées in best ever shape.

Domenica Beech, Vic ★★★ Flashy new BEECH producer with est v'yds. Exuberant, spicy SHIRAZ. Textural MARSANNE. NEBBIOLO in process of stealing show.

Eden Road r w Well-made SHIRAZ, CHARD, CAB SAUV from Hilltops, TUMBARUMBA, CAN DISTRICT regions.

Eden Valley SA BAR's closest neighbour. Hilly region to e, home to Chris Ringland,

HENSCHKE, PEWSEY VALE, Radford, TORZI MATTHEWS and others; racy RIES, (perfumed, bright) SHIRAZ, CAB SAUV of top quality.

Elderton Bar V, SA r w (br) (sp) ★★ Old vines; rich, oaked CAB SAUV, SHIRAZ. All bases covered. Some organics/bio. Rich reds in excellent form.

Eldorado Road Ruth, Vic r ★★ Pet project of winemaker Paul Dahlenburg. DURIF, SHIRAZ, NERO D'AVOLA all show elegance, power not mutually exclusive.

Eldridge Estate Mor P, Vic r w ★★★ Winemaker David Lloyd is a fastidious experimenter. PINOT N, CHARD worth the fuss. Varietal GAMAY really quite special.

Epis Mac, Vic r w ★ (PINOT N) Long-lived Pinot N; elegant CHARD. Cold climate. Powerful at release; complexity takes time.

Evans & Tate Marg R, WA r w ★ Focus almost entirely on value end of market, but does a v.gd job. SHIRAZ, CAB SAUV, CHARD, SAUV BL. Aspirational wines can be gd too.

Mount Pleasant's had five chief winemakers in 98 yrs. Buy new chief Adrian Sparks a comfy chair.

Faber Vineyards Swan V, WA r ★★★ (Res SHIRAZ) 11' 12' 14' 15 John Griffiths is a guru of WA winemaking. Home estate redefines what's possible for SWAN V Shiraz. Polished power.

Fighting Gully Road Beech, Vic r w ★★ Touchstone producer of BEECH. CHARD, AGLIANICO, TEMPRANILLO kicking goals. Quality just starting to change up a gear.

Flametree Marg R, WA r w ★★ Exceptional CAB SAUV; spicy, seductive SHIRAZ; CHARD often compelling.

Fraser Gallop Estate Marg R, WA r w ★★ Concentrated CAB SAUV, CHARD, (wooded) SEM/SAUV BL. Cab has been particularly strong in recent yrs.

Freycinet Tas r w (sp) ★★★ (PINOT N) 10' 12' 13' 16 Pioneer family winery on TAS's e coast producing dense Pinot N, gd CHARD, excellent Radenti sparkling.

Garagiste Mor P, Vic r w ★★★ CHARD, PINOT N of intensity, finesse. Quality always seems to be high or higher. Multi-v'yd blends really take value cake.

Geelong Vic Region w of Melbourne. Cool, dry climate. Best names: BANNOCKBURN, Bellarine Estate, BY FARR, LETHBRIDGE, CLYDE PARK. Provenance.

Gemtree Vineyards McL V, SA r (w) ★★ Warm-hearted SHIRAZ alongside TEMPRANILLO and other exotica, linked by quality. Largely bio.

Giaconda Beech, Vic r w ★★★★ (CHARD) 10' 11' 14' 15' 16 (SHIRAZ) 10' 13' 14' 15' In mid-80s Rick Kinzbrunner walked up a steep, rock-strewn hill and came down a winemaking legend. In the process he kickstarted BEECH region. Australian Chard royalty. Tiny production of powerhouse wines.

Giant Steps Yarra V, Vic r w ★★★ Top single-v'yd CHARD, PINOT N, SHIRAZ. Vintages 14' 15' 17' 18 all exciting for three main varieties.

Glaetzer-Dixon Tas r w ★★★ Nick Glaetzer turned his family history on its head by setting up camp in cool TAS. Euro-style RIES, Rhôney SHIRAZ, meaty PINOT N. Strength to strength.

Glaetzer Wines Bar V, SA r ★ Big, polished reds with eye-catching packaging to match. V-ripe old-vine SHIRAZ led by iconic Amon-Ra.

Goulburn Valley Vic Temperate region in mid-Vic. Full-bodied, earthy table wines. MARSANNE, CAB SAUV, SHIRAZ the pick, MITCHELTON, TAHBILK perpetual flagbearers. Aka Nagambie Lakes.

Grampians Vic Temperate region in nw Vic previously known as Great Western. High-quality spicy SHIRAZ, sparkling Shiraz. Home to SEPPELT (for now), BEST'S, MOUNT LANGI, The Story.

Granite Belt Qld High-altitude, (relatively) cool, improbable region just n of Qld/NSW border. Spicy SHIRAZ, rich SEM, eg. Boireann, Golden Grove.

Grant Burge Bar V, SA r w (br) (sw) (sp) ★ Smooth red/white from best grapes of Burge's large v'yd holdings. Acquired by ACCOLADE in 2015.

Great Southern WA Remote cool area at bottom left corner of Oz; Albany, Denmark, Frankland River, Mount Barker, Porongurup are official subregions. 1st-class RIES, SHIRAZ, CAB SAUV. Style, value here.

Grosset Clare V, SA r w ★★★★ (RIES) 10' 15' 17' 18 (Gaia) 05' 12' 13' 14' 15 Fastidious winemaker. Foremost Oz Ries, lovely CHARD, v.gd *Gaia* CAB SAUV/MERLOT. Beetrooty PINOT N.

Gundog Estate Can, NSW r w ★ Highly aspirational SEM SHIRAZ from CAN, HUN V.

Hahndorf Hill Ad H, SA r w ★★ Much experimentation across wide range, but makes fascinating fist of GRÜNER V, and has made variety its own in Oz.

Hardys r w (sw) sp ★★★ (Eileen CHARD) 12' 15' 16 (Eileen SHIRAZ) 06' 10' 12' 15 Historic company now part of ACCOLADE. Chard excellent. Shiraz not far off.

Heathcote Vic The region's 500-million-yr-old Cambrian soil has great potential for high-quality reds, esp SHIRAZ. Now that the excitement has abated, it's turning out excellent full-bodied reds.

Henschke Eden V, SA r w ★★★★ (SHIRAZ) 04' 06' 12' 13 (CAB SAUV) 04' 06' 10' Pre-eminent 150-yr-old family business known for delectable Hill of Grace (Shiraz), v.gd Cab Sauv, red blends, gd whites, scary prices and more. Wonderful producer.

Hentley Farm Bar V, SA r ★★ Consistently produces SHIRAZ of immense power, concentration – wall-of-flavour territory – though importantly in a (generally) fresh, almost frisky, context.

Hewitson SE Aus r (w) ★★ (*Old Garden Mourvèdre*) 10' 12' 14' Dean Hewitson sources parcels off the "oldest MOURVÈDRE vines on the planet". V.gd SHIRAZ at various price levels.

Houghton Swan V, WA r w ★★★ (Jack Mann) 08' 11' 12' 14' 15' Once-legendary winery of Swan Valley nr Perth. Part of ACCOLADE. Inexpensive white blend was long *a national classic*. V.gd CAB SAUV, SHIRAZ, etc. sourced from GREAT SOUTHERN, MARG R. Jack Mann Cab blend is seriously gd.

Howard Park WA r w ★★ (RIES) 12' 14' 17 (CAB SAUV) 09' 10' 11' 12' 13' 14 Scented Ries, CHARD; earthy Cab. Second label *MadFish* v.gd value. PINOT N improving.

Hunter Valley NSW It makes no sense but it works. Sub-tropical coal-mining area 160-km (100-miles) n of Sydney. Mid-weight, earthy SHIRAZ, gentle SEM can live for 30 yrs. Arguably most terroir-driven styles of Oz. MOUNT PLEASANT, Brokenwood, ANDREW THOMAS, *Tyrrell's* (esp) the pillars.

Inkwell McL V, SA r (w) ★★ High polish, high opinion, high character. Full house of intriguing wines, mostly SHIRAZ-based.

Jacob's Creek Bar V, SA r w (br) (sw) sp ★ Owned by Pernod Ricard. Almost totally focused on various tiers of uninspiring-but-reliable Jacob's Creek wines, covering all varieties, prices. New red range, aged in whisky barrels, proves that bourbon, Coke and wine aren't always dissimilar.

Jasper Hill Hea, Vic r w ★ (SHIRAZ) 09' 10' 17 Emily's Paddock Shiraz/CAB FR blend, Georgia's Paddock Shiraz from dry-land estate are intense, burly, long-lived and bio. NEBBIOLO to watch.

Jericho Ad H, SA, McL V, SA r w ★★ Excellent fruit selection and skilled winemaking produce a suite of modern, tasty, well-presented wines, esp SHIRAZ, TEMPRANILLO.

Henschke turns 150
Eden Valley winery HENSCHKE, most famous for its (v.) old-vine Hill of Grace SHIRAZ, has its 150th birthday. Hill of Grace v'yd was planted in 1860. The 1st Henschke wines were offered for sale in 1868. The 1st wine to be labelled Hill of Grace didn't come until 1958; the current 13 vintage was the 55th release. The vines, now approaching 160 yrs old, are still productive and still make the rare-as-hens-teeth wine – 13 has limit of one bottle/customer.

Jim Barry Clare V, SA r w ★★ Great v'yds provide v.gd RIES, McCrae Wood SHIRAZ and richly robed, pricey, oaked-to-the-devil The Armagh Shiraz.

John Duval Wines Bar V, SA r ★★★ John Duval – former maker of PENFOLDS Grange – makes *delicious Rhône reds* of great intensity, character.

Kalleske r ★★ Old family farm at Greenock, nw corner of BAR V, makes rather special single-v'yd SHIRAZ among many other intensely flavoured things. Bio/organic.

Katnook Estate Coon, SA r w (sw) (sp) ★★ (Odyssey CAB SAUV) 05' 10' 13 Pricey icons Odyssey, Prodigy SHIRAZ. Concentrated fruit slathered in oak.

Kilikanoon Clare V, SA r w ★★ RIES, SHIRAZ excellent performers. Luscious, generous, beautifully made. Sold to Chinese investment group in 2017.

King Valley Vic Altitude range 155–860m (509–2821ft) has massive impact on varieties, styles. Over 20 brands, headed quality-wise by BROWN BROTHERS, Chrismont, Dal Zotto, PIZZINI (esp).

Kirrihill Clare V, SA r w ★ V.gd CAB SAUV, SHIRAZ, RIES at, often, excellent prices.

Knappstein Wines Clare V, SA r w ★ Reliable RIES, SHIRAZ and CAB SAUV. Sold by LION NATHAN to ACCOLADE in 2016. Treading water for now, but always has some gd-value offerings.

Kooyong Mor P, Vic r w ★★ PINOT N, *superb Chard* of harmony, structure. PINOT GR of charm. High-quality single-v'yd wines.

Lake Breeze Lang C, SA r (w) ★★ Succulently smooth, gutsy, value SHIRAZ, CAB SAUV; has mid-level wines thoroughly licked.

Lake's Folly Hun V, NSW r w ★★ (CHARD) 13' 14' (CAB SAUV) 13' 14' 16 Founded by surgeon Max Lake, the pioneer of HUN V Cab Sauv. Chard often better than Cab blend.

Langmeil Bar V, SA r w ★★ Holder of some of the world's oldest SHIRAZ vines (planted mid-1800s), plus other old v'yds, all employed to produce full-throttle Shiraz, GRENACHE, CAB SAUV.

Larry Cherubino Vines Fra R, WA r w ★★★ Intense SAUV BL, RIES, *spicy Shiraz*, polished CAB SAUV. Ambitious label now franking its early promise in full. Expansive range.

Leasingham Clare V, SA r w Once-important brand now a husk of its former self, at best. Owned by ACCOLADE.

Leeuwin Estate Marg R, WA r w ★★★★ (CHARD) 10' 13' **14' 15** Iconic producer. All about Chard. Full-bodied, age-worthy Art Series rendition. SAUV BL, RIES less brilliant. *Cab Sauv* occasionally v.gd.

Leo Buring Bar V, SA w ★★ 02' 05' 13' 14' Part of TWE. Exclusively RIES; Leonay top label, *ages superbly*. Maybe a step behind where it once was.

Lethbridge Vic r w ★★★ Small, stylish producer of CHARD, SHIRAZ, PINOT N, RIES. Forever experimenting. Cool climate but wines are meaty, substantial.

Limestone Coast Zone SA Important zone, incl Bordertown, COON, Mt Benson, Mt Gambier, PADTHAWAY, Robe, WRATTONBULLY.

Lindemans r w ★ Owned by TWE. Low-price Bin range now main focus, far cry from former glory. Lindemans' COON Trio reds still okay.

Why do some Aussie reds taste of eucalyptus? Oil from trees blows onto grapes, gets in vats.

Luke Lambert Yarra V, Vic ★ Off-beat producer of variable but at times excellent (cool-climate mostly) SHIRAZ, PINOT N, NEBBIOLO.

Macedon and Sunbury Vic Adjacent regions: Macedon with higher elevation, Sunbury nr Melbourne airport. Quality from BINDI, CRAIGLEE, CURLY FLAT, EPIS, Hanging Rock.

Mac Forbes Yarra V, Vic ★★★ Mover and shaker of YARRA V. Myriad (in both number, styles) single-v'yd releases, mainly PINOT N, CHARD, RIES.

> **Can-do attitude**
> In 2018, wine-in-a-can arrived as a noticeable force in Australia. A great idea. If you take wine camping or trekking or on a picnic, you have to carry out the empty bottle. You can crush the empty can and it weighs almost nothing. Cans are recyclable, give perfect protection against light, and are quick to cool.

McHenry Hohnen Marg R, WA ★★ Among best producers of MARG R CHARD, on rise too. Gd train to catch.

McLaren Vale SA Beloved maritime region on s outskirts of Adelaide. Big-flavoured reds in general but BRASH HIGGINS, CHAPEL HILL, CORIOLE, GEMTREE, INKWELL, SC PANNELL, WIRRA WIRRA and growing number of others show elegance too. SHIRAZ the hero but varietal GRENACHE the big quality mover.

McWilliam's SE Aus r w (br) (sw) ★★ Family-owned. Hanwood, MOUNT PLEASANT key pillars. Sale of EVANS & TATE in 2017 a curious move.

Main Ridge Estate Mor P, Vic r w ★★ Rich, age-worthy CHARD, PINOT N. Founder Nat White is legend of MOR P wine; hard to imagine place without him. Changed hands in 2015.

Majella Coon, SA r (w) ★★ As reliable as the day is long. Opulent SHIRAZ, CAB SAUV. Essence of modern COON.

Margaret River WA Temperate coastal area s of Perth. Powerful CHARD, structured CAB SAUV, spicy SHIRAZ. CULLEN, DEVIL'S LAIR, DEEP WOODS ESTATE, FRASER GALLOP, LEEUWIN ESTATE, MOSS WOOD, VOYAGER ESTATE and many others. Great touring (and surfing) region.

Marius McL V, SA r ★★★ Varietal SHIRAZ and blends of dramatic concentration. Quality in inverse proportion to fuss; latter kept to a min.

Mayford NE Vic, Vic r w ★★★ Tiny v'yd in private, hidden valley. Put ALPINE VALLEYS region on map. SHIRAZ, CHARD, exciting spice-shot TEMPRANILLO.

Meerea Park Hun V, NSW r w ★ Brothers Garth and Rhys Eather create age-worthy SEM, SHIRAZ often as single-v'yd expressions.

Mike Press Wines Ad H, SA r (w) ★★ Tiny production, tiny pricing. CAB SAUV, SHIRAZ, CHARD, SAUV BL. Crowd favourite of bargain hunters.

Mitchelton Goulburn V, Vic r w (sw) ★★ Stalwart producer of CAB SAUV, SHIRAZ, RIES, plus speciality of *Marsanne*, ROUSSANNE. Top spot to visit; fancy new hotel set among those fab river red gums.

Mitolo r ★ Quality SHIRAZ, CAB SAUV. Heroic style.

Montalto Mor P, Vic r w ★★★ For some yrs was nice restaurant and gallery. Recently, wine quality skyrocketed. Firmly "must try" of MOR P. Single-v'yd releases top-notch.

Moorilla Estate Tas r w (sp) ★★ Pioneer nr Hobart on Derwent River. Gd CHARD, RIES; PINOT N. V.gd restaurant, extraordinary art gallery. Recently acquired nearby DOMAINE A.

Moorooduc Estate Mor P, Vic r w ★★★ Long-term producer of stylish, sophisticated CHARD, PINOT N. Just a bit special.

Moppity Vineyards Hilltops, NSW r w ★★ Stern, tannic SHIRAZ/VIOGNIER, CAB SAUV (Hilltops). Elegant CHARD (TUMBARUMBA). Quality ambitions but best known as a value producer.

Mornington Peninsula Vic Coastal area 40 km (25 miles) se of Melbourne. Quality boutique wineries abound. Cool, windy climate. PINOT N, CHARD, PINOT GR. Wine/surf/beach/food playground. ELDRIDGE ESTATE, GARAGISTE, KOOYONG, MAIN RIDGE ESTATE, MONTALTO, STONIER, TEN MINUTES BY TRACTOR and more. A rising star.

Morris NE Vic (r) (w) br ★★★ RUTH producer of Oz's (the world's?) greatest dessert *Muscats*, TOPAQUES. Owned by CASELLA.

Moss Wood Marg R, WA r w ★★★ (CAB SAUV) 05' 12' 13' 14' 15 MARG R's most opulent (red) wines. SEM, CHARD, super-smooth *Cab Sauv*. Oak-and-fruit-rich.

Mount Horrocks Clare V, SA r w ★★ Fine dry RIES, sweet Cordon Cut Ries. SHIRAZ, CAB SAUV in fine form.

Mount Langi Ghiran Gra, Vic r w ★★★★ (SHIRAZ) 10' 12' 13' 14' 15 Rich, peppery, *Rhône-like Shiraz*. Excellent Cliff Edge Shiraz. Special patch of dirt. Special run of form.

Mount Majura Can, NSW r w ★★ Leading TEMPRANILLO producer. RIES, SHIRAZ, CHARD all gd. Reds sturdy, spicy.

Mount Mary Yarra V, Vic r w ★★★★ (PINOT N) 13' 14' 15' 16 (Quintet) 10' 14' 15' 16 Late Dr. Middleton made tiny amounts of suave CHARD, vivid Pinot N, elegant CAB SAUV blend. All age impeccably. Remarkably, post-Dr. era has brought improvement, if anything.

Mount Pleasant Hun V, NSW ★★★ Old HUN V producer owned by MCWILLIAM'S, now re-invigorated. ■B single-v'yd SEMS (esp *Lovedale*), SHIRAZ.

Mudgee NSW Region nw of Sydney. Earthy reds, fine SEM, full CHARD. Gd quality but needs a hero.

Murdoch Hill Ad H, SA r w ★★ Stunningly peppery PINOT N; SYRAH. Just keeps on producing hits.

Murray Valley SA Vast irrigated v'yds. Key figure in climate-change discussions.

Ngeringa Ad H, SA r w ★ Perfumed PINOT N, NEBBIOLO. Rhôney SHIRAZ. Savoury rosé. Bio.

Nick Spencer Can, NSW r w ★★ CAN and Gundagai-based former EDEN ROAD winemaker. CHARD and red blend (SHIRAZ/TEMPRANILLO/TOURIGA/CAB SAUV) of particular interest.

Ochota Barrels Bar V, SA r w ★★ Quixotic producer making hay with (mostly) old-vine GRENACHE, SHIRAZ from MCL V, BAR V.

O'Leary Walker Clare V, SA r w ★★ Low profile but excellent quality. CLARE V RIES, CAB SAUV standout. MCL V SHIRAZ oak-heavy but gd.

Orange NSW Cool-climate, high-elevation region. Lively SHIRAZ (when ripe), but best suited to (intense) aromatic whites and CHARD.

Out of Step Yarra V, Vic r w ★★★ Took on YARRA V SAUV BL and won. Now doing likewise with CHARD, PINOT N and NEBBIOLO from various v'yds. Only the brave.

Padthaway SA V'zd SHIRAZ, CAB SAUV. Rarely mentioned but important region. Soil salinity ongoing issue.

Paringa Estate Mor P, Vic r (w) ★★★ Maker of irresistible PINOT N, SHIRAZ. Fleshy, fruity, flashy styles.

Passing Clouds Bendigo, Vic ★★ Pioneer of modern era of Vic wine. Off radar for many yrs but burst back in 2016 with a gloriously elegant, textured signature CAB blend. Gd form since.

Paxton McL V, SA r ★ Prominent organic/bio grower/producer. Ripe but elegant SHIRAZ, GRENACHE.

Pemberton WA Region between MARG R and GREAT SOUTHERN; initial enthusiasm for PINOT N replaced by RIES, CHARD, SHIRAZ.

Australian Prosecco sales rocketing: here grape variety, not region. Italians v. cross.

Penfolds r w (br) ★★★★ (Grange) 86' 90' 96' 04' 06' 08' 10' 12' 14 (CAB SAUV Bin 707) 96' 02' 05' 06' 10' 12' 15' 16 and of course *St Henri*, "simple" SHIRAZ. Originally Adelaide, now SA. Oz's best warm-climate red wine company. Superb *Yattarna* CHARD, Bin Chard now right up there with reds.

Petaluma Ad H, SA r w sp ★★ (RIES) 11' 12' 13' 17 (CHARD) 12' 16 (CAB SAUV COON) 05' 08' 12' Seems to miss ex-owner/creator Brian Croser. Gd but low-key now.

Peter Lehmann Vines Bar V, SA r w (br) (sw) (sp) ★★ Well-priced wines incl easy RIES.

Luxurious/sexy Stonewell SHIRAZ among many others (r w). Heroic Peter L died 2013; company sold 2014 to CASELLA (Yellow Tail).

Pewsey Vale Ad H, SA w ★ V.gd RIES, standard and (aged-release) The Contours, grown on lovely tiered v'yd.

Pierro Marg R, WA r w ★★★ (CHARD) 13′ 14′ 15′ 16 Producer of expensive, tangy SEM/SAUV BL and full-throttle Chard.

Pipers Brook Tas r w sp ★★★ (RIES) 09′ 13′ (CHARD) 13′ 14 Cool-area pioneer, gd Ries, *restrained Chard and sparkling* from Tamar Valley. Second label: Ninth Island. Owned by Belgian Kreglinger family.

For every 100m (328ft) rise in v'yd altitude, there's a temperature drop of 0.6–0.7°C (1.1°F). Can be useful.

Pizzini King V, Vic r ★★ (SANGIOVESE) 14′ 15′ 16 A leader of Italian varieties in Oz, esp NEBBIOLO, SANGIOVESE (recently stepped up a gear). Dominant KING VALLEY producer.

Primo Estate SA r w dr (sw) ★★ Joe Grilli's many successes incl rich MCL V SHIRAZ, tangy COLOMBARD, potent Joseph CAB SAUV/MERLOT and (exceptionally) complex sparkling Shiraz.

Punch Yarra V, Vic r w ★★★ Lance family ran Diamond Valley for decades. When they sold, they retained close-planted PINOT N v'yd. It can grow detailed, decisive, age-worthy wines.

Pyrenees Vic Central Vic region making rich, often minty reds. Blue Pyrenees, Dalwhinnie, Dog Rock, Summerfield, Mount Avoca, TALTARNI leading players, though it's also a happy hunting ground for assorted small producers.

Ravensworth Can, NSW r w ★★ Suddenly in hot demand for various wine experiments. SANGIOVESE best-known but there's a buzz over skin-contact whites and GAMAY Noir.

Riverina NSW Large-volume irrigated zone centred on Griffith.

Robert Oatley Wines Mudgee, NSW r w ★ Ambitious venture of ROSEMOUNT ESTATE creator Robert Oatley. Quality/price ratio usually well-aligned.

Rockford Bar V, SA r (w) sp ★★★ Sourced from various old, low-yielding v'yds; reds best; iconic Basket Press SHIRAZ and noted *sparkling Black Shiraz*.

Rosemount Estate r w Once the pacesetter. Periodically loses its way but reds can be gd.

Ruggabellus Bar V, SA r ★★ Causing a stir. Funkier, more savoury version of BAR V. Old oak, min sulphur, wild yeast, whole bunches/stems. Blends of CINSAULT, GRENACHE, MATARO, SHIRAZ.

Rutherglen & Glenrowan Vic Two of four regions in warm ne Vic zone, justly famous for sturdy reds, magnificent fortified dessert wines.

Rymill Coon, SA r ★★ Well-est. Ever-reliable across range, CAB SAUV is clear winner.

St Hallett Bar V, SA r w ★★→★★★ (Old Block) 08′ 12′ 13′ 14 Old Block SHIRAZ the star; rest of range is smooth, sound, stylish. ACCOLADE-owned.

Saltram Bar V, SA r w ★ Value Mamre Brook (SHIRAZ, CAB SAUV) and (rarely sighted) No.1 Shiraz are leaders. Main claim to fame is uniquitous Pepperjack Shiraz.

Samuel's Gorge McL V, SA r ★★ Justin McNamee makes (at times) stunning GRENACHE, SHIRAZ, TEMPRANILLO of character and place.

Savaterre Beech, Vic r w ★★★ (PINOT N) 10′ 12′ 13′ 16 Excellent producer of full-bodied CHARD, meaty Pinot N, close-planted SHIRAZ, and SAGRANTINO.

Schmolzer & Brown Beech, Vic r w ★★ CHARD, PINOT N and rosé of intense, spice-drenched interest.

SC Pannell McL V, SA r ★★★ Excellent (spicy, whole-bunch-fermented) SHIRAZ (often labelled SYRAH) and (esp) GRENACHE-based wines. NEBBIOLO to watch. Meticulous.

Sentio Beech, Vic r w ★★ Picks eyes out of various cool-climate regions to produce compelling CHARD, PINOT N, SHIRAZ.

Seppelt Gra, Vic r w br sp ★★★ (St Peter's SHIRAZ) 08' 10' 12' 13' 14' 16 Historic name owned by TWE. Impressive CHARD, RIES, (esp) peppery Shiraz.

Seppeltsfield Bar V, SA r br National Trust Heritage Winery bought by Warren Randall (2013). Fortified wine stocks back to 1878.

Serrat Yarra V, Vic r w ★★★★ Micro-v'yd of noted winemaker Tom Carson (YABBY LAKE) and wife Nadege. Complex, powerful, precise SHIRAZ/VIOGNIER, PINOT N, CHARD.

Seville Estate Yarra V, Vic r w (SHIRAZ) 10' 14' 15' 17 Excellent CHARD, spicy Shiraz, delicate PINOT N. Yarra v pioneer still showing 'em how it's done.

Sir Ian Botham's new wines mark top cricket yrs. Will Aussies like reminders of 1981 Ashes Series?

Shadowfax Vic r w ★→ More than just a tourist adjunct to the historic Werribee Park. V.gd CHARD, PINOT N, SHIRAZ. Never a bad wine.

Shaw & Smith Ad H, SA r w ★★★ Savvy outfit. Crisp **harmonious** SAUV BL, complex M3 CHARD and, surpassing them both, *Shiraz*. PINOT N slowly improving.

Shy Susan Tas r w ★★ New range by winemaker Glenn James, former maker of top-end HARDYS and PENFOLDS whites. CHARD, RIES, PINOT N particularly strong, age-worthy initial releases. Gorgeous packaging.

Simao & Co Ruth, Vic r w ★★★ Young Simon Killeen, of STANTON & KILLEEN family, makes scrumptious TEMPRANILLO, UGNI BL, SHIRAZ and more. Personality+.

Sorrenberg Beech, Vic r w ★★★ No fuss but highest quality. SAUV BL/SEM, CHARD, (Australia's best) GAMAY, B'x blend. One of great "in the know" wineries of Oz.

Southern NSW Zone NSW Incl CAN, Gundagai, Hilltops, TUMBARUMBA. Savoury SHIRAZ; lengthy CHARD.

Spinifex Bar V, SA r w ★★★ Bespoke BAR V producer. Complex SHIRAZ, GRENACHE blends. Routinely turns out rich-but-polished reds.

Stanton & Killeen Ruth, Vic (r) br ★★ Fortified vintage is dominant attraction.

Stefano Lubiana S Tas r w sp ★★★ Beautiful v'yds on banks of Derwent River, 20 mins from Hobart. Excellent PINOT N, sparkling, MERLOT, CHARD. Homely but driven and ambitious. Bio.

Stella Bella Marg R, WA r w ★★★ Humdinger wines. CAB SAUV, SEM/SAUV BL, CHARD, SHIRAZ, SANGIOVESE/Cab Sauv. Sturdy, characterful.

Stoney Rise Tas r w ★★★ Joe Holyman used to be a world-class wicketkeeper, but his efforts with PINOT N, CHARD long put his cricket in shade.

Stonier Wines Mor P, Vic r w ★★★ (CHARD) 15' 17 (PINOT N) 12' 15' 17 Consistently gd; Res notable for elegance. Pinot N in particularly fine form, tense, resonant. Myriad single-v'yd releases now.

Sunbury Vic See MACEDON AND SUNBURY.

Swan Valley WA Birthplace of wine in the w, 20 mins n of Perth. Hot climate makes strong, low-acid wines. FABER V'YDS leads way.

Tahbilk Goulburn V, Vic r w (MARSANNE) 06' 14' 16' 17 (SHIRAZ) 04' 10' 12' 16 Historic Purbrick family estate: long-ageing reds, also some of Oz's best old-vine **Marsanne**. Res CAB SAUV can be v.gd. Rare 1860 Vines Shiraz. For lovers of rustic.

Taltarni Pyrenees, Vic r w sp ★★ SHIRAZ, CAB SAUV in gd shape. Long-haul wines but jackhammer no longer required to remove tannin from your gums.

Tapanappa SA ★★★★ WRATTONBULLY collaboration between Brian Croser, Bollinger, J-M Cazes of Pauillac. Splendid CAB SAUV blend, SHIRAZ, MERLOT, CHARD. Surprising *Pinot N* from Fleurieu Peninsula.

Tar & Roses Hea, Vic r w ★★ SHIRAZ, TEMPRANILLO, SANGIOVESE of impeccable polish, presentation. Modern success story. 2017 death of co-founder Don Lewis a great loss but quality remains strong.

Tarrawarra Estate Yarra V, Vic r w ★★ (Res CHARD) 12' 13' 17 (Res PINOT N) 12' 13' 17 Moved from hefty, idiosyncratic to elegant, long. Res generally a big step up on standard.

Tasmania Cold island region with hot reputation. Outstanding sparkling, PINOT N, RIES. V.gd CHARD, SAUV BL, PINOT GR. Future looks bright.

Taylors Wines Clare V, SA r w ★ Large-scale production led by RIES, SHIRAZ, CAB SAUV. Exports under Wakefield Wines brand.

Ten Minutes by Tractor Mor P, Vic r w ★★★ Wacky name, smart packaging, even better wines. *Chard, Pinot N both excellent* and will age. Style meets substance.

Teusner Bar V, SA r ★★ Old vines, clever winemaking, pure fruit flavours. Leads a BAR V trend towards "more wood, no good".

Thousand Candles Yarra V, Vic r w ★★ V'yd to-die-for. Beautiful site producing beautiful wines. Delicate PINOT N, spicy SHIRAZ, lively field-blend. Cool climate. Quality on steady march forward.

Tim Adams Clare V, SA r w ★ Ever-reliable (in gd way) RIES, CAB SAUV/MALBEC blend, SHIRAZ and (full-bodied) TEMPRANILLO.

Tolpuddle Tas ★★★ SHAW & SMITH bought this outstanding 1988-planted v'yd in TAS's Coal River Valley in 2011. Scintillating PINOT N, CHARD in lean, lengthy style.

Topaque Vic Replacement name for iconic RUTH sticky "Tokay", thanks to EU; 10 yrs on and it's still hard to find anyone who likes the new name.

Torbreck Bar V, SA r (w) ★★★ Dedicated to (often old-vine) Rhône varieties led by SHIRAZ, GRENACHE. Ultimate expression of rich, sweet, high-alc style. Quality has cruised through internal ructions unaffected.

Torzi Matthews Eden V, SA r ★★ Aromatic, stylish, big-hearted SHIRAZ. Value RIES. Incredible consistency yr-on-yr.

Tripe.Iscariot Marg R, WA r w ★★ Hard to spell, easy to drink. Complex whites/reds by its own design. Impossible accurately to pigeonhole; part of natural wine movement.

Tumbarumba NSW Cool-climate NSW region tucked into Australian Alps. Sites 500–800m (1640–2625ft). CHARD the star. PINOT N long way behind, unlikely ever to catch up.

Turkey Flat Bar V, SA r p ★★★ Top producer of bright-coloured rosé, GRENACHE, SHIRAZ from core of 150-yr-old v'yd. Controlled alc and oak. New single-v'yd wines. Old but modern.

TWE (Treasury Wine Estates) Aussie wine behemoth. Dozens of well-known brands: COLDSTREAM HILLS, DEVIL'S LAIR, LINDEMANS, PENFOLDS, ROSEMOUNT, SALTRAM, WOLF BLASS, WYNNS among them.

Two Hands Bar V, SA r ★★★ Big reds and many of them. They've finally turned the volume down a fraction and the glory of the fruit seems all the clearer/louder.

Tyrrell's Hun V, NSW r w ★★★★ (SEM) 13' 14' 15' 16' 17' 18 (Vat 47 CHARD) 14' 15' 16' 17' 18 Oz's greatest maker of Sem, Vat 1 now joined with series of individual v'yd or subregional wines. *Vat 47*, Oz's 1st Chard, continues to defy climatic odds. Outstanding old-vine 4 Acres SHIRAZ, Vat 9 Shiraz. One of the true greats.

Vasse Felix Marg R, WA r w ★★★ (CHARD) 13' 14' 15' 16 (CAB SAUV) 10' 11' 12' 14' With CULLEN, pioneer of MARG R. Elegant Cab Sauv for mid-weight balance. Complex/funkified Chard. Returning to estate-grown roots.

Rob Mann, rolled-gold royalty of WA wine, now has his own label: Corymbia.

Voyager Estate Marg R, WA r w ★★ Big volume of (mostly) estate-grown, rich, powerful SEM, SAUV BL, (esp) CHARD and CAB SAUV/MERLOT.

Wantirna Estate Yarra V, Vic r w ★★★ Regional pioneer showing no sign of slowing down. CHARD, PINOT N, B'x blend all excellent. Small on quantity, big on quality.

Wendouree Clare V, SA r ★★★★ Treasured maker (tiny quantities) of powerful, tannic, concentrated reds, based on CAB SAUV, MALBEC, MATARO, SHIRAZ. Recently moved to screwcap; the word "longevity" best defined with a picture of a Wendouree red. Beg, borrow or steal.

West Cape Howe Denmark, WA r w ★ Affordable, flavoursome reds the speciality.

Westend Estate Riverina, NSW r w ★★ Thriving family producer of **tasty bargains**, esp Private Bin SHIRAZ, Durif. Recent cool-climate additions gd value.

Willow Creek Mor P, Vic r w ★★ Gd gear. Impressive producer of CHARD, PINOT N in particular. Power and poise.

Wirra Wirra McL V, SA r w (sw) (sp) ★★ (RSW SHIRAZ) 04' 05' 10' 12' (The Angelus CAB SAUV) 10' 12' 14' 15 High-quality, concentrated wines in flashy livery. The Angelus Cab Sauv named Dead Ringer outside Australia.

Wolf Blass Bar V, SA r w (br) (sw) (sp) ★★ (Black Label CAB SAUV blend) 06' 08' 12' 13' 14 Owned by TWE. Not the shouty player it once was but still churns through an enormous volume of clean, inoffensive wines.

Woodlands Marg R, WA r (w) ★★ 7 ha of 40-yr-old+ CAB SAUV among top v'yds in region, plus younger but v.gd plantings of other B'x reds. Reds of brooding impact.

Wrattonbully SA Important grape-growing region in LIMESTONE COAST ZONE; profile lifted by activity of TAPANAPPA, Terre à Terre, Peppertree.

Wynns Coon, SA r w ★★★★ (SHIRAZ) 10' 12' 14' 16 (CAB SAUV) 04' 05' 06' 12' 13' 14' 15 TWE-owned coon classic. RIES, CHARD, Shiraz, Cab Sauv all v.gd, esp Black Label Cab Sauv (15' release one for the ages), **John Riddoch Cab Sauv**. Recent single-v'yd releases are the icing.

Yabby Lake Mor P, Vic r w ★★★ Made its name with estate CHARD, PINOT N, boosted with single-site releases, now spice-shot SHIRAZ builds reputation yet more.

Yalumba Bar V, SA, SA r w sp ★★★ 169 yrs young, family-owned. **Full spectrum of high-quality wines** from budget to elite single-v'yd. Entry level Y Series v.gd value.

Yangarra Estate McL V, SA r w ★★★★ Conventional in some ways, inventive in others. Whatever it takes to make great wine. Full box and dice here, across most price points. Varietal GRENACHE particularly strong.

Yarraloch Yarra V, Vic r w ★★ CHARD can be to die for. Also capable of exceptional PINOT N.

Yarra Valley Vic Historic area just ne of Melbourne. Growing emphasis on v. successful CHARD, PINOT N, SHIRAZ, sparkling. Understated, elegant CAB SAUV.

Yarra Yering Yarra V, Vic r w ★★★ (Dry Reds) 05' 06' 15' 17 One-of-a-kind YARRA V pioneer. Powerful PINOT N; deep, herby CAB SAUV (Dry Red No.1); SHIRAZ (Dry Red No.2). Luscious daring flavours (r w).

Yellow Tail NSW See CASELLA.

Yeringberg Yarra V, Vic r w ★★★★ (MARSANNE/ROUSSANNE) 13' 14' 15 (CAB SAUV) 05' 10' 12' 13' 14' 15 Historic estate still in hands of founding (1862) Swiss family, the de Purys. Extremely small quantities of v.high-quality CHARD, Marsanne, Roussanne, Cab Sauv, PINOT N.

Yering Station / Yarrabank Yarra V, Vic r w sp ★★ On site of Vic's 1st v'yd; replanted after 80-yr gap. Snazzy table wines (Res CHARD, PINOT N, SHIRAZ, VIOGNIER); Yarrabank (sparkling wines in joint venture with Champagne Devaux).

The thrill of Tasmania

Train your glasses on Tassie. There's been a buzz about Tassie wine for 30 yrs, but it has only been in the past handful that a few tiny producers have achieved high-class PINOT N. We're into exciting territory. Est names like BAY OF FIRES, FREYCINET, Meadowbank, MOORILLA, PIPERS BROOK, STEFANO LUBIANA have been joined and/or surpassed by CHATTO, Dr Edge, GLAETZER-DIXON, Holyman, Hughes & Hughes, Lisdillon, Pooley, Sailor Seeks Horse, Small Island, Stargazer, TOLPUDDLE, Two Tonne Tasmania and others. Many of these wines are only a barrel or two, but hooley dooley, are they gd.

New Zealand

Abbreviations used
in the text:

Auck   Auckland
B of P Bay of Plenty
Cant   Canterbury
Gis   Gisborne
Hawk   Hawke's Bay
Hend   Henderson
Marl   Marlborough
Mart   Martinborough
Nel   Nelson
N/C Ot North/Central Otago
Waih   Waiheke Island
Waip   Waipara Valley
Wair   Wairarapa

Five million glasses of NZ wine are consumed around the world each day. As well as Britain – a long-term enthusiast – Americans have also developed a strong appetite for Marlborough's punchy, penetrating style of Sauvignon Blanc. The US is now its richest market in dollar terms. In Australia, the biggest-selling of all white wines is Oyster Bay Marlborough Sauvignon Blanc. But NZ has no more producers than six years ago and its rising stream of bulk-wine exports has triggered concern at top levels about unofficial blending with cheaper wines from other countries. Hence the 2018 launch of Appellation Marlborough Wine. The group's members agree to use exclusively Marlborough grapes in their Sauvignon Blancs and to bottle their wines within NZ. Another welcome sign is that Chardonnay and Cabernet Sauvignon – two varieties that were prestigious in the 80s but were eclipsed by Sauvignon, Pinot Gris, Pinot Noir and Merlot – are back in vogue, with Chardonnay expanding its presence in the deep south and Cabernet Sauvignon exciting renewed interest in Hawke's Bay.

Recent vintages

2018 Hottest-ever summer, destructive storms in April. Ripe, less
   herbaceous Marl Sauv Bl. Disease widespread, but some gd wines
   from early pickings.
2017 Challenging vintage, with rain before harvest. C Ot more successful.
2016 Ripe, tropical fruit-flavoured Marl Sauv Bl. In Hawk, excellent Chard
   but autumn rain hit Merlot.
2015 Aromatic, vibrant Marl Sauv Bl. Fragrant, charming, rather than powerful,
   reds in Hawk.

Akarua C Ot r (p) (w) (sp) ★★★ PINOT NS: outstanding Bannockburn 17'; floral, drink-young Rua (briefly oak-aged) 17'; esp powerful The Siren 16. Lively fizz, incl complex Vintage Brut 11; vivacious Brut NV; strawberryish Rosé Brut NV.

Allan Scott Marl (r) (p) w (sp) ★★ Family firm. Lively RIES 17; tropical SAUV BL 18; gently oaked CHARD 17'. Upper-tier: Generations range. Fruit-packed C OT PINOT N (labelled Scott Base) 17'.

Alpha Domus Hawk r w ★★ Family winery in Bridge Pa Triangle. Elegant The Skybolt CHARD 16. Rich, B'x-style reds, esp MERLOT-based The Navigator 14 and v. classy AD CAB SAUV The Aviator 15'. Generous Barnstormer SYRAH 16. The Pilot: drink young. AD is top range (savoury CHARD 16').

Amisfield C Ot r (p) (w) ★★★ Full-bodied PINOT GR 17; classy RIES (dry 17 and medium-sweet 8'); tangy SAUV BL 18'; off-dry Pinot Rosé 18', graceful PINOT N 16 (RKV Res is powerful, Rolls-Royce model 15'). Lake Hayes is label to drink young.

Astrolabe Marl (r) w ★★→★★★ Characterful wines from Simon Waghorn. Ripely herbal SAUV BL 18. Dry PINOT GR 17 and ALBARIÑO 17; intense CHENIN BL 17'. Dry and medium-dry RIES; peachy CHARD. Long PINOT N 16.

Ata Rangi Mart r (p) (w) ★★★★ Much respected family affair. PINOT N 13' 14' 15' 16' is a NZ classic; finely scented (1st vines 1980). Delicious younger-vine Crimson Pinot N 16. Notable Craighall CHARD 15' 16 (planted 1983); full Lismore PINOT GR 17. Nutty, partly oak-aged Raranga SAUV BL 17.

Auckland Largest city (n, warm, cloudy) in NZ; 0.9% v'yd area. Head offices of many big producers. Nearby wine districts: Kumeu/Huapai/Waimauku (long est); newer (since 80s): Matakana, Clevedon, WAIH (island v'yds, v. popular with tourists). Savoury B'x blends in dry seasons 13' 14, bold SYRAH 13' 14 is fast-expanding and rivals HAWK for quality; underrated CHARD 15; promising ALBARIÑO, PINOT GR. Wet yrs recently.

Auntsfield Marl r w ★★→★★★ Consistently impressive wines from site of region's 1st (1873) v'yd (replanted 1999). Intense, partly barrel-fermented SAUV BL 18; fleshy CHARD, esp single-block Cob Cottage 16', bold, flavour-packed PINOT N 16'.

Awatere Valley Marl Key subregion (pronounced *Awa-terry*), with few wineries, but huge v'yd area (more than HAWK), pioneered in 1986 by VAVASOUR. YEALANDS is key producer. Slightly cooler, drier, windier, less fertile than WAIRAU VALLEY, with racy, ("tomato stalk") SAUV BL (rated higher by UK than US critics); vibrant RIES, PINOT GR; slightly herbal PINOT N.

Babich Marl r w ★★★→★★★★ NZ's oldest family-owned wine producer (1916), Croatian origin. HAWK, MARL v'yds; wineries in AUCK, MARL. Age-worthy Irongate from GIMBLETT GRAVELS: CHARD and B'x-like Irongate CAB/MERLOT/CAB FR 13' 14'. Biggest seller: weighty Marl SAUV BL. Top red: stylish The Patriarch (B'x-style, MALBEC-influenced) 13'.

Blackenbrook Nel r w ★★ Small winery with impressive aromatic whites, esp Alsace-style GEWURZ; PINOT GR. Punchy SAUV BL; generous CHARD; graceful PINOT N. Second label: St Jacques.

Black Estate Cant r w ★★ Small organic WAIP producer with mature (1994) vines. Intense Home V'yd CHARD; savoury, supple PINOT N; outstanding Damsteep PINOT N.

Blank Canvas Marl r w ★★ Owned by Matt Thomson (ex-SAINT CLAIR) and Sophie Parker-Thomson. Aromatic SAUV BL; light RIES; complex PINOT N.

Borthwick Hend r w ★★ V'yd at Gladstone with Paddy Borthwick brand. Punchy SAUV BL; citrus CHARD; peachy PINOT GR; full-flavoured Pinot Rose. Rich PINOT N.

Brancott Estate Marl r (p) (w) ★→★★★ Major brand of PERNOD RICARD NZ that replaced Montana worldwide (except in NZ). Top wines: Letter Series eg. fleshy "B" Brancott SAUV BL 16'; rich "O" CHARD; classy "T" PINOT N. Huge-selling, value Sauv Bl. New Identity range: subregional focus. Living Land: organic. Flight: plain, low alc. Top-value, lively, bottle-fermented Brut Cuvée.

Brightwater Nel (r) w ★★ Impressive whites, esp intense SAUV BL; medium-dry RIES; gently oaked CHARD; fresh PINOT GR. Smooth PINOT N. Top: Lord Rutherford (incl ripe Sauv Bl; refined, tight CHARD).

Canterbury NZ's 5th-largest wine region; most v'yds in relatively warm n WAIP district (increasingly called North Cant). Greatest success with aromatic RIES (since mid-80s) and rich PINOT N. Emerging strength in Alsace-style PINOT GR. SAUV BL heavily planted, but often minor component in other regions' wines.

Carrick C Ot r w ★★★ Bannockburn winery with organic focus. Classy RIES (dry, medium); elegant CHARD, esp EBM; partly-oak-aged PINOT GR. PINOT N, built to last. Attractive, drink-young Unravelled Pinot N. Top Excelsior Pinot N **14'** rich, smooth.

Central Otago C Ot (r) **16** 17' (w) **16** 17 High-altitude, dry inland region (now NZ's 3rd largest) in s of S Island, with many tiny producers. Sunny, hot days, v. cold nights. Most vines in Cromwell Basin. Crisp RIES, PINOT GR; fast-growing interest in tight-knit CHARD; famous PINOT N (78%+ v'yd area) is buoyantly fruity, with drink-young charm; older vines yielding more savoury wines. Excellent Pinot N rosé and traditional-method fizz.

Chard Farm C Ot r w ★★ Pioneer winery; fleshy, dry PINOT GR; scented RIES; mid-weight PINOT N (fruity River Run; single-v'yd The Tiger, The Viper more complex). Drink-young Rabbit Ranch Pinot N. Mata-Au Pinot N is sweet-fruited, signature red **15**.

C Ot and Marl have same number of producers, but C Ot's are mostly tiny, Marl's small to colossal.

Church Road Hawk r (p) w ★★→★★★ PERNOD RICARD NZ winery with historic HAWK roots. Buttery CHARD; partly oak-aged SAUV BL; Alsace-style PINOT GR; dark MERLOT/ CAB SAUV; delicious, drink-young SYRAH (all great value). Impressive Grand Res wines. McDonald Series, between standard and Grand Res, offers eye-catching quality, value (incl Chard, Syrah, Cab Sauv, Merlot **14**). New, delicate, dry Gwen Rosé. Prestige TOM selection, incl powerful Merlot/Cab Sauv **14'**; Chard **14'** (on grand scale); v. fragrant Syrah **14'**.

Churton Marl r w ★★ Elevated Waihopai Valley site with bone-dry SAUV BL; age-able, oak-aged Best End Sauv Bl; sturdy VIOGNIER **15**; savoury PINOT N (esp The Abyss: oldest vines, greater depth **13'**). Sweet, compelling PETIT MANSENG.

Clearview Hawk r (p) w ★★→★★★ Coastal v'yd at Te Awanga (also drawing grapes from inland) renowned for hedonistic, oaky Res CHARD (Beachhead Chard is excellent junior version); rich Enigma (MERLOT-based), Old Olive Block (CAB SAUV/ MALBEC/CAB FR blend). Top value Cape Kidnappers Merlot.

Clos Henri Marl r w ★★→★★★ Organic producer, founded 2001 by Henri Bourgeois of Sancerre. Weighty SAUV BL from stony soils, one of NZ's best; sturdy, savoury PINOT N (on clay). Second label: Bel Echo (reverses variety/soil match). Third label: Petit Clos, from young vines. Distinctive, satisfying wines, priced right.

Cloudy Bay Marl r w sp ★★★ Large-volume, still classy SAUV BL (weighty, dry, some barrel-ageing) is NZ's most famous wine, complex CHARD, supple PINOT N classy too. Stylish Pelorus sparklings, rose and NV. Te Koko (oak-aged Sauv Bl) has strong personality. More involvement in C OT for Te Wahi Pinot N (fleshy, rich **14'** **15'**, **16**). Owned by LVMH.

Constellation New Zealand Auck r (p) w ★→★★ Largest producer of NZ wine, previously Nobilo Wine Group, now owned by Constellation Brands (New York-based). Strong in US market (KIM CRAWFORD MARL SAUV BL is no.1-selling NZ wine.) Strength mainly in solid, moderately priced wines (esp Sauv Bl) under Kim Crawford, Monkey Bay, NOBILO and SELAKS brands.

Cooper's Creek Auck r w ★★→★★★ Innovative medium-sized producer with gd value from several regions, incl flavoury home-v'yd MONTEPULCIANO. Toasty Swamp Res HAWK CHARD; gd SAUV BL, RIES; MERLOT; easy-drinking PINOT N; rich SYRAH (esp SV Chalk Ridge Hawk Syrah). Res is top range; SV (Select V'yd) range is mid-tier. NZ's 1st: ARNEIS, GRÜNER V, ALBARIÑO, MARSANNE.

Craggy Range Hawk r (p) w ★★★→★★★★ High-profile winery, top restaurant and large v'yds in HAWK, MART. Stylish CHARD, PINOT N; excellent mid-range MERLOT, SYRAH from GIMBLETT GRAVELS; dense Sophia (Merlot); show-stopping Syrah Le Sol 14' 15' 16'; sturdy The Quarry (Cab Sauv); fragrant Aroha (Pinot N) 14' 15' 16'.

Delegat Auck r w →★ Large listed company (two million cases/yr+), still controlled by Delegat family. Owns v'yds (2000 ha) in HAWK, MARL; three wineries (incl AUCK). Hugely successful OYSTER BAY brand, esp tangy SAUV BL, plummy MERLOT, excellent dry ROSÉ. Top-value Delegat range: citrus CHARD; full Sauv Bl; vibrant Merlot; savoury PINOT N. (Also owns Barossa Valley Estates).

Delta Marl ★★→★★★ Owned by SAINT CLAIR. V.gd-value PINOT N, slightly salty SAUV BL; Hatters Hill range a step up.

Destiny Bay Waih r ★★→★★★ Expatriate Americans make classy, high-priced (but cheaper to Patron Club members) brambly, silky B'x-style reds. Flagship is savoury Magna Praemia (mostly CAB SAUV). Mystae is mid-tier: lush. Destinae: softly textured, for earlier drinking.

Deutz Auck sp ★★★ Champagne house gives name to refined, great-value fizz from MARL by PERNOD RICARD NZ. Popular Brut NV has min 2 yrs on lees. Much-awarded Blanc de Blancs is vivacious, piercing. Crisp Rosé NV; outstanding, harmonious Prestige (disgorged after 3 yrs), mostly CHARD.

Dog Point Marl r w ★★★ Grower Ivan Sutherland and winemaker James Healy make incisive, age-worthy, oak-aged SAUV BL (Section 94); CHARD (elegant); complex PINOT N 13' 14' 15 16, all among region's finest. Larger-volume, but v.gd unoaked Sauv Bl, organic (2017).

Dry River Mart r w ★★★ Small pioneer winery, now US-owned. Reputation for elegant, long-lived whites: savoury CHARD; intense dry RIES; oily PINOT GR (NZ's 1st outstanding example); heady GEWURZ; late-harvest whites; graceful, youthful PINOT N.

Elephant Hill Hawk r (p) w ★★→★★★★ Stylish winery/restaurant on coast at Te Awanga, also draws grapes from inland. Rich CHARD; bold MERLOT/MALBEC; supple SYRAH. Outstanding Res range, incl Chard. Top pair: Airavata Syrah (notably dense, complex); Hieronymus (flowing, blended r).

Escarpment Mart r (w) ★★★ Australian-owned, with pioneer winemaker Larry McKenna (ex-MARTINBOROUGH V'YD). Known for savoury PINOT N. Top label: Kupe. Single-v'yd, old-vine reds esp gd. MART Pinot N is regional blend. Lower-tier: The Edge.

NZ's fastest-growing wine style abroad is rosé – up by 400%+ over 10 yrs.

Esk Valley Hawk r p w ★★→★★★★ Owned by VILLA MARIA. Acclaimed MERLOT-based blends (esp Winemakers Res 14' 16'; excellent Merlot/MALBEC/CAB. Supple SYRAH (rich Res). Popular Merlot Rosé; barrel-fermented CHARD superb value; full-bodied VERDELHO. Striking flagship red Heipipi The Terraces: spicy, single-v'yd blend, Malbec/Merlot/CAB FR.

Fairbourne Marl ★★ NZ's only SAUV BL specialist. Tightly structured, bone-dry, hand-picked from elevated, n-facing slopes on s side of WAIRAU VALLEY.

Felton Road C Ot r w ★★★★ Celebrated winery at Bannockburn, best-known for PINOT N, but RIES, CHARD notably classy too. Bold yet graceful Pinot N Block 3 15' 17', more powerful Block 5 15' 17' from The Elms V'yd; intense Ries (dr s/sw); citrus Chard (esp Block 2); key label is Bannockburn Pinot N, four-v'yd blend. Other fine single-v'yd Pinot N: Calvert (nr winery), Cornish Point (6-km/4-miles away).

Buy your icons now
Over past decade, prices of mid-priced wines have not risen. How about NZ's "icon" wines? Bad news – at least for consumers. Average price of such prestigious reds as FELTON ROAD Block 5 PINOT N, TE MATA Coleraine and TRINITY HILL Homage SYRAH has climbed 40% over past decade. As world increasingly wakes up to fact NZ can make distinguished wines, these prices likely to keep climbing.

Forrest Marl r (p) w ★★ Mid-size business. Runaway success with The Doctors' MARL SAUV BL, low alc (9.5%), delicate, tangy acidity. Wide range of attractive, value Marl whites; floral rosé; v.gd-value PINOT N. Tatty Bogler: complex C OT and WAITAKI VALLEY wines.

Framingham Marl (r) w ★★→★★★ Owned by Sogrape (*see* Portugal). Strength in aromatic whites: intense *Ries (esp organic Classic)* from mature vines. Perfumed PINOT GR, GEWURZ. Vibrant CHARD. Subtle SAUV BL; lush Noble RIES; silky PINOT N. Rare F Series wines (incl Old-Vine Ries and brilliant botrytized sweet whites), full of personality.

Fromm Marl r w ★★★ Swiss-owned. Distinguished PINOT N, esp rare, organic, hill-grown Clayvin V'yd 15' 16'. Fromm V'yd, sturdier, firmer. Stylish Clayvin CHARD. Earlier-drinking La Strada range, incl rich Pinot N; tangy SAUV BL; fleshy PINOT GR; excellent rosé.

Gibbston Valley C Ot r (p) w ★★★ →★★★ Pioneer with original v'yd at Gibbston. Most v'yds now at Bendigo. Strong name for PINOT N, esp smooth GV Collection. Silky Le Maitre (17 best ever), mostly from 1st vines planted in 80s. Racy GV RIES, full-bodied GV PINOT GR, classy CHARD (esp China Terrace). Gold River Pinot N: drink-young charm.

Giesen Cant (r) w ★★ Family winery making huge volume, tangy, ripely herbaceous MARL SAUV BL. Light RIES (value), classy, single-v'yd Gemstone Ries. Multi-region PINOT GR also gd value. Bold The Brothers (mid-tier) Sauv Bl, barrel-fermented The August Sauv Bl. Fast-improving PINOT N. Recently leased famous Clayvin V'yd and bought Ara brand.

Gimblett Gravels Hawk Defined area (800 ha planted, mostly since early 80s) of old river bed, mostly free-draining, low-fertility soils noted for rich B'x-style reds (mostly MERLOT-led, but stony soils also suit CAB SAUV – recent renewed interest). And super SYRAH. Best reds are world-class. Also age-worthy CHARD, gd MARSANNE/VIOGNIER.

Gisborne NZ's 5th-largest region (biggest in 70s/80s), on e coast of N Island. Abundant sunshine but often rainy; fertile soils. Key is CHARD (fragrant, soft in youth, but best mature well). Excellent GEWURZ, CHENIN BL, VIOGNIER; MERLOT, PINOT GR more variable. Interest in ALBARIÑO (rain-resistant). Top wines from MILLTON.

Gladstone Vineyard Wair r w ★★ Largest producer in n WAIR. Tropical SAUV BL (incl wooded Sophie's Choice); weighty, spicy PINOT GR; v.gd RIES; vibrant VIOGNIER; excellent dry rosé. Fruit-packed PINOT N. 12,000 Miles is lower-priced, early-drinking range.

Grasshopper Rock C Ot r ★★→★★★ Estate-grown at Alexandra by PINOT N specialist. Subregion's finest red 14' 17': harmonious, cherry, spice, dried-herb flavours. Age-worthy, great value.

Greenhough Nel r w ★★→★★★ One of region's best; scented Apple Valley RIES 16, organic SAUV BL 18, consistently gd CHARD 17, PINOT N 16. Top label: Hope V'yd (organic Chard 16'; old-vine PINOT BL is NZ's finest 15'; mushroomy Pinot N 15').

Greystone Waip (r) w ★★★ Star producer (also owns MUDDY WATER), partly organic, with aromatic whites (dry and medium RIES, Alsace-style PINOT GR; classy CHARD, oak-aged SAUV BL); PINOT N (scented). Thomas Brothers is top, notably Pinot N.

Greywacke Marl r w ★★★ Distinguished wines from Kevin Judd, ex-CLOUDY BAY. Flavour-packed SAUV BL; weighty, age-worthy CHARD; fleshy, rich PINOT GR; gently sweet RIES; silky PINOT N. Barrel-fermented Wild Sauv full of personality.

Grove Mill Marl r w ★★ Attractive, gd-value whites with WAIRAU VALLEY sub-regional focus: ripe SAUV BL; generous CHARD; oily-textured PINOT GR; slightly sweet RIES. Smooth PINOT N (Owned by Foley Family Wines.)

Hans Herzog Marl r w ★★★ Warm, stony, organic v'yd with many varieties planted. Sturdy MERLOT/CAB; firm PINOT N. Creamy CHARD; apricot-coloured PINOT GR; oak-aged SAUV BL; weighty VIOGNIER. Classy TEMPRANILLO, MONTEPULCIANO. Sold under Hans brand in the EU, US.

Hawke's Bay NZ's 2nd-largest region (12.6% v'yd area). Long history (since 1850s) of wine in sunny, dryish climate. Classy MERLOT and CAB SAUV-based reds in favourable vintages; SYRAH (vibrant plum, pepper) fast-rising star; peachy CHARD; rounded SAUV B (suits oak); NZ's best VIOGNIER. Alsace-style PINOT GR, promising PINOT N from cooler, elevated, inland districts, esp Mangatahi and Central Hawk. *See also* GIMBLETT GRAVELS.

Huia Marl (r) w (sp) ★★ V.gd, partly oak-aged, organic SAUV BL; rounded PINOT GR. Lower tier: Hunky Dory (incl The Tangle: gd, all-purpose blend, Pinot Gr/ GEWURZ/RIES).

Hunter's Marl (r) w (sp) ★★→★★★ Pioneer winery, strength in whites. Crisp SAUV BL. Oak-aged Kaho Roa. Vibrant CHARD. Excellent fizz Miru Miru NV (esp late-disgorged Res) RIES (off-dry), GEWURZ, PINOT GR (dry) all rewarding, value. Easy-drinking PINOT N.

Invivo Auck (r) w ★★ Fast-expanding young producer with aromatic MARL SAUV BL; citrus Marl PINOT GR; savoury C OT PINOT N. Recent focus on celebrity labels, esp "chief winemaker" Graham Norton's Own Sauv Bl (easy-drinking).

Isabel Marl r w ★★ Formerly distinguished SAUV BL producer. After quality and financial problems, bought by Australian supermarket giant Woolworths 2014. Classy SAUV BL, vibrant CHARD auspicious signs.

Johanneshof Marl (r) w sp ★★ Small winery acclaimed for perfumed GEWURZ (one of NZ's finest). Lively Blanc de Blancs fizz; v.gd RIES, PINOT GR.

Jules Taylor Gis, Marl (r) (p) w ★★ Stylish, gd value. Refined, partly barrel-aged MARL CHARD. Delicious Marl SAUV BL (incisive); generous PINOT N. Complex top wines: OTQ ("On The Quiet").

Kim Crawford Hawk ★→★★ Brand owned by CONSTELLATION NEW ZEALAND. Easy-drinking (with "Res" on capsule, but not label), incl high-impact MARL SAUV BL (huge seller in US); floral PINOT GR; fruity HAWK MERLOT; generous Marlb PINOT N. Top range: Small Parcels, incl fragrant CHARD.

Kumeu River Auck (r) w ★★★ Complex Estate CHARD is multi-site blend; value. Top, single-v'yd Mate's V'yd Chard (planted 1990) is more opulent; single-v'yd Hunting Hill Chard a rising star: notably refined, tight-knit. Lower-tier Village Chard is great value (17 incl HAWK fruit.) New Hawk SAUV BL, mineral. Refined Hunting Hill PINOT N.

Lawson's Dry Hills Marl (r) (p) w ★★→★★★ Best-known for intense SAUV BL, exotic GEWURZ. Fast-improving, gd-value CHARD 17' and PINOT N. Top range: The Pioneer (outstanding Gewurz). New Res range: searching Sauv Bl; slightly buttery CHARD; savoury Pinot N.

Lindauer Auck ★→★★ Hugely popular (in NZ), low-priced fizz, esp bottle-fermented Lindauer Brut Cuvée NV. Latest batches: easy-drinking, slightly nutty. Special Res (2 yrs lees) offers complexity, value. Ever-expanding range, with low-alc, single-variety bottlings.

Mahi Marl r w ★★ Stylish, complex wines: punchy, SAUV BL (part oak-aged); gd-value CHARD (esp Twin Valleys V'yd); weighty PINOT GR; floral rosé; fragrant PINOT N.

Man O' War Auck r w ★★ Largest v'yd on WAIHEKE ISLAND. Penetrating Valhalla CHARD; full-flavoured PINOT GR from adjacent Ponui Island; tangy SAUV BL. Minerally Gravestone (Sauv Bl/SEM). Reds incl generous MERLOT/CAB/MALBEC/PETIT VERDOT; delicious Death Valley Malbec; spicy Dreadnought SYRAH.

Marisco Marl r w ★★ Waihopai Valley producer (owned by Brent Marris, ex-WITHER HILLS) with two brands, The Ned and Marisco The King's Series. Impressive Marisco The King's Favour SAUV BL; punchy The Ned Sauv Bl. Gd CHARD, PINOT GR, PINOT N.

Marlborough NZ's dominant region (68% plantings) at top of S Island; 1st vines in modern era planted 1973 (SAUV BL in 1975.) Hot, sunny days and cold nights give aromatic, crisp whites and PINOT N-based rosés. Intense Sauv Bl, from sharp, green capsicum to ripe tropical fruit (some top wines faintly oak-influenced). Fresh RIES (recent wave of sweet, low-alc wines); some of NZ's best PINOT GR, GEWURZ; CHARD is slightly leaner than HAWK but more vibrant and can mature well. High-quality, gd-value fizz and classy botrytized Ries. Pinot N underrated, top examples (from n-facing clay hillsides) among NZ's finest. Interest stirring in ALBARIÑO, GRÜNER V.

Martinborough Wair Small, prestigious district in S WAIR (foot of N Island). Cold, s winds reduce yields, warm summers, usually dry autumns, free-draining soils. Success with several white grapes (SAUV BL, PINOT GR both widely planted), but esp acclaimed since mid-to-late 80s for long-lived PINOT N (higher % of mature vines than other regions).

Martinborough Vineyard Mart r (p) (w) ★★★ Pioneer winery; famous PINOT N (refined Home Block). Classy Home Block CHARD; intense Manu RIES; gd-value Te Tera range (crisp SAUV BL, supple Pinot N). Owned by American Bill Foley (2014). Lower-tier: Russian Jack.

Matawhero Gis r (p) w ★★ Former star GEWURZ producer of 80s, now different ownership. Unoaked Single V'yd CHARD; weighty oak-fermented Irwin Chard. Perfumed Gewurz; scented PINOT GR; plummy MERLOT; promising ALBARIÑO; fruity, smooth Rosé.

Matua Auck r w ★→★★★ Producer of NZ's 1st SAUV BL in 1974 (from AUCK grapes) long known as Matua Valley. Now owned by TWE. Most are pleasant, easy-drinking. Impressive, luxury range of Single V'yd wines, incl pure Sauv Bl; v. classy ALBARIÑO; powerful CHARD; dense MERLOT/MALBEC 14'; SYRAH 14'.

Maude C Ot r w ★★ Consistently gd, scented PINOT GR; outstanding RIES (dry, medium) from mature vines at Mt Maude V'yd, at Wanaka. Finely textured PINOT N, esp age-worthy Mt Maude.

Mills Reef B of P r w ★★→★★★ Easy-drinking wines from estate v'yds in GIMBLETT GRAVELS and other HAWK grapes. Top Elspeth range incl age-worthy CHARD; fine-textured B'x-style reds and SYRAH. Res range (r w) typically gd value. 2018 release of two prestige 13 reds, labelled Arthur Edmund, at $350 each: stylish Syrah and CAB/MERLOT.

Millton Gis r (p) w ★★→★★★★ Region's top wines from NZ's 1st organic producer. Arresting, hill-grown, single-v'yd Clos de Ste Anne range: CHARD, CHENIN BL, VIOGNIER, SYRAH, PINOT N in favourable seasons. Long-lived, partly barrel-fermented CHENIN BL (honeyed in wetter vintages) is one of NZ's finest. Drink-young range: Crazy by Nature (gd value). Classy, new La Cote Pinot N.

> ### Greenish
> NZ's "clean, green" image helps to promote its wine, but only 6% v'yd is certified organic: not far ahead of global average of 4.5%. MILLTON led the way in 80s. Interest in organic production now intensifying, esp in C OT, where over 16% v'yd has organic status.

Misha's Vineyard C Ot r w ★★ Large v'yd at Bendigo. Scented PINOT GR; RIES (dry Lyric, slightly sweet Limelight); age-worthy SAUV BL; classy dry rosé. PINOT N: High Note (graceful).

Mission Hawk r (p) w ★★ NZ's oldest wine producer; 1st vines 1851; 1st sales 1890s; still owned by Catholic Society of Mary. Wide range of gd-value regional varietals, with V'yd Selection next up the scale. Res range incl excellent MERLOT, CAB SAUV, SYRAH, MALBEC, CHARD, SAUV BL. Top label: Jewelstone (delicate Chard; floral Syrah). Also owns large v'yd in AWATERE VALLEY. Purchased NGATARAWA (2017).

Mordillo C Ot r w ★★ Rising star at Bendigo with dry RIES. Fragrant PINOT N. Complex Bella Res Pinot N.

Mount Edward C O r w ★★ Small, respected, organic producer with citrus CHARD; racy RIES; complex CHENIN BL; refined PINOT N.

Mount Riley Marl r p) w ★★ Medium-sized, gd-value family firm. Punchy SAUV BL; fine PINOT GR, off-dry RIES, gently oaked CHARD, drink-young PINOT N. Top range is Seventeen Valley (biscuity Chard).

Mt Beautiful Cant w ★★ Large v'yd at Cheviot, n of WAIP. Toasty CHARD; fleshy PINOT GR; invitingly scented RIES; herbaceous SAUV BL; complex PINOT N.

Mt Difficulty C O r (p) w ★★★ Quality producer with extensive v'yds at Bannockburn, now owned by US billionaire Bill Foley. Typically powerful PINOT N (16' slightly lighter). Roaring Meg is popular Cromwell Basin blend for early drinking. Single V'yd Growers Series reds incl plummy Havoc Farm Gibbston. Consistently classy whites (esp RIES, PINOT GR).

1st vines planted in NZ were in top of North Island. But British army galloped over them.

Mud House Cant r w ★★→★★★ Large, Australian-owned, MARL-based producer (also owns v'yds in WAIP, C OT). Brands: Mud House, Waipara Hills, Hay Maker (lower tier). Regional blends incl gd-value Marl SAUV BL; scented Marl PINOT GR, medium-dry WAIP RIES; vibrant PINOT N. Excellent Single V'yd collection (Home Block Waipara Pinot Gr) and Estate range (youthful Claim 431 C Ot PINOT N).

Nautilus Marl r w sp ★★→★★★ Medium-sized, rock-solid range, owned by S Smith & Sons (*see* Yalumba, Australia). Top: herbaceous SAUV BL, classy CHARD; graceful Southern Valleys PINOT N; weighty PINOT GR; yeasty NV sparkler (min 3 yrs on lees), one of NZ's best. Excellent new GRÜNER V; ALBARIÑO.

Nelson Small region (3.1% planting) w of MARL; climate wetter (damp in 16 17 18) but equally sunny. Clay soils of Upper Moutere hills (full-bodied wines) and silty WAIMEA plains (more aromatic). SAUV BL is most extensively planted, but also strength in aromatic whites, esp RIES, PINOT GR, GEWURZ; also gd (sometimes outstanding) CHARD, PINOT N.

Neudorf Nel r (p) w ★★★→★★★★ Smallish winery with big reputation. Refined, citrus Moutere CHARD 15' 16' one of NZ's greatest; excellent Rosie's Block Chard. Superb *Moutere Pinot N*; lightly oaked SAUV BL; off-dry PINOT GR; RIES (dr s/sw) also top flight. Classy new ALBARIÑO.

No. 1 Family Estate Marl sp ★★ Family-owned company of regional pioneer Daniel Le Brun, ex-Champagne. No longer controls Daniel Le Brun brand (owned by Lion). Specialist in v.gd fizz, esp citrus CHARD-based NV, Cuvée No 1. Top end, vigorous Cuvée Virginie.

Nobilo Marl *See* CONSTELLATION NEW ZEALAND.

Obsidian Waih r p) w ★★ V'yd in Onetangi: stylish B'x blend Res The Obsidian; rounded Res CHARD, dense Res SYRAH. 2nd tier incl spicy Estate MONTEPULCIANO. Attractive MERLOT-based rosé.

Oyster Bay Marl r w sp ★★ From DELEGAT. A marketing triumph: huge sales in UK, US, Australia. Vibrant, easy-drinking, mid-priced wines with touch of class from MARL, HAWK. Marl SAUV BL is biggest seller, 1.5 million cases/yr. Citrus Marl CHARD; medium-bodied Hawk PINOT GR; plum/spice Marl PINOT N, plummy Hawk MERLOT, easy-drinking fizz, gd dry rosé.

Palliser Mart r w ★★ →★★★ One of district's largest and best; multiple shareholders. Excellent SAUV BL; v. elegant CHARD; bubbly (best in MART); harmonious PINOT N. Top wines: Palliser Estate. Lower tier: Pencarrow (great value, majority of output).

Pegasus Bay Waip r w ★★★ Pioneer family firm with superb range: powerful CHARD; complex SAUV BL/SEM; medium RIES (big seller); exotic GEWURZ; silky PINOT N (esp mature-vine Prima Donna). S Island's best MERLOT/CAB SAUV (dense Maestro). Lovely sweet Ries, Sauv Bl, MUSCAT. Second label: Main Divide, top value, esp PINOT GR.

Peregrine C Ot r w ★★ Vibrant, flavoursome whites: dryish PINOT GR; Rastaburn RIES; gd NV sparkling. Refined PINOT N. Charming organic ROSÉ. 2nd tier: Saddleback.

Pernod Ricard NZ Auck r (p) w sp ★ →★★★ One of NZ's largest producers, formerly Montana. Wineries in AUCK, HAWK, MARL. Extensive co-owned v'yds for Marl whites, esp huge-selling BRANCOTT ESTATE SAUV BL. Major strength in fizz, esp big-selling DEUTZ Marl Cuvée. Wonderful value CHURCH ROAD reds and CHARD. Other key brands: STONELEIGH.

Puriri Hills Auck r (p) ★★ →★★★ Classy, long-lived MERLOT-based reds (with CAB FR, CARMENÈRE, CAB SAUV, MALBEC) from Clevedon 10' 13'. Distinctly B'x-like. Fragrant Estate red. Res is impressive, with more new oak. Top label is lush Pope. Second label: Mokoroa.

Pyramid Valley Cant r w ★★ →★★★ Tiny elevated limestone v'yd at Waikari, bought in 2017 by US-investor Brian Sheth and viticulturist Steve Smith (ex-CRAGGY RANGE). Estate-grown wines (rare, high-priced, strong personality), incl floral PINOT N (Angel Flower, Earth Smoke); citrus CHARD. Classy Growers' Collection wines (incl PINOT BL, CAB FR) from other regions.

Quartz Reef C Ot r w sp ★★ →★★★ Small, quality, bio producer with superb dry PINOT GR; fragrant, savoury, supple Bendigo Estate PINOT N. Stylish, yeasty, *lively fizz*: gd Vintage Blanc de Blancs.

Rapaura Springs Marl ★★ Skilfully crafted, gd-value (r w), esp Res range: CHARD, PINOT GR, SAUV BL, PINOT N.

Rippon Vineyard C Ot r w ★★ →★★★ Pioneer v'yd on shores of Lake Wanaka; arresting view and wines. Fragrant, savoury style. Mature Vine PINOT N, from vines planted 1985–91; Jeunesse Pinot N from younger vines. Tinker's Field Pinot N: oldest vines, age-worthy. Slowly evolving whites, esp outstanding Mature Vine RIES.

Rockburn C Ot r (p) w ★★ Mouthfilling, dry PINOT GR, light RIES. Harmonious PINOT N blended from Cromwell Basin (mostly) and GIBBSTON grapes. Popular Stolen Kiss: vibrant rosé. Second label: Devil's Staircase.

Sacred Hill Hawk r w ★★ →★★★ Mid-size producer. Acclaimed Riflemans CHARD 16', powerful but refined, from inland, elevated site. Wine Thief Chard: from same v'yd, more toasty, upfront. Long-lived Brokenstone MERLOT, Helmsman CAB/Merlot and Deerstalkers SYRAH from GIMBLETT GRAVELS. Punchy MARL SAUV BL, delicious, gd-value HAWK Merlot/Cab Sauv. Halo and Res: mid-tier.

Saint Clair Marl r (p) w ★★ →★★★ Largest family-owned producer in region; 1st vintage 1994. Acclaimed for pungent SAUV BL from relatively cool sites in lower WAIRAU VALLEY – esp punchy Wairau Res. Res is top selection; then array of impressive, 2nd-tier Pioneer Block (single v'yds); then gd-value, large volume regional blends: Sauv Bl, RIES, PINOT GR, GEWURZ, CHARD, GRUNER V, MERLOT (HAWK), PINOT N. 4th tier is Vicar's Choice.

Seifried Estate Nel (r) w ★★ Region's 1st and biggest winery, family-owned. Best known for medium-dry RIES, GEWURZ. Gd value, often excellent SAUV BL, CHARD.

Easy-drinking Würzer. Best: Winemakers Collection (esp Sweet Agnes Ries, creamy Chard). Old Coach Road: 3rd tier. Whites better than reds.

Selaks Marl r w ★→★★ Old producer of Croatian origin, now a brand of CONSTELLATION NEW ZEALAND. Solid, easy-drinking Premium Selection range. Gd-value Res HAWK CHARD, rosé, MERLOT/CAB, SYRAH. Recently revived top Founders range, esp complex Chard. New The Taste Collection range: Buttery Chard.

Seresin Marl r w ★★★→★★★★ Quality organic producer. Winery building and adjacent v'yd (but not brand or other v'yds) sold 2018. Sophisticated SAUV BL one of NZ's finest; generous CHARD. Savoury PINOT N, partly wood-aged PINOT GR. Bone-dry sparklings. Res: top range. 3rd tier Momo (v.gd quality/value). Complex, fine-textured, distinctive wines.

Sileni Hawk r (p) w ★★ Large producer, sold to investment company (2018). Strong recent focus on HAWK PINOT N. Top wines: bold Exceptional Vintage CHARD, SYRAH, MERLOT. Strong, mid-range Estate Selection, incl buttery The Lodge Chard; generous Triangle Merlot; floral Plateau Pinot N. Then Cellar Selection.

Smith & Sheth Cru Hawk r w ★★ Partnership of Steve Smith (ex-CRAGGY RANGE) and billionaire Brian Sheth. All single-v'yd wines. Complex HAWK CHARD; weighty MARL SAUV BL; savoury Hawk SYRAH. Practise saying it.

Spy Valley Marl r (p) w ★★→★★★ High achievers; extensive v'yds. Flavoury whites (dryish RIES, GEWURZ, soft PINOT GR) superb value; impressive SAUV BL, CHARD, PINOT N. Classy top selection: Envoy (oak-aged Pinot Gr; scented Ries; complex Outpost Pinot N).

Staete Landt Marl r w ★★ V'yd at Rapaura (WAIRAU VALLEY): refined CHARD; top-flight Annabel SAUV BL; weighty PINOT GR, savoury PINOT N; peppery SYRAH. Second label: Map Maker (gd value).

Starborough Family Estates Marl (r) w ★★ Family-owned v'yds in AWATERE and WAIRAU VALLEYS. SAUV BL, fleshy. Fresh CHARD. Scented PINOT GR. Elegant PINOT N. NB: not to be confused with Starborough brand controlled by Gallo.

Stonecroft Hawk r w ★★ Small organic winery. NZ's 1st serious SYRAH (1989). Youthful Res Syrah; Crofters Syrah: drink-young charm. Sturdy Ruhanui (MERLOT/CAB SAUV). Lush, v. rich Old-Vine GEWURZ. Refined CHARD. NZ's only ZIN.

Stoneleigh Marl r (p) w ★★ Owned by PERNOD RICARD NZ. Based on relatively warm Rapaura v'yds. Gd large-volume MARL whites: popular SAUV BL; easy-drinking RIES, slightly buttery CHARD. Top wines: Rapaura Series (esp intense Sauv Bl; smoky Chard; rich PINOT GR; flavourful PINOT N). New Wild Valley range, using indigenous yeasts: delicious Pinot Gr, rosé.

Stanyridge Waih r w ★★★→★★★★ Boutique winery, known since mid-80s for exceptional CAB SAUV-based blend, Larose, one of NZ's greatest. Airfield, little brother of Larose. Dense, Rhône-style, SYRAH-based blend, Pilgrim; Faithful Syrah, made for early drinking. Super-charged Luna Negra MALBEC.

Te Awa Hawk r w ★★→★★★ GIMBLETT GRAVELS v'yd now owned by VILLA MARIA and site of Kidnapper winery. Complex CHARD; refined MERLOT/CAB; stylish SYRAH. Fruity TEMPRANILLO. Left Field range: easy-drinking, gd value.

Biggest varieties in NZ? Sauv Bl, Pinot N, Chard. Made up 88%+ of 2018 harvest.

Te Kairanga Mart r w ★★ One of district's oldest, largest wineries, much-improved since purchase by American Bill Foley in 2011. Weighty PINOT GR; SAUV BL; fragrant PINOT N (value); delicious rosé. Runholder is mid-tier (graceful Pinot N). Top-tier is John Martin: complex CHARD; harmonious Pinot N.

Te Mata Hawk r w ★★★→★★★★ Winery of highest repute (1st vintage 1895) run by Buck family since 1974. Coleraine (CAB SAUV/MERLOT/CAB FR blend) **13' 14' 15'** has rare breed, great longevity (98 vintage currently in full stride). Much lower-priced Awatea Cabs/Merlot also classy, more forward. ***Bullnose Syrah*** among

NZ's finest. Elegant Elston CHARD. Classy, oak-aged SAUV BL: Cape Crest. Fleshy Zara VIOGNIER. Estate V'yds range for early drinking.

Terra Sancta C Ot r (p) (w) ★★ Bannockburn's 1st v'yd, founded 1991 as Olssens. V.gd-value, drink-young Mysterious Diggings PINOT N; mid-tier savoury Bannockburn Pinot N; lovely Slapjack Block Pinot N (from district's oldest vines). Scented, full PINOT GR; outstanding Pinot N Rosé arguably NZ's finest.

Te Whare Ra Marl r w ★★ Label: TWR. Small WAIRAU VALLEY producer, some of region's oldest vines, planted 1979. Known for highly perfumed, organic GEWURZ; vibrant SAUV BL, RIES (dry "D", medium "M").

Tiki Marl (r) w ★★ McKean family own extensive v'yds in MARL, WAIP. Punchy Marl SAUV BL, esp Single V'yd; fleshy Waipara PINOT GR; rich Single Vineyard HAWK CHARD, generous Koru Waipara PINOT N. Second label: Maui.

Romeo Bragato (government viticulturalist) 1st offered Sauv Bl vines for sale in 1907. Took off slowly.

Tohu r w ★★ Maori-owned venture with extensive v'yds in MARL, NEL. Racy AWATERE VALLEY SAUV BL; complex, barrel-fermented Mugwi Res Sauv Bl; vibrant Marl CHARD; strong RIES; refined Blanc de Blancs fizz; moderately complex PINOT N.

Trinity Hill Hawk r (p) w ★★→★★★ Highly regarded producer, US-owned since 2014. Refined, B'x-style blend The Gimblett 15'; stylish GIMBLETT GRAVELS CHARD 16'. Prestigious Homage SYRAH 14' 15' 16, Rhôney *Marsanne/Viognier*, Impressive TEMPRANILLO. Lower-tier, "white label" range gd value, esp drink-young MERLOT.

Two Paddocks C Ot r (w) ★★ Actor Sam Neill makes several PINOT NS. Single-v'yd Res range: First Paddock (more herbal, from cool Gibbston district), Last Chance (riper, from warmer Alexandra). Latest is perfumed The Fusilier, grown at Bannockburn.

Two Rivers Marl r (p) w ★★ Classy Convergence SAUV BL. Vibrant CHARD; rich rosé. Supple Tributary PINOT N. Second label: Black Cottage (v.gd value).

Urlar Wair r w ★★ Small organic producer with complex, oak-aged PINOT GR; scented RIES; vigorous SAUV BL; engaging PINOT N.

Valli C Ot ★★→★★★ Superb range of complex, single-v'yd PINOT N (fragrant Gibbston, ripe Bendigo, savoury Bannockburn, scented WAITAKI). Also racy Waitaki RIES.

Vavasour Marl r w ★★→★★★ Planted 1st vines in AWATERE VALLEY (1986). Now US-owned by Foley Family Wines. Vibrant, deep CHARD (Anna's V'yd, from oldest vines, esp tight, layered); best-known for weighty SAUV BL. Also lovely ROSE; generous PINOT N.

Vidal Hawk r w ★★→★★★ Est 1905, owned by VILLA MARIA since 1976. Top Legacy range: smoky CHARD; spicy SYRAH; superb CAB SAUV/MERLOT; great-value mid-tier Res range.

Villa Maria Auck r (p) w ★★→★★★ NZ's largest fully family-owned winery; president Sir George Fistonich; daughter Karen chairs the board. New CEO appointed 2018. Also owns ESK VALLEY, TE AWA, VIDAL. Wine-show focus, with glowing success. Distinguished top ranges: Res (express regional character) and Single V'yd (reflect individual sites); Cellar Selection: mid-tier (less oak) excellent, superb value; 3rd-tier, volume Private Bin wines can also be v.gd. Small volumes of v.gd ALBARIÑO, VERDELHO, GRENACHE, MALBEC. New icon red, Ngakirikiri The Gravels 13': CAB SAUV-based, v. youthful.

Waiheke Island r (w) ★★→★★★ Lovely, sprawling island in Auckland's Hauraki Gulf (with temperatures moderated by the sea). Pioneered by Goldwater 1978. Biggest producer by far is MAN O' WAR. Initial acclaim was for stylish CAB SAUV/MERLOT blends; more recently for dark, bold SYRAH. Popular tourist destination with many helipads.

Waimea Nel r (p) w ★★ One of region's largest and best-value producers, sold in

2017 to investment fund. Punchy SAUV BL, fragrant PINOT GR, perfumed GEWURZ. V gd honeyed RIES, punchy ALBARIÑO. Full-bodied PINOT N. Spinyback is 2nd tier.

Waipara Valley Cant CANT's key subregion, n of Christchurch (86% plantings). High profile for PINOT N, RIES. Currently repositioning itself as "North Canterbury", after name confusion in export markets.

Wairarapa NZ's 7th-largest wine region (not to be confused with WAIP. *See* MART. Also incl Gladstone subregion in n (slightly higher, cooler, wetter). Driest, coolest region in N Island; strength in whites (SAUV BL, PINOT GR most widely planted, also gd RIES, GEWURZ, CHARD) and esp PINOT N (savoury from relatively mature vines). Starting to promote itself as "Wellington Wine Country".

Wairau River Marl r (p) w ★★ Gd whites: punchy SAUV BL; rich PINOT GR; scented ALBARIÑO. Res is top label: single-v'yd Sauv Bl; weighty VIOGNIER; smoky CHARD; fragrant PINOT N.

Wairau Valley Marl MARL's largest subregion (1st v'yd planted 1873; modern era since 1973). Vast majority of region's cellar doors. Three important side valleys to s: Brancott, Omaka, Waihopai (known collectively as Southern Valleys). SAUV BL thrives on stony, salty plains; PINOT N on clay-based, n-facing slopes. Strong recent criticism by district council of many wine producers on environmental grounds.

Waitaki Valley C Ot Slowly expanding subregion in N Ot, with cool, frost-prone climate. Handful of producers. V. promising PINOT N (but can be leafy); racy PINOT GR, RIES.

Whitehaven Marl r (p) w ★★ Medium-sized producer. Flavour-packed, gd-value SAUV BL big seller in US. Rich GEWURZ; citrus CHARD; oily PINOT GR; off-dry RIES; v.gd dry rosé from PINOT N; sturdy Pinot N.

Wither Hills Marl r w ★★ Big producer, owned by Lion brewery. Popular, gd-value wines: lively SAUV BL (single v'yd Rarangi is intense); fleshy PINOT GR; generous CHARD (esp Single V'yd Benmorven); gd-value, finely balanced, Single V'yd Taylor River PINOT N.

Wooing Tree C Ot r (p) w ★★ Single v'yd, mostly reds. Bold PINOT N (Beetle Juice is delicious, drink-young style). Powerful Sandstorm Res Pinot N. Weighty CHARD. Less "serious" wines, all from Pinot N, incl delicious dry rosé, Blondie (faintly pink, off-dry white), Tickled Pink (sweet, raspberry/plum).

Yealands Marl r (p) w ★★ NZ's biggest "single v'yd", at AWATERE VALLEY site, now owned by utility company, Marlborough Lines. Convicted and fined $400,000 in 2018 for "deliberate, deceptive and sustained" breaches of the Wine Act, involving added sugar in wines exported to Europe. Partly estate-grown, mostly MARL wines. Past high profile for sustainability, but most wines not certified organic. Single V'yd range: lingering SAUV BL; scented PINOT GR; generous PINOT N. Lower-priced range: Peter Yealands: top value. Other key brands: Babydoll, Crossroads, The Crossings.

Ambitious Prices

From its shingly Mere Road v'yd, in the GIMBLETT GRAVELS of HAWK, MILLS REEF has produced a stream of classy CAB SAUV-, MERLOT- and SYRAH-based reds since the mid-90s under its NZ$50 Elspeth label. Now comes a new pair of flagship reds, priced at NZ$350. After tasting the wines "blind" against famous French reds, Mills Reef decided they were of similar quality. About 1000 bottles each were made of Mills Reef Arthur Edmund Cabernet/Merlot 2013 and Arthur Edmund Syrah 2013. One wine judge rated them highly, but behind other top 2013 Hawk reds retailing at NZ$50. Another NZ critic, although "shocked" by the price, awarded the Cab/Merlot a perfect score.

South Africa

OLIFANTS RIVER

Cederberg
Citrusdal

Groot Berg
Swartland
Darling
COASTAL REGION Breedekloof **KLEIN KAROO** Qudtshoorn
Wellington **BREEDE** Tulbagh Calitzdorp
Voor Paardeberg **RIVER**
Cape Paarl **VALLEY** Robertson
Town Durbanville Franschhoek Breede
Stellenbosch Swellendam
Constantia Caledon
Elgin Overberg/Elandskloof
Hemel-en-Aarde
Walker Bay **CAPE SOUTH COAST**
Bredasdorp *Indian Ocean*
Elim

Atlantic Ocean

Abbreviations used in the text:		**Rdg/Up/V**	Ridge/Upper/Valley
Bre	Breedekloof	**Oli R**	Olifants River
C'dorp	Calitzdorp	**Pie**	Piekenierskloof
Cape SC	Cape South Coast	**Rob**	Robertson
Ced	Cederberg	**Sla**	Slanghoek
Coast	Coastal Region	**Stell**	Stellenbosch
Const	Constantia	**Swa**	Swartland
Ela	Elandskloof	**Tul**	Tulbagh
Elg	Elgin	**V Pa**	Voor Paardeberg
Fran	Franschhoek	**Wlk B**	Walker Bay
Hem	Hemel-en-Aarde...	**Well**	Wellington

The workhorse grape in the past was Steen, alias Chenin Blanc. It was the base, inter alia, of the Cape's very passable "Sherry", its main export. Veteran vineyards still have plenty; the irony is that the workhorse now makes some of the country's very best wines. We are spoilt for choice, though. There is juicy Sauvignon Blanc, firm, fresh Chardonnay, locally rare varieties like Vermentino, forgotten heirlooms such as Palomino and lab-engineered exotics like Therona. The best white blends from Swartland have few rivals anywhere. Reds used to be less exciting; recently they have become finer, fresher and less wood-reliant, as winemakers explore earlier picking times; clay, concrete or ceramic for maturation; and other kinds of wood. There are old-vine bottlings worthy of contemplation too. And, if gorgeously packaged, pricey rosé floats your yacht, that is now a thing. This cornucopia has a dark side: many sobering questions need to be answered – around sustainability, eco-degradation, ongoing drought, social justice, to name a few. S Africa is not alone in this, but perhaps more aware of it.

Recent vintages

2018 3rd successive drought yr. Concentrated, flavourful wines though probably not for long cellaring.

2017 Quality, character comparable to 2015. Accessible young, possibly peaking earlier too.

2016 Extreme conditions favoured later-ripening varieties, cooler areas. Many excellent wines, to drink while waiting for 2015.

2015 Among greats exceptional flavour, balance, intensity. Slow starting, structure for long ageing.

2014 Cooler, wetter yr; lighter, elegant wines; earlier-drinking.

AA Badenhorst Family Wines W Cape r (p) w (sp) ★★→★★★★ Cousins Adi and Hein Badenhorst's winery on Paardeberg Mtn epitomizes new S Africa dynamism. Gnarled vines, ambient yeasts, old oak for mostly Med blends, CHENIN BL, heirloom varieties eg. CINSAULT, PALOMINO. New orange (skin-contact) wine Riviera in exceptional-value everyday range Secateurs.

Alheit Vineyards W Cape (r) w ★★★★ Breathtaking old-vine and heritage-variety expressions by husband-and-wife Chris and Suzaan Alheit. Multi-region CHENIN BL, SEM Cartology 14' 15', Chenin Bl (Magnetic N Mtn Makstok 13' 15', Radio Lazarus 12' 15' and new Fire By Night, Huilkrans, Nautical Dawn), SEM La Colline 15' 17', field-blend Vine Garden 15' from HEM home farm. Each new release a revelation. Stylish earlier-drinking Flotsam & Jetsam.

Anthonij Rupert Wyne W Cape r (p) w (br) sp ★→★★★ International businessman Johann Rupert honours late brother in extensive, increasingly impressive portfolio from own v'yds in DARLING, SWA, Overberg and stately home farm (and cellar door) L'Ormarins nr FRAN. Best: flagship Anthonij Rupert and site-specific Cape of Gd Hope. Jean Roi Rosé part of mini-boom in premium pinks.

Ataraxia Wines W Cape r w ★★★ Top-drawer CHARD 15' and newer PINOT N by grower/co-owner Kevin Grant on Skyfields farm, with remarkable chapel-like cellar door overlooking HEM.

Babylonstoren W Cape r (p) w (sp) ★→★★★ C17 Cape Dutch farm nr PAARL (name means Tower of Babel) stylishly restored by Karen Roos, ex-*Elle Decoration* editor, and media-giant husband Koos Bekker. B'x red Nebukadnesar 15' heads ever more impressive line-up.

Bartho Eksteen W Cape r p w sw sp ★★★ HEM-based Bartho Eksteen specializes in Rhône varieties and SAUV BL, mentors young growers/distillers under Wijnskool/Tree of Knowledge banner.

Bartinney Private Cellar Stell r (p) w (sp) ★→★★★ Rising star on precipitous Banhoek Valley slopes, family-owned; original CAB SAUV 14' 15', CHARD 15' since joined by equally riveting Res versions. "Lifestyle" range Noble Savage. New upscale sibling brand Montegray.

Beau Constantia Const w ★★ Elegant B'x/Rhône varieties and blends from steep mtn v'yds planted by Du Preez family owners in early 2000s.

Beaumont Family Wines Bot R r w br (sw) ★★→★★★ Excellent handcrafted wines from charming rustic estate. Rare solo-bottled MOURVÈDRE 10' 15', elegant Hope Marguerite CHENIN BL 12' 15' 16' 17', recent Chenin Bl-based New Baby 15'.

BEE (Black Economic Empowerment) Initiative aimed at increasing wine-industry ownership and participation by previously disadvantaged groups.

Beeslaar Wines Stell r ★★★★ KANONKOP winemaker's personal take on PINOTAGE 13' 14' 16'. Refined, rather special.

Bellingham Coast r w ★★→★★★ Enduring DGB brand with fascinating low-volume, high-class The Bernard Series (incl hen's-teeth-scarce monovarietal ROUSSANNE 15') and Homestead Series with v.gd old-vine CHENIN BL.

Beyerskloof W Cape (p) (w) (br) ★→★★★ SA's PINOTAGE champion, nr STELL. Ten versions of grape on offer (11, incl spirit used to fortify Port-style Lagare Cape Vintage). Powerful varietal Diesel 13' 16', trio of CAPE BLENDS. Even PINOTAGE burgers at cellar-door bistro. Also classic CAB SAUV/MERLOT Field Blend 09' 14'.

Boekenhoutskloof Winery Fran r (p) w sw ★→★★★★ Top FRAN winery; showing

Collective catapult for Cabernet
Inside S Africa, "STELL" and "top-flight CAB SAUV" are pretty much synonymous. Internationally, not so much. Which is why there is a new association, Stellenbosch Cabernet Collective (Stellenboschcabernet. co.za), with more than 30 member wineries aiming to spread overseas awareness of the quality, terroir diversity and long pedigree of varietal Cab as produced in the local wine industry's heartland. Sustained and focused effort have seen S African CHENIN BL producers transform their Cinderella grape into a princess, and these Cab-growing colleagues are striving for similar success through public tastings, participation in auctions and shows, social and print promotion, and more. Take your own counter-clockwise taste trip around the area with the following members: BARTINNEY, JORDAN, KAAPZICHT, KANONKOP, LE RICHE, RUSTENBERG, RUST EN VREDE, STARK-CONDÉ, VILLIERA, WARWICK.

exemplary quality, consistency over past quarter-century with *Syrah* 09' 12' 15' (now entirely SWA fruit); *FRAN CAB SAUV* 08' 09' 11' (also-excellent newer STELL version); old-vines *Sem*; Med-style-red Chocolate Block 17'; superior-quaffing Porcupine Ridge, Wolftrap lines. *See* PORSELEINBERG.

Bon Courage Estate Rob r (p) w (br) sw (s/sw) sp ★→★★★ Broad family-grown range led by Inkará reds; stylish trio of Brut MCC; aromatic desserts (RIES, MUSCAT).

Boplaas Family Vineyards W Cape r w br (sp) (sw) ★→★★★ Wine-growers Carel Nel and daughter Margaux at C'DORP, known for Port styles: Cape Vintage Res 09' 12', Tawny. Recent emphasis on unfortified Portuguese grapes (r w).

Boschendal Wines W Cape r (p) w (sw) sp ★→★★★ Famous, photogenic estate nr FRAN under DGB stewardship, noted for SHIRAZ, SAUV BL, CHARD and MCC.

Botanica Wines W Cape r (p) w (sw) ★★→★★★★ By STELL-based American Ginny Povall. Superlative Mary Delany CHENIN BL 12' 14' 15' 16' 17' from old w-coast bush vines; PINOT N partly from HEM; SEM 15' ex-ELG; VIOGNIER *vin de paille* NV from Stell.

Bouchard Finlayson Cape SC r w ★★→★★★★ V. fine PINOT N grower in HEM. Galpin Peak 13' 15' and barrel-selection Tête de Cuvée. Impressive CHARD (Crocodile's Lair, ex-Ela vines and Missionvale), exotic red Hannibal 10' 11'.

Breedekloof Large (c.13,000 ha) inland district; mostly bulk- and entry-level; pockets of high-quality: Bergsig, OLIFANTSBERG, O?PSTAL, Stofberg Family.

Bruce Jack Wines W Cape r p w (sp) ★→★★★ Never a dull moment at FLAGSTONE founder Bruce Jack's solo venture based on Appelsdrift farm nr Napier. Endlessly creative Portuguese-French-Italian blends, varietals, rosé and bubbly. Delightful labels by artist wife, Penny.

Buitenverwachting W Cape r (p) w sw (sp) ★★→★★★ Classy family winery in CONST. Standout CHARD 14', Husseys Vlei SAUV BL 13', B'x red Christine 09'. Labelled Bayten for export.

Calitzdorp KLEIN KAROO DISTRICT (c.335 ha) climatically similar to the Douro, known for Port styles and latterly unfortified Port-grape blends (r w) and varietals eg. BOPLAAS, DE KRANS.

Cape Blend Usually red with PINOTAGE component; occasionally CHENIN BL blend, or simply wine with "Cape character". Try Alvi's Drift, BEAUMONT, BEYERSKLOOF, KAAPZICHT, KWV, OPSTAL.

Cape Chamonix Wine Farm Fran r w (sp) ★★→★★★ Excellent winemaker-run mtn property. Distinctive PINOT N, PINOTAGE, CHARD, SAUV BL, B'x blends (r w) and CAB FR, all worth keeping.

Capensis W Cape w ★★★ S Africa-US venture, GRAHAM BECK's Antony Beck and Jackson Family's Barbara Banke. Luxurious multiregion CHARD 15'.

Cape Point Vineyards (r) w (sw) ★★★→★★★★ Outstanding producer at Noordhoek, way s on CAPE TOWN peninsula. Complex, age-worthy SAUV BL/SEM Isliedh 12' 16' 17', CHARD, Sauv Bl. Gd-value label Splattered Toad. New sibling venture Cape Town Wine Company (r w sp).

Cape Rock Wines W Cape r (p) w ★★ →★★★ OLI R's leading boutique grower, noted for personality-packed, strikingly packaged Rhône and Port-grape blends (r w).

Cape South Coast Cool-climate "super REGION" (c.2600 ha) comprising DISTRICTS of Cape Agulhas, ELG, Overberg, Plettenberg Bay, Swellendam and WLK B, plus standalone WARDS Herbertsdale, Lower Duivenhoks River, Napier, Stilbaai East.

Cape Town DISTRICT (c.2700 ha) covering Cape Town city, its peninsula and CONST, DUR, Hout Bay, Philadelphia WARDS.

Catherine Marshall Wines W Cape r w (br) ★★★ Cool-climate (chiefly ELG) specialist Cathy M and partners focus mostly on PINOT N, MERLOT, SAUV BL, CHENIN BL; delightful dry, mineral RIES.

Cederberg Tiny (c.100 ha) high-altitude standalone WARD in Cederberg mtns. Mainly SHIRAZ, SAUV BL. Driehoek and CEDERBERG PRIVATE CELLAR sole producers.

Cederberg Private Cellar Ced, Elim r (p) w sp ★★ →★★★★ Nieuwoudt family with perhaps S Africa's highest (CED) and most s (ELIM) v'yds. Elegant intensity in CAB SAUV, PINOT N, rare Bukettraube, CHENIN BL, SAUV BL, SEM, MCC, SHIRAZ (incl exceptional CWG bottling Teen die Hoog 10' 11').

Central Orange River Standalone N Cape "mega WARD" (c.9300 ha). Hot, dry, irrigated; mainly whites, fortified. Major producer is Orange River Cellars.

Charles Fox Cap Classique Wines Elg sp ★★★ Champagne-style bubbly house, complete with French consultant winemaker; six classic, delicious Bruts incl new pair of NV Res sp w.

Coastal Largest REGION (c.43,000 ha), incl sea-influenced DISTRICTS of CAPE TOWN, DARLING, STELL, SWA, and, since 2018, previously standalone ward Lamberts Bay. Confusingly, also non-coastal FRAN, PAARL, TUL, WELL.

Colmant Cap Classique & Champagne W Cape sp ★★★ →★★★★ Belgian family *méthode traditionnelle* sparkling specialists at FRAN. Brut and Sec Res, Rosé, CHARD, new Absolu Zero Dosage; all MCC, NV and excellent.

Constantia Scenic CAPE TOWN WARD (c.430 ha) on cool Constantiaberg slopes, S Africa's 1st and among most-famous fine-wine areas, revitalized in recent yrs by GROOT, KLEIN CONST *et al*.

Constantia Glen Const r w ★★★ Waibel-family-owned gem on upper reaches of Constantiaberg. Superb B'x blends (r w) and varietal SAUV BL.

Constantia Uitsig Const r w br sp ★★★ Premium v'yds, cellar producing mostly still whites, MCC. Consistent, striking, individual SEM 12' 14' 15'.

Creation Wines Cape SC r w ★★ →★★★★ Elegant modernity in family-owned/-vinified range of B'x, Rhône, Burgundy varietals and blends. V.-fine new Cool Climate CHENIN BL.

CWG (Cape Winemakers Guild) Independent, invitation-only association of 47 top growers. Stages benchmarking annual auction of limited premium bottlings.

Dalla Cia Wine & Spirit Company W Cape r w ★★ →★★★ Reputable 3rd-generation family vintners/distillers at STELL. Flagship: pricey "Supertuscan" Teano.

Darling DISTRICT (c.2800 ha) around this w-coast town. Best v'yds in hilly Groenekloof WARD. Cloof, Darling Cellars, Groote Post/Aurelia, Mount Pleasant, Ormonde, Withington bottle under own labels; most other fruit goes into 3rd-party brands.

David & Nadia Swa r w ★★★★ Sadie husband and wife follow natural-winemaking principles of SWA Independent Producers. Exquisite Rhône-style-red Elpidios, GRENACHE N, CHENIN BL (varietals and blend Aristargos 12' 13' 14' 15'), SEM, newer PINOTAGE, mostly from old vines. Assistant winemaker André Bruyns' own label, City on a Hill, also v. finely crafted.

De Krans Wines W Cape r (p) w br (sp) ★ →★★★ Nel family v'yds at C'DORP noted for Port styles (esp Vintage Res 08' 09' **10'** 11' 12' 13' 16') and fortified MUSCAT. Latterly success with unfortified Port grapes.

Delaire Graff Estate W Cape r (p) w (br) (sw) (sp) ★ →★★★★ UK diamond merchant Laurence Graff's eyrie v'yds, winery and tourist destination nr STELL. Gem-encrusted portfolio headed by premium-priced, age-worthy CAB SAUV Laurence Graff Res 09' 12' 13'.

Delheim Wines Coast r (p) w sw (s/sw) (sp) ★ →★★★ Eco-minded family winery nr STELL. Vera Cruz SHIRAZ, PINOTAGE; cellar-worthy, best-yrs CAB SAUV-driven Grand Res, scintillating Edelspatz botrytis RIES **13'** 15'.

DeMorgenzon Stell r (p) w (sw) (sp) ★★ →★★★★ Hylton and Wendy Appelbaum's manicured property hitting high notes with B'x, Rhône varietals and blends, CHARD, CHENIN BL. Occasional Chenin Bl The Divas 13' 17' is spectacular.

De Toren Private Cellar Stell r ★★★ Now majority Swiss owned, with consistently flavourful B'x Fusion V 09' 15' and earlier-maturing MERLOT-based Z; light-styled Délicate.

De Trafford Wines Coast r w sw ★★★ →★★★★ Boutique grower David Trafford with track record for bold yet harmonious wines. B'x/SHIRAZ Elevation 393, CAB SAUV, Blueprint SYRAH **12'** 15', CHENIN BL (dry and *vin de paille*). See SIJNN.

De Wetshof Estate Rob r w sw sp ★★★ Famed CHARD pioneer and exponent; five versions (oaked/unwooded, still/sparkling) topped by single-v'yd The Site.

DGB W Cape Long-est, WELL-based producer/wholesaler, owner of high-end brands The Bernard Series and BOSCHENDAL, also easy-drinking Bellingham, Brampton, Douglas Green.

Diemersdal Estate W Cape r (p) w ★ →★★★ DUR family farm excelling with various site/row-specific SAUV BL (incl skin-fermented Wild Horseshoe), red blends, PINOTAGE, CHARD and S Africa's 1st/only commercial GRÜNER V.

Estimated 20% local wineries wholly or partly owned by non-S African nationals.

Diemersfontein Wines W Cape r (p) w ★ →★★★ Family wine estate, restaurant and guest lodge at WELL, esp noted for full-throttle Carpe Diem range. PINOTAGE created emulated "coffee style". BEE brand is Thokozani.

Distell W Cape S Africa's biggest drinks company, in STELL. Owns or has interests in many brands, spanning styles/quality scales. *See* DURBANVILLE HILLS, FLEUR DU CAP, JC LE ROUX, NEDERBURG WINES.

District *See* GEOGRAPHICAL UNIT.

Dorrance Wines W Cape r (p) w ★★ →★★★ French-toned, family-owned, with one of only two cellars in Cape Town city (reason to visit). Gorgeous SYRAH, CHARD, CHENIN BL.

Durbanville Cool, hilly WARD (c.1350 ha) in CAPE TOWN DISTRICT, best-known for pungent SAUV BL; also MERLOT, white blends. Corporate co-owned DURBANVILLE HILLS and many family ventures eg. newer Canto, with rare SHIRAZ MCC among other sparklers.

Durbanville Hills Dur r (p) w (sw) (sp) ★ →★★★ Owned by DISTELL, local growers and staff trust, with awarded PINOTAGE, CHARD, SAUV BL. V.gd newer B'x blend Tangram (r w).

Eagles' Nest Coast r (p) w ★ →★★★ CONST family winery with reliably superior MERLOT, VIOGNIER, SHIRAZ. Also vibrant SAUV BL, cellar-door-only Little Eagle Rosé.

Edgebaston W Cape r w ★★ →★★★ V'yds, cellar nr STELL owned by David Finlayson, scion of esteemed Cape wine family. V.gd GS CAB SAUV 14', old-vine Camino Africana series, classy early-drinkers. With resident winemaker, produces rare solo TEMPRANILLO and fine GRENACHE under Van der Merwe & Finlayson label.

Eikendal Vineyards W Cape r w ★★★ Back-to-form Swiss-owned property nr STELL.

SOUTH AFRICA

B'x red Classique MERLOT, newer vintage-blend Charisma (r). Always-excellent CHARD now part of trio: multi-site, bush-vine, single-clone.

Elgin Cool-climate DISTRICT (c.755 ha) recognized for SAUV BL, CHARD, PINOT N; also exciting SYRAH, RES and MCC. Mostly family boutiques, incl one of only two certified-bio wineries in S Africa, Elg Ridge (other is REYNEKE in STELL).

Elim Cool-climate WARD (c.140 ha) in most S DISTRICT, Cape Agulhas, producing aromatic SAUV BL, white blends, SHIRAZ. Also grape source for majors like KWV and boutiques eg. Flying Cloud.

Look for Certified Heritage V'yd bottle sticker for old-vine (35 years+) wines.

Ernie Els Wines W Cape r (p) (w) ★→★★★★ S Africa's star golfer's wine venture nr STELL; long-lived varietal and blended CAB SAUV under Signature and Proprietor's labels, earlier-ready Big Easy range (r w). Co-proprietor Baron Hans von Staff-Reitzenstein also owns, and is restoring nearby Stellenzicht to former glory.

Estate Wine Wine grown, made and bottled on "units registered for the production of estate wine". Not a quality designation.

Fable Mountain Vineyards W Cape r p w ★ →★★★★ Reputed TUL grower and sibling of MULDERBOSCH. Exceptional SHIRAZ (varietal and blend), white blend, Rhône-grape rosé. New special sites/vintages Small Batch Series, easy-drinking Raptor Post range.

Fairview Coast r w (br sw) (sp) ★→★★★ Dynamic, innovative owner Charles Back, with smorgasbord of varietal, blended, single-v'yd and terroir-specific bottlings under Fairview, Spice Route, Goats do Roam and trimmed La Capra brands.

FirstCape Vineyards W Cape r p w sp ★→★★ DYA Hugely successful export joint venture of five local co-ops and UK's Brand Phoenix, with entry-level wines in more than a dozen ranges, some sourced outside S Africa.

Flagstone Winery W Cape r (p) w (br) ★→★★★ High-end producer at Somerset W, owned by Accolade Wines, with impressive PINOTAGE, SAUV BL, B'x white, luxe new Velvet Red Blend. Sibling to mid-tier Fish Hoek, entry-level KUMALA.

Fleur du Cap W Cape r (p) w sw ★→★★★ DISTELL premium label, incl v.gd Series Privée Unfiltered (formerly "Unfiltered Collection"), always-stellar botrytis dessert and B'x red Laszlo.

Foundry, The Stell, V P. r w ★★★→★★★★ MEERLUST winemaker Chris Williams' own brand, with wine-partner James Reid; v.gd Rhône varietals: GRENACHE BL 12' 13' 15'.

Franschhoek Valley Huguenot-founded DISTRICT (C.1240 ha) known for CAB SAUV, CHARD, SEM, MCC. Boasts some of S Africa's oldest vines; watch for bottlings by ALHEIT, BOEKENHOUTSKLOOF, Eikehof, MULLINEUX/Leeu Passant (CINSAULT), Rickety Bridge, Yardstick (SEM).

Free State Province, GEOGRAPHICAL UNIT. The Bald Ibis is sole producer, in e highlands.

Gabriëlskloof W Cape r (p) w (sw) ★→★★★ Star winemaker Peter-Allan Finlayson vinifies this expanding and improving line-up, headed by Landscape Series (CAB FR, SYRAH, old-vine CHENIN BL, B'x white), plus own excellent Crystallum PINOT N, CHARD in family-owned cellar nr Bot R.

Geographical Unit (GU) Largest of the four main WO demarcations: E, N and W Cape, KWAZULU-NATAL, Limpopo and newer FREE STATE. The other WO delineations (in descending size): REGION, DISTRICT, WARD.

Glen Carlou Coast r (p) w (sw) ★→★★★ 1st-rate family-owned cellar, v'yds, art gallery, restaurant nr PAARL, hailed for B'x-red styles, single/multisite CHARD.

Glenelly Estate Stell r w ★→★★ Former Ch Pichon-Lalande (*see* B'x) owner May-Eliane de Lencquesaing's "retirement" v'yds and cellar. Impressive flagships Lady May (B'x red) and Estate Res duo (B'x/SHIRAZ, CHARD). Superior-value Glass Collection.

GlenWood Coast r w (sw) ★★★ Meticulous FRAN grower with acclaimed prestige label Grand Duc (SYRAH, CHARD, B'x white, botrytis SEM).

Graham Beck W Cape sp ★★★ Front-ranker nr ROB focused exclusively on MCC bubbly. Seven bottlings (vintage/NV; Brut, Sec, Demi-Sec) led by superb *Chard Cuvée Clive*.

Grangehurst Stell r p ★★→★★★ Small-batch specialist known/valued for long bottle-ageing at cellar before release. CAB SAUV and blends, CAPE BLEND Nikela and PINOTAGE. Lovely dry rosé.

Groot Constantia Estate Const r (p) w (br) sw (sp) ★★→★★★★ Historic property and tourist mecca in S Africa's original fine-wine area, with suitably serious wines, esp MUSCAT de Frontignan Grand Constance (14') helping restore CONST dessert to C18 glory.

Hamilton Russell Vineyards Swa, Hem V r (p) w ★★→★★★★ Admired cool-climate pioneer and burgundy-style specialist in HEM. Elegant PINOT N 12' 15', long-lived CHARD 11' 12' 15' under HRV label. Super SAUV BL, PINOTAGE (varietal and blend), Sauv Bl/Chard in S Right and Ashbourne livery. Now new venture in Oregon.

Hartenberg Estate W Cape r w (sw) ★→★★★ Welcoming STELL family farm never disappoints with SHIRAZ, (several varietals and new blend, The Megan); B'x red, CHARD, RIES (semi-dry, botrytis); gd-value Alchemy blends (r w).

Haskell Vineyards W Cape r w ★★→★★★ US-owned v'yds, cellar nr STELL serially awarded for trio of mono-site SYRAH, single-v'yd CHARD and red blends. V.gd sibling label Dombeya.

Hemel-en-Aarde Trio of cool-climate WARDS (Hem V, Up Hem, Hem Rdg) in WLK B DISTRICT, producing outstanding PINOT N, CHARD, SAUV BL.

Hermanuspietersfontein Wynkelder W Cape r p w ★★→★★★ Leading SAUV BL and B'x/Rhône blend (r w) specialist; creatively markets physical and historical connections with seaside resort Hermanus; sources (esp fresh CABS) mostly from cool site Sunday's Glen close by.

Iona Vineyards Cape SC r w ★★→★★★ Co-owned by staff, with high-altitude v'yds in ELG. Excellent blends (SHIRAZ-based and B'x white), CHARD, SAUV BL (now also wooded version), PINOT N, new 8+8 RIES. Cut-above lifestyle brand Sophie & Mr P.

JC le Roux, The House of W Cape sp ★→★★★ S Africa's largest specialist fizz producer at STELL, DISTELL-owned. Best labels are PINOT N, Scintilla and Brut NV, all MCC.

Jean Daneel Wines W Cape r w ★★→★★★ Family winery at Napier producing high-powered Director's Signature Series, esp B'x red, CHENIN BL.

Joostenberg Wines Paarl r w sw ★★→★★★ Ever-improving family range, organic-grown. SYRAH, CHENIN BL; some gems in experimental Small Batch Collection. Partner, with STARK-CONDÉ, in stylish everyday MAN Family Wines brand.

Jordan Wine Estate W Cape r (p) w (sw) (sp) ★→★★★★ Family winery nr STELL offering consistency, quality, value, from entry Chameleon to immaculate CWG bottlings. Flagship CHARD Nine Yards and B'x red Cobblers Hill. Setting up to produce traditional-method bubbly in England.

Northern Cape growers find their Shangri-la

Picture a semi-desert the size of Germany, with summer rain (and attendant viticultural challenges), bitter cold and searing heat. Wine-growing paradise this may not be, yet a tiny handful of family boutiques is beating the odds with steadily rising quality, excitement and a sense of place. Try Super Single V'yds' character-packed NEBBIOLO, SYRAH, TEMPRANILLO and wooded RIES from vines at Sutherland, S Africa's coldest and nr-highest site; and Lowerland (literally meaning "Verdant Land", hinting at its location further n on fertile Orange/Gariep River banks), with TANNAT, VIOGNIER, COLOMBARD (still and MCC sparkling), grown organically and vinified by top young W Cape winemakers.

Julien Schaal Cape SC w ★★★ Alsace vigneron Julien Schaal and wife Sophie handcraft thrilling CHARD from cool-grown ELG and HEM parcels.

Kaapzicht Wine Estate Stell r (p) w (sw) ★★→★★★ Family winery in STELL; widely praised top range Steytler (best-yrs CAPE BLEND Vision 12', PINOTAGE, B'x r Pentagon, old-vines CHENIN ■. The 1947 13' 14' 16'). Newer Skuinsberg CINSAULT 15'.

Kanonkop Estate Coast r (p) ★★→★★★★ Decades-long undisputed "First Growth" status, mainly with PINOTAGE ("regular" 09' 10', and old-vines Black Label 16'), B'x-blend Paul Sauer 14' 15' and CAB SAUV. Insatiable demand for 2nd-tier Kadette (CAPE BLEND, dry rosé, PINOTAGE).

Grenache vines can need half as much water as Syrah. No-brainer.

Keermont Vineyards Stell r w sw ★★★ Neighbour (and supplier of some grapes to) DE TRAFFORD, on steep STELL Mtn slopes. SHIRAZ and CHENIN BL (single-v'yd and blended), newer MERLOT.

Ken Forrester Wines W Cape r (p) w sw (s/sw) (sp) ★→★★★ With international drinks giant AdVini as partner, STELL vintner/restaurateur Ken F concentrates on Med varieties, CHENIN BL (dry, off-dry, botrytis). Unputdownable budget line-up, Petit.

Klein Constantia Estate W Cape r (p) w sw sp ★★→★★★★ Iconic property, re-energized and -focused on S.UV BL, with ten different varietal bottlings, and on luscious, cellar-worthy non-botrytis MUSCAT de Frontignan Vin de Constance 12' 13' 14' 15' (best ever?), convincing re-creation of legendary C18 CONST sweet dessert.

Kleine Zalze Wines ▼ Cape r (p) w sp ★→★★★★ STELL-based star with brilliant CAB SAUV, SHIRAZ, CHENIN BL, SAUV BL in Family Res and V'yd Selection ranges. Exceptional value in Cellar Selection series.

Klein Karoo Mainly semi-arid REGION (c.2200 ha) known for fortified, esp Port style in C'DORP. Revived old vines beginning to feature in young-buck bottlings eg. Ron Burgundy Wines' Patatsfontein CHENIN BL 15', Le Sueur Wines' Chenin Bl.

Krone W Cape (p) sp ★→★★★ Refined, classic MCC, incl recently introduced RD 02'. Made at revitalized Twee Jonge Gezellen Estate in TUL.

Kumala W Cape r (p) w sw/sw (sp) ★→★★★ DYA Major entry-level export label, and sibling to premium FLAGSTONE and mid-tier Fish Hoek. All owned by Accolade Wines.

KwaZulu-Natal Province and demarcated GEOGRAPHICAL UNIT on e coast; summer rain; sub-tropical/tropical climate in coastal areas; cooler in central Midlands plateau, home to Abingdon, Highgate wineries and, further n, central Drakensberg area, where dramatic mtn spires backdrop Cathedral Peak Estate.

KWV W Cape r (p) w Lr (sw) (s/sw) (sp) ★→★★★ Formerly national wine co-op and controlling body, today one of S Africa's biggest producers and exporters, based in PAARL. Reds, whites, sparkling, Port styles and other fortified under more than a dozen labels, headed by serially decorated The Mentors.

Lammershoek Winery Coast r (p) w ★→★★★ Influential in recent SWA/S African evolution, early emphasis on old vines, organic cultivation, "natural" practices, etc. Lots happening in The Mysteries range, eg. ultra-rare solo HÁRSLEVELŰ.

La Motte W Cape r w sw sp ★★→★★★ Graceful winery and cellar door at FRAN owned by the Koegelenberg-Rupert family. Old World-styled B'x, Rhône varietals, blends, CHARD, SAUV BL, MCC, VIOGNIER *vin de paille*.

Leeu Passant *See* MULLINEUX.

Le Lude Méthode Cap Classique Fran sp ★★★ Celebrated, innovative sparkling-only house, family-owned. Premium-priced offering incl CHARD/PINOT N Agrafe, 1st in S Africa to undergo 2nd fermentation under cork closure.

Le Riche Wines Stell r (w) ★★★ Fine CAB SAUV-based boutique wines, handcrafted by Christo le Riche, son of recently retired founder Etienne. Also elegant CHARD.

MCC (Méthode Cap Classique) EU-friendly name for bottle-fermented sparkling, one of SA's major success stories; c.350 labels and counting.

Meerlust Estate Stell r w ★★★★ Historic family-owned v'yds, cellar. Elegance, restraint in flagship Rubicon 09' 10' 15', among S Africa's 1st B'x reds; excellent MERLOT, CAB SAUV, CHARD, PINOT N.

Miles Mossop Wines Coast r w sw ★★★ Former TOKARA wine chief Miles Mossop's own brand; consistently splendid red and white blends, botrytized CHENIN BL.

Morgenster Estate W Cape r (p) w (sp) ★ →★★★ Prime Italian-owned wine/olive farm nr Somerset West, advised by Bordelais Pierre Lurton (Cheval Blanc). Classically styled Morgenster Res 11' 15' and second label Lourens River Valley (both B'x r). Old-country varieties in Italian Collection, Single Varietal range.

Mount Abora Vineyards Swa r w ★★★ "SWA chic" epitomized in naturally fermented, old-vine CINSAULT, Rhône red blend, bush-vine CHENIN BL 14' 16', vinified by Johan Meyer, whose non-interventionist approach is also evident in own brands Mother Rock, Force Majeure, JH Meyer Signature.

Mulderbosch Vineyards W Cape r w (sp) ★★ →★★★ Highly regarded STELL winery, sibling to FABLE MTN V'YDS, with headlining 1000 Miles SAUV BL, trio of single-block CHENIN BL, hugely popular CAB SAUV rosé.

Mullineux & Leeu Passant W Cape r w sw ★★★ →★★★★ Chris M and US-born wife Andrea with investor Analjit Singh transform SWA SHIRAZ, **Chenin Bl** and handful of compatible varieties into ambrosial blends and monovarietals based on soil type (granite, quartz, schist), CWG bottlings and *vin de paille*. Newer, wider-sourced Leeu Passant portfolio – Dry Red and two CHARD (ex-STELL and Overberg) – equally sublime. Also California boutique brand Fog Monster.

Mvemve Raats Stell r ★★★★ Mzokhona Mvemve, S Africa's 1st qualified black winemaker, and Bruwer Raats (RAATS FAMILY): stellar best-of-vintage B'x blend, MR de Compostella 09' 13' 15'.

Nederburg Wines W Cape r (p) w ss s/sw (sp) ★ →★★★★ Among S Africa's biggest (two million cases) and best-known brands, PAARL based, DISTELL owned. Excellent Two Centuries flagship (CAB SAUV 10' 14' 15'), Manor House, Heritage Heroes, Ingenuity ranges. Small Private Bins for annual Nederburg Auction, incl CHENIN BL botrytis Edelkeur 09' 10' 12'. Low-priced quaffers, still and sparkling.

Neil Ellis Wines W Cape r w (sw) ★ →★★★★ Pioneer STELL-based négociant sourcing cooler-climate parcels for site expression. Masterly Terrain Specific range, esp Jonkershoek Valley CAB SAUV 10' 15' and Pie GRENACHE 15'. New Palomino-based blend Op Sy Moer 1st foray into orange wine.

N Cape ward Prieska = "place of the lost nanny goat" in (admirably succinct) Griqua.

Newton Johnson Vineyards Cape SC r (p) w (sw) ★ →★★★★ Acclaimed family winery in UP HEM. Top Family V'yds PINOT N 10' 11' 12' 13' 14' 15' 17', **Chard**, SAUV BL, Granum SYRAH/MOURVÈDRE, from own and partner v'yds; S Africa's 1st commercial ALBARIÑO. Lovely botrytis CHENIN BL L'illa, ex-ROB; entry-level brand Felicité.

Olifantsberg Family Vineyards W Cape r (p) w ★★ →★★★ BRE's Dutch-owned rising star, focused on Rhône grapes (r w), PINOTAGE, CHENIN BL on mtn slopes. SHIRAZ-based Silhouette 14', sophisticated Blanc from mostly ROUSSANNE/GRENACHE/VGR.

Olifants River W-coast REGION (c.9700 ha). Warm valley floors, conducive to organics, and cooler, fine-wine-favouring sites in Citrusdal Mtn DISTRICT and its WARD, Pie, plus, nr the Atlantic, Bamboes Bay, Koekenaap.

Opstal Estate Sla r p w (sw) ★ →★★★ BRE's quality leader, family-owned, in mtn amphitheatre. Fine CAPE BLEND (r, stellar new w), old-vines CHENIN BL, SEM.

Orange River Cellars *See* CENTRAL ORANGE RIVER.

Paarl Historic DISTRICT (c.8900 ha) with new WARD, Agter Paarl, w of PAARL town. Diverse styles, approaches; best results with Med varieties (r w), CAB SAUV, PINOTAGE, CHENIN BL. Major kosher producers (Backsberg, Simonsvlei, Zandwijk/ Kleine Draken) based here.

Paul Cluver Estate Wines Elg r w sw s/sw ★★ →★★★ Area's pioneer, Cluver family-owned/run; convincing PINOT N (incl "everyday" Village bottling), elegant CHARD, knockout RIES (botrytis 11' 17' and new oak-brushed semi-dry version).

Porseleinberg Swa r ★★★★ BOEKENHOUTSKLOOF-owned, organically farmed v'yds and cellar with expressive SYRAH 12' 14' 16'. Handcrafted, incl ethereal front label printed on-site by winemaker.

Raats Family Wines Stell r w ★★★ →★★★★ Pure-fruited CAB FR and CHENIN BL, oaked and unwooded, incl exceptional newer Eden single-v'yd bottlings. Vinified by STELL-based Bruwer Raats and cousin Gavin Bruwer Slabbert, also partners in B Vintners, unearthing vinous gems locally and in WLK B. *See* MVEMVE RAATS.

Radford Dale W Cape r w (sw) ★ →★★★ STELL venture with eclectic Australian-French-S African UK ownership; formerly "The Winery of Good Hope". Creative, compatible blend of styles, influences, varieties and terroirs. Instant hit with newer Thirst range – juicy, lower-alc CINSAULT, GAMAY, CLAIRETTE varietals. Winemaker Jacques de Klerk's SWA Reverie CHENIN BL a subtle beauty.

Rall Wines Coast r w ★★★ →★★★★ Donovan Rall among original SWA "revolutionaries". New: S Africa's only Cinsault Blanc, from miniscule old WELL parcel, showing house's understatement.

Region *See* GEOGRAPHICAL UNIT.

Reyneke Wines W Cape r w ★ →★★★ Leading certified-bio producer nr STELL; apt Twitter handle (and wine brand) "Vine Hugger". Luminous SHIRAZ, CHENIN BL, SAUV BL, newer limited-release, barrel-selected CAB SAUV 15'.

Oldest soil in S Africa Malmesbury Shales, formed when it was where Canada is now, 650 million yrs ago.

Richard Kershaw Wines W Cape r w ★★★ →★★★★ Heralded UK-born MW Richard Kershaw's refined PINOT N, SYRAH and CHARD from ELG fruit; consituent sites showcased in separate Deconstructed bottlings. Newer GPS and Smuggler's Boot spotlight further-flung areas and innovative techniques respectively.

Rijk's Coast r w sp ★ →★★★ TUL pioneer with multiple tiers of varietal SHIRAZ, PINOTAGE, CHENIN BL; v.gd CHARD MCC.

Robertson Valley Low-rainfall inland DISTRICT with nine existing WARDS newly redrawn and five added; c.12,000 ha; lime soils; historically gd CHARD, desserts; more recently SAUV BL, SHIRAZ, CAB SAUV. Major cellars, eg. GRAHAM BECK, ROBERTSON WINERY and many family boutiques, incl recently reborn Mont Blois.

Robertson Winery Rob r p w sw s/sw sp ★ →★★ Consistency, value throughout extended portfolio. Best: Constitution Rd (SHIRAZ, CHARD).

Rupert & Rothschild Vignerons W Cape r w ★★★ Top v'yds and super-cellar nr PAARL owned by Rupert family and Baron Benjamin de Rothschild. Baron Edmond and Classique (both er blends), CHARD Baroness Nadine.

Rustenberg Wines W Cape r (p) w (br) (sw) ★ →★★★★ Venerable family cellar and v'yds nr STELL. Beautiful site, gardens. Flagship is CAB SAUV Peter Barlow 12' 15'. Outstanding red blend John X Merriman, savoury SYRAH, single-v'yd Five Soldiers CHARD, CHENIN BL-based *vin de paille*.

Rust en Vrede Wine Estate W Cape r (w) sw ★ →★★★★ STELL owner Jean Engelbrecht's powerful, pricey offering, incl Rust en Vrede red varietals, blends; Cirrus SYRAH joint venture with California's Silver Oak; Stell Res range; Donkiesbaai PINOT N, CHENIN BL (dry and *vin de paille*); v.gd Guardian Peak wines.

Sadie Family Wines Stell, Swa, Oli R r w ★★★★ Revered winemaker Eben Sadie's traditionally made portfolio. Columella (SHIRAZ/MOURVÈDRE) 09' 10' 15' 16', a Cape benchmark; complex multivariety white Palladius 12' 14' 15' 16'; ground-breaking Old Vines series, celebrating S Africa's vinous heritage in eight profound, pure-fruited wines.

Saronsberg Cellar W Cape r (p) w (sw) sp ★→★★★ Art-adorned TUL family estate with awarded B'x blends (r), Rhône varieties, blends (r w), bracing CHARD MCC.

Savage Wines W Cape r w ★★★ Star winemaker Duncan Savage ranges far and wide from cellar in Cape Town city for thrillingly understated wines featuring mostly Med varieties. NEW CHENIN BL Never Been Asked To Dance (17') ex-PAARL and remote Malgas is jaw-droppingly gd.

Shannon Vineyards Elg r w (sw) ★★★→★★★★ Arguably S Africa's top MERLOT, also cracking PINOT N, SAUV BL, SEM, rare botrytis Pinot N, grown by brothers James and Stuart Downes, vinified at/by NEWTON JOHNSON.

Sijnn Mal r p w ★★★ DE TRAFFORD co-owner David Trafford and partners' pioneering venture on CAPE SOUTH COAST. Pronounced "Seine". Stony soils, maritime climate, distinctive varietals and blends, brilliant rosé. Winemaker Charla Haasbroek's partly amphora-vinified eponymous brand equally compelling.

Simonsig Estate W Cape r w (br) (sw) (s/sw) sp ★→★★★ Malan family estate nr STELL admired for consistency and lofty standards. Pinnacle wine is powerful mtn CAB SAUV The Garland; v. fine SYRAH Merindol, PINOTAGE Red Hill; S Africa's original MCC, Kaapse Vonkel, still a delicious celebrator.

Spier W Cape r p w (sw) (sp) ★★→★★★ Large, multi-awarded winery and tourist magnet nr STELL. Flag-bearer Frans K Smit ("regular" B'x/SHIRAZ and B'x-only for CWG Auction), Creative Block, 21 Gables and new organic ranges, in particular, show meticulous wine-growing.

Spioenkop Wines W Cape r w ★★★ High-spirited Belgian Koen Roose and family on ELG estate named for Second Boer War battle zone. V.gd individual PINOTAGE, CHENIN BL, new single-v'yd PINOT N Gandhi.

Springfield Estate Rob r w ★→★★★ Cult grower Abrie Bruwer with traditionally vinified CAB SAUV, CHARD, SAUV BL, B'x-style red, PINOT N. Quaffable white blend.

Stark-Condé Wines Stell r w ★★★ →★★★★ Boutique vigneron José Conde with CWG protégé winemaker Rudger van Wyk in STELL's Alpine Jonkershoek. Exceptional CAB SAUV, SYRAH and Field Blend (w) in Three Pines, Stark-Condé ranges.

Steenberg Vineyards W Cape r (p) w sp ★★→★★★ Top CONST winery, v'yds and chic cellar-door, GRAHAM BECK-owned; SAUV BL, Sauv Bl/SEM blend, MCC, polished reds incl rare varietal NEBBIOLO.

Stellenbosch University town, demarcated wine DISTRICT (c.12,500 ha) and heart of wine industry – Napa of SA. Many top estates, esp for reds, tucked into postcard mtn valleys and foothills; extensive wine tasting, accommodation, restaurants.

Stellenbosch Vineyards W Cape r w (sw) (sp) ★→★★★ Big-volume winery with impressive Flagship range (eg. new age-worthy blend Right Bank), geeky (and gd) Limited Release line-up incl vanishingly rare, locally developed grape Therona. Budget range Welmoed.

Storm Wines U Hem, Hem V, Hem Rdg r w ★★★ PINOT N and CHARD specialist Hannes Storm expresses his favoured HEM sites with precision and sensitivity.

Sumaridge Wines W Cape r (p) w ★★→★★★ UK-owned cool-climate v'yds, cellar recently showing improved form; fine PINOT N, CHARD, new B'x white Klip Kop.

Swartland Trendy, internationally-praised COASTAL DISTRICT, with two new wards completing official demarcation of its most famous landmark, Paardeberg Mtn (3rd, earlier-gazetted WARD, Voor Paardeberg, is in PAARL). C.10,000 ha of mostly shy-bearing, unirrigated bush-vines produce concentrated, distinctive, fresh wines. Source of fruit for many others, often with stellar results.

Testalonga Swa r w ★★→★★★ Out-there SYRAH, GRENACHE, CARIGNAN, HÁRSLEVELŰ, CHENIN BL by extreme non-interventionist Craig Hawkins under El Bandito/Baby Bandito labels. Every sip a surprise.

Thelema Mountain Vineyards W Cape r (p) w (s/sw) (sp) ★→★★★★ STELL-based pioneer of S Africa's modern wine revival, still a beacon of quality, consistency;

CAB SAUV, MERLOT **Les**, B'x red Rabelais. Extensive Sutherland v'yds in ELG broaden repertoire, eg. new Res GRENACHE N, PETIT VERDOT, CHARD.

Thorne & Daughters Wines W Cape r w ★★★→★★★★ John T Seccombe and wife Tasha's wines, some from v. old vines, marvels of purity, refinement. Debut Cat's Cradle CHENIN BL and Man In The Moon CLAIRETTE BL epitomize Bot R vintners' hypnotic cerebral yet-sensual styling and emphasis on heirloom varieties.

Tokara W Cape r (p) w (sw) (sp) ★→★★★★ Wine, food, art showcase nr STELL. V'yds also in ELG. Gorgeous Director's Res blends (r w); elegant CHARD, SAUV BL. Newer CAB SAUV Res 13' 15, CAB FR, Chard MCC.

Tulbagh Inland DISTRICT (c.1000 ha) historically associated with still white and bubbly, latterly also beefy reds, some sweeter styles.

Uva Mira Mountain Vineyards Stell r w ★★★ Helderberg eyrie v'yds and cellar reaching new heights under owner Toby Venter, CEO of Porsche SA. Brilliant line-up incl newer SYRAH plus longtime performers CHARD, SAUV BL.

Vergelegen Wines Stell r w (sw) ★★★→★★★★ 2nd Cape governor Van der Stel's mansion, immaculate v'yds/wines/camphor trees, stylish cellar-door at Somerset West, owned by Anglo American. Powerful CAB SAUV V, sumptuous B'x blend GVB Red, perfumed SAUV BL/SEM GVB White, age-worthy Sem Res.

Vilafonté Paarl r ★★★ California's Zelma Long (ex-Simi) and Phil Freese (ex-Mondavi viticulturist) partnering ex-WARWICK Mike Ratcliffe. Trio of deep-flavoured B'x blends given distinctiveness by CAB SAUV, MERLOT or MALBEC predominance.

Spate of recent additions has seen number of demarcated (WO) areas rise to 124.

Villiera Wines Elg, Stell, Hem Rdg r w (sw) (s/sw) sp ★→★★★ Grier family v'yds and winery nr STELL with exceptional quality/value ratio, esp brut MCC bubbly quintet (incl low-alc).

Vondeling V Pa r (p) w w sp ★→★★★ UK-owned, sustainability-focused; Paardeberg foothills. Eclectic offering incl one of S Africa's few méthode ancestrale bubblies.

Walker Bay Highly regarded maritime DISTRICT (c.1000 ha); WARDS HEM, Bot River, Sunday's Glen, Stanford Foothills. PINOT N, SHIRAZ, CHARD, SAUV BL standout.

Ward Smallest of the wo demarcations. *See* GEOGRAPHICAL UNIT.

Warwick Estate W Cape r (p) w (sp) ★★→★★★★ Tourist-cordial property on STELL outskirts, now US-owned and incorporating ex-DISTELL estate Uitkyk. V. fine CAB SAUV, CAB FR, CHARD, B'x blend Professor Black (w, previously varietal SAUV BL).

Waterford Estate W Cape r (p) w (sp) (sp) ★→★★★★ Stylish family winery nr STELL; awarded cellar door. Savoury Kevin Arnold SHIRAZ, elegant CAB SAUV, intricate Cab Sauv-based flagship The Jem 12' 14'. Fascinating experiments in Library Collection, eminently/immediately drinkable Pecan Stream trio.

Waterkloof Elg, Stell r (p) w sp ★→★★★ British wine merchant Paul Boutinot's organic v'yds, winery and cantilevered cellar door nr Somerset West. Top tiers: Waterkloof, Circle of Life, Seriously Cool and Astraeus MCC. Lower-priced quality under False Bay, Peacock Wild Ferment labels.

Wellington Warm-climate DISTRICT (c.4000 ha) bordering PAARL and SWA, now with quintet of wards, reflecting general trend towards regionality and terroir expression. Growing reputation for PINOTAGE, SHIRAZ, chunky red blends, CHENIN BL. Stars: Bosman Family, DIEMERSFONTEIN, Mischa, Welbedacht.

Wine of Origin (WO) S Africa's "AC" but without French restrictions. Certifies vintage, variety, area of origin. Opt-in sustainability certification additionally aims to guarantee eco-sensitive production. *See* GEOGRAPHICAL UNIT.

Worcester Sibling DISTRICT (c.6400 ha) to ROB, BRE in Breede River basin. Mostly bulk produce for export but bottled wines of Arendskloof, Alvi's Drift, Conradie, Leipzig, Stettyn, Survivor (by Overhex International) and Tanzanite are taste-worthy, mostly family-made exceptions.

Wine flavour

How, what, why?

Wine flavour changes. Wine today does not taste as it did in 1950, far less 1850, or 1550. And how it tasted before that can only be guesswork.

Why is this? Cold fermentation, keen amateurs will say. Better hygiene. Climate change. Yes, all of those. But not just those. The latest change in wine flavour is a swing against obvious oak taste, which surged into fashion in the 80s. Now the fashionable tasting notes are "mineral" or "saline". It's a massive turnaround in the flavour in favour.

There, I've said it: fashion. We like new things, and get tired of old ones. But what is leading fashion? Not, initially, consumer demand. Yes, when we first tasted the vanilla flavours of new oak back in the 80s they tasted different and expensive and for a while we wanted more – but until they were put in front of us we didn't know they existed.

The wine grapes grown now are not always the same as they were before phylloxera, and often totally different to those grown in the Middle Ages. Why? Surely a good vine is a good vine? Why have so many vines simply disappeared? We can construct family trees of vines, but the further you go back the more gaps there are. We mostly do not know what vines were being grown in the past – or what their wine tasted like.

Climate swings in the past have affected what vines are grown; so have trade patterns and, above all, shifting political and commercial power. It's no coincidence that major wine regions are near major cities, and often on rivers. There's no point in making fine wine without a wealthy urban market. And then you have to aim for the wine that that market wants to drink.

What we're going to look at in this year's supplement is why wine tastes the way it does today, and how it might change in the near future. How much comes from grape variety – and why those grape varieties? How much comes from manipulation in the cellar? Where is climate change leading us? And how does terroir, the deity to which we are all supposed to bow, fit in?

The how, what and why of wine flavour is a big subject. We'll see how far we can get in 16 pages.

Fashions in flavour
From oak to salt

This is the biggest change that most of us have seen: from the vogue for new-oak flavours of vanilla and toast, to the current mode of invisible oak or none. The highest compliment you can pay a wine now is to say it is "mineral" or "salty" – these are also useful words when you can't think of anything to say, incidentally.

But this change went hand in hand with another massive change: the switch to cellar hygiene and temperature-controlled fermentation. These are not glamorous subjects, but they eradicated the flavour of dirt from wine. As recently as the late 80s it was perfectly possible to visit the more rustic sort of French cellar and be told that what you were tasting was terroir. It wasn't terroir. It was generally dirty barrels, "brett" (*see* opposite) and oxidation – or all three. Dirt, and what are now considered bacterial infections and winemaking faults, have been elements in wine flavour probably since people started making wine. In a sense we are the first to know what "clean" wine tastes like.

I use inverted commas because there's another change afoot. Just when wine had reached a level of technical perfection that meant people were beginning to complain that you couldn't tell where a wine came from or which grape it was made from, because everything was focused on ticking the laboratory-analysis boxes, along came natural wine to bring us back down to earth. The extreme wing of this movement holds that there is no such thing as a wine fault: everything is part of the journey of the wine. This is accidental winemaking, claiming authenticity because it's accidental – rather like claiming that the turkey you've just burnt for Christmas lunch is more authentic than one cooked according to the recipe.

Not all natural wine is the equivalent of burnt turkey, I should add: I have tasted many wonderful natural wines, often made in clay amphorae in ways the ancient world would recognize. But here's a question: Pinot Noir (to take the most obvious example) made in amphorae does not taste like the Pinot Noir we know. It does not have the seductive incense-and-spice fruit, the compelling aromas, the silky texture. Amphorae, to my palate, narrow the differences between grape varieties and bring a greater sameness of flavour – but it's a different sort of flavour. Aficionados might argue that if my palate were more tuned in I would see more differences; they may be right. It's important to have an open mind; but wine flavour, you see, is not fixed. Different grape varieties taste different because they are both structurally different (thicker or thinner skins, more or fewer pips) and because they are chemically different, but these differences can themselves be emphasized or eroded by soil, climate, viticulture and winemaking. Wine flavour is what we decide it should be.

And while we're on the subject of faults – for a wine to be oxidized is considered a fault (by conventional winemakers, that is); so is reduction, so is cork taint, so is brett, and so are various other things. These usually only became labelled as faults when a way of avoiding them was invented. (Cork taint is the exception; there the fault was recognized and complained of for years before the cork industry addressed it.) Technicians can argue that volatile acidity is a fault – yet a hint of it can lift an old wine into greatness. Only when cold fermentation became available did we recognize that the stewed-fruit flavour and lack of aroma that comes with overheated fermentation was unattractive. "Sweaty saddles" was a normal tasting note for Hunter Valley Shiraz, until one day it was decided that this was caused by brett, and brett was bad.

What is brett? It's short for brettanomyces, which is a kind of yeast, albeit not one deliberately used in grape fermentation. When it's present in a wine it produces a range of compounds that can smell like sticking plaster, or farmyards, or horses, or indeed sweaty saddles. The anti-brett movement started in the US and moved to Australia, and in both it's a cardinal sin, even though some of the world's greatest wines – Penfolds Grange, sometimes, plenty of southern French wines – have it at noticeable levels. Wines with low acidity are at particular risk, so it's usually a warm-climate problem. Some drinkers enjoy its savoury, feral, funky notes (and it's considered a positive attribute in some beers) while others regard even a hint as a sign of disastrously incompetent winemaking. Certainly it changes the flavour of wine. For better or for worse? These things can be personal; I like it; you turn up your nose.

Barrel staves, shaped with heat and water: toasting has a big effect on wine flavour.

Terroir
Can you taste the salt of the earth?

Site gives flavour. You only have to look at how the afternoon fog rolls into the Napa Valley, or how the soil and slope changes every few metres in Canada's Okanagan Valley, to see how obvious that is. Site matters.

Everything about a site matters. Terroir, classically, is defined as the combination of soil, climate and exposure to the sun that makes each vineyard unique. The hand of man is part of it too: vineyards have had their terroir adjusted – by drainage, by windbreaks, by soil fertilization and sometimes pH adjustment (in Spain's Galicia the tradition was to throw shellfish shells into the vineyards) – for as long as people have planted vines. More or less sun and more or less wind or rain or cloud cover will affect wine flavour: ripeness, yes, but also skin thickness and berry size and thus flavour concentration and tannins. Wines from warm, sunny years are richer and more opulent than wines from cool years. Cool nights are just as important as warm days for the ideal combination of ripeness and freshness: hot nights mean low acidity.

What people talk about most, though, is soil. Think of the solid chalk of Champagne, or the gravel of the Médoc, the clay-limestone of the Côte d'Or or the slate of the Mosel. Wines don't taste of these things directly – when someone says a wine tastes "mineral" or "salty" that only makes sense as a description of a flavour, in the same way as "cherry" or "plum". It is not to be taken literally.

So, what is the effect of soil on wine flavour? Basically, it's drainage and nutrients. Well-drained soils – gravelly ones, for example, or chalk – are warmer. They warm up faster in spring and give the vines a better start, so grapes ripen better. Shallow soils can mean smaller canopies, more sun on the grapes and thus richer flavours; deeper soils can mean bigger canopies, more shading and fresher flavours. The gradations of flavour of, say, Pinot Noir, from bright, fresh, savoury red cherry through lush black cherry to, at the overripe end, plum jam, are the flavours of different degrees of ripeness. It's why winemakers set such store by picking at exactly the right moment.

Having said that, different soils can affect structure and tannins too. Clay gives weight; chalk gives an elegant line of acidity, which is subtly different to the acidity from other soils, even though the laboratory analysis may look the same. Schist gives what soil specialist Pedro Parra calls " horizontal structure"; he finds, too, that granite gives tension. Volcanic soils seem to reveal themselves in a particular sparky energy in the wine. Germany's Ürziger Würzgarten vineyard is famous for the spicy taste it imparts to its Rieslings (the clue is in the name). Sometimes particular grapes are happiest on a particular soil type: in Austria, top Grüner Veltliner is planted on loess, Riesling on rock.

In NZ's Marlborough the most fertile silt soils give the most pungent wines high in thiols (*see* p.328–9 for an explanation of these), while the gravelly soils with fewer nutrients give more methoxypyrazines and greener flavours. In Sancerre, where the soils can be divided into chalky *caillottes* for finesse and aroma, chalky-clay *terres blanches* for richness and freshness and flinty silex for a certain liveliness, flavours are different again. The box on p.92 gives some examples.

Could you make a Sancerre style in Marlborough, or vice versa? You could certainly adapt the style of each region to resemble the other to some extent. Many producers in Europe have been influenced by the bright fruit of the New World, and it's possible to make a Sonoma Coast Chardonnay that would pass for good burgundy. Styles change with fashion, as we've seen. But to make an outright copy of another region is to deny your own terroir. Serious winemakers want to explore the differences between this vineyard and that, this hillside and that, not obliterate them.

When Nigel Greening of NZ's Felton Road, for example, has identified a character that comes from a particular vineyard, he will seek to emphasize it in blending, so that the wines labelled as that vineyard taste of that vineyard. "When we select for Cornish Point," he says, "we taste all the Cornish Point vats and select those that taste most like Cornish Point, and blend them. It's about 'place-ness'."

Blending is not the only cellar decision to affect wine flavour. We'll look at some of the others next.

Rocky terraces overlooking Austria's Wachau and the Danube.

The effects of temperature
Ripe, riper, ripest

Temperature – climate, if you prefer – dictates ripeness, and ripeness dictates flavour. If you think of cool-climate flavours you think of fresh, sappy, citrus notes in whites, aromatic red fruit in reds, and a fresh crunchiness; warm-climate flavours tend towards peach in whites, black fruits in reds, and more opulence.

That's it at its simplest. But what is a warm climate for one grape might be a cool one for another; as a general rule, the best wines are made at the climatic margin for a given grape: where it will ripen, but not overripen. Late-ripening grapes need warmer climates than earlier-ripening ones: an early-ripener like Merlot in a warm climate will give flabby, soupy wines. The Montepulciano grape, usually thought of as being suited to the warm vineyards of southern Italy, actually needs a cooler climate in order to reach sugar ripeness and phenolic ripeness – and thus ripe tannins with reasonable alcohol – at much the same time. In a hot site you either pick in August and have harsh green tannins, or much later and have 16% alcohol.

This is what climate is largely about, when it comes to flavour. Sugar comes from sun and warmth. It develops quickly, in the right conditions. Tannic ripeness, however, demands time. It won't be hurried. So in the wrong climate the sugar can be going through the roof, but if the tannins are green, the winemaker has to wait. And wait. And wait. By the time the tannins are ripe, the sugar might give 15% alcohol. The world's great terroirs are usually those that give tannin ripeness and sugar ripeness at roughly the same time: silky tannins with no green, rustic flavours, and 13–14% alcohol. But with climate change, even in those great terroirs, the gap can be widening.

The world is getting warmer. Picking dates are earlier, sugar levels are higher. This, given that for much of the 20th century, getting grapes ripe even in the finest vineyard could be a problem, could be good news. Bordeaux is reliably ripe every year; gone are the green, hard vintages when tannins took ten years or more to become approachable. In Germany there hasn't been a really bad vintage for decades. Champagne can now make vintage wines almost every year, instead of just three or four times in a decade. Alsace's flirtation with ever-sweeter wines has subsided into a realization that dryness and ripeness can go together. English wine actually has a chance of being financially viable – how about that?

So: warmer summers. Hooray. Region after region has edged further inside its climatic comfort zone. It's all win, isn't it? When you focus on flavour, you realize how thin the margin of error can be. The sweet spot for top quality on the Côte d'Or, says our Burgundy correspondent Jasper Morris, has moved 50m (164ft) higher up the hillside. However, growers have plenty of tools in their armoury yet:

Cool-climate flavours: strawberries, red cherries, red plums.

leaving on the secondary clusters to delay ripening of the main clusters; leaving on leaves for shade; adjusting ploughing times. They've learnt a lot about how to manage heat.

Or take Mosel Kabinett. Some of the vineyards that growers relied on for this pure, fresh, light wine – the essence of Riesling, some would say – are now too warm, and produce something much bigger and riper. So cooler vineyards, perhaps facing away from the sun, or tucked into chilly side valleys – vineyards that were abandoned years ago as being too cold – are being replanted.

The most obvious example, though, of how climate affects flavour is Syrah. Or Shiraz, if you prefer. The two names sum up its dual character: black olives, stones, wild herbs, roses in the Northern Rhône; soy and black chocolate in the Barossa Valley. (*See* p.285 for a snapshot of different Shiraz flavours in Australia.) The Northern Rhône isn't usually thought of as cool, but it's as cool as Syrah wants. And if you overdo things in the Barossa (and it has happened, believe it or not) you go from soy to such dense, black, pruney chewiness that you'd be hard put to know what grape variety you're tasting. "Dead fruit" is the Australian name for that flavour: grapes left too long on the vine in a hot climate.

In too cool a climate, grapes don't develop their full aromas and flavours. In too hot a climate, they lose them and end up all tasting alike. What all winemakers seek is the climate that will allow each grape perfect expression.

But what is that expression? Who decides? And what happens when they change their minds?

Grape variety
The single greatest factor

What does Chardonnay taste like? We can all make a stab at that one. Um, cream? Smoke? Nuts? Stone fruit? Not bad. What about tropical fruit and butterscotch? Or salt and chalk and lemon rind? Chardonnay can taste of all these. And it complicates the picture: grape variety is certainly the greatest single influence on wine flavour. But who says what a grape tastes like?

I mentioned Pinot Noir on p.322, and how making it in an amphora changes pretty well everything about it. With Chardonnay you don't have to go that far. Australian Chardonnay, back in the day, wowed us all with its broad, lush pineapple and cream flavours. Then, quite suddenly, it changed. Now Australian Chardonnay is tight, lean and fresh. Growers started picking earlier and making wine with less contact with oxygen – that immediately means higher acidity and less toastiness. But of course the climate has to allow you to do that and still have ripe grapes. You can never escape the part played by climate.

The current fashion in Chardonnay is for a smoky struck-match note on the nose; it originated in Burgundy, and anybody who admired the style of the Côte d'Or took note. It can be imitated; it's a winemaking flavour, not a terroir one: it comes from reductive winemaking (ie. winemaking that avoids oxygen). *See* p.99 for some examples.

Sauvignon is also pretty varied in flavour – think of Sancerre, all tight and tense citrus, and Marlborough, pungent gooseberries, passion fruit and box. The flavours of Sauvignon Blanc are more thoroughly understood than those of most grapes.

Talk about them, and the word "thiols" invariably crops up, along with "methoxypyrazine". (There's no avoiding a bit of techy stuff here.)

Struck match is a winemaking flavour, not a terroir one.

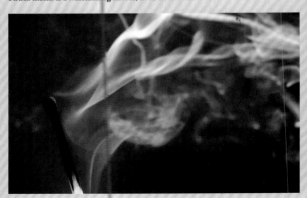

The latter give green flavours: grass and green pepper, and they crop up in unripe Cabernet Sauvignon too. Thiols give those tropical-fruit and passion-fruit notes. Thiols are especially important in Marlborough Sauvignon, and they might derive from the site or they might derive from machine-harvesting: nobody is quite certain. The box on p.92 gives examples of each.

Other grapes have their own characteristic compounds: peppery-tasting rotundone, which is found in Syrah; floral, citrus-tasting terpenes, found in Gewurztraminer.

The point of this, though, is not a chemistry lesson, although the reason that different grapes taste different is because they have a different chemical make-up: some are higher in this compound, others in that. Instead it's to show that those descriptors people come up with are not overfanciful: your "peach" might be my "apricot", and your "rosemary" might be my "medicinal", but we're both struggling to express the same thing. They're the flavour of the grape, but they are modified or emphasized by climate (Cabernet Sauvignon loses those green-pepper flavours as it ripens, and if it's unripe it's horrid), by terroir and especially by winemaking. The winemaker can subdue the varietal flavours of the grape, or emphasize them, to reflect what he or she wants, and we'll look at that on p.330–1.

Not all winemakers want the flavour of the grape to shine through. In Burgundy and in many other top vineyards, the grape is regarded as simply the conduit for the terroir. So a Burgundian winemaker wants to make not a Pinot Noir but a Pommard, and not just a Pommard but a Pommard Rugiens, that expresses precisely the character of those few hectares of hillside, and indeed the character of his few ares of it, since no vineyard, even in Burgundy, is completely homogeneous. They seek not fruit-forward varietal flavours but the particular character they have discovered in that vineyard over the years; but what terroir is and why it matters is a subject for p.324–5.

Another way of suppressing the varietal character of individual grapes is by growing and making a field blend – that is, different vines, perhaps six or ten of them, planted together, picked on the same day and fermented together. Most wines were field blends once; it was an insurance against frost. If one variety was wiped out, another, later budding, might survive. Having almost died out, field blends are now a bit of a cult, especially in the vineyards of Vienna and parts of Portugal: *see* the Austria and Portugal chapters for some examples.

What do they taste like? Winey, is the answer. Not a very helpful one, maybe, but while you could have a guess at the varieties in them, they taste far more than the sum of their parts: more complex, more interesting. Fermenting the same grapes separately and blending them later does not have the same result. It's the magic of winemaking – and we'll look at that on p.330–1.

Winemaking
The great manipulation?

Wine does not make itself. Or rather, it can if you throw grapes into an amphora, put the lid on and come back in a few months. Such winemaking is the height of fashion (or was a moment ago). It can occasionally produce glorious results. Or horrible ones.

But, even to do that is to take a decision. Winemaking is a series of decisions, and each one affects the flavour of the final wine. The date of picking is the first one: once the grapes are off the vine the die is cast. The final wine can never be better than the grapes.

Red wines, as we know, get their colour and tannins from fermentation with the skins and pips. But do you press whole bunches, or crush everything and put it into the vat as a sort of slurry? It's a flavour decision. Whole-cluster fermentation is fashionable for Pinot Noir in particular, for the extra spice, weight and colour it gives; you can spot the flavour, blind. Used to excess it can mask terroir. Oh, you think: whole-cluster. But where from? Do you macerate the skins with the juice before fermentation and, in the case of whites, before pressing? It gives more aromas (because they're in the skins too) but sometimes too much tannin. A naturally tannic white grape like Verdicchio, to take one, doesn't take happily to skin contact.

And yeasts: they may be too small to see, but they're important. Indeed they're vital to your brand's identity. Once a couple of Médoc châteaux swapped yeasts as a trial; they rapidly reverted to their own. If you're making Sauvignon Blanc you can choose a yeast that will emphasize the thiols (see p.328–9; we've met thiols before). There are yeasts to emphasize most flavours you can think of. Or you can choose a neutral yeast; or you can let the juice ferment with the indigenous yeasts on the skins and in the winery. This last, while risky (you never know what mix of yeasts you have, or what might happen) gives a distinct flavour – less obviously fruity, more, well, winery and mineral.

Length of fermentation: yes, that affects flavour as well. A longer fermentation means rounder wines. So does temperature. If you ferment cold you get crisp, fresh fruit flavours: sometimes boringly so, if it's too cold. But too hot and you lose aromas and risk stewed flavours. The type of fermentation vessel affects flavour too: new oak will give vanilla flavours; old oak will give less or no oak flavour, but will still give some extra roundness and weight. Steel gives tight, crisp wines. Clay amphorae give a wet-clay note and a delectable texture. Concrete is newly popular again for doing none of the above. There's no harm in glass fibre, either.

And the malolactic fermentation, that transmutes one sort of acid to another: to do or not to do? It affects flavour, big time.

All these decisions – and there are more, plenty more – can be used to mask vineyard character or to reveal it. Too much extraction of tannins

Hands-on winemaking, or non-interventionist?

gives the sort of impenetrable chewiness that is mercifully less fashionable now. Overacidification in hot climates can give artificial-tasting, disjointed acidity. And too much new oak, for example, clouts you with the vanilla flavour we all know.

And while we're on the subject of oak: you can buy oak barrels that will emphasize many different aspects of your wine – structure, length, mid-palate weight. Burgundy growers will often choose different coopers for different vineyards, because every cooper has a signature too. Where is the oak grown? The forest, and the climates in different parts of that forest make a difference. Oak with a tight grain might tighten up a broad, ripe wine; oak with a more open grain might flatter a tighter, leaner wine. The length of drying time for the wood affects the flavour precursors in the staves; so does the climate in which it was dried. Even the species of oak tree – sessile or pedunculate – matters for flavour. The choice of how toasted it is in the making (they use fire to bend the staves) is another topic worth 1000 words. Concrete is simpler.

So, when winemakers describe themselves as "non-interventionist", what exactly does that mean? It doesn't mean they avoid these decisions, because they're unavoidable. Usually it means less extraction of tannins, less insistence on analytical perfection, perhaps indigenous yeasts – but all winemaking is interventionist, unless it's of the chuck-the-grapes-in-an-amphora kind.

In the end, with a good winemaker, these decisions should be invisible in the glass. Winemakers are not stupid, and there is nothing wrong with trusting them on the decisions they make – if we like the wine. But when we buy the wine we have to decide when to drink it. That's a flavour decision that we have to make for ourselves.

From youth to old age
How flavour evolves

Young wines taste different from old wines. The popular idea is that older is better, and certainly smarter; the trouble is, it's not necessarily nicer. All wines have a lifespan of youth, maturity and old age, and as winemaking techniques have changed, so have the best times to drink most wines.

The flavours of youth are "primary" flavours of fruit, acidity, tannin and sometimes oak. What happens as wine matures is that the tannins soften, the oak gets tucked more neatly into the wine so it shows less, and the fruit flavours change. Whites get more honeyed in taste; reds more savoury and herbal and eventually gain notes of undergrowth and leather – one hopes of the finest, silkiest, most beautifully aromatic leather. Eventually great reds and whites come to taste and sometimes even look pretty similar. Whites darken with age, reds lighten.

The decision we have to take is at what point to interrupt this process. Young wines are (or are meant to be) delicious, and because modern winemaking is aimed at producing wines that can be drunk earlier – yes, even for long-lived reds like Rhônes or Bordeaux – the tannins are "approachable" – or non-aggressive – younger, and the balance should be there right from the start. The oak, if there is some, might sometimes be obtrusive at first, however. The only period to avoid if you can is adolescence, when wines close up and become unfriendly and inexpressive; getting past that period is really what cellaring these days is about.

When adolescence hits varies with each wine. Fine Riesling doesn't suffer from it; Verdicchio can, a bit; red burgundy does, to the point of annoyance. Pinot Noir can be glorious in extreme youth: so aromatic and seductive that you may wonder why you need to age it at all, but

You don't actually need to age burgundy this long.

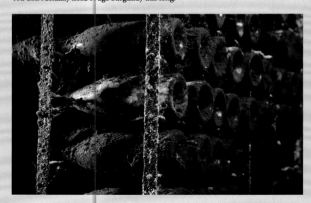

its adolescence can be unpredictable. Cabernet always takes time to settle down.

Most people are drinking white burgundy younger than they used to, because everybody is still nervous of premature oxidation, or "premox". This affliction was noticed with the 1995 and 1996 vintages, which often turned brown and old well before their time. Many winemakers have views on what causes it (cutting back on the sulphur is one), and some say the problem is solved; but there are still fingers crossed. So, if you don't want to lose those youthful flavours of citrus and cream and smoke, don't leave them too long.

We haven't mentioned sparkling wines so far, and they're a subject in themselves. Not all fizz is made to be aged, but good Champagne certainly is, and so is top English bubbly. Here the tightness and freshness, the assertive lemon peel and nuts of the young wine will soften into brioche and confit fruit, then into cream, honey, chocolate and toast, and at last undergrowth and mushrooms. The very young flavours can be too tight, too inexpressive; a good non-vintage wine will benefit from another six months to a year before being drunk. A good vintage wine will need ten years at least (some are not even released before ten years), and the best will live for decades and still astonish with their freshness and complexity.

Ah, complexity. That boon of age – sometimes. There's a difference between wine that merely lasts and wine that improves, and gains from the experience. Priorat of the chewiest, densest kind, which tasted of cherries in brandy when it was young, aged within a few years to flavours of prunes in brandy, and it was hard to see that this was an improvement. Priorat now has lightened up, and we'll see. Ageing ability is always about more than mere size and muscle. Riesling, for example, starts light, tight and citrus and opens up to become honeyed and infinitely layered. Sweeter Spätlesen and Auslesen, given enough age, become less sweet: the sweetness is absorbed into the wine (how is a mystery), while the freshness remains.

Most fortifieds are ready to drink when bottled – pre-aged, we could call them. You buy them with the flavours you want. Amontillado, Palo Cortado and Oloroso Sherries become ever darker and more concentrated with barrel-age, with increasingly pungent flavours of nuts, bitter chocolate, coffee, burnt toast, dried fruit and citrus peel: they're the flavours of slow oxidation over many years. Once they're in the bottle, that's it. Tawny Port, at ten years old, still has some juicy bounciness to it; by 20 years old, nuts and spice dominate. Vintage Port follows a similar trajectory but takes longer, and has more weight, power, fruit and spice at all ages. By about 60 years you'll find notes of marmalade and sandalwood – if you want to wait that long. If not, drink Late Bottled Vintage or LBV.

You'll find lots of food and wine matches, for wines of all ages, on p.27. But what we don't talk about there is the effect of decanting, and of different glasses, on flavour. So turn to p.336...

Flavour A-Z
Some frequently found flavours

Apple: can be green (cool-climate white) or stewed/baked (warm climate, especially Chenin Blanc).

Apricot: in Viognier, sometimes Albariño, Petit Manseng, Croatian Zilavka.

Balsamic: especially high-quality reds from warmish climates, eg. Bolgheri. Comes from low levels of volatile acidity.

Beeswax: comes with age, especially Sémillon, white Rioja.

Bitterness: from tannins. A touch adds freshness to Champagne and other whites.

Blackberry: in warm-climate red, eg. Barossa; especially Grenache.

Blackcurrant: typical of ripe Cab Sauv.

Butter: winemaking flavour, from lees-ageing of eg. Champagne, also from malolactic fermentation.

Cherry: goes from red cherry to black with increasing ripeness; especially Pinot Noir, but widely found.

Chocolate: black chocolate in warm-climate red, especially Syrah, some Italians. Can be from oak.

Citrus: can be lemon or lemon peel, or orange peel, or grapefruit. Usually ripe cool-climate: Champagne often tastes of citrus. Fine Riesling can start with limes and mature towards oranges. Orange peel in mature Port. Pink grapefruit in pale rosés.

Coconut: from unsubtle and overenthusiastic use of oak. Rarer now.

Coffee/mocha: usually from oak.

Damson: flavour of ripeness in reds. Riper than plum, much riper than cherry.

Eucalyptus: can come from the trees: eucalyptus oil blows onto grapes, stays on skins during fermentation. Hence a flavour of red.

Fruitcake: ripe Merlot. Typical tasting note for St-Émilion.

Fruity: fruit flavours listed here usually come from esters – in grapes, but especially from reactions during fermentation and ageing.

Graphite: ("lead pencil") in reds. Often goes with good quality.

Green (bell) pepper: flavour of methoxypyrazines in unripe Cabernet.

Herbal / garrigue: wild herbs, thyme and fennel, from ripeness levels. Pinot Noir that is slightly too ripe can have these notes; so can eg. Douro, leading some winemakers to say these flavours come from surrounding vegetation.

Herbal / green / grass: slightly underripe Sauvignon Blanc and Cabernet Sauvignon. From methoxypyrazines in the grapes, lessens with ripeness.

Honey: especially on mature Riesling, develops with age.

Lavender: especially Grenache. Sometimes good Southern Rhône whites. From terpenes in the grapes.

Leather: comes to most oak-aged reds in the end. A flavour of age.

Leafiness: fresh note found on young whites, especially those of no great character.

Liquorice: usually in hot-climate red.

Marmalade: especially mature Port, young and mature Sauternes. Comes from ripeness/noble rot/age.

Mineral / salt: does not come from minerals in the soil or salt on the wind. From sulphur compounds. Winemakers regard it as part of terroir expression.

Mint: like eucalyptus; less aggressive. Often found on Cabernet Sauvignon, probably at a particular level of ripeness.

Mushroom: from age. Champagne and many wines taste mushroomy after many years. Should be fresh mushroom; a dirty mushroomy smell is a fault.

Oily: whites especially Viognier, Sauvignon Blanc: derived from too hot a summer and imperfect balance, and perhaps too much skin contact.

Peach: on many whites, especially Chardonnay; from ripeness (riper than green apple).

Pepper: black pepper especially on Syrah, comes from rotundone in the grape. White pepper is a character of eg. Grüner Veltliner.

Raspberry: from ripeness in cool-climate reds. Riper than strawberry, not as ripe as cherry. From raspberry ketone.

Redcurrant: especially Malbec. In coolish-climate reds.

Rose: especially Syrah, Muscat, Gewurztraminer, some more showily than others. From terpenes in the grapes.

Savoury: in much mature red, usually to its benefit; can indicate low levels of brett.

Smoke: a struck-match nose is a flavour of reductive winemaking, often found on white burgundy and much imitated elsewhere.

Soupy: not exactly a flavour. Means lack of tannin definition, blurred flavours. Goes with low acidity, from overripeness, usually on red but not always: hot-climate white can be soupy too if the grape is unsuited to the climate.

Soy: especially Shiraz. Comes from a hot climate.

Spice: can be from the grape, from oak or from ageing. Clove = oak.

Strawberry: on cool-climate reds; cooked strawberry indicates overripeness.

Tea: typical of Sangiovese; gives a nice edge. Very Italian.

Toast: from oak, or from oxidization: mature Champagne can take on a toasty note even if it hasn't seen oak, as can Semillon. Burnt toast is a flavour of long oxidation, especially on old Oloroso Sherry.

Toffee: especially low-acidity reds. Typical of Merlot.

Truffle: sounds expensive, often on expensive red. From age rather than price, though.

Undergrowth (French "sous-bois"): from age.

Vanilla: from new oak, and too much of it. Was fashionable a while ago; no longer.

Violets: usually warmish-climate reds, especially Petit Verdot, Graciano, good Tannat, Rhône. Much loved.

Serving wine
Do you need glasses?

This is where sceptics stop reading. There are so many differing bits of advice on decanting, so much talked about shapes of glasses, so much about temperature; it's enough to make anyone give up and simply serve everything as it comes.

One can worry too much about serving. But temperature makes a huge, even existential, difference to flavour: too cold, and wines are hard and ungiving. Too warm, and they turn soupy. You don't need a thermometer in the end; if they come to the table too cold, they'll soon warm in the glasses, and then the flavour will blossom and the wine will sing for its supper.

Need you decant? Only old wines that have thrown a deposit. But decanting changes flavours; whether you prefer your red vigorous, tight and just-uncorked, or more open and more supple after an hour in a decanter is up to you. It can help young reds, though it's not a substitute for ageing; young, tight red will open up in a decanter, but it will still taste young. Very old wines are a lottery. They can fade right away, or reveal depths you never expected.

You don't need to have umpteen different glass shapes, either, whatever glassmakers tell you. But what you do need to do is invest in a really good basic shape: and use it for everything, if you wish. Zalto glasses emphasize aroma and are wonderful, but if they seem too expensive to risk breaking, that angular shape is being copied by others now. Jancis Robinson backs a one-glass-for all policy – and very elegant it is too. Tight, narrow glasses don't flatter wine, even Champagne: wine in a narrow glass will taste narrow. Wine needs a decently wide bowl to say anything at all. Nobody in Champagne now serves it in flutes. Go for Riedel's Riesling/Zinfandel glass (I use their water glass), or, more cheaply, Spiegelau's red wine glass. Put those Paris goblets in the recycling bin, and don't even think of using tumblers. They're not cool; just a waste of decent wine.

Decanting changes flavours – and so do glasses.

A little learning...

A few technical words

The jargon of laboratory analysis is often seen on back labels. It creeps menacingly into newspapers and magazines. What does it mean? This hard-edged wine talk is very briefly explained below.

Acidity is both fixed and volatile. **Fixed** is mostly tartaric, malic and citric, all from the grape, and lactic and succinic, from fermentation. Acidity may be natural or (in warm climates) added. **Volatile (VA)**, or acetic acid, is formed by bacteria in the presence of oxygen. A touch of VA is inevitable, and can add complexity. Too much = vinegar. Total acidity is fixed + VA combined.

Alcohol content (mainly ethyl alcohol) is expressed as per cent (%) by volume of the total liquid. (Also known as "degrees".) Table wines are usually between 12.5–14.5%; too many wines go as high as 16% these days.

Amphora the fermentation vessel of the moment, and the last 7000 years. Remove lid, throw in grapes, replace lid, return in six months. Risky: can be wonderful or frankly horrible.

Barriques small (225-litre) oak barrels, as used in Bordeaux and across the world for fermentation and/or ageing. The newer the barrel, the stronger the smell and taste of oak influence; French oak is more subtle than American. The fashion for overpowering wine of all sorts with new oak has waned; oak use is now far more subtle across most of the globe.

Biodynamic (Bio) viticulture uses herbal, mineral and organic preparations in homeopathic quantities, in accordance with the phases of the moon and the movements of the planets. Sounds like voodoo, but some top growers swear by it. NB: "bio" in French means organic too, but here it means biodynamic.

Malolactic fermentation occurs after the alcoholic fermentation, and changes tart malic acid into softer lactic acid. Can add complexity to red and white alike. Often avoided in hot climates where natural acidity is low and precious.

Micro-oxygenation is a widely used bubbling technique; it allows controlled contact with oxygen during maturation. Softens flavours and helps to stabilize wine.

Minerality a tasting term to be used with caution: fine as a descriptor of chalky/ stony flavours; often wrongly used to imply transference of minerals from soil to wine, which is impossible.

Natural wines are undefined, but start by being organic or biodynamic, involve minimal intervention in the winery and as little sulphur as possible; sometimes none. Can be excellent and characterful, or oxidized and/or dirty. An element of emperor's new clothes may creep in.

Old vines give deeper flavours. No legal definition: some "vieilles vignes" turn out to be c.30 years. Should 50+ to be taken seriously.

Orange wines are tannic whites fermented on skins, perhaps in amphorae. Caution: like natural wines, some are good, some not.

Organic viticulture prohibits most chemical products in the vineyard; organic wine prohibits added sulphur and must be made from organically grown grapes.

Pét-nat (pétillant naturel) bottled before end of fermentation, which continues in bottle. Slight residual sugar, quite low alcohol. Dead trendy.

pH is a measure of acidity: the lower the pH, the sharper the acidity. Wine is normally 2.8–3.8. High pH can be a problem in hot climates. Lower pH gives better colour, helps stop bacterial spoilage and allows more of the SO_2 to be free and active as a preservative. So low is good in general.

Residual sugar is that which is left after fermentation has ended or been stopped, measured in grams per litre (g/l). A dry wine has almost none.

Sulphur dioxide (SO_2) added to prevent oxidation and other accidents in wine-making. Some combines with sugars, etc. and is "bound". Only "free" SO_2 is effective as a preservative. Trend worldwide is to use less. To use none is brave.